Renault 16 Owners Workshop Manual

by J H Haynes
Member of the Guild of Motoring Writers
and Peter G Strasman

Models covered:
Renault 16 De Luxe and Grande Luxe; 1470 cc
Renault 16 L, TL and TS; 1565 cc
Renault 16 TX; 1647 cc
Covers 4- and 5-speed manual gearbox, and automatic transmission

ISBN 0 85696 847 1

ABCDE
F

Printed in England *(081 - 2N3)*

Haynes Publishing Group
Sparkford Nr Yeovil
Somerset BA22 7JJ England

Haynes Publications, Inc
861 Lawrence Drive
Newbury Park
California 91320 USA

British Library Cataloguing in Publication Data

Strasman, Peter G.
Renault 16 owners workshop manual.–3rd ed.
(Owners Workshop Manual)
1. Renault automobile
I. Title
629.28'722 TL215.R4
ISBN 0–85696–847–1

Acknowledgements

Thanks are due to Renault, particularly their organisation in the United Kingdom, for their assistance with technical material and certain illustrations.

Further thanks are due to several owners of the Renault 16 who have been most kind in answering our questions and advancing information unasked.

Thanks are also due to Castrol who provided lubrication information, and to the Champion Sparking Plug Company who supplied the illustrations showing the various spark plug conditions.

Felix Nicholson should not be forgotten, for without his help in sorting out the text, laying it out and generally being of assistance, this manual would not have been possible.

About this manual

Its aims

The aim of this manual is to help you to get the best value from your car. It can do so in several ways. It can help you decide what work must be done (even should you choose to get it done by a garage), provide information on routine maintenance and servicing, and give a logical course of action and diagnosis when random faults occur. However, it is hoped that you will use the manual by tackling the work youself. On simpler jobs it may even be quicker than booking the car into a garage, and going there twice to leave and collect it. Perhaps most important, a lot of money can be saved by avoiding the costs the garage must charge to cover its labour and overheads.

The manual has drawings and descriptions to show the function of the various components so that their layout can be understood. Then the tasks are described and photographed in a step-by-step sequence so that even a novice can do the work.

Its arrangement

The manual is divided into fourteen Chapters, each covering a logical sub-division of the vehicle. The Chapters are each divided into Sections, numbered with single figures, eg 5; and the sections into paragraphs (or sub-sections), with decimal numbers following on from the Section they are in, eg 5.1, 5.2, 5.3 etc.

It is freely illustrated, especially in those parts where there is a detailed sequence of operations to be carried out. There are two forms of illustration: figures and photographs. The figures are numbered in sequence with decimal numbers, according to their position in the Chapter: eg Fig 6.4 is the 4th drawing/illustration in Chapter 6. Photographs are numbered (either individually or in related groups) the same as the Section or sub-section of the text where the operation they show is described.

There is an alphabetical index at the back of the manual as well as a contents list at the front.

References to the 'left' or 'right' of the vehicle are in the sense of a person in the driver's seat facing forwards.

Unless otherwise stated, nuts and bolts are removed by turning anti-clockwise, and tightened by turning clockwise.

Vehicle manufacturers continually make changes to specifications and recommendations, and these, when notified, are incorporated into our manuals at the earliest opportunity.

Whilst every care is taken to ensure that the information in this manual is correct, no liability can be accepted by the authors or publishers for loss, damage or injury caused by any errors in, or omissions from, the information given.

Introduction to the Renault 16

In 1965 when the Renault 16 was introduced the Renault Company were producing small cars only, in anything like large quantities; the Renault 8 and Dauphine and the Renault 4. The Renault 4 was their first serious attempt at a front wheel drive car and it has proven to be very successful. Spurred on by this they designed the Renault 16 as an attack at the medium sized, medium priced saloon market. Based on the Renault 4 with gearbox in front of the engine, fwd, torsion bar suspension, 5 doors and flat chassis pan they enlarged it all, created distinctive angular styling and produced a totally new all aluminium engine. Its immediate attraction to the French market soon showed itself as only it could in France.

Because of its extreme interior comfort, silence, economy and lively performance as well as its large luggage capacity it soon created its own market in other countries. It started the vogue for the saloon/estate car - a saloon car to look at yet with the capacity of an estate car. This formula for success has been well copied by other manufacturers since 1965. Its design allows it always to behave like a lively saloon car whether it is loaded or not for the Renault policy of long suspension travel accompanied with soft but well damped suspension well manages to keep an equilibrium under most conditions.

Such is the distinctive styling of the Renault 16, it is now instantly recognisable no matter where it is, and such is the overall success of the car both as a saleable vehicle and as a very attractive and comfortable car to ride in, the manufacturers will be hard pressed to supersede it with another model significantly better.

Contents

RENAULT 16 TL

RENAULT 16 TS

Buying spare parts and vehicle identification numbers

Buying spare parts

Spare parts are available from many sources; our advice is as follows:

Officially appointed vehicle main dealers – This is the best source of parts which are peculiar to your vehicle and are otherwise not generally available (eg complete cylinder heads, internal transmission components, badges, interior trim etc). It is also the only place at which you should buy parts if your vehicle is still under warranty. To be sure of obtaining the correct parts it will always be necessary to give the storeman your vehicle's engine and chassis number, and if possible, to take the 'old' part along for positive identification. Remember that many parts are available on a factory exchange scheme – any parts returned should always be clean! It obviously makes good sense to go straight to the specialists on your vehicle for this type of part, for they are best equipped to supply you.

Other dealers and auto accessory stores – These are often very good places to buy materials and components needed for the maintenance of your vehicle (eg oil filters, sparking plugs, bulbs, fan belts, oils and greases, touch-up paint, filler paste etc). They also sell general accessories, usually have convenient opening hours, charge lower prices and can often be found not far from home.

Motor factors – Good factors will stock all of the more important components which wear out relatively quickly (eg clutch components, pistons, valves, exhaust systems, brake cylinders/pipes/hoses/seals/shoes and pads etc). Motor factors will often provide new or reconditioned components on a part exchange basis – this can save a considerable amount of money.

Vehicle identification numbers

Modifications are a continuing and unpublished process in vehicle manufacture. Spare parts manuals and lists are compiled on a numerical basis, the individual vehicle numbers being essential to identify correctly the component required.

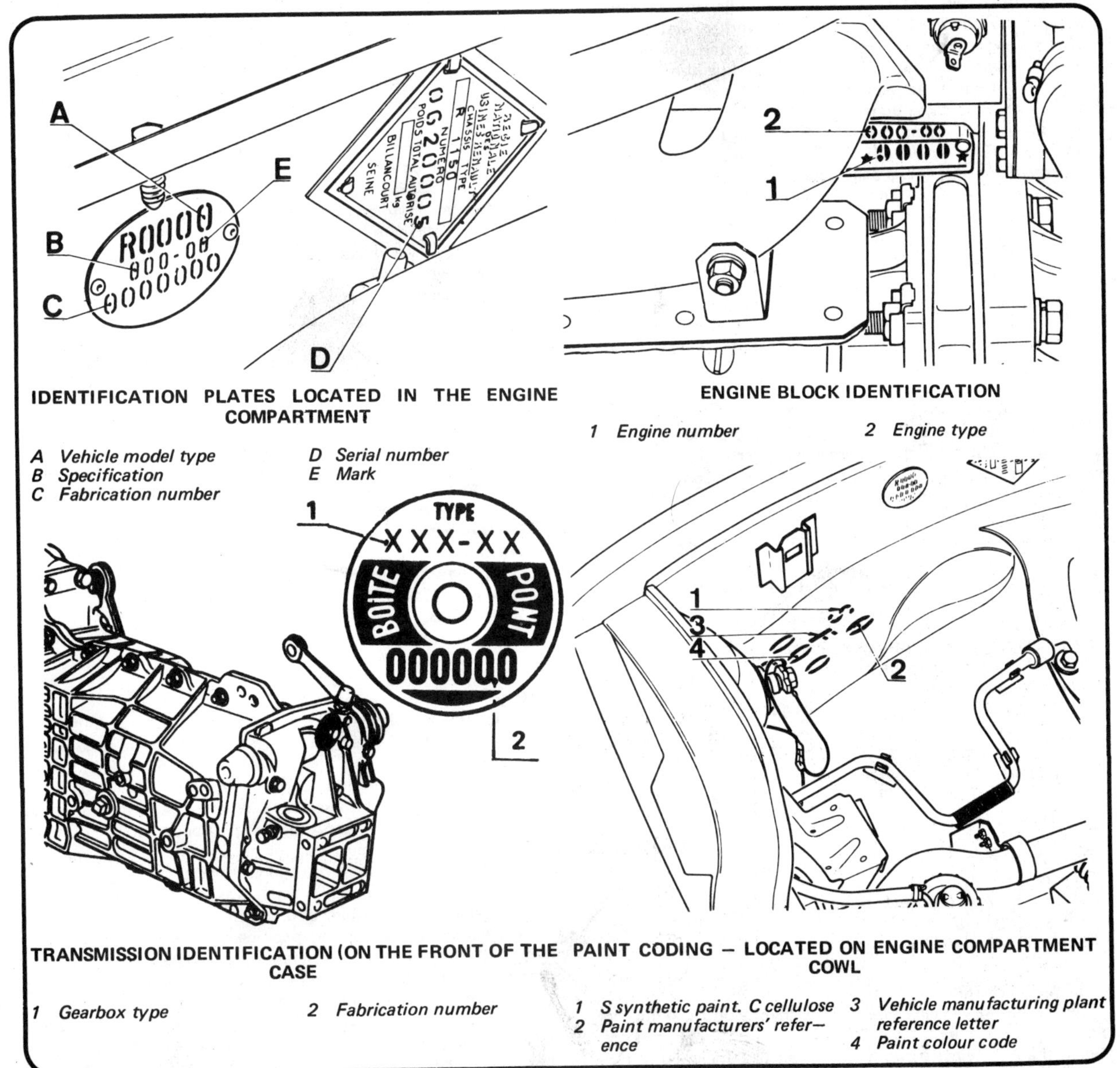

IDENTIFICATION PLATES LOCATED IN THE ENGINE COMPARTMENT

A Vehicle model type
B Specification
C Fabrication number
D Serial number
E Mark

ENGINE BLOCK IDENTIFICATION

1 Engine number *2 Engine type*

TRANSMISSION IDENTIFICATION (ON THE FRONT OF THE CASE

1 Gearbox type *2 Fabrication number*

PAINT CODING – LOCATED ON ENGINE COMPARTMENT COWL

1 S synthetic paint. C cellulose
2 Paint manufacturers' reference
3 Vehicle manufacturing plant reference letter
4 Paint colour code

Tools and working facilities

Introduction

A selection of good tools is a fundamental requirement for anyone contemplating the maintenance and repair of a motor vehicle. For the owner who does not possess any, their purchase will prove a considerable expense, offsetting some of the savings made by doing-it-yourself. However, provided that the tools purchased are of good quality, they will last for many years and prove an extremely worthwhile investment.

To help the average owner to decide which tools are needed to carry out the various tasks detailed in this manual, we have compiled three lists of tools under the following headings: *Maintenance and minor repair, Repair and overhaul,* and *Special.* The newcomer to practical mechanics should start off with the *Maintenance and minor repair* tool kit and confine himself to the simpler jobs around the vehicle. Then, as his confidence and experience grows, he can undertake more difficult tasks, buying extra tools as, and when, they are needed. In this way a *Maintenance and minor repair* tool kit can be built-up into a *Repair and overhaul* tool kit over a considerable period of time without any major cash outlays. The experienced do-it-yourselfer will have a tool kit good enough for most repair and overhaul procedures and will add tools from the *Special* category when he feels the expense is justified by the amount of use these tools will be put to.

It is obviously not possible to cover the subject of tools fully here. For those who wish to learn more about tools and their use there is a book entitled *How to Choose and Use Car Tools* available from the publishers of this manual.

Maintenance and minor repair tool kit

The tools given in this list should be considered as a minimum requirement if routine maintenance, servicing and minor repair operations are to be undertaken. We recommend the purchase of combination spanners (ring one end, open-ended the other): although more expensive than open-ended ones, they do give the advantages of both types of spanner.

Combination spanners - 10, 11, 12, 13, 14, 17 mm
Adjustable spanner - 9 inch
Engine sump/gearbox drain plug
Spark plug spanner (with rubber insert)
Spark plug gap adjustment tool
Set of feeler gauges
Brake adjuster spanner (where applicable)
Brake bleed nipple spanner
Screwdriver - 4 in long x ¼ in dia (flat blade)
Screwdriver - 4 in long x ¼ in dia (cross blade)
Combination pliers - 6 inch
Hacksaw, junior
Tyre pump
Tyre pressure gauge
Oil can
Fine emery cloth (1 sheet)
Wire brush (small)
Funnel (medium size)

Repair and overhaul tool kit

These tools are virtually essential for anyone undertaking any major repairs to a motor vehicle, and are additional to those given in the *Maintenance and minor repair* list. Included in this list is a comprehensive set of sockets. Although these are expensive they will be found invaluable as they are so versatile - particularly if various drives are included in the set. We recommend the ½ in square-drive type, as this can be used with most proprietary torque wrenches. If you cannot afford a socket set, even bought piecemeal, then inexpensive tubular box spanners are a useful alternative.

The tools in this list will occasionally need to be supplemented by tools from the *Special* list.

Sockets (or box spanners) to cover range in previous list
Reversible ratchet drive (for use with sockets)
Extension piece, 10 inch (for use with sockets)
Universal joint (for use with sockets)
Torque wrench (for use with sockets)
'Mole' wrench - 8 inch
Ball pein hammer
Soft-faced hammer, plastic or rubber
Screwdriver - 6 in long x 5/16 in dia (flat blade)
Screwdriver - 2 in long x 5/16 in square (flat blade)
Screwdriver - 1½ in long x ¼ in dia (cross blade)
Screwdriver - 3 in long x 1/8 in dia (electricians)
Pliers - electricians side cutters
Pliers - needle nosed
Pliers - circlip (internal and external)
Cold chisel - ½ inch
Scriber
Scraper
Centre punch
Pin punch
Hacksaw
Valve grinding tool
Steel rule/straight edge
Allen keys
Selection of files
Wire brush (large)
Axle-stands
Jack (strong scissor or hydraulic type)

Special tools

The tools in this list are those which are not used regularly, are expensive to buy, or which need to be used in accordance with their manufacturers' instructions. Unless relatively difficult mechanical jobs are undertaken frequently, it will not be economic to buy many of these tools. Where this is the case, you could consider clubbing together with friends (or a motorists' club) to make a joint purchase, or borrowing the tools against a deposit from a local garage or tool hire specialist.

The following list contains only those tools and instruments freely available to the public, and not those special tools produced by the vehicle manufacturer specifically for its dealer network. You will find occasional references to these manufacturers' special tools in the text of this manual. Generally, an alternative method of doing the job without the vehicle manufacturers' special tool is given. However, sometimes, there is no alternative to using them. Where this is the case and the relevant tool cannot be bought or borrowed, you will have to entrust the work to a franchised garage.

Valve spring compressor
Piston ring compressor
Balljoint separator
Universal hub/bearing puller
Impact screwdriver
Micrometer and/or vernier gauge
Carburettor flow balancing device (where applicable)
Dial gauge
Stroboscopic timing light
Dwell angle meter/tachometer
Universal electrical multi-meter
Cylinder compression gauge
Lifting tackle
Trolley jack
Light with extension lead

Buying tools

For practically all tools, a tool factor is the best source since he will have a very comprehensive range compared with the average garage or accessory shop. Having said that, accessory shops often offer excellent quality tools at discount prices, so it pays to shop around.

Remember, you don't always have to buy the most expensive items on the shelf, but it is always advisable to steer clear of the very cheap tools. There are plenty of good tools around at reasonable prices, so ask the proprietor or manager of the shop for advice before making a purchase.

Care and maintenance of tools

Having purchased a reasonable tool kit, it is necessary to keep the tools in a clean serviceable condition. After use, always wipe off any dirt, grease and metal particles using a clean, dry cloth, before putting the tools away. Never leave them lying around after they have been used. A simple tool rack on the garage or workshop wall, for items such as screwdrivers and pliers is a good idea. Store all normal spanners and sockets in a metal box. Any measuring instruments, gauges, meters, etc., must be carefully stored where they cannot be damaged or become rusty.

Take a little care when tools are used. Hammer heads inevitably become marked and screwdrivers lose the keen edge on their blades from time-to-time. A little timely attention with emery cloth or a file will soon restore items like this to a good serviceable finish.

Working facilities

Not to be forgotten when discussing tools, is the workshop itself. If anything more than routine is to be carried out, some form of suitable working area becomes essential.

It is appreciated that many an owner mechanic is forced by circumstances to remove an engine or similar item, without the benefit of a garage or workshop. Having done this, any repairs should always be done under the cover of a roof.

Wherever possible, any dismantling should be done on a clean flat workbench or table at a suitable working height.

Any workbench needs a vice: one with a jaw opening of 4 in (100 mm) is suitable for most jobs. As mentioned previously, some clean dry storage space is also required for tools, as well as lubricants, cleaning fluids, touch-up paint and so on which become necessary.

Another item which may be required, and which has a much more general usage, is an electric drill with a chuck capacity of at least 5/16 in (8 mm). This, together with a good range of twist drills, is virtually essential for fitting accessories such as mirrors and reversing lights.

Last, but not least, always keep a supply of old newspapers and clean, lint-free rags available, and try to keep any working area as clean as possible.

Spanner jaw gap comparison table

Jaw gap (in)	Spanner size
0.250	$\frac{1}{4}$ in AF
0.276	7 mm
0.313	$\frac{5}{16}$ in AF
0.315	8 mm
0.344	$\frac{11}{32}$ in AF; $\frac{1}{8}$ in Whitworth
0.354	9 mm
0.375	$\frac{3}{8}$ in AF
0.394	10 mm
0.433	11 mm
0.438	$\frac{7}{16}$ in AF
0.445	$\frac{3}{16}$ in Whitworth; $\frac{1}{4}$ in BSF
0.472	12 mm
0.500	$\frac{1}{2}$ in AF
0.512	13 mm
0.525	$\frac{1}{4}$ in Whitworth; $\frac{5}{16}$ in BSF
0.551	14 mm
0.563	$\frac{9}{16}$ in AF
0.591	15 mm
0.600	$\frac{5}{16}$ in Whitworth; $\frac{3}{8}$ in BSF
0.625	$\frac{5}{8}$ in AF
0.630	16 mm
0.669	17 mm
0.686	$\frac{11}{16}$ in AF
0.709	18 mm
0.710	$\frac{3}{8}$ in Whitworth; $\frac{7}{16}$ in BSF
0.748	19 mm
0.750	$\frac{3}{4}$ in AF
0.813	$\frac{13}{16}$ in AF
0.820	$\frac{7}{16}$ in Whitworth; $\frac{1}{2}$ in BSF
0.866	22 mm
0.875	$\frac{7}{8}$ in AF
0.920	$\frac{1}{2}$ in Whitworth; $\frac{9}{16}$ in BSF
0.938	$\frac{15}{16}$ in AF
0.945	24 mm
1.000	1 in AF
1.010	$\frac{9}{16}$ in Whitworth; $\frac{5}{8}$ in BSF
1.024	26 mm
1.063	$1\frac{1}{16}$ in AF; 27 mm
1.100	$\frac{5}{8}$ in Whitworth; $\frac{11}{16}$ in BSF
1.125	$1\frac{1}{8}$ in AF
1.181	30 mm
1.200	$\frac{11}{16}$ in Whitworth; $\frac{3}{4}$ in BSF
1.250	$1\frac{1}{4}$ in AF
1.260	32 mm
1.300	$\frac{3}{4}$ in Whitworth; $\frac{7}{8}$ in BSF
1.313	$1\frac{5}{16}$ in AF
1.390	$\frac{13}{16}$ in Whitworth; $\frac{15}{16}$ in BSF
1.417	36 mm
1.438	$1\frac{7}{16}$ in AF
1.480	$\frac{7}{8}$ in Whitworth; 1 in BSF
1.500	$1\frac{1}{2}$ in AF
1.575	40 mm; $\frac{15}{16}$ in Whitworth
1.614	41 mm
1.625	$1\frac{5}{8}$ in AF
1.670	1 in Whitworth; $1\frac{1}{8}$ in BSF
1.688	$1\frac{11}{16}$ in AF
1.811	46 mm
1.813	$1\frac{13}{16}$ in AF
1.860	$1\frac{1}{8}$ in Whitworth; $1\frac{1}{4}$ in BSF
1.875	$1\frac{7}{8}$ in AF
1.969	50 mm
2.000	2 in AF
2.050	$1\frac{1}{4}$ in Whitworth; $1\frac{3}{8}$ in BSF
2.165	55 mm
2.362	60 mm

Routine maintenance

Maintenance is essential to ensure safety and it is desirable for the preservation of the appearance and retention of the value of the vehicle. Although oiling and greasing have now become unnecessary due to the development of sealed and grease packed components, the need for routine cleaning and inspection is still essential to minimise rust, corrosion and mechanical wear.

The summary below gives a schedule of routine maintenance operations. The items in **bold type** affect the owner's **safety** and are vital, the other operations are designed to combat depreciation.

250 miles (400 km) or weekly, whichever occurs first

STEERING

Check tyre pressures
Examine tyres for wear

BRAKES

Try an emergency stop
Check the handbrake on a steep incline

LIGHTS AND ELECTRICAL COMPONENTS

Check the correct operation of all lights
Check the operation of the flasher units
Check the operation of the brake stop lamp
Check the operation of the windscreen wiper and washer
Check the operation and efficiency of the horn

Cooling system expansion bottle, maximum and minimum levels

ENGINE COMPARTMENT
Check the oil level in the sump
Check the coolant level in the expansion bottle
Check the windscreen washer bottle level
Check the battery electrolyte level

1000 miles (1600 km) or monthly whichever occurs first

Check for free play in the steering
Check the brake hydraulic fluid level in the reservoir

3000 miles (5000 km) or six monthly, whichever occurs first

STEERING
Check all steering linkages and balljoints for signs of damage or wear
Examine the steering rack for signs of oil leakage

BRAKES
Examine front disc pads for wear and renew if necessary
Adjust rear brakes or renew shoes if adjustment near limit
Check rigid hydraulic pipes for corrosion and renew
Check flexible hydraulic hoses for perishing or rubbing marks and renew if necessary
Probe vent hole in fluid reservoir cap
Check security of rubber hoses to servo unit (if fitted)

SUSPENSION
Check security of suspension component securing nuts and bolts
Check telescopic damper mountings.
Check dampers for fluid leakage, if evident, renew.

FRONT DRIVE SHAFTS
Check rotational play not excessive
Check for play in drive shaft joints
Check for oil leakage from differential housing around drive shafts. Renew seals if oil leaks evident

ENGINE
Drain sump and refill with correct grade of oil
Check ignition timing
Check valve clearances
Check spark plug gaps, renew if necessary
Check distributor points gap, renew points if burned
Check alternator and water pump drive belt tensions and adjust if required. Check for belt deterioration

CLUTCH
Check for correct free movement

GEARBOX (manual)
Check oil level

GEARBOX (automatic)
Check oil level as described in Chapter 7

9 000 miles (15 000 km) or annually (additional to 3 000 mile (5 000 km) check list

BODYWORK
Examine the underbody for rust and corrosion, repair damaged undersealing
Oil locks and hinges

FUEL SYSTEM
Clean fuel pump filter and sediment bowl
Clean carburettor bowl of sediment
Renew air filter element.

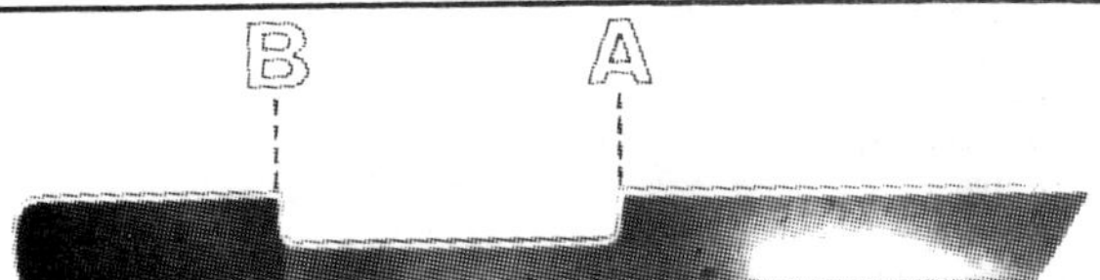

Engine oil dipstick. A maximum. B minimum. Never allow level to fall below B

Battery filler plugs and windscreen washer bottle

Hydraulic brake fluid resevoir

Air filter (early type). A securing wing nut. B cover. C element. D body

Air filter (later type). E air pre-heater. F flap lever. 1 summer position. 2 winter position.

BATTERY

Clean terminals and smear with petroleum jelly

Remove earth strap connections to body, scrape locations and retighten

Examine battery case for signs of leakage, if evident repair or renew

ELECTRICAL SYSTEM

Check alignment of headlamps

Fit new windscreen wiper blades

COOLING SYSTEM

Check all rubber hoses for deterioration and renew if necessary

Check strength of coolant anti-freeze mixture

GEARBOX/TRANSMISSION UNIT

Drain and refill with correct grade of oil

EXHAUST SYSTEM

Check for leaks and renew sections as required

HUBS

Fill with heavy wheel bearing grease

General servicing notes

All nuts and bolts are metric and a set of suitable spanners and sockets is essential for all servicing and overhaul operations. Screws used for certain detachable components may be POZIDRIV type or TACL type. Screwdrivers for the former are readily available but for the latter, a special screwdriver will be required, obtainable from a Renault dealer. The TACL type screw incorporates a nylon washer for sealing and non-scratch purposes.

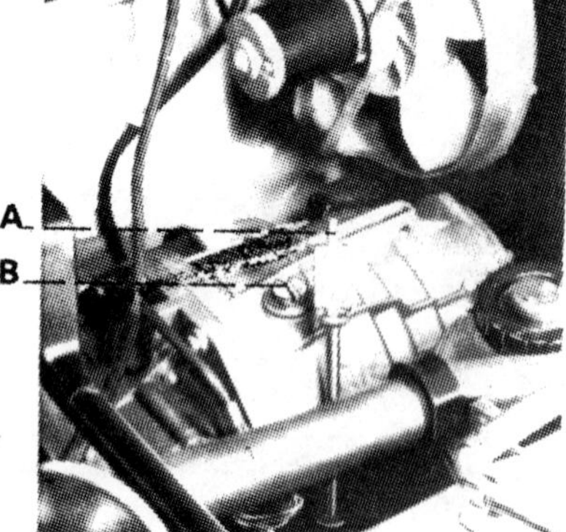

Automatic gearbox drain plugs C and D. A dipstick. B filler

Dipstick	1 minimum mark 2 maximum mark	engine COLD
	2 minimum mark 3 maximum mark	engine HOT

Static ignition timing marks

Checking the distributor contact breaker points gap. A adjustment tab. B locking screw. C points gap.

Bearing cap removed from hub. Half fill with grease

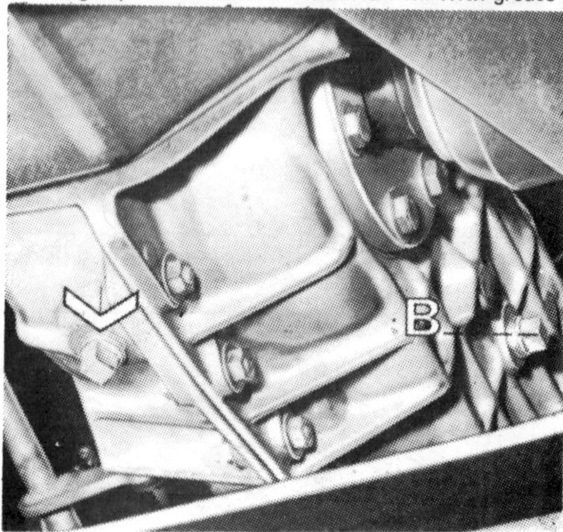

Manual gearbox drain plug and combined filler/level plug B.

Chapter 1 Engine

For modifications, and information applicable to later models, see Supplement at end of manual

Contents

Specifications

Vehicle type	**R.1150 (16)**		**R.1151 (16TS - manual)** **R.1154 (16TS - automatic)**		**R.1152 (16L and TL - manual)** **R.1153 (16TL - automatic)**	
Engine type (HC)	697 - 01		807 - 01		821 - 02	
(LC)	697 - 02		807 - 02			
	R.1153					
Engine type (HC)	821 - 01					
ENGINE						
Type	697 - 01	697 - 02	807 - 01	807 - 02	821 - 01	821 - 02
No. of cylinders	4		4		4	
Valve positions	in - line		in - line		in - line	
BHP at 5000 rev/min	63	60			71	
at 5200 rev/min						70
at 5750 rev/min			87.5	81.5		
Max. torque at 2800 rev/min	81	76				
(lb/ft) at 3000 rev/min			90	88	87	85
Compression ratio	8.6	7.6	8.6	7.6	8.6	8.6

Bore: in	2.992	3.032	3.032	
mm	76	77	77	
Stroke: in	3.189	3.307	3.307	
mm	81	84	84	
Firing order	1 3 4 2	1 3 4 2	1 3 4 2	
Cubic capacity cc...	1470	1565	1565	
Static ignition advance (degress)	0 ± 1	0 ± 1	0 ± 1	0 ± 1
Idling speed rev/min	600 - 700	650	600 in 'A'	675

	607	807	821
Cylinder head depth			
Standard in	3.175	3.681	3.207
mm	80.65	93.50	81.45
Minimum after planning			
in	3.163	3.670	3.195
mm	80.35	93.20	81.15
Liner bottom dia. in	3.228	3.248	3.248
mm	82	82.5	82.5
Liner bore in	2.992	3.032	3.032
mm	76	77	77
Liner projection after correct base seal fitted			
in	0.006 - 0.0081	0.006 - 0.008	0.006 - 0.008
mm	0.15 - 0.20	0.15 - 0.20	0.15 - 0.20

Liner seal	Base diameter 3.228 in (82mm)	3.248 in (82.5mm)
Thickness		
Blue spot in	0.08	0.08
mm	0.003	0.003
Red spot in	0.10	0.10
mm	0.004	0.004
Green spot in	0.12	0.12
mm	0.0047	0.0047

Crankshaft

No. of main bearings	5
Main bearing shells	807/821 aluminium-tin 697 white metal
End plug	0.002 to 0.009 in (0.05 to 0.23 mm)
Thrust washer availability	0.110 in (2.80 mm) 0.114 in (2.90 mm) 0.116 in (2.95 mm)
Main bearing journal diameter	2.158 in (54.8 mm)
Regrind diameter for oversize shell bearings.	
Roll hardened crankshaft	(807 and 821 types) 2.148 in (54.55 mm) (697 type) 2.138 in (54.30 mm)
Regrind tolerances	(807 and 821 types) 0.0005/0.00004 in (0.013/0.001 mm) (697 type) 0.0005/0.00012 in (0.013/0.003 mm)
Crankpin diameter	1.890 in (48 mm)
Regrind diameter for oversize shell bearings	
Roll hardened crankshaft	(807 and 821 types) 1.880 in (47.75 mm) (697 type) 1.870 in (47.50 mm)
Regrind tolerances	(all types) 0.0007/0.0001 in (0.018/0.002 mm)

Connecting rods

Bearing shells	(807 and 821 types) aluminium/tin (697 type) white metal

Pistons

Type	Alloy
Gudgeon pin length	(697 type) 2 5/8 in (67 mm) (807 and 821 types) 2 11/16 in (68 mm)
Gudgeon pin diameter	0.787 in (20 mm)
Fitting method	Press fit in small end, floating in piston

Piston Rings

Number	3 (two compression, one oil control)

Valves

Head diameter (inlet)	697 and 821 types 1.378 in (35 mm) 807 type 1.575 in (40 mm)
(exhaust)	697 and 821 types 1.220 in (31 mm) 807 type 1.392 in (35.35 mm)

Stem diameter (all engine types) inlet		
inlet and exhaust	0.315 in (8.00 mm)	
Seat widths		
inlet	(type 697 and 821)	0.051/0.063 in (1.3/1.6 mm)
	(type 807)	0.059/0.071 in (1.5/1.8 mm)
exhaust	(all types)	0.067/0.079 in (1.7/2 mm)
Valve guide internal diameter	0.315 in (8 mm)	
External diameter, standard	0.512 in (13 mm)	
Oversize (identified by one groove)	0.516 in (13.10 mm)	
Oversize (identified by two grooves)	0.522 in (13.25 mm)	

Valve timing	697 and 821 types	807 type
Inlet valve opens	10° BTDC	21° BTDC
Inlet valve closes	42° ABDC	59° ABDC
Exhaust valve opens	46° BBDC	59° BBDC
Exhaust valve closes	10° ATDC	21° ATDC

Minimum valve lift		
Inlet	(697 and 821 types)	0.319 in (8.11 mm)
Exhaust		0.295 in (7.50 mm)
Inlet	(type 807)	0.342 in (8.69 mm)
Exhaust		0.342 in (8.69 mm)

Valve springs		
Type		
Single	(697 type)	
Double	(807 and 821 type)	
Free length	(697 type)	1 29/32 in (48.4 mm)
External	(807 type)	1 29/32 in (48.4 mm)
Internal		1 33/64 in (38.4 mm)
External	(807 type, early)	2 9/64 in (54.3 mm)
Internal		1 3/4 in (44.7 mm)
External	(807 type, later)	2 9/64 in (54.3 mm)
Internal		1 27/32 in (46.8 mm)

Camshaft		
Number of bearings	4	
End-float	0.002 to 0.0045 in (0.05 to 0.12 mm)	
Flange clearance	0.002 to 0.0047 in (0.05 to 0.12 mm)	

Valve clearances		
Inlet	0.008 in (0.20 mm)	
Exhaust	0.010 in (0.25 mm)	
Tappet diameter, standard	0.472 in (12 mm)	
oversize	0.480 in (12.20 mm)	
Push rod length	(697 and 821 types)	3 15/32 in (88 mm)
Inlet	(807 type)	7 in (178 mm)
Exhaust		4 11/32 in (110 mm)
Pushrod diameter	(all types)	0.236 in (6 mm)
Oil capacity (engine)	7 pts (4 litres) (8½ US pints)	
Oil pressure at 650 rev/min	30 - 35 lb/in2	

TORQUE WRENCH SETTINGS	lbf ft	kgf m
Cylinder head (Stage 1 & 2) COLD		
697 and 821 types	50 - 55	6.9 – 7.6
807 type	55 - 60	7.6 – 8.3
Stage 3 (50 minutes after cooling from operating temp.)		
697 and 821 types	55 - 60	7.6 – 8.3
807 type	60 - 65	8.3 – 9.0
Rocker arm pillar nuts and bolts	15 - 20	2.1 – 2.8
Crankshaft main bearing cap bolts	45	6.2
Connecting rod bearing cap bolts	30	4.1
Crankshaft sprocket bolt	45 - 58	6.2 – 8.0
Crankcase oilway screwed plugs: 8 mm	60	8.3
4.5 mm	30	4.1
Flywheel securing bolts	40	5.5
Manifold securing bolts and nuts: (697 and 821 types)	10 - 20	1.4 – 2.8
(807 type) inlet	20 - 25	2.8 – 3.4
exhaust	15 - 25	2.1 – 3.4

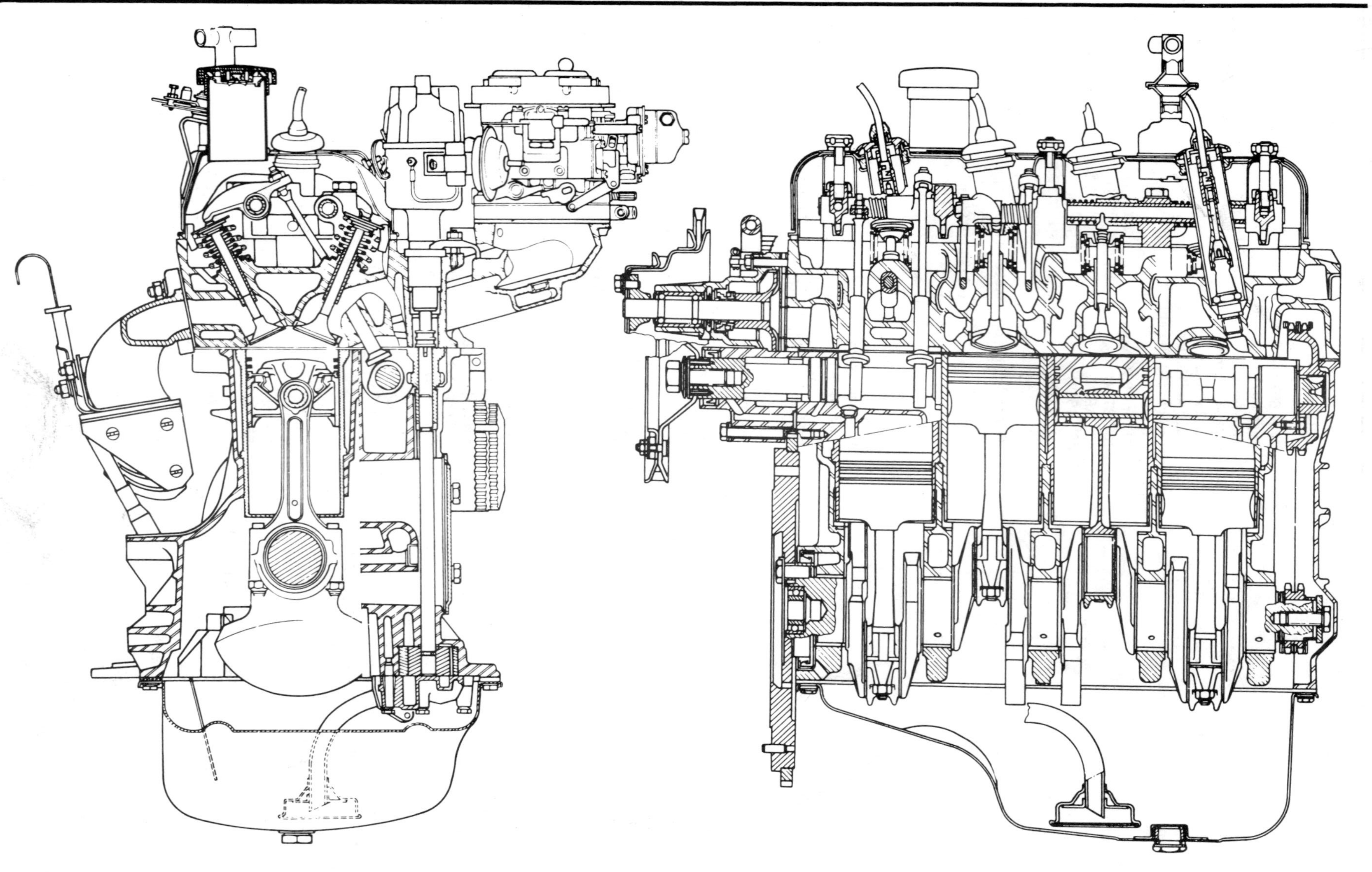

Fig.1.1 Sectional views of the type 807 engine

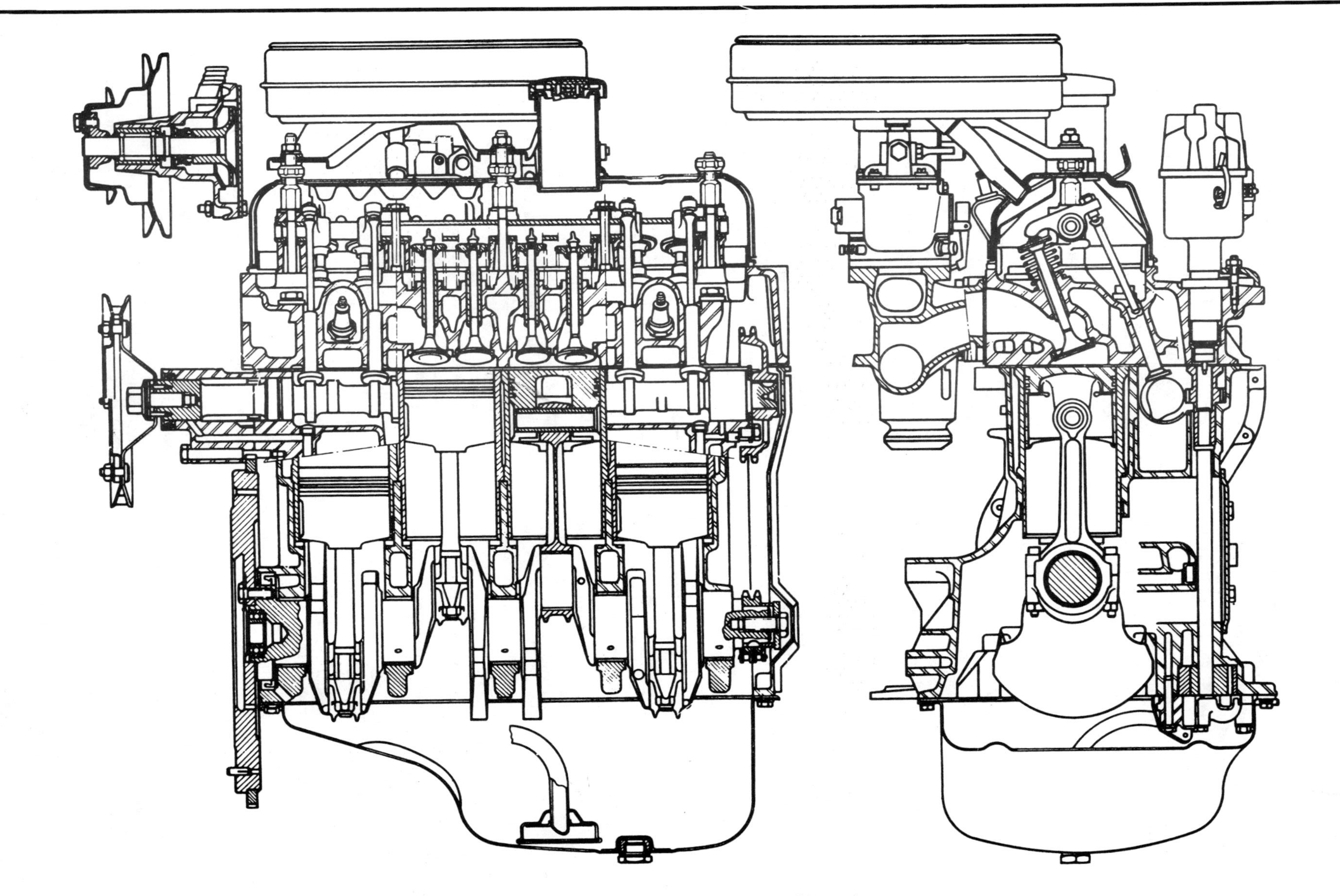

Fig.1.2 Sectional views of the types 697 and 821 engines

1 General description

1 The engines fitted to the four models covered by this manual are basically similar in design but vary in detail. Reference should be made to Specifications before proceeding with this chapter in order to establish the exact type of engine fitted to a particular model vehicle.
2 The type 697 engine is supplied in low or high compression form as is also the type 807. The type 821 engine is high compression only.
3 All types of engine are four cylinder, in-line units mounted at the front of the vehicle. The gearbox is located ahead of the engine unit and is integral with the final drive unit which connects through drive shafts to the front road wheels.
4 From the foregoing description it will be apparent that the flywheel and clutch are located at the forward end of the engine block and the timing gear at the rear.
5 Cooling is by a conventionally front mounted radiator and water circulation system.
6 Major castings are of light alloy and the cylinder block is fitted with wet liners.
7 A five bearing crankshaft is used and the bearings themselves are of renewable shell type.
8 Overhead valves are fitted to all engines and are operated by pushrods and tappets from the camshaft. Except for the type 807 engine which has valves mounted in vee formation, all valves are mounted in-line.
9 The camshaft also operates the fuel pump by means of an eccentric and the distributor and oil pump through geared drive.
10 A full set of metric spanners and sockets is required for servicing the engine and in view of the possibility of stripping threads in the alloy castings, the torque tightening figures given in Specifications must be strictly adhered to.
11 Sectional views of the type 807 and 697/821 engines are shown in Figs.1.1 and 1.2.

2 Major operations with engine in position in vehicle

1 Where major overhaul or servicing is required it will be wise to remove the complete engine/gearbox-transmission unit and obtain the ease of access provided by mounting the unit on a bench. However, the following operations may be carried out with the engines still in place in the vehicle.
2 Removal of the cylinder head. Attention to valves, rocker gear and pushrods.
3 Removal of the sump, permitting attention to the cylinder liners, pistons, piston rings, connecting rods and big-ends and oil pump.
4 Removal of the engine ancillaries including the distributor and starter motor.

3 Major operations with the engine/gearbox removed

1 Due to the front mounted location of the gearbox, overhaul or servicing of the following components can only be undertaken after removal of the gearbox* or engine/gearbox-transmission combined assembly and the gearbox/transmission unit separated from the engine.
2 Timing gear, chain and cover.
3 Camshaft and tappets (cam followers).
4 Crankshaft main bearings.
5 Crankshaft.
6 Flywheel*
7 Clutch assembly*

These components may be serviced after gearbox removal leaving the engine in position.

4 Method of engine removal

1 As previously explained, although the front mounted gearbox-transmission unit may be removed (Chapter 6) leaving the engine in position in the vehicle, the engine can only be withdrawn complete with the gearbox-transmission unit and this combined assembly will obviously be very heavy and necessitate the use of a hoist and the help of an assistant.
2 Where the car has seen considerable service and the engine compartment is very dirty then an application of grease solvent such as 'Gunk' prior to removal will be worthwhile.
3 Obtain a trolley type jack and assemble to hand all necessary spanners, freeing fluid and rags. Place clean containers of adequate capacity ready to receive the coolant and oils which will require draining.

5 Engine/gearbox-transmission unit - removal

1 Raise the bonnet and remove the check strap (photo).
2 Prop the bonnet lid open as far as it will go using a piece of wood or alternatively disconnect the fingers and remove the lid completely (photo).
3 Detach the spring from the spare wheel clip (photo).
4 Remove the spare wheel.
5 Disconnect the HT and LT leads from the coil noting the location of the LT lead tags for exact replacement (photo). On some models, the coil is mounted on the spare wheel carrier.
6 Remove the spare wheel carrier securing bolts and withdraw the carrier (photos).
7 Disconnect the battery earth (negative) lead (photo).
8 Drain the cooling system as described in Chapter 2, retaining the coolant if required for further use.
9 Drain the oil from the engine/gearbox unit (photo).
10 Remove the radiator as described in Chapter 2, ensuring the leads to the fan motor and temperature transmitter unit are first disconnected (photo). The hose clips are not suitable for re-use and the opportunity should be taken to renew them with worm-drive types.
11 Remove the air cleaner and disconnect the controls from the carburettor (photo). With 1150/697 and 1152/821 engined models, up to 1968, disconnect the accelerator return spring, the accelerator linkage and swivel lever and detach the cable from the cylinder head clip, Fig.1.3. On models produced after 1968, remove the accelerator return spring, cable and cable locknut connection on the rocker box cover.
12 Disconnect the fuel line from the inlet pipe of the fuel pump and the return pipe to the fuel tank (photo). Plug the pipes to prevent fuel loss.
13 Mark the electrical leads to the alternator for correct replacement and detach them, Fig.1.4.
14 Remove the bolt from the adjustment strap to alternator connection and loosen the mounting bolts (photo).
15 Push the alternator in towards the engine so that the alternator drive belt may be removed (photo).
16 Remove the alternator mounting bolts and withdraw the unit (photo).
17 Where applicable, disconnect the earth link strap which is fitted between the transmission case and the body frame (photo).
18 If the Renault lifting tool is to be used, disconnect the cylinder block earth screw (photo).
19 Disconnect the lead to the oil pressure transmitter unit (photo).
20 Disconnect the leads from the starter motor (photo). Where access to the terminals is difficult, it will be preferable to wait until the engine has been lifted out from its mountings by about 8 inches (203.2 mm) before disconnecting the leads.
21 If the Renault lifting tool is to be used, unscrew and remove the starter motor upper securing bolt.
22 Where fitted, disconnect the leads to the reverse lamp switch (photo).
23 Disconnect the heater hoses from their connections with the water pump and cylinder head, Fig.1.5 (photo).
24 If the carburettor is to be removed, disconnect the two water hoses.
25 Disconnect the engine breather hoses.
26 Where applicable, disconnect the vacuum hose from the inlet manifold (photo).
27 With 1151/807 engined models, remove the flame trap capsule and pipe.

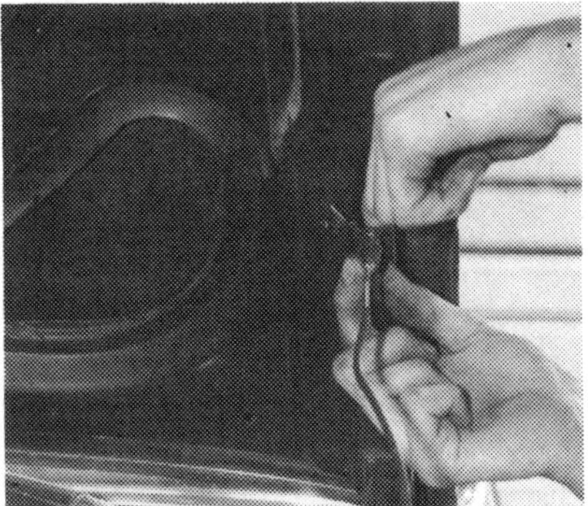
5.1 Removing bonnet check strap

5.2 Propping the bonnet lid

5.3 Spare wheel carrier clip spring

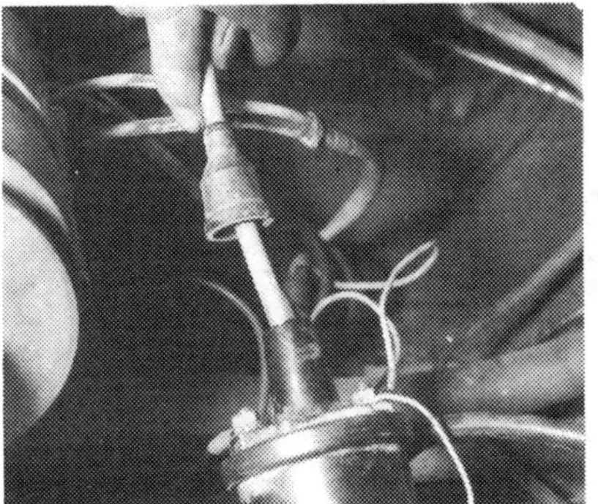
5.5A Removal of HT leads

5.5B Removal of LT leads

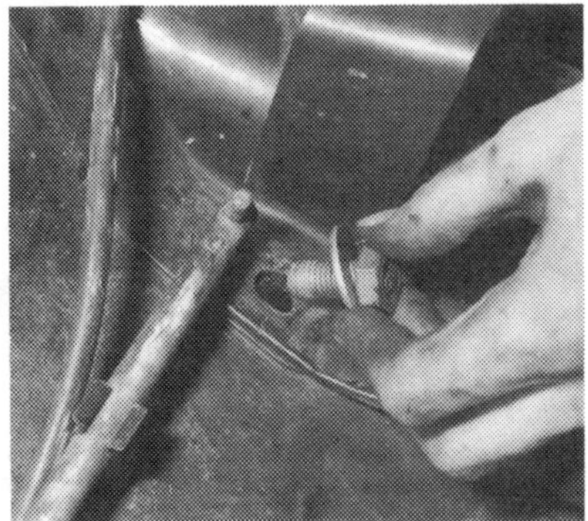
5.6A Removing the spare wheel carrier bolt

5.6B Removing the spare wheel

5.7 Disconnecting battery earth (negative) lead

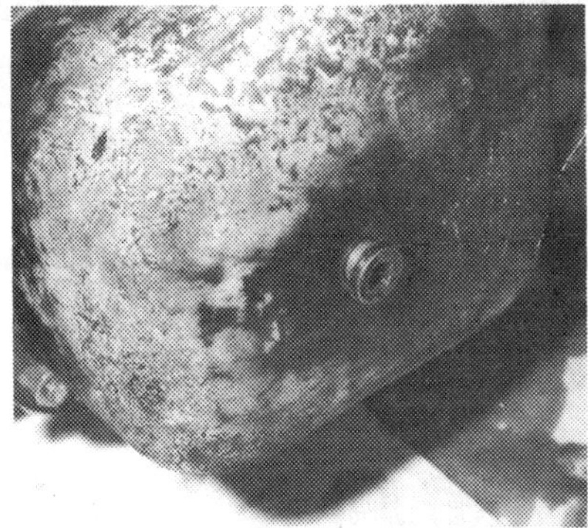
5.9 Sump drain plug

5.10 Water temperature transmitter lead

5.11 Air cleaner removal

5.12 Removing the fuel lines from the fuel pump

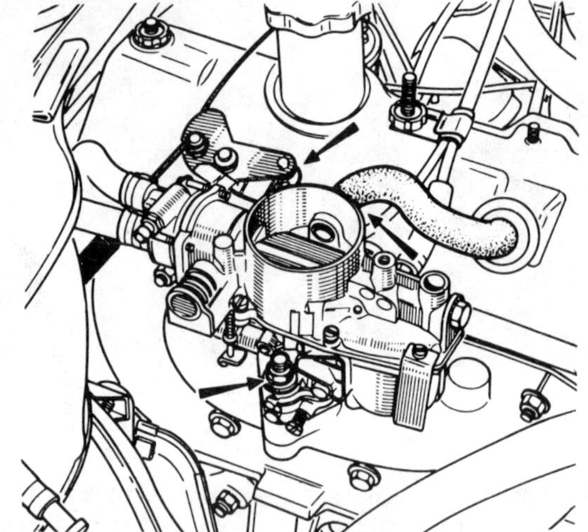

Fig.1.3. The accelerator cable and swivel linkage

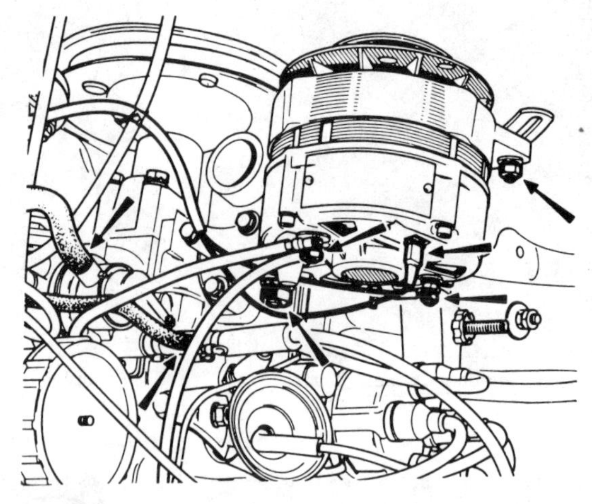

Fig.1.4 Alternator leads and adjustment strap bolt

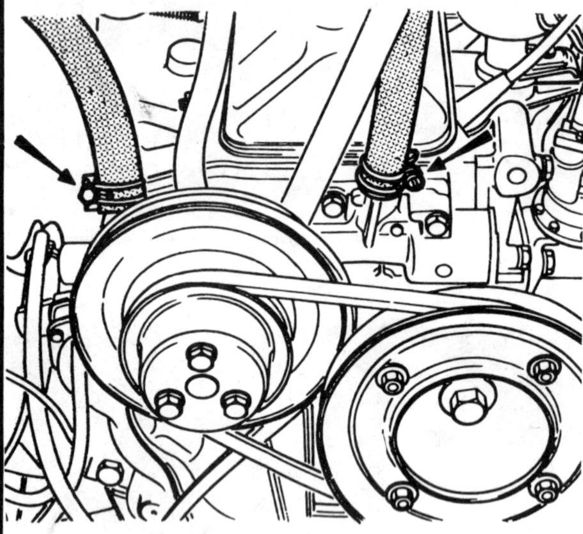

Fig.1.5 Heater hose connections

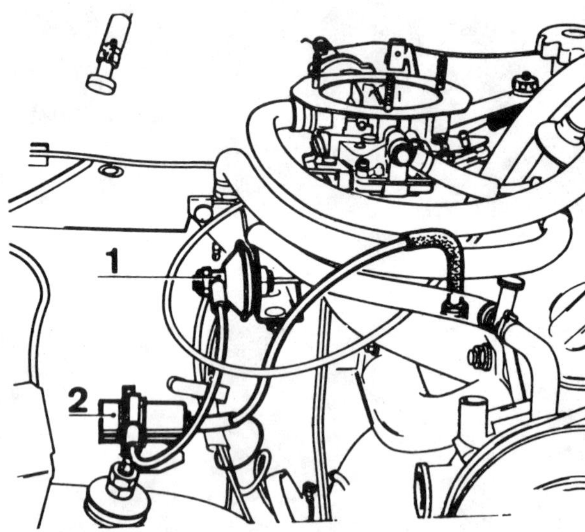

FIG.1.6 COMPONENTS OF THE ANTI-POLLUTION DEVICE FITTED TO MODEL 1152 FOR THE USA

1 Capsule *2 Solenoid flap valve*

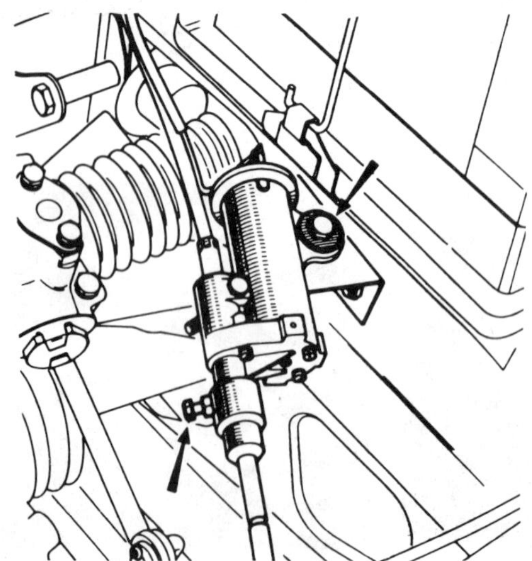

Fig.1.7 Speedometer cable driven centrifugal switch, part of the anti-pollution device

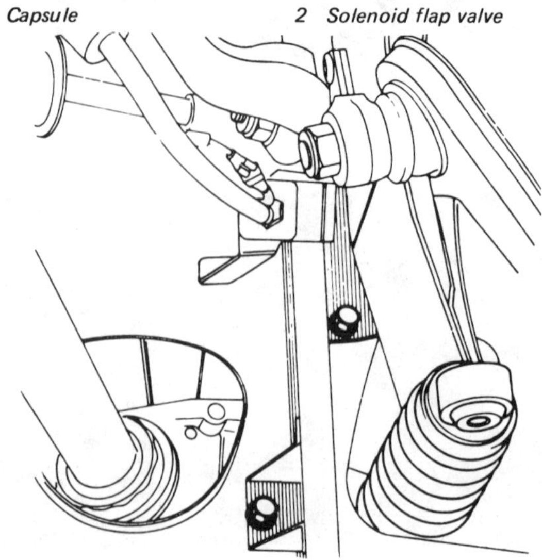

Fig.1.8 Two of the four steering crossmember securing bolts

5.14 Loosening the alternator adjustment strap bolt

5.15 Removing the alternator driving belt

5.16 Removing the alternator mounting bolt

5.17 Disconnecting an earthing strap

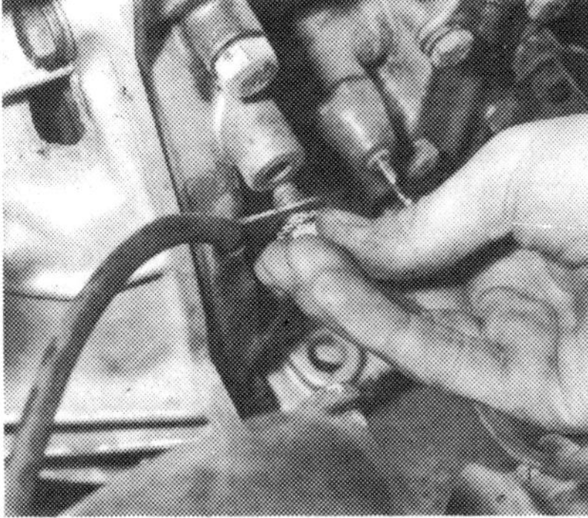
5.18 Unscrewing the cylinder block earth screw

5.19 Detaching the oil pressure transmitter lead.

5.20 The starter motor leads

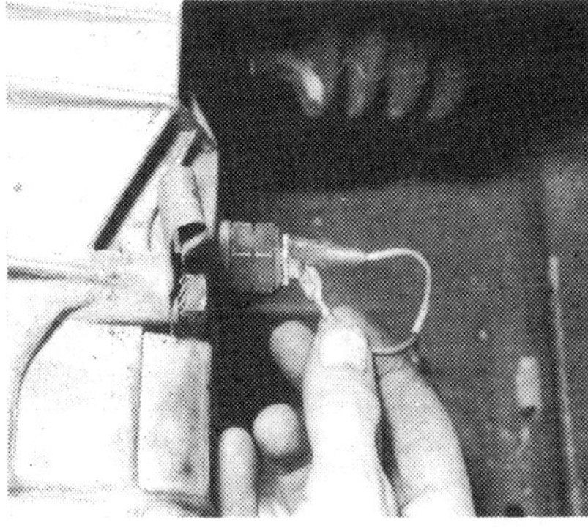
5.22 The reversing lamp switch and leads

5.23A Heater hose connection to water pump

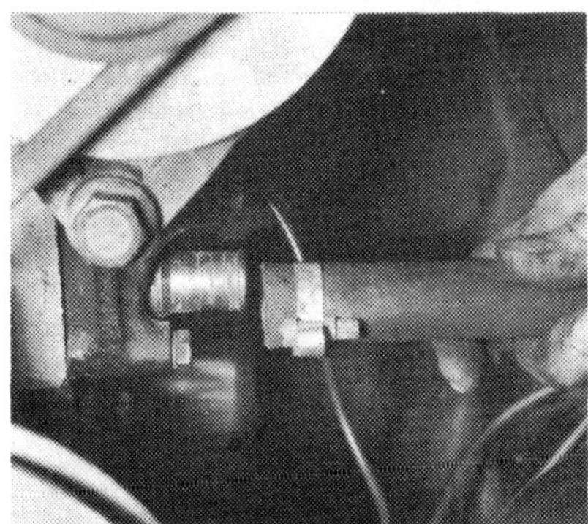
5.23B Heater hose connection to cylinder block

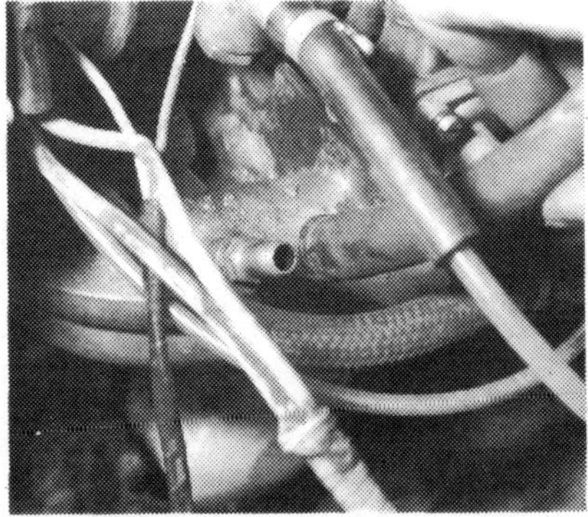
5.26 Vacuum hose connection to inlet manifold

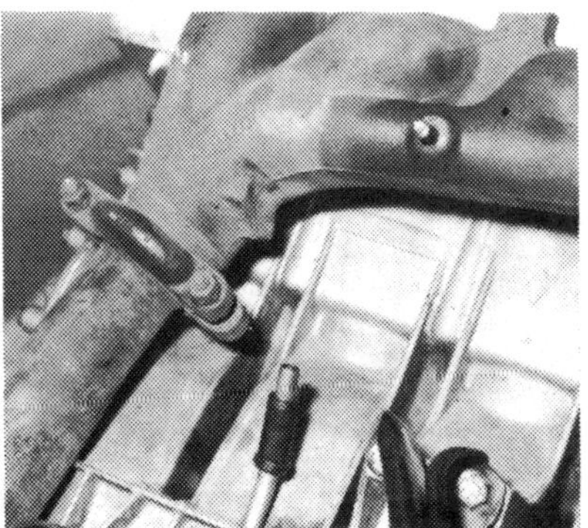
5.29A Exhaust manifold to downpipe clamp

28 Model 1152 models (North American Market) are fitted with anti-pollution devices. Pull the pipe from the capsule (1) Fig.1.6 and the vacuum pipe from the solenoid flap valve (2). A full description of this system is given in Chapter 3, Section 26.
29 Disconnect the manifold to exhaust pipe clamp and remove the bottom retaining bolt (photos). Alternatively, disconnect the downpipe from the exhaust pipe. Remove the manifold heat shield.

30 Refer to Fig.1.7 and release the locknut and bolt which secure the speedometer drive cable in the switch (1152 only models). Remove the switch securing bolt and swing the switch unit aside. On other models release the cable directly from the gearbox in similar manner (photos).
31 The steering rack unit must now be removed as it is located above the gearbox-transmission unit. Loosen the road wheel nuts, jack up the front of the car securely and remove the road wheels. Remove the two steering arm to rack eye bolts (photo). This is achieved by first moving the steering to full lock and removing the bolt which is accessible, then turn to full opposite lock and withdraw the second bolt.
32 Refer to Fig.1.8 and unscrew and remove the four bolts (two only shown one side) which secure the steering unit supporting crossmember to the engine compartment sides. The bolt heads are accessible from below the wheel arches (photo).
33 Unscrew and remove the two nuts and bolts which secure the steering column upper section to the flexible coupling (photo). Remove the steering gear assembly from its location by using a twisting action to the pinion end as arrowed in Fig.1.9. Prior to removal of the steering rack, the lower section of the steering column should be rotated until the steering rack eyes are sufficiently retracted to permit withdrawal of the pinion end of the gear. The pinion end of the steering rack will be either left or right when viewed from the front of the car to provide right or left hand steering respectively.
34 Refer to Fig.1.10 and disconnect the link arm on the gear-change lever (photo).
35 Remove the two bolts which retain the gearchange lever to the gearbox and move the lever to one side, hooking it to the battery tray. Remove the linkage pivot bolt (photo).
36 Disconnect the clutch operating cable from the clutch release lever and the cable sleeve stop, Fig.1.11.
37 Unscrew the two bolts from the front mounting pad (gear-change lever side - left or right according to left or right hand steering) and free the two anchor washers (photo). Remove the two bolts which connect the mounting pad to the front housing and withdraw the mounting pad and bracket (photos). It may be advisable at this stage to employ a second jack to support the transmission case. Do not allow the jack lifting platform to damage the light alloy ribs of the case, use a packing piece to obviate this.
38 Remove the radiator locating bracket (photo).

39 The drive shafts must now be freed from the transmission. Drive out the spring roll pins (photo) which secure the shafts to the transmission sun wheels, using a suitable drift, Fig.1.12. The flexible couplings will become disengaged once they are pulled and immediately the roll pins are removed, restraining clips must be used to keep the couplings in engagement. Suitable clips are supplied with new drive couplings but a length of wire and a worm drive clip will provide a good substitute. Compress the couplings by hand pressure and wrap the wire round, securing the two ends to the drive shaft by the clip Fig.1.13.
40 With the drive couplings now restrained, use the scissors type jack (supplied with the car) to prise the transmission away from the body frame, Fig.1.14, (photo). By placing the jack first on one side and then the other, each drive shaft may be released from engagement with the transmission sun wheels (photo).
41 Refit the front road wheels and lower the car carefully, remembering that there are two jacks in position and the transmission mounting pad has been removed.
42 The only remaining connections to the power unit should be the rear mountings and the starter cables (if these have not previously been disconnected). Check that this condition prevails.

43 Prepare a lifting attachment. This may be a rope passed over the starter motor on one side of the engine and passing between the sump and clutch cover on the other (photos). Alternatively, make up a lifting bar to bolt into the starter motor upper bolt hole and the cylinder block earth bolt hole. On no account use any other bolts or points of attachment to lift the engine as the alloy construction will either cause the threads to strip or break or distort the point of attachment.
44 Raise the hoist just sufficiently to take the weight of the engine /transmission unit and allow the jacks to be removed.
45 Refer to Fig.1.15 and remove the mounting pad bolts from either side of the engine.
46 Hoist the engine slowly and carefully and when it is withdrawn by about 8 inches (203.2 mm) the starter cables may be disconnected if they have not previously been so removed due to inacessibility.
47 Check for fouling of engine ancillaries and guide the lifting rope past the steering column (photo).
48 Raise the front (gearbox) end of the unit as high as possible and continue hoisting until the complete unit clears the engine compartment (photo).
49 If a mobile hoist is used, roll it away with the unit suspended or if a static hoist is used, roll the car backwards until the unit can be lowered to the ground (photo).

6 Engine/automatic gearbox-transmission unit - removal

1 The procedure given in the preceding section for engine/gearbox-transmission unit removal will generally apply to model 1153 (TA) automatic gearbox – type 821 engined vehicles but the following instructions must also be implemented.
2 Refer to Fig.1.16 and disconnect the speedometer cable (T) the gearchange control arm, (V) the governor cable (G) the combination plug from the electronic gear selection unit (C). Also remove the housing earth wire, the pipe to the vacuum capsule (D) and lift the wiring harness from its clips.
3 The drive shafts cannot be withdrawn from the transmission sun wheels until the suspension units are tilted outwards to provide sufficient room for their withdrawal. In order to tilt the suspension units, the suspension upper ball joints must first be disconnected by using wedges or a ball joint extractor, Fig.1.17. Before tilting the suspension, detach the brake caliper unit to avoid straining the flexible brake hose.
3 Before lowering the car back onto its road wheels (paragraph 33, section 5 of this Chapter) reconnect the upper suspension arm ball joint.

7 Engine ancillaries - removal

1 Unscrew and remove the inlet/exhaust manifold assemblies complete with carburettor from 697 and 821 type engines. On 807 type engines which have crossflow design heads, the inlet and exhaust manifolds are fitted on opposite sides of the engine and are removed individually (photos). The distributor, fuel pump and rocker box cover must be removed before the inlet manifold can be removed from the type 807 engine.
2 Unscrew and remove the fuel pump securing nuts and lift the fuel pump away.
3 Unscrew and remove the sparking plugs.
4 Unscrew and remove the oil pressure transmitter unit and oil pressure transmitter switch from their cylinder block locations.
5 Remove the distributor from its location in the cylinder block (photo). Unscrew the securing nut and lift it from its recess, (photo).
6 Remove the water pump (as described in Chapter 2) and drive belts.
7 Unscrew the oil filter.
8 Withdraw the dipstick.
9 Remove the starter motor bolts and withdraw the starter (photo).

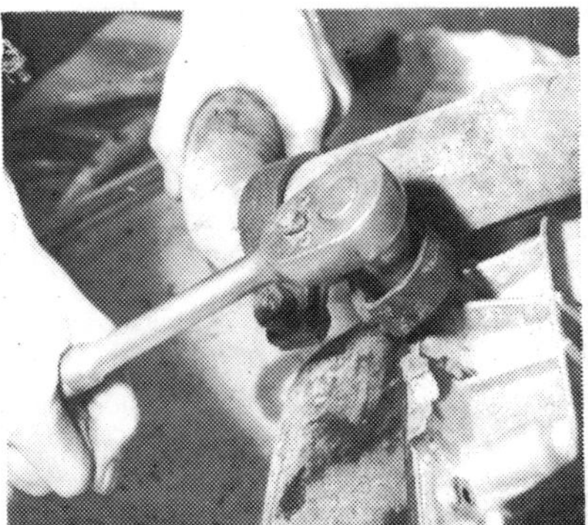
5.29B Exhaust pipe bottom securing bolt

5.30A Unscrewing the speedometer cable locating bolt

5.30B Withdrawing the speedometer cable from the gearbox

5.32 Steering crossmember securing bolts

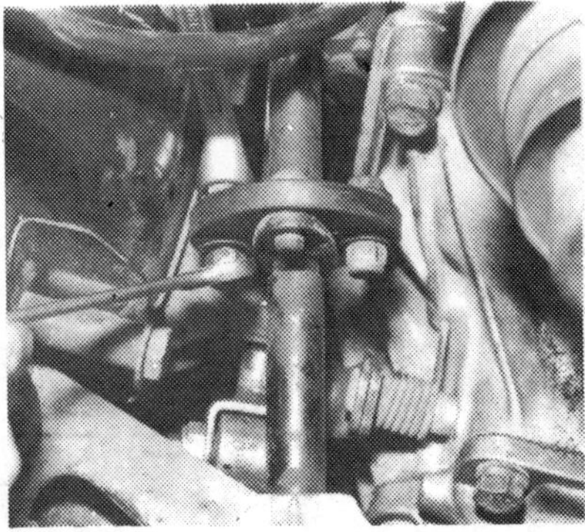
5.33 Removing steering flexible coupling bolt

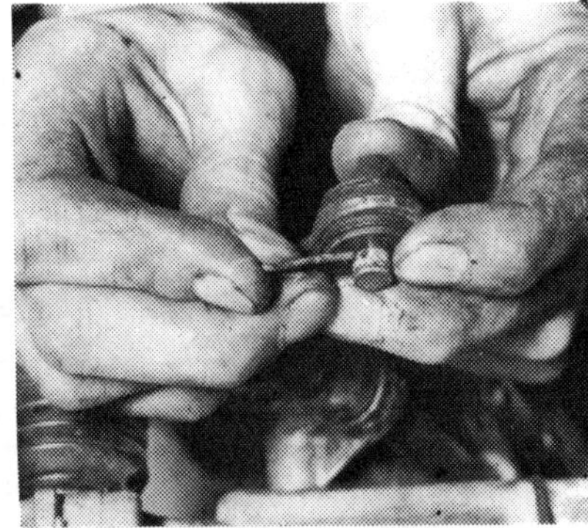
5.34 Gearchange lever to link arm connection

5.35 Removing the gearchange pivot bolt

5.37A Removing a front mounting securing nut

5.37B Withdrawing anchor washer from front mounting

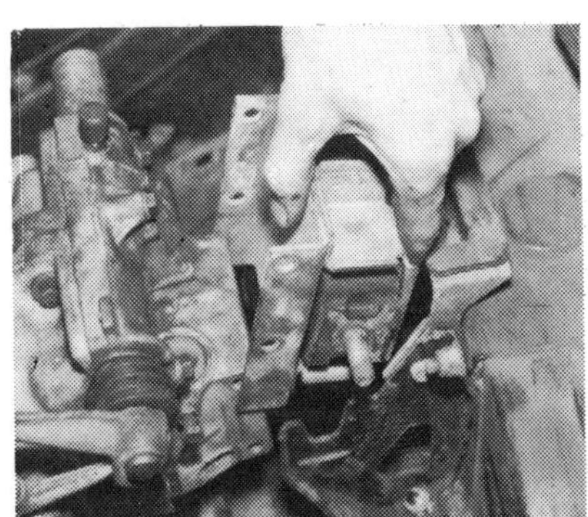
5.37C Removing the front mounting

5.38 Radiator locating bracket

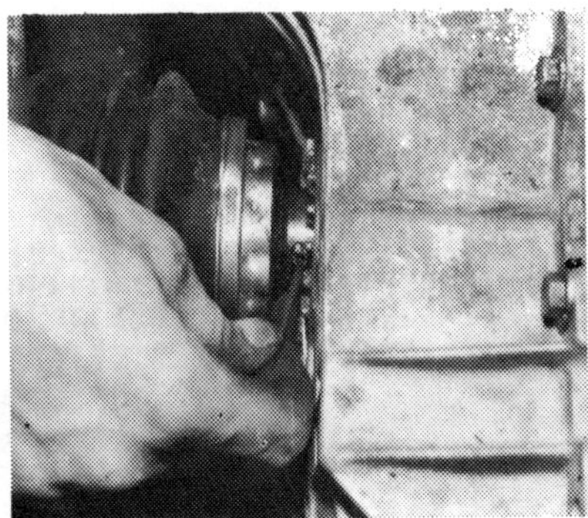
5.39 Removal of a spring roll pin from a drive shaft

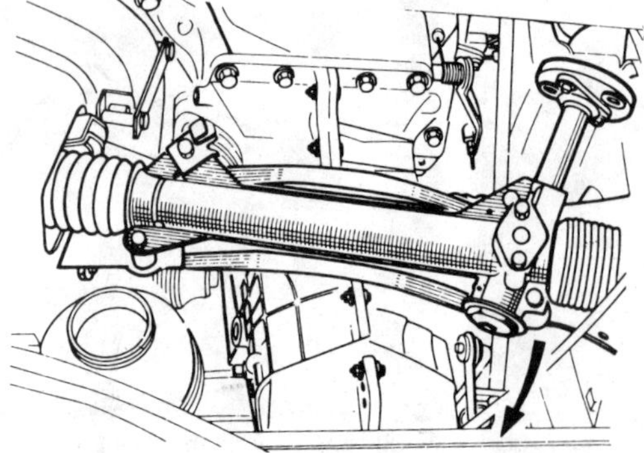

Fig.1.9 Removing the steering unit/crossmember assembly

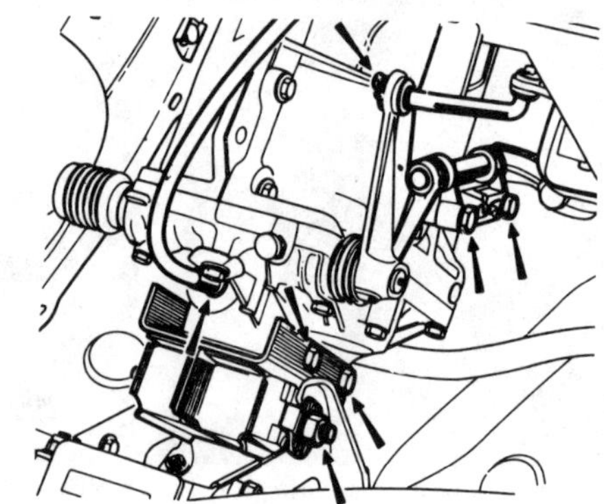

Fig.1.10 Gear change lever link arm and front mounting connections

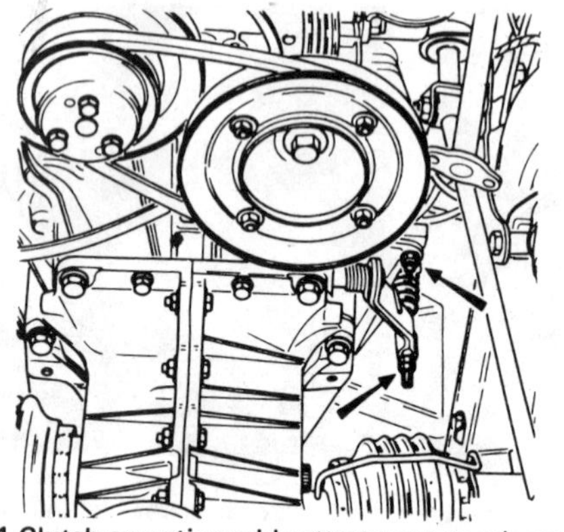

Fig.1.11 Clutch operating cable attachment to release lever

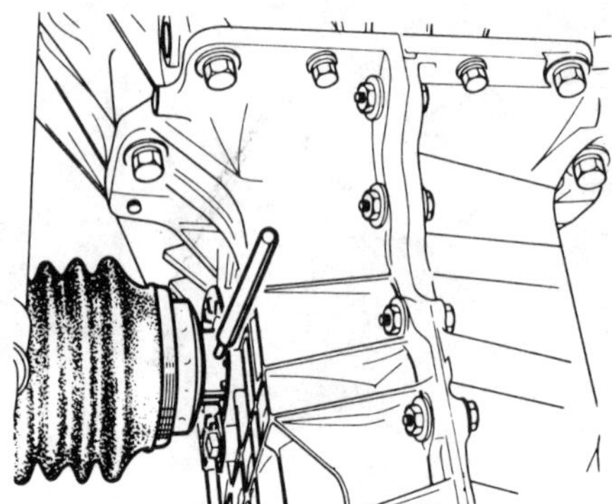

Fig.1.12 Removing a drive shaft roll pin

Fig. 1.13 Drive shaft joint with restraining clip

Fig. 1.14 Prising the power unit in order to remove the drive shaft connection to the transmission unit sun wheel.

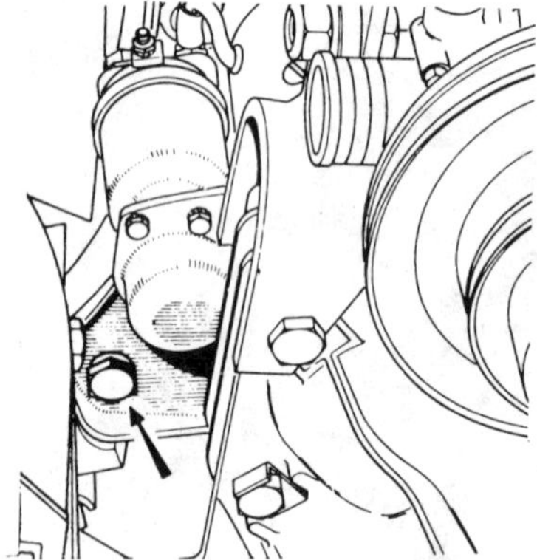

Fig. 1.15 An engine side mounting pad securing bolt

FIG.1.16 AUTOMATIC TRANSMISSION MODELS (MODEL 1153) POINTS OF DISCONNECTION (ADDITIONAL TO THOSE FOR OTHER MODELS) PRIOR TO ENGINE/TRANSMISSION REMOVAL

Key

C Electronic gear selection unit
D Vacuum capsule
G Governor cable
T Speedometer cable
V Gearchange control arm

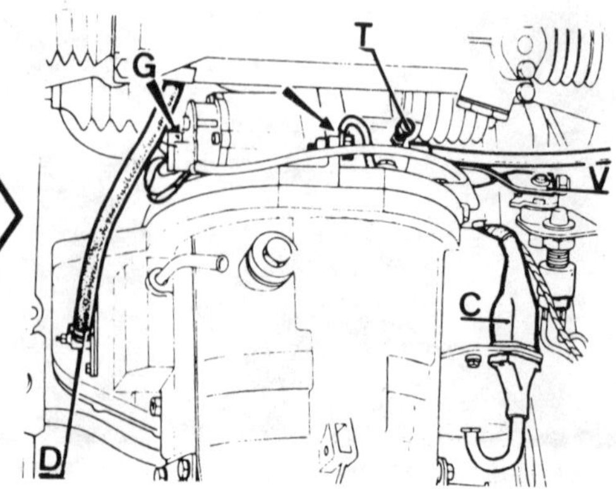

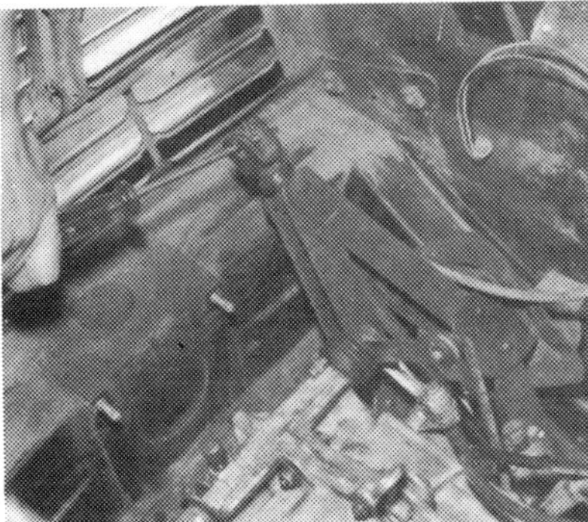

5.40A Prising the transmission unit to free the drive shafts

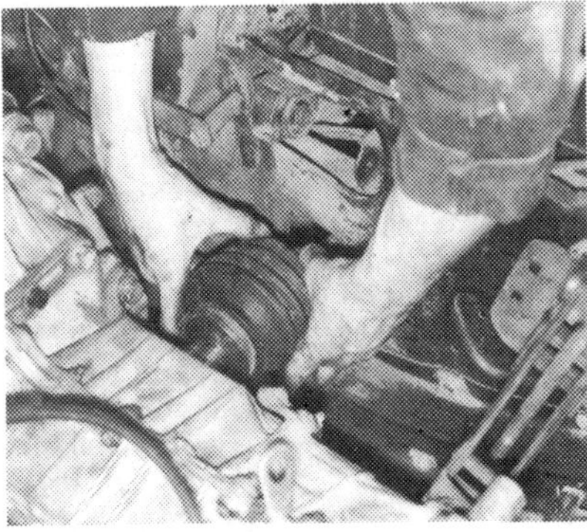

5.40B Pulling the drive shafts from engagement with the sun wheels

5.43A Placing lifting ropes in position

5.43B Placing lifting ropes in position

5.47 Starting to remove the engine/transmission unit

5.48 Hoisting the engine/transmission unit from the engine compartment

5.49 Lowering the engine/transmission unit to the ground

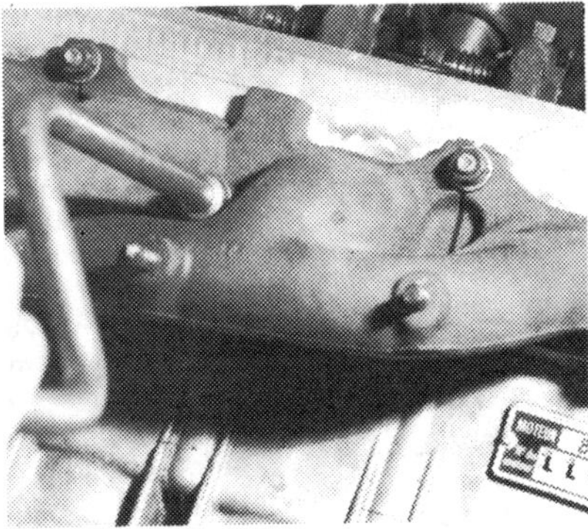

7.1A Removing the 807 type exhaust manifold

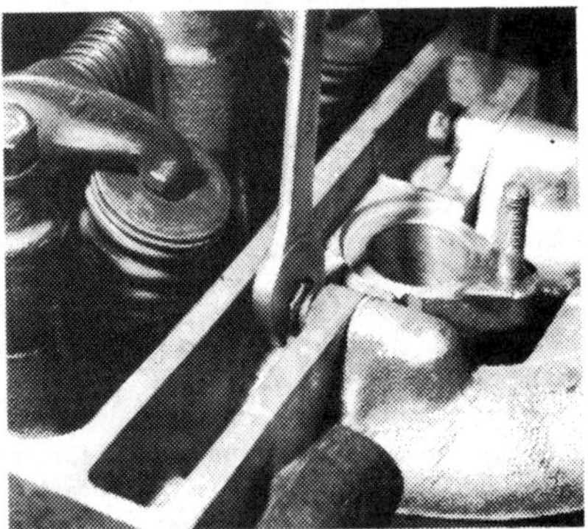

7.1B Removing the 807 type inlet manifold

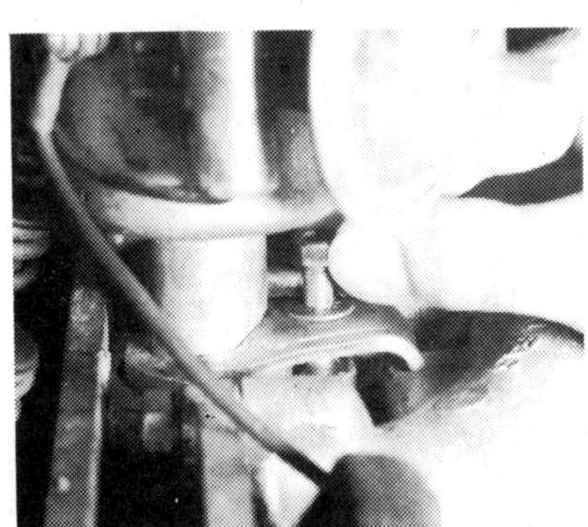

7.5A Removing the distributor securing nut

7.5B Removing the distributor from its location

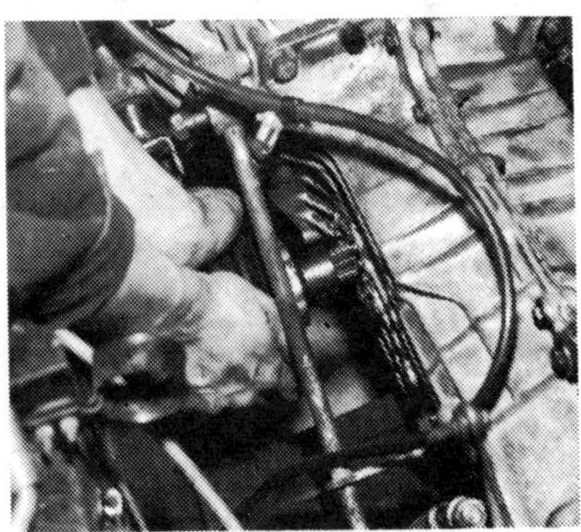

7.9 Removing the starter motor

8 Engine/gearbox-transmission - separation (part 1 - MANUAL)

1 Remove the securing bolts from the flywheel housing to engine front face.
2 Pull the gearbox-transmission unit straight out from the engine unit. Take the weight of the gearbox during withdrawal so that at no time does the weight of this unit hang upon the input shaft of the gearbox while it is still engaged with the splines of the clutch driven plate (photo).
3 Mark the (now exposed) clutch pressure plate cover in relation to its position on the flywheel for exact refitting.
4 Slacken the clutch cover securing bolts in diametrically opposite sequence, a turn at a time until all diaphragm spring pressure is relieved (photo). Fully unscrew the bolts and remove them. Withdraw the pressure plate assembly and driven plate. Do not allow either component to fall during removal and keep oil and grease from the friction surfaces of the driven plate (photo).
5 The engine is now stripped of ancillary components and is ready for dismantling.

8 Engine/gearbox-transmission - separation (part 2 - AUTOMATIC)

1 Remove the securing bolts from the convertor housing to engine front plate.
2 Pull the automatic transmission unit straight out from its connection with the engine.
3 Refer to Fig.1.18 and fit on retaining plate to avoid displacement of the convertor from the gearbox.

9 Engine dismantling - general

1 Prior to dismantling the engine, assemble a supply of rags, tins, brushes, paraffin and masking tape for part identification purposes. Pencil and paper is essential to make sketches **before** dismantling an assembly.
2 As each component is removed, keep like parts together or in strict sequence for such items as tappets, rockers, valves and push rods.
3 Check for mating and identification marks on bearing caps **before** dismantling. If they are not marked, centre punch them or use quick drying paint so that they are fitted in their original position and the right way round.
4 As each component is removed, wash it in paraffin and remove any carbon or corrosion. Checks for wear cannot be accurate if the part is covered in carbon or congealed oil!
5 Do not attempt to save gaskets during the dismantling process. Order a complete top and bottom overhaul set well in advance of requirement. This also applies to oil seals and valve springs as they are seldom held in stock by other than Renault main dealers.
6 As bolts and studs are removed, check the condition of their threads also the tapped holes. Renew any bolts which have suspect threads but where the holes in the alloy engine castings have had their threads stripped then they will either have to be drilled out and re-tapped to an oversize or a patent thread insert used. Take professional advice before taking this action as in many cases the thickness of metal involved may not permit a larger hole to be tapped.

10 Cylinder head - removal (Type 697 and 821 engines)

1 Unscrew and remove the three rocker box cover retaining nuts and lift off the cover.
2 Unscrew the three studs and two bolts which secure the rocker shaft pillars, Fig.1.19. Unscrew each of these a turn or two at a time in alternate sequence to avoid any possibility of distortion to the shaft by the pressure of the compressed valve springs.
3 Lift off the rocker shaft assembly. Remove the water pump to camshaft pulley drive belt as described in Section 14.
4 Withdraw the push rods and place them in strict sequence for correct replacement.
5 Unscrew the cylinder head bolts, Fig.1.20. Unscrew them a turn or two at a time working from the centre bolts outwards to avoid any possibility of distortion to the head.
6 At this stage, if the cylinder head is pulled directly upwards, the 'wet' cylinder liners will also be drawn upwards as they will almost certainly be stuck to the underside of the cylinder head. Movement of the liners in this way will break the seals at the bottom of the liners and where major dismantling is being carried out, renewal of the seals is no problem. Where top overhaul only is being undertaken, then the following procedure must be strictly followed. Temporarily screw in one of the centre cylinder head bolts finger tight and then tap the sides of the cylinder head with a plastic or hide faced mallet. Withdraw the bolt and move the head until it begins to swivel about its locating dowel showing that the liner seal to the head has been broken.
7 Remove the centre bolt, lift the head sufficiently far to enable the tappets to be withdrawn (keep them in strict order for replacement) and then lift the head right off.
8 Withdraw the fuel pump push rod and oil seal.
9 Remove the tappet chamber seal.
10 Where further dismantling is not required, liner clamps should be fitted similar to those shown in Fig.1.21, their purpose being to keep the liner bottom seals unbroken during further overhaul operations and decarbonising. Simple clamps may be devised, held in position by temporarily screwing in the cylinder head bolts.

11 Cylinder head - removal (type 807 engine)

1 The removal procedure described in the preceding section will generally apply but the detail differences are covered in the following operations.
2 Remove the three rocker box securing nuts (photo).
3 Remove the rocker box cover (photo).
4 Remove the rubber washers and cups from the sparking plug tubes (photos) the water pump to camshaft pulley drive belt (Section 14).
5 Unscrew the rocker arm adjusting screws Fig.1.22 and lift out the pushrods, keeping them in strict order (photo). Unscrew and remove the cylinder head bolts working from the centre outwards a turn or two at a time. These bolts serve as combined rocker pillar and cylinder head bolts and once they are removed the rocker shaft assembly may be lifted away. The pair of bolts which retain the rear most rocker pillars cannot be fully withdraw as they impinge upon the engine bulkhead. Use an elastic band to support them as shown in Fig.1.23 during removal (forward) of the rocker shaft assembly.
6 Carry out operations described in paragraphs 6–10 inclusive in the preceding section.

12 Cylinder head, rocker gear and valves - dismantling (type 807)

1 Provided care is exercised, the water pump, water temperature transmitter and alternator bracket need not be removed from the cylinder head during operations described in this section.
2 Drift out the spring roll pins which retain the rocker shafts to their pillars, Fig.1.24.
3 Slide off the rocker arms and springs and clean them and place them in order for replacement. Do not remove the concave plugs from the shaft ends.
4 All valves can be removed with the aid of a conventional type spring compressor, except No 1 inlet. For this, obtain a piece of tubing or an open ended spanner (photo). With the head laid flat on a bench and using a small block of wood or metal within the combustion head (photo) to prevent the valve dropping, press down on the spring until the split collets, Fig.1.25 can be removed.
5 Lift off the valve spring top cups, the springs and the base washers (photo).
6 Withdraw each valve from its guide and keep it in strict order for correct replacement.

8.2 Withdrawing the gearbox-transmission unit

8.4A Slackening the clutch cover bolts

8.4B Withdrawing the clutch pressure plate and driven plate

11.2 Unscrewing the rocker box cover nuts

11.3 Removing the rocker box cover

11.4A Removing the sparking plug tube washers

11.4B Removing the sparking plug tube cups

11.5 Lifting out the push rods

12.4A Compressing a valve spring with a piece of tubing

12.4B Supporting the valve heads with a block

12.5A Removing valve top cup and spring

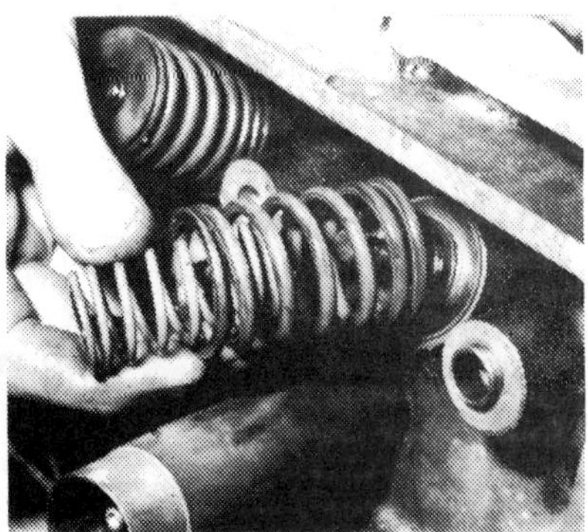
12.5B Removing the inner valve spring

Fig.1.17 Upper ball joint fitted with extractor

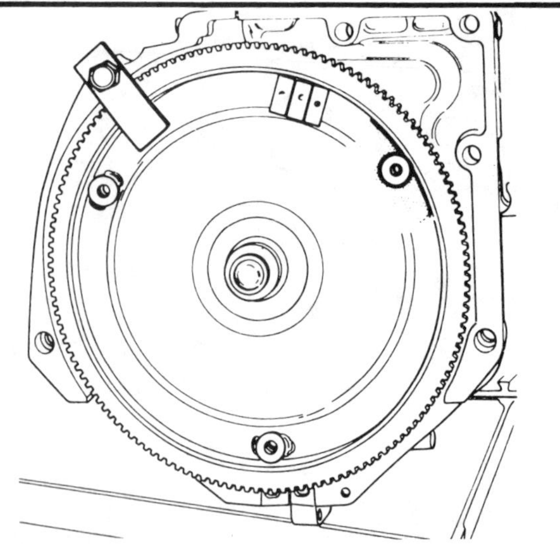
Fig.1.18 Automatic transmission convertor temporary retaining plate

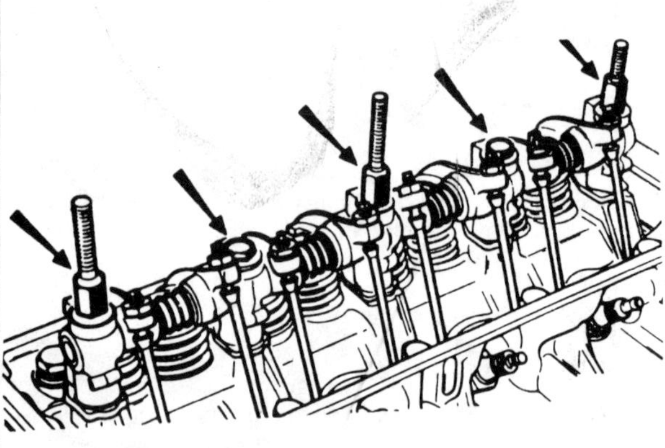
Fig.1.19 Rocker securing bolts and nuts on type 697 and 821 engines

Fig.1.20 Cylinder head bolts on type 697 and 821 engines

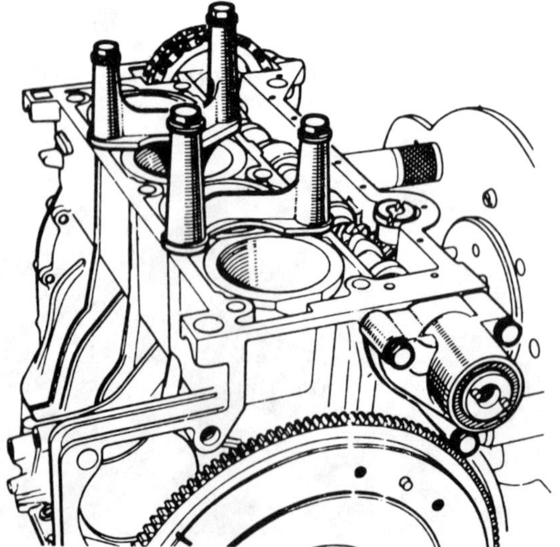
Fig.1.21 Liner clamps in position

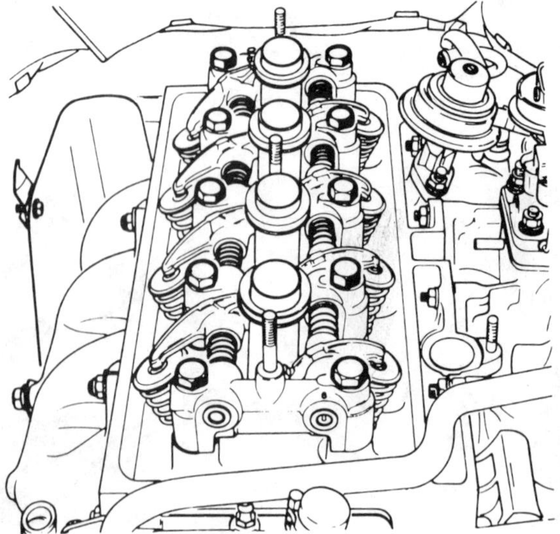
Fig.1.22 Combined rocker pillar and cylinder head bolts on a type 807 engine

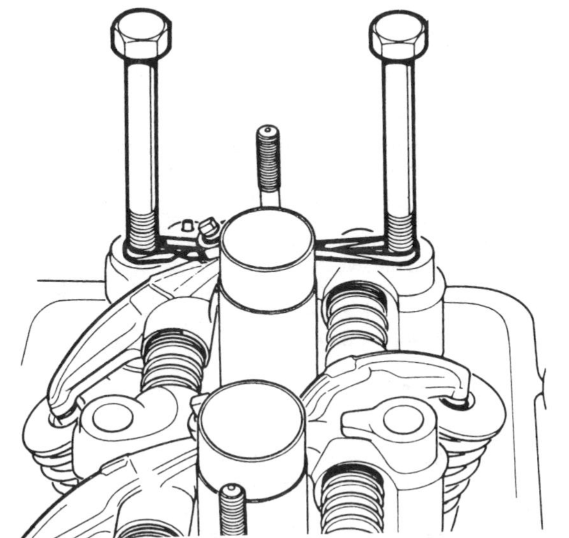
Fig.1.23 Retaining the two end cylinder head bolts in the partly withdrawn position on a type 807 engine

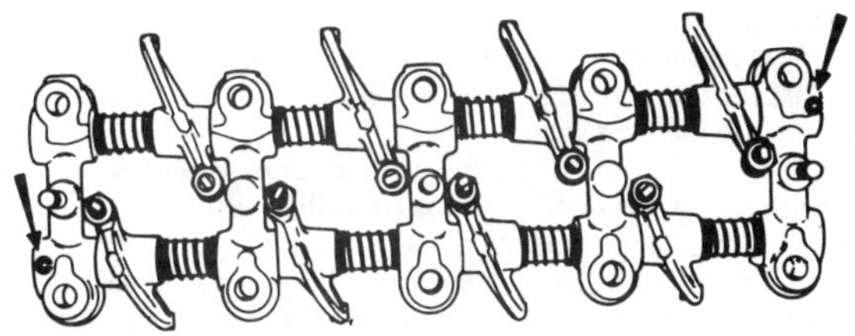
Fig.1.24 Type 807 rocker shaft securing roll pin positions

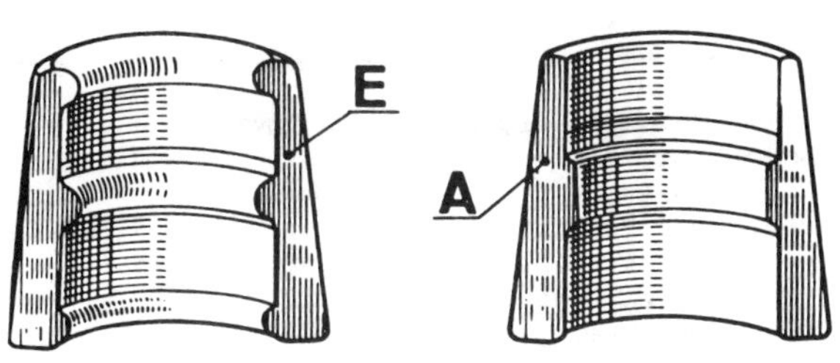

FIG.1.25 VALVE COLLETS

A Inlet type *E Exhaust type*

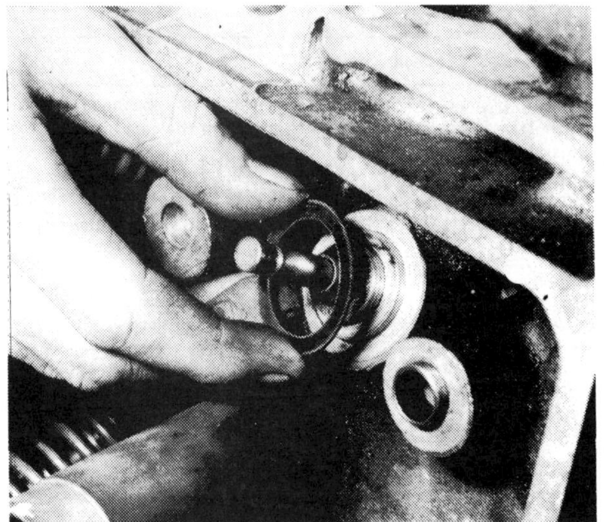
12.5C Removing the valve base washers

15.2 The flywheel securing bolts

15.3 Removing the flywheel

13 Cylinder head, rocker gear and valves - dismantling (types 697/821)

1 Removal of the in-line type valves and rocker shaft assembly follows a procedure similar to that described in the preceding section for vee-inclined valves..
2 Note the location of the shaft retaining spring roll pins.
3 Do not remove the concave plugs from the shaft ends.
4 Remove the valve assemblies using a normal clamp type spring compressor and taking great care that the valves are kept in sequence for correct replacement into their original guides. Remove No 1 inlet as previously explained.

14 Camshaft and water pump pulleys - removal

1 Unscrew and remove the four bolts from the camshaft pulley outer flange. Remove the pulley adjusting shims.
2 Detach the drive belt from the water pump pulley and then remove the three bolts which secure the water pump pulley to the pump shaft flange.

15 Flywheel - removal

1 As explained in section 3, attention may be given to the flywheel, with the engine still in position in the car, the gearbox-transmission only having been removed.
2 Bend down the tabs of the securing bolt lockwashers and unscrew each of the seven bolts, Fig.1.26 (photo).
3 Pull the flywheel straight off and do not knock the starter ring gear teeth during handling (photo).

16 Automatic transmission - convertor driving plate - removal

1 The procedure described in the preceding section applies to the removal of the torque convertor driving plate which is fitted instead of a flywheel with automatic transmission, Fig.1.27. Note convertor/plate mating marks for exact replacement.

17 Sump - removal

1 The sump can be removed while the engine is still in position in the car.
2 Ensure that the engine oil has been drained and unscrew and remove the sump securing bolts. Remove them a turn or two at a time in diametrically opposite sequence.
3 Withdraw the sump and discard the gasket.

18 Oil pump - removal

1 Accessible after removal of the sump, the oil pump is secured to the crankcase by five fixing bolts.
2 Refer to Fig.1.21 and withdraw the oil pump/distributor drive from its engagement with the camshaft.
3 Unscrew and remove the pump securing bolts and remove the pump taking care not to damage the gauze filter, Fig.1.28 or rotors (photo).

19 Timing cover, gear and camshaft - removal

1 Refer to Fig.1.28 and unscrew and remove the thirteen timing cover bolts (photo). Note any difference in length in the bolts and mark them for correct replacement.
2 Lift the cover away to expose the timing chain and gear.
3 Refer to Fig.1.29 and insert a 3 mm Allen key in the chain tensioner cylinder retaining screw, having first bent back the screw lock tab. Turn the screw in a clockwise direction until the pad assembly is withdrawn from contact with the timing chain.
4 Unscrew and remove the two tensioner securing screws and remove the tensioner assembly (photo).
5 Refer to Fig.1.30 and unscrew and remove the crankshaft sprocket retaining bolt. If the crankshaft tends to rotate during this operation, use a 'slogger' type spanner. Remove the washer and thrust ring.
6 Unscrew and remove the four nuts from the two chain anti-flail guards and remove them.
7 Bend down the tabs on the camshaft flange securing bolt lockwashers and unscrew and remove the bolts. Remove the camshaft bearing (3 bolts) from the flywheel end of the engine (photo).
8 Refer to Fig.1.31 and using either an extractor similar to the one shown or two levers behind the crankshaft sprocket, withdraw the crankshaft sprocket complete with duplex chain. At the same time the camshaft flange (integral with camshaft) must be eased from its location to keep the chain as straight as possible. When the crankshaft sprocket has been withdrawn past the end of the crankshaft, then the chain may be removed from both the crankshaft and camshaft sprockets.
9 Withdraw the camshaft taking great care not to damage the camshaft bearing surfaces during the operation (photo).
10 Should components of the chain tensioner have worn or require attention, the component fitting sequence is shown.

20 Piston/liner assemblies, connecting rods and big-end bearings - removal

1 These components may be removed with the engine in position in the car, if required, after removal of the cylinder head and sump.
2 It is important that where the existing cylinder liners are to be replaced, they are identified for position. Mark the top edges with quick drying paint to indicate each liner's position in the line and also its orientation so that it will be refitted exactly the same way round.
3 Check the numbering of the connecting rods and the big-end caps. These should run from 1 to 4 from the clutch end of the engine and are marked on the camshaft side of the unit, Fig.1.32. In the event of these components not being marked, then dot punch them in such a way that the bearing caps will be fitted the correct way round when the mating marks are adjacent (photo).
4 Unscrew and remove the big-end bearing cap nuts.
5 Withdraw the big-end bearing caps complete with shell bearings.
6 Withdraw each cylinder liner/piston/connecting rod assembly upwards from the cylinder block (photo). The lower liner seals will be broken during this operation and must be cleaned from the liner and block mating faces. The seals are supplied colour identified to show thickness but it is unlikely that the original identification marks will still be visible and the seal refitting procedure must be carried out on reassembly as described in section 45 of this Chapter.
7 After removal of each connecting rod, temporarily refit its matching bearing cap and shell bearing.
8 Withdraw each connecting rod/piston assembly from its cylinder liner. Do not allow the piston rings to spring outwards during removal from the liners but restrict them with the fingers to avoid breakage.

21 Piston rings - removal

1 Removal of rings from their grooves is an operation calling for care as they are of cast construction and will snap if opened too wide.
2 Cut three pieces of thin sheet tin (or use three old feeler gauges) and prise the open ends of the ring apart with the thumb nails just enough to permit the first strip of tin (or feeler) to be slid behind the ring. Slide in the other two pieces of tin and position them equidistantly round the periphery of the piston. The

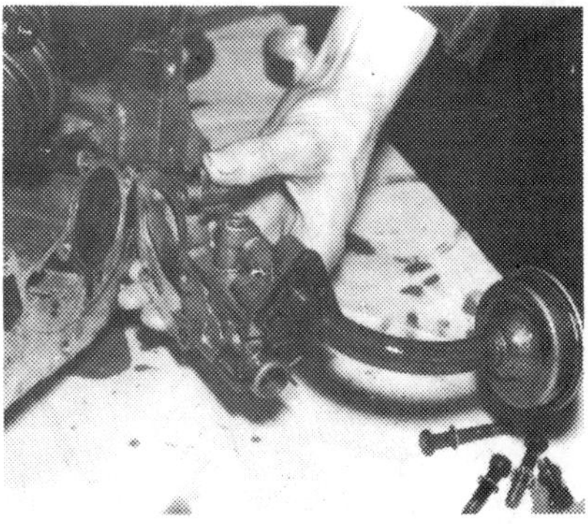
18.3 Removing the oil pump

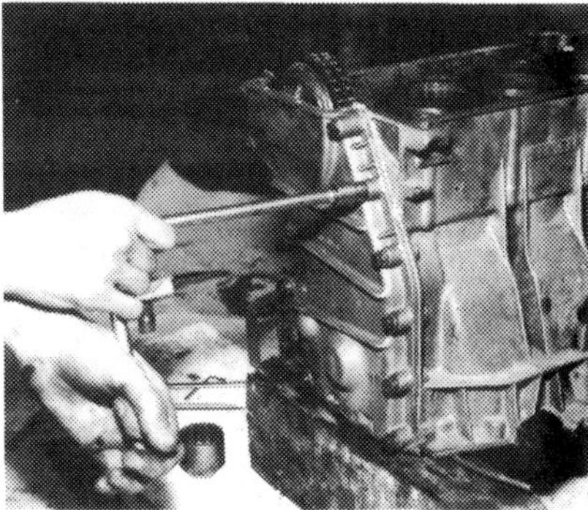
19.1 Unscrewing the timing cover bolts

19.4 Unscrewing the timing chain tensioner assembly

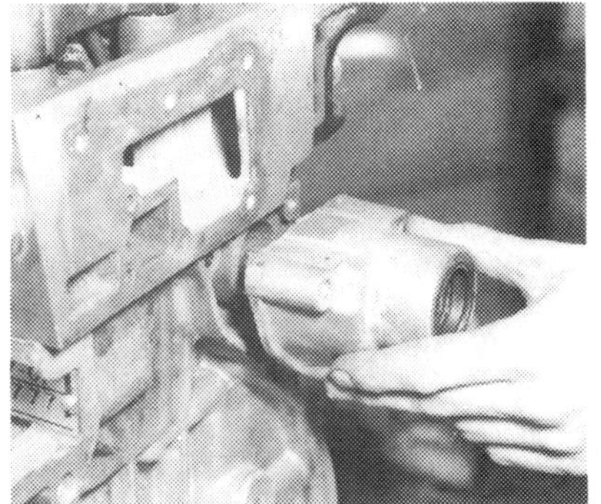
19.7 Removing the camshaft bearing

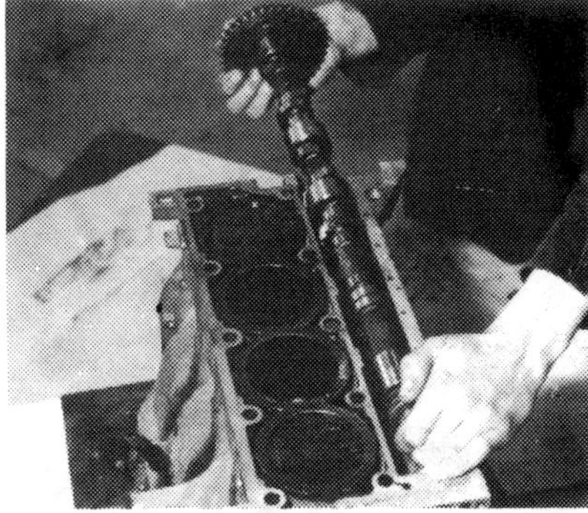
19.9 Lifting the camshaft from its location

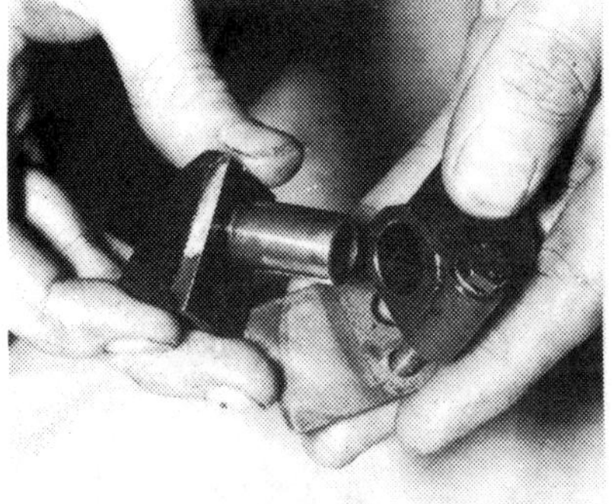
19.10A Components of the timing tensioner

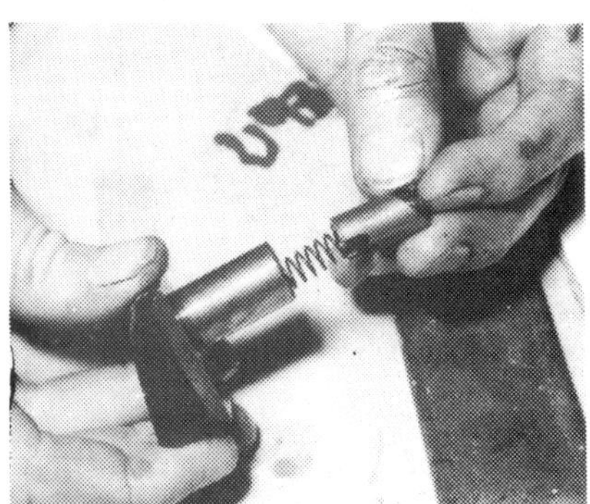
19.10B Components of the timing tensioner

20.3 Big-end mating and alignment marks

20.6 Withdrawing a piston/liner assembly from the block

23.2 Marking a main bearing cap

24.8 Inserting oil pump rotors into their crankcase location

24.9 Checking rotor clearance of the oil pump

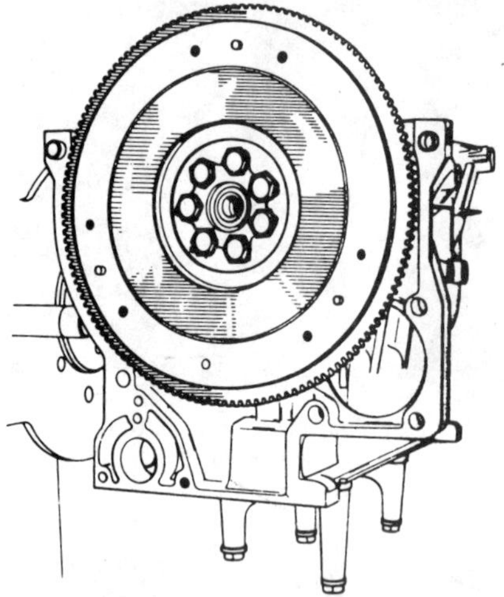

Fig.1.26 Flywheel securing bolts and locking plate

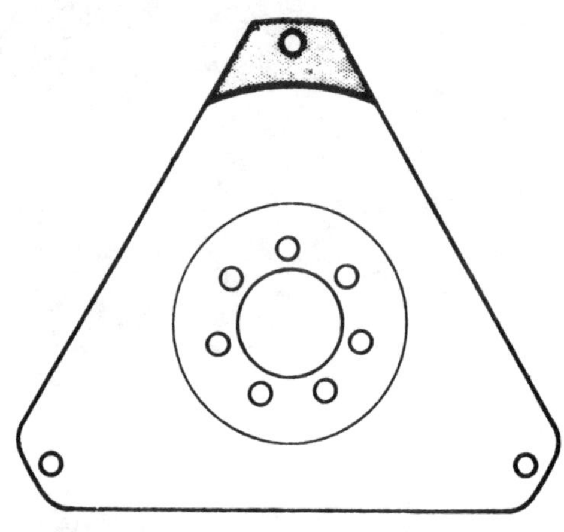

Fig.1.27 Torque convertor driving plate fitted to the crankshaft instead of flywheel, with automatic transmission vehicles

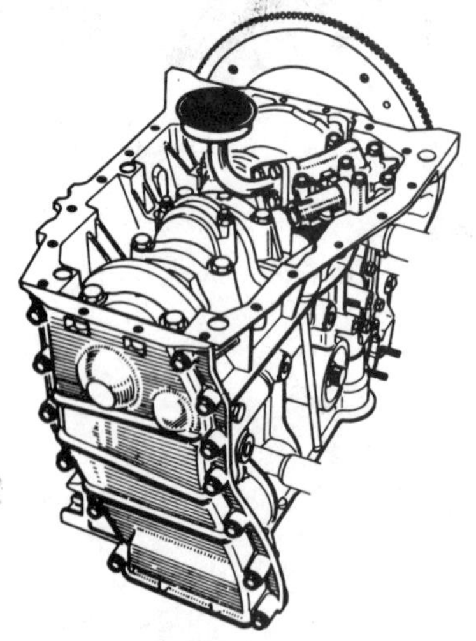

Fig.1.28 Location of the oil pump

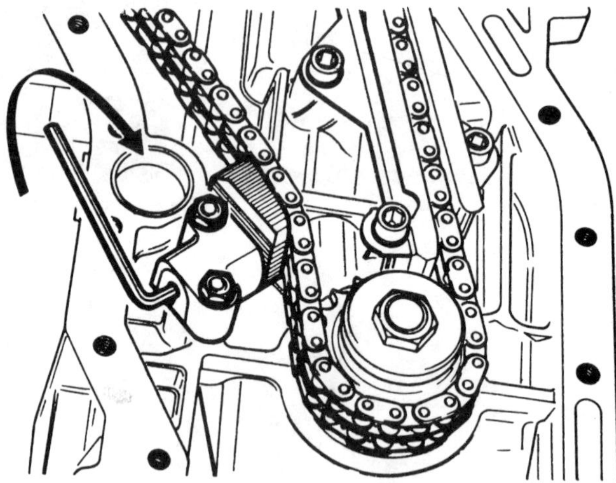

Fig.1.29 Using Allen key to withdraw tensioner pad from chain

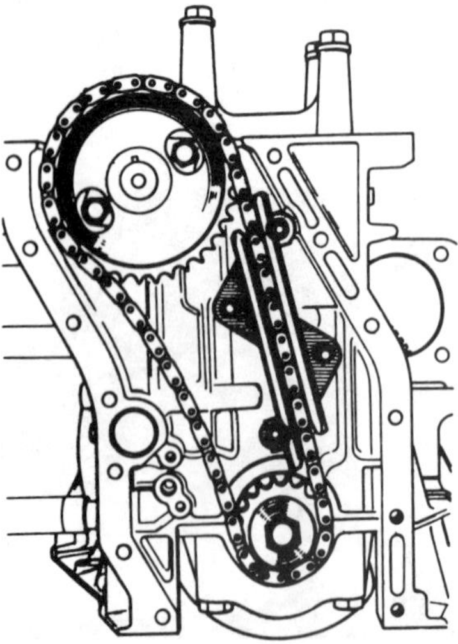

Fig.1.30 Location of timing chain guards

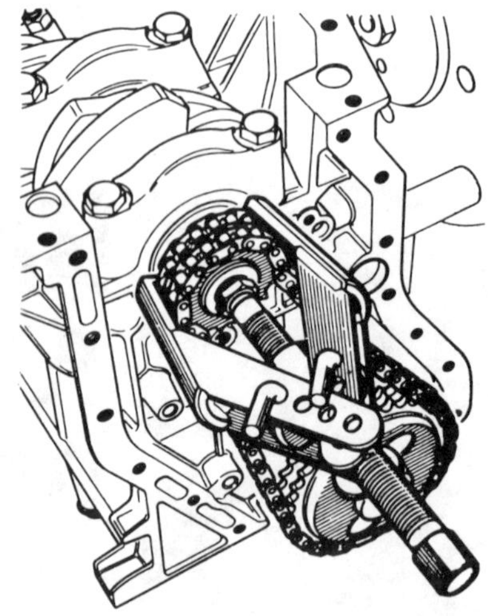

Fig.1.31 Using an extractor to remove the crankshaft sprocket

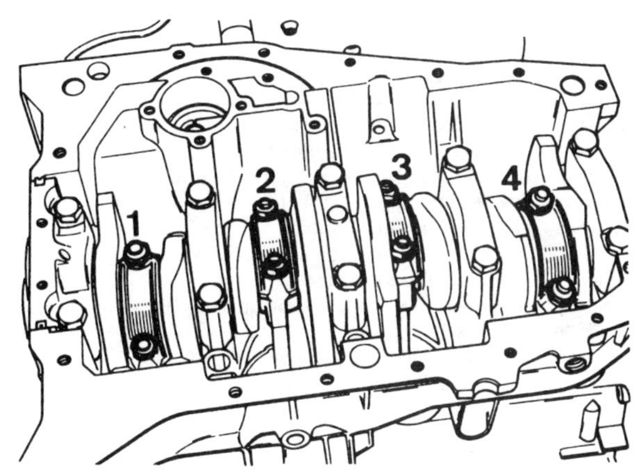

Fig.1.32 Big-end cap numbering (on crankshaft side for correct location)

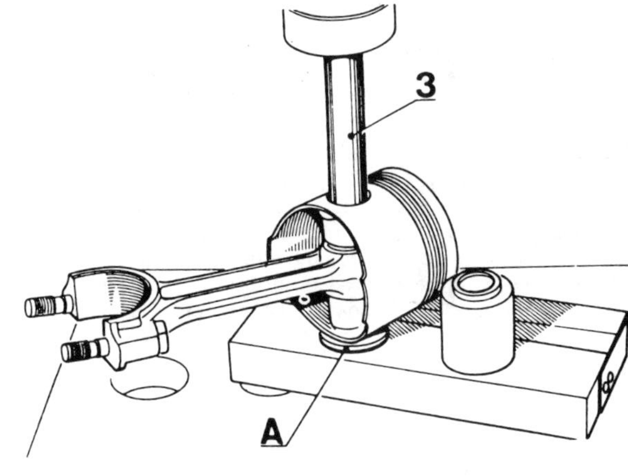

FIG.1.33 SPECIAL TOOLS REQUIRED FOR GUDGEON PIN FITTING

A is insertion limit guide 3 press and mandrel

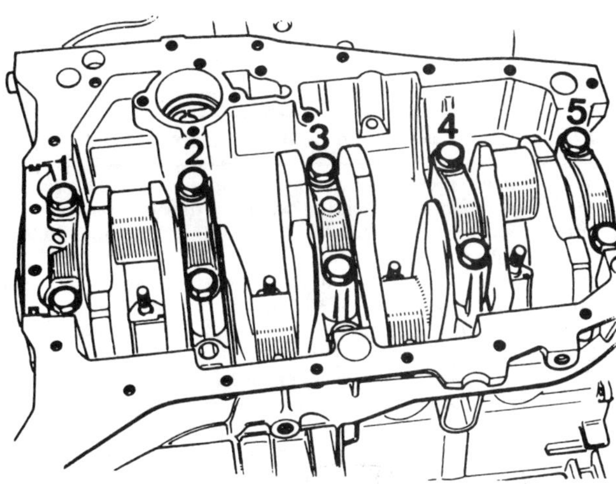

Fig.1.34 Main bearing numbering, caps and crankcase (on crankshaft side for correct location)

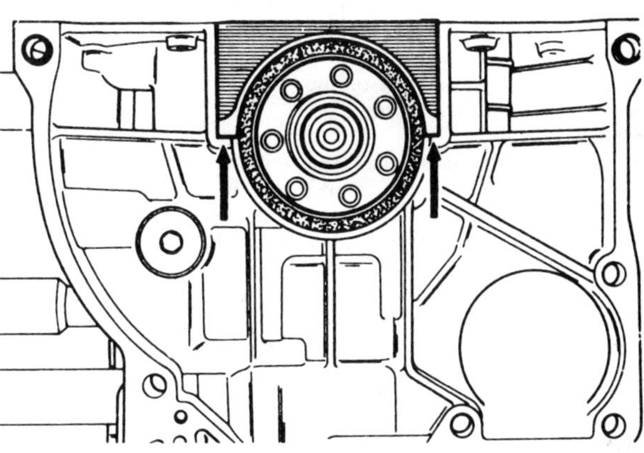

Fig.1.35 Direction to tap No.1 main bearing cap to release it

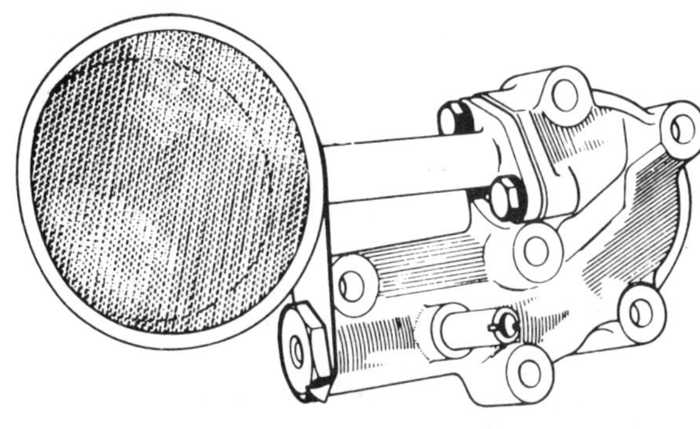

Fig1.36 Oil pump fitted to type 697 engines of early manufacture

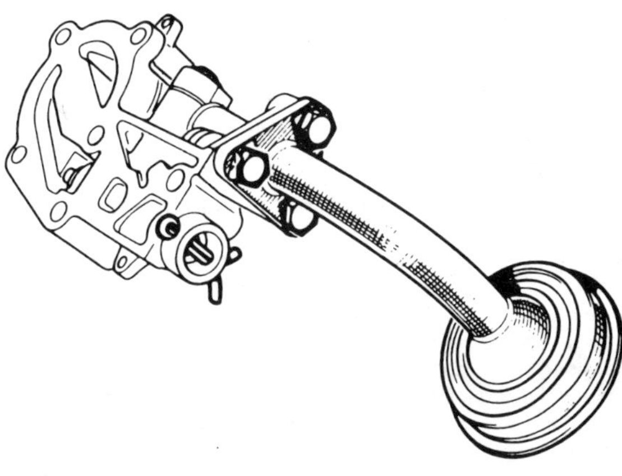

Fig.1.37 Later type oil pump

piston ring may now be drawn off as the strips will permit it to ride safely over the lands and other grooves of the piston.

22 Gudgeon pin - removal

1 The gudgeon pins fitted to these engines are an interference fit in the connecting rod small end but a running fit in the piston. It is preferable that the removal or fitting of gudgeon pins be left to a Renault agent as the connecting rod must first be heated to 250°C (482°F) and a press and special guide tools employed, Fig.1.33.

23 Crankshaft and Main bearings - removal

1 Invert the engine block so that the sump flange is uppermost.
2 Mark the five main bearing caps in sequence from the front either by dot punching or using quick drying paint, Fig.1.34, (photo). Ensure that the position of the mating marks on both the caps and crankcase will automatically ensure their correct orientation on refitting.
3 Unscrew and remove the main bearing cap bolts and remove all the caps except no.1, which cannot be removed by hand pressure.
4 Refer to Fig.1.35 and tap the no. 1 main bearing cap in the direction indicated by the arrows.
5 Remove the seal.
6 Remove the two bearing side seals.
7 With model 821 engines, remove the two white metal type thrust washers from either side of the centre main bearing.
8 Carefully lift out the crankshaft from the halves of the crankcase bearings.
9 Unless the shell bearings are to be renewed, they may be left in position but temporarily screw on the bearing caps which will give some measure of protection to the shell bearings during further servicing operations on the engine block.

24 Oil pump - overhaul

1 The design of the oil pump may vary in type according to date of engine manufacture. Fig.1.36 shows the type fitted to early model 697 engines and the later type oil pump is shown in Fig.1.37, this being fitted to all other types of engine of later manufacture.
2 With early type pumps, bend back the locking tab and unscrew and remove the relief valve screwed plug.
3 Withdraw the spring, guide and ball.
4 Unscrew and remove the two strainer flange securing bolts and lift the pipe and strainer assembly away.
5 With the later type pumps, unscrew and remove the three strainer/pipe assembly securing bolts.
6 Remove the split pin from the relief valve orifice and withdraw the cup, spring, guide and piston, Fig.1.38.
7 Examine and clean all components. Any scored parts or weak springs should be renewed. If a new oil pump assembly is to be fitted instead of an earlier type, then this will necessitate the fitting of a later type domed sump.
8 The inner oil pump rotor was probably removed at the time of removing the pump from the crankcase. Both rotors should now be tested for wear by trying them in position in the crankcase housing (photo).
9 Using feeler gauges, test the lobe clearance, with the rotors held in two different positions, Fig.1.39, and check that the clearances fall within the tolerances quoted (photo). In the event of wear having occurred, renew the rotors as a matched pair. Scoring or wear of the lobe surfaces is usually due to neglect of oil and filter changes.

25 Oil filter - removal and replacement

1 The oil filter is of canister, screw-in, throw away type located on the left hand side of the crankcase.
2 The old filter may be very tight to remove and by prising a screwdriver against one of the filter case notches it may be possible to lever it undone (photo).
3 If this fails use a small chain wrench or a worm drive clip to which two bolts have been riveted or welded. After tightening the worm drive screw fully, pressure against the bolts will unscrew the filter from its base.
4 Before fitting a new filter, grease the surface of the rubber sealing gasket and screw it in by hand (photo) until it seats then screw in a further quarter turn by hand. Do not screw the filter in by using a wrench or tool.
5 Start the engine, check for leaks and top up the engine oil level as necessary.

26 Engine components - examination for wear

With the engine stripped down and all parts thoroughly cleaned, it is now time to examine every thing for wear. The following items should be checked and where necessary renewed or renovated as described in the following sections.

27 Crankshaft - examination and renovation

1 Examine the crankpin and main journal surfaces for signs of scoring or scratches. Check the ovality of the crankpins at different positions with a micrometer. If more than 0.001 inch (0.0254 mm) out of round, the crankpins will have to be reground. It will also have to be reground if there are any scores or scratches present. Also check the journals in the same fashion. Specialist engineering firms will carry out this work and supply new shell bearings to the correct undersizes.
2 There are certain differences in hardening between the various engine type crankshafts and it is imperative that the proposed regrinding matches the figures given in Specifications. Figs.1.40 and 1.41 show points of identification for type 821 engines and 697/807 types.

28 Big-end and main bearings - examination and renovation

Big end bearing failure is accompanied by a noisy knocking from the crankcase and a slight drop in oil pressure. Main bearing failure is accompanied by vibration which can be quite severe as the engine speed rises and falls and a drop in oil pressure.

Bearings which have not broken up, but are badly worn, will give rise to low oil pressure and some vibration. Inspect the big-ends, main bearings, and thrust washers for signs of general wear, scoring, pitting and scratches. The bearings should be matt grey in colour. With lead indium bearings should a trace of copper colour be noticed the bearings are badly worn as the lead bearing material has worn away to expose the indium underlay. Renew the bearings if they are in this condition or if there is any sign of scoring or pitting.

The undersizes available are designed to correspond with the regrind sizes, ie, .010 inch (0.254 mm) bearings are correct for a crankshaft reground .010 undersize. The bearings are in fact slightly more than the stated undersize as running clearances have been allowed for during their manufacture.

Very long engine life can be achieved by changing big-end bearings at intervals of 30,000 miles (48,000 km), irrespective of bearing wear. Normally crankshaft wear is infinitesimal and a change of bearings will ensure mileages of between 100,000 to 120,000 miles (160,000 to 192,000 km) before crankshaft regrinding becomes necessary. Crankshafts normally have to be reground because of scoring due to bearing failure.

Never file the bearings caps to try and take up bearing wear.

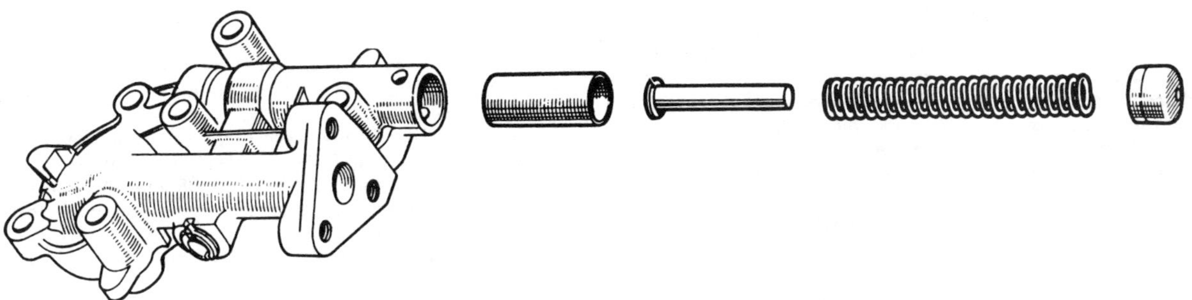

Fig.1.38 Later type oil pump components

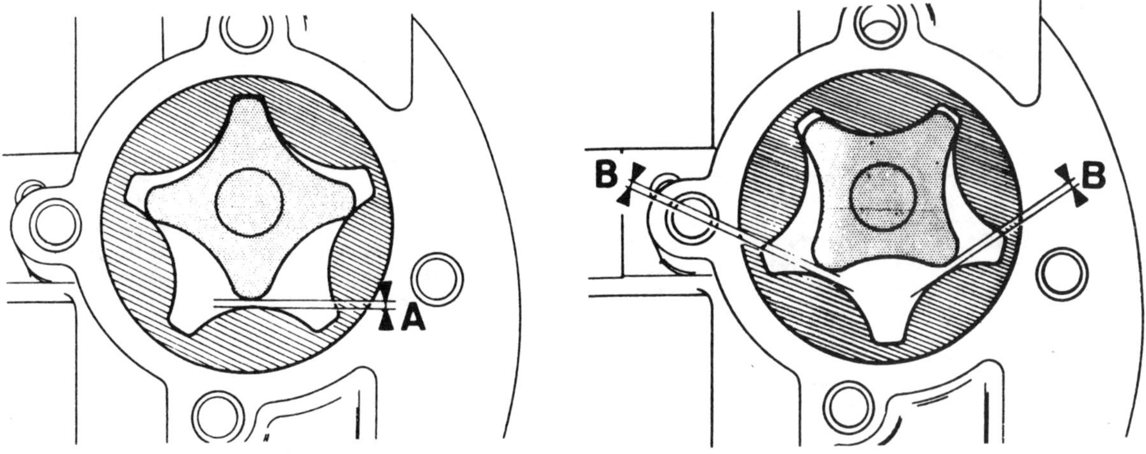

FIG.1.39 OIL PUMP ROTOR CLEARANCES TO BE CHECKED IN TWO DIFFERENT POSITIONS

A = 0.002 to 0.012 in (0.04 to 0.29 mm)
B = 0.001 to 0.006 in (0.02 to 0.14 mm)

25.2 Unscrewing the oil filter

25.4 Greasing the oil filter gasket prior to screwing in by hand

29 Cylinder liners - examination and renovation

1 The cylinder bores must be examined for taper, ovality, scoring and scratches. Start by carefully examining the top of the cylinder bore. If they are at all worn a very slight ridge will be found on the thrust side. This marks the top of the piston ring travel. The owner will have a good indication of the bore wear prior to dismantling the engine, or removing the cylinder head. Excessive oil consumption accompanied by blue smoke from the exhaust is a sure sign of worn cylinder bores and piston rings.
2 Measure the bore diameter just under the ridge with a micrometer and compare it with the diameter at the bottom of the bore, which is not subject to wear. If the differences between the two measurements are more than 0.006 inch (0.1524 mm) then it will be necessary to fit new pistons and liner assemblies. If no micrometer is available remove the ring from a piston and place the piston in each bore in turn about ¾ inch below the top of the bore. If an 0.010 inch (0.254 mm) feeler gauge can be slid between the piston and the cylinder wall on the thrust side of the bore then remedial action must be taken.
3 Should the liners have been disturbed they must be completely removed from the cylinder block and new seals fitted otherwise once the seals have been disturbed the chances are that water will leak into the sump.

30 Pistons and piston rings - examination and renovation

If the old pistons are to be refitted carefully remove the piston rings and then thoroughly clean them. Take particular care to clean out the piston ring grooves. At the same time do not scratch the aluminium in any way. If new rings are to be fitted to the old pistons then the top ring should be stepped so as to clear the ridge left above the previous top ring. If a normal but oversize new ring is fitted it will hit the ridge and break because the new ring will not have worn in the same way as the old, which will have worn in union with the ridge.

Before fitting the rings on the pistons each should be inserted approximately 3 inches (76.2 mm) down the cylinder bore and the gap measured with a feeler gauge.

This should be between 0.015 inch (0.3810 mm) and 0.038 inch (0.9652 mm). It is essential that the gap should be measured at the bottom of the ring travel, as if it is measured at the top of a worn bore and gives a perfect fit, it could easily seize at the bottom. If the ring gap is too small rub down the ends of the ring with a very fine file until the gap, when fitted, is correct. To keep the rings square in the bore for measurement line each up in turn by inserting an old piston in the bore upside down, and use the piston to push the ring down about 3 inches (76.2 mm). Remove the piston and measure the piston ring gap.

When refitting new pistons and rings to new liners the piston ring gap can be measured at the top of the bore as the bore will not now taper. It is not necessary to measure the side clearance in the piston ring grooves with the rings fitted as the groove dimensions are accurately machined during manufacture. When fitting new oil control rings to old pistons it may be necessary to have the groove in this instance widened by machining to accept the new wider rings.

31 Connecting rod and gudgeon pin - examination and renovation

1 A visual check only can be carried out to observe whether any movement or play can be seen when the piston is held still and the connecting rod pushed and pulled alternately.
2 If there has been evidence of small end knock with the engine at normal working temperature then the connecting rod/piston assembly should be taken to a Renault dealer as special tools are required to dismantle and refit these components.

32 Camshaft and camshaft bearings - examination and renovation

1 Examine the chain sprockets. If these are worn or the teeth are hooked, drift out the two securing pins and press off the sprocket.
2 Check the clearance between the camshaft and the flange as shown in Fig.1.42. Use feelers to measure the gap which should be between 0.002 and 0.0047 inch (0.05 and 0.12 mm). If the clearance is incorrect, the flange will have to be pressed off and a new one pressed on.
3 If the sprocket is removed for any reason, it must always be renewed.
4 If the camshaft is renewed as an assembly, then the distributor drive pinion must also be renewed as both components are supplied as matched pairs.
5 The camshaft front bearing contains two oil seals as shown in Fig.1.43. They should both be renewed and a check made that there is no wear in the actual bearing itself.

33 Tappets - examination and renovation

Examine the bearing surface of the mushroom tappets which lie on the camshaft. Any indentation in this surface or any cracks indicate serious wear and the tappets should be renewed. Thoroughly clean them out, removing all traces of sludge. It is most unlikely that the sides of the tappets will prove worn, but, if they are a very loose fit in their bores and can readily be rocked, they should be exchanged for new units. It is very unusual to find any wear in the tappets, and any wear is likely to occur at a very high mileages.

34 Valves and valve seats - examination and renovation

1 Examine the heads of the valves for pitting and burning, especially the heads of the exhaust valves. The valve seatings should be examined at the same time. If the pitting on valve and seat is very slight the marks can be removed by grinding the seats and valves together with coarse, and then fine, valve grinding paste. Where bad pitting has occurred to the valve seats it will be necessary to recut them and fit new valves. If the valve seats are so worn that they cannot be recut, then it will be necessary to recut them and fit new valves. If the valve seats are so worn that they cannot be recut, then it will be necessary to fit new valve seat inserts. These latter two jobs should be entrusted to the local Renault agent or engineering works. In practice it is very seldom that the seats are so badly worn that they require renewal. Normally, it is the exhaust valve that is too badly worn for replacement, and the owner can easily purchase a new set of valves and match them to the seats by valve grinding.
2 Valve grinding is carried out as follows. Smear a trace of coarse carborundum paste on the seat face and apply a suction grinder tool to the valve head. With a semi-rotary motion, grind the valve head to its seat, lifting the valve occasionally to redistribute the grinding paste (photo). When a dull matt even surface finish is produced on both the valve seat and the valve, wipe off the paste and repeat the process with fine carborundum paste, lifting and turning the valve to redistribute the paste as before. A light spring placed under the valve head will greatly ease this operation. When a smooth unbroken ring of light grey matt finish is produced on both valve and valve seat faces, the grinding operation is completed.
3 Scrape away all carbon from the valve head and the valve stem. Carefully clean away every trace of grinding compound, taking great care to leave none in the ports or in the valve guides. Clean the valves and valve seats with a paraffin soaked rag then with a clean rag, and finally, if an air line is available, blow the valves, valve guides and valve ports clean.

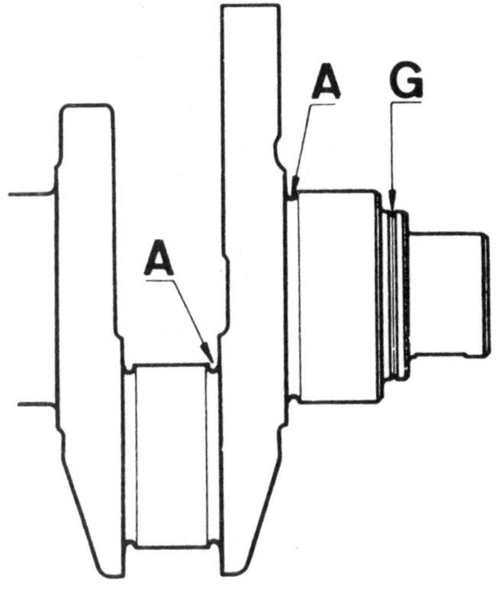

FIG.1.40 CRANKSHAFT IDENTIFICATION DRAWING (TYPE 821 ENGINE)

A = Under cuts
G - single groove for 821 - 02 engine
G - twin grooves for 820 - 01 engine

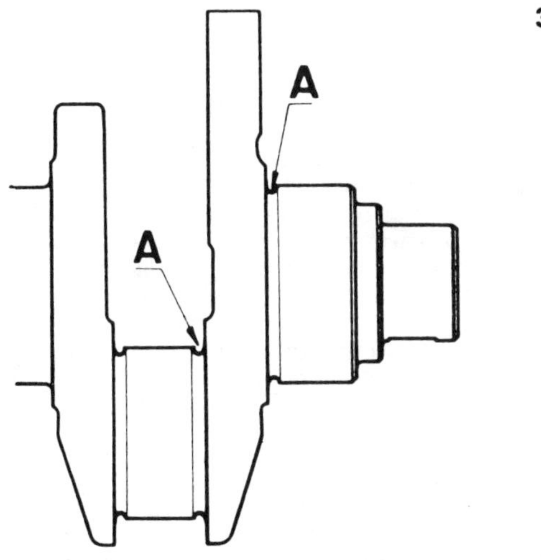

FIG.1.41 CRANKSHAFT IDENTIFICATION DRAWING (TYPE 697 AND 807 ENGINES)

A = Undercuts. no grooves on main journal

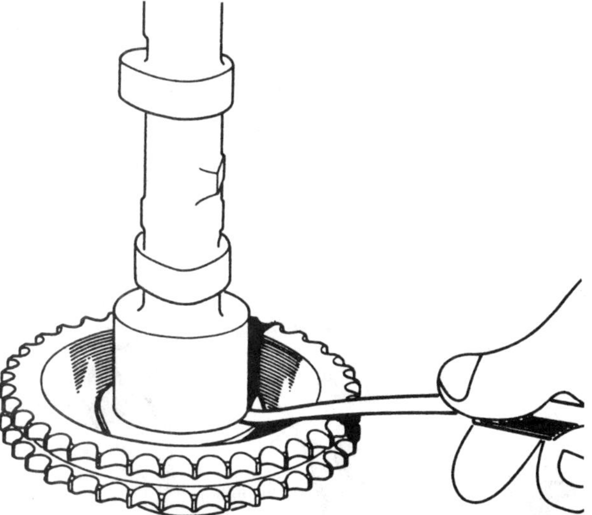

Fig.1.42 Checking the camshaft flange clearance

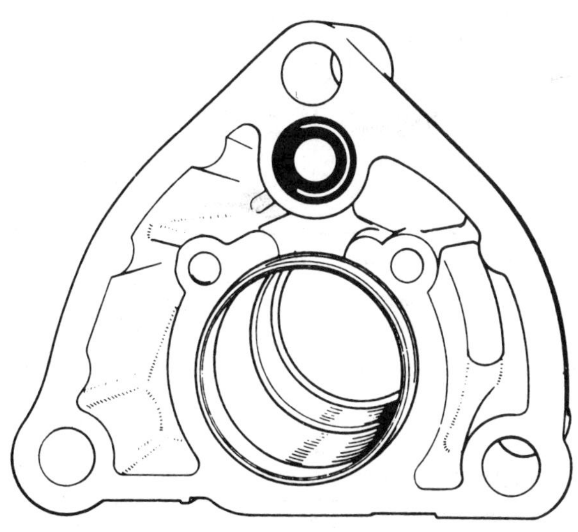

Fig.1.43 Camshaft front bearing showing oil seals

34.2 Grinding in a valve

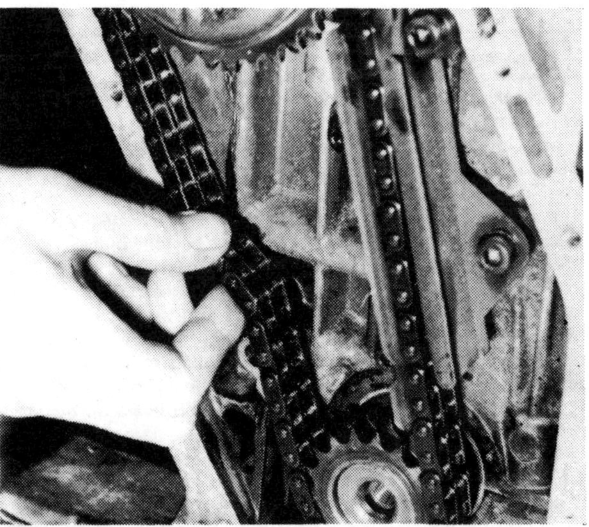

36 Testing timing chain wear

35 Valve guides - examination and renovation

1 Examine the valve guides internally for wear. If the valves are a very loose fit in the guides and there is the slightest suspicion of lateral rocking using a new valve, then new guides will have to be fitted. If the valve guides have been removed compare them internally by visual inspection with a new guide as well as testing them for rocking with a new valve.
2 Valve guide renewal should be left to a Renault agent who will have the required press and mandrel. Work of this kind in a light alloy head without the correct tools can be disastrous.

36 Timing gears and chain - examination and renovation

Examine the teeth on both the crankshaft gearwheel and the camshaft gearwheel for wear. Each tooth forms an inverted 'V' with the gearwheel periphery, and if worn, the side of each tooth under tension will be slightly concave in shape when compared with the other side of the tooth, ie, one side of the inverted 'V' will be concave when compared with the other. If any sign of wear is present the gearwheels must be renewed.

Examine the links of the chain for side slackness and renew the chain if any slackness is noticeable when compared with a new chain (photo). It is a sensible precaution to renew the chain at about 30,000 miles (48,000 km) and at a lesser mileage if the engine is stripped down for a major overhaul. The actual rollers on a very badly worn chain may be slightly grooved.

37 Timing chain tensioner - examination and renovation

1 If the timing chain is badly worn it is more than likely that the tensioner will be too.
2 Examine the side of the tensioner which bears against the chain and renew it if it is grooved or ridged.

38 Cylinder block - examination and renovation

1 Check for cracks. The cost of welding the alloy material must be weighed against a new casting. Threaded holes which have stripped, may have proprietary thread inserts installed to rectify.

39 Rockers and rocker shaft - examination and renovation

Check the shaft for straightness bv rolling it on the bench. It is most unlikely that it will deviate from normal, but, if it does, then a judicious attempt must be made to straighten it. If this is not successful purchase a new shaft. The surface of the shaft should be free from any worn ridges caused by the rocker arms. If any wear is present, renew the shaft. Wear is only likely to have occurred if the rocker shaft oil holes have become blocked.

Check the rocker arms for wear of the rocker bushes, for wear of the adjusting ball ended screws. Wear in the rocker arm bush can be checked by gripping the rocker arm tip and holding the rocker arm in place on the shaft, noting if there is any lateral rocker arm shake. If shake is present, and the arm is very loose on the shaft, a new bush or rocker arm must be fitted.

Check the tip of the rocker arm where it bears on the valve head for cracking or serious wear on the case hardening. If none is present reuse the rocker arm. Check the lower half of the ball on the end of the rocker arm adjusting screw. On high performance engines wear on the ball and top of the pushrod is easily noted by the unworn 'pip' which fits in the small central oil hole on the ball. The larger this 'pip' the more wear has taken place to both the ball and the pushrod. Check the pushrods for straightness by rolling them on the bench. Renew any that are bent.

40 Flywheel starter ring - examination and renovation

1 If the teeth on the flywheel starter ring are badly worn, or if some are missing, then it will be necessary to remove the ring. This is achieved by splitting the ring with a cold chisel. The greatest care should be taken not to damage the flywheel during this process.
2 To fit a new ring heat it gently in boiling water. With the ring at this temperature, fit it to the flywheel with the front of the teeth facing the flywheel register. The ring should be tapped gently down onto its register and left to cool naturally when the shrinkage of the metal on cooling will ensure that it is a secure and permanent fit. Great care must be taken not to overheat the ring, as if this happens, the temper of the ring will be lost.
3 Note carefully that the chamfered side of the teeth on the ring must provide a lead in to the starter motor drive and must be fitted the correct way round.
4 Do not attempt to renew the starter ring gear on the torque convertor fitted to an automatic gearbox (model R1153 vehicle) Leave it to a specialist or exchange the convertor as an assembly - see Chapter 7.

41 Cylinder head and piston crowns - decarbonisation

This can be carried out with the engine either in or out of the car. With the cylinder head off carefully remove with a wire brush and blunt scraper all traces of carbon deposits from the combustion spaces and the ports. The valve head stems and valve guides should also be freed from any carbon deposits. Wash the combustion spaces and ports down with petrol and clean the cylinder head surface free of any gasket cement or foreign matter with the Renault product 77-01-390-107.

Clean the pistons and top of the cylinder bores. If the pistons are still in the block then it is essential that great care is taken to ensure that no carbon gets into the cylinder bores as this could scratch the cylinder walls or cause damage to the piston and rings. To ensure this does not happen, first turn the crankshaft so that two of the pistons are at the top of their bores. Stuff rag into the other two bores or seal them off with paper and masking tape. The waterways should also be covered with small pieces of masking tape to prevent particles of carbon entering the cooling system and damaging the water pump.

There are two schools of thought as to how much carbon should be removed from the piston crown. One school recommends that a ring of carbon should be left round the edge of the piston and on the cylinder bore wall as an aid to low oil consumption. Although this is probably true for early engines with worn bores, on later engines the thought of the second school can be applied, which is that for effective decarbonisation all traces of carbon should be removed.

If all traces of carbon are to be removed, press a little grease into the gap between the cylinder walls and the two pistons which are to be worked on. With a blunt scraper carefully scrape away the carbon from the piston crown, taking great care not to scratch the aluminium. Also scrape away the carbon from the surrounding lip of the cylinder wall. When all carbon has been removed, scrape away the grease which will now be contaminated with carbon particles, taking care not to press any into the bores. To assist prevention of carbon build-up the piston crown can be polished with a metal polish such as Brasso. Remove the rags or masking tape from the other two cylinders and turn the crankshaft so that the two pistons which were at the bottom are now at the top. Place a rag or masking tape in the cylinders which have been decarbonised and proceed as just described.

If a ring of carbon is going to be left round the piston then this can be helped by inserting an old piston ring into the top of the bore to rest on the piston and ensure that carbon is not accidentally removed. Check that there are no particles of carbon in the cylinder bores. Decarbonising is now complete.

42 Engine reassembly - general

1 To ensure maximum life with minimum trouble from a rebuilt engine, not only must everything be correctly assembled, but all the parts must be spotlessly clean, all the oilways must clear, locking washers and spring washers must always be fitted where indicated and all bearing and other working surfaces must be thoroughly lubricated during assembly. Before assembly begins renew any bolts or studs, the threads of which are in any way damaged, and whenever possible use new spring washers.
2 Check the core plugs for signs of weeping and renew any that are suspect.

3 To do this drive a punch through the centre of the core plug.

4 Using the punch as a lever lift out the old core plug.

5 Thoroughly clean the core plug orifice and using a thin headed hammer as an expander firmly tap a new core plug in place, convex side facing out.

6 Apart from your normal tools, a supply of clean rag, an oil can filled with engine oil (an empty plastic detergent bottle thoroughly cleaned and washed out will invariably do just as well), a new supply of assorted spring washers, a new set of gaskets and a torque spanner should be collected together.

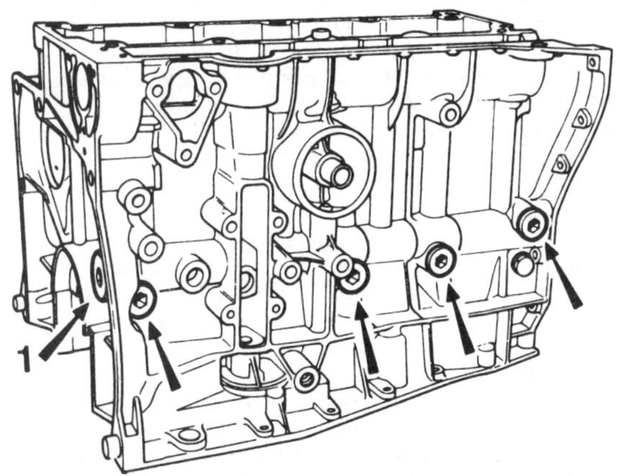

Fig.1.44 Oilways socket screws

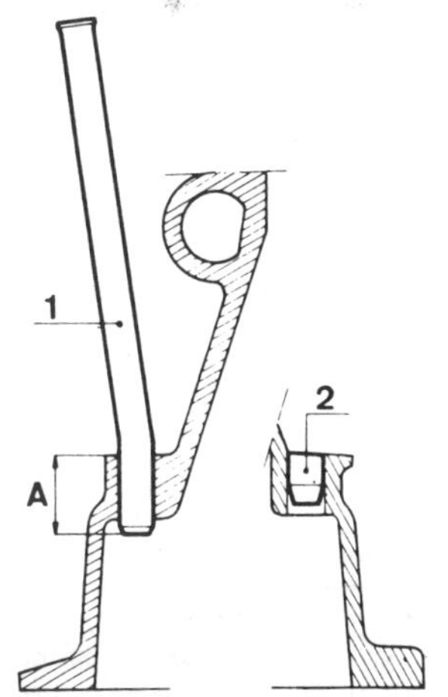

FIG.1.46 FITTING OF DIPSTICK TUBE AND BLANKING PLUG TO TYPE 697 AND 821 ENGINES

1 Dipstick tube
2 Blanking plug
A 47/64 in (18.5 mm)

43 Cylinder block - preparation for reassembly

1 Where regular oil changing has been neglected or a bearing has broken up then it will be wise to clean out the oilways of the block using wire to probe and a paraffin syringe and finally blowing through with air from a tyre pump or a compressed air line.
2 Access to the oilways is obtained by unscrewing and removing the socket screws arrowed in Fig.1.44. When refitting these plugs tighten to a torque of 30 lbf ft (4.1 kgf m) except no. 1 which should be tightened to 60 lbf ft (8.3 kgf m).
3 Check the projection of the oil filter attachment stud, this should project as shown in Fig.1.45. Adjust if necessary by screwing in or out, taking great care not to damage the threads in the process.
4 On 697 and 821 type engines note the position of the dipstick tube (left hand side) and blanking plug (right hand side) and ensure that thev are positioned correctly as shown in Fig.1.46.
5 On 807 type engines, the dipstick and plug are reversed as shown in Fig.1.47.
6 Type 697 engines of late manufacture are fitted with cylinder blocks of similar type to those used in the 807 and 821 engines. This type of cylinder block has shorter depth (2 9/16 inch, 65mm) tapped holes to accommodate the two rearmost cylinder head bolt holes. When using an early type cylinder head with original bolts, then the bolts must either be shortened or packing washers or distance pieces used to prevent them 'bottoming'.

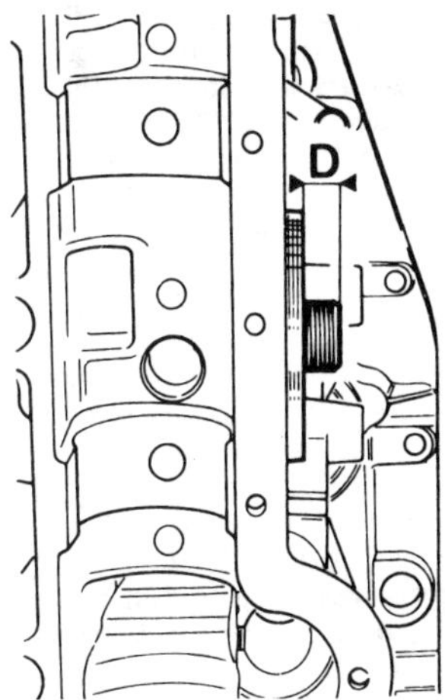

FIG.1.45 CORRECT PROJECTION OF THE OIL FILTER STUD

D = 3/8 to 1/2 in (9.5 to 12.5 mm)

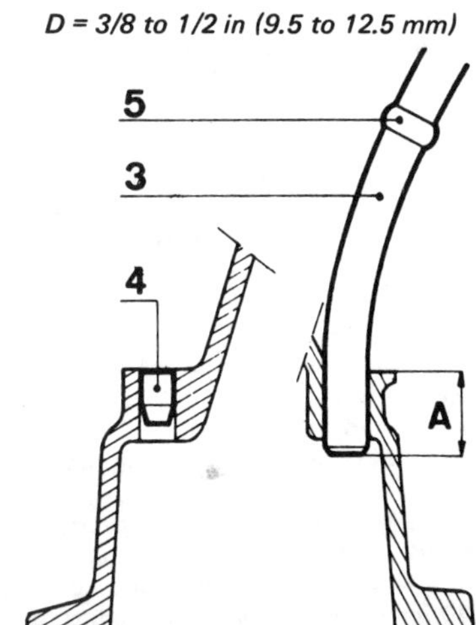

FIG.1.47 FITTING OF DIPSTICK TUBE AND BLANKING PLUG TO TYPE 807 ENGINE

3 Dipstick tube
4 Blanking plug
5 Seam
A 47/64 in (18.5 mm)

44 Engine reassembly - crankshaft

1 Fit the upper sections of the main bearing shells into their crankcase locations (photo). These are the oil holes and grooves. Ensure that the locating tags engage correctly with the cut-outs in the bearing recesses.
2 Stick the two thrust washers into place, one on either side of the centre main bearing (photo). Use grease to hold them in position and ensure that the white metalled sides face the crankshaft webs.
3 Oil the bearings and crankshaft journals and lay the crankshaft carefully in position in the crankcase (photo).
4 Fit the lower halves (plain) sections of the shell bearings to the main bearing caps (photo). Oil the seals and fit them (bolts, finger tight) to main bearings 2, 3, 4 and 5, not no.1. On type 821 engines, the centre main bearing has a locating dowel and the thrust washers should have locating tabs.
5 Check the crankshaft end-float. This may be done by using either a dial gauge or feeler gauges and prising the crankshaft first in one direction and then the other. The total permissible end-float must be between 0.002 and 0.009 inch (0.05 and 0.23 mm) and if outside these tolerances, then the thrust washers must be changed for ones of different thickness as listed in Specifications.
6 With type 697 engines, check the size of the front bearing cap oil hole, Fig.1.48. It should be 0.472 in (12 mm) in diameter. If it is smaller than this, drill it out and deburr the ends of the hole.
7 With its shell bearing in position, fit the front main bearing cap (no.1) and screw in the bolts, finger tight (photo). Refer to Fig.1.49 and measure the gap 'C'. If the gap is less than 0.197 in (5 mm) obtain two seals 0.201 inch (5.1 mm) thick, if greater, obtain two seals 0.213 inch (5.4 mm) thick (colour identified by white spots).
8 If the two side seals into position in the front main bearing cap (photo). The seal groove must be to the outside and projecting by approximately 0.008 inch (0.2032 mm) as shown in Fig.1.50.
9 Fitting of the front main bearing cap is critical. Obtain two studs (10 mm x 150) and temporarily screw them into the crankcase. Tape the side seals (photo) to protect them during fitting and then carefully slide the bearing cap down the two studs, Fig.1.51. When the bearing cap is almost home, check that the side seals are still projecting, withdraw the protective tape and studs and fit the securing bolts (photo).
10 Tighten all main bearing cap bolts to a torque of 45 lb ft (67 kg m) (photo).
11 Renew the crankshaft front oil seal. Remove the old seal and then start the new seal into place using the fingers only (photo). The seal lips are very delicate and great care must be taken to avoid damaging them. Drive it into position by using a piece of tubing of appropriate diameter (photo).

45 Engine reassembly - pistons, connecting rods, liners

1 As previously explained, the fitting of the pistons to the connecting rods will have been carried out by the Renault agent due to the difficulty of removing and inserting the gudgeon pin. Check that the pistons have been fitted correctly however by noting that the arrows on the piston crowns will face towards the front ot the engine when the connecting rod identification markings are facing the camshaft.
2 Locate the shell bearings in the connecting rod and cap big-end bearings (photo).
3 Fit the piston rings squarely into their respective liner bores, one at a time and push them half way down the bores. Measure the ring gaps with a feeler gauge, these should not be less than 0.010 inch (0.2540 mm). Remove and file or grind the ring ends if necessary. Keep the sets of three rings once measured, identified for fitting to the relative liner.
4 Fit the piston rings to each piston. Use the method described for removal in section 21. Note that the top ring is the thinner one (oil control) and the two compression rings are marked GOE-TOP on their face.
5 Liberally oil the rings and ring grooves and turn the rings so that the gaps are at three different points of circle (photo).
6 Attention must now be given to fitting the liners. If the original liners are being fitted and the bottom liner seals were identified by their colour coding on dismantling then it is a single matter to fit new seals of identical colour coding. Where new liners are being fitted or where it was not possible to identify the original seals, then the following procedure must be carried out.
7 Establish whether the liner diameter at its bottom end is 3.228 inch (82 mm) or 3.248 inch (82.5 mm) and obtain a selection of bottom seals (one of each from the sizes listed in specifications).
8 Smear a little grease onto the seating section of the liner and slide on a seal. Press the liner into position by hand. Maintaining hand pressure, place a steel straightedge across the top of the liner and with feelers measure the gap between the top face of the cylinder block and the undersurface of the straightedge. This gap is equivalent to the protrusion of the cylinder liner above the top face of the block and should measure 0.006 to 0.008 inch (0.15 to 0.20 mm). Try different seal thicknesses until the protrusion is correct: Remember to take the measurement with the liner in two different positions and if the measurement differs greatly, take an average. Where original liners are being refitted, place the liners so that the locating marks made before removal are correctly aligned. Repeat the foregoing operations on the remaining three liners and mark them so that during final assembly they will take up the positions which they held during seal measurement.
9 Oil the interior of the liner bore and then using a clamp (photo) slide the piston/connecting rod assembly into the liner. The use of plenty of oil and striking blows with the hand will facilitate this operation (photo). Ensure that fitting takes into account the liner, piston crown and connecting rod alignment marks so that the piston will not have to be rotated in its bore which will cause the staggered ring gaps to line up with each other and cause gas blow-by (photo).
10 Grease the seat of the liner and check that the correct bottom seal is in position (photo). Place the liner/piston/connecting rod assembly into position in the cylinder block with all locating marks correctly aligned (piston crown arrow facing front, connecting rod numbers facing camshaft, liner positioning marks correct).
11 Oil the crankpins and pull each connecting rod down so that the respective (numbered) big-end bearing cap complete with shell bearing can be fitted to the crankpin and the big-end bolts tightened to a torque of 30 lbf ft (4.1 kgf m). Washers are not fitted under the big-end nuts (photos).
12 Fit the remaining three piston/liner assemblies in the same way and then apply clamps to keep the liners and seals in position during the remaining engine reassembly operations, Fig.1.21.

46 Oil pump - refitting

1 Locate the inner (complete with drive shaft) and outer rotors in the crankcase recess.
2 Fit the oil pump body and screw in and tighten the securing bolts (photo).
3 For further operations with the engine in an upright position, stand the lower faces of the crankcase on blocks of wood in order to protect the oil pump and strainer from damage.

47 Camshaft and timing gear - reassembly

1 With the engine in an upright position, oil the camshaft bearing surfaces in the crankcase. Slide the camshaft into position but projecting from the face of the engine by approximately 3 inches (76.2 mm).
2 Place the chain on the camshaft sprocket.
3 Fit the crankshaft sprocket within the loop of the timing chain (photo).
4 By turning the crankshaft and the camshaft and repositioning the crankshaft sprocket teeth in the links of the chain, a position

44.1 Fitting a main bearing shell

44.2 Fitting a crankshaft thrust washer

44.3 Fitting the crankshaft

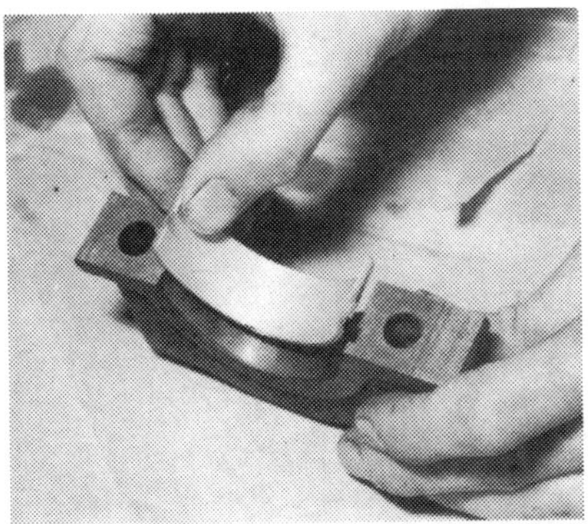
44.4 Fitting a shell to a main bearing cap

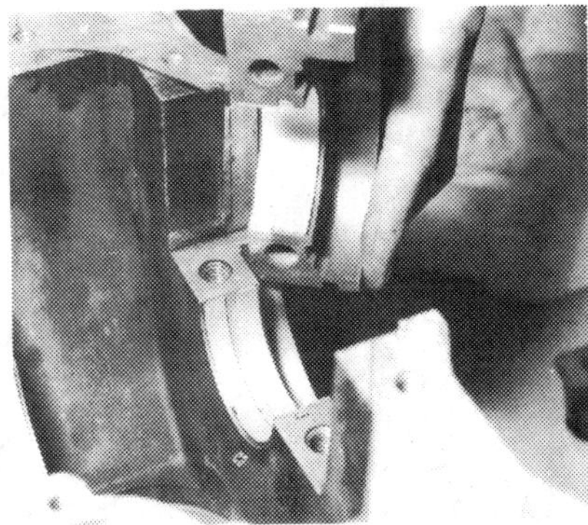
44.7 Fitting the front main bearing cap

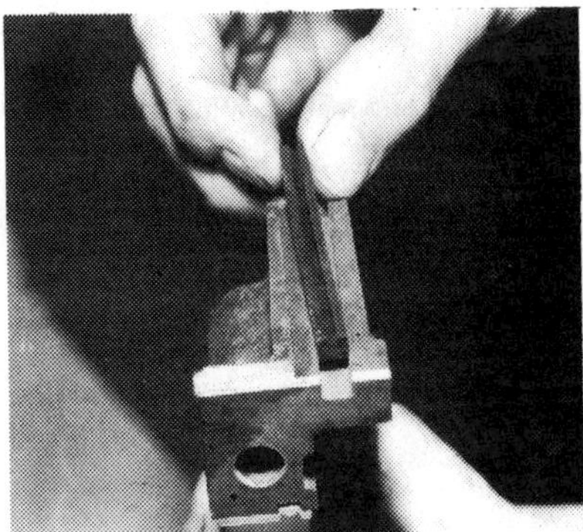
44.8 Fitting the front main bearing side seals

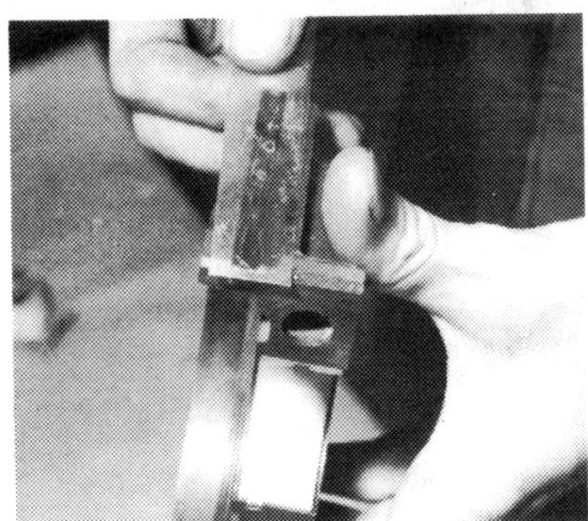
44.9A Taping the main bearing side seals

44.9B Withdrawing protective tape from the front main bearing side seals

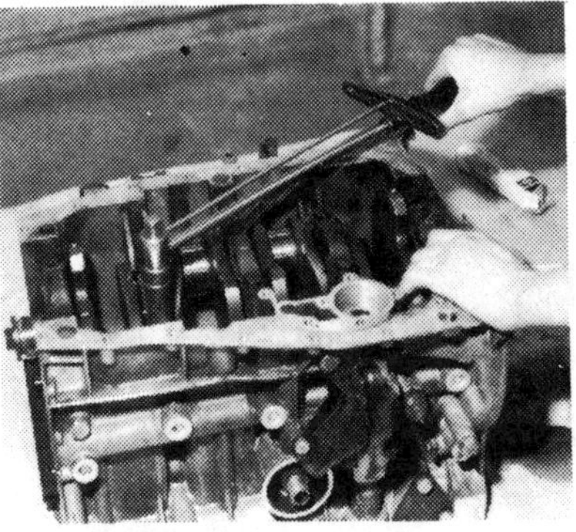
44.10 Tightening a main bearing cap bolt

44.11A Locating a crankshaft front oil seal

44.11B Driving home the crankshaft front oil seal

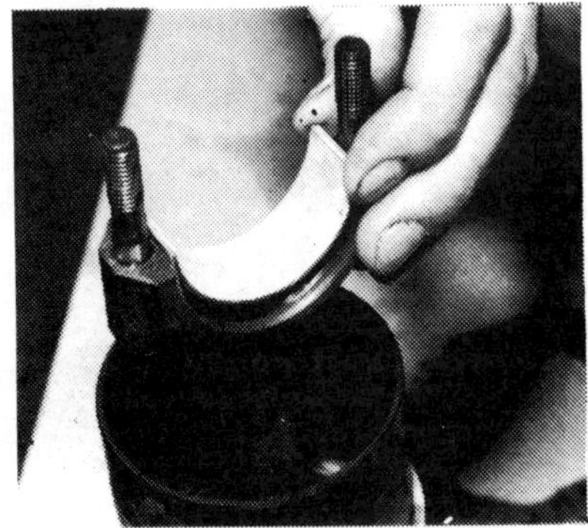
45.2 Fitting a big-end bearing shell

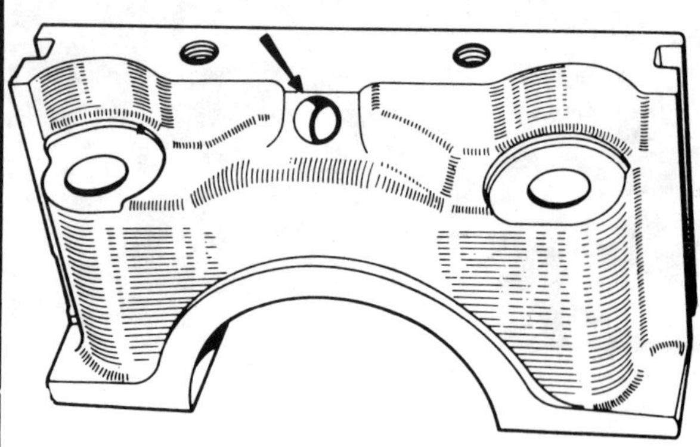

Fig.1.48 Front main bearing cap on type 697 engine (oil hole arrowed)

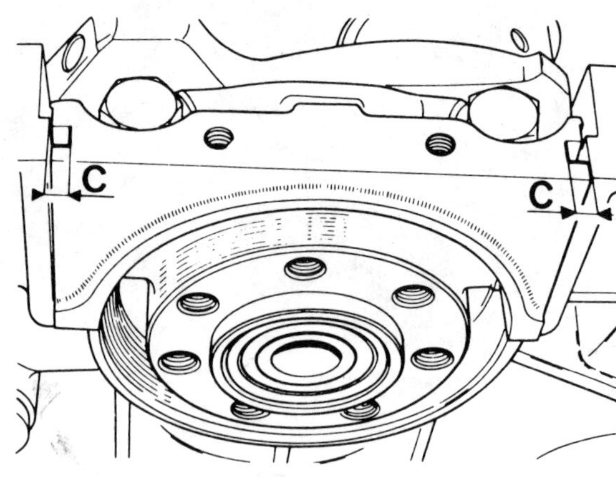

Fig.1.49 No.1 main bearing cap fitted to measure seal gap (C)

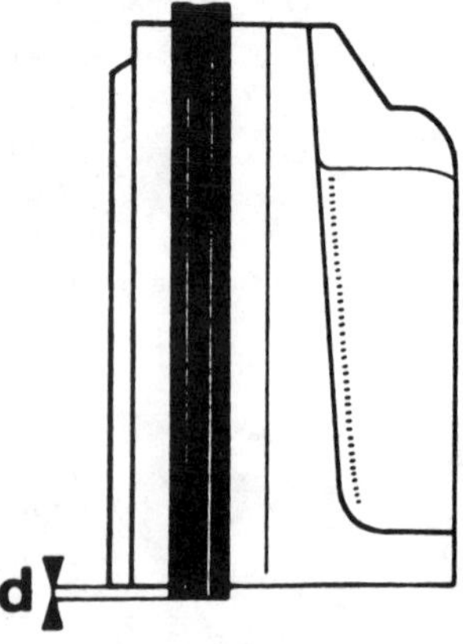

Fig.1.50 No.1 main bearing cap seal projection (D)

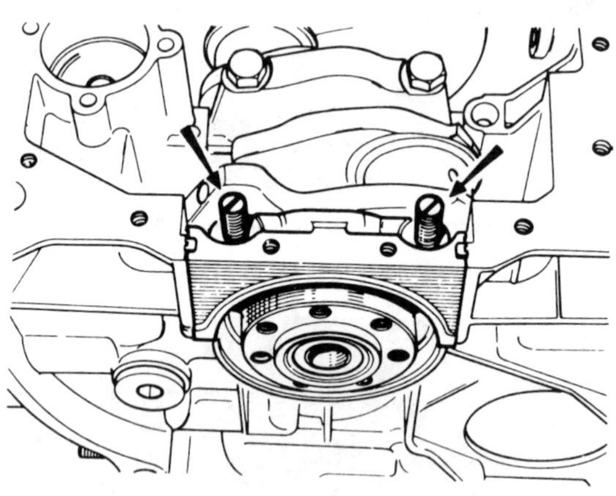

Fig.1.51 Locating studs temporarily fitted to No.1 main bearing cap

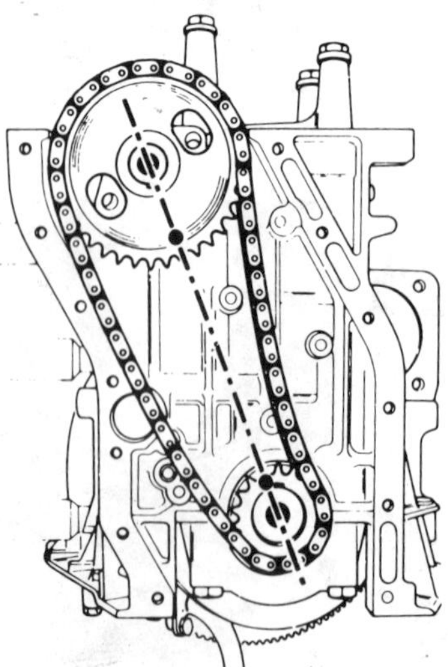

Fig.1.52 Correct alignment of camshaft and crankshaft sprockets

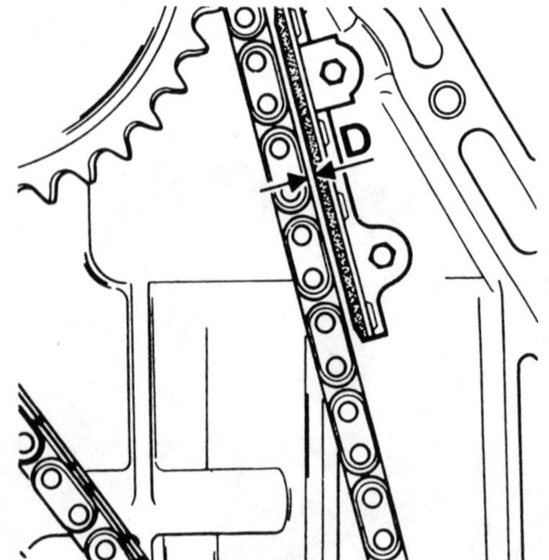

Fig.1.53 Timing chain to guard clearance (0.032 in 0.8 mm)

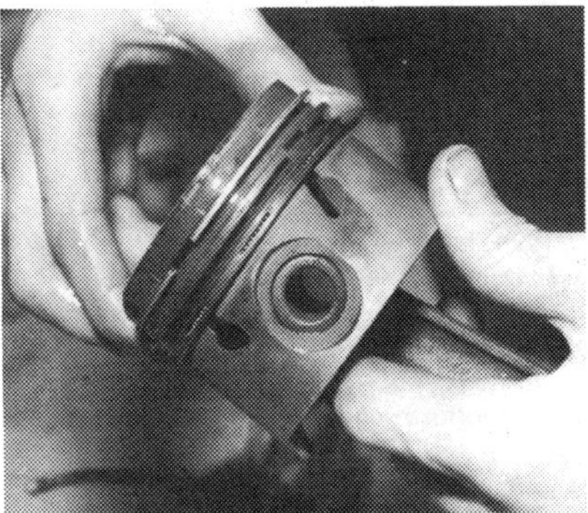
45.5 Correctly fitted piston rings

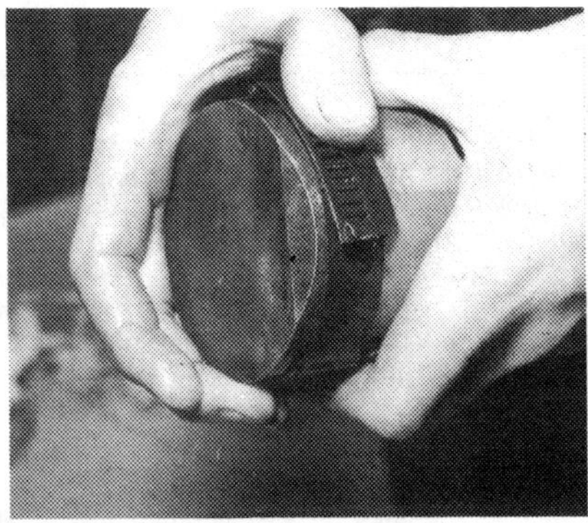
45.9A Fitting a piston ring clamp

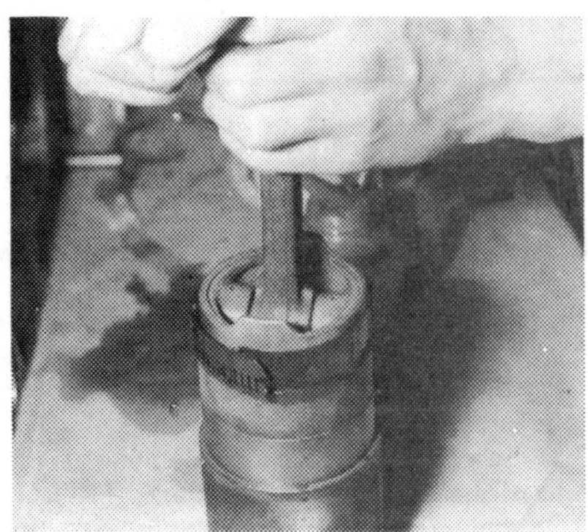
45.9B Sliding the piston/connecting rod assembly into its liner

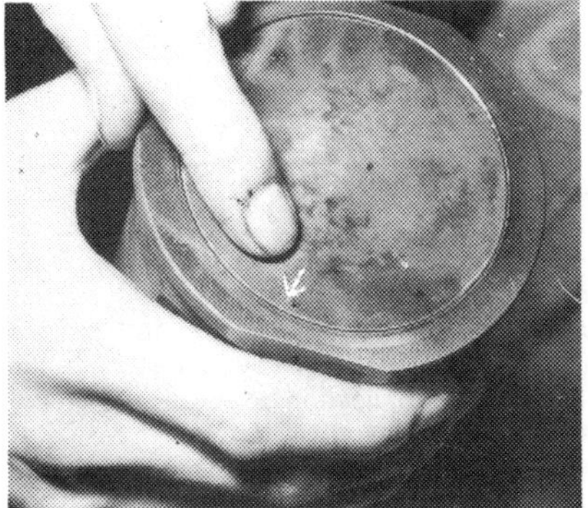
45.9C Piston crown directional arrow (faces front of engine)

45.10. Locating a liner bottom seal

45.11A. Oiling the crankpins

45.11B Fitting a big-end bearing cap

46.2 Fitting the oil pump securing bolts

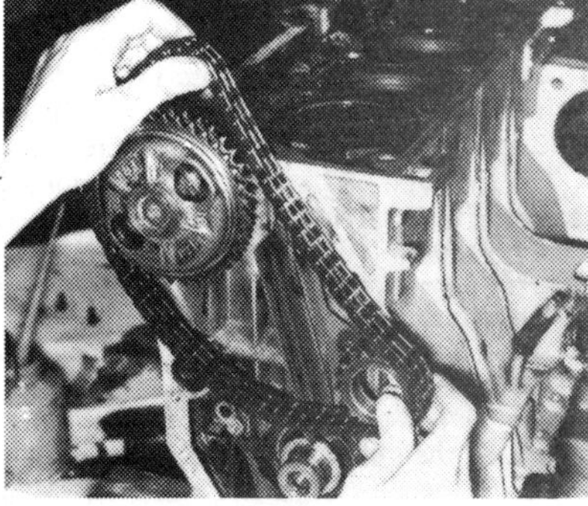
47.3 Fitting crankshaft sprocket to timing chain

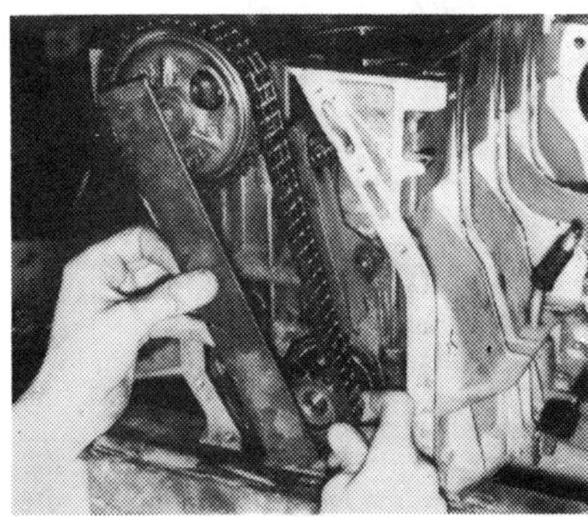
47.4 Checking alignment of timing marks

47.5 Driving the crankshaft sprocket home

47.6 Fitting the crankshaft sprocket bolt

will be reached where the crankshaft sprocket can be slid onto its key and the timing marks on both sprockets will be in exact alignment with the shaft centres as shown in Fig.1.52 (photo).

5 Drive on the crankshaft sprocket using a tubular drift and at the same time push in the camshaft to its final position, keeping the chain as straight as possible (photo).

6 Fit the distance piece, thrust washer and bolt to the crankshaft, tightening the bolt to a torque of 45 to 58 lbf ft (6.2 – 8.0 kgf m) (photo).

7 Screw in the two camshaft flange bolts and bend down the tabs of the locking plates (photo).

8 Locate the plunger and spring into the slipper of the chain tensioner.

9 Fit the tensioner assembly (two bolts) together with its thrust plate (photo).

10 Insert a 0.118 in (3mm) Allen key into the retaining cylinder and turn clockwise until the slipper just touches the chain (photo). Remove the key and lock the cylinder bolt (photo).

11 Fit the chain anti-flail guards (one on Type 697 engine) so that there is a parallel gap between the guard and the chain of 0.032 inch (0.8 mm) as shown in Fig.1.53.

12 Stick new timing cover gaskets into position with grease and fit the cover and securing bolts finger tight (photo). Check that the edge of the timing cover is in alignment with the cylinder head mating surface of the crankcase before finally tightening the timing cover bolts.

13 Using a new gasket fit the camshaft front bearing (photo) which has been fitted with new seals as described in section 32. Fit the camshaft pulley so that the roll pins have their gaps as shown in Fig.1.54. Tightening the pulley belt will pull the roll pins into position.

48 Sump - refitting

1 Cut off the parts of the front (no. 1) main bearing side seals which were left standing proud.

2 Smear the mating faces of the crankcase with grease and stick the sump gaskets in position so that the bolt holes align.

3 Offer up the sump and screw all the bolts in finger tight. Tighten fully in diametrically opposite sequence.

4 Check the security of the sump drain plug.

5 On the type 697 engine a flat or domed type sump pan may be met with in service. If a flat type is renewed with a domed type, then a different pattern oil pump strainer must be fitted.

49 Distributor drive gear - refitting

1 Turn the engine so that no. 1 piston is at TDC (firing) this will position the cams at number 4 cylinder in balance and no. 1 cams with their circular profiles uppermost.

2 Insert the oil pump/distributor drive gear to mesh with the camshaft gear as follows (Photo) with type 697 and 821 engines the slot must be parallel with the centre of the engine and the small D segment nearest the camshaft, Fig.1.55. With type 807 engines, position the drive so that the small D segment is nearest the camshaft and the slot at an angle of 53° (A) as shown in Fig.1.56. An additional guide to location is provided by the flat (P).

3 Pour some engine oil into the cavity below the camshaft.

50 Valves - reassembly

1 Apply engine oil to the valve stems and slide them back into their original position in the cylinder head.

2 Fit the base washers, the valve springs and the spring cap. (photo).

3 Using a compressor, compress the valve springs so that the split collets may be located in the recess in the valve stem. (photo) The use of a little grease will help to keep the collets in position while the compressor is released. Note the different types of collets used for inlet and exhaust valves, Fig.1.25.

4 Once all the valves have been reassembled, tap the ends of the stems with a soft faced hammer to ensure that the collets are correctly seated.

51 Rocker shafts - reassembly

1 With type 697 and 821 engines simply slide on the pillars, rocker arms and springs in the order shown in Fig.1.57. Note that the rocker shaft holes should be towards the pushrod side and the pillar bolt holes must align with the holes in the shaft to permit passage of the retaining bolts.

2 With type 807 engines, commence by sliding the two shafts into the pillar which is fitted at the clutch end, Fig.1.58 noting that both this pillar and all the others will have their machined faces towards the clutch end of the engine when finally installed. Fit the roll pin to secure the inlet valve rocker shaft. Fit the components to both shafts and then secure the exhaust valve rocker shaft with a roll pin (Fig.1.24). The correct location of the type 807 rocker gear is shown diagrammatically in Fig. 1.59.

3 During assembly of both types of rocker gear, oil the components liberally.

52 Cylinder head - refitting

1 Ensure that the cylinder head and cylinder block mating faces are scrupulously clean.

2 Insert the tappets into their original cylinder head locations and tap each one lightly to retain them in their bores when the head is being lowered (photo). Application of some stiff grease to the tappets will assist their retention.

3 Tap the cylinder head locating dowel into position in the top face of the cylinder block. Remove the liner clamps.

4 Clean out the cylinder block blind bolt holes as any trapped oil will prevent correct head fitting.

5 The following operations require extreme accuracy and care, if the fitting of the cylinder head is to give a leak-free installation and the maintenance of good performance. **Do not use gasket cement.**

6 Carefully position a new gasket on the top face of the cylinder block. Check that all the bolt and water holes are clear. (Photo)

7 Fit the rubber seal round the edge of the tappet chamber ensuring that its ends dovetail into (not overlap) the cylinder head gasket. It should be noted that with type 697 engines two different designs of tappet chamber seals are available according to the number of cylinder bolt holes (5 or 9 holes) and the appropriate type of seal should be ordered in advance of requirement.

8 With type 807 engines, the rocker shaft assemblies should be positioned on the cylinder head before it is installed. With other types of engine, fit the cylinder head and then install the rocker assembly.

9 Lower the cylinder head extremely carefully into position on the block and then check the alignment of the distributor hole by testing the distributor in position and adjusting the head fractionally until the distributor is a perfect sliding fit into its location. Install the sparking plug tubes.

10 Smear the cylinder head bolt threads with heavy grease and screw them into position. Note that the two shorter ones are located at the timing cover end. If the cylinder head is being refitted with the engine in position in the car, remember to insert the two rearmost bolts into the rocker pillars and retain them with an elastic band (Fig.1.23) **before** installing the head (80) engine (photo).

11 Oil the washers which are fitted under the cylinder head bolt heads and then screw in all the bolts finger tight.

12 Using a torque wrench, tighten the cylinder head bolts in three separate stages and in the sequence shown in Fig.1.60 (the illustration shows the combined rocker pillar/cylinder head bolts on the type 807 engine (Photo)). With the 697/821 engines, the cylinder head bolts do not secure the rocker pillars but should be tightened in the same relative order.

Stage 1. Tighten to 30 lbf ft (4.2 kgf m) COLD.

Stage 2. Tighten to 50 – 55 lbf ft (6.9 – 7.6 kgf m) for type 697 and 821 engines, tighten to 55 – 60 lbf ft (7.6 – 8.3 kgf m) for

47.7 Tightening the crankshaft flange bolts

47.9 Fitting the timing chain tensioner securing bolts

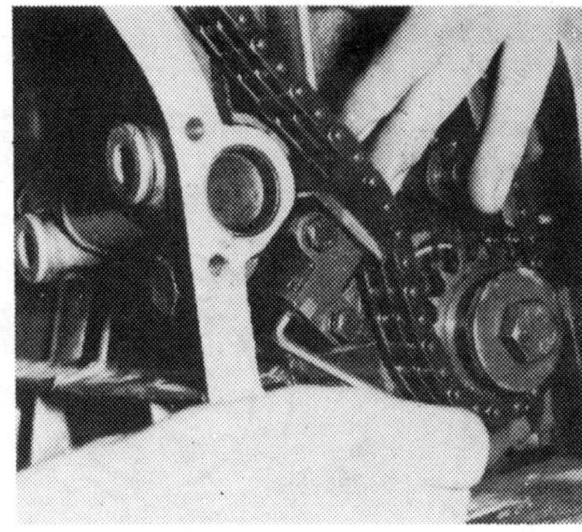
47.10A Adjusting the timing chain tensioner

47.10B Bending the timing chain tensioner bolt tab

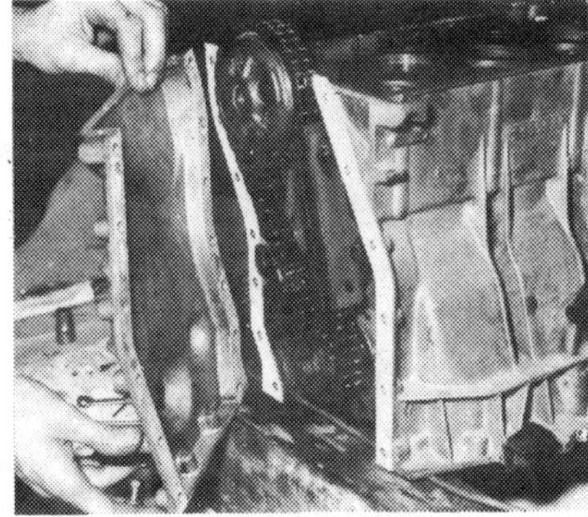
47.12 Fitting a timing cover gasket

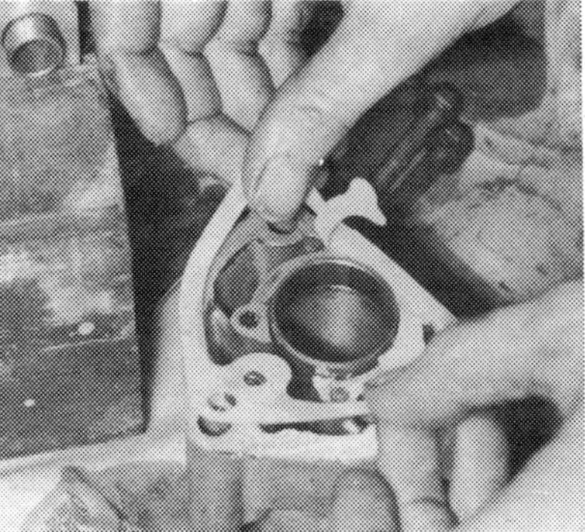
47.13 Fitting a camshaft bearing gasket

48.2 Correct location of the sump gasket

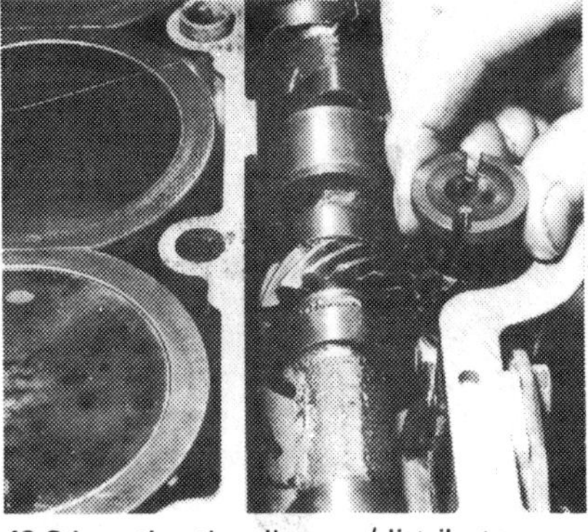
49.2 Inserting the oil pump/distributor drive

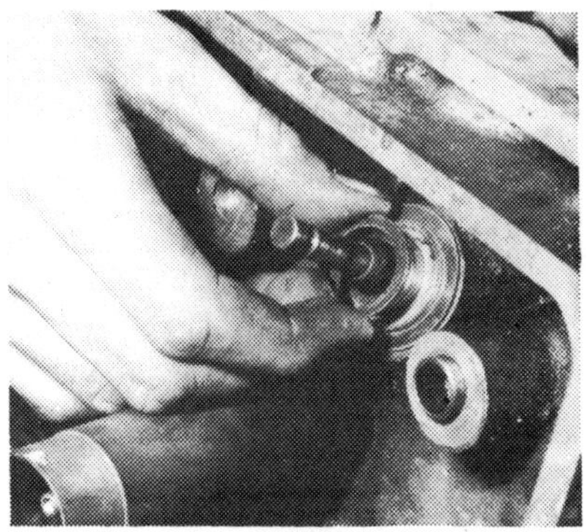
50.2 Fitting a valve spring base washer

50.3 Fitting the valve collets

52.2A Inserting the tappets

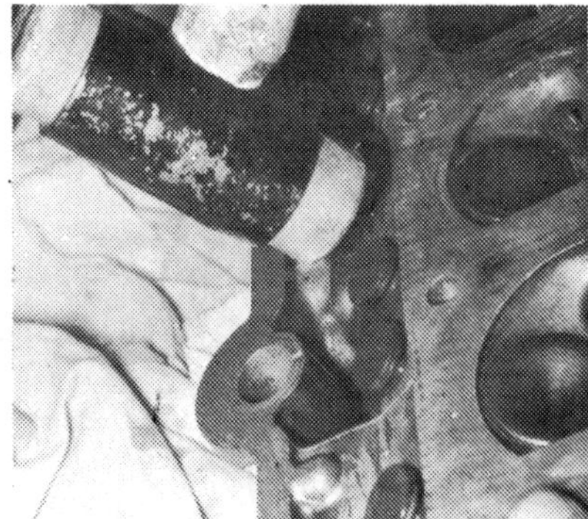
52.2B Tapping the tappets to retain them in position

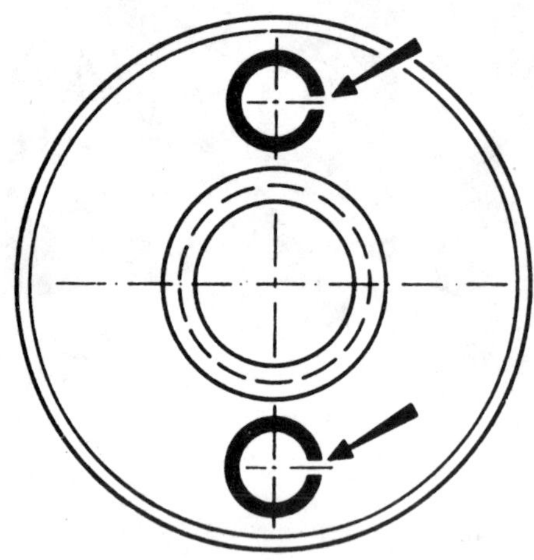

Fig.1.54 Correct gap position of camshaft roll pins

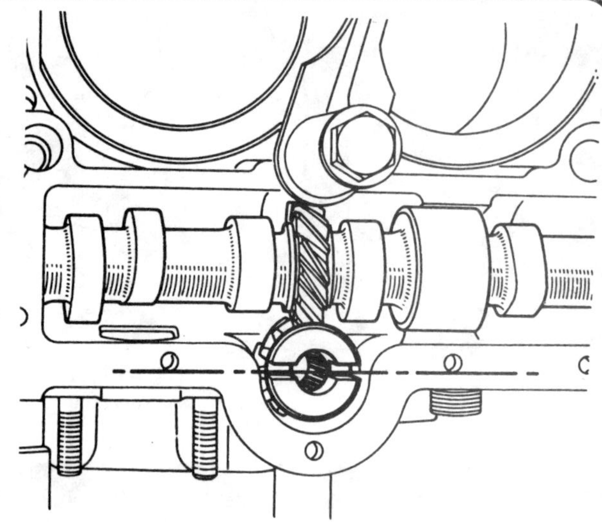

Fig.1.55 Smaller segment location on distributor drive shaft (type 697 and 821 engines)

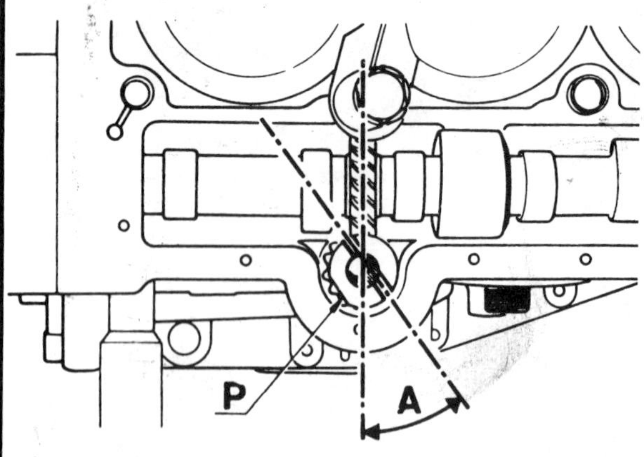

Fig.1.56 Smaller segment location on distributor drive shaft (type 807 engines) A is 53° P is flat

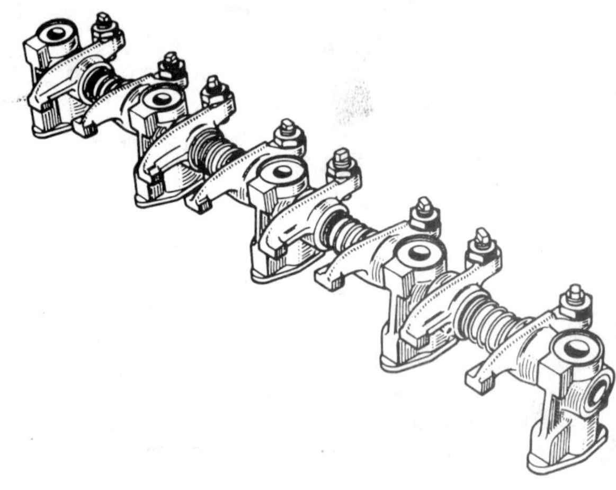

Fig.1.57 Components of the rocker shaft correctly fitted (type 697 and 821)

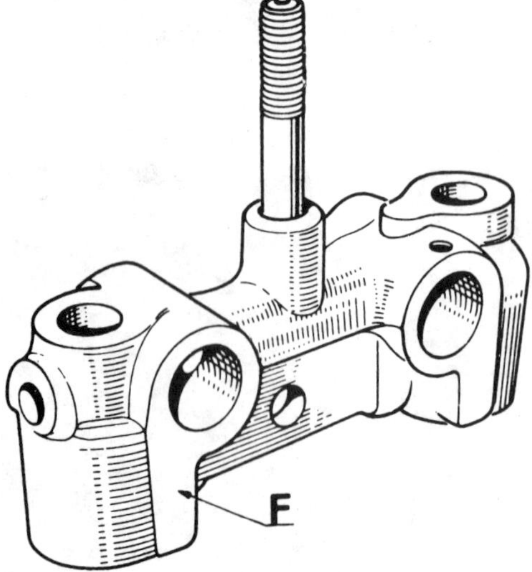

Fig.1.58 Rocker pillar (type 807 engine) F is machined face

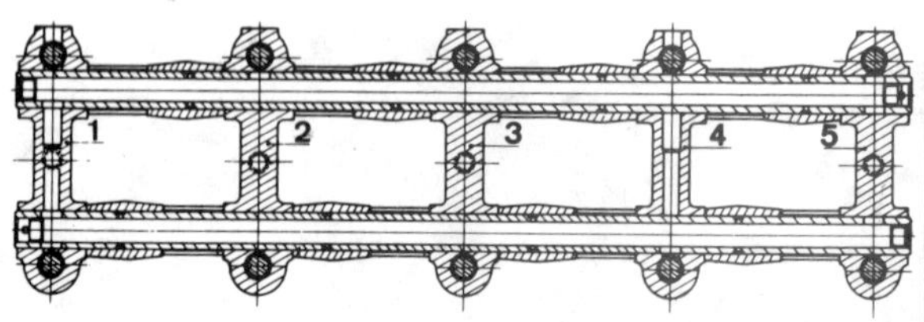

FIG.1.59 ROCKER GEAR FITTED TO TYPE 807 ENGINE

Rocker pillars 1 and 4 are similar but 1 has roll pin hole
Rocker pillars 2, 3 and 5 are similar but 5 has roll pin hole
Rocker pillar 4 has no stud hole

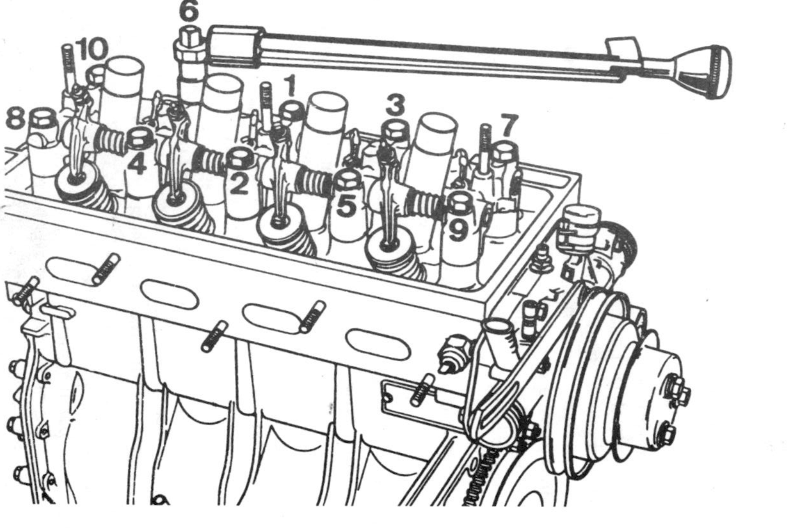

Fig.1.60 Cylinder head bolt tightening sequence

52.6 Locating a new cylinder head gasket

52.10 Installing the rocker gear and end bolts (807 type engine)

52.12 Tightening the dual purpose rocker pillar/cylinder head bolts on a type 807 engine

type 807 engines. COLD.
Stage 3. Start the engine and let it reach normal running temperature, switch off and allow it to cool for 50 minutes. Tighten 807 bolts to 60 – 65 lbf ft (8.3 – 9.0 kgf m) and 697 and 821 bolts to 55 – 60 lbf ft (7.6 - 8.3 kgf m).
13 After the first 300 miles (500 km) repeat the stage 3 operations and re-check the valve clearances.
Note that before tightening a bolt to a specified torque, the bolt should first be unscrewed by a quarter of a turn.
14 With type 697 and 821 engines, install the rocker shaft assembly, tightening the securing nuts to a torque of 15 – 20 lbf ft (2.1 – 2.8 kgf m).
15 Fit the pushrods, ensuring that they are returned to their original locations. Push rod installation is achieved by pushing each rocker arm against its shaft coil spring to obtain access to the push rod hole in the cylinder head. In some cases, it may be necessary to slack off the adjuster screw and locknut completely and to rotate the engine in order to bring the tappet to its lowest point of travel before the push rod can be fitted. Note that the push rods fitted to the type 807 engine are of different length, the shorter ones being the inlet ones and the longer ones the exhaust ones.

53 Valve/Rocker clearances - adjustment

1 Final and precise adjustment of the valve stem to the rocker arm clearances will be carried out with the engine temperature as described for Stage 3 cylinder head bolt tightening in the preceding section. Approximate settings made when the engine is on the bench will require rotation of the engine and this may be done by turning the exposed flywheel or connector plate. When the engine is in the car and a manual gearbox is fitted, top gear should be engaged and the starting handle dog utilised or a front road wheel jacked up and turned. With automatic transmission cars, neither of these methods are possible and 'inching' the engine while using the starter motor will have to be resorted to. The engine can also be turned by using a spanner on the camshaft pulley securing nut.
2 Turn the engine by means of one of the methods described until no. 1 piston is at T.D.C. on the compression stroke. This may be ascertained by placing a finger over no. 1 plug hole and feeling the build-up of pressure. A rod placed in the plug hole will indicate the highest point of travel of the piston which will be for all practical purposes T.D.C.
Both valves for that particular cylinder will now be fully closed and the clearances should be checked using feeler gauges (photo). The correct clearances are INLET 0.008 in (0.20 mm) EXHAUST 0.010 in (0.25 mm).
3 If the clearance requires adjustment, loosen the locknut, and with the feeler in position turn the adjuster screw until the feeler blade is nipped and will not move. Now unscrew the adjuster until the feeler blade is a stiff sliding fit. Tighten the locknut and recheck the clearance. (photo).
4 Repeat the adjustment procedure on the other valves bearing in mind the engine firing order (1 - 3 - 4 - 2) as if the cylinders are tackled in this sequence, much less engine turning will be required. With type 807 engine the inlet valves are on the right when viewed from the front of the car. With type 697 and 821 engines, inlet valves are 2 - 3 - 6 - 7 and exhaust valves 1 - 4 - 5 - 8 when counted from the front of the car.

54 Inlet and exhaust manifolds - refitting (type 807 engine)

1 Clean the mating faces of both inlet and exhaust manifolds and the cylinder block.
2 Ensure that the distributor, rocker cover and fuel pump have not yet been fitted as the manifolds cannot be located with these components in position.
3 Check that the coolant passages are clear in the inlet manifold and free from scale and sludge.
4 Fit the four small gaskets to the inlet manifolds (dry), checking that the water passages are clear (photo).
5 Fit the single gasket to the exhaust manifold (photo) again dry without the application of jointing compound.
6 Locate the manifolds on their studs and fit the plain washers, lock washers and nuts, tightening them to (exhaust 15 – 25 lbf ft/ 2.1–3.4 kgf m) and (inlet 20–25 lbf ft/2.8–3.4 kgf m). (photo).
7 When securing the exhaust manifold, attach the heat sheild and dipstick tube.

55 Inlet and exhaust manifolds - refitting (types 697/821)

1 With these types of engine, the inlet and exhaust manifold is combined assembly, Fig.1.61.
2 Fit the gasket and tighten the nuts and bolts to 10 - 20 lbf ft (1.4 - 2.8 kgf m)

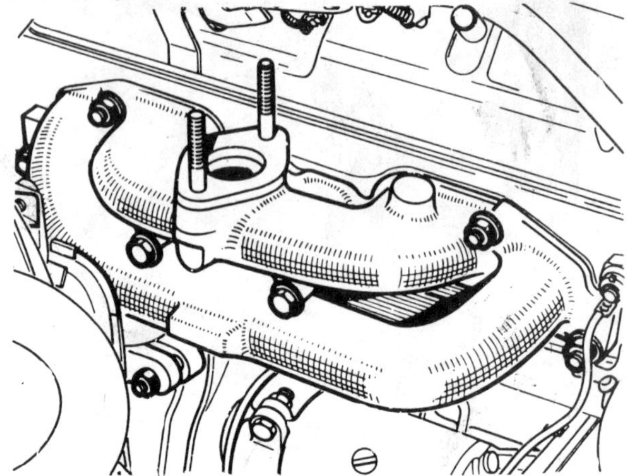

Fig.1.61 Inlet and exhaust manifold bolts and nuts (type 697 and 821 engines)

56 Flywheel and clutch - reassembly

1 Carefully clean the mating faces of the flywheel and the camshaft flange.
2 Check that the oil drain hole from the flywheel recess is clear by probing with wire.
3 Locate the flywheel on the crankshaft flange and fit a new lockplate and screw in one bolt to retain the components (photo).
4 Screw in the remaining bolts, finger tight. Tighten them in diametrically opposite sequence to 40 lbf ft (5.5 kgf m) holding the flywheel against the direction of rotation if necessary, but inserting a screwdriver in the ring gear and levering against the gearbox mating dowel (photo).
5 Secure the securing bolts by bending up the tabs of the locking plate (photo).
6 Place the clutch friction disc against the face of the flywheel, ensuring that the friction disc centre splined hub has its longest boss towards the gearbox.
7 Fit the pressure plate assembly in position on the flywheel and screw in the securing bolts finger tight. Now tighten each bolt in diametrically opposite sequence just two turns each.
8 With the driven plate (friction disc) only under slight pressure it must be centralised. Use an old gearbox primary shaft stepped dowel or a screwdriver and centralise the splined hub with the spigot bush in the flywheel (photo). The object of this operation is to enable the gearbox primary shaft to pass through the driven plate hub and engage with the flywheel spigot bush. If the plate is not exactly central, the force of the pressure plate when finally tightened down will not permit the plate to move sideways order to create the correct alignment.
9 Fully tighten the pressure plate cover bolts.
10 The components of the clutch, including the release mechanism should all be checked (before fitting to the engine) as described in Chapter 5.

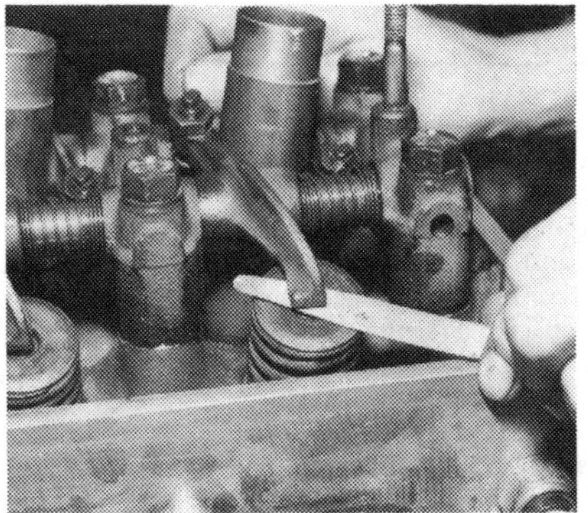
53.2 Checking a valve clearance

53.3 Adjusting a valve clearance

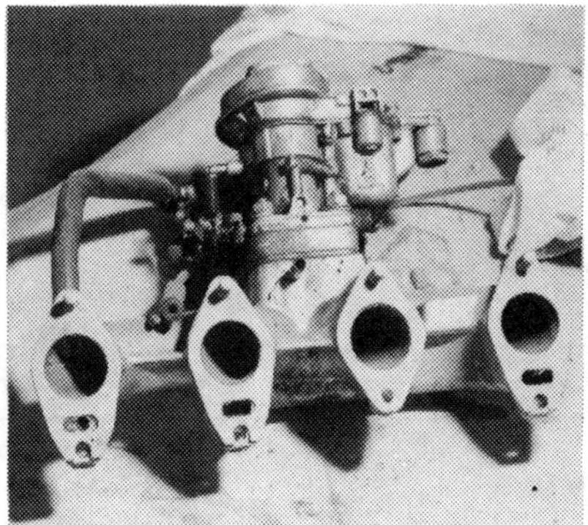
54.4 Inlet manifold, type 807 engine

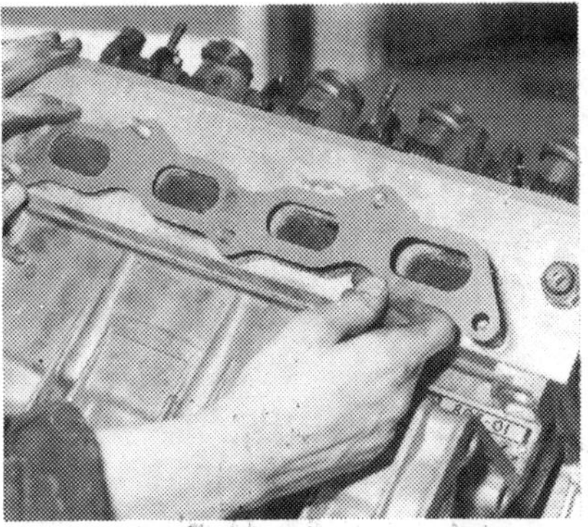
54.5 Exhaust manifold gasket, type 807 engine

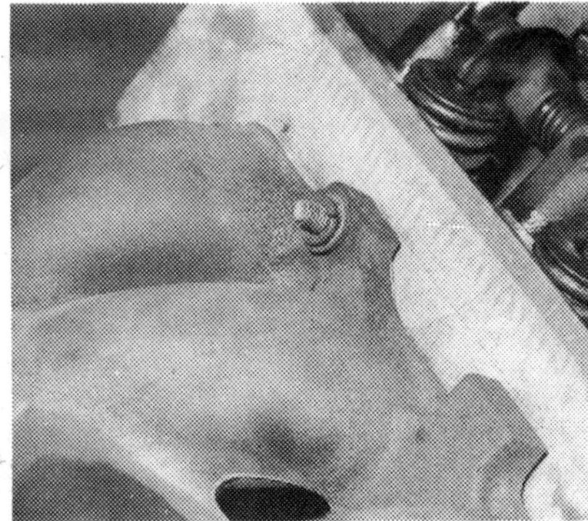
54.6 Exhaust manifold stud showing plain and lock washer

56.3 Fitting a flywheel lockplate and bolt

56.4 Tightening the flywheel securing bolts

56.5 Bending the flywheel bolt locking plate tabs

56.8 Centralising the clutch driven plate

57.2 Mating the gearbox/transmission with the engine

57.3 Final location of the gearbox and engine

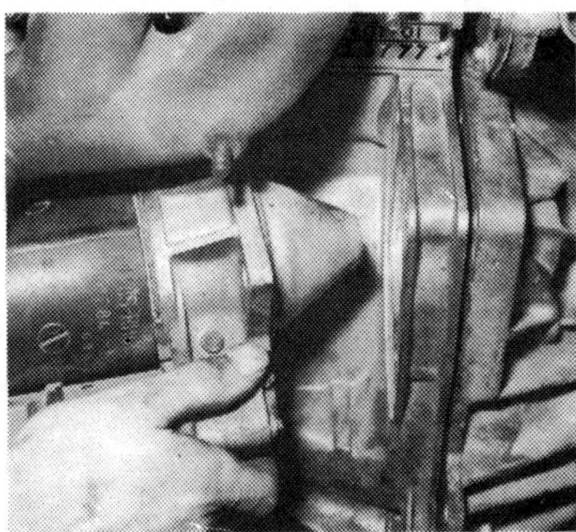
57.4 Fitting the starter motor

11 With model 1153TA vehicles which are fitted with automatic transmission, the connector plate will be fitted to the camshaft as opposed to a flywheel and clutch mechanism. Fuller details of the components concerned are given in Chapter 7 together with full fitting procedure.

57 Engine to gearbox/transmission - refitting

1 Check that the release bearing and lever are correctly located as described in Chapter 5.
2 Adequately support the engine and gearbox/transmission units at the same relative height so that the gearbox primary shaft will slide in horizontally into the splined hub of the friction disc (photo).
3 The help of an assistant to keep the engine still will be useful. Keep the gearbox - transmission quite level and push it into engagement with the engine. In order to engage the primary shaft of the gearbox with the driven plate splines and finally with the flywheel bush, it may be necessary to turn the gearbox unit slightly or to raise or lower it fractionally, but on no account allow the weight of the gearbox - transmission unit to hang upon the clutch assembly while the primary shaft is passing through it and support it at all times (photo).
4 Refit the bell housing securing bolts and fit the starter motor (lower securing bolts only) (photo).
5 Locate the rocker cover using a new gasket if required.
6 The combined engine/gearbox - transmission unit is now ready for refitting to the engine compartments.
7 Before coupling an automatic gearbox, remember to remove the connector retaining plate fixed on dismantling.

58 Engine - replacement

1 Clean the engine compartment and tie back any cables and wires.
2 Check the condition of the engine (two) rear mountings and the single mounting which supports the front of the gearbox. If the rubber shows signs of deterioration or is oil soaked, renew them (photo).
3 Fit the rope slings or lifting attachment.
4 Using the hoist or crane, lift the unit into the engine compartment at a steep angle with the gearbox end pointing upwards (photo).
5 When the unit has been manoeuvred to within 8 inches (203.2 mm) approximately of its final location, fit the starter motor leads (photo).
6 Continue to move the unit until the rear mounting bolts can be fitted. Use a screwdriver to align the mounting holes so that the bolts will pass through the holes easily without damaging the threads (photo).
7 With the weight of the engine still held by the hoist, use the scissors type jack as used for removal (section 5 paragraph 40) to refit the drive shafts. Remember to lubricate the splines with Molykote grease, use new roll pins (photo) sealing the ends with recommended sealer and, above all, keep the restraining clips in position on the shafts until the front gearbox mounting has been connected. Should you inadvertently pull the drive joints apart, refer to Chapter 8 for the refitting procedure.
8 Place a jack under the gearbox - transmission unit and remove the lifting tackle. Carefully lower the unit so that the front gearbox mounting can be connected (photo).
9 Remove the jack, fit the radiator support bracket, and the radiator (photo).

59 Ancillaries and connections - refitting and remaking

1 This is a reversal of removal and disconnection operations listed in section 5 of this Chapter.
2 The following groups of components are given as a check list and any specific fitting procedure is described in the following paragraphs.

Cooling system

3 Connect the radiator hoses (photo).
4 Connect the heater hoses.
5 Connect the manifold water hoses.
6 Refill the cooling system as described in the next Chapter.

Fuel System

7 Refit the air cleaner.
8 Refit the accelerator linkage (photo).
9 Refit the engine breather hose (photo).
10 Refit the vacuum hoses (distributor and brake servo).
11 Refit the fuel pipes to pump, carburettor and tank. (photo)
12 Refit exhaust manifold to pipe.
13 On type 807 engines, fit the flame trap capsule and pipe

Steering gear

14 Refit the steering gear crossmember assembly (photo).
15 Re-connect the steering eye bolts
16 Reconnect the steering column flexible joint (photo).

Transmission

17 Reconnect the gearchange link arm and pivot bolt (photo).
18 Reconnect the clutch cable to release arm and adjust the clutch free movement (see Chapter 5).
19 Refit the speedometer drive cable to gearbox and centrifugal

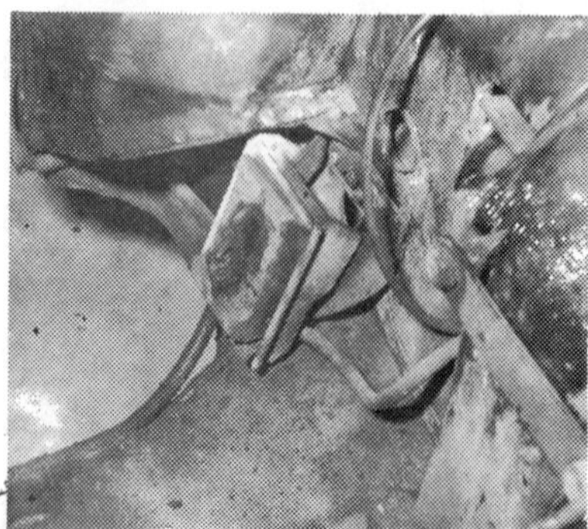
58.2 Engine mounting showing signs of deterioration

58.4 Hoisting the engine/transmission unit into the car

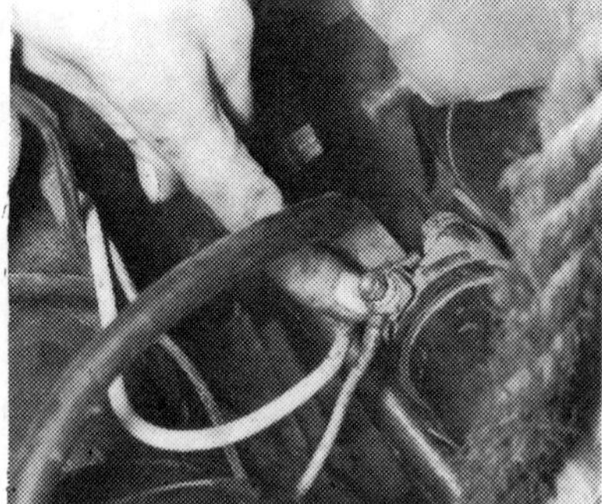
58.5 Fitting the starter motor leads

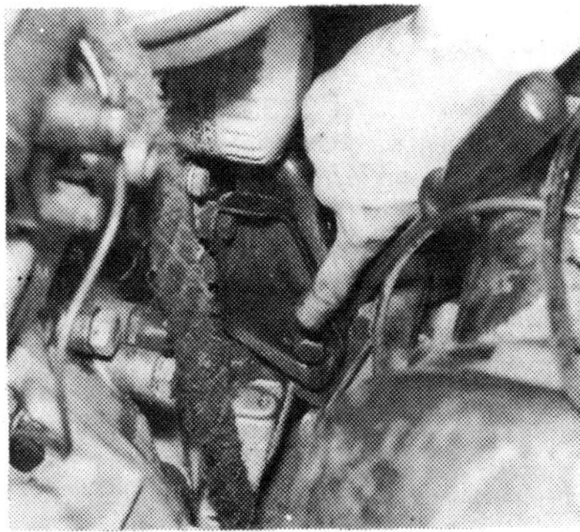
58.6 Prising the engine mountings to align the bolt holes

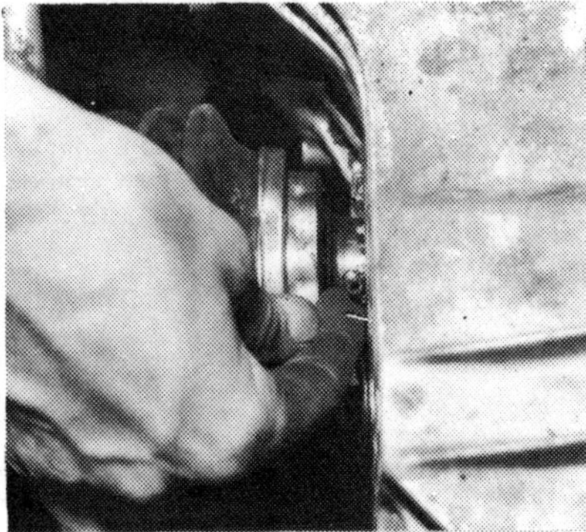
58.7 Fitting a roll pin to a drive shaft

58.8 Connection of the gearbox front mounting

58.9 The radiator and fan in position

59.3 Connecting the radiator hoses

59.8A Refitting the accelerator linkage

59.8B Accelerator cable bracket on rocker box cover

59.9 Engine breather hose

59.11 Refitting the fuel pipes to carburettor

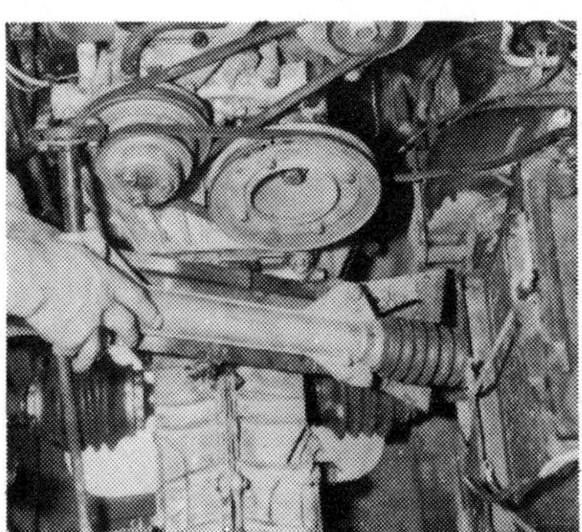
59.14 Refitting the steering assembly attached to its crossmember

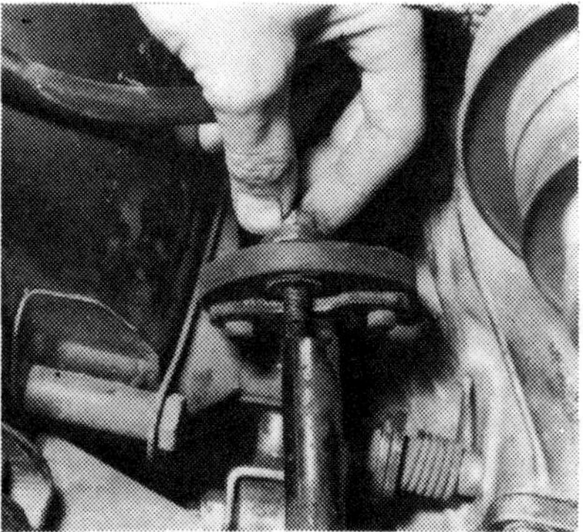
59.16 Reconnecting the steering column flexible joint

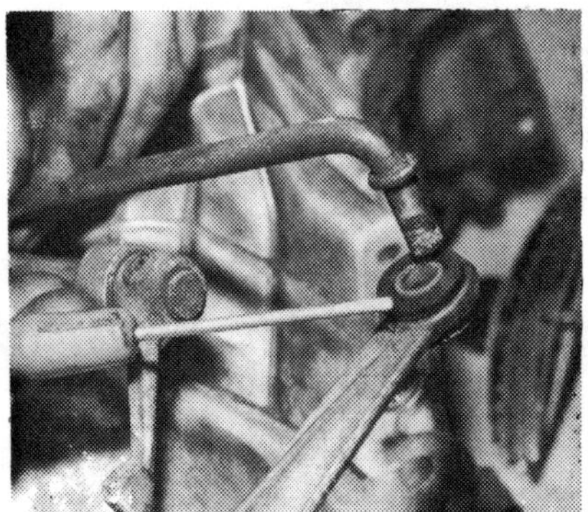
59.17a Connecting the gearchange lin' arm

switches (photo).
20 With automatic transmission, reverse the disconnection procedure given in section 6 of this Chapter.

Electrical

20 Connect the earth straps.
21 Connect oil and water transmitter leads.
22 Alternator leads and alternator to its mountings.
23 Connect the radiator cooling fan leads.
24 Fit the sparking plugs and coil.
25 Fit the distributor (photo). The distributor should only require dropping into its recess and turning the shaft until the large and small segments of the drive shaft mate. This will automatically provide the correct engine timing and can be checked by fitting the rotor arm and noting that it is pointing to no. 1 plug contact in the distributor cap when the engine is in the position of no.1 piston at T.D.C on compression stroke. Where the timing is incorrect, then refer to section 49 and refit the distributor drive shaft to the camshaft as fully described.
26 Connect the HT and LT ignition leads.
27 Connect the battery (photo).

Drive belts

28 The two drive belts (camshaft to water pump and water pump to alternator) must be fitted with care to avoid early destruction of belts and heavy loading of water pump or alternator bearings. Release the alternator strap adjuster bolt and push the alternator in towards the engine. Slip the belt over the alternator and water pump pulleys and then prise the alternator away from the engine until the belt is fairly taut. Tighten the adjuster strap bolt when the belt can be pushed and pulled in the centre of its longest run to give a total deflection of between 5/32in and 15/64 in (4 to 6 mm) for new belts on type 697 and 821 engines. For type 807 engines, the deflection is 1/8 in to 11/64 in (3 to 4.5 mm). Where belts are being refitted which have seen previous service then the deflection should be 9/32 in to 3/8 in (7 to 9.5 mm) and 13/64 in to 5/16 in (5 to 8 mm) respectively.
29 Fit the primary drive belt to the water pump pulley. Fit the camshaft belt driving pulley flange within the loop of the belt and then fit the pulley flange to the end of the camshaft. Refit any shims and fit the securing nuts finger tight only. Tighten the camshaft pulley nuts whilst rotating the engine. The correct mid-way deflection of the water pump to the camshaft belt is a total of 5/32 in (3.96 mm) for those fitted to type 697 and 821 engines and 1/8 in (3.2 mm) for belts fitted to type 807 engines. Where this deflection is incorrect, loosen the camshaft pulley flange nuts slightly and prise the flange away from the water pump at the same time turning the engine. Retighten the nuts when belt tension is correct.
30 Fit the spare wheel carrier, the spare wheel and the bonnet.

60 Engine - initial start up after major overhaul

1 Refill the engine and gearbox - transmission units with the correct grade and quantity of oil. (photo)
2 Check that there is fuel in the tank and turn the engine over on the starter to prime the fuel pump.
3 Start the engine with the carburettor set to a fast tick over and then inspect for leaks.
4 Give the car a test run and with the engine at the normal working temperature adjust the carburettor as described in Chapter 3.
5 Check the torque of the cylinder head bolts as described for stage 3 section 52, adjust the valve clearances.
6 Repeat the operations described in the preceding paragraph after 500 miles (800 km) and change the engine oil.

59.17b Connecting the pivot bolt

59.19 Reconnecting the speedometer cable

59.25 Fitting the distributor

59.27 Connecting the battery earth lead

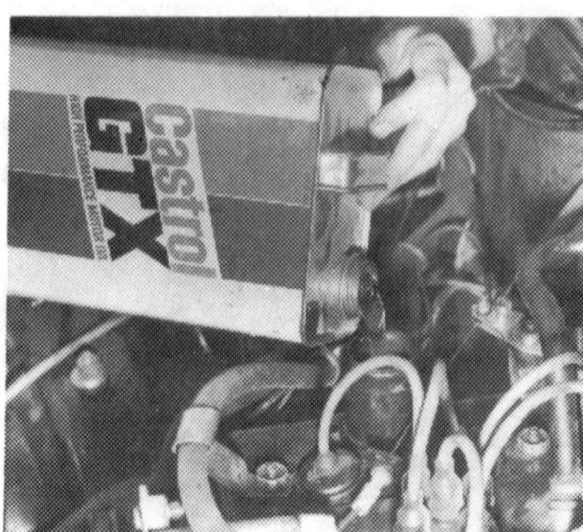

60.1A Filling the engine with oil

60.1B Filling the gearbox/transmission unit.

61 Fault diagnosis

Symtom	Reason/s	Remedy
No current at starter	Flat or defective battery	Charge or replace battery. Push - start car.
	Loose battery leads	Tighten both terminals and earth ends of earth lead.
	Defective starter solenoid or switch or broken wiring	Run a wire direct from the battery to the starter motor or by - pass the solenoid.
	Engine earth strap disconnected	Check and retighten strap.
Current at starter motor	Jammed starter motor drive pinion	Place car in gear and rock from side to side. Alternatively, free exposed square end of shaft with spanner.
	Defective starter motor	Remove and recondition.
No spark at sparking plug	Ignition damp or wet Ignition leads to spark plugs loose	Wipe dry the distributor cap and ignition leads. Check and tighten at both sparkplug and distributor cap ends.
	Shorted or disconnected low tension leads	Check the wiring on the CB and SW terminals of the coil and to the distributor.
	Dirty, incorrectly set, or pitted contact breaker points	Clean, file smooth, and adjust.
	Faulty condenser	Check contact breaker points for arcing, remove and fit new.
	Defective ignition switch	By - pass switch with wire.
	Ignition leads connected wrong way round	Remove and replace leads to spark plugs in correct order.
	Faulty coil	Remove and fit new coil.
	Contact breaker point spring earthed or broken	Check spring is not touching metal part of distributor. Check insulator washers are correctly placed. Renew points if the spring is broken.
No fuel at carburettor float chamber or at jets	No petrol in petrol tank	Refill tank!
	Vapour lock in fuel line (In hot conditions or at high altitude)	Blow into petrol tank, allow engine to cool, or apply a cold wet rag to the fuel line.
	Blocked float chamber needle valve	Remove, clean, and replace.
	Fuel pump filter blocked	Remove, clean, and replace.
	Choked or blocked carburettor jets	Dismantle and clean.
	Faulty fuel pump	Remove, overhaul, and replace.
Excess of petrol in cylinder or carburettor flooding	Too much choke allowing too rich a mixture to wet plugs	Remove and dry sparking plugs or with wide open throttle, push - start the car.
	Float damaged or leaking or needle not seating	Remove examine, clean and replace float and needle valve as necessary.
	Float lever incorrectly adjusted	Remove and adjust correctly.
No spark at spark plug	Ignition failure - Sudden	Check over low and high tension circuits for breaks in wiring
	Ignition failure - Misfiring precludes total stoppage	Check contact breaker points, clean and adjust. Renew condenser if faulty.
	Ignition failure - In severe rain or after traversing water splash	Dry out ignition leads and distributor cap.
No fuel at jets	No petrol in petrol tank	Refill tank.
	Petrol tank breather choked	Remove petrol cap and clean out breather hole or pipe.
	Sudden obstruction in carburettor(s)	Check jets, filter, and needle valve in float chamber for blockage.
	Water in fuel system	Drain tank and blow out fuel lines.

Chapter 2 Cooling system

For modifications, and information applicable to later models, see Supplement at end of manual

Contents

Specifications

Radiator	Copper or steel, tube and fin
System type	Sealed, thermo-syphon with water pump assistance and electric fan with thermal switch control
Capacity - Model R1150	10 pints (5.8 litres)
Models R1151 and R1154	12 pints (6.8 litres)
Models R1152 and R1153	11½ pints (6.6 litres) 14 U.S. pints
Thermostat opening temperature	84°C (183°F)
Fan thermal switch	
Fan operates at	92°C (197.6°F)
Fan cuts out at	82°C (179.6°F)

1 General description

1 The system is of pressurised type and sealed but with the inclusion of an expansion bottle to accept coolant displaced from the system when hot and to return it when the system cools.
2 Coolant is circulated by thermosyphon action and is assisted by means of the impeller in the belt driven water pump.
3 A thermostat is fitted in the outlet of the water pump. When the engine is cold, the thermostat valve remains closed so that the coolant flow which occurs at normal operating temperatures through the radiator matrix is interrupted.
4 As the coolant warms up, the thermostat valve starts to open and allows the coolant flow through the radiator to resume.
5 The engine temperature will always be maintained at a constant level (according to the thermostat rating) whatever the ambient air temperature and the use of a muff or shield in front of the radiator is quite superfluous.
6 The coolant circulates around the engine block and cylinder head and absorbs heat as it flows and travels in an upward direction and out into the radiator to press across the matrix. As the coolant flows across the radiator matrix, air flow created by the forward motion of the car cools it and it returns via the bottom tank of the radiator to the cylinder block. This is a continuous process, assisted by the water pump impeller.
7 In hot climates or when the car is travelling slowly or stationary, an electrically driven radiator fan cuts in by means of a thermostatically controlled switch actuated by the pre-determined temperature of the coolant.
8 The car interior heater operates by means of water from the cooling system.
9 Certain carburettors fitted to the Renault 16 are fitted with water connections from the cooling system for the purpose of choke operation or hot spot heating and the models are dealt with in Chapter 3.

2 Cooling system - draining

1 If the coolant is known to be in clean condition and of the correct constituency of antifreeze mixture, arrange suitable containers to hand before commencing draining.
2 Where one object of draining is to flush the system then it is to be recommended that the engine is at normal operating temperature as sludge and dirt will then be in suspension and more readily removed. If the engine is drained hot, flush with hot water not cold or distortion or cracking of internal engine components may occur.
3 Set the facia heater control to HOT (photo).
4 Remove the air vent valve from the expansion bottle (photo).
5 Open the drain tap under the radiator and drain plug. The coolant will flow slowly at first and as the expansion bottle empties it will flow faster. At this stage, unscrew and remove the radiator filler cap. This is rather inaccessible and situated below the grille support crossmember (photo).
6 Open the water pump bleed screw (photo).
7 Open the heater bleed screw (this is at the end of a short flexible pipe emerging from the engine bulkhead) (photo).
8 Open the carburettor bleed screw (where applicable) (photo).
9 Blowing through each (open) bleed screw will assist removal of all the coolant from the system.

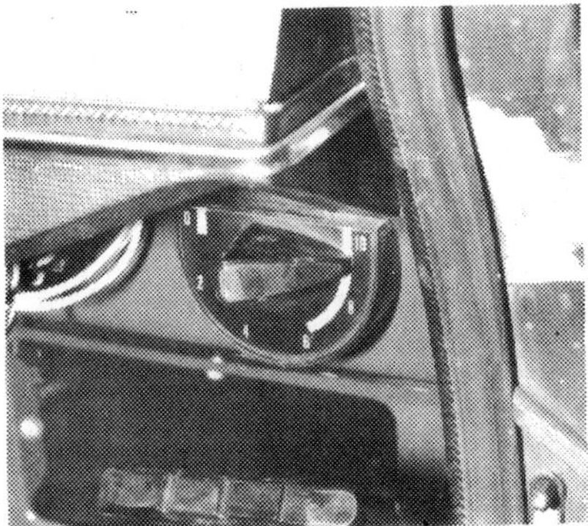

2.3 Facia heater control

2.4 Removing air vent valve from expansion bottle

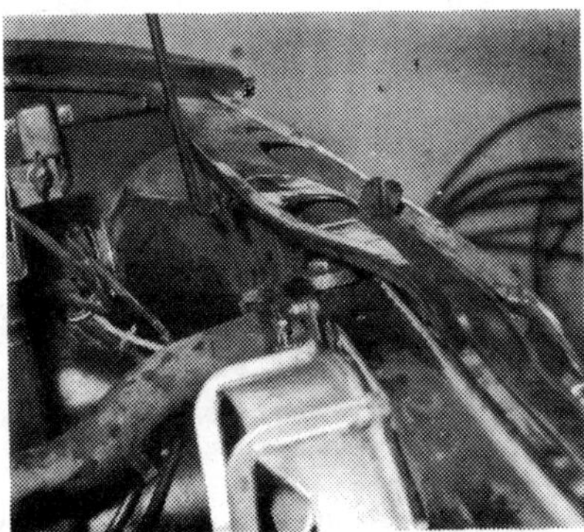

2.5 Location of radiator filler cap

2.6 Opening water pump bleed screw

2.7 Heater bleed screw

2.8 Carburettor bleed screw

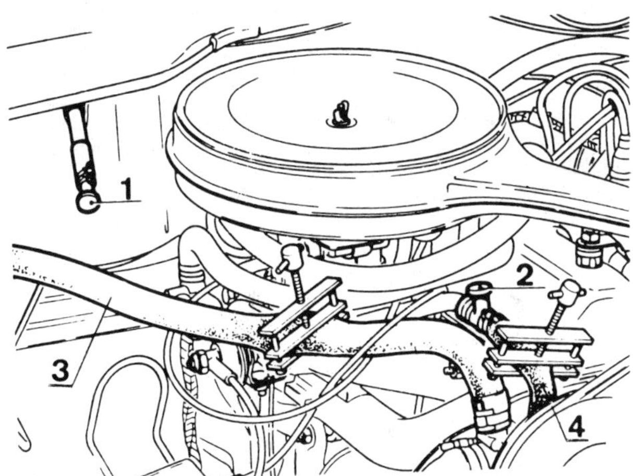

FIG.2.1 BLEED SCREW AND HOSE CLAMP LOCATIONS FOR FILLING COOLING SYSTEM (TYPE 697 AND 821 ENGINES)

Key

1 *Heater bleed screw*
2 *Carburettor bleed screw*
3 *Heater hose*
4 *Carburettor heater hose*

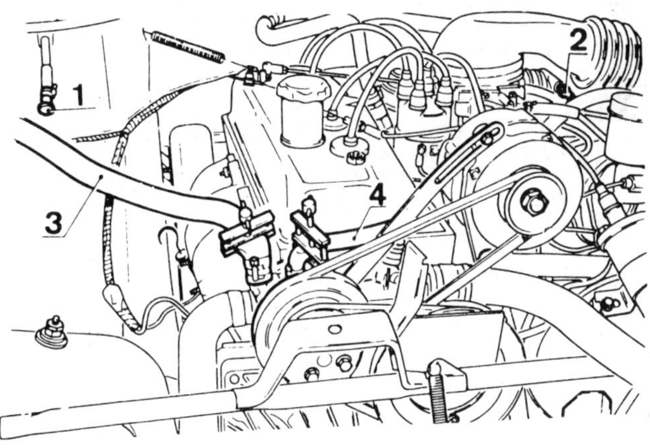

FIG.2.2 BLEED SCREW AND HOSE CLAMP LOCATIONS FOR FILLING COOLING SYSTEM (TYPE 807 ENGINE)

Key

1 *Heater bleed screw*
2 *Carburettor bleed screw*
3 *Heater hose*
4 *Carburettor heater hose*

3 Cooling system - flushing

1 Remove the thermostat from its water pump location as described in Section 8.
2 Temporarily reconnect the hose to the water pump outlet.
3 Check that the drain plugs are open and that the heater control is on HOT.
4 Insert a hose in the radiator filler cap and flush through until the water emerges clean. Use hot water if the engine was drained hot.
5 The accumulation of sludge or scale may necessitate removal of the radiator (Section 6) and reverse flushing. This is carried out by inverting the radiator matrix and placing a hose in the outlet pipe so that water flows in a reverse direction to normal.
6 The use of chemical descaler should only be used in a cooling system if scale and sluge formation are severe and then adhere strictly to the manufacturers instructions.
7 Leakage of the radiator or cooling system may be temporarily stopped by the use of a proprietary sealant but in the long term, a new cylinder head or other gasket, water pump, hoses or radiator matrix must be installed. Do not attempt to solder a radiator yourself. The amount of local heat required will almost certainly melt adjacent joints. Take the radiator to a specialist or exchange it for a reconditioned unit.

4 Cooling system - filling

1 Have ready a sufficient quantity of coolant mixture as described in Section 5. Close the radiator and block taps.
2 Turn the heater control lever to HOT.
3 Fill the expansion bottle 1.3/16 inch (30 mm) above the maximum mark (photo).
4 Fit the expansion bottle cap and valve. The seal must be fitted between the screw cap and the valve (photo).
5 Refer to Figs.2.1 or 2.2 according to engine type and check that bleed screws (1) heater and (2) carburettor are open.
6 Fill the system with coolant by pouring it into the radiator via the filler cap (photo).
7 When the radiator is full, clamp the hoses as close as possible to the water pump as shown in Figs.2.1 and 2.2. Suitable clamps may be made up quite simply or small G clamps used with two small strips of plywood to protect the hoses.
8 Start the engine and run at a fast tickover.
9 Continue to fill the radiator and when water emerges from all the bleed screws instead of hissing air, close them. Do not re-open them.
10 Remove the clamps.
11 Top up the radiator and fit the radiator cap.
12 When the engine has cooled, check the level in the expansion bottle and top up if necessary. If coolant passes through the expansion bottle valve at any time then the valve must be renewed.

5 Coolant and antifreeze mixture

1 The original coolant in the sealed system is of 'long-life' type and with antifreeze characteristics. It is preferable to mix a new coolant solution every year however, as apart from the antifreeze properties, rust and corrosion inhibitors (essential to a light alloy engine) will after this period of usage, tend to lose their effectiveness.
2 Mix the antifreeze with either distilled or rain water in a clean container. Drain and flush the system as previously described and pour in the new coolant. Do not allow an antifreeze mixture to come in contact with vehicle paintwork and check the security of all cooling system hoses and joints as antifreeze mixture has a searching action (photo).
3 The following amounts of antifreeze (as a percentage of the total coolant - see specification) will give positive protection down to the specified temperatures.

Percentage of antifreeze	Protection to (°C)
50%	−37
40%	−25
30%	−16
25%	−13
20%	−9
15%	−7
10%	−4

A mixture of less than 20% strength is not recommended as anti-rust and anti-corrosion action is not effective.

6 Radiator and electric cooling fan - removal

1 Drain the cooling system as described in Section 2.
2 Remove the spare wheel from the engine compartment and disconnect the battery earth terminal.
3 Disconnect the top radiator hose (photo).
4 Disconnect the bottom radiator hose (photo).
5 Unscrew and remove the vent valve assembly from the expansion bottle.
6 Disconnect the 'Lucar' type terminals from the fan temperature switch on the radiator (photo).
7 Disconnect the fan motor leads from the relay located at the side of the radiator.
8 Take out the two bolts with their washers and rubber mountings which secure the radiator mounting feet in position (photo). The use of a long socket drive is the easiest way to remove these bolts (photo).
9 Lift the radiator and fan assembly from the engine compartment (photo).
10 Note the expansion bottle vent valve and hose which will be attached to the radiator during removal and check that they are not damaged.
11 Refitting is a reversal of removal, but note the tongue which is attached to the bottom of the radiator and must engage during refitting with the rubber lined socket (photo).
12 After refitting, refill the system as described in Section 4.

7 Radiator cooling fan - removal and dismantling

1 The fan may be removed from the radiator without removing the radiator from the engine. This has the obvious advantage of avoiding draining and refilling the cooling system.
2 Disconnect the battery earth terminal.
3 Disconnect the two fan motor leads from the relay beside the radiator.
4 Refer to Fig.2.4 and unscrew and remove the four securing screws which retain the fan assembly to the radiator.
5 The fan normally has a very long trouble-free life and apart from the renewal of brushes, any wear occuring in other components will indicate the need for an exchange replacement unit.
6 Refer to Fig.2.3 and unscrew and remove the nut (7) which secures the fan blades to the drive shaft. This has a left hand thread and the nut should be unscrewed in a clockwise direction. Pull the fan straight off its shaft.
7 Unscrew and remove the two bolts (8) now exposed by removal of the fan blades, which secure the fan cage to the electric motor and separate these two major components.
8 Unscrew and remove the two motor cover bolts (1) lift off the cover and inspect the brushes. Where these are well worn, renew them by unsoldering the old and resoldering the new at the soldering points, arrowed in Fig.2.5.

8 Thermostat - removal, testing and replacement

1 The thermostat is located within the outlet pipe of the water pump housing (photo). The thermostat unit is itself retained within the rubber hose by a hose clip and the rubber hose is in

4.3 Expansion bottle level mark

4.4 Expansion bottle cap correctly located

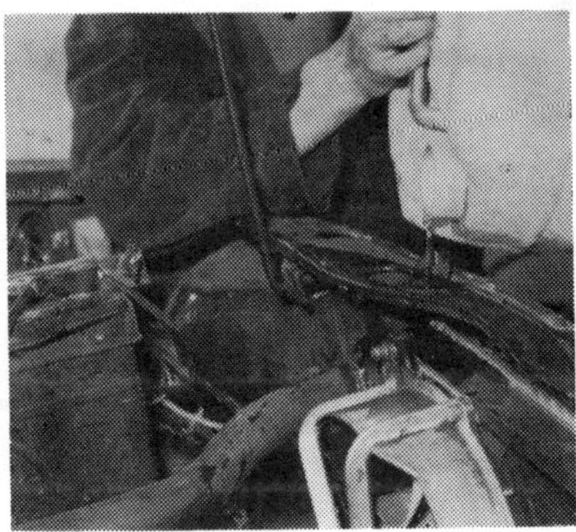
4.6 Filling the cooling system

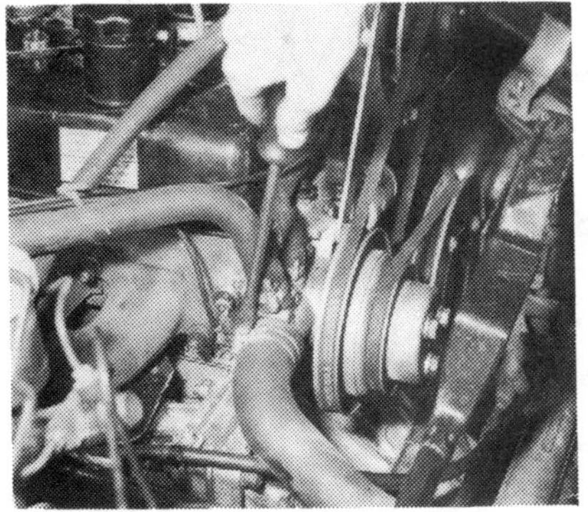
5.2 Checking security of a hose clip

6.3 Disconnecting the radiator top hose

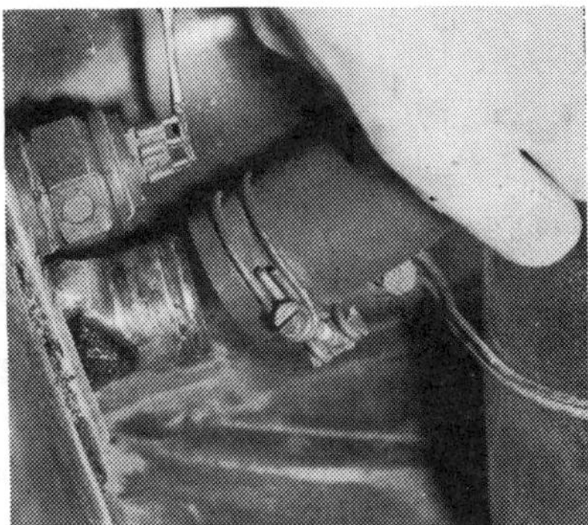
6.4 Disconnecting the radiator bottom hose

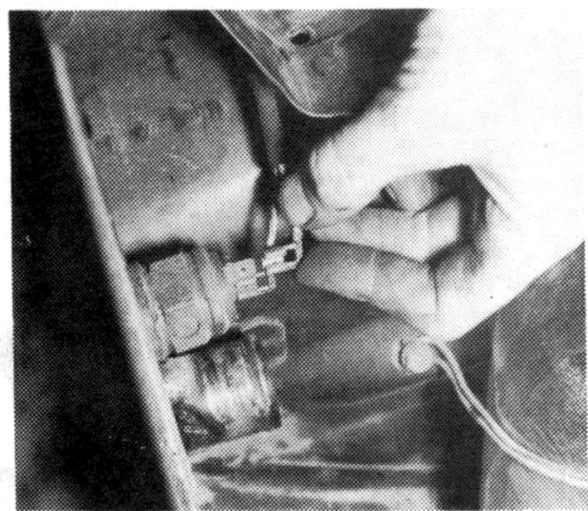
6.6 The radiator fan thermal switch terminals

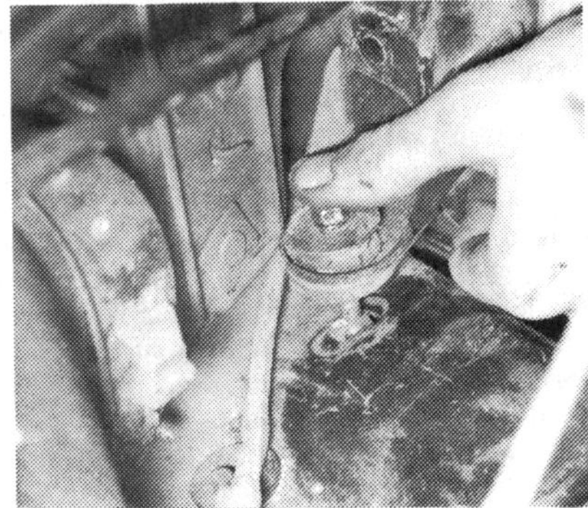
6.8A Radiator mounting

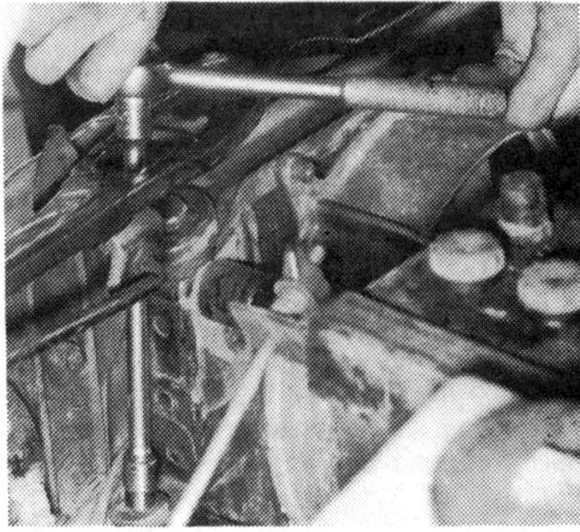
6.8B Unscrewing a radiator mounting bolt

6.9 Removing radiator and fan assembly

6.11 Radiator bottom locating tongue

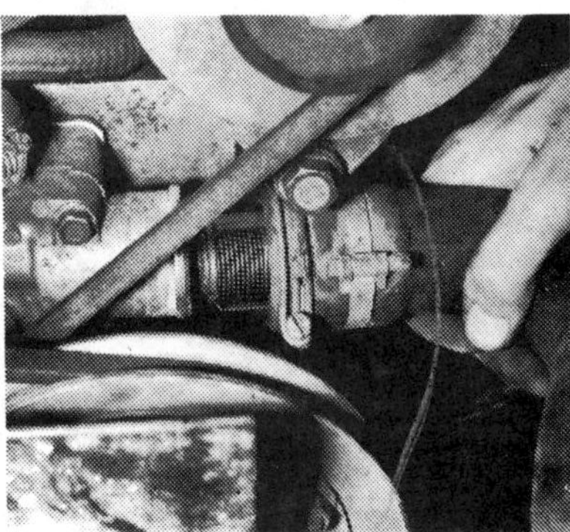
8.1 Thermostat location in water pump outlet hose

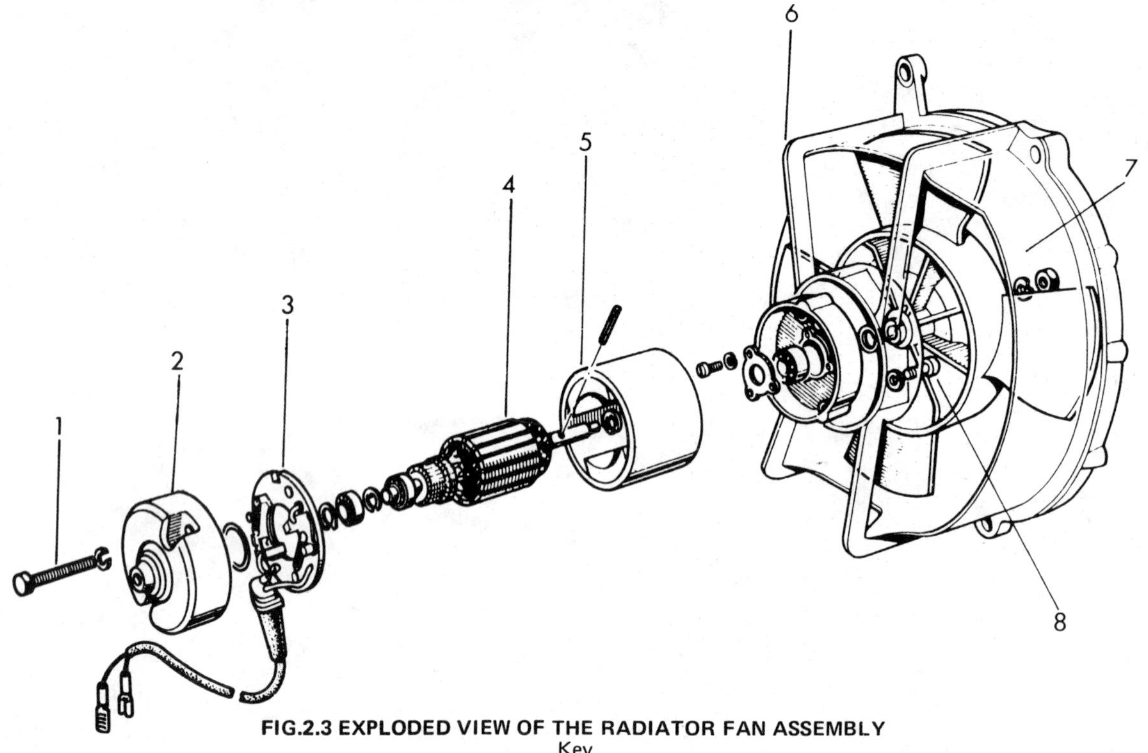

FIG.2.3 EXPLODED VIEW OF THE RADIATOR FAN ASSEMBLY

Key

1 Motor cover bolt
2 Motor cover
3 Brush plate
4 Armature
5 Stator
6 Fan cage
7 Fan securing nut
8 Cage to motor securing bolt

turn secured to the water pump outlet tube by another clip. Both clips must be loosened in order to extract the thermostat completely.

2 Before removing the thermostat, drain sufficient coolant so that the system level falls below the top radiator hose. Carry out this partial draining procedure just as described in Section 2.

3 Suspend the thermostat in a pan of water in which a thermometer has been placed. The thermostat should commence opening within 3 or 4 degrees of its specified opening temperature (75°C) and continue to its fully open position at the specified temperature. Transfer the fully open thermostat to cold water and observe that it closes within 20 seconds. If the unit does not operate correctly within the specified temperatures, renew it.

4 Refitting is a reversal of removal but ensure that the bleed hole is pointing upwards (opposite the lug on the water pump body, Fig.2.6).

5 Fill the system as described in Section 4.

9 Water pump - removal and replacement

1 The water pump is not designed for servicing or overhaul and should leakage occur from the shaft gland or the bearings become worn or noisy, then the pump should be renewed on an exchange basis.

2 Partially drain the cooling system as described in Section 2, and disconnect the five hoses from the water pump (Fig.2.7).

3 Slacken the alternator mounting bolts and adjustment strap bolts and push the unit in towards the engine so that the drive belt may be slipped from the pulleys.

4 Unscrew and remove the four nuts and bolts which secure the two halves of the camshaft pulley together. The camshaft to water pump belt may now be removed followed by the water pump to alternator belt.

5 Unscrew and remove the three bolts which secure the water pump pulley in position.

6 Unscrew and remove the water pump securing bolt which also retains the alternator adjustment strap.

7 Unscrew and remove the water pump securing bolts (photo).

8 Do not loosen the nuts which are visible as these retain the pump backing plate in position.

9 Tap the pump assembly forward to break its seal with the front face of the cylinder block and withdraw the pump.

10 Unscrew and remove the backing plate securing bolts and detach the pump from the plate.

11 Inspect the interior of the pump for signs of corrosion or erosion of the impeller which can give rise to overheating. As previously explained, should the impeller have deteriorated or the bearings show evidence of wear, renew the pump complete.

12 Fitting the pump is a reversal of removal but ensure that the mating surfaces are absolutely clean and use new gaskets (dry) between pump and backing plate and backing plate and engine block (photo).

13 Connect all hoses, making sure that the one containing the thermostat is not tightened until it is checked to see that the thermostat bleed hole is pointing upwards (photo).

14 Refill the cooling system as described in Section 4.

15 Adjust the drive belt tension as described in the next section.

10 Drive belts - removal, fitting and adjustment

1 Two drive (vee section) belts are used, the primary one drives the water pump front pulley from the camshaft pulley and the alternator is driven by a second belt running between the water pump rear pulley and the alternator driving pulley.

2 The belts can be adjusted independently but the rear one can only be removed after withdrawal of the front belt (photo).

3 Inspect the condition of the belts periodically and renew them if they show signs of fraying or have stretched so that available adjustment has been fully taken up.

4 Belts are correctly adjusted when a total deflection of between 1/8 and 3/8 inch (3 and 9.5 mm) can be obtained by moderate thumb pressure at the centre of the longest run (see Chapter 1 for belt deflection table).

5 To adjust the camshaft to water pump belt, remove the four nuts and bolts which secure the two halves of the camshaft pulley together. Shims are located between the two halves and

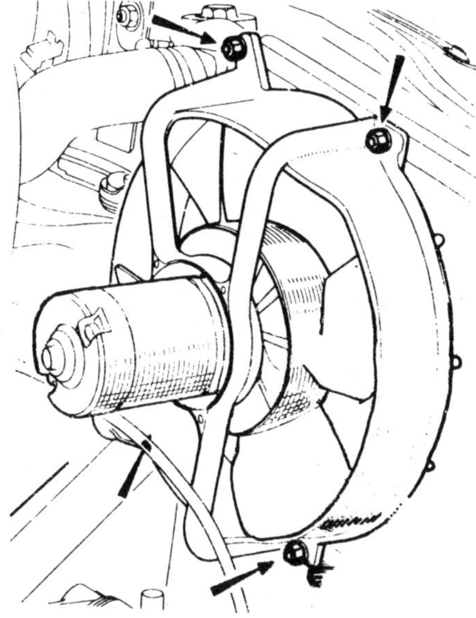

Fig.2.4 The radiator fan assembly securing screws

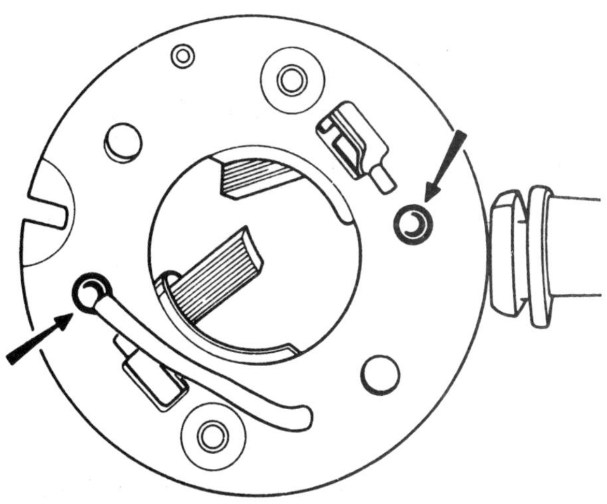

Fig.2.5 Brush soldering points on brush baseplate of radiator fan electric motor

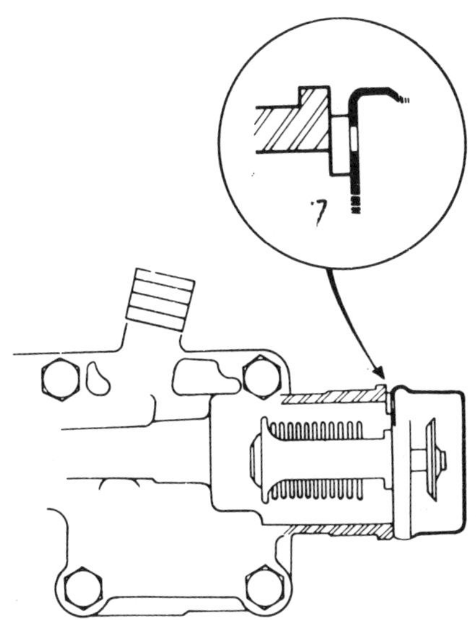

Fig.2.6 Correct location of thermostat bleed hole

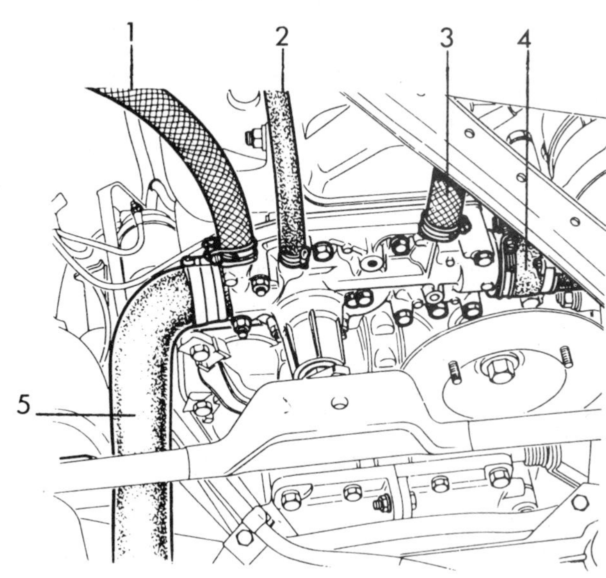

FIG.2.7 LOCATION OF WATER PUMP HOSES

Key

1 Heater
2 Carburettor
3 Heater
4 Outlet (thermostat
5 Inlet (from radiator)

9.7. Unscrewing the water pump assembly bolts

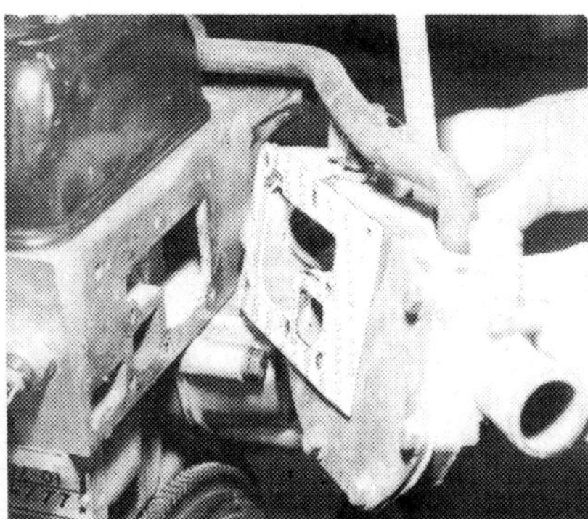

9.12 Fitting the water pump to the cylinder block face

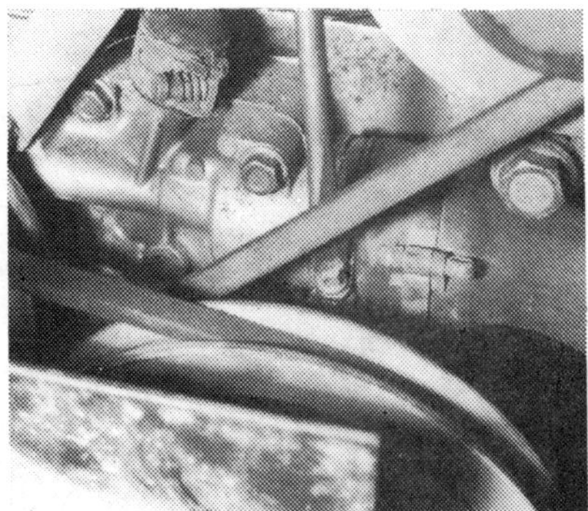

9.13 Tightening the thermostat enclosing hose clip

by adjusting the number of shims the tension of the belt will be varied once the two halves of the pulley are bolted up as the operation effectively widens or narrows the pulley belt gap. Place the unused shims on the outside of the pulley and retain them for future use by means of the pulley nuts and bolts. Always check that the belt is not trapped between the pulley flange halves and rotate the engine two or three times and again check the belt tension before finally tightening the pulley bolts.
6 To adjust the water pump rear pulley to alternator driving belt, slacken the alternator strap bolts, the two mounting bolts and prise the alternator away from the engine until the belt tension is correct. Do not slacken the bolts too much but just enough to permit the alternator to swivel stiffly. Retighten the alternator mounting and strap bolts.

11 Engine water temperature transmitter - testing

1 The transmitter may either be a thermal switch (models R.1150–R.1152 or R.1153) or a thermal bulb indicator (model R.1151). It is screwed into the right hand side of the cylinder head just to the rear of the water pump.
2 Ideally, the unit should be checked by removing it and placing it in a vessel to make operating tests but as the cooling system will have to be drained and refilled if this is done, an alternative is to run the engine to obtain the desired temperature checks with the radiator blanked off.
3 With a thermal switch, blank off the radiator, and run the engine.
4 Use a test bulb between the transmitter unit 'Lucar' type terminal and earth and check the temperature of the cylinder block or water pump with a thermometer held in contact with their surfaces. When the temperature reaches approximately 92°C (197.6°F) then the test bulb should light up as the temperature approaches or passes (within a margin of 5°C–9°F) this figure. Switch off the engine and as the coolant temperature drops to 82°C (179.6°F), the lamp should go out.
5 If the transmitter unit operates correctly, then the fault must lie within the connecting wiring or indicator bulb. If the unit does not operate correctly, renew it and this will necessitate draining and refilling the system.
6 With a thermal bulb type temperature gauge any fault will necessitate the renewal of the complete gauge - bulb assembly as it is a sealed assembly

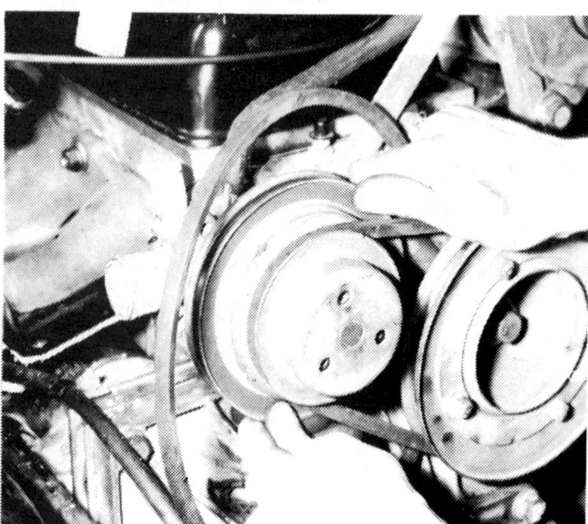

10.2 Slipping off the water pump pulley and belt to enable the rear belt to be removed

12 Radiator fan temperature switch - testing

1 The thermal type switch which controls the operation of the electric radiator fan is mounted in the right hand tank of the radiator. Ideally, tests to the switch should be carried out after it has been removed from its location. If this is done, the cooling system will have to be drained and refilled and the following alternative method may be substituted.
2 Connect a test bulb as shown in Fig.2.8 and with the engine cold, it should not light up.
3 Start the engine and blank off the radiator to ensure quick warming up.
4 Hold a thermometer in contact with the radiator and when the temperature reaches 92°C (197.6°F) the bulb should light up (allow a margin of 5°C either side).
5 Switch off the engine and allow the temperature of the radiator to drop to 82°C (179°F) when the light should go out. Differential between lamp ON or OFF should be 6–20°C (42.8–68°C).
6 If the switch does not operate within the test limits, renew it and this will necessitate draining and refilling the cooling system.
7 If the switch does operate correctly, then the fault must lie in the fan assembly or the connecting wiring or relay.

13 Expansion bottle - removal and refitting

1 The valve assembly in the expansion bottle screwed lid is only designed to pass air and if coolant comes into contact with it, then it must be renewed. This may be carried out without having to drain the system if the following procedure is observed.
2 Remove the spare wheel and apply a clamp to the hose which leads from the expansion bottle to the radiator as shown in Fig.2.9.
3 Unscrew the valve cap, using a spanner if necessary.
4 Unscrew the bottle retaining strap screw and remove the bottle if it is necessary to clean out or renew the bottle.
5 To install, place the bottle in position and locate and engage the securing strap and retaining screw and spring (photo). Screw in the retaining screw until its head just touches the end of the coil spring, then back it off one turn.
6 Fill the bottle to the 'maximum' mark and locate the valve, seal and screw caps (seal fits between valve and bottle neck).
7 Remove the hose clamp.

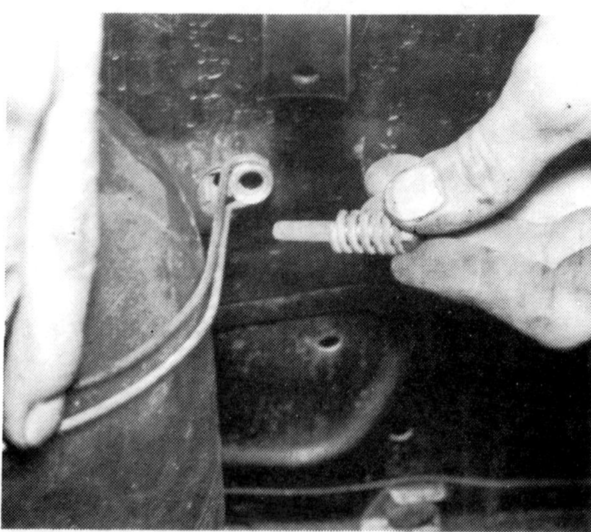

13.5 Expansion bottle securing strap and sprung retaining bolt

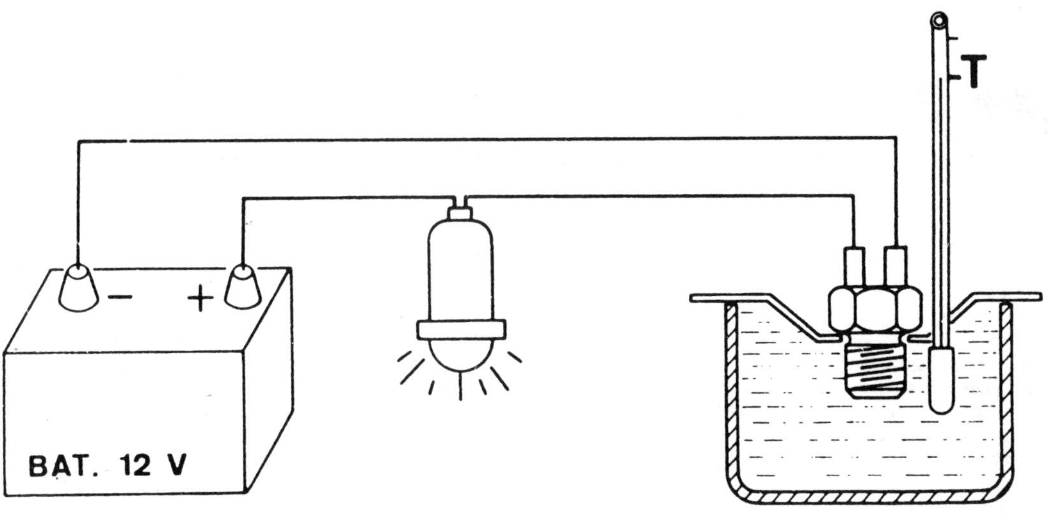

Fig.2.8 Testing circuit for radiator fan thermal switch

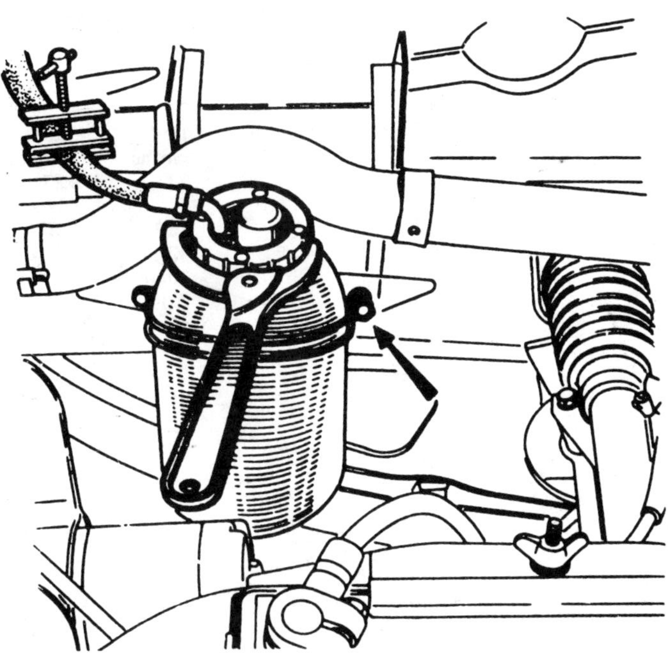

Fig.2.9 Clamping the hose, unscrewing the securing strap screw and the screw lid prior to removal of the expansion bottle

Chapter 3 Fuel system

For modifications, and information applicable to later models, see Supplement at end of manual

Contents

Specifications

Fuel pump ... SEV mechanical, driven from camshaft eccentric

Carburettors

Solex 35 DISA

Carburettor index number	319 and 319–1	365 and 365–1	370 and 365–2 1st setting	2nd setting	376 and 376–1	366
Choke tube	27	27	27	27	26.5	26.5
Main jet	140	142.5	142.5	142.5	142.5	142.5
Air compensator	135	160	160	150	155	145
Idling jet	50	42.5	42.5	42.5	50	50
Spring loaded needle valve	1.5 mm	1.5 mm	1.5 mm	2 mm	1.7 mm	1.7 mm
Float	7.3 g	7.3 g	7.3 g	7.3 g	7.3 g	7.3 g
Accelerator pump	50	40	40	40	50	50
Pump stroke	5 mm (13/64 in)	3 mm (1/8 in)	3 mm (1/8 in)	3 mm (1/8 in)	3 mm (1/8 in)	3 mm (1/8 in)

Zenith 36 IF

Carburettor index number	V10 005	V10 006
Choke tube	27	27
Main jet	135	145
Air compensator	100	100
Idling jet	40	40
Needle valve	1.5 mm	1.5 mm
Float		
Accelerator pump	40	40
Accelerator pump stroke		
Initial throttle butterfly opening	1 mm (0.040 in)	1 mm (0.040 in)

Solex 35 DITA

Carburettor index number	382 and 382–1	388	387 and 387–1	405 and 405–1	406
Choke tube	26.5	26.5	26.5	26.5	26.5
Main jet	140	140	140	140	140

Carburettor index number	382 and 382–1	388	387 and 387–1	405 and 405–1	406
Air compensator	155	145	155	155	145
Idling jet	50	50	50	50	50
Spring loaded needle valve	1.7 mm	1.7 mm	1.7 mm	1.7 mm	1.7 mm
Float	7.3 gr.	7.3 gr.	7.3 gr.	7.3 gr.	7.3 gr.
Accelerator pump	50	50	50	50	50
Pump stroke	3 mm (1/8 in)	3 mm (1/8 in)	3 mm (1/8 in)	3 mm (1/8 in)	3 mm (1/8 in)

Weber 32 DAR	1st barrel	2nd barrel
Choke tube	24	26
Main jet	145	150
Air compensator	180	140
Idling jet	50	80
Needle valve	1.75 mm	
Float	11 grams	
Initial throttle butterfly opening	1.2 mm (0.047 in)	
Float level	5 mm (13/64 in)	

Solex 26–32 DIDSA 3	1st barrel	2nd barrel
Choke tube	23.5	26
Main jet	120	140
Air compensator	125	130
Idling jet	65 with damper	95
Needle valve	1.7 mm	
Float	7.3 frams	
Accelerator pump	40	
Accelerator pump Stroke	2.5 mm (3/32 in)	

Weber 32 DIR 8 Mk 600	1st barrel	2nd barrel
Choke tube	24	24
Main jet	140	140
Air compensator	190	165
Idling jet	45	70
Needle valve	1.75 mm	
Float	11 grams	
Initial opening of throttle butterfly	0.047 in	
Float level	7 mm (9/32 in)	
Float travel	8 mm (5/16 in)	

Fuel tank capacity ... 11 imperial gallons 13 U.S. gallons 50 litres

Torque wrench settings

Inlet exhaust manifold (type 697/821 engine)	10 – 20 lbf ft (1.4 – 2.8 kgf m)
Inlet manifold (type 807 engine)	20 – 25 lbf ft (2.8 – 3.4 kgf m)
Exhaust manifold (type 807 engine)	15 – 25 lbf ft (2.1 – 3.4 kgf m)

1 General description

1 The fuel system comprises a rear mounted fuel tank, a mechanically operated fuel pump, driven from the camshaft, a carburettor and all necessary fuel lines, air cleaner and exhaust system.

2 A number of different types of carburettor are fitted according to vehicle and engine type and date of manufacture.

Vehicle	R1150	R1151	R1153	R1152 (USA)
Engine	697	807	821–01	821–02
Carburettor				
Early (up to) (1966)	Solex 35 DISA or Zenith 36 IF	Weber 32 DAR	Weber 32 DIR	Solex 26–32 DIDSA
Later	Solex 35 DITA			
Very late	Solex 35 DISA or Zenith 36 IF			

3 The Zenith type 36 IF has a water heated base hot spot.

4 The Solex 35 DITA has an automatic choke controlled by hot water from the cooling system. The Solex 35 DISA, the Weber 32 DAR the Solex 26 and the Weber 32 DIR 8 all have connections to the cooling system for base hot-spot heating.

5 Model R.1152 vehicles are fitted with anti-pollution device to reduce the formation of unburnt hydrocarbons and

carbon oxides in the exhaust gases.
6 All vehicles are fitted with a crankcase fume rebreathing device.

2 Air cleaner - removal, servicing and replacement

1 The air cleaner may be one of two types according to year of manufacture, a dry paper element type of circular design, Fig.3.1 or an oil wetted gauze type with rubber connecting duct to the carburettor (photo).
2 The paper element type cleaner is in three sections, lid (B), element (C) and body (D) all held together by a bolt and wing nut (A).
3 Every 12,000 miles (20000 km) renew the element. In very dusty conditions, renew it more frequently. The air cleaner lid need only be removed for this operation, but if the complete air cleaner assembly must be removed then the securing clamp at the carburettor throat should be loosened.
4 With the oil wetted type of air cleaner, loosen and detach the rubber trunking from the carburettor throat and then unscrew the two nuts from the air cleaner mounting bracket (photo).
5 Wash the filter gauze in paraffin and when dry, re-oil.
6 Refitting is a reversal of removal.

3 Fuel pump - routine servicing

1 The fuel pump is bolted to the left hand side of the crankcase, just forward and below the distributor mounting. It is driven by a cam on the forward end of the camshaft.
2 Check that the fuel hoses are secure to the pump inlet and outlet pipes and the circle of screws which secure the pump flanges together are tight.
3 Every 5000 miles (8000 km) remove the cover securing screw (the method of securing the cover varies according to pump model and may be a bar type retainer as shown in Fig.3.2).
4 Clean the sediment chamber and wash the gauze filter in clean fuel.
5 When refitting the cover, check the condition of the gasket and renew if necessary, do not overtighten the cover screw or bolt.

4 Fuel pump - testing

1 Uncouple the fuel pipe at its connection with the carburettor.
2 Spin the engine on the starter and observe if a well defined spurt of petrol is ejected from the hose. If this occurs then the fuel pump is serviceable.
3 An alternative test method is to remove the pump from its location and place a thumb over the inlet port and actuate the operating lever. A substantial suction should be felt and heard if the pump is in good order.
4 Where these tests prove positive then lack of fuel at the carburettor must be due to blocked fuel lines, blocked tank vent or a sticky carburettor inlet valve.

5 Fuel pump - removal, dismantling, reassembly and refitting

1 Disconnect the pump inlet fuel line and plug the fuel line so that fuel does not escape from the tank.
2 Disconnect the pump fuel line to the carburettor.
3 Unscrew and remove the two pump to crankcase securing bolts and washers. Withdraw the pump and retain any gaskets or insulating washers which are fitted between the pump flange and the engine block.
4 If the pump has seen considerable service it will almost certainly be realistic to exchange it for a factory reconditioned unit.
5 If it is decided to repair the pump then before dismantling, file an alignment mark across the edges of the two mating flanges to facilitate reassembly.
6 Remove the cover and filter and the flange screws and separate the two halves of the pump body (Fig. 3.3).
7 Withdraw the diaphragm by disengaging the operating rod from the pump operating lever.
8 The diaphragm and valve assemblies may be renewed if necessary as these components are available in kit form.
9 If wear has occurred in the operating lever or its spindle, then a new pump unit should be obtained.
10 Reassembly is a reversal of dismantling but ensure that the valves are correctly orientated and staked in position.
11 When refitting the fuel pump to the engine block, take care to engage the operating lever correctly with the camshaft before bolting up.

6 Carburettors - types and applications (R1150/697 engine)

1 Vehicle model R1150 fitted with a type 697 engine may be fitted with one of five different model carburettors according to date of manufacture.
2 Very early models are fitted with a Solex 35 DISA carburettor (Fig.3.4) which is of downdraught type incorporating manually operated choke and base heated by water from the cooling system. This carburettor may be encountered in one of five versions some of which include crankcase oil fume emission rebreathing connections and alternative choke controls. The exact type and index number of individual carburettors is marked on a plate attached to one of the float chamber securing screws. It is most important to check the index number against the jet and valve specification table given in Specifications.
3 The Zenith 36 IF carburettor is fitted to cars produced during 1966 and to the latest models. It is a downdraught carburettor with manually operated choke and base heated by water from the cooling system (Fig.3.5).
4 Cars produced after 1966 may also be fitted with a Solex 35 DITA (Fig.3.6). It is a downdraught carburettor with thermostatically (automatic) controlled choke which is actuated by water from the cooling system. Modified versions of this carburettor may be encountered which are designed for high altitude use or with over-riding cold setting control for the choke (Fig.3.7).

7 Carburettors - types and applications (R1151S/807 engine)

1 This type of vehicle is fitted with a Weber 32 DAR carburettor which is a twin choke, downdraught model having a thermostatically (automatic) controlled choke flap actuated by water from the cooling system (Fig.3.8).
2 Two versions of this carburettor may be encountered, one with a single choke flap or one having a choke flap for each choke tube.

8 Carburettors - types and applications (R1152/821 engine)

1 This model car, expressly modified for the North American market is fitted with a Solex 26–32 DIDSA carburettor. This is a twin choke, downdraught carburettor with manually operated choke operating on the first choke tube only. The base is heated by water from the cooling system (Fig.3.9). The index number is marked on a plate attached to a float chamber screw and this must be checked against the jet and valve specification given in Specification section of this Chapter.
2 The carburettor has connections for an anti-pollution device, fully described in Section 26 of this Chapter.

9 Carburettors - types and applications (R1153TA/821 engine)

1 This vehicle, which is fitted with an automatic gearbox uses

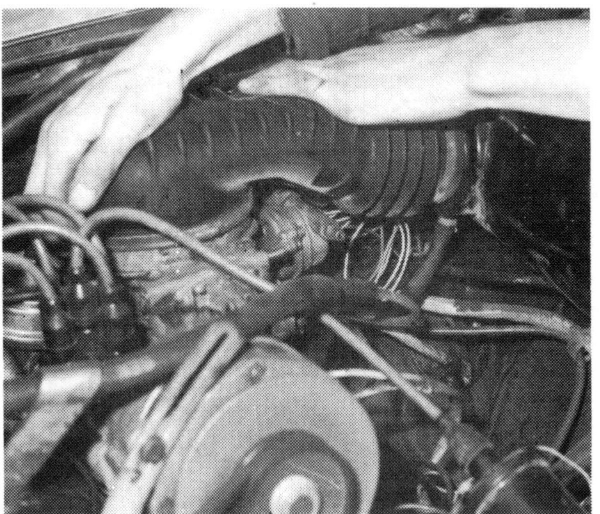

2.1 Disconnecting the air cleaner ducting from the carburettor

2.4 Air cleaner mounting brackets

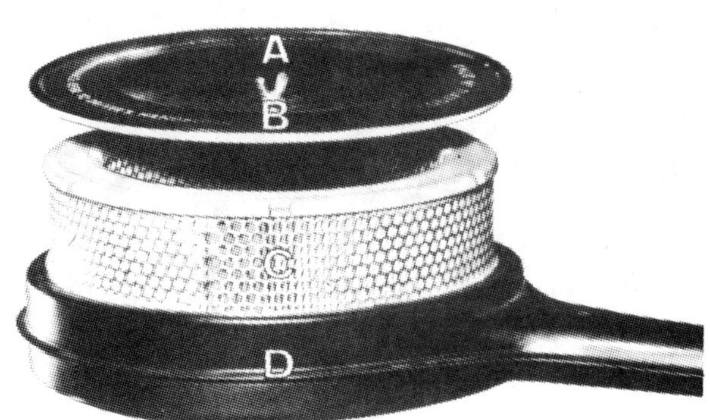

FIG.3.1 PAPER ELEMENT TYPE OF AIR CLEANER

A Wing nut
B Lid
C Element
D Body

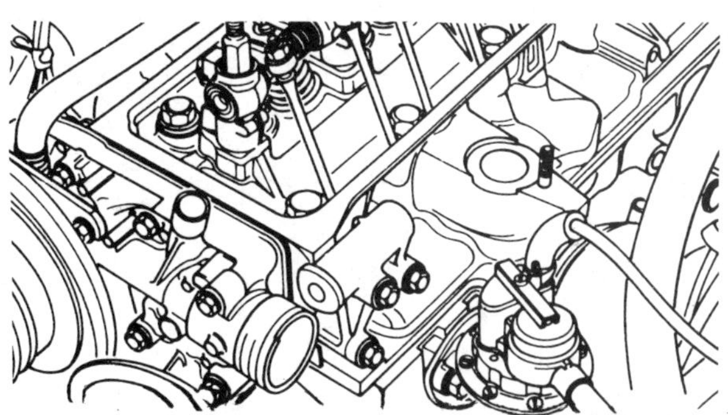

Fig.3.2 Location of mechanical fuel pump

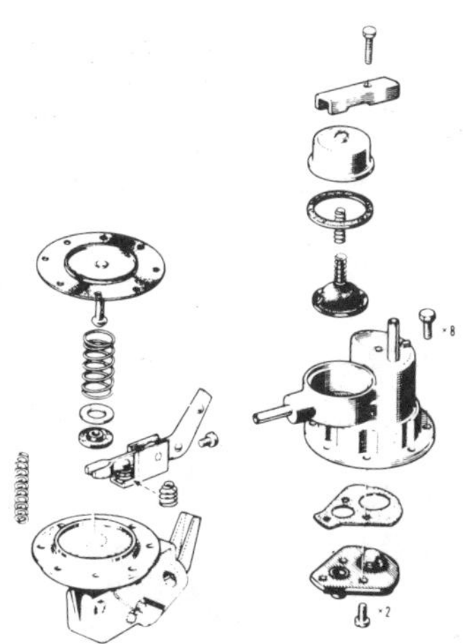

Fig.3.3 Exploded view of SEV type fuel pump

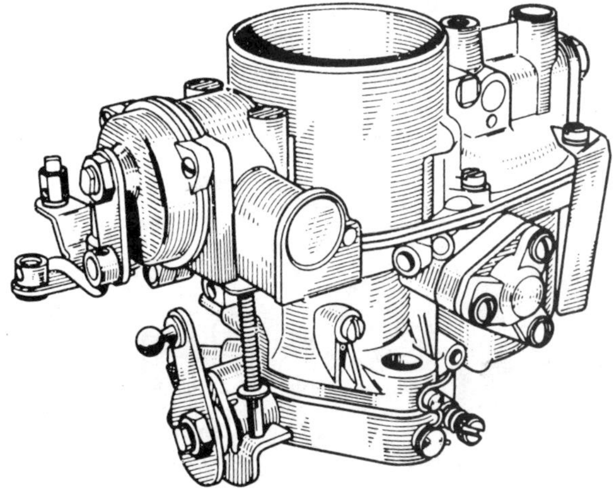

Fig.3.4 Solex type 35 DISA carburettor

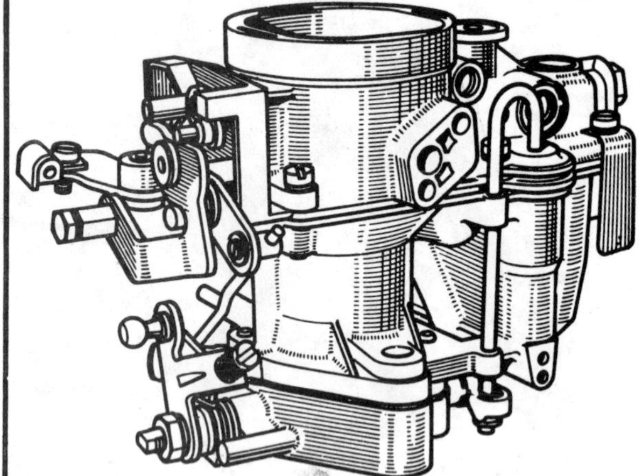
Fig.3.5 Zenith type 36 IF carburettor

Fig.3.6 Solex type 35 DITA carburettor

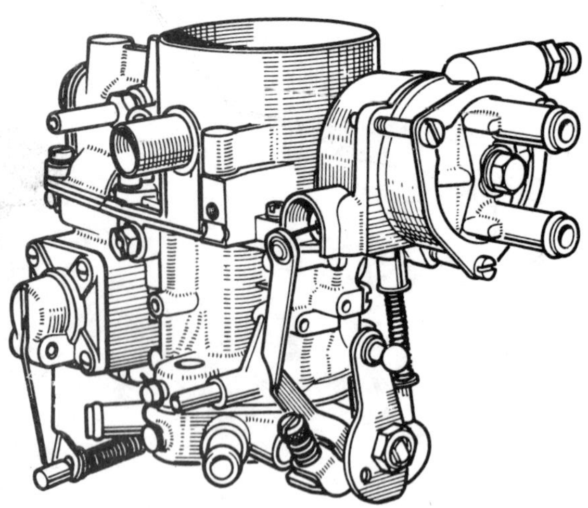
Fig.3.7 Solex type 35 DITA (modified) with overriding choke control

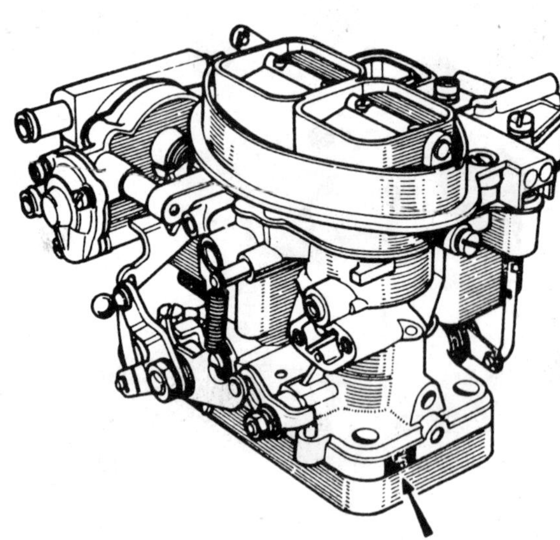
Fig.3.8 Weber type 32 DAR carburettor

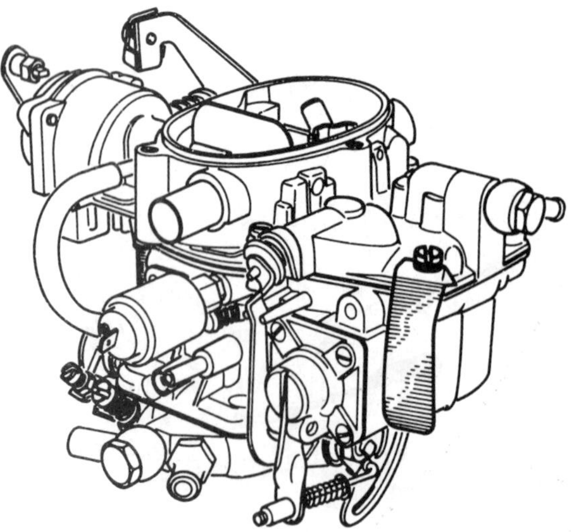
Fig.3.9 Solex type 26 - 32 DIDSA carburettor

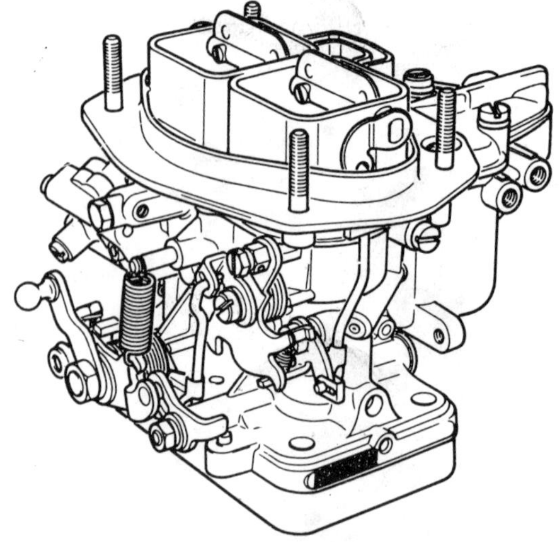
Fig.3.10 Weber type DIR 8 Mk 600 carburettor

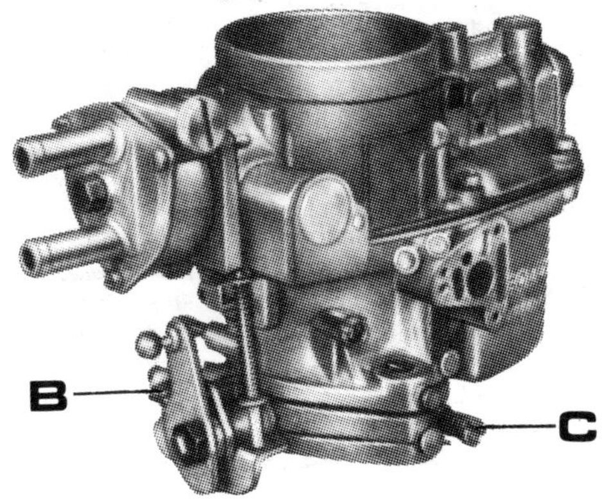

FIG.3.11 SOLEX 35 DISA ADJUSTMENT SCREWS

B Throttle butterfly screw *C Mixture screw*

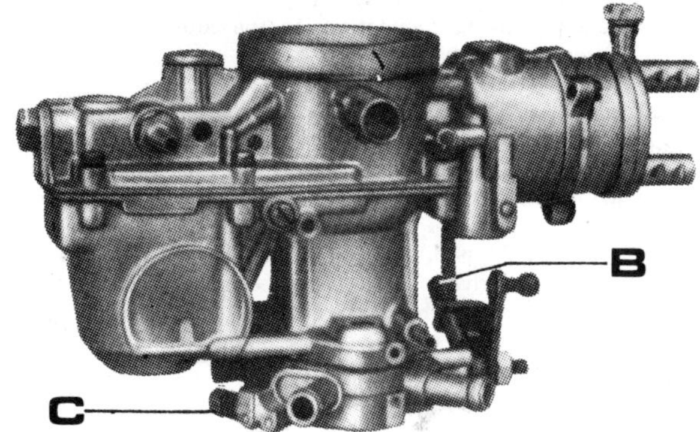

FIG.3.12 ZENITH 36 IF ADJUSTMENT SCREWS

B Throttle butterfly screw *C Mixture screw*

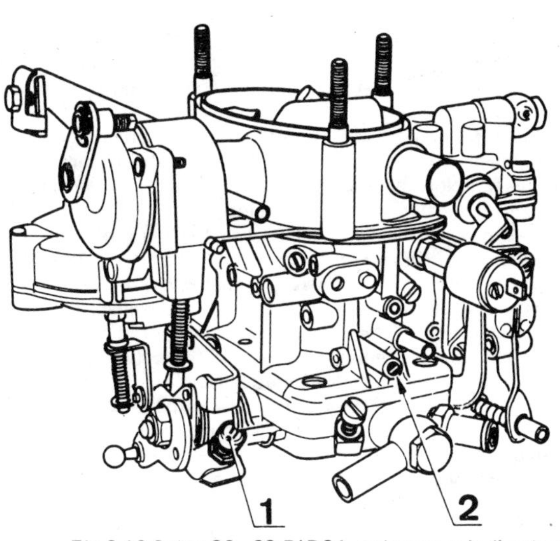

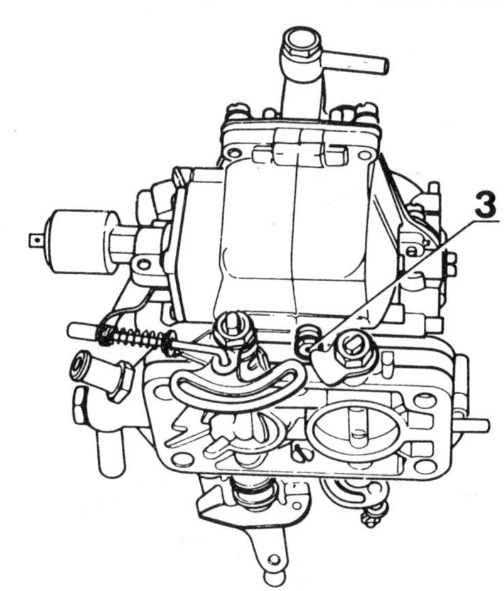

Fig.3.13 Solex 26 - 32 DIDSA carburettor indicating factory pre-set screws 1 - 2 - 3 which must not be altered

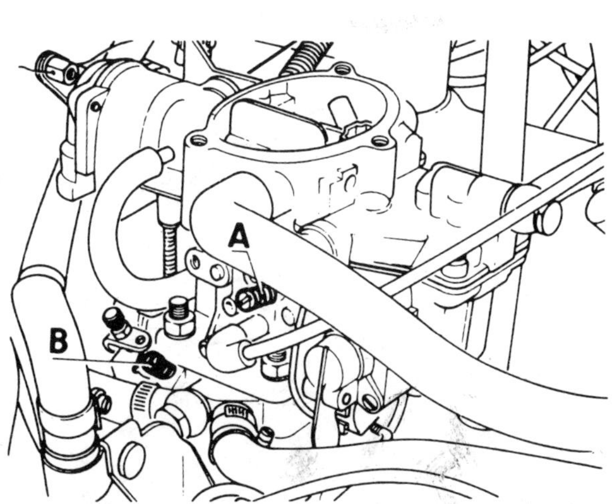

FIG.3.14 SOLEX 26 - 32 DIDSA ADJUSTMENT SCREWS

A Air screw *B Fuel screw*

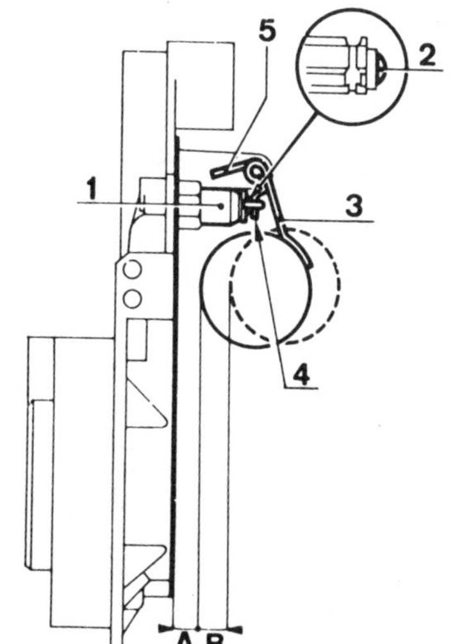

FIG.3.15 DIAGRAM FOR FLOAT ADJUSTMENT – WEBER 32 - DAR

1 Inlet needle valve
2 Valve ball
3 Float arm tongue
4 Float tab
A and B float travel

a Weber DIR 8 Mk 600 carburettor (Fig.3.10).

2 This is a twin choke, downdraught type with manually operated choke, having connections to the cooling system for heating the carburettor base.

10 Solex 35 DISA - adjustment

1 Run the car until the engine is at normal operating temperature.

2 Refer to Fig.3.11 and turn the throttle butterfly screw (B) until a slightly faster than normal idling speed is obtained.

3 Screw in (clockwise) the mixture screw (C) until the engine starts to run unevenly ('hunts') then unscrew it just enough to permit the engine to run smoothly.

4 Re-adjust the screw (B) if necessary to acquire the desired tickover.

11 Zenith 36 IF - adjustment

1 Adjustment should be carried out in a manner similar to that described in the preceeding section for the Solex 35 DISA but refer to Fig.3.12 for the location of the two adjustment screws.

12 Solex 35 DITA - adjustment

1 The method of adjustment of this carburettor is similar to that described for the Solex 35 DISA in Section 10.

13 Solex 26–32 DIDSA - adjustment

1 The method of adjustment of this carburettor differs from other types of Solex carburettors as no throttle butterfly screw is fitted. Two screws are provided however, one to control the air flow (air screw) and one to vary the mixture (fuel screw).

2 Refer to Fig.3.14 and carry out the following operations after the engine has reached full working temperature.

3 Turn the air screw (A) until the engine is running at 700 rev/min. This point may be ascertained by connecting an electric rev counter to the distributor or jacking up one of the front road wheels securely and engaging top gear and comparing the speedometer reading with the required engine revolutions (700 rev/min approximate 10 mph/16 km/h).

4 Turn the fuel screw (B) until the idling speed reaches its maximum and will go no higher whichever way the screw is rotated.

5 Now turn the air screw again until the engine settles to 700 rev/min.

6 Again turn screw (B) until the idling speed is at maximum and will go no higher whichever way the screw is turned.

7 Repeat operations 5 and 6 one further time and finally turn screw (B) until the engine speed drops to 675 rev/min which is the recommended idling speed. DO NOT TOUCH ANY OTHER SCREWS ON THIS CARBURETTOR AS THEY ARE FACTORY PRE-SET (Fig.3.13.).

14 Weber 32 DAR - adjustment

1 With this type of carburettor, two adjustment screws are fitted. One is the throttle plate lever screw and the other the volume control screw which acts only on the first choke tube.

2 Operate the engine until normal running temperature is attained.

3 Screw in the throttle plate screw until a fast tickover is obtained.

4 Adjust the volume control screw until the engine runs evenly without any sign of 'hunting' or unevenness.

5 Unscrew the throttle plate screw until the desired tickover speed is obtained and then re-adjust the volume control screw if necessary.

6 Where the conditions of weak or rich mixture are encountered or where satisfactory slow running adjustment cannot be obtained, check the fuel level in the float chamber.

7 Remove the carburettor from the engine (see Section 17) and remove the carburettor cover and gasket. Hold the cover assembly vertically so that the float will hang down and the valve closure tab will be in light contact with the inlet valve ball (Fig.3.15).

8 Using a steel rule, measure distance A (face of cover gasket to face of float) which should be 13/64 inch (5 mm). If the measurement differs from that recommended, bend the tongue (3) but ensuring that the arm (4) remains at right angles to the needle valve centre line.

9 Gently check the float travel (B) which should be 5/16 inch (8 mm). If incorrect, bend tongue (5).

15 Weber 32 DIR 8 Mk 600 - adjustment

1 This type of carburettor is fitted with two fuel adjustment screws, one for each choke tube and an air screw. Ideally this unit should be adjusted by using a vacuum gauge connected to the inlet manifold. Set the air screw to a point where the engine (at normal operating temperature) runs at a fast tickover. Adjust the two fuel screws until the highest vacuum gauge reading is obtained. Adjust the air screw to obtain the desired tickover.

2 If a vacuum gauge is not available, screw in both fuel adjustment screws, connecting the number of turns of each before full closure. Open each screw equally the average number of turns originally calculated for closure.

3 Set the engine to fast tickover using the air screw.

4 Open each fuel screw one half turn at a time until the engine begins to 'hunt' or run unevenly then close each screw by the same amount until the tickover speeds up and smooths out.

5 Finally, reset the air screw to give the desired tickover speed.

NOTE: Before removal of any type of carburettor, the water hose connections to the carburettor base or thermostatic choke housing must be clamped as near the carburettor as possible to prevent loss of coolant and admission of air to the cooling system when the hoses are disconnected. Failure to observe this procedure will necessitate bleeding and refilling the system as described in Chapter 2. Suitable clips or clamps for the purpose may be made up similar to the ones illustrated in Chapter 2 and this Chapter.

16 Solex and Zenith carburettors - removal and refitting

1 Disconnect the battery and remove the air cleaner from the carburettor as described earlier in this Chapter.

2 Refer to Fig. 3.16 and disconnect the pump to carburettor fuel pipe.

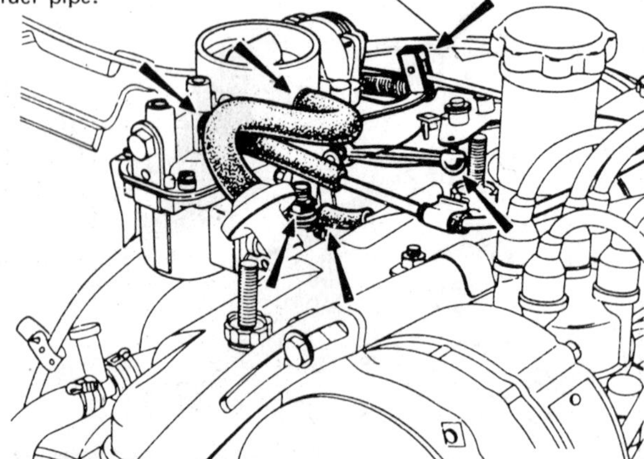

Fig.3.16 Disconnection points prior to removal of Solex or Zentih type carburettors

3 Disconnect the vacuum pipe.
4 Disconnect the vacuum capsule pipe.
5 Disconnect the throttle linkage.
6 With manually operated choke versions, disconnect the choke control at the carburettor.
7 With thermostatically operated choke versions, clamp the water hose (water pump to carburettor base) close to its connection with the carburettor and then disconnect the hose. Failure to clamp the hose will necessitate bleeding the cooling system after the carburettor is refitted.
8 Disconnect the water hose which runs between the base of the carburettor and the cylinder head (manual choke) or between the thermostatic choke housing and the cylinder head (automatic choke models).
9 Unscrew and remove the two carburettor flange fixing nuts and washers and withdraw the carburettor from the inlet manifold.
10 Refitting is a reversal of removal, but check the coolant level and unscrew the carburettor bleed screw to allow any trapped air to emerge. Tighten the bleed screw immediately water is expelled. Use new flange gaskets when refitting the carburettor to the manifold.

17 Weber 32 DAR - removal and refitting

1 Disconnect the battery earth terminal.
2 Disconnect the air filter trunking from the carburettor.
3 Refer to Fig.3.17 and disconnect the throttle linkage, the pump to carburettor fuel pipe and the vacuum pipe.
4 Fit clamps to the two water hoses which connect to the carburettor (water pump to base and thermostatic choke housing to inlet manifold) and then disconnect the hoses (photo).
5 Unscrew and remove the four carburettor flange fixing nuts and lift the carburettor from the inlet manifold.
6 Replacement is a reversal of removal, but check the coolant level and unscrew the carburettor bleed screw to allow any trapped air to emerge. Tighten the bleed screw immediately water is expelled. Use new flange gaskets when refitting the carburettor to the inlet manifold.

18 Solex 26–32 DIDSA - removal and refitting

1 Disconnect the battery earth terminal.
2 Disconnect the air cleaner ducting from the carburettor.
3 Refer to Fig.3.18 and disconnect the pump to carburettor fuel pump.
4 Disconnect the vacuum pipe.
5 Disconnect the idling speed damper wire.
6 Disconnect the choke cable and throttle linkage.
7 Disconnect the vacuum capsule pipe.
8 Disconnect the rebreathing pipe (fume emission) from the carburettor and then unscrew the nut which secures the rebreather valve and lift it complete with hoses from its location.
9 Refer to Fig.3.19 and clamp the two water hoses which connect with the carburettor base. Disconnect the two hoses.

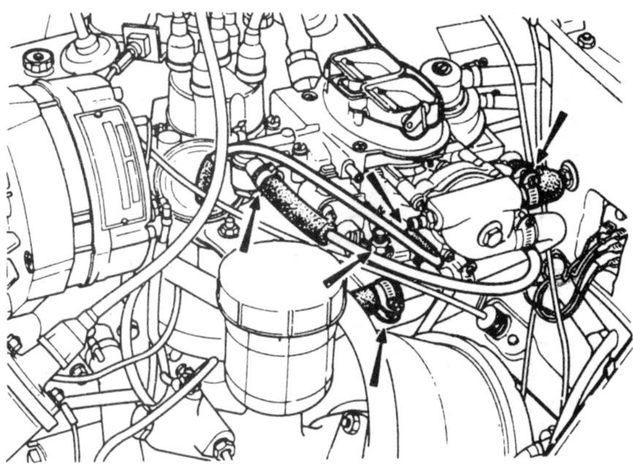

Fig.3.17 Disconnection points prior to removal of Weber 32 -DAR carburettor

17.4 Removing a carburettor water heater hose

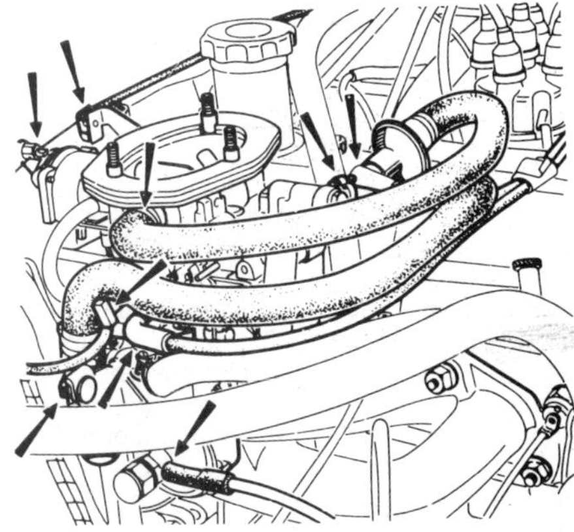

Fig.3.18 Disconnection points prior to removal of Solex 26 - 32 DIDSA carburettor

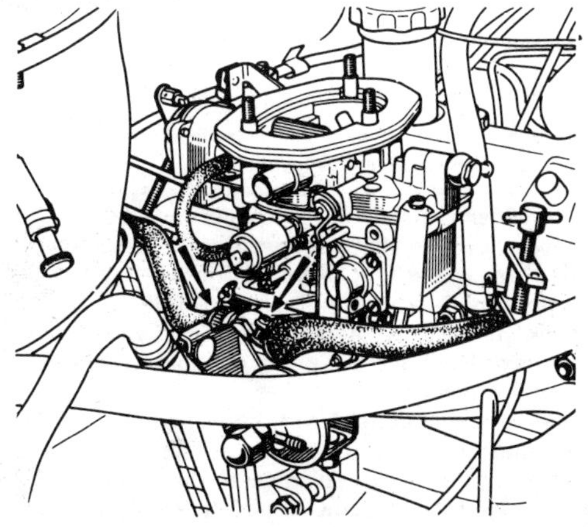

Fig.3.19 Disconnecting the carburettor water heater hoses on the Solex 26 - 32 DIDSA

10 Unscrew the four carburettor flange fixing nuts and withdraw the carburettor complete with vacuum capsule support plate.
11 Refitting is a reversal of removal, but check the coolant level and unscrew the carburettor bleed screw to allow any trapped air to emerge. Tighten the bleed screw immediately water is expelled. Use new flange gaskets when refitting the carburettor to the inlet manifold

19 Weber 32 DIR 8 Mk 600 - removal and refitting

1 Disconnect the battery earth terminal.
2 Remove the air cleaner.
3 Refer to Fig.3.20 and disconnect the pump to carburettor fuel pipe.
4 Disconnect the vacuum pipe.
5 Disconnect the choke cable and throttle linkage.
6 Clamp the two water hoses which are attached to the base of the carburettor to prevent water loss and disconnect them.
7 Unscrew and remove the carburettor flange fixing nuts and detach the automatic transmission control cable clip.
8 Lift the carburettor from the inlet manifold.
9 Refitting is a reversal of removal, but check the coolant level and unscrew the carburettor bleed screw to allow any trapped air to emerge. Tighten the bleed screw immediately water is expelled. Use new flange gaskets when refitting the carburettor to the inlet manifold.

20 Solex 35 DISA - dismantling and reassembly

1 Unscrew and remove the six screws and washers which retain the upper body to the carburettor main assembly. Note the lengths and locations of the screws for exact replacement.
2 Remove the float swivel pin and remove the float.
3 Clean any sediment from the float chamber and check the security of the inlet valve in its seat. Do not remove any of the washers behind the inlet valve body nut or the fuel level will be altered.
4 Servicing of the carburettor should be restricted to removal, cleaning, checking against specification and refitting the jets. Do not attempt to remove the choke or throttle butterflies. If their spindles are worn then renew the carburettor on an exchange basis.
5 Refer to Fig.3.21 and using screwdrivers of compatible size, unscrew the jets indicated. Blow the jets through using a tyre pump, never probe them with wire.
6 The level of the fuel in the float chamber will be maintained correctly, provided washers have not been removed or additional ones fitted.
7 The accelerator pump stroke should be checked in specifications section according to index number and the swan neck of the operating rod bent carefully if it is necessary to adjust the travel.
8 Reassembly is a reversal of dismantling, use a new cover gasket.

21 Zenith 36 IF - dismantling and reassembly

1 Unscrew and remove the six screws and washers which retain the upper body to the carburettor main assembly. Note the lengths of the screws for exact replacement.
2 Remove the float lever and spindle and the float.
3 Check the security of the inlet needle valve located in the cover, but do not remove it unless evidence of flooding indicates the need for renewal.
4 Interconnecting control rods between cover and main body may be disconnected but do not attempt to remove the choke or throttle butterflies or spindles. If these are worn then it is preferable to exchange the complete unit for a factory reconditioned one.
5 Refer to Fig.3.22 and remove the jets using spanners and screwdrivers of appropriate close-fitting sizes. Blow the jets through with a tyre pump, never probe with wire.
6 Refitting is a reversal of dismantling. Use a new cover gasket if required.

22 Solex 35 DITA - dismantling and reassembly

1 The procedure is similar to that for the Solex 35 DISA described in Section 20, but the following must be noted. The thermostatically (water heated) controlled choke is not repairable and must be renewed as an assembly if it becomes faulty. Before removing it, observe the alignment marks which appear on the top of the thermostatic choke housing and the carburettor cover. These must be in alignment when fitting the new unit.
2 Refer to Fig.3.23 for location of carburettor jets.

23 Weber 32 DAR - dismantling and reassembly

1 Unscrew and remove the upper body screws and withdraw the upper assembly which contains the needle valve and choke control mechanism.
2 Empty the float cnamber and remove the float, taking care to retain the needle from the valve.
3 Do not dismantle the choke butterflies or spindles unless essential. Check the security of the inlet valve, but do not add or remove any of the washers located beneath it.
4 Disconnect the accelerator pump linkage from the throttle valve spindle and dismantle the pump.
5 If the automatic choke has failed, remove the complete unit and fit a new one.
6 Refer to Fig.3.24 and remove the jets. Clean them by blowing air from a tyre pump through them, never use wire to probe them.
7 Reassembly is a reversal of dismantling, but use new gaskets and check that any interconnecting linkage is correctly located.

24 Solex 26–32 DIDSA - dismantling and reassembly

1 This carburettor is fitted to engines having emission control of the exhaust gases and any dismantling should be restricted to renewing the cover gasket, float or inlet needle valve and removing, cleaning and refitting the jets shown in Fig.3.25. All other settings are set to precise limits during manufacture and must not be altered, Fig.3.13.

25 Weber 32 DIR 8 Mk 600 - dismantling and reassembly

1 Dismantling and reassembly are similar to that described for the Weber type 32 DAR carburettor and reference should be made to Section 23.
2 The position of the jets is shown in Fig.3.26 and the method of adjusting the float is identical to that described in Section 14.

26 Exhaust anti-pollution device - description

1 The R1152 model car, built specifically for the North American market incorporates a device to reduce the formation of unburnt hydrocarbons and carbon oxides in the exhaust gases during deceleration and so comply with current regulations.
2 Basically, the type 821–02 engine has been modified to include special pistons with less clearance between crown and cylinder head, special inlet manifold and cylinder head ports and a twin choke carburettor having vacuum controlled linkage. A special device is fitted to hold the throttle butterfly slightly open during deceleration and an ignition distributor having a modified centrifugal and vacuum advance curve.
3 The main components and layout of the device are shown in Fig.3.28.

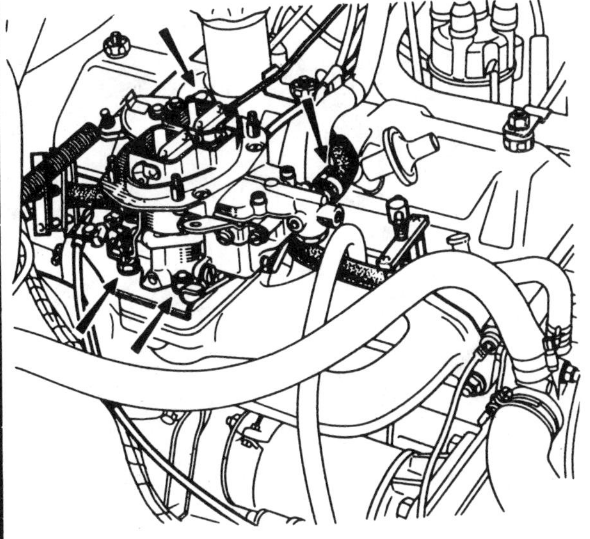

Fig.3.20 Disconnection points prior to removal of the Weber 32 - DIR 8 Mk 600 carburettor

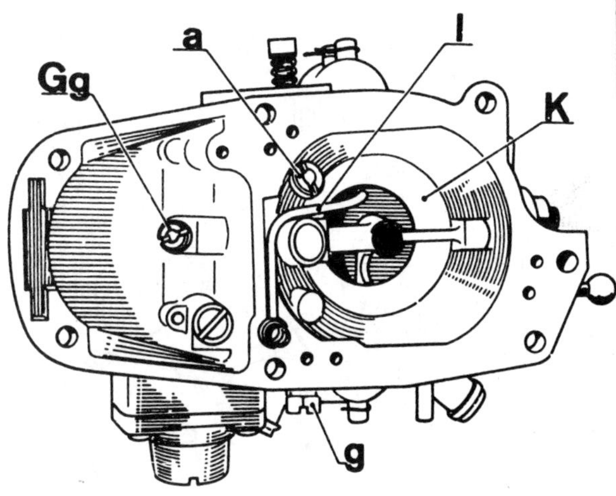

FIG.3.21 LOCATION OF JETS IN SOLEX 35 DISA

a Air compensator
Gg Main jet
g Idling jet
I Accelerator pump
k Choke

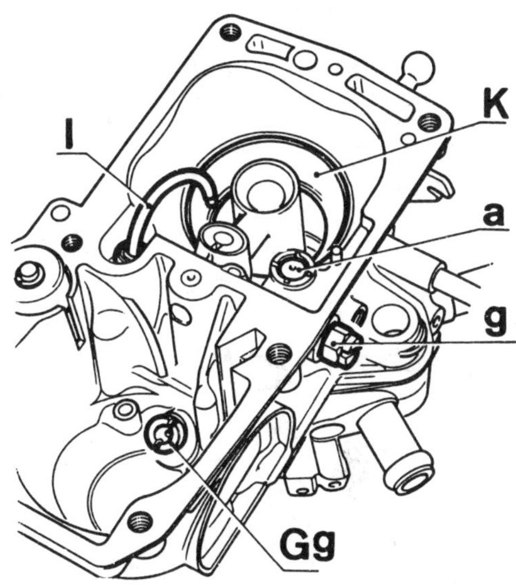

Fig.3.22 Location of jets in Zenith 36 IF carburettor. Key as for Fig.3.21

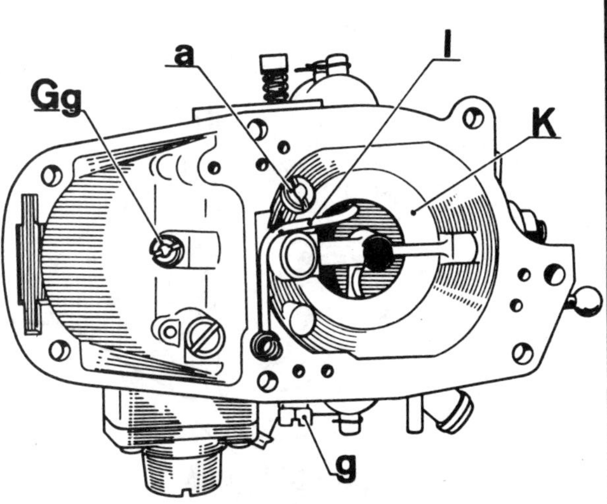

Fig.3.23 Location of jets in Solex 35 DITA carbruettor. Key as for Fig.3.21

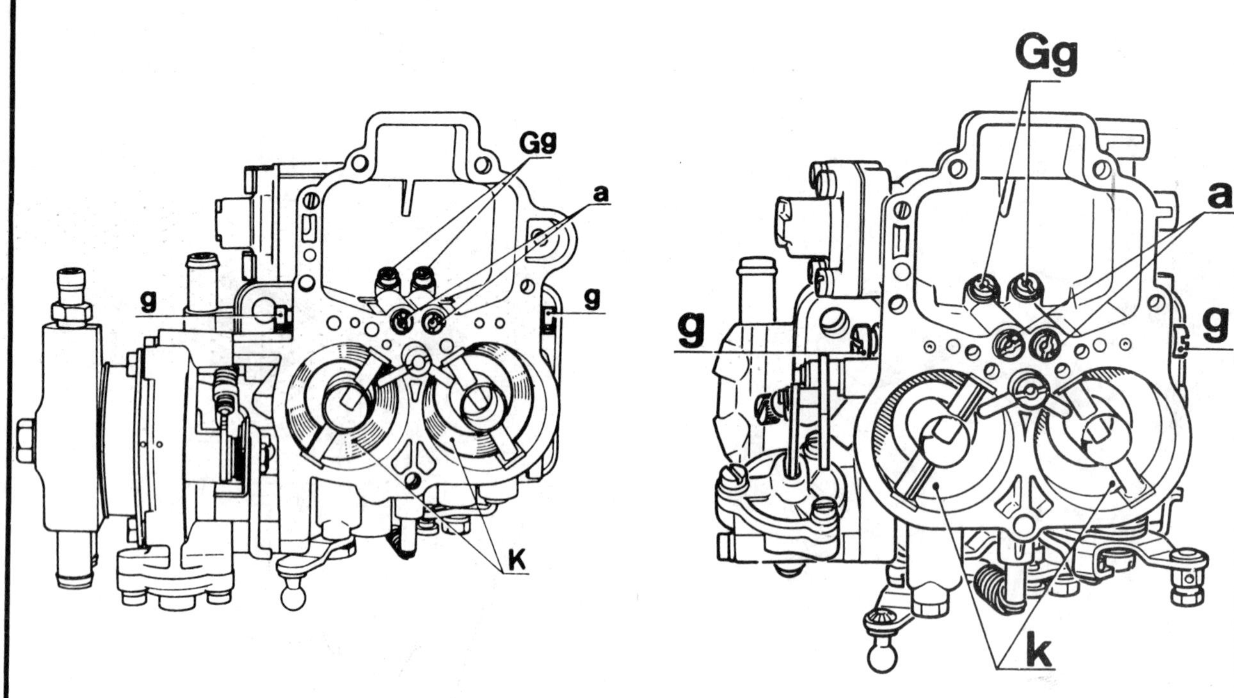

Fig.3.24 Location of jets in Weber 32 DAR carburettor. Key as for Fig.3.21

Fig.3.25 Location of jets in Solex 26 - 32 DIDSA carburettor. Key as for Fig.3.21

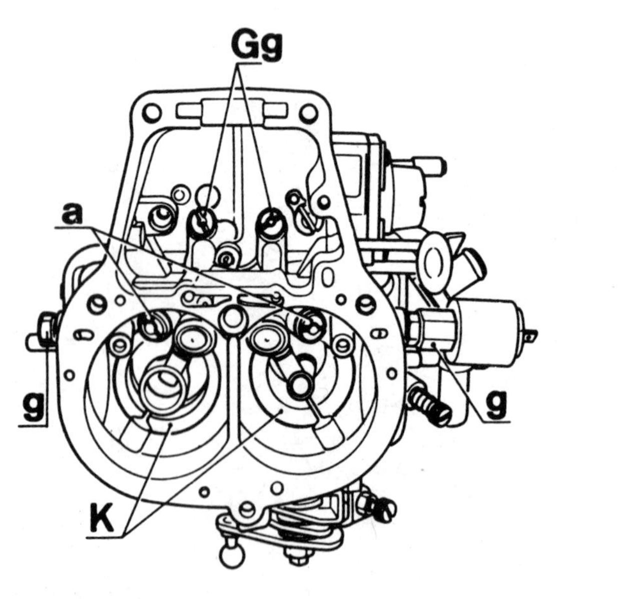

Fig.3.26 Location of jets in Weber 32 DIR 8 Mk 600 carburettor Key as for Fig. 3 – S

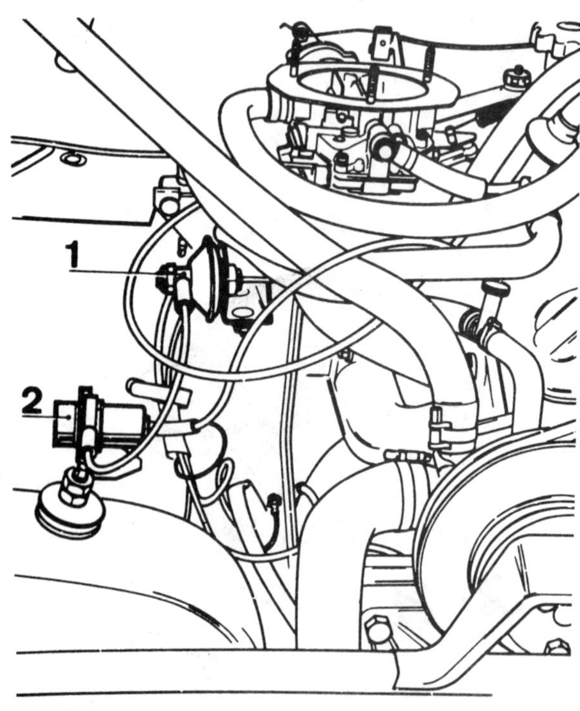

Fig.3.27 Location of the vacuum capsule (1) and solenoid flap valve (2) fitted to the exhaust emission control system

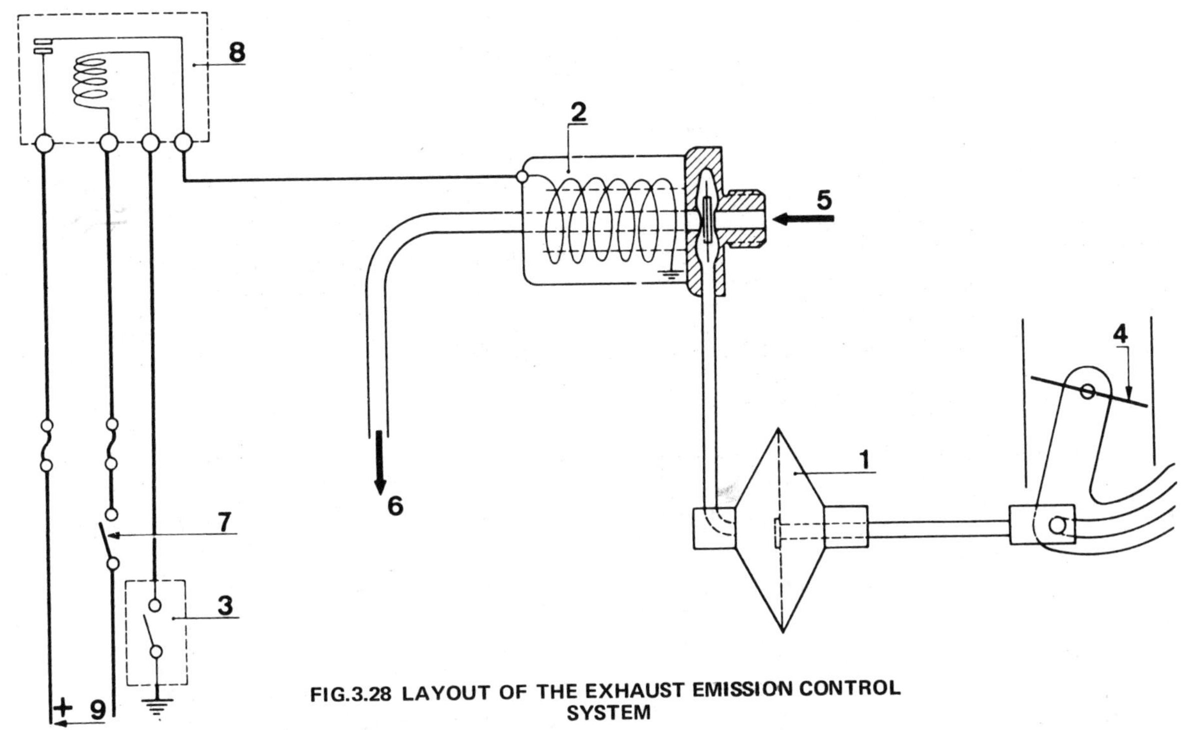

FIG.3.28 LAYOUT OF THE EXHAUST EMISSION CONTROL SYSTEM

1 Vacuum capsule
2 Solenoid flap valve
3 Centrifugal switch
4 Throttle butterfly
5 Outlet to atmosphere
6 To inlet manifold
7 Ignition switch
8 Solenoid flap vlave relay
9 Lead to battery +

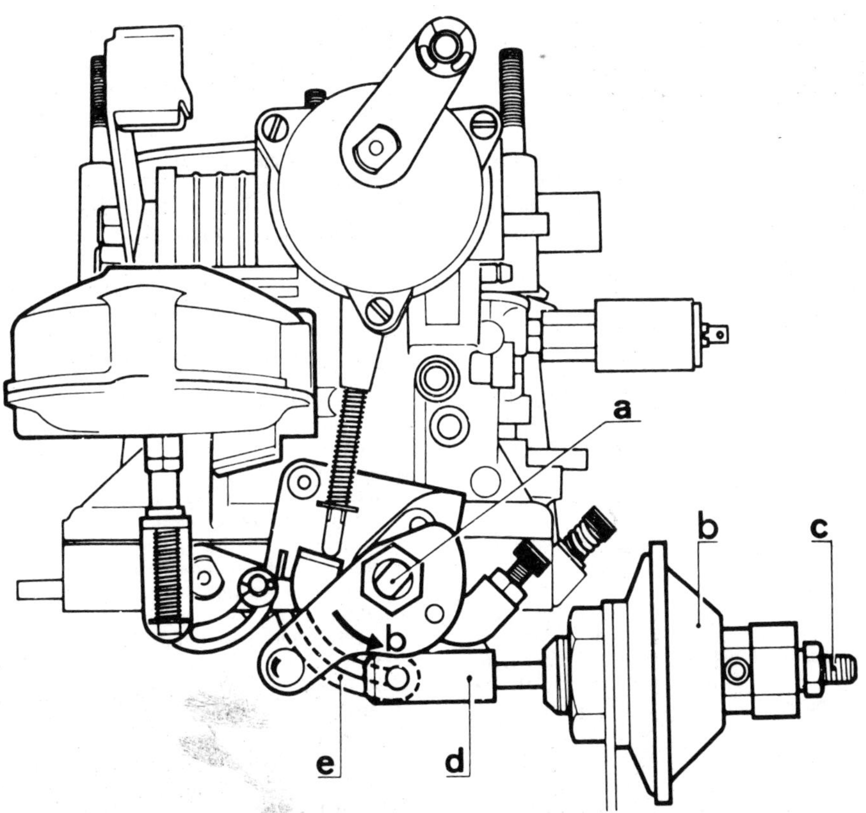

FIG.3.29 DIAGRAM OF OPERATING PRINCIPLE OF EXHAUST EMISSION CONTROL SYSTEM

a) Spindle
b) Capsule
c) Adjuster screw
d) Forked end operating rod
e) Quadrant

27 Exhaust anti-pollution device - principle of operation

1 The capsule (1) Fig.3.29 is connected to the carburettor linkage. Inlet manifold depression acts upon the capsule diaphragm which causes the fork end rod (d) to move and turn the quadrant (e) and spindle (a). This movement causes the first choke tube butterfly to open but the amount of travel is controlled by adjuster screw (c).

2 Whilst vacuum is applied to the capsule diaphragm, partial opening of the butterfly is maintained even when the accelerator pedal is released. The vacuum is applied or cut off by the medium of a solenoid flap valve (2) Fig.3.27.

3 The solenoid flap valve is connected in series between the inlet manifold and the capsule (1) and is actuated by the centrifugal switch, Fig.3.30.

4 The centrifugal switch (3) is operated by the speedometer cable which according to its speed of rotation opens or closes a set of points. The points close when the vehicle speed drops to 16 mph (27 km/h) and vacuum is no longer applied to the capsule and the engine operates at normal idling speed.

5 The points of the centrifugal switch open as the vehicle speed reaches 23 mph (37.5 km/h) and the solenoid flap valve opens to permit vacuum to again be applied to the capsule diaphragm. The carburettor butterfly is held partially open although the accelerator pedal is completely released.

6 In order to maintain engine operational sensitivity and to ensure that the second carburettor choke tube is brought into action to match engine demands without the creation of flat spots or delay, the linkage connected to the vacuum capsule through the medium of the forked control rod, quadrant and plate is so designed and interconnected that the transition from first to second choke tube is smooth and without any hesitation.

28 Exhaust anti-pollution device - adjustment

1 Run the engine until normal operating temperature is reached.

2 If the car is fitted with an electric revolution counter, then adjustment is simple, if not attempt to obtain one for temporary connection to the distributor. Where this is not possible, jack up the front of the car securely and with top gear engaged rely upon an assistant to check the speedometer readings which are given as approximating to the required engine revolutions for the purpose of adjustment.

3 Refer to Fig.3.14 and turn screw A until the engine is rotating at 700 rev/min (10 mph/16 km/h). Now turn the mixture screw B until the idling speed reaches its maximum.

4 Repeat the previous procedure so that the engine will be left running at 700 rev/min (10/16 km/h).

5 Turn the mixture screw B clockwise until the engine speed drops to 675 rev/min (9mph/14.5 km/h). If the operations have been accurately carried out then the emission of carbon monoxide will be at its lowest level.

6 With the engine at normal operating temperature and idling speed disconnect the lead to the solenoid flap valve.

7 Refer to Fig.3.31 and holding nut (C) still, unscrew the protective cover from the capsule.

8 Still holding nut (C) unscrew the locknut (D).

9 Use a 3 mm Allen key, turn the adjusting screw (E) until the engine is idling at 1300 to 1400 rev/min. Unless an electric rev counter is available, this operation will again call for jacking up of the front of the car, with top gear engaged and reading off the comparative mph from the speedometer (20–25 mph–32 to 40 km/h).

10 Retain adjusting screw in its new position and tighten locknut (D) by hand.

11 Holding nut (C) still, tighten locknut (D).

12 Reconnect the lead to the solenoid flap valve.

13 Finally, check the moment of points opening and closure within the centrifugal switch. This is carried out by connecting a test lamp between the solenoid flap valve terminal and a good earthing point. Allow plenty of wire to permit the test bulb to be positioned within the car.

14 Start the engine and run it until normal operating temperature is reached (indicated when radiator fan switches itself on).

15 Check that the engine idling speed is within 650 to 700 rev/min as previously set.

16 Drive the car on the road until it reaches 25 mph (40 km/h), release the accelerator pedal and note the speed of the car when the temporary test bulb lights up, this should be 16 mph (27 km/h). If the test bulb fails to illuminate, accelerate to 25 mph (40 km/h), again release the accelerator pedal and apply the brakes to slow down the engine revolutions until the test bulb lights and then read off the vehicle speed from the speedometer. Where the light still does not come on, check the following fault check list.

Test lamp does not illuminate

Check circuit continuity then check relay and switch by substitution.

Test lamp will not extinguish and abnormal idling speed

Disconnect vacuum pipe from capsule and plug the end of the pipe. If normal idling speed is not restored by this action, check the solenoid flap valve by substitution. If the solenoid flap valve is serviceable, check that the free movement between the forked rod (d) and the quadrange (e) Fig.3.29 is 1/16 inch (1.6 mm). Adjust the clearance if necessary by moving the vacuum capsule. Check the throttle linkage and accelerator cable for tight spots and general freedom of movement.

Engine remains at normal idling speed when it should be on fast idle (throttle butterfly held slightly open)

Jack up one front wheel, start engine and select 'Drive', accelerate slowly until speedometer registers 35 mph (56 km/h). With an assistant observing the vacuum capsule ensure that the vacuum capsule forked end operating rod exerts a pull on the 'fast idle' carburettor linkage. Where no movement is observed, detach the lead from the solenoid flap valve and if 'fast idle' then occurs, the fault must lie in the circuit, switch or relay. If 'fast idle' is still not obtained, connect the vacuum capsule directly to the inlet manifold. If still no improvement, unscrew the adjusting screws. Finally, renew the capsule if previous checks have failed.

17 Circuit diagram and wiring colour code for the anti-pollution device are shown in Fig.3.33.

29 Crankcase fume emission - rebreathing device

1 All types of engine are fitted with this device to reduce the emission of fumes from the crankcase to atmosphere.

2 The system, Fig.3.34 comprises a circuit of hoses with a valve incorporated. When the engine is running, crankcase fumes are drawn up through a tie piece mounted on the rocker box cover and sucked through one of the two hoses which connect with the carburettor and the inlet manifold.

3 The direction of fume flow in controlled by a valve (D) which is mounted on the inlet manifold. The valve operates according to the level of vacuum in the induction manifold. With wide throttle openings (low vacuum) fumes are directed to the inlet manifold. With the throttle nearly closed (high vacuum) the fumes re-enter the engine through the carburettor hose connection.

4 A flame trap (B) is fitted to prevent a flash back from the carburettor reaching the crankcase and causing a secondary explosion.

5 Servicing is limited to checking the security of the hose unions and very occasionally removing and washing the valve and flame trap in paraffin and shaking dry.

30 Fuel gauge and transmitter unit - fault finding

1 If the fuel gauge fails to give a reading with the ignition on

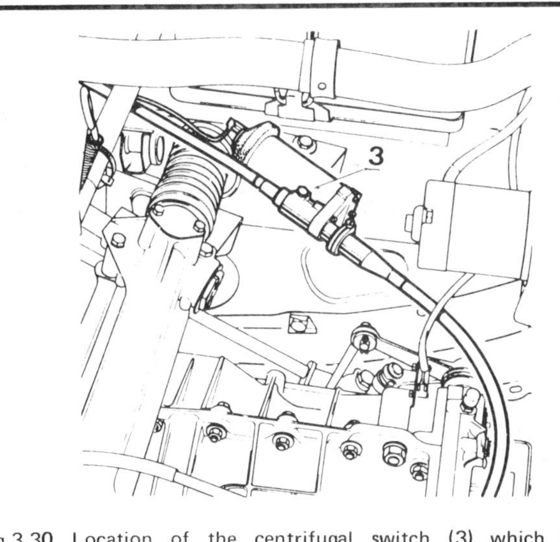

Fig.3.30 Location of the centrifugal switch (3) which is incorporated in the exhaust emission control system

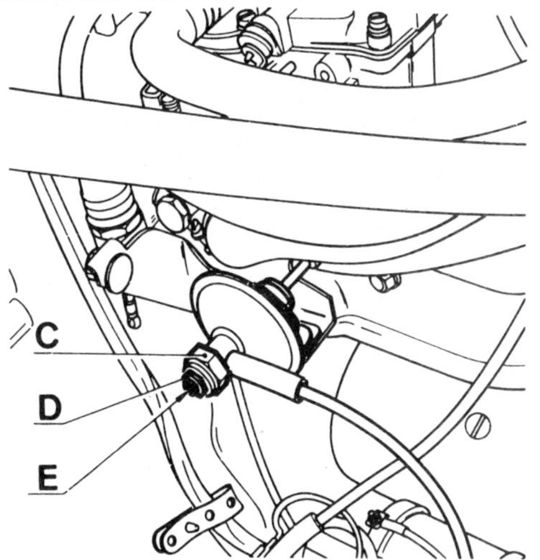

FIG.3.31 ADJUSTMENT OF THE CAPSULE FITTED TO THE EXHAUST EMISSION CONTROL SYSTEM

C Body nut
D Lock nut
E Adjuster screw

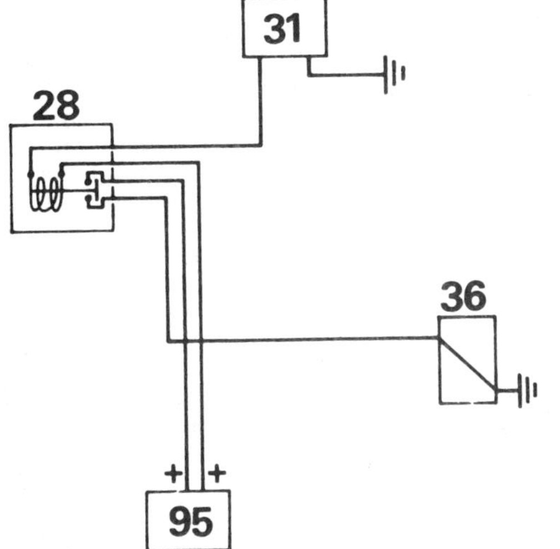

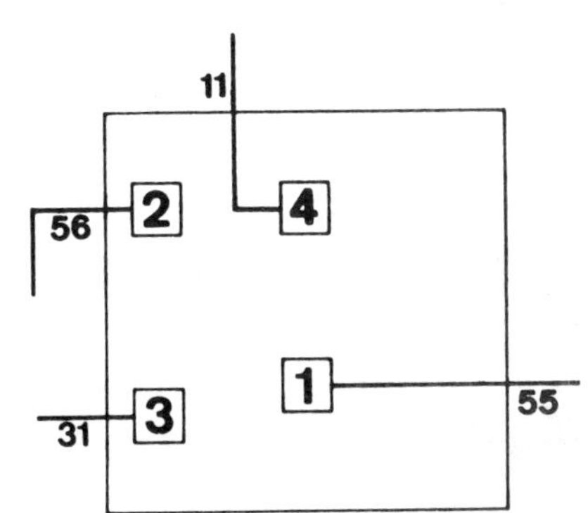

FIG.3.33 CIRCUIT DIAGRAM FOR THE EXHAUST EMISSION CONTROL SYSTEM

Key	*Component*	*Wire*	*Colour*
28	*Solenoid flap valve relay*	*11*	*Grey*
31	*Centrifugal switch*	*31*	*Red*
36	*Solenoid flap valve*	*55*	*Yellow*
95	*Junction box*	*56*	*Beige then green*

FIG.3.34 CRANKCASE FUME EMISSION RE BREATHING DEVICE SYSTEM

A Hose (carburettor to flame trap)
B Flame trap
C Hose (inlet manifold valve to rocker cover)
D Valve

or reads 'FULL' all the time, then a check must be made to see if the fault is in the gauge, sender unit, or wire in between.
2 Turn the ignition on and disconnect the wire from the fuel tank sender unit. Check that the fuel gauge needle is on the empty mark. To check if the fuel gauge is in order now earth the fuel tank sender unit wire. This should send the needle to the full mark.
3 If the fuel gauge is in order check the wiring for leaks or loose connections. If none can be found, then the sender unit will be at fault and must be renewed.

31 Fuel tank cleaning

1 With time it is likely that sediment will collect in the bottom of the fuel tank. Condensation, resulting in rust and other impurities, will usually be found in the fuel tank of any car more than three or four years old.
2 When the tank is removed it should be vigorously flushed out and turned upside down and, if facilities are available, steam cleaned.

32 Fuel tank - removal and refitting

1 The fuel tank is fitted into a recess pressed into the floor of the luggage boot.
2 Either arrange to remove the tank when there is a very low level of fuel or syphon the fuel into a container.
3 Disconnect the battery earth terminal and the fuel transmitter lead from the tank unit.
4 Disconnect the fuel feed pipe from the tank outlet pipe.
5 Disconnect the fuel filler flexible pipe from the rigid tank section of pipe.
6 Unscrew and remove the fuel tank flange securing bolts and then cut round the mastic sealing bead and withdraw the tank upwards through the boot.
7 Refitting is a reversal of removal, but scrape the old sealing mastic from the mating flanges and apply a bead of new sealer so that the fuel tank flange seats into it before the retaining bolts are screwed in and tightened.

33 Exhaust system - description, removal and replacement

1 The exhaust system is conventional in design but it must be remembered that the manifold assembly differs according to engine type. With R1151 (TS) cars which are fitted with type 807 engines, inlet and exhaust manifolds are fitted on opposite sides of the engine. With all other types the inlet and exhaust manifolds are on the same side of the engine.
2 The manifold connects to the exhaust system by means of a clamp on the down pipe.
3 It is usual to find that the silencer box or rear section of the system corrodes first and requires renewing. The down pipe and front section will normally outlast two or three replacements of the rest of the system.
4 The sections requiring renewal can be purchased separately and the old sections may be removed by disconnecting the pipe joints. This operation can be very difficult due to the effects of rust and heat and it will probably be easier to jack up the car securely and to remove the exhaust system complete. Apply freeing fluid liberally to all joints and remove the pipe clips if necessary by cutting through the bolts with a hacksaw. Now drive a cold chisel down each of the longitudinal slots in each overlapping section of pipe (photo). The two pipes should now be capable of separation using a twisting motion. Where this does not succeed, cut the pipe through with a hacksaw first

33.4 Fitting new silencer to existing exhaust pipe

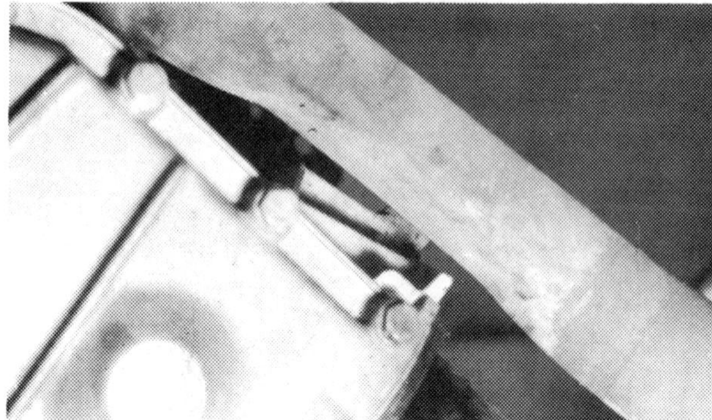
33.6 Exhaust down pipe shaped to clear transmission casing

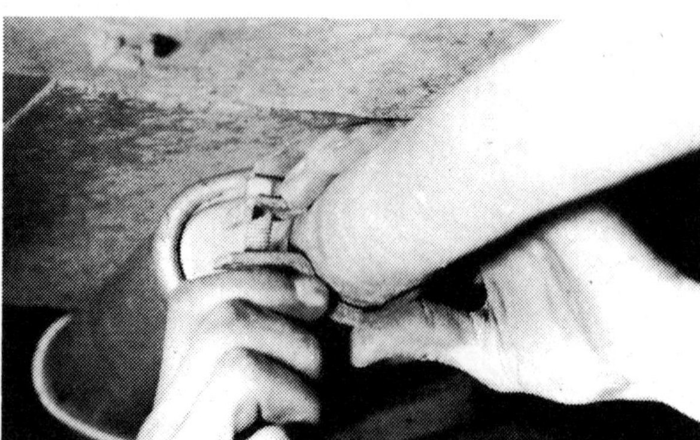
33.7 Fitting a one piece exhaust pipe clip

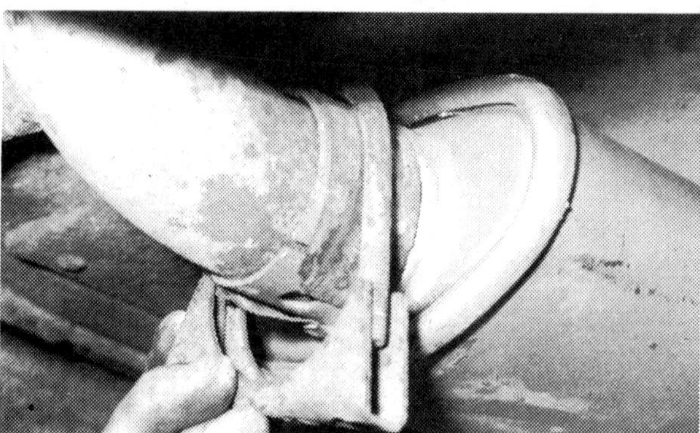
33.8 Fitting a two piece exhaust pipe clip

measuring the new unit to ensure that too much is not cut off. The internal or external overlapping section of pipe may then be hacksawed off. Saw carefully lengthwise so that no damage is caused to the section of pipe which is being retained for further use.

5 Before refitting the system, assemble new exhaust pipe clips and chamfer the ends of the cut sections of pipe so that they will enter the overlapping joints easily.

6 Fit the down pipe first tightening the clamp and lower pipe support nut. Note the depression in the bend of the pipe to accommodate the transmission casing (photo).

7 If one piece pipe clips are being used, then slide these on before connecting the next section (photo) and tighten the clamp bolt and nut only finger tight. A little grease applied to the joints will facilitate the entry of the pipe sections and alignment of the system.

8 Where two piece pipe clips are used then these can be located after the complete system is assembled and attached to the support straps (photo).

9 When the exhaust system is fitted together and supported on its straps, check it for alignment and twist each section if necessary so that the silencer or rear section are not so close to the body frame or floor panels or wheel arches which might cause knocking during periods of engine vibration or flexing on the systems resilient mountings.

10 When the alignment is satisfactory, fully tighten the pipe clips to cause a good gas tight seal to be made.

34 Fuel system - fault finding

There are three main types of fault the fuel system is prone to, and they may be summarised as follows:-

a) Lack of fuel at engine.
b) Weak mixture.
c) Rich mixture.

35 Lack of fuel at engine

1 If it is not possible to start the engine, first positively check that there is fuel in the fuel tank, and then check the ignition system as detailed in Chapter 4. If the fault is not in the ignition system then disconnect the fuel inlet pipe from the carburettor and turn the engine over by the starter relay switch.

2 If petrol squirts from the end of the inlet pipe, reconnect the pipe and check that the fuel is getting to the float chamber. This is done by unscrewing the bolts from the top of the float chamber, and lifting the cover just enough to see inside.

3 If fuel is there then it is likely that there is a blockage in the starting jet, which should be removed and cleaned.

4 No fuel in the float chamber, is caused either by a blockage in the pipe between the pump and float chamber or a sticking float chamber valve. Alternatively on the Weber twin choke carburettor the gauze filter at the top of the float chamber may be blocked. Remove the securing nut and check that the filter is clean. Washing in petrol will clean it.

5 If it is decided that it is the float chamber valve that is sticking, remove the fuel inlet pipe, and lift the cover, complete with valve and floats, away.

6 Remove the valve spindle and valve and thoroughly wash them in petrol. Petrol gum may be present on the valve or valve spindle and this is usually the cause of a sticking valve. Replace the valve in the needle valve assembly, ensure that it is moving freely, and then reassemble the float chamber. It is important that the same washer be placed under the needle valve assembly as this determines the height of the floats and therefore the level of petrol in the chamber.

7 Reconnect the fuel pipe and refit the air cleaner.

8 If no petrol squirts from the end of the pipe leading to the carburettor then disconnect the pipe leading to the inlet side of the fuel pump. If fuel runs out of the pipe then there is a fault in the fuel pump, and the pump should be checked as has already been detailed.

9 No fuel flowing from the tank when it is known that there is fuel in the tank indicates a blocked pipe line. The line to the tank should be blown out. It is unlikely that the fuel tank vent would become blocked, but this could be a reason for the reluctance of the fuel to flow. To test for this, blow into the tank down the fill orifice. There should be no build up of pressure in the fuel tank, as the excess pressure should be carried away down the vent pipe.

36 Weak mixture

1 If the fuel/air mixture is weak there are six main clues to this condition:-

a) The engine will be difficult to start and will need much use of the choke, stalling easily if the choke is pushed in.
b) The engine will overheat easily.
c) If the sparking plugs are examined (as detailed in the section on engine tuning), they will have a light grey/white deposit on the insulator nose.
d) The fuel consumption may be light.
e) There will be a noticeable lack of power.
f) During acceleration and on the overrun there will be a certain amount of spitting back through the carburettor.

2 As the carburettors are of the fixed jet type, these faults are invariably due to circumstances outside the carburettor. The only usual fault likely in the carburettor is that one or more of the jets may be partially blocked. If the car will not start easily but runs well at speed, then it is likely that the starting jet is blocked, whereas if the engine starts easily but will not rev, then it is likely that the main jets are blocked.

3 If the level of petrol in the float chamber is low this is usually due to a sticking valve or incorrectly set floats.

4 Air leaks either in the fuel lines, or in the induction system should also be checked for. Also check the distributor vacuum pipe connection as a leak in this is directly felt in the inlet manifold.

5 The fuel pump may be at fault as has already been detailed.

37 Rich mixture

1 If the fuel/air mixture is rich there are also six main clues to this condition:-

a) If the sparking plugs are examined they will be found to have a black sooty deposit on the insulator nose.
b) The fuel consumption will be heavy.
c) The exhaust will give off a heavy black smoke, especially when accelerating.
d) The interior deposits on the exhaust pipe will be dry, black and sooty (if they are wet, black and sooty this indicates worn bores, and much oil being burnt.).
e) There will be a noticeable lack of power.
f) There will be a certain amount of back-firing through the exhaust system.

2 The faults in this case are usually in the carburettor and the most usual is that the level of petrol in the float chamber is too high. This is due either to dirt behind the needle valve, or a leaking float which will not close the valve properly, or a sticking needle.

3 With a very high mileage (or because someone has tried to clean the jets out with wire), it may be that the jets have become enlarged.

4 Occasionally it is found that the choke control is sticking or has been maladjusted.

5 Again, occasionally the fuel pump pressure may be excessive so forcing the needle valve open slightly until a higher level of petrol is reached in the float chamber.

Chapter 4 Ignition system

For modifications, and information applicable to later models, see Supplement at end of manual

Contents

Specifications

Firing order 1 3 4 2

Ignition system ... ... 12v, battery, coil, camshaft driven distributor

Distributor - Index Number ... ...

Vehicle type	Compression ratio 8:6	Compression ratio 7:6	Static ignition timing °BTDC
R1150 1966, 1967, 1968	4159 or 4160	4163, 4164, 4193, 4194	0 ± 1
R1150 1969 model	4239 or 4240	4193, 4194	0 ± 1
R1151 1968 model	4215 or 4217		2 ± 1
R1151 1969 model	4235, 4236, 4231, 4232	4237, 4238	0 ± 1
R1152 all years	4219, 4220, 4329, 4330		0 ± 1
R1153 all years (except U.S.)	4219, 4220, 4298, 4299		6 ± 1

Contact breaker gap ... ... 0.016 to 0.020 in (0.4 to 0.5 mm)

Spark plugs

Model R1150	AC 45XL or MARCHAL 35HS
Model R1151	AC 44XL, CHAMPION N3
Model R1152	AC 42XLS, CHAMPION N5
Model R1153	AC 42XLS, CHAMPION N5
Spark plug gap	0.024 in (0.6 mm)
Coil type	Ducellier 2765A (12v)

1 General Description

In order that the engine may run correctly it is necessary for an electrical spark to ignite the fuel/air mixture in the combustion chambers at exactly the right moment in relation to engine speed and loading. The ignition system is based on feeding low tension voltage from the battery to the coil where it is converted to high tension voltage. The high tension voltage is powerful enough to jump the gap between the electrodes of the sparking plugs in the cylinders many times a second under high compression, providing that the system is in good condition and all the adjustments are correct.

The system is divided into two circuits; the low tension and high tension.

The low tension (sometimes called primary) circuit consists of the battery, lead wire to the control box, lead from the control box to the ignition switch, lead from ignition switch to the coil low tension windings (SW or + terminal) and from the coil low tension windings (CB or – terminal) to the contact breaker points and condenser in the distributor.

The high tension circuit comprises the high tension or secondary windings in the coil, the heavily insulated lead from the coil to the distributor cap centre contact, the rotor arm, and the leads from the four distributor cap outer contacts (in turn) to the sparking plugs.

Low tension voltage is stepped up by the coil windings to high tension voltage intermittently by the operation of the contact points and the condenser in the low tension circuit. High tension voltage is then fed via the centre contact in the distributor cap to the rotor arm.

The rotor arm rotates clockwise at half engine revolutions inside the cap and each time it comes in line with one of the outer contacts in the cap the contact points open and the high voltage is discharged jumping the gap from rotor arm to contact and thence along the plug lead to the centre electrode of the plug where it jumps the other gap - sparking in the process - to the outer plug electrode and thence to earth.

The static timing of the spark is adjusted by revolving the outer body of the distributor in relation to the distributor shaft. This alters the position at which the points open in relation to the position of the crankshaft (and thus the pistons).

The timing is also altered automatically by a centrifugal device which further alters the position of the complete points mounting assembly in relation to the shaft when engine speed increases, and by a vacuum control working from the inlet manifold which varies the timing according to the position of the throttle and consequently load on the engine. Both of these automatic alterations advance the timing of the spark at light loads and high speeds. The mechanical advance mechanism consists of two weights, which move out from the distributor shaft as engine speed rises due to centrifugal force. As they move out, so the cam rotates relative to the shaft and the contact breaker opening position is altered.

The degree to which the weights move out is controlled by springs, the tension of which significantly controls the extent of the advance to the timing.

The vacuum advance device is a diaphragm and connecting rod attached to the cam plate. When the diaphragm moves in either direction the cam plate is moved, thus altering the timing. The diaphragm is actuated by depression (vacuum) in the inlet manifold and is connected by a small bore pipe to the carburettor body above the throttle flap.

2 Routine Maintenance

1 Every 3000 miles (5000 km) snap back the spring clips which hold the distributor cap in position and lift off the cap (photo).

2.1 Removing distributor cap

2 Pull the rotor arm from its spindle.

3 Apply a smear of petroleum jelly to the high points of the square contact breaker cam and apply two or three drops of engine oil to the felt pad which is located within the recess at the top of the cam spindle.

4 Apply two or three drops of oil through the holes in the base plate in order to lubricate the centrifugal weight mechanism.

5 Check the contact breaker gap and condition of the points as described in Section 4.

6 Remove, clean and adjust the spark plugs as described in Section 13.

7 Wipe the external surfaces of all HT leads, and ignition components with a petrol moistened rag to remove oil film which might cause tracking. Wipe the inside of the distributor cap with a clean, dry non-fluffy rag.

8 Examine the condition of the ignition lead insulation periodically and renew them if signs of cracking or deterioration are observed.

3 Firing Sequence and Ignition Lead Positions

1 The firing order is 1 3 4 2. The distributor rotor revolves clockwise and the HT plug lead positions are as shown in the figure.

2 The procedure for removing and refitting the distributor drive gear and the correct meshing with the camshaft is fully described in Chapter 1.

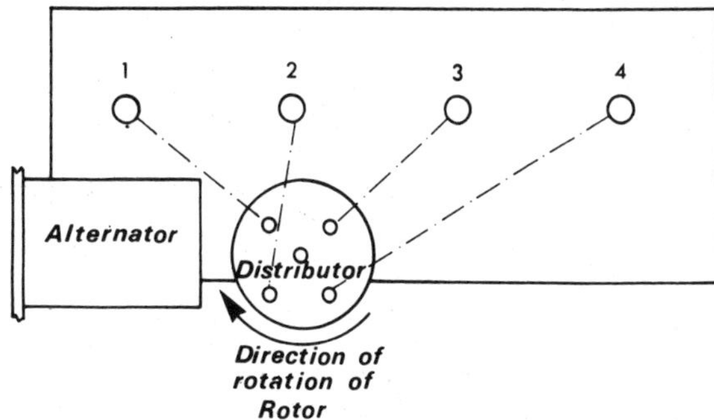

Fig.4.1 Sparking plug HT lead connections

4 Distributor Contact Breaker Points - Adjustment

1 Snap back the distributor cap clips and remove the cap.

2 Pull off the rotor arm and remove the spark plugs (to facilitate rotation of the engine).

3 Either use the starting handle (if fitted) or jack up one of the front wheels and turn it (after engaging top gear) so that any one of the cam high points opens (fully) the contact breaker points. On automatic cars use the camshaft pulley wheel to turn the engine. Ensure that the fibre heel of the spring contact breaker arm is on the highest point of the cam.

4 Slacken the screw which secures the fixed contact breaker plate to the distributor base plate and move the fixed contact breaker until, using feeler gauges the cap between the points is between 0.016 and 0.020 inch (0.4 to 0.5 mm), (photo).

5' Tighten the locking screw and re-check the gap. Ideally, the feeler gauge should just fall by its own weight when in position between the points and the gap is correct.

6 Refit the rotor, distributor cap and spark plugs and their leads.

5 Contact Breaker Points - Removal, Servicing, Refitting

1 At the time of checking the contact breaker points gap, examine the faces of the points for burning. Such burning

usually takes the form of a 'pip' on one point and a 'crater' or depression on the other. With later types of hollow points the effects of arcing or burning are not so apparent. Severe burning of the contact faces is usually due to a faulty condenser or to poor earth connections from the battery or engine or transmission earthing straps.
2 Remove the spring clip from the contact swivel post and withdraw the insulating washer.
3 Unscrew the nut and locknut from the LT terminal on the outside of the distributor body (photo). Only unscrew the terminal nuts sufficiently far to enable the spade connector and lead from the contact breaker arm to be slipped out from beneath the head of the terminal bolt located on the inside of the distributor body.
4 Press the spring arm of the contact breaker inwards and disengage it from its securing anchor. Withdraw the contact breaker arm assembly from its swivel post.
5 Unscrew and remove the fixed contact securing screw and remove the contact breaker arm.
6 The faces of both contact points should be dressed on an oilstone, keeping them perfectly square and ensuring that all pips and depressions are removed. Where severe burning has occurred or the faces have been ground on previous occasions and have become thin, renew them.
7 Clean the faces of old or new points with methylated spirit before fitting in order to remove oil or protective grease.
8 Refitting is a reversal of removal but ensure that the fibre washers located above and below the spring arm breaker are in position and do not overtighten the LT terminal nuts.
9 Adjust the gap as described in the preceding section.

6 Condenser - Removal, Testing, Replacement

1 Faulty ignition resulting in misfiring and uneven running can be caused by a faulty condenser which is mounted externally on the body of the distributor.
2 If the contact breaker points show signs of excessive burning and pitting on the faces of the contacts it is an indication that the condenser has probably broken down and should be renewed.
3 To check the efficiency of the condenser remove the distributor cap and rotor arm. Then rotate the engine so that the points are closed - that is with the breaker arm resting between two high points on the cam.
4 Switch on the ignition and with a non-conductive article such as a splinter of wood, move the contacts open by levering on the spring of the moving breaker. If there is a severe flashing spark it indicates that the condenser has probably failed.
5 An additional test to confirm condenser failure is to open the points (this can be done by placing a piece of paper of postcard between the contacts) and disconnecting the condenser lead from the breaker terminal post. Then put a voltmeter or 12v bulb with two wander leads between the terminal post and the condenser lead. Switch on the ignition and if there is a reading or the bulb lights the condenser is faulty and must be replaced.
6 To renew the condenser, detach the wire from the terminal post, remove the mounting screw and replace the old unit with a new one. Check that arcing has been virtually eliminated by testing as already described.

7 Distributor - Removal and Replacement

1 Disconnect the HT leads from the spark plugs and between the distributor cap and the coil.
2 Disconnect the LT lead from the terminal on the side of the distributor body. Pull off the hose from the vacuum unit.
3 The method of retaining the distributor in the cylinder block varies according to model and may be by lever plate secured by one of the distributor pillar studs (photo), or a lock screw and nut screwed into the distributor drive shaft housing. Disconnect the appropriate component and withdraw the distributor.
4 Refitting is a reversal of removal and provided the distributor drive shaft has not been removed, the ignition timing will automatically be correct when the unit is replaced as the large and small shaft segments will engage to give the correct timing position.
5 If the distributor drive shaft has been withdrawn or partially withdrawn and rotated, then it will be necessary to refit the driving gear as described in Chapter 1 before the distributor unit is located in the engine block.

8 Distributor - Dismantling and Reassembly

1 Remove the distributor cap, rotor, contact breaker arms and externally mounted condenser all as previously described.
2 Remove the retaining spring (1) from the end of the drive shaft (references are to Fig 4.3)
3 Withdraw the pin (2) and slide off the washers and bush from the drive shaft.
4 Remove the baseplate securing screws and withdraw the baseplate (3).
5 The cam plate assembly (4) complete with counterweights and springs may now be withdrawn upwards through the distributor body.
6 If wear is evident in the bushes, counterweight holes or the springs are stretched then it will be economical to exchange the complete distributor unit for a factory exchange one. Ensure that the replacement unit carries the same index number as the original. The appropriate index numbers, and vehicle and engine applications, are listed in the specifications section of this chapter.
7 Reassembly is a reversal of dismantling but clean and lubricate all components first.

9 Ignition - Timing (Models R.1150–R.1151–R1152)

1 Jack up the front left hand road wheel, engage top gear and turning the road wheel in the forward direction of rotation, rotate the engine until the mark on the flywheel aligns with the zero mark on the clutch housing. It will be found easier to turn the engine if the spark plugs are first removed. Check that the distributor rotor is pointing towards No. 1 spark plug electrode in the distributor cap. If it is pointing to No.4 electrode, rotate the crankshaft a further 360°.
2 The position of the flywheel is now correct for the models R.1150 – R.1151 (1969 model) and R.1152. For R.1151 (1968 model) continue to turn the engine until the flywheel mark is opposite an estimated 2 degree mark on the casing.
3 Connect a 12v test bulb between the distributor LT terminal and a good earth and switch on the ignition.
4 Loosen the distributor clamp according to type and turn the distributor body in an anticlockwise direction until the test bulb lights up. If the distributor is turned too far inadvertently, turn the distributor sharply back to its original position and carry out the setting operation again as it is important that the timing point shall be reached by turning the distributor in an anticlockwise direction only.
5 Retighten the distributor securing device, remove the test bulb and switch off the ignition. Fit the distributor cap and HT leads.

10 Ignition Timing - (Model R.1153)

1 The ignition timing on vehicles fitted with automatic transmission may be set by using a test lamp or by stroboscope.
2 Remove the spark plugs and connect a test bulb between the LT terminal on the distributor case and earth.
3 Turn the engine by means of the camshaft pulley in a direction opposite to that of normal rotation (as approved), until the timing mark on convertor, visible through an aperture in the convertor housing, is in alignment with the housing 6° mark.
4 Switch on the ignition and having loosened the distributor fixing, rotate the distributor until the bulb just goes out. During this operation keep the distributor shaft cam turned anti-

4.2 Checking contact breaker gap

5.3 Distributor LT terminal

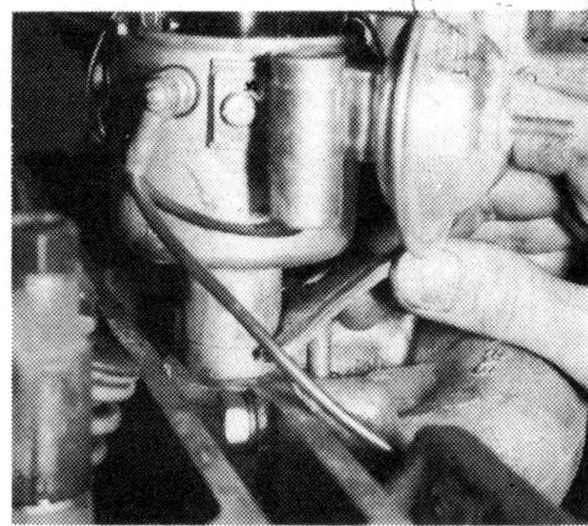

7.3 Distributor fixing plate

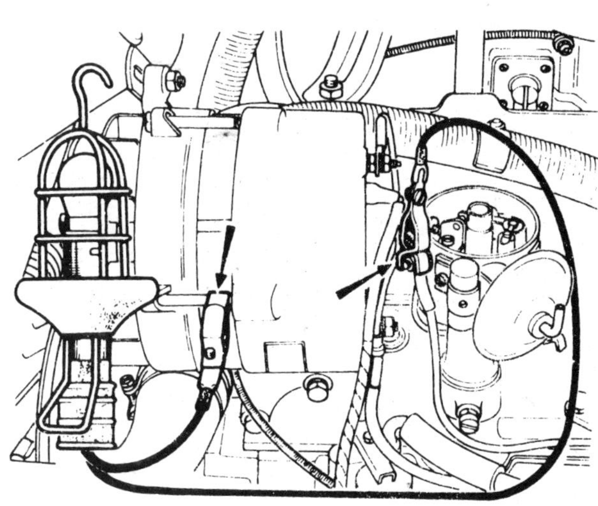

Fig.4.2 Test bulb connected for timing the ignition. Distributor fixing screw and locknut also shown

Fig.4.3 Timing marks, visible through convertor housing aperture on automatic transmission model vehicles. Direction and method of movement of camshaft pulley is shown

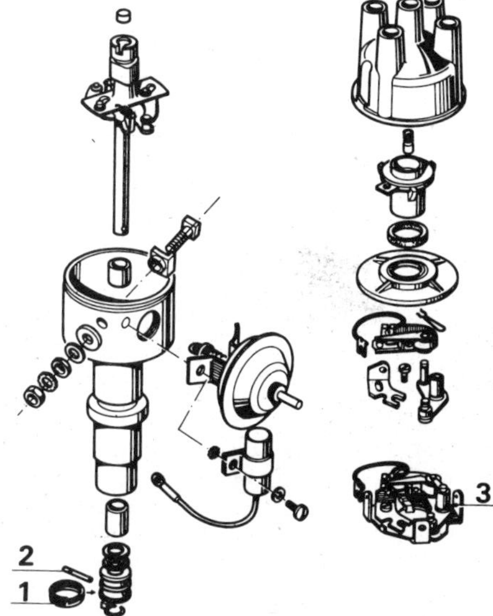

FIG.4.4 EXPLODED VIEW OF THE DISTRIBUTOR

1 Shaft pin retaining spring
2 Retaining pin
3 Contact breaker base plate

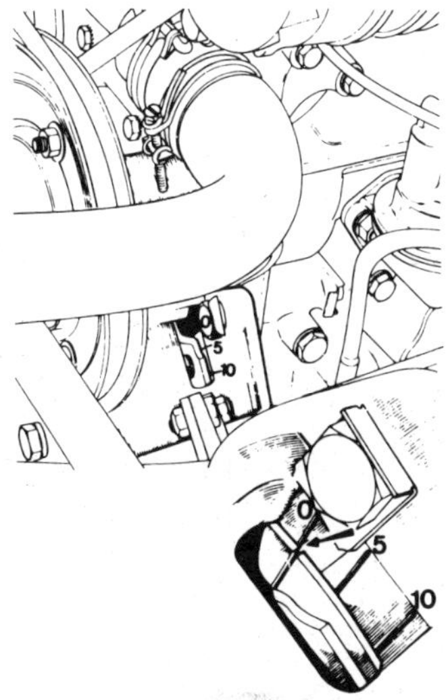

Fig.4.5 Timing marks, visible through clutch housing aperture on manually operated gearbox vehicles

clockwise in order to take up any slack in the mechanical advance mechanism.

5 Switch off the ignition and tighten the distributor clamp.

6 If a stroboscopic lamp is used, connect the red (+) and the black (—) to the battery. Connect the HT lead to number 1 or 4 spark plug or to the coil.

7 Disconnect the vacuum pipe from the distributor.

8 Run the engine at a slow tickover (750 rpm) and unclip the distributor fixing device.

9 Illuminate the TDC mark on the convertor and then rotate the distributor until the convertor mark appears to be in stationary alignment with the 6° mark on the housing.

10 Switch off the engine.

11 Tighten the distributor fixing.

12 Remove the stroboscopic lamp and connections.

11 The Coil

1 This is located close to the battery.

2 It is essential that the LT leads and the leads to the rev counter and idling speed damper (emission fume control) should be correctly connected as shown.

3 Check occasionally, the security of the main HT lead in the coil socket.

12 The Ignition/Steering Lock Switch

1 A combined multiple position ignition starter and steering anti-theft lock is provided on all vehicles. On the R.1150 and R.1151 there is a four position switch (NEIMAN). With R.1152 models a 'DAVAUTO' three position switch is fitted and with R.1153 models a Neiman type switch is fitted but the starter position is over-riden by the selector lever switch operating only when in the N or P positions associated with automatic transmission.

2 Wiring arrangement of the switches used in manual gearbox cars is shown in the figure.

3 Never remove the key from the ignition lock while the vehicle is in motion.

13 Spark Plugs - Servicing, Adjustment, Engine Condition Indications

1 Regular servicing of the spark plugs is essential to economical and top engine performance. Cleaning and adjustment of the spark plugs is described in the 'Routine Maintenance' section of this manual.

2 The appearance and condition of the spark plugs gives a very good indication of the state of tune and wear of the power unit as shown in the figure.

3 Spark plugs should be renewed at or before a maximum operating life of 9000 miles (15 000 km) as their sparking efficiency under compression will almost certainly be much reduced after such a mileage.

4 Do not experiment with other than the specified grades of plug but when renewing them check that the manufacturers specification has not changed in the light of operating experience.

14 Fault Finding

1 Engine troubles normally associated with, and usually caused by faults in, the ignition system are:—

a) Failure to start when the engine is turned.

b) Uneven running caused by misfiring or mistiming.

c) Even running at low engine speed and misfiring when engine speeds up or is under the load of acceleration of hill climbing.

d) Even running at higher engine speeds and misfiring or stoppage at slow speed.

For a) First check that all wires are properly connected and dry. If the engine fails to catch when turned on the starter do not continue turning or the battery will be flattened and the problem made worse. Remove one spark plug lead from a plug and turn the engine again and see if a spark will jump from the end of the lead to the top of the plug or the engine block. It should jump a gap of ¼ inch with ease. If the spark is there, ensure that the static ignition timing is correct and then the fuel system. If there is no spark at the plug lead proceed further and remove the HT lead from the centre of the distributor which comes from the coil. Try again by turning the engine to see if a spark can be obtained from the end. If there is a spark the fault lies between the contact in the distributor cap and the plug. Check that the rotor arm is in good condition and making proper contact in the centre of the distributor cap and that the plug leads are properly attached to the cap. The four terminals inside the cap should be intact, clean and free from corrosion. If no spark comes from the coil HT lead, check next that the contact breaker points are clean and the gap is correct. If there is still no spark obtainable it may be assumed that the low tension circuit is at fault. To check the low tension circuit properly it is best to have a voltmeter handy or a 12v bulb in a holder with two wander leads attached. The procedure now given is arranged so that the interruption in the circuit - if any - can be found. Starting at the distributor, put one of the two leads from the tester (be it lamp or voltmeter) to the moving contact terminal and the other to earth. A reading (or light) indicates that there is no break in the circuit between the ignition switch and the contact points. Check next that the condenser is ok as described in Section 6. If this is satisfactory it means that the coil is not delivering HT to the distributor and must therefore be renewed. If there is no LT reading on the first check point repeat the test between the CB (—) terminal of the coil and earth. If a reading is now obtained there must be a break in the wire between the CB (—) terminal and the contact points. If there is no reading at this second check point repeat the test between the SW (+) terminal of the coil and earth. If this produces a reading then the low tension post of the coil windings must be open- circuited and the coil must be renewed. If there is no reading at this third check point there must be a break between the ignition switch and the coil. If this is the case, a temporary lead between the + terminals of both coil and battery will provide the means to start the engine until the fault is traced.

For b) Uneven running and misfiring should be checked first by ensuring that all HT wires are dry and properly connected. Ensure also that the leads are not short circuiting to earth against metal pipework or the engine itself. If this is happening an audible click can usually be heard from the place where the unwanted spark is being made.

For c) If misfiring occurs at high speeds the points gap is too small or the spark plugs need renewal due to failure under more severe operating pressures.

For d) If misfiring is occuring at low engine speeds and the engine runs satisfactorily at high speed, the points gap is probably the cause - being too great.

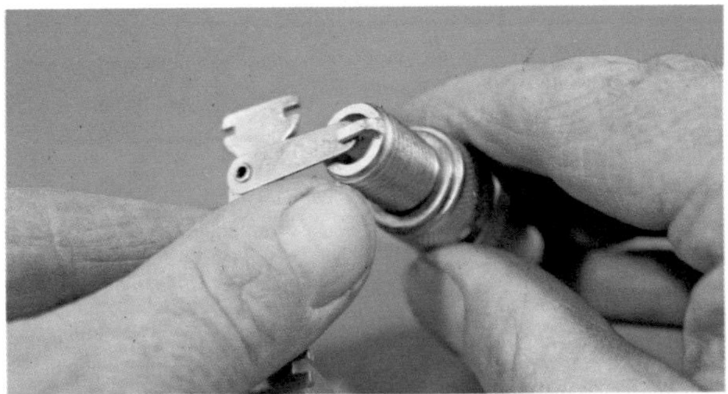

Measuring plug gap. A feeler gauge of the correct size (see ignition system specifications) should have a slight 'drag' when slid between the electrodes. Adjust gap if necessary

Adjusting plug gap. The plug gap is adjusted by bending the earth electrode inwards, or outwards, as necessary until the correct clearance is obtained. Note the use of the correct tool

Normal. Grey-brown deposits, lightly coated core nose. Gap increasing by around 0.001 in (0.025 mm) per 1000 miles (1600 km). Plugs ideally suited to engine, and engine in good condition

Carbon fouling. Dry, black, sooty deposits. Will cause weak spark and eventually misfire. Fault: over-rich fuel mixture. Check: carburettor mixture settings, float level and jet sizes; choke operation and cleanliness of air filter. Plugs can be re-used after cleaning

Oil fouling. Wet, oily deposits. Will cause weak spark and eventually misfire. Fault: worn bores/piston rings or valve guides; sometimes occurs (temporarily) during running-in period. Plugs can be re-used after thorough cleaning

Overheating. Electrodes have glazed appearance, core nose very white – few deposits. Fault: plug overheating. Check: plug value, ignition timing, fuel octane rating (too low) and fuel mixture (too weak). Discard plugs and cure fault immediately

Electrode damage. Electrodes burned away; core nose has burned, glazed appearance. Fault: pre-ignition. Check: as for 'Overheating' but may be more severe. Discard plugs and remedy fault before piston or valve damage occurs

Split core nose (may appear initially as a crack). Damage is self-evident, but cracks will only show after cleaning. Fault: pre-ignition or wrong gap-setting technique. Check: ignition timing, cooling system, fuel octane rating (too low) and fuel mixture (too weak). Discard plugs, rectify fault immediately

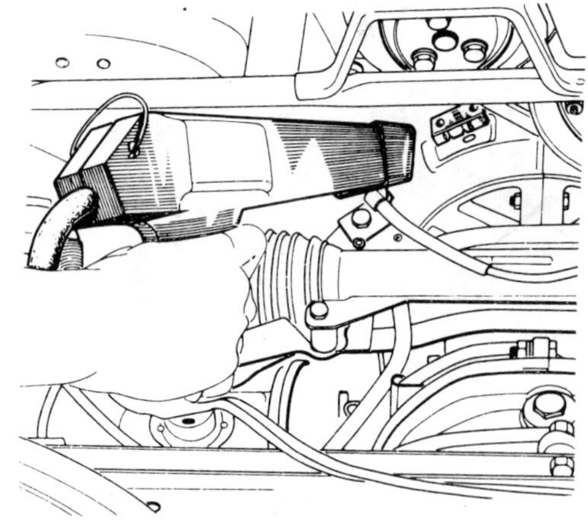

Fig.4.6 Using a stroboscope to check the ignition timing on an automatic transmission model.

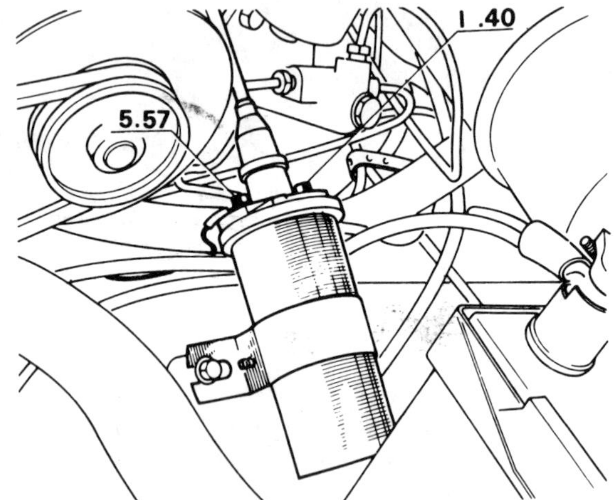

FIG.4.7 LOCATION AND CONNECTIONS OF THE COIL

5 Lead to ignition switch
57 Lead to idling speed damper
1 LT lead to distributor
40 Lead to rev. counter

FIG.4.8 THE IGNITION/STEERING LOCK SWITCH

Position 00 Steering locked
0 Steering unlocked (for pushing vehicle)
1 Ignition on (steering unlocked)
2 Starter operates (ignition on, steering unlocked)

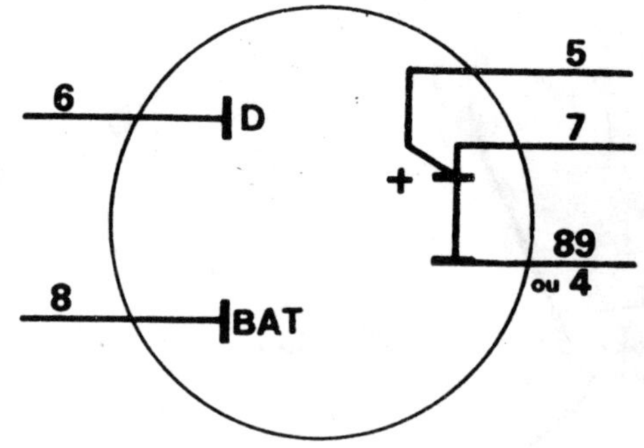

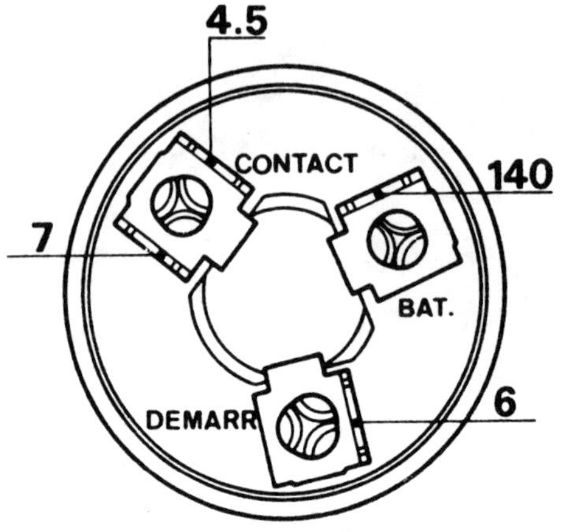

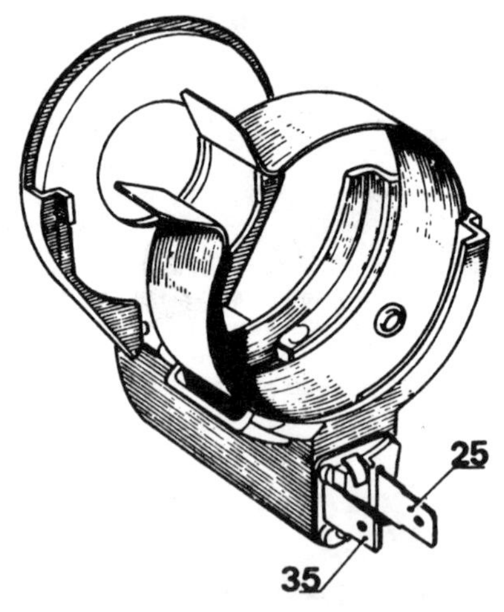

FIG. 4.9 WIRING ARRANGEMENTS FOR IGNITION/ STEERING LOCK SWITCHES

Upper - NEIMAN four position - terminals
4 regulator +
5 Coil
6 Starter relay
7 Fuse
8 Switch + from battery
8-9 Feed to voltmeter

Centre DAVAUTO three position - terminals
4 regulator +
5 Coil
6 Starter relay
7 Fuse
140 Feed + from battery

Lower - NEIMAN - illumination - terminals
25 +
35 — (earth)

Chapter 5 Clutch

For modifications, and information applicable to later models, see Supplement at end of manual

Contents

Specifications

Type	Single dry plate with diaphragm spring pressure plate
Identification	200D
Friction disc thickness	0.304 in (7.7 mm)
Release bearing	Ball, grease sealed
Clutch free movement	5/64 - 1/8 in (2 - 3 mm)

1 General Description

1 All manual gearbox models are fitted with a single dry plate diaphragm clutch. The clutch assembly comprises a pressure plate and cover which is bolted to the face of the flywheel and contains the diaphragm spring and fulcrum rings.

2 The clutch driven plate (friction disc) is free to slide along the splined first motion shaft of the gearbox and is held in position between the machined faces of the flywheel and pressure plate by the force of the diaphragm spring. The friction lining material is riveted to the driven plate which incorporates a spring cushioned hub to absorb rotational transmission shocks and ensure smooth clutch engagement.

3 The circular diaphragm spring is mounted on shouldered pins and held in place in the cover by fulcrum rings. The spring is held to the pressure plate by steel clips.

4 The clutch is actuated by cable from a pendant type foot pedal. The cable actuates the release arm which in turn pushes the release bearing (ball bearing sealed type), forwards to bear against the release plate to move the centre of the diaphragm spring inwards.

5 The diaphragm spring is sandwiched between two annular rings which act as fulcrum points. As the centre of the spring is pushed in, the outside of the spring is pushed out which causes the pressure plate to move backwards and cease contact with the driven plate (friction disc).

6 When the clutch pedal is released, the diaphragm spring forces the pressure plate into contact with the high friction linings on the driven plate and at the same time pushes the driven plate slightly forward on its splines to engage its friction lined surfaces with the flywheel. The driven plate is now firmly sandwiched between the pressure plate and the flywheel in order that the drive is taken up and transmitted without significant power loss or slip.

7 As the lining material wears due to frictional abrasion, the pressure plate automatically moves closer to the friction disc to compensate. The arrangement obviates the necessity for regular clutch adjustment, provided the clearance is correctly set originally or after dismantling or reassembly, as described in Section 2.

8 The correct clutch assembly may be identified by checking the type number which is located as shown in the figure. A sectional diagram of the clutch assembly is also given.

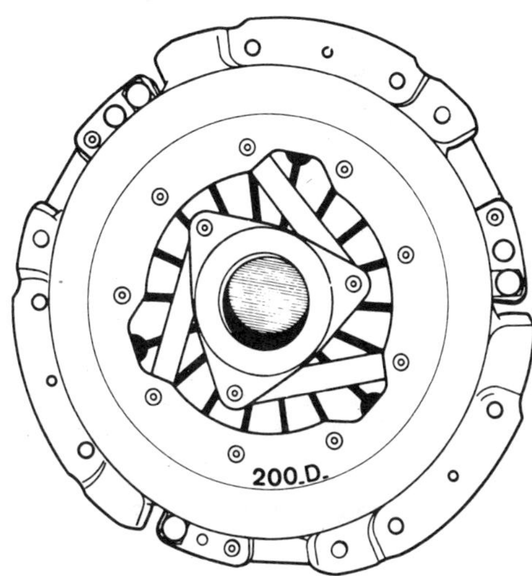

Fig.5.1 Clutch pressure plate cover showing position of type index number

2 Clutch Clearance - Adjustment

1 Loosen the locknut on the threaded end of the clutch operating cable. (References are to Fig 5.3)
2 Unscrew or screw up the adjusting nut (2) until there is a free movement of between 5/64 and 1/8 inch (2 to 3 mm) at the lowest point of the clutch operating lever arm. The measurement can most easily be made by holding a rule against the transmission case and noting the dimensions with the arm first lightly pushed inwards and then pulled outwards.
3 When the correct free movement is obtained, tighten the locknut.
4 For those vehicles which are fitted with a protective undertray, the cable locknut must be reached with a socket fitted to a universal jointed drive and the adjuster nut held in position with a long open ended spanner.

3 Clutch Pedal - Removal and Replacement

1 Remove the left hand glove compartment in order to gain access to the pedal shaft. The compartment is retained to the facia by self-tapping screws.
2 Release the pedal return spring by unhooking it.
3 Detach the pedal to shaft retaining clip and withdraw the pedal from its shaft.
4 The clutch cable forked clevis may now be detached from the pedal.
5 Refitting is a reversal of dismantling but grease the pedal shaft sleeve before reassembly and check the clearance (section 2).
6 The tension type pedal spring has been replaced (as a spare) by a coil type spring which fits round the pedal shaft sleeve.

4 Clutch Cable - Removal and Refitting

1 Disconnect the clutch cable from the release lever arm by unscrewing and removing the cable adjuster and locknuts.
2 Remove the clutch outer cable stop attachment from the clutch housing and push the cable from the stop attachment.
3 Remove the clutch pedal (Section 3) and detach the clutch cable from it.
4 Cut through the bead of sealing compound at the point where the cable passes through the engine compartment bulkhead. Withdraw the cable assembly into the car interior.
5 Refitting is a reversal of removal, but fit the cable into the clutch housing stop attachment before connecting the cable to the foot operating pedal.
6 Apply fresh sealant to the bulkhead cable entry and adjust the clutch free movement (Section 2).

5 Clutch - Removal and Component Inspection

1 Withdraw the gearbox as described in Chapter 6.
2 Mark the position of the clutch pressure plate cover in relation to its location on the face of the flywheel.

3 Unscrew the clutch cover securing bolts. These should be unscrewed in diametrically opposite sequence, a few turns at a time until the diaphragm spring pressure is released and the pressure plate assembly can be withdrawn. During withdrawal of the pressure plate assembly, do not let the driven plate fall.
4 Examine the driven plate friction linings for wear and loose rivets. Check the disc for distortion, cracks, broken hub springs or worn splines in its hub. The surface of the linings may be highly glazed but provided the woven pattern of the friction material can be clearly seen, then the plate is serviceable. Any sign of oil staining will indicate renewal of the driven plate and investigation and rectification of the oil leak (probably crankshaft front main bearing and seals) being required.
5 Check the amount of wear which has taken place on the friction linings and, if they are worn level with or to within 1/16 inch (1.6 mm) of the heads of the securing rivets, the driven plate should be renewed as an assembly. Do not attempt to re-line it yourself as it is rarely successful.
6 Examine the machined faces of the flywheel and the pressure plate and if scored or grooved, renew both components on a factory exchange basis.
7 Check the segments of the pressure plate diaphragm spring for cracks and renew the assembly if apparent.
8 Where clutch engagement has been fierce or clutch slip has occurred in spite of the driven plate being in good condition, renew the pressure plate assembly complete.
9 Check the clutch release bearing which is located in the fork of the release lever. See that it spins freely without shake or slackness and that its pressure face is not scored or chipped Where renewal is needed, refer to Section 7.

6 Clutch - Refitting

1 Clean the machined face of the flywheel with a petrol soaked rag.
2 Locate the driven plate on the face of the flywheel so that the longer projection of the splined hub is on the gearbox side.
3 Locate the pressure plate assembly on the flywheel (sandwiching the driven plate) so that the cover/flywheel mating marks are in alignment.
4 Screw in the securing bolts in diametrically opposite sequence until they are slightly more than finger tight.
5 The driven plate must now be centralised by inserting either an old gearbox first motion shaft or a suitably stepped mandrel or dowel which will pass through the hub of the driven plate and engage with the spigot bush in the centre of the flywheel. As the pressure plate securing bolts have not yet been tightened, the insertion of the centralising tool will cause the driven plate to move sideways or up and down as necessary until it is centralised. Try the tool in two or three different positions to ensure perfect centralising and to enable the gearbox first motion shaft to pass through the clutch driven plate during refitting of the gearbox to the engine.
6 Fully tighten the pressure plate assembly to flywheel bolts in diametrically opposite sequence.
7 Refit the gearbox to the engine as described in Chapter 6.
8 Adjust the clutch free movement as described in Section 2.

7 Clutch Release Bearing - Removal and Refitting

1 Remove the gearbox as described in Chapter 6.
2 Withdraw the pins which secure the release fork to the cross shaft. An extractor may be needed for this operation, similar to the one shown in the figure, although the use of a lever having a rounded forked end may suffice. The pins may be one of two types which are shown in another figure.
3 The fork may now be swung round on its shaft to enable the release bearing to be removed. Alternatively, the release cross shaft may be withdrawn and the fork/bearing assembly removed for separation on the bench.
4 The release bearing should be drawn from its retaining hub using a suitable extractor.
5 Press the release bearing onto its hub and fit the complete release fork assembly to the release cross shaft. Rotate the fork until the holes are in alignment with those in the cross shaft and press in the retaining pins so that in their final position, their shoulders will be standing 1/32 inch (1 mm) proud.
6 The clutch release ball bearing is grease sealed and requires no lubrication during its service life.
7 Refit the gearbox as described in Chapter 6 and adjust the clutch free movement.

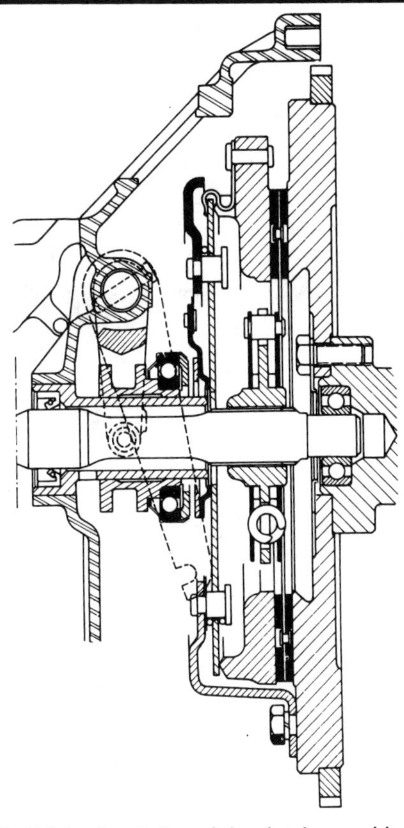

Fig.5.2 Sectional view of the clutch assembly

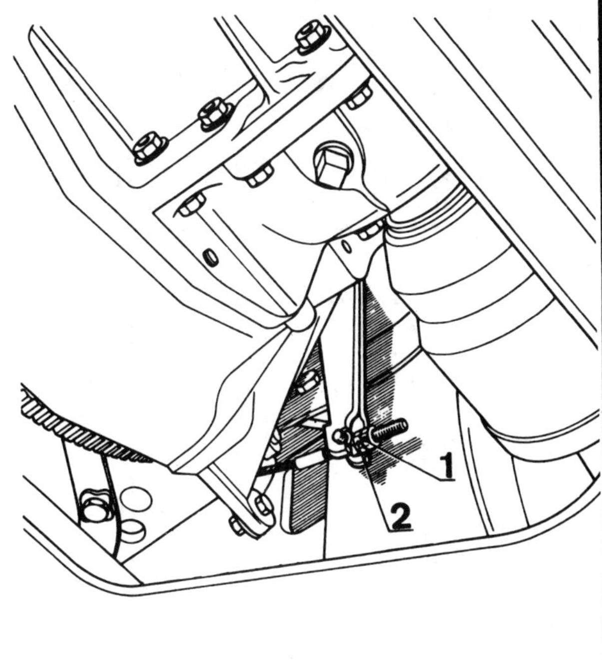

FIG.5.3 CLUTCH CABLE TO RELEASE ARM CONNECTION

1 Locknut *2 Adjuster nut*

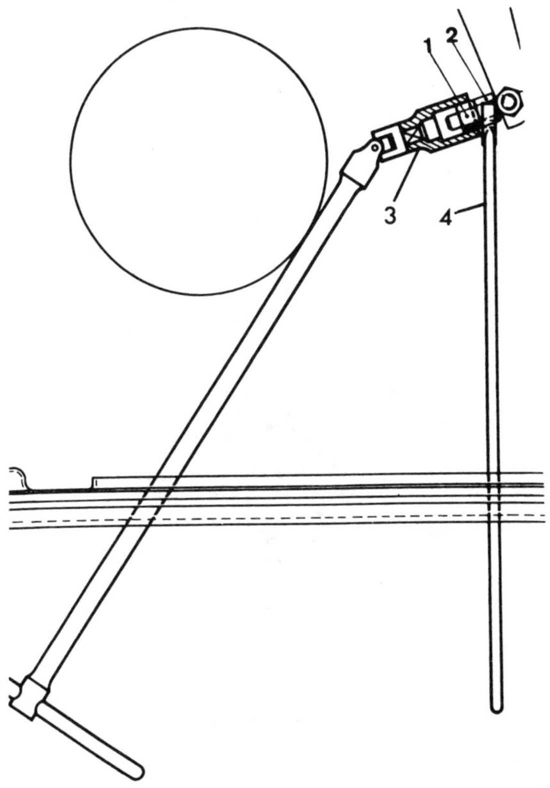

FIG.5.4 ADJUSTING CLUTCH CABLE NUTS ON CARS FITTED WITH AN UNDER TRAY

1 Locknut
2 Adjuster nut
3 Universal jointed socket wrench
4 Open ended spanner

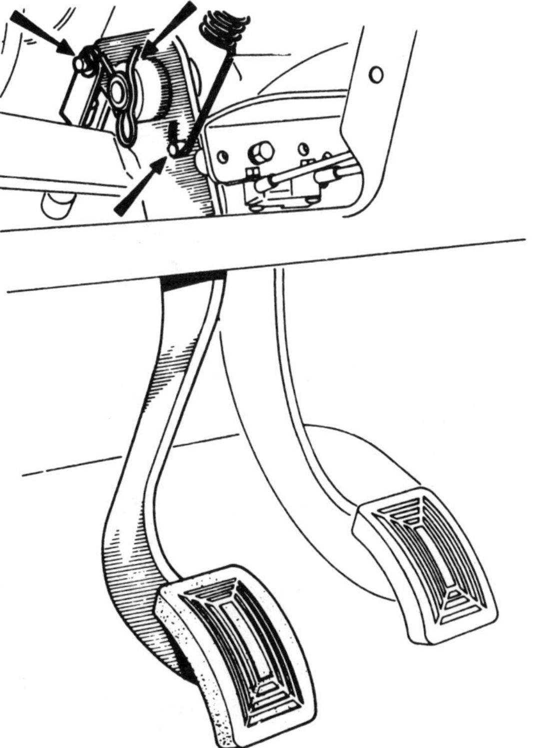

Fig.5.5 Clutch operating pedal, showing pedal return spring (early type) pedal to shaft retaining clip and cable clevis.

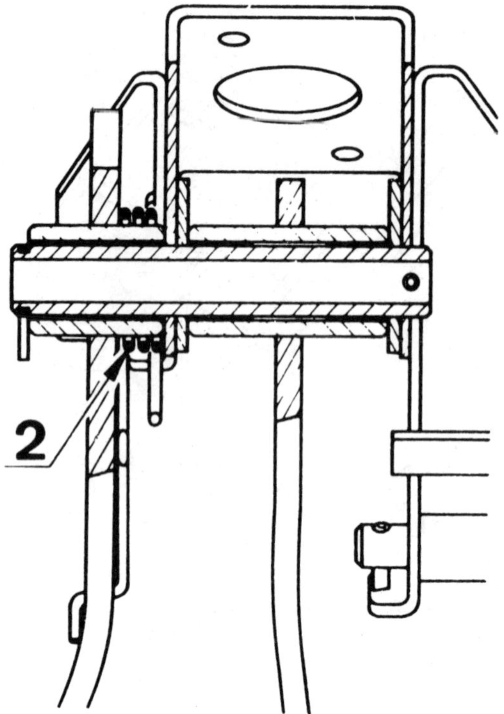

Fig.5.6 Later type pedal return spring (2)

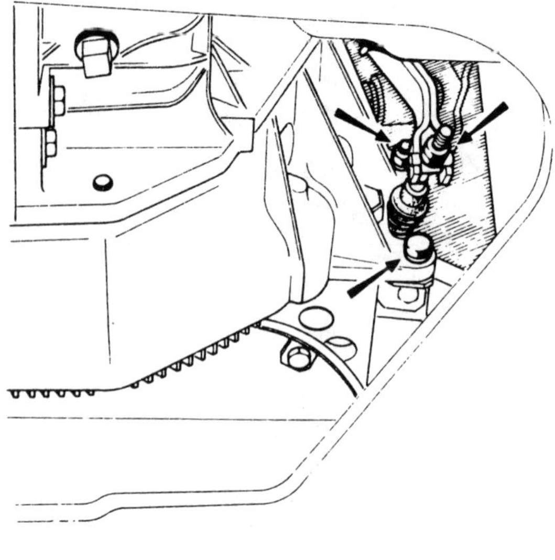

Fig.5.7 Clutch cable stop securing bolts on bell housing

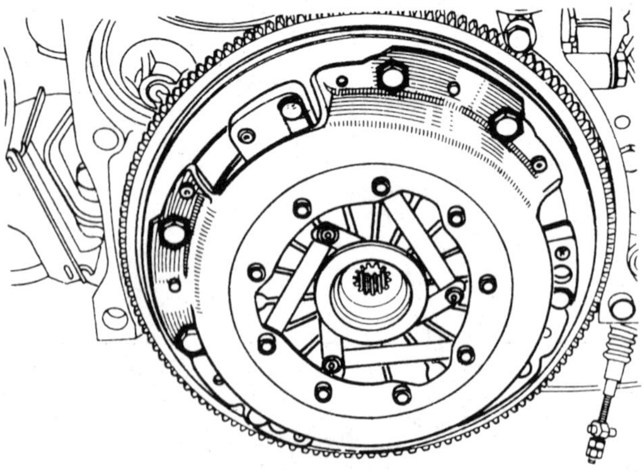

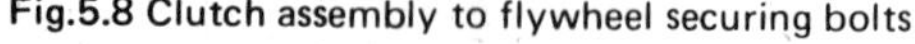

Fig.5.8 Clutch assembly to flywheel securing bolts

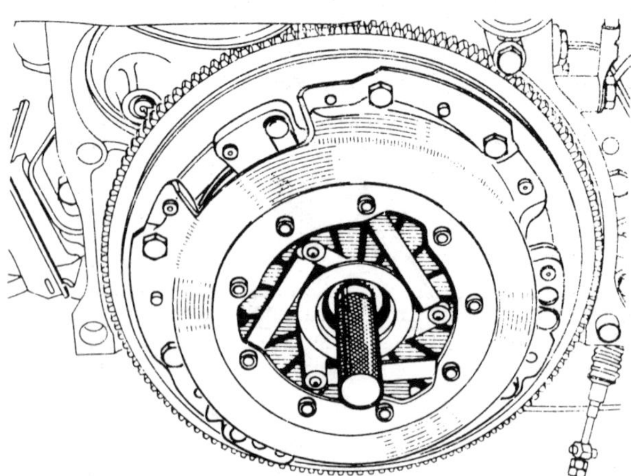

Fig.5.9 Centralising the clutch driven plate using a dowel

8 Clutch Spigot Bearing - Removal and Replacement

1 This is of ball bearing, grease sealed, type and is located in the crankshaft flange to which the flywheel is bolted. The bearing supports the nose of the gearbox first motion shaft after the shaft has passed through the clutch assembly and flywheel.
2 Remove the gearbox (Chapter 6).
3 Remove the clutch assembly from the flywheel (Section 5).
4 Remove the flywheel (Chapter 1).
5 Using an expanding type of bearing puller, extract the bearing assembly from its recess in the crankshaft/flywheel flange.
6 The new bearing is supplied pre-greased so do not clean it but fit it as supplied using a suitable tubular drift to bear upon the outer track of the bearing.
7 Refit the flywheel (Chapter 1).
8 Refit and centralise the clutch assembly (Section 6).
9 Refit the gearbox (Chapter 6) and adjust the clutch free movement (Section 2).

9 Gearbox First Motion Shaft Oil Seal - Renewal

1 The seal is located in a recess at the rear of the clutch release bearing guide through which the gearbox first motion shaft passes.
2 Evidence of oil on the clutch assembly or driven plate may be due to a defective first motion shaft oil seal.
3 Remove the gearbox (Chapter 6).
4 Separate the clutch bellhousing from the gearbox (photo).
5 The oil seal, now exposed, should be prised from its location (photo).
6 With Model R.1150 vehicles check that a 0.315 inch (8 mm) drain hole has been drilled at the base of the release bearing tubular guide as arrowed in the figure.
7 Where this is not apparent, one should be drilled ensuring that it is in alignment with the centre line of the gearbox and the hole edges are deburred on completion of drilling.
8 Drive a new oil seal into position, using a tubular drift and ensuring that the lips of the seal point towards the gearbox.
9 Fit the clutch bellhousing to the gearbox, first taping the splines of the first motion shaft to prevent the oil seal lips being cut as the bellhousing passes over the shaft.
10 Fit the gearbox to the engine (Chapter 6).
11 Adjust the clutch free movement.

10 Clutch Faults

There are four main faults to which the clutch and release mechanism are prone. They may occur by themselves or in conjunction with any of the other faults. They are clutch squeal, slip, spin and judder.

11 Clutch Squeal - Diagnosis and Cure

1 If on taking up the drive or when changing gear, the clutch squeals, this is a sure indication of a badly worn clutch release bearing.
2 As well as regular wear due to normal use, wear of the clutch release bearing is much accentuated if the clutch is ridden, or held down for long periods in gear, with the engine running. To minimise wear of this component the car should always be taken out of gear at traffic lights and for similar hold-ups.
3 The clutch release bearing is not an expensive item, but difficult to get at.

12 Clutch slip - Diagnosis and Cure

1 Clutch slip is a self-evident condition which occurs when the clutch friction plate is badly worn, the release arm free travel is insufficient, oil or grease have got onto the flywheel or pressure plate faces, or the pressure plate itself is faulty.
2 The reason for clutch slip is that, due to one of the faults listed above, there is either insufficient friction from the driven plate to ensure solid drive.
3 If small amounts of oil get onto the clutch, they will be burnt off under the heat of clutch engagement, and in the process, gradually darkening the linings. Excessive oil on the clutch will burn off leaving a carbon deposit which can cause quite bad slip, or fierceness, spin and judder.
4 If clutch slip is suspected, and confirmation of this condition is required, there are several tests which can be made.
5 With the engine in second or third gear and pulling lightly up a moderate incline, sudden depression of the accelerator pedal may cause the engine to increase its speed without any increase in road speed. Easing off on the accelerator will then give a definite drop in engine speed without the car slowing.
6 In extreme cases of clutch slip the engine will race under normal acceleration conditions.
7 If slip is due to oil or grease on the linings a temporary cure can sometimes be effected by squirting carbon tetrachloride into the clutch. The permanent cure is, of course, to renew the clutch driven plate and trace and rectify the oil leak.

13 Clutch Spin - Diagnosis and Cure

1 Clutch spin is a condition which occurs when there is too little or no free movement at the release arm or cable or there is an obstruction in the clutch either on the primary gear splines, or in the operating lever itself, or the oil may have partially burnt off the clutch linings and have left a resinous deposit which is causing the clutch disc to stick to the pressure plate or flywheel.
2 The reason for clutch spin is that due to any, or a combination of, the faults just listed, the clutch pressure plate is not completely freeing from the centre plate even with the clutch pedal fully depressed.
3 If clutch spin is suspected, the condition can be confirmed by extreme difficulty in engaging first gear from rest, difficulty in changing gear, and very sudden take-up of the clutch drive at the fully depressed end of the clutch pedal travel as the clutch is released.
4 If these points are checked and found to be in order then the fault lies internally in the clutch, and it will be necessary to remove the clutch for examination.

14 Clutch Judder - Diagnosis and Cure

1 Clutch judder is a self-evident condition which occurs when the gearbox or engine mountings are loose or too flexible, when there is oil on the faces of the clutch friction plate, or when the clutch pressure plate has been incorrectly adjusted.
2 The reason for clutch judder is that due to one of the faults just listed, the clutch pressure plate is not freeing smoothly from the friction disc, and is snatching.
3 Clutch judder normally occurs when the clutch pedal is released in first or reverse gears, and the whole car shudders as it moves backwards or forwards.

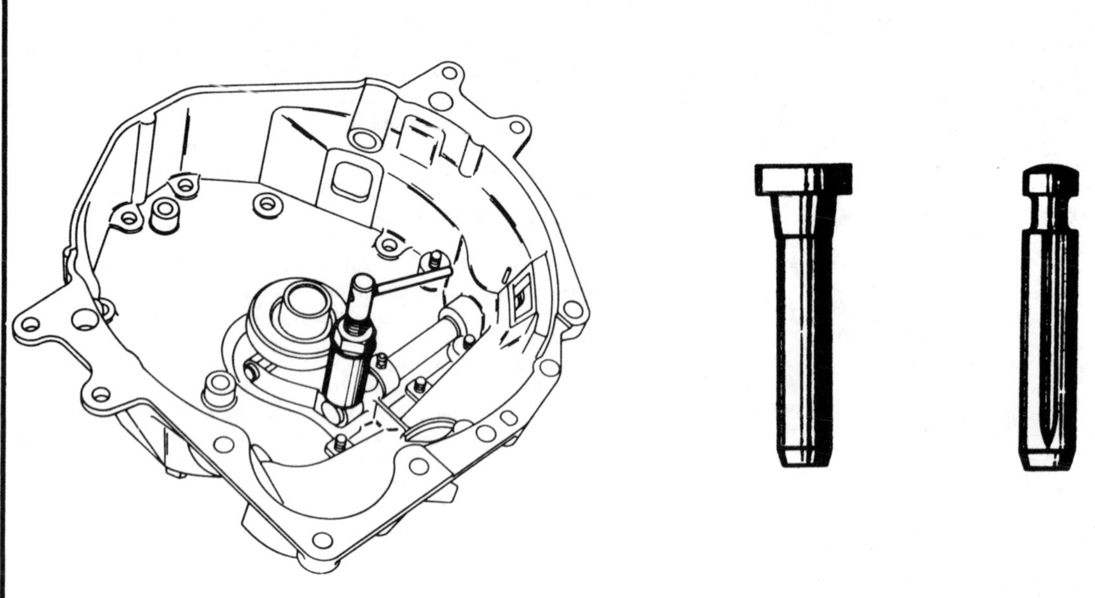

Fig.5.10 Removing the release fork to cross shaft securing pins with an extractor

Fig.5.11 Alternative types of release fork to cross shaft securing pins

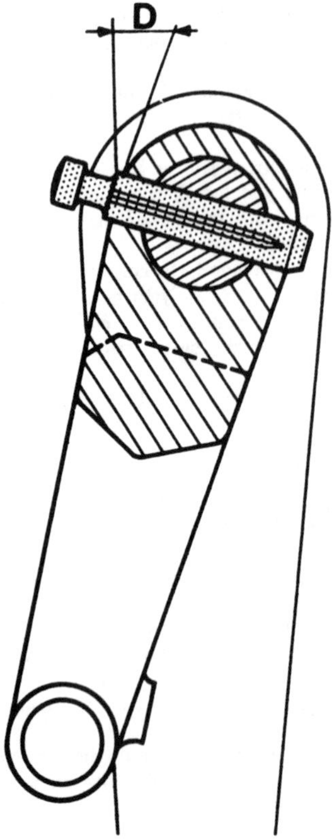

Fig.5.12 Shoulder projection of correctly located release fork to cross shaft retaining pins. D = 1/32 in (1 mm)

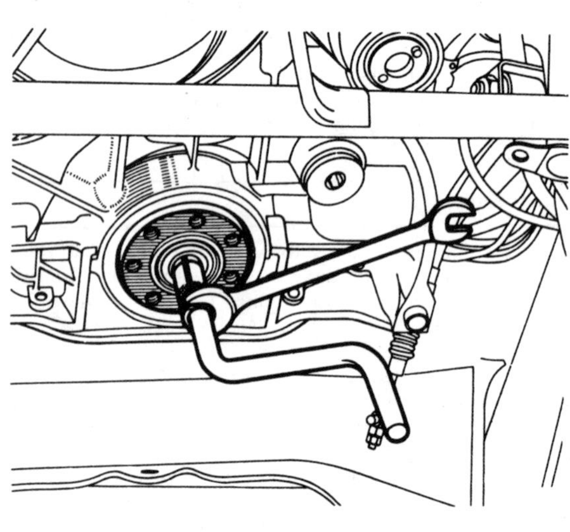

Fig.5.13 Withdrawing the first motion shaft spigot ball bearing from the flywheel mounting flange of the crankshaft, using an expanding type of extractor

With differential adjustment by nuts

Index	Steering LH	RH	Crown wheel and pinion	Pinion Protrusion
336 - 06 336 - 07	X	 X	9 x 34 Normal	51.6 mm (2.032")
336 - 12 336 - 13	X	 X	9 x 34 Normal	51.6 mm (2.032")
336 - 14 336 - 15	X	 X	8 x 34	53 mm (2.087")

Commencing with the 1968 model
New reverse gear position
Up to January 1968

Index	Steering LH	RH	Crown wheel and pinion	Pinion Protrusion
336 - 20 336 - 21	X	 X	9 x 34 Normal	51.6 mm (2.032")
336 - 22 336 - 23	X	 X	9 x 34 Normal	51.6 mm (2.032")
336 - 24 336 - 25	X	 X	8 x 34	53 mm (2.087")

From January 1968 to October 1968
Fitting of a strengthened crown wheel and pinion (9 x 34)

Index	Steering LH	RH	Crown wheel and pinion	Pinion Protrusion
336 - 30 336 - 31	X	 X	9 x 34 Strengthened	53 mm (2.087")
336 - 32 336 - 33	X	 X	9 x 34 Strengthened	53 mm (2.087")
336 - 24 336 - 25	X	 X	8 x 34	53 mm (2.087")

From November 1968
Fitting of a strengthened clutch housing

Index	Steering LH	RH	Crown wheel and pinion	Pinion Protrusion
336 - 34 336 - 35	X	 X	9 x 34 Strengthened	53 mm (2.087")
336 - 36 336 - 37	X	 X	9 x 34 Strengthened	53 mm (2.087")
336 - 24 336 - 25	X	 X	8 x 34	53 mm (2.087")

From February 1969
Addition of a tapped boss for fitting a reverse light switch

Index	Steering LH	RH	Crown wheel and pinion	Pinion Protrusion
336 - 40 336 - 43	X	 X	9 x 34 Strengthened	53 mm (2.087")
336 - 41 336 - 42	X	 X	9 x 34 Strengthened	53 mm (2.087")

336 - 44	X (LH)		8 x 34	53 mm
336 - 45		X (RH)		(2.087")

Gearboxes with indexes 14-15-24-25-44 and 45 are fitted with 697 - 02 engine having a 7.6 to 1 compression ratio.

Model R1151
from vehicle No. 1

Index	Steering LH	RH	Crown wheel and pinion	Pinion Protrusion
336 - 34	X		9 x 34	53 mm
336 - 35		X	strengthened	(2.087")
336 - 36	X		9 x 34	53 mm
336 - 37		X	strengthened	(2.087")

From February 1969
Addition of a tapped boss for fitting a reverse light switch

Index	Steering LH	RH	Crown wheel and pinion	Pinion Protrusion
336 - 40	X		9 x 34	53 mm
336 - 43		X	strengthened	(2.087")
336 - 41	X		9 x 34	53 mm
336 - 42		X	strengthened	(2.087")

R1152
From vehicle No. 1

Index	Crown wheel and pinion	Pinion protrusion
336 - 36 Followed by 336 - 34	9 x 34 strengthened	53 mm (2.087")

From February 1969
Addition of a tapped boss for fitting a reverse light switch

Index	Crown wheel and pinion	Pinion protrusion
336 - 40	9 x 34 strengthened	53 mm (2.087")

Torque Wrench Settings

	lbf ft	kgf m
Crownwheel bolts (0.394 in - 10 mm dia.)	70	9.7
Crownwheel bolts (0.434 in - 11 mm dia.)	60 - 80	8.3 – 11.0
Differential side cover plate bolts	15	2.1
Gearbox housing bolts (0.276 in - 7 mm dia.)	15	2.1
Gearbox housing bolts (0.315 in - 8 mm dia.)	20	2.8
Reverse swivel lever pivot bolt	20	2.8
Gearshift hand control ball joint nut ... ... (5/32 in - 4 mm thick)	10	1.4
Gearshift hand control ball joint nut ... ... (9/32 in - 7 mm thick)	15	2.1
Gearshift pivot pin bolt	20	2.8
Gearshift control mechanism (gearbox end) bolts	10	1.4

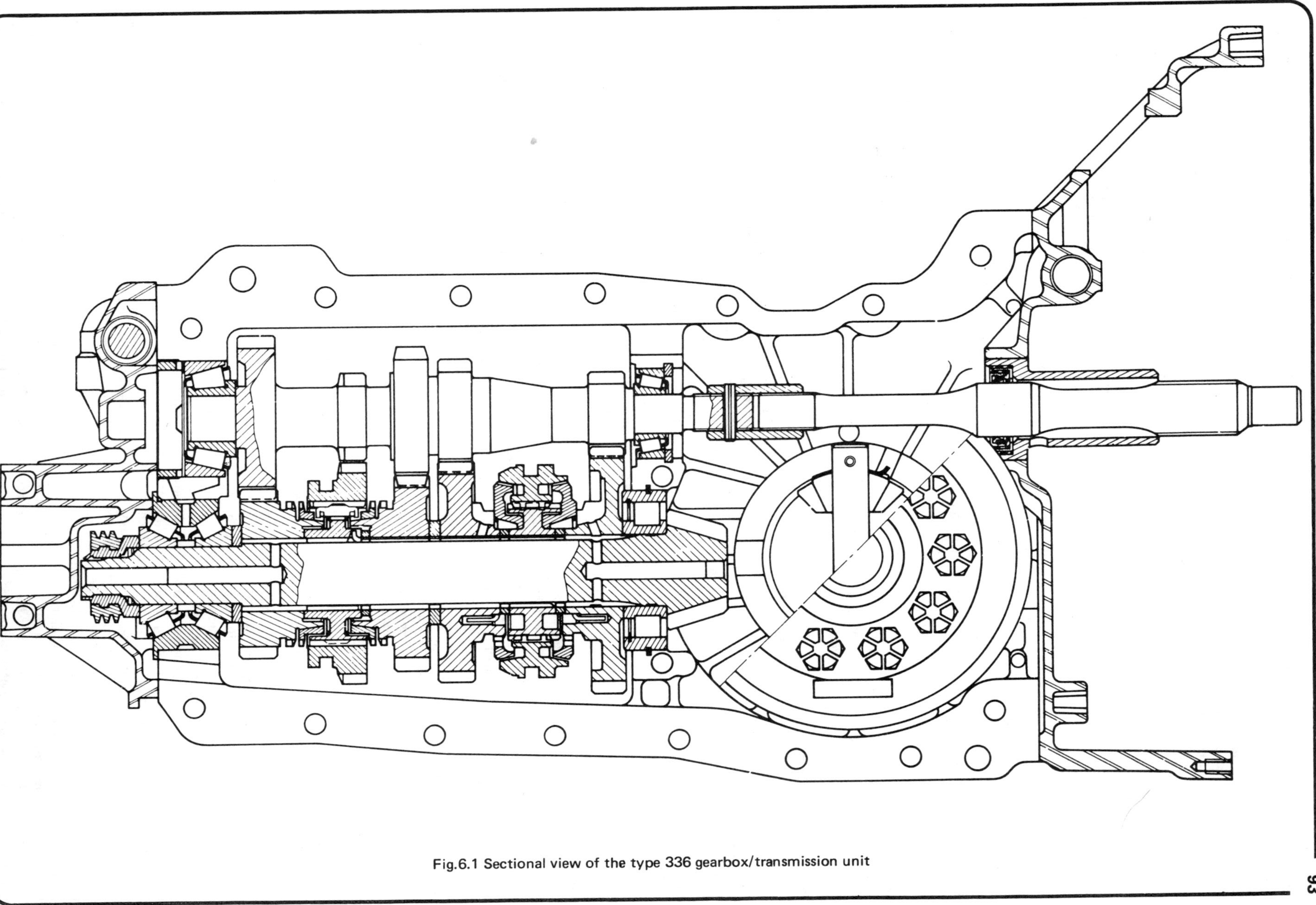

Fig.6.1 Sectional view of the type 336 gearbox/transmission unit

1 General Description

1 A type 336 gearbox is fitted to all models except the R1153 and R1154 which have automatic transmission (described in the following Chapter).
2 The type, index and serial numbers are shown on a plate bolted to the front of the gearbox. (Fig 6.2)..
3 The gearbox housing is of pressure die-cast aluminium construction, fabricated in two halves.
4 Four forward speeds, all with synchromesh, are incorporated and one reverse gear.
5 The crownwheel and pinion final drive and differential are integral with the gearbox and the complete unit is located ahead of the engine at the front of the car. A sectional view of the gearbox/transmission unit (viewed from the left hand side of the car) is given in Fig. 6.1.
6 Certain detail modifications have been made according to date of manufacture and are as follows but they are dealt with in detail in the appropriate section of this Chapter.

Model R1150 up to 1968
Index 02, 03, 10,11 - differential adjustment by shims.
Index 06, 07, 12, 13, 14, 15 - differential adjustment by nuts.
Index 20, 21, 22, 23, 24, 25 - new reverse gear location.

January 1968 to October 1968
Index 30, 31, 32, 33, 24, 25 - crownwheel and pinion strengthened.

November 1968 on
Index 24, 25, 34, 35, 36, 37 - clutch bellhousing strengthened.

February 1969 on
Index 34, 35, 36, 37, 40, 41, 42, 43, 44, 45 - reverse light switch boss incorporated.

Gearboxes with the following index numbers are only fitted to vehicles having a 697 - 02 engine (7.6 : 1 compression ratio).

Model R1152
Index 34, 36 - strengthened crownwheel and pinion.
Index 40 - reverse light switch boss incorporated.
7 The gearchange is steering column mounted and the control mechanism is by rods and levers to the gearbox front housing in which the gearshift fork lever and shaft are located.

2 Gearbox/Transmission - Removal and Refitting

1 It is assumed that the gearbox is to be removed from the car leaving the engine in position. Where the engine and gearbox/transmission unit are to be removed as a combined assembly, then reference should be made to Chapter 1.
2 Disconnect the battery and remove the spare wheel from the engine compartment.
3 Drain the gearbox by removing plug B. The removal of plug A will help to speed the operation.
4 Where necessary, remove the clutch shield.
5 Remove the radiator fan and shroud (see Chapter 2).
6 Disconnect the battery lead from its fixing clamp on the steering box and then disconnect it at its terminal.
7 Remove the spare wheel support crossmember.
8 The radiator need not be disconnected and this will obviate the necessity of draining and refilling the cooling system (Chapter 2). Using a clamp, pinch the flexible pipe which runs between the radiator and the expansion bottle. Unscrew the expansion bottle cap. The radiator securing bolts may now be removed and the radiator swung up and over the engine with all hoses still connected. Do not strain the hoses but support the radiator just clear of the gearbox/transmission.
9 With R1152 models only, disconnect the speedometer drive cable (1) from the centrifugal switch and having removed the switch securing bolt, swing the switch to one side.
10 Turn the steering wheel to full left lock (ignition key in position O) and remove the connecting bolt from the steering arm to steering end fitting.
11 Turn the steering to full right lock and remove the left hand connecting bolt.
12 Remove the camshaft pulley front flange and the shims. Pull off the drive belt and remove the pulley inner flange.
13 Unscrew and remove the four bolts which secure the steering cross member to the engine compartment sides.
14 Disconnect the steering column flexible coupling and with full right lock, remove the steering assembly in the direction of the arrow shown.
15 Disconnect the reverse light wires (if fitted).
16 Disconnect the speedometer cable, the gearchange control lever linkage.
17 Remove the two bolts which secure the gearchange control to the gearbox and swing the control to one side (photo).
18 Support the gearbox on a jack and then remove the two nuts and two bolts which secure the front mounting pad. Remove the pad and its bracket.
19 Using a suitable drift, drive out the drive shaft roll pins.
20 Fit securing clips to each drive shaft joint to prevent them becoming dismantled.
21 Using a scissors type jack located between the gearbox and left hand frame side member, prise the gearbox until the drive shaft can be disconnected from the sunwheel. Repeat on the right hand side.
22 Disconnect the clutch operating cable from the release lever and remove the cable stop attachment from the clutch bell-housing.
23 Support the engine with another jack and then unscrew and remove the clutch bellhousing to engine bolts.
24 Unscrew the starter motor securing bolts and withdraw the starter as far as possible.
25 Carefully pull the gearbox/transmission unit as far forward as is necessary to disengage the first motion shaft from the flywheel and clutch assembly. It is strongly emphasised that at no time during this operation must the weight of the gearbox hang upon the first motion shaft while it is engaged with the clutch assembly. Failure to observe this will probably necessitate a new clutch assembly and driven plate. Always provide adequate support until the first motion shaft has passed through the clutch assembly.
26 The gearbox front face may now be lifted up, (taking care not to damage the radiator temporarily located above the engine) and then the complete gearbox/transmission unit removed in a vertical position from the engine compartment.
27 Refitting the gearbox/transmission is a reversal of removal but the following points must be noted.
28 Grease the first motion shaft splines sparingly.
29 Centralise the clutch driven plate as described in Chapter 5.
30 Grease the transmission sunwheel splines.
31 Use new drive shaft roll pins and seal each end with recommended sealer.
32 Adjust the clutch free movement, Chapter 5.
33 Adjust the water pump drive belt, Chapter 2.
34 Refill the gearbox with the correct grade and quantity of lubricant.
35 Should it be necessary to fit a new clutch bellhousing, those of later or replacement manufacture have a thicker engine mating flange which will necessitate the fitting of longer starter motor securing bolts and a modified clutch shield (without rubber seal).

3 Gearbox/Transmission - Dismantling

1 Unscrew and remove the six clutch bellhousing to gearbox securing bolts.
2 Unscrew and remove the reverse light switch (if fitted).
3 Unscrew and remove the eight gearbox front housing bolts (photo). Lift away the front housing but take care to retain the first motion shaft bearing adjusting shims and distance piece

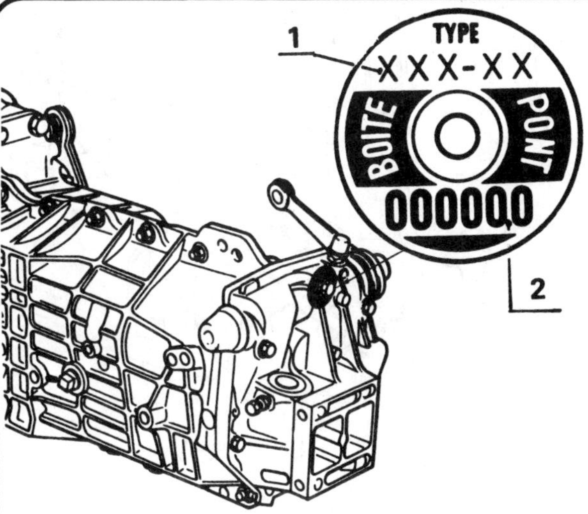

Fig.6.2. Location of gearbox/transmission unit index plate

1 Type *2 Serial number*

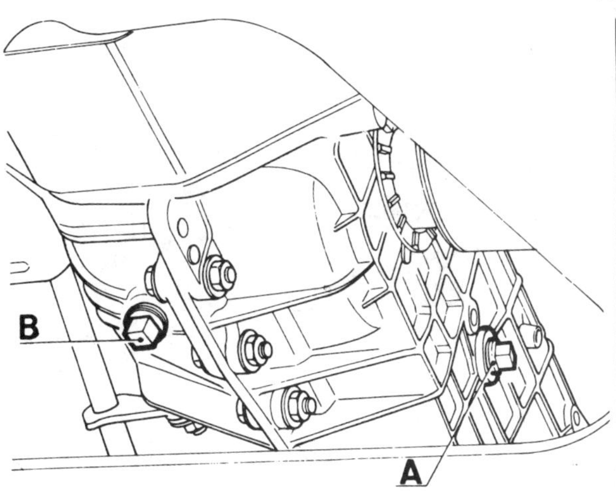

2.3 Gearbox filler (A) and drain (B) plugs

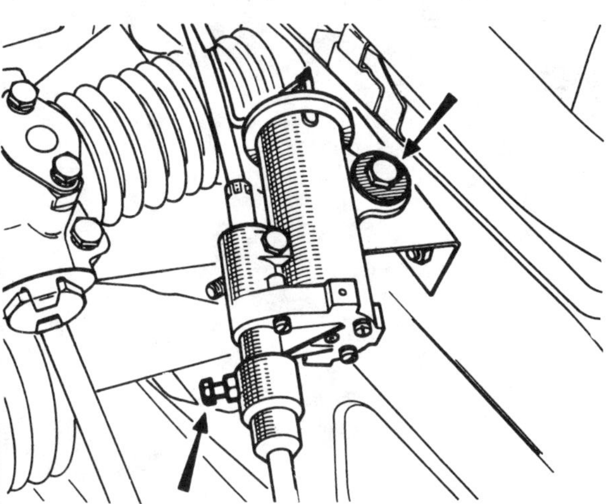

2.9 Speedometer cable and centrifugal switch securing bolts

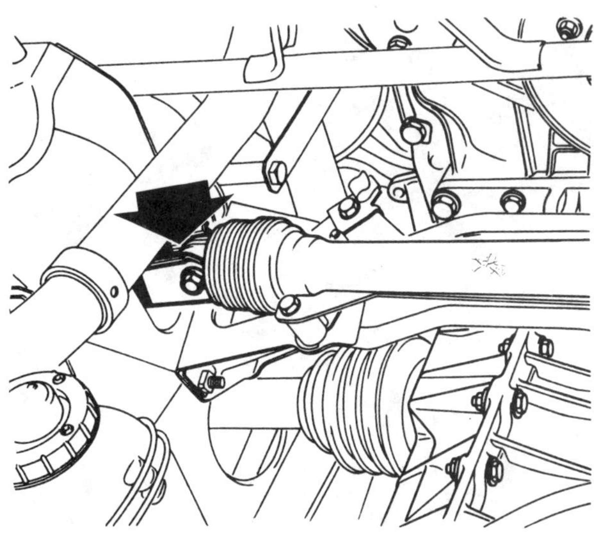

2.10 Steering arm to eye connecting bolt

2.12 Camshaft pulley and drive belts

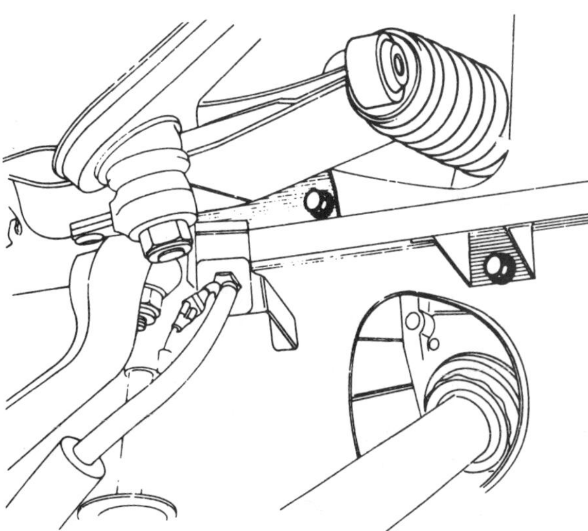

2.13 Steering crossmember to engine compartment side securing bolts (one side - 2 bolts only shown)

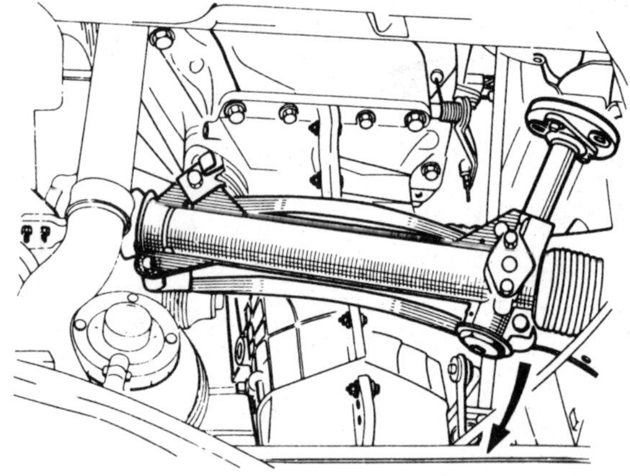

2.14 Steering gear removal from engine compartment

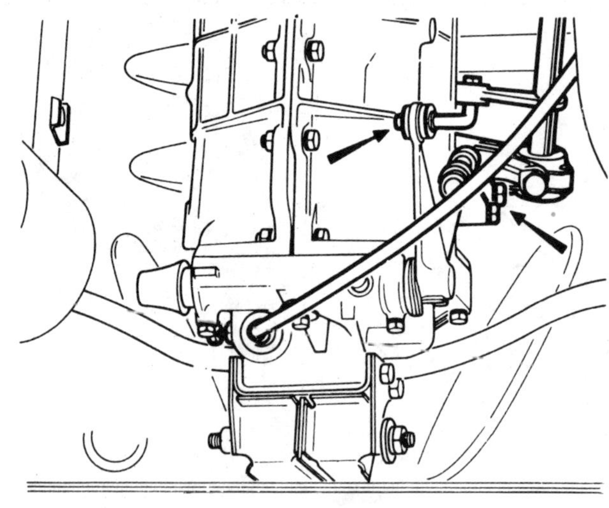

2.16 Gearchange control removal points

2.17A Disconnecting gearchange control

2.17B Disconnecting gearchange control

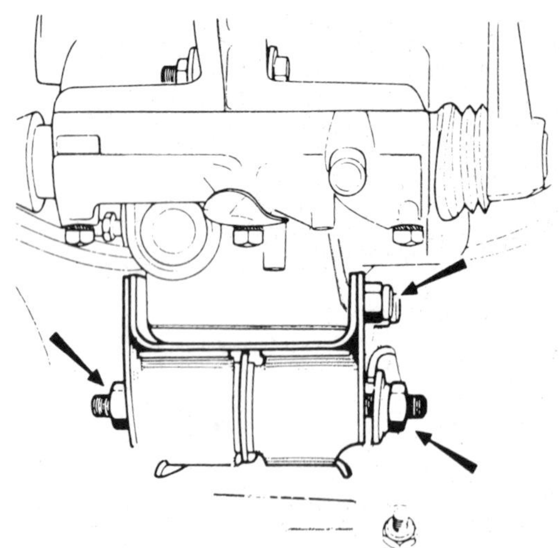

2.18 Gearbox front mounting bolts

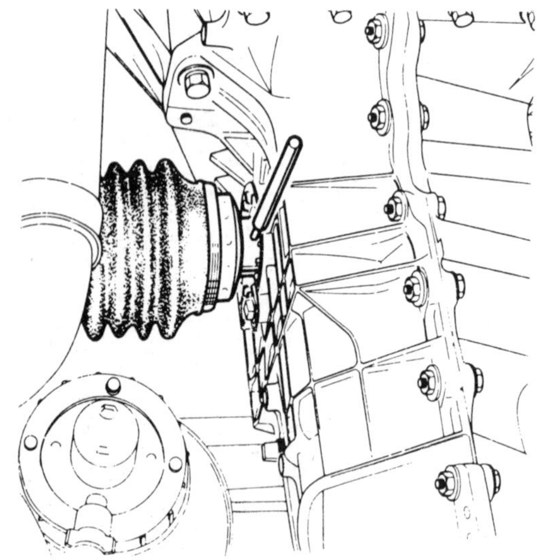

2.19 Drifting out the sun wheel to drive shaft roll pins

2.20 Retaining clip fitted to drive shaft

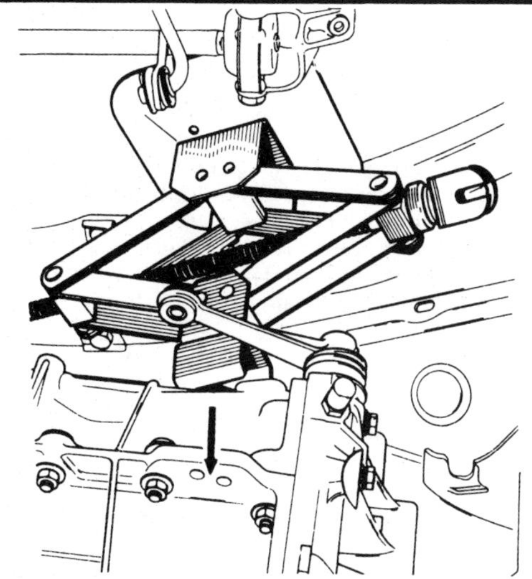
2.21 Using a jack to prise the gearbox/transmission unit and facilitate removal of the drive shafts

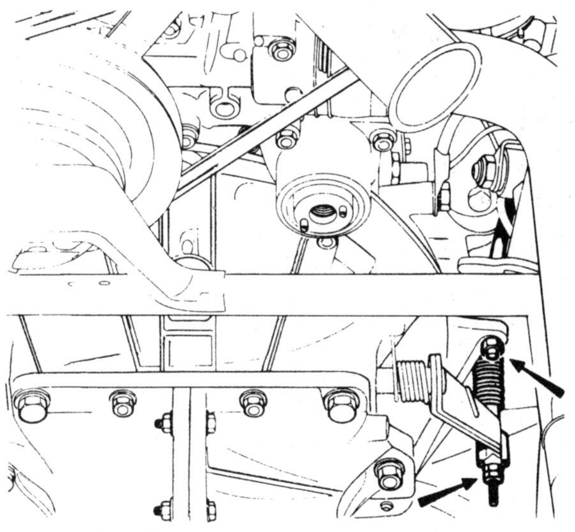
2.22 Clutch operating cable fixings

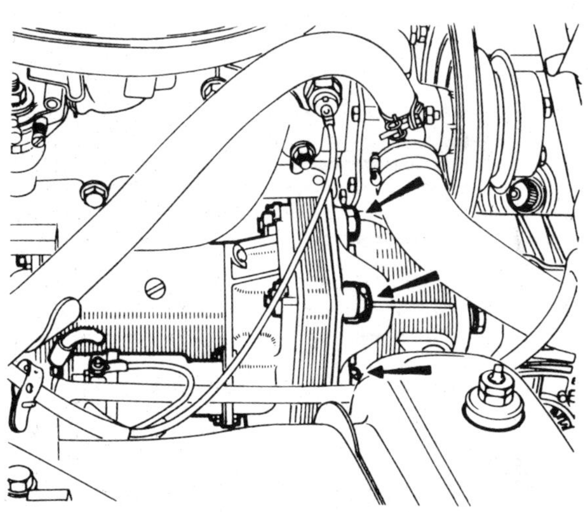
2.24 Starter motor securing bolts

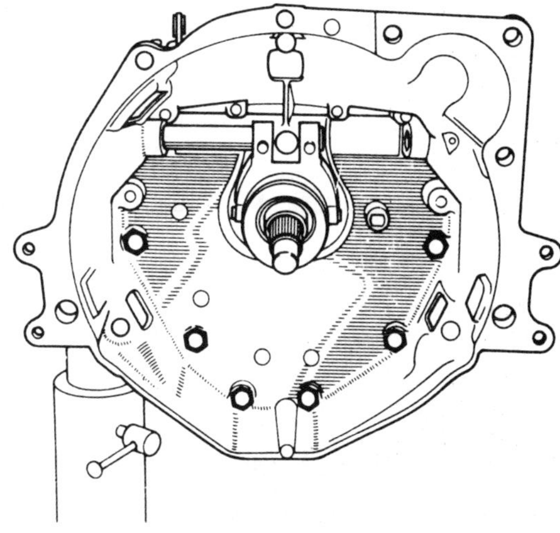
3.1 Clutch bell housing to gearbox securing bolts

3.3 Removing gearbox front housing bolts

which will be released.

4 Remove the differential adjusting nut locking tab (photo).

5 Unscrew the differential adjusting nut using a brass drift (photo). Where the differential bearings are adjusted by means of shims then the side covers should be marked before removal and the bearing tracks pressed out of the side covers.

6 Remove the fifteen bolts and nuts which secure the two halves of the gearbox housing together and separate them (photo). Unscrew the bolts evenly, working from the centre towards each end.

7 Lift out the mainshaft gear train and peg which locks the double taper roller bearing outer cage from one half of the gearbox housing.

8 Lift out the first motion shaft and the differential (photo).

9 From the other half of the gearbox, drive out the roll pin which secures the 3rd and 4th speed fork to the selector shaft. Remove the fork and shaft but take care to retain the locking ball and spring. Remove the locking disc located between the two shafts.

10 Select first gear and slide back reverse gear as far as possible. Drift out the roll pin which secures the 1st and 2nd gear fork to the shaft.

11 Remove the fork and shaft but retain carefully the locking ball and spring.

12 Unscrew the reverse gear swivel lever pin and remove the swivel lever.

13 Drift out the reverse gear shaft positioning roll pin. The shaft will have to be rotated during this operation and the roll pin finally extracted with the aid of a pair of pliers.

14 Remove the reverse gear wheel retaining circlip.

15 Withdraw the shaft, gear wheel, thrust washer and guide, carefully retaining the locking ball and spring.

16 The gearbox is now dismantled into its major components and unless the appropriate presses and bearing extractors are available, further dismantling operations should be entrusted to a service station having the necessary equipment. Makeshift methods or brute force will not work with the fine tolerances needed in a modern gearbox.

17 All components should be brushed clean in a paraffin bath. Examine the gears for wear or chipping of teeth. Check the shaft bearings, synchroniser units, circlips and detent balls and springs should be renewed.

18 Separate the first motion shaft from the layshaft by drifting out the securing circlip.

19 Using a bearing extractor remove the bearing from the differential side of the layshaft.

20 Remove the bearing from the other end of the layshaft.

21 Grip the mainshaft in a vice by positioning the first gear wheel in the jaws which have been adequately protected with wood packing pieces (photo).

22 Select first gear and unscrew the pinion and speedometer drive retaining nut. The flats on a 32 mm open ended spanner will have to be ground down in order to fit this nut (photo).

23 From the mainshaft, lift the double taper roller bearing (1) the pinion protrusion adjusting washer (2), the fourth speed gear (3) and ring (4) the 3rd and 4th speed synchroniser sleeve (5) and keys (mark the position of the synchro sliding gear relative to the hub) (photos). References are to Fig 3.23.

24 Extract the 3rd and 4th speed synchroniser hub from the mainshaft (photo). A special Renault extractor will be needed.

25 Remove the gear wheel thrust washer retaining key (arrowed), the 3rd gear thrust washer and the 3rd speed gear and its ring.

26 Remove the second gear thrust washer (1) the second speed gear and ring (2) the 1st and 2nd synchromesh sleeve (3) marking its position relative to the hub and the thrust washer for 1st and 2nd synchro hub.

27 Again using a suitable extractor, remove the 1st and 2nd gear synchro hub.

28 Remove 1st gear synchro ring, 1st gear thrust washer and 1st speed gear.

29 After removal of the 1st speed gear it must be noted that the roller bearing inner track is bonded to the mainshaft and renewal will necessitate replacement of the mainshaft/bearing assembly (see section 5). With strengthened crownwheel and pinion assemblies, a clip should be used to prevent the outer track being dislodged and releasing the rollers.

4 Differential Unit - Dismantling

1 Using a suitable puller, extract the bearings from each side of the differential. Two of the crownwheel securing bolts may first have to be removed.

2 Unscrew and remove all the crownwheel securing bolts. These are of self-locking type and must not be re-used.

3 Drift out the roll pin which secures the planet wheel shaft to the differential housing.

5 Crownwheel and Pinion - Matching

1 The crownwheel and pinion are supplied as matched pairs and cannot be renewed separately. The mainshaft incorporates the pinion and roller bearing and as neither of these can be removed, any wear in these items will necessitate renewal of both the mainshaft assembly and the crownwheel.

2 Identical index marks are located on matched components as shown in the figure.

6 Pinion and Synchro Hub - Matching

1 The synchromesh hubs must be matched with the final drive pinion. If the synchromesh units are in good order and are to be used again but the pinion and crownwheel are to be renewed then the pinion and crownwheel must be ordered after the following calculations have been made.

2 Conversely where the pinion and crownwheel are to be used again but the synchromesh units are worn and are to be renewed, carry out similar calculations before ordering new synchromesh units.

3 Using a micrometer measure the distance across two splines on the final drive pinion. Take several similar measurements across different sets of splines around the synchro hub seating and take an average of the varying measurements.

4 Refer to the following table and order either new pinion and crownwheel assemblies or synchroniser units by colour code.

Average two spline measurement	Colour matching code
0.6539 to 0.6547 inch 16.61 to 16.63 mm	blue
0.6551 to 0.6559 inch 16.64 to 16.66 mm	yellow

7 Synchromesh Units

1 As previously described, the synchromesh hub and sleeve should be marked as shown in the figure, before dismantling. In the case of new units, these are already marked. Any marking should be made on the chamfered side of the 1st/2nd synchromesh sliding gear so that it will be visible after fitting the hub to the pinion/mainshaft.

2 The 3rd/4th synchromesh unit should be assembled in the following manner. Fit on to the hub the three keys, and the two springs (insert the end of the springs into the same key with the non-hooked ends located on either side of it).

3 Fit the sliding gear sleeve in the correct position so that its peripheral groove is on the opposite side to the hub notch also the alignment mark on the sleeve (made prior to dismantling) is in line with the one on the hub.

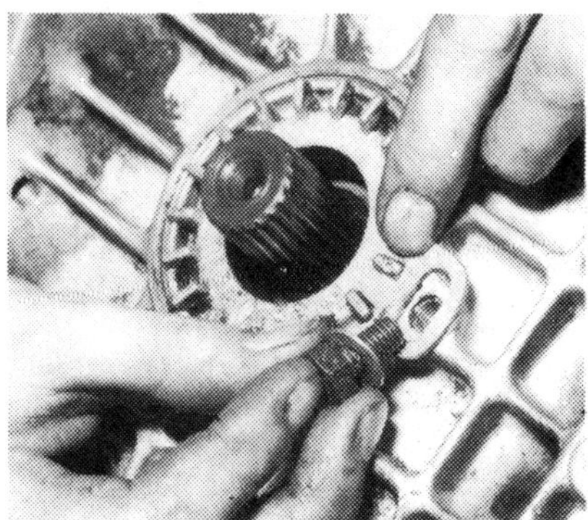

3.4 Differential adjustment nut locking tab and bolt

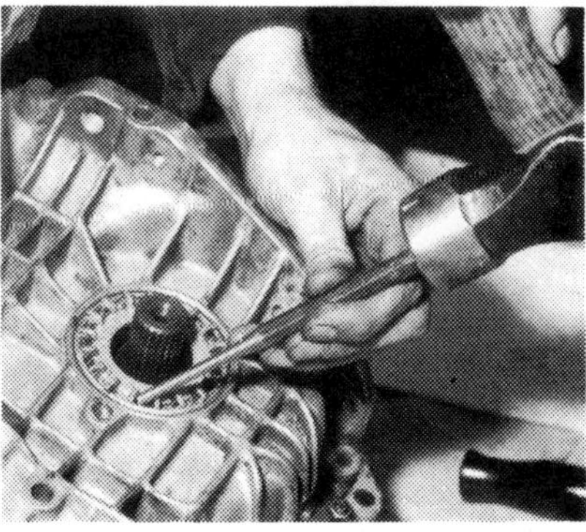

3.5 Moving differential nut using a drift

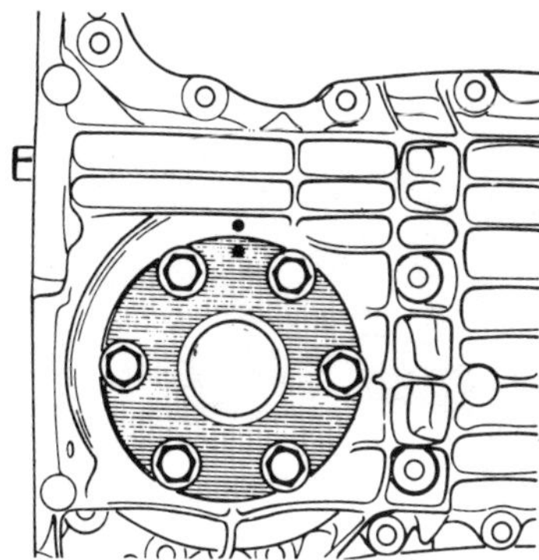

3.5A Side cover plates, alignment marks and securing bolts

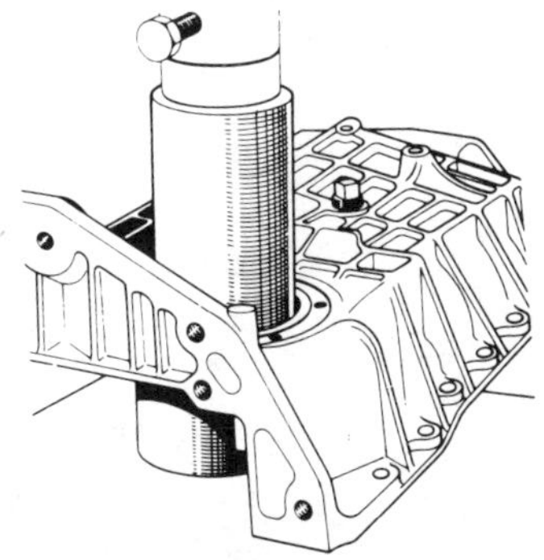

3.5B Pressing out the differential bearing outer tracks from the gearbox/transmission unit

3.6 Gearbox housing securing bolts

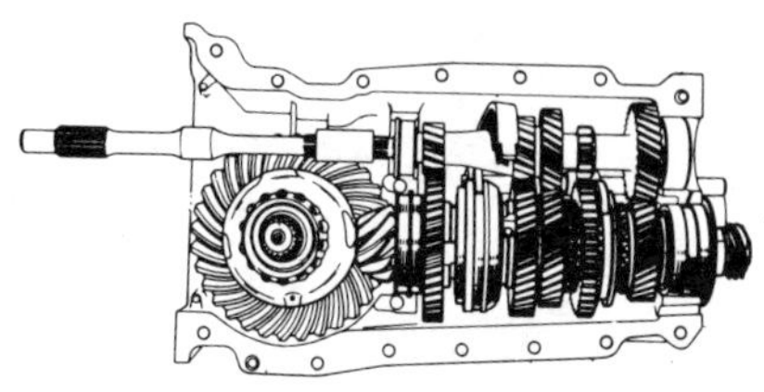

3.7 View of differential, pinion drive shaft /mainshaft and first motion/layshaft in position in the gearbox

3.8 The pinion drive shaft/mainshaft removed from the gearbox

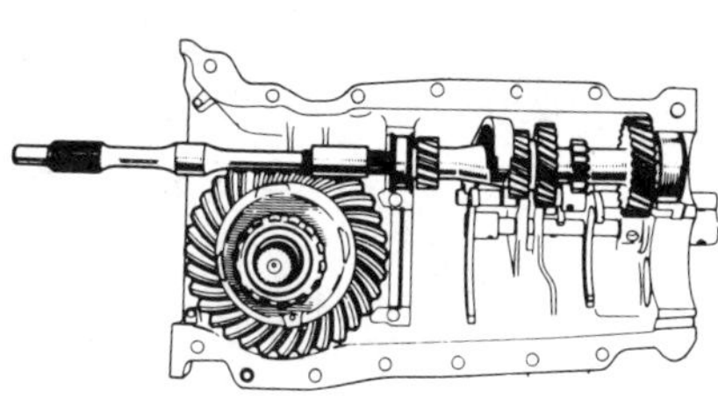

3.8A Lifting first motion shaft from gearbox

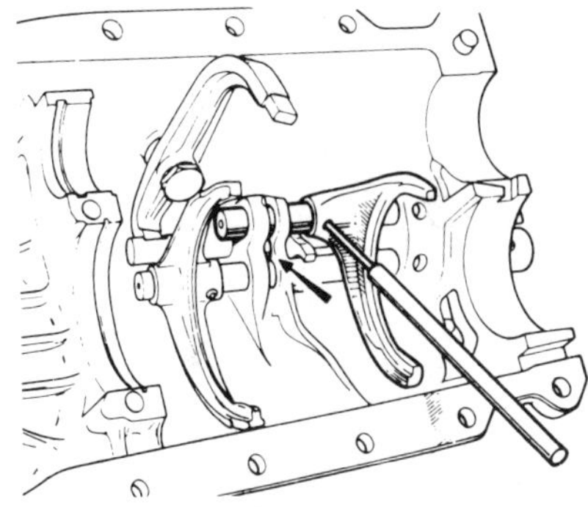

3.9 Driving out the 3rd/4th selector fork rollpin (locking disc arrowed)

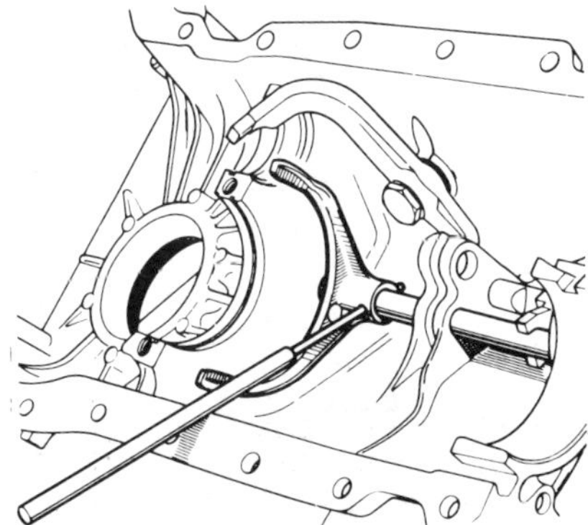

3.10 Driving out the 1st/2nd selector fork roll pin

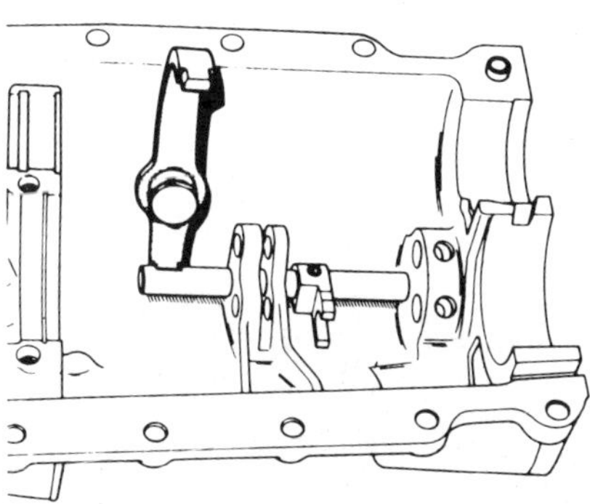

3.12 The reverse gear swivel lever pin

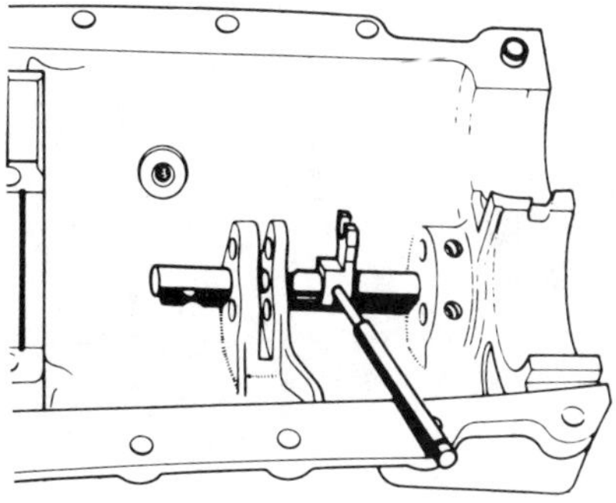

3.13 Driving out the reverse gear shaft locating roll pin

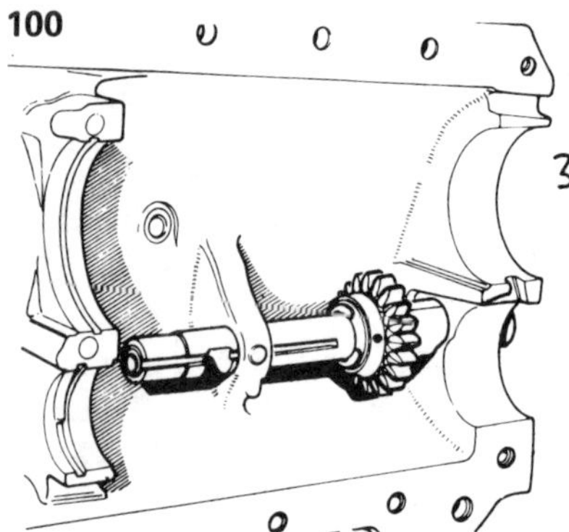

3.14 The reverse gearwheel and retaining circlip

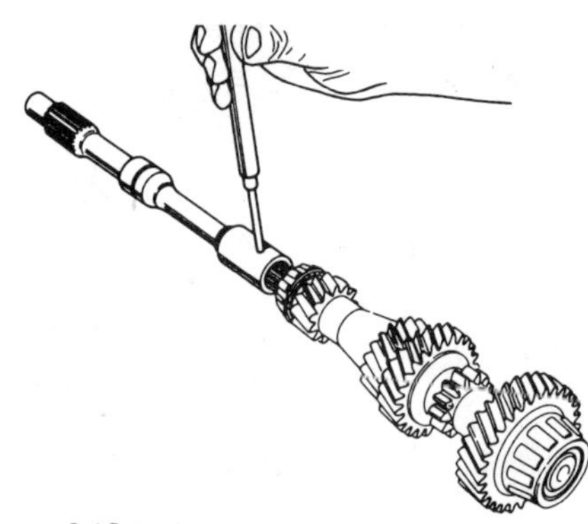

3.18 Drifting out the first motion (primary) shaft to layshaft retaining circlip

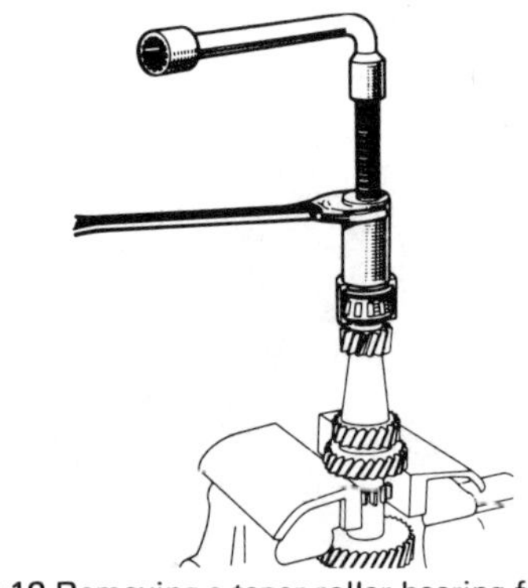

3.19 Removing a taper roller bearing from the layshaft

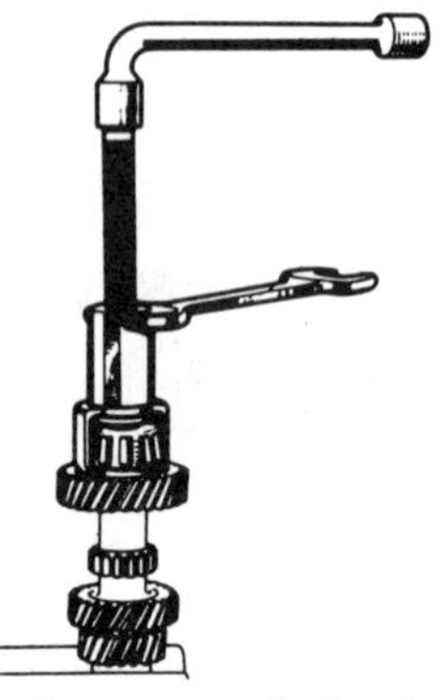

3.20 Removing a taper roller bearing from the layshaft

3.21 Gripping mainshaft prior to dismantling

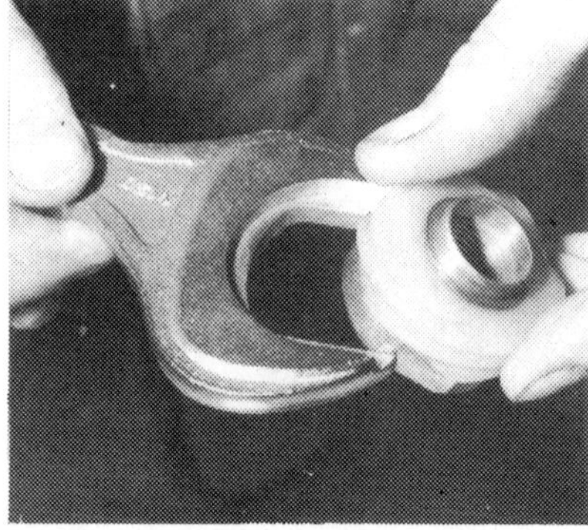

3.22 Modified spanner to fit speedometer drive nut

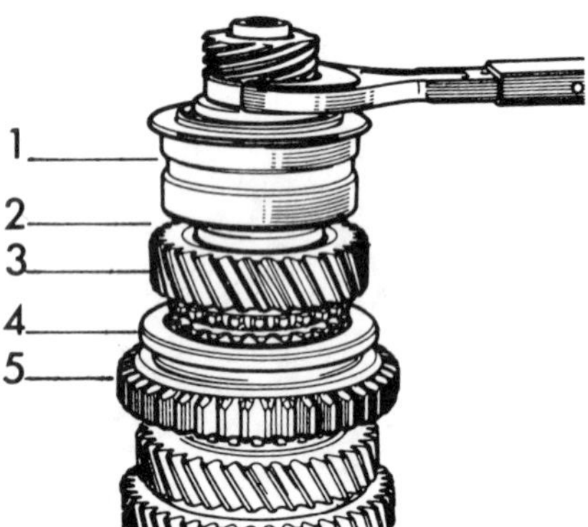

3.23 Unscrewing the pinion/speedometer drive retaining nut

3.23A Removing 3rd/4th speed synchroniser sleeve

3.23B Removing 3rd/4th speed synchro. hub keys

3.24 3rd/4th speed synchro. hub fitted to mainshaft showing close proximity to 3rd speed ring

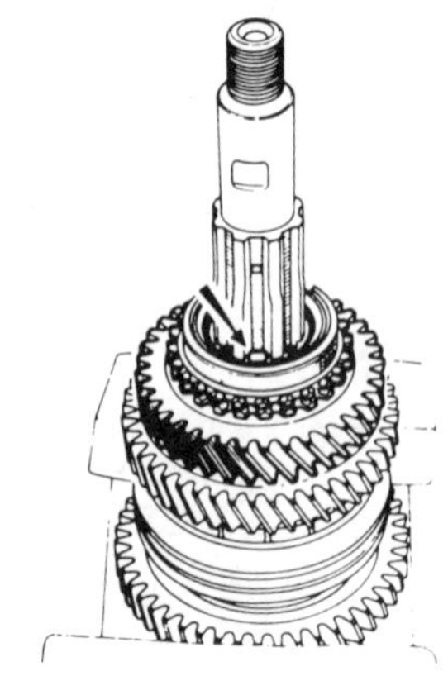

3.25 Mainshaft showing gear wheel thrust washer retaining key (arrowed)

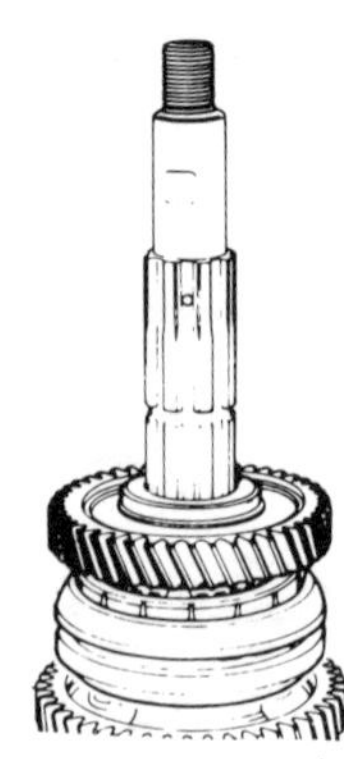

3.26 Mainshaft showing: (1) thrust washer. (2) 2nd speed gear and ring. (3) 1st/2nd speed synchro sleeve

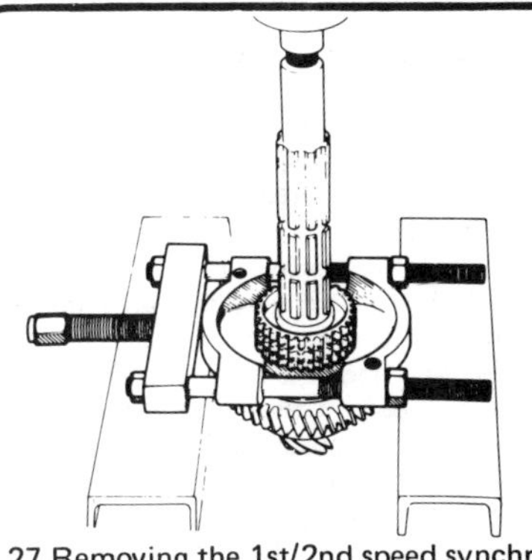

3.27 Removing the 1st/2nd speed synchro hub

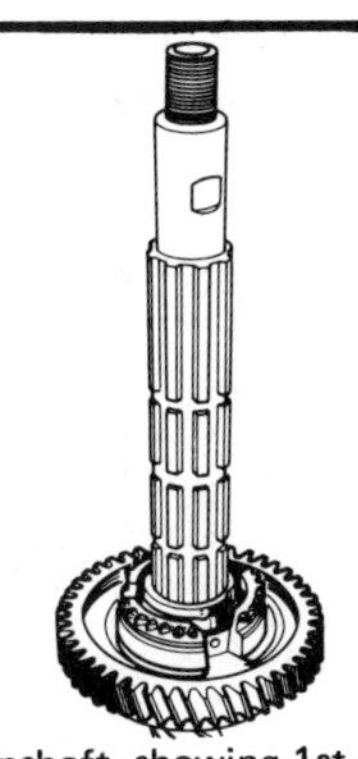

3.28 Mainshaft, showing 1st speed gear, synchro ring and thrust washer

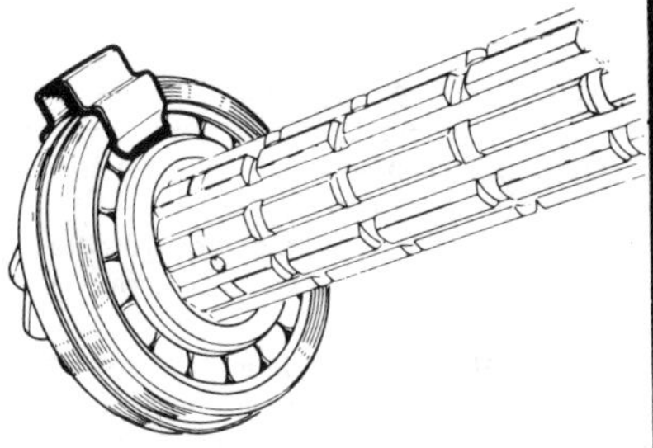

3.29 Temporary clip fitted to pinion drive shaft end bearing

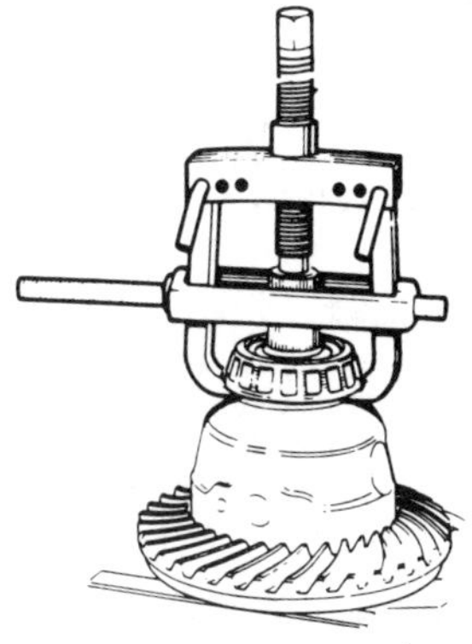

4.1A Extracting the roller bearings from the differential

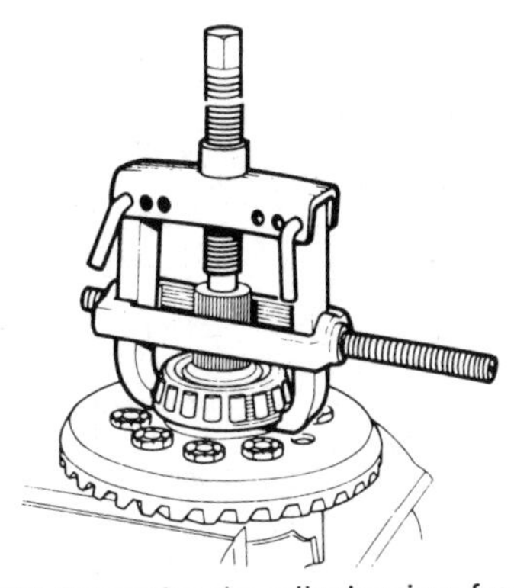

4.1B Extracting the roller bearings from the differential

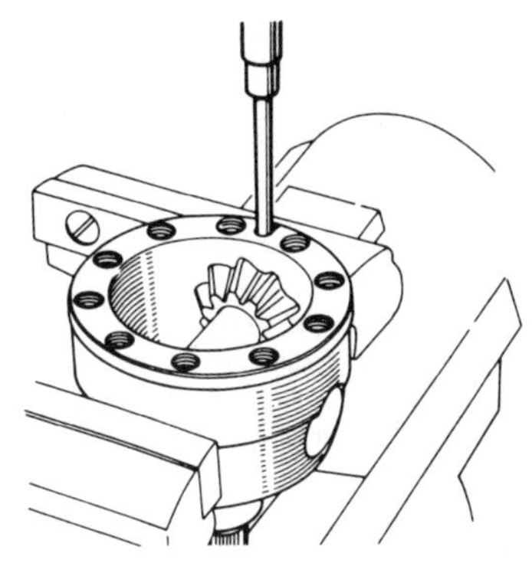

4.3 Drifting out the differential sunwheel retaining roll pins

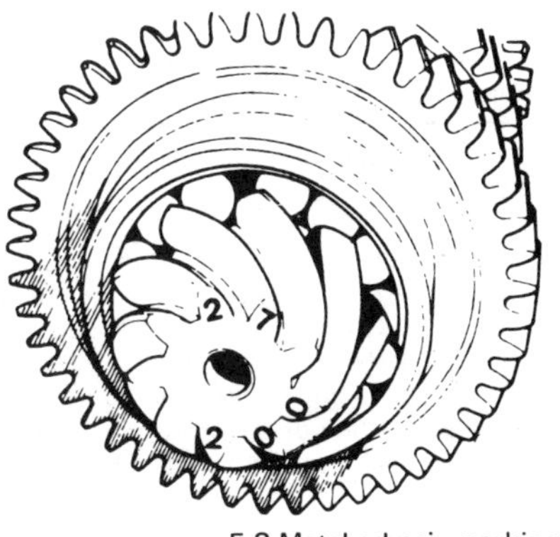

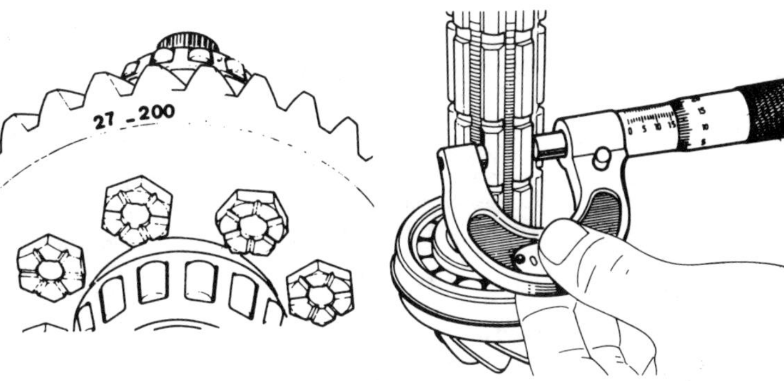

5.2 Matched pair markings on the pinion and crownwheel

6.3 Taking a measurement for colour code calculation

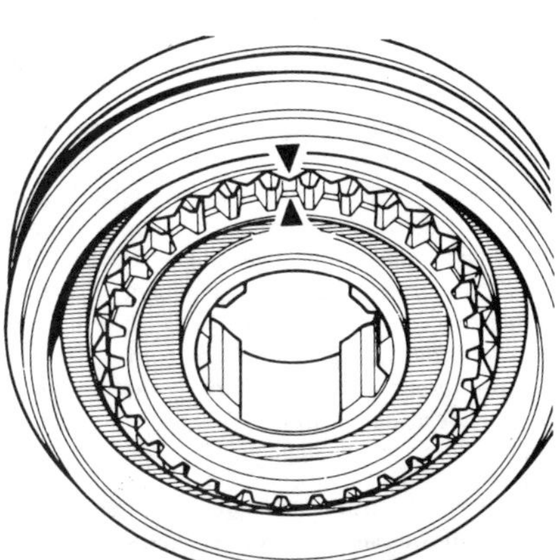

7.1 Synchro hub and sleeve alignment marks

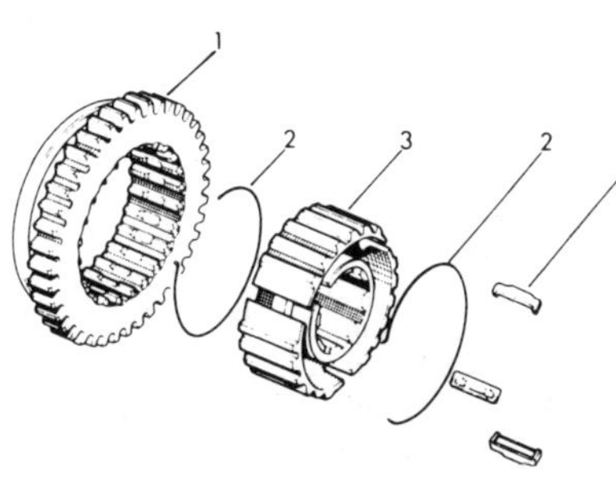

7.2 Components of the 3rd/4th synchro unit: (1) Sleeve. (2)Spring. (3) Hub. (4) Keys

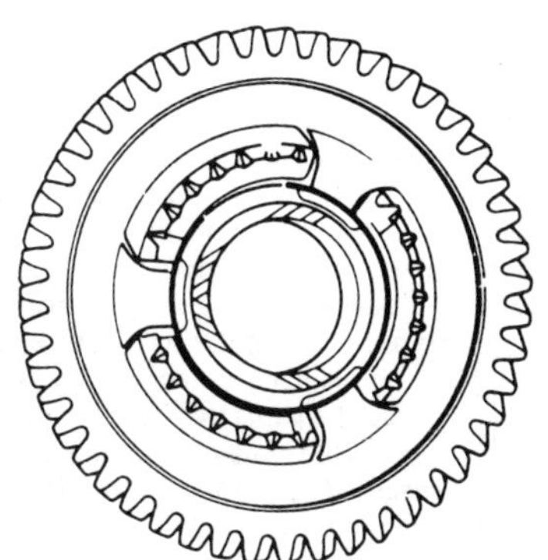

8.1 Correct location of spring on the 1st speed gearwheel

8 Pinion Driveshaft/Mainshaft - Reassembling

1 Fit the synchro spring on the 1st speed gearwheel so that it covers the three notches.
2 Take the final drive pinion/mainshaft assembly (which will be fitted with its roller bearing as a captive component) and fit the 1st gearwheel and its ring.
3 Fit the 1st speed gearwheel thrust washer.
4 Turn the thrust washer and lock it in position by means of a dummy key. The key may be made from an old washer retaining key by cutting off its curved end. Make sure that the dummy key is placed in a groove having an oil hole.
5 Remove any clip which was temporarily attached to secure the roller bearing assembly together.
6 Place the 1st/2nd speed synchro hub in a domestic oven and heat it to 250o C (482o F). When the correct temperature has been reached, remove the hub and press it onto the splined drive pinion shaft until the hub touches the thrust washer. As the hub is pressed onto the shaft, ensure that the dummy key slides through one of the grooves in the hub and the chamfered side of the hub splines face towards the pinion teeth. During this operation, hold the synchro ring control with its lugs below the level of the thrust washer to avoid damage to the synchro spring. Keep the pressure on the synchro hub until it has cooled down and then remove the press and the dummy key.
7 Fit the 1st/2nd synchro sleeve to its hub so that the marks are in alignment and the chamfer on the side facing the 2nd speed gearwheel.
8 Fit the thrust washer, turning it so that its splines align with those of the pinion drive shaft.
9 Fit the synchro spring to the 2nd speed gearwheel in a similar manner to that for the 1st speed gearwheel.
10 Fit the second speed gearwheel and its ring.
11 Fit the 2nd gear thrust washer, aligning its splines with those of the pinion drive shaft.
12 Fit the 3rd speed gearwheel and its ring, the thrust washer (splines in alignment with those of the pinion drive shaft).
13 Fit the retaining key for the gearwheel thrust washers, inserting it in a groove having an oil hole.
14 Using a press, fit the 3rd/4th speed synchro unit (assembled) until it just touches the 3rd speed gear wheel thrust washer. Ensure that the notch on the (3rd gearwheel side) is in alignment with the retaining key. The hub of the 3rd/4th synchro unit must not be heated but fitted cold.
15 Check that the three notches on the synchro ring are in line with the three retaining keys.
16 Fit the 4th speed gearwheel and its ring (photo).
17 Fit the pinion protrusion adjusting washer (photo).
18 Fit the double taper roller bearing and the speedometer drive gear (photos).
19 Support the assembled pinion drive/mainshaft in a vice with jaws protected with wooden strips. Grip the assembly by the first speed gearwheel.
20 Using a torque wrench or the previously filed down spanner and a spring balance (the spanner must be 12 in - 305 mm in length) tighten the speedometer drive gear to 75 — 85 lbf ft (10.4 — 11.7 kgf m) (photo). Do not lock the speedo drive gear at this stage as the correct pinion protrusion adjustment has yet to be carried out, as described in Section 11.
21 Remove the shaft assembly from the vice and check the play which exists between the 3rd speed gear synchro and the rim of the synchro hub. During the measurement operation, ensure that the synchro ring is hard up against the gearwheel cone with the gearwheel pressed against the synchro hub. Check the 4th speed synchro ring to hub play in a similar manner. Any deviation from the specified tolerance will indicate incorrect assembly or worn synchro units.

9 Differential - Reassembly

1 Insert into the housing (1) the impregnated washer having its oil groove facing the sunwheel. References are to Fig. 6.3.
2 Fit the spacer washer (2) followed by the sunwheel (3). Dip all components in EP80 oil prior to reassembly. Normally a spacer washer 0.77 to 0.079 in (1.96 to 2 mm) thick will be used but where excessive play is observed between the sunwheel and planet wheel teeth then a thicker washer is available 0.080 to 0.082 in (2.03 to 2.07 mm) in thickness.
3 Fit the planet wheels (4) and their thrust washers (5) ensuring that the washer tags locate in the holes in the housing.
4 Insert the planet wheel shaft (6) ensuring that its hole aligns with the one in the differential housing.
5 Fit a new planet wheel shaft securing roll pin and drift it into position. Roll pins of 0.158 in (4 mm) or 0.197 in (5 mm) diameter may be encountered and the receiving hole size should be established before ordering new roll pins.
6 Locate the second sunwheel within the crownwheel and then, using new self-locking bolts, bolt the crownwheel to the differential housing.
7 Tighten the crownwheel bolts to a torque of 70 lbf ft (9.7 kgf m) for bolts of 0.394 in (10 mm) diameter or 60 — 80 lbf ft (8.3 — 11.0 kgf m) for those of 0.434 in (11 mm) diameter; (Fig.)
8 Fit the new 'O' ring oil seals to the sunwheels (photo).
9 At this stage, hold one sunwheel quite still and turn the other. Wind a piece of cord round the shaft of the sunwheel and attach it to a spring balance. The force required to turn it should be between 10 and 15 lbf ft (1.4 and 2.1 kgf m).
10 Fit the differential taper roller bearings by using a suitable press.

10 Layshaft - Reassembly

1 This consists of pressing on the taper roller bearings at each end of the shaft.

11 Gearbox/Transmission - Adjustment prior to Reassembly

Before the gearbox/transmission can be reassembled, the following adjustments must be carried out.

(a) Pinion Protrusion

1 Lay the mainshaft/pinion drive shaft into the gearbox housing and measure the distance between the face of the pinion and the centre line of the crownwheel. This is a complex operation and it is preferable to leave it to a Renault Dealer. Where it is decided to carry out the adjustment then a tool will be required to simulate the centre line of the crownwheel. Such a tool may be made up by utilising old sunwheel taper roller bearings and a steel round bar
2 Locate the mainshaft/pinion drive shaft within the gearbox housing and secure both housing halves together but with the bolts only finger tight.
3 Temporarily fit the gearbox front housing to hold the double taper roller bearing track ring in position.
4 Insert the crownwheel simulating tool and a spacer of predetermined length resting against the face of the pinion.
5 Reference should now be made to the following table and the pinion protrusion measured. If a spacer is used, then feeler gauges may be utilised, otherwise measure the distance with a vernier gauge or a dial or cylinder bore dial gauge. Whichever method of measurement is employed remember that half the diameter (radius) of the crownwheel simulator tool shaft must be added to the pinion face to shaft surface measurement in order to determine the required pinion face to crownwheel centre line dimension A.

6 Where dimension A does not conform to specification, dismantle the gearbox half housings, unscrew the speedometer drive gear from the mainshaft/pinion drive shaft assembly and substitute a washer of different thickness beneath the double taper roller bearing. Re-check dimension A. Pinion protrusion adjustment washers are available in thicknesses between 0.138 and 0.162 in (3.50 and 4.10 mm) in steps of 0.002 in (0.05

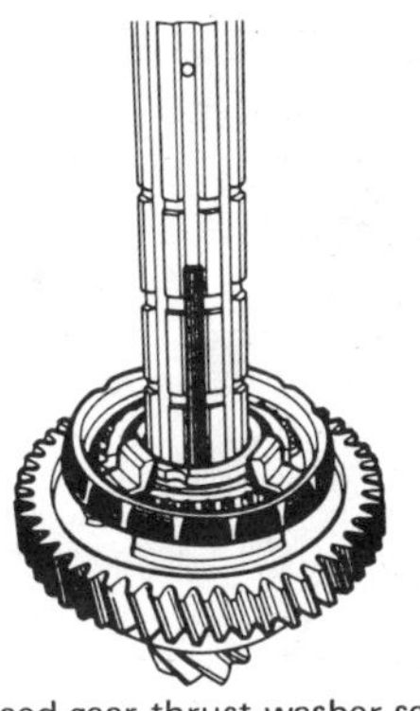

8.4A 1st speed gear thrust washer secured by dummy key

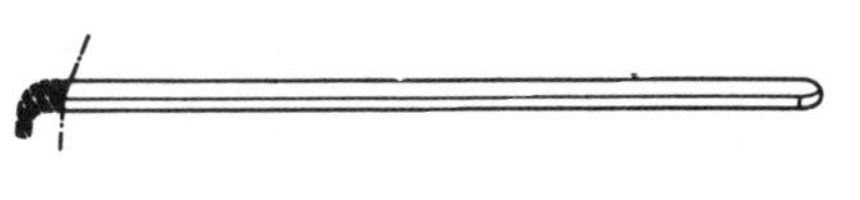

8.4B Diagram for making dummy key

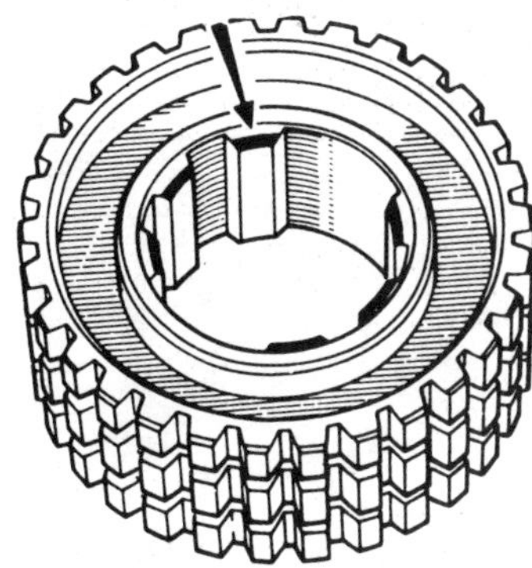

8.6 1st/2nd speed synchro hub showing chamfered side

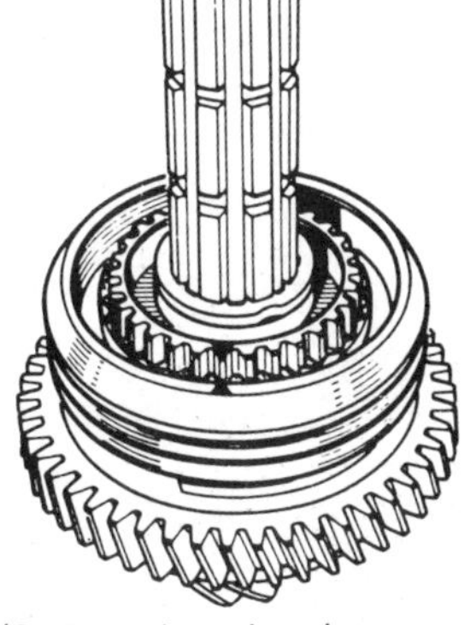

8.7 1st/2nd speed synchro sleeve correctly fitted to its hub

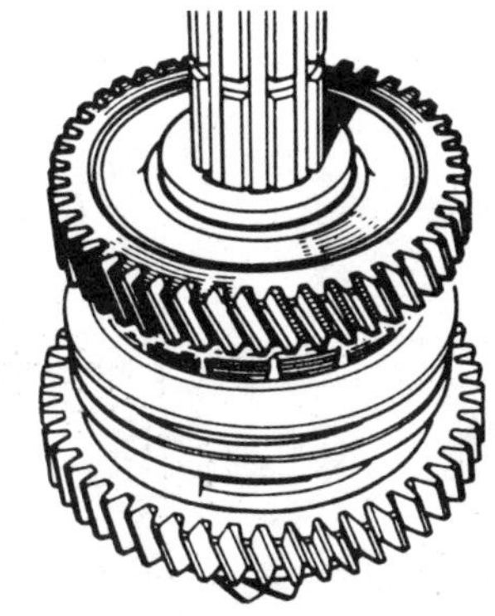

8.11 Correct alignment of 2nd speed thrust washer

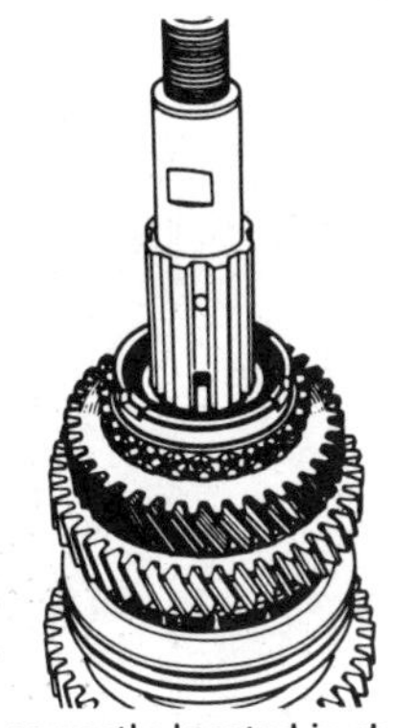

8.13 Key correctly located in shaft groove which incorporates an oil hole

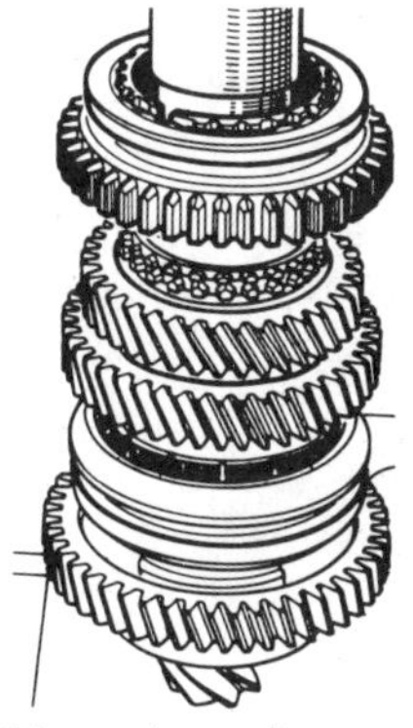

8.14 3rd/4th synchro unit correctly located having notch in alignment with retaining key

8.16 Fitting 4th speed gear and ring to mainshaft

8.17 Fitting pinion protrusion adjusting washer to mainshaft

8.18A Fitting double taper roller bearing to mainshaft

8.18B. Fitting speedo drive gear to mainshaft

8.20 Tightening the speedo drive gear

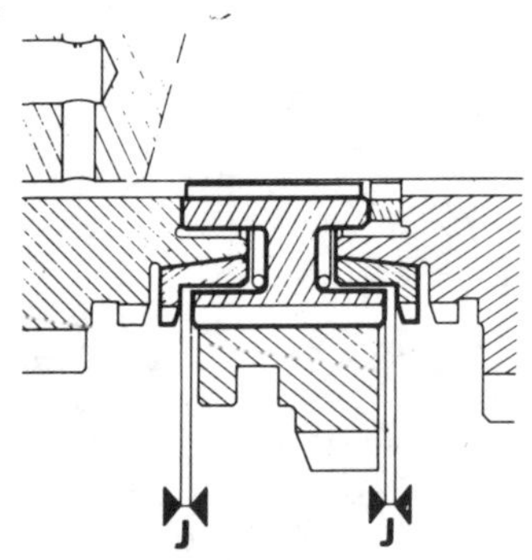

8.21 Diagram for checking play between 3rd speed synchro and rim of synchro hub. J = 0.008 in (20 mm)

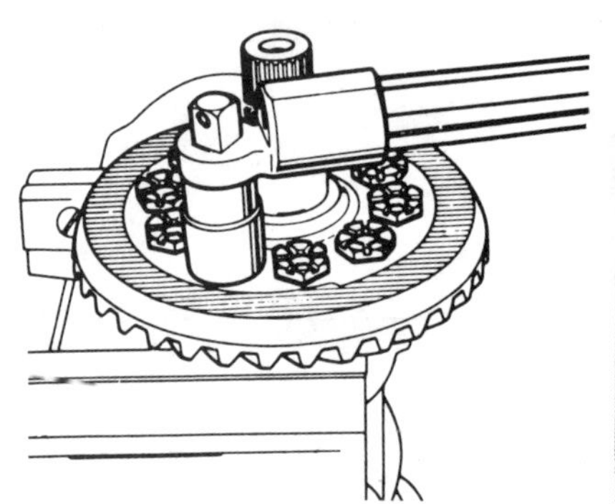

9.7 Tightening the crownwheel self locking bolts

9.8 Sun wheel 'O' ring seals

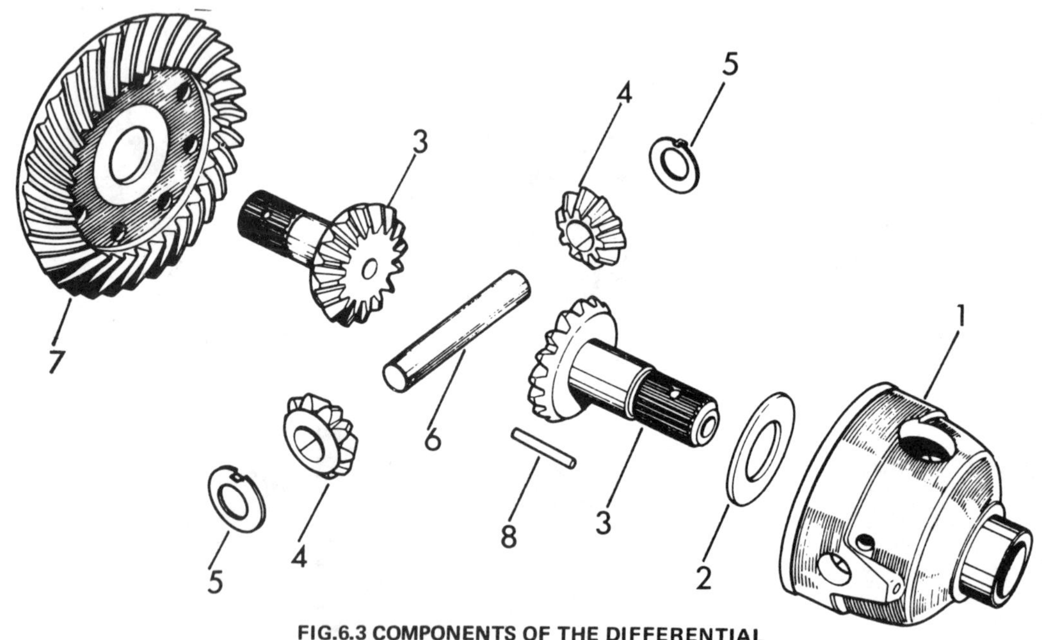

FIG.6.3 COMPONENTS OF THE DIFFERENTIAL

1 Housing	*4 Planet wheel*	*7 Crownwheel*
2 Spacer washer	*5 Thrust washer*	*8 Pin*
3 Sun wheel	*6 Shaft*	

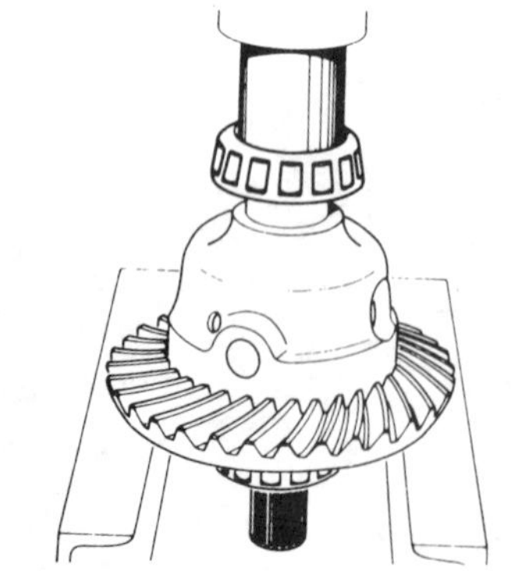

9.10 Pressing on the differential bearings

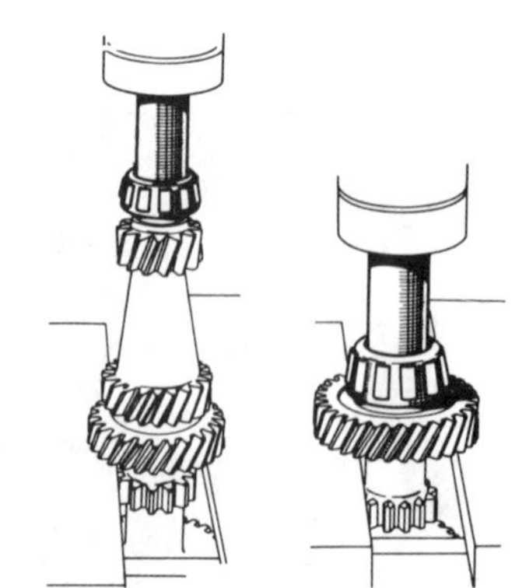

10.1 Pressing on the layshaft bearings

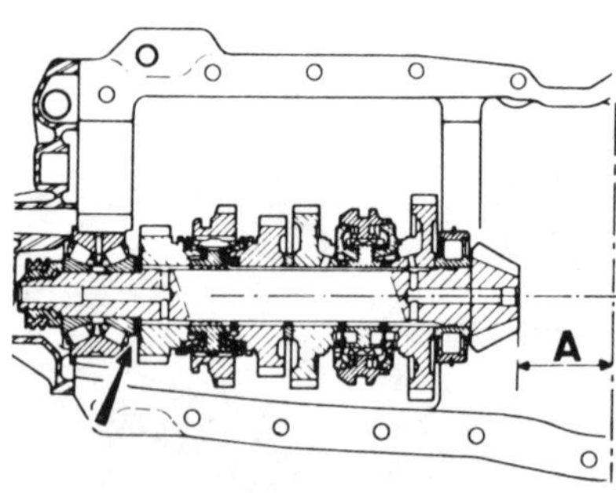

11.1A Diagram for measuring pinion protrusion. (A) see text. Thrust washer arrowed

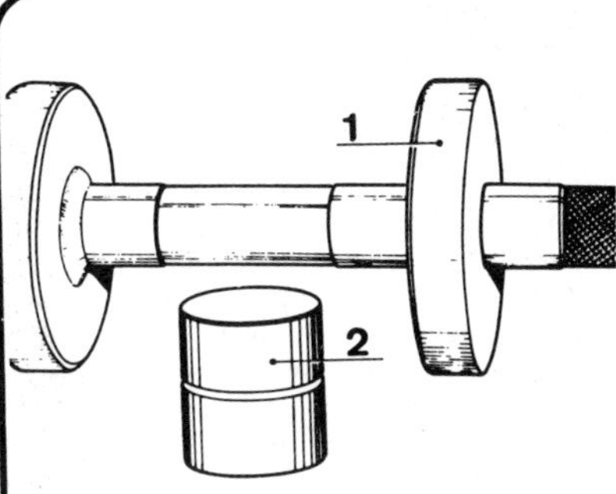

11.1B Tool (1) and spacer (2) used for pinion protrusion measurement

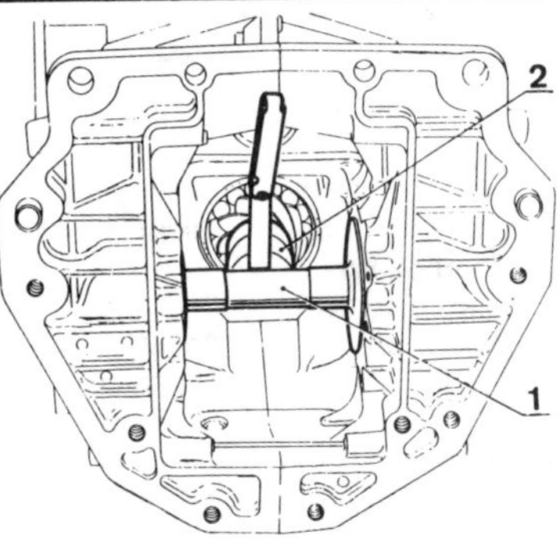

11.4 Measuring the pinion protrusion with feeler gauges. Key as 11.1B

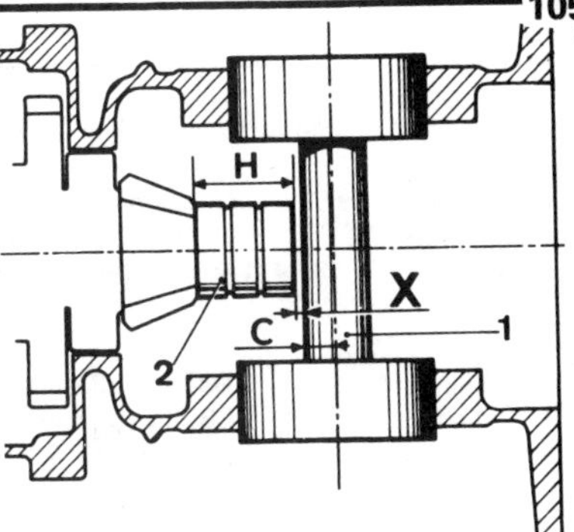

11.5 Pinion protrusion measuring diagram with tools in position. 1 Tool. 2 Spacer. H length of spacer. C radius of tool shaft. X pinion protrusion

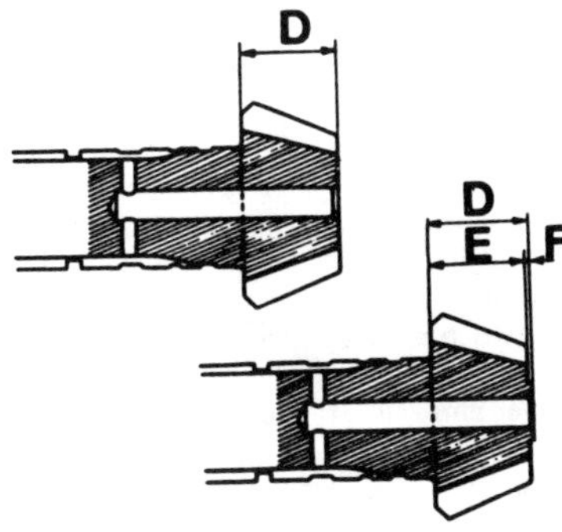

11.6 Alternative types of pinion. D overall dimension. F projection

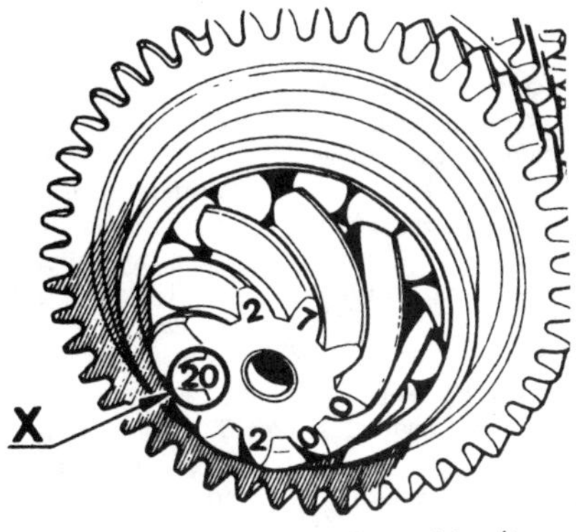

11.7 Pinion face undersize marking (in circle)

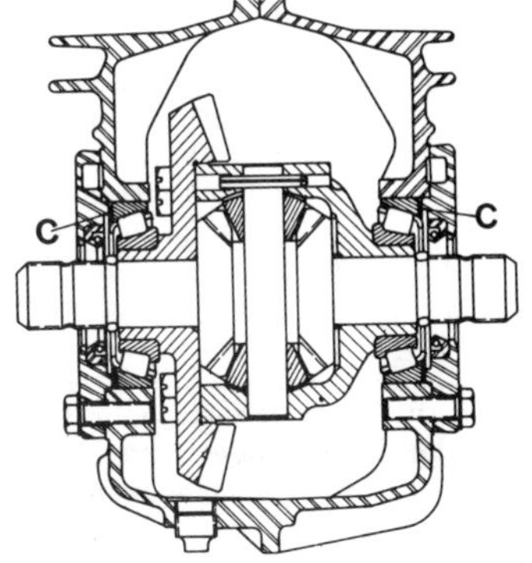

11.B.2 Differential side cover shim packs (C)

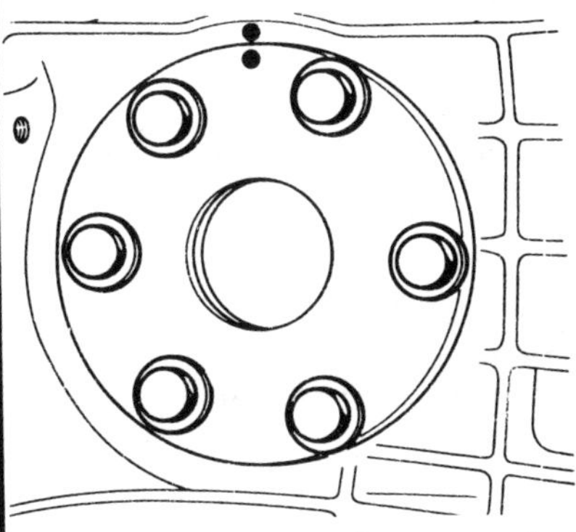

11.B.5 Side cover plate alignment marks and retaining bolts

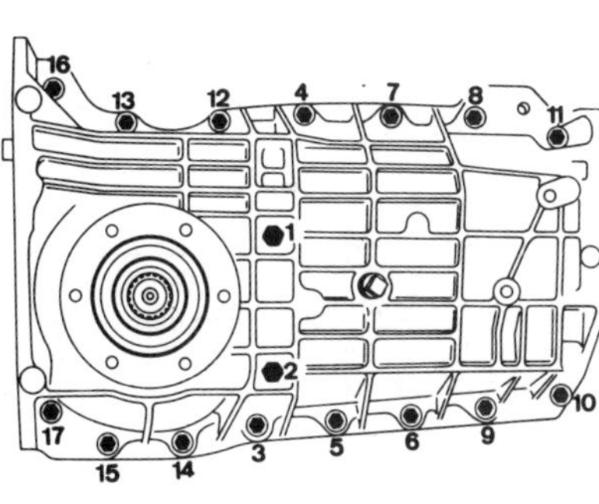

11.B.8 Gearbox/transmission housing bolt tightening sequence

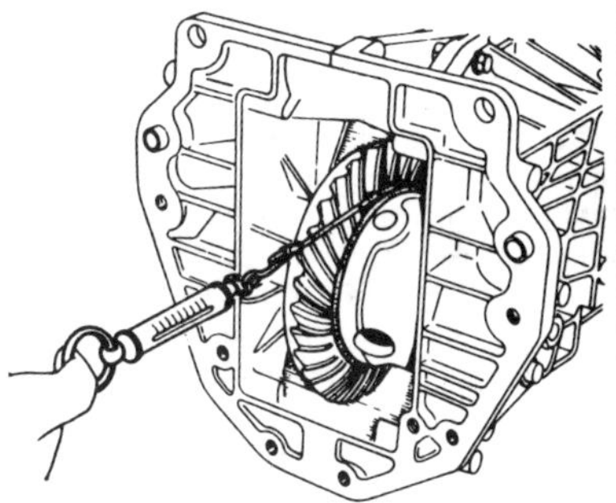

11.B.12 Checking the differential bearing adjustment

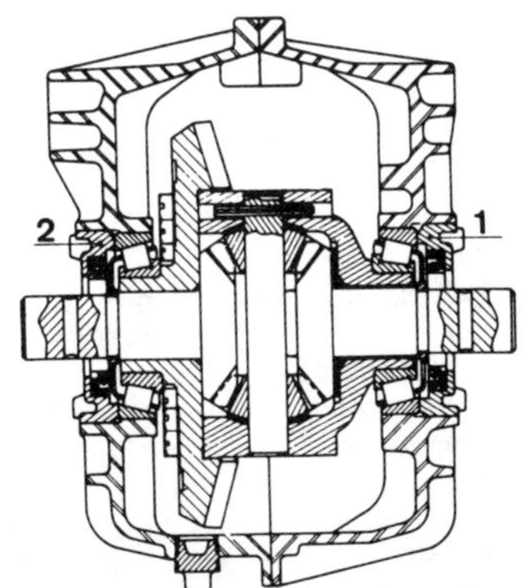

11.B13A Sectional view of differential with bearings adjusted by nuts

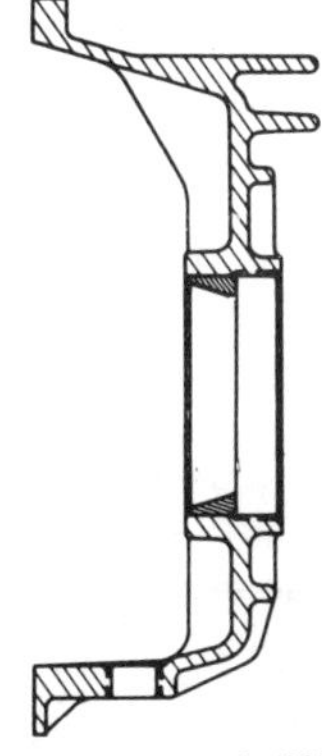

11.B.13B Correct location of differential bearing track rings, just below inner housing faces on nut adjustment type unit

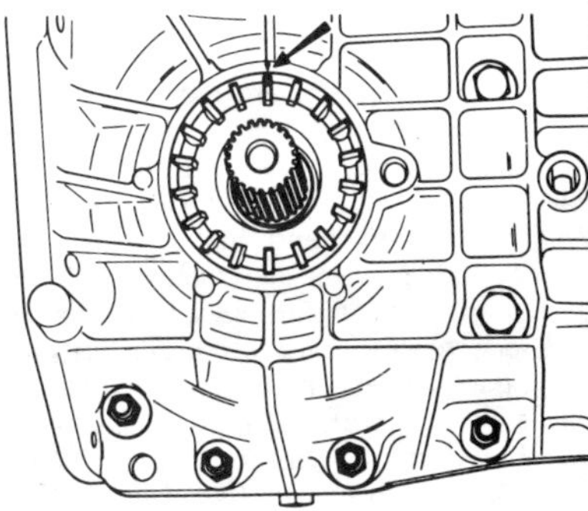

11.B.15 Adjuster nut position marks made after adjustment

mm). The washers are arrowed in Fig 11.1A.

Crownwheel Type	Dimension A	
9 x 34 normal	2.032 in (51.60 mm)	
9 x 34 normal	1.988 in (50.50 mm)	Gearbox type 336.02 up to number 5997 only*
9 x 34 heavy duty	2.087 in (53 mm)	
8 x 34 normal	2.087 in (53 mm)	

*All measurements should be made from the face extremity. Two different forms of pinion may be encountered.

7 Where a pinion is encountered which has a number in a circle engraved upon its end face then dimension A will be as specified in the table plus the encircled number (expressed as hundredths of a millimetre).

8 When pinion protrusion adjustment is complete, lock the speedometer drive gear.

(b) Differential Bearings

1 Adjustment of the differential bearings is carried out either by means of shims or nuts according to date of manufacture.

2 With the shim type, the shim packs are located between the bearing track rings and the side cover plate.

3 Fit the bearing track ring to the left hand housing but do not push it fully home.

4 Fit the shim pack which was removed on dismantling and the paper gasket.

5 Fit the side cover plate with mating marks in alignment.

6 Tighten the cover plate bolts to 15 lbf ft (2.1 kgf m).

7 Fit the differential assembly (complete with roller bearings) into the left hand half of the gearbox housing.

8 Fit the right hand half of the gearbox housing and secure it to the other half by inserting and tightening all the retaining bolts to 15 lbf ft (2.1 kgf m) 0.276 in (7 mm) bolts and 20 lbf ft (2.8 kgf m) for 0.315 in (8 mm) diameter bolts.

9 Fit the differential roller bearing track ring to the right hand half of the housing.

10 If the original differential roller bearings are being refitted, replace the shims and paper gasket removed on dismantling.

11 Gradually tighten the side cover plate securing bolts. If the differential becomes stiff to turn before the bolts are fully tightened, then remove some shims. Conversely add shims if it rotates too freely. Shims are available in the following thicknesses: 0.004 in (0.10 mm) 0.008 in (0.20 mm) 0.010 in (0.25 mm) 0.020 in (0.50 mm) 0.040 in (1 mm).

12 Where new differential roller bearings are being installed, then they must be pre-loaded. Adjust the shim packs until using a piece of cord and a spring balance, the force required to start the differential rotating is between 2 and 7 lb (0.91 and 3.2 kg). (Fig.)

13 Where differential bearings are adjusted by means of nuts the nuts are screwed in or out as required. Ensure that the bearing track rings are located slightly below the inner faces of the housing.

14 Adjust and check by cord and spring balance as previously described for shim type units. Remember original bearings require no preload, new bearings do.

15 When adjustment is correct, mark the position taken up by the nuts and then dismantle the gearbox housings.

(c) Layshaft Bearings

1 Place the roller bearing track rings (2 and 3) and the adjusting washer (1) onto the layshaft. References are to 11.C.1.

2 Into the left hand half of the gearbox housing, fit the layshaft and the mainshaft/pinion shaft assembly.

3 Using a steel straight edge and feeler gauges, check that the B to D and A to C gearwheel face offsets are equal, as indicated in the figure. Where this is not the case, change the adjusting washer (1) (photo). These are available in varying thicknesses - 0.079 in (2 mm) 0.089 in (2.25 mm) 0.098 in (2.50 mm) 0.108 in (2.75 mm) 0.118 in (3 mm) 0.128 in (3.25 mm) 0.138 in (3.50 mm) 0.148 in (3.75 mm) 0.158 in (4 mm)

4 When the correct adjustment has been obtained, place the right hand half of the gearbox housing in position but do secure it to the left hand section.

5 Fit the adjustment shims (C) and spacer (4) which were removed on dismantling.

6 The layshaft should turn freely without any end play and the spacer should project above the housing face by 0.008 in (0.2 mm) which is the thickness of the front housing paper gasket. Check the projection (F) using a steel rule and feeler gauges. Adjust if necessary by altering the shim pack (C) thickness. Shims are available in thicknesses 0.004 in (0.10 mm) 0.008 in (0.20 mm) 0.020 in (0.50 mm) 0.040 in (1.01 mm).

7 When adjustment is correct, separate gearbox and remove layshaft.

12 Front Housing - Dismantling and Reassembly

1 The front housing will not normally have to be dismantled unless wear has occurred or the rubber bellows have deteriorated. It should however be closely inspected at this stage and any necessary servicing carried out before the assembly is fitted to the main gearbox/transmission unit.

Models up to 1968

2 Remove the speedometer drive gear and sleeve, noting that the latter is fitted with an 'O' ring seal.

3 Remove the breather (photo).

4 Drive out the roll pins which secure the external control lever to the cross shaft.

5 Remove the control lever and pull off the bellows.

6 Drive out the two roll pins which secure the internal control lever to the cross shaft (photo). The lever and cross shaft may now be withdrawn.

7 Reassembly is a reversal of dismantling but use new roll pins and note that at both cross shaft locations an outer and inner pin is used. Particular care must be taken to ensure that the outer roll pin slot is at right angles to the shaft centre line and the inner roll pin slot is at right angles to the outer pin slot.

Models 1968 onwards

8 The method of dismantling and reassembling the front housing is similar to that for earlier models but additional internal and cross shaft components are incorporated.

13 Gearbox - Reassembly

1 The adjustments described in the preceding section having been carried out, final assembly of the gearbox/transmission unit may now start.

2 Insert the reverse selector shaft and fork (hub towards differential) into the gearcase.

3 Pin the fork to the reverse shaft (photo).

4 Fit the reverse swivel lever engaging its slot in the reverse shaft. Tighten the pivot bolt to a torque of 20 lbf ft (2.8 kgf m) (photos).

5 Fit the 1st/2nd gear selector shaft detent ball and spring followed by the 1st/2nd selector fork (hub towards gearchange lever end) and pin it to the selector shaft (photos).

6 Fit the locking disc between the selector shafts (photos).

7 Fit the 3rd/4th selector shaft detent ball and spring (photos).

8 Insert the 3rd/4th selector shaft and fork (hub towards differential) and pin it to the shaft (photo).

9 Into the right hand half of the gearbox housing, fit the reverse gearshaft locking ball and spring (photo). Springs of two different lengths may be encountered 3/4 in (19 mm) and 15/32 in (29 mm). The springs are not interchangeable and the shorter spring is only fitted in housings which have no boss on the spring location.

10 Locate the reverse idler shaft in the gearbox housing (photo).

11 Fit the reverse idler gear to the shaft (projecting hub towards differential) followed by the thrust washer (bronze face towards reverse gear (photo).

12 Push the reverse idler shaft assembly fully home and fit the circlip (photo).

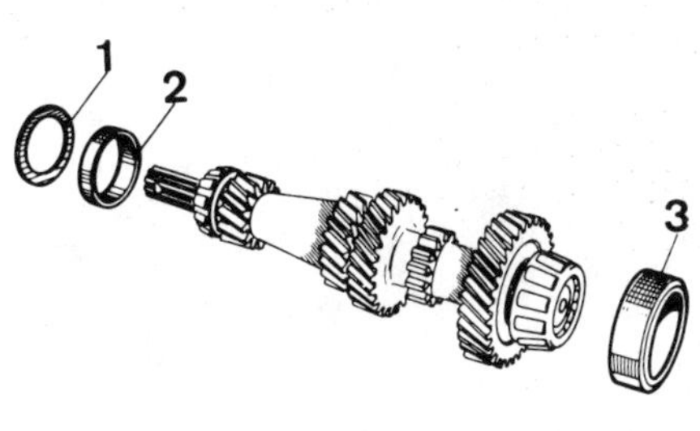

11.C1 Components of the layshaft. 1 Adjustment washer. 2 & 3 Bearing track rings

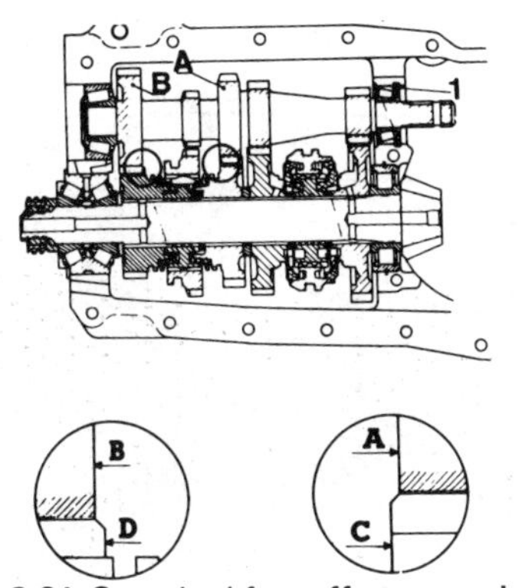

11.C.3A Gearwheel face offset measuring diagram. 1 Adjustment washer

11.C.3B Layshaft adjusting washer and recess

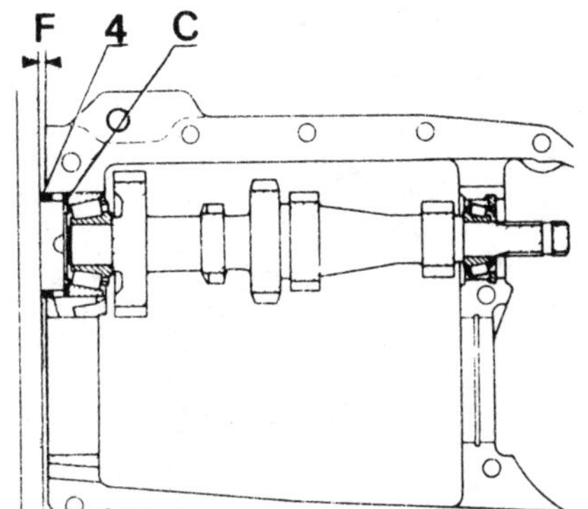

11.C.5 Layshaft in position with shims (C) and spacer (4)

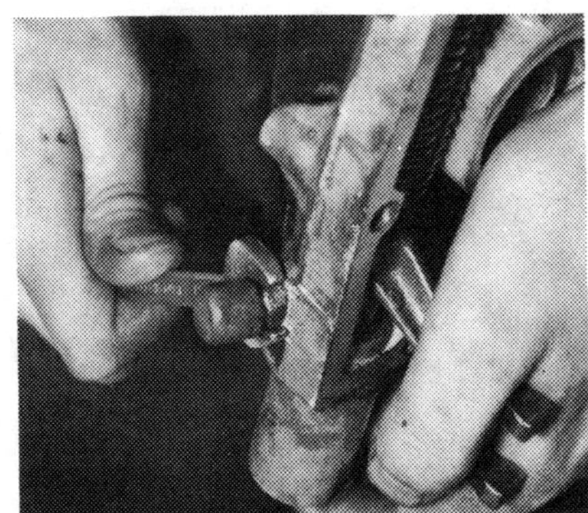
12.3 Removing breather from front housing

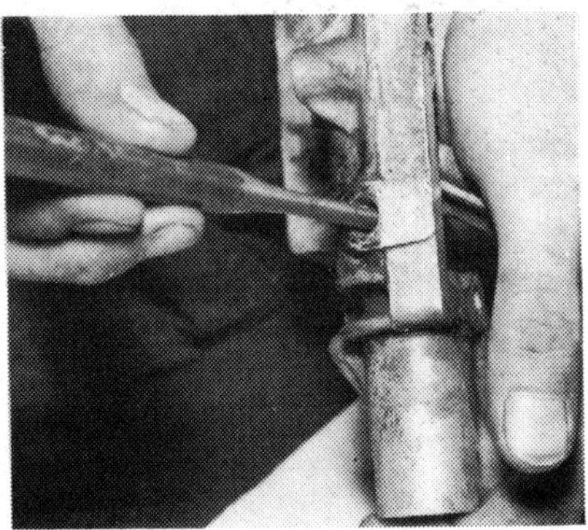
12.6 Drifting out front housing cross shaft roll pin

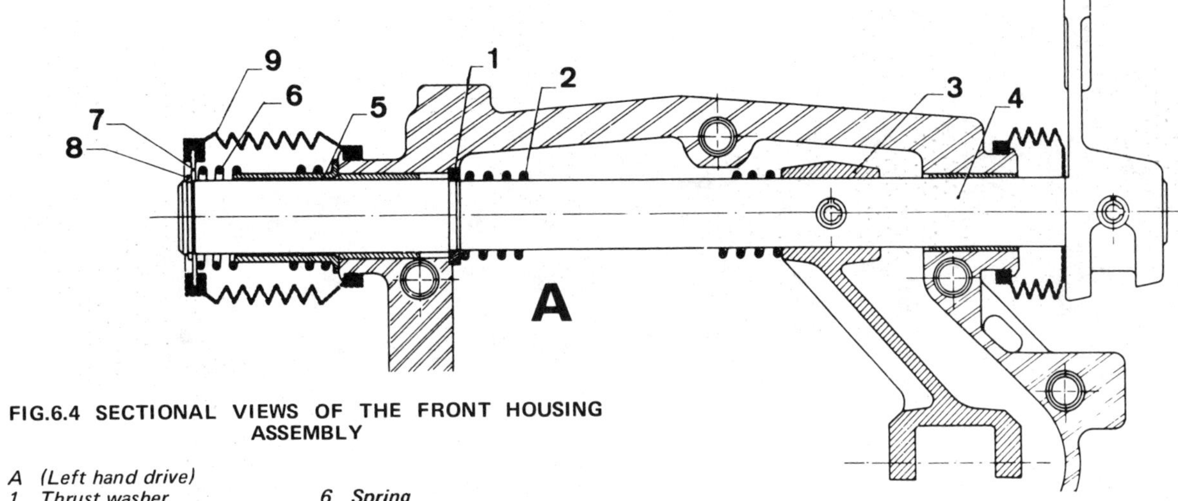

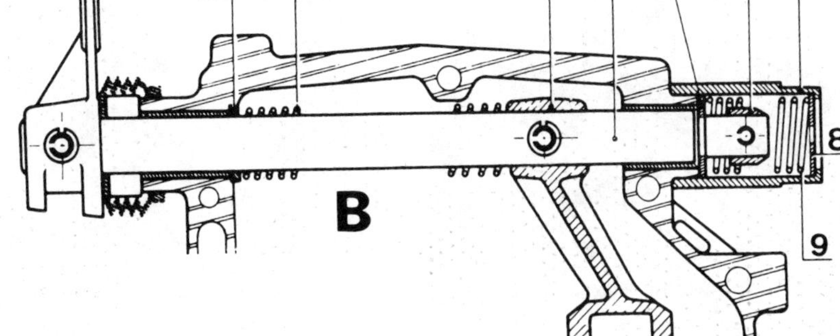

FIG.6.4 SECTIONAL VIEWS OF THE FRONT HOUSING ASSEMBLY

A (Left hand drive)
1 Thrust washer
2 Spring
3 Lever
4 Cross shaft
5 Cup thrust washer
6 Spring
7 Washer
8 Circlip
9 Rubber bellows

B (right hand drive)
1 Thrust washer
2 Spring
3 Lever
4 Cross shaft
5 Washer
6 Sleeve
7 End cap
8 Washer
9 Spring

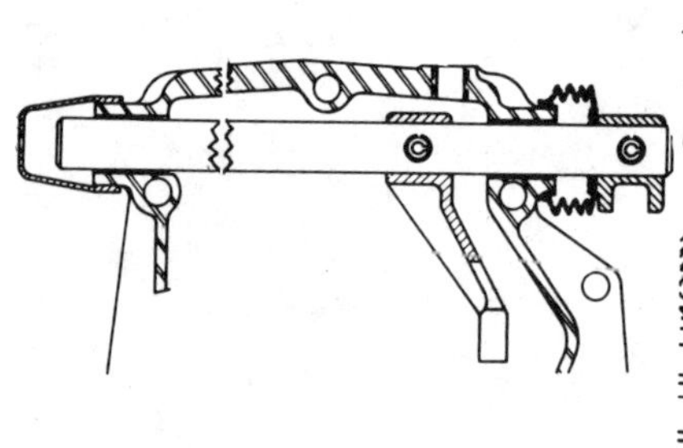

12.7 Front housing assembly showing correct alignment of shaft roll pins

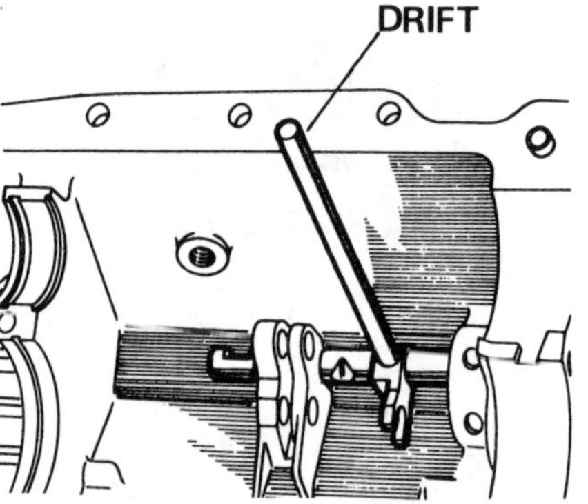

13.2 Correct location of reverse selector fork on shaft

13.3 Fitting fork to reverse shaft with roll pin

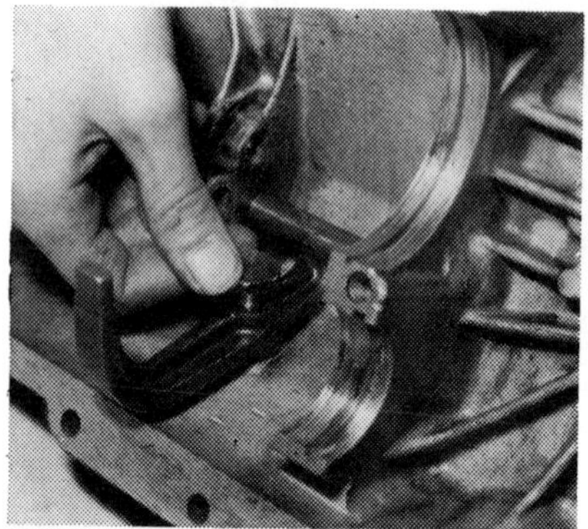

13.4A Screwing in reverse swivel lever bolt

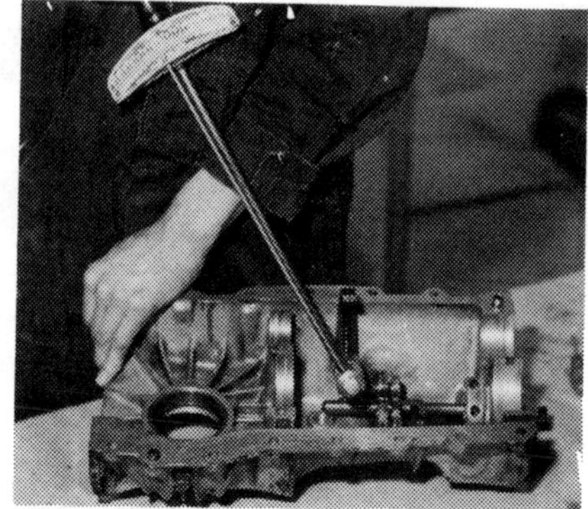

13.4B Tightening reverse swivel lever bolt to correct torque

13.5A Fitting 1st/2nd gear selector shaft ball

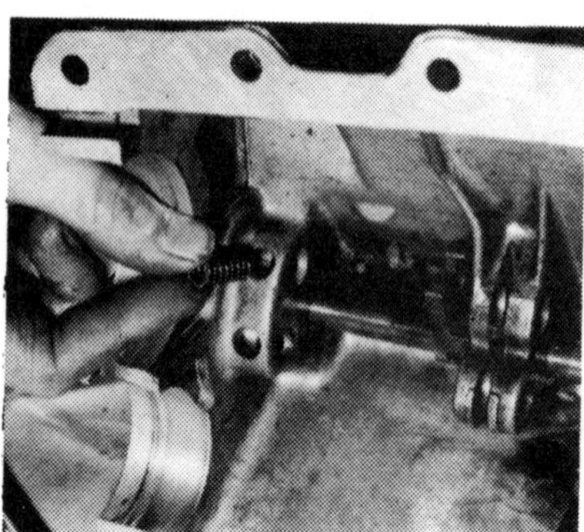

13.5B Fitting 1st/2nd gear selector shaft spring

13.5C Pinning 1st/2nd gear selector fork to shaft

13.6 Fitting locking disc between selector shafts

13.7A Fitting 3rd/4th selector shaft ball

13.7B Fitting 3rd/4th selector shaft spring

13.8. Pinning 3rd/4th selector fork to shaft

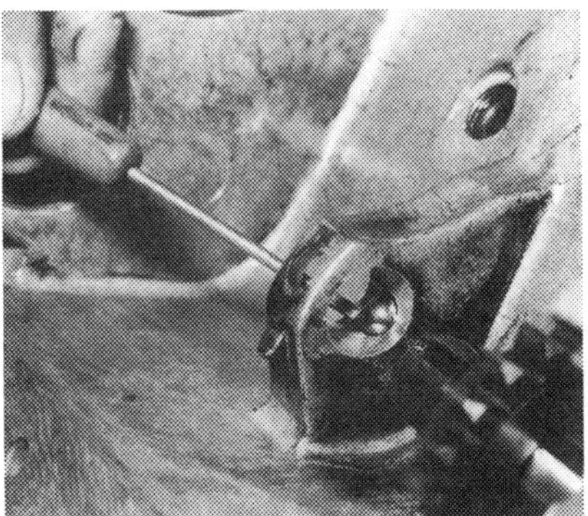
13.9 Fitting reverse gear shaft locking ball

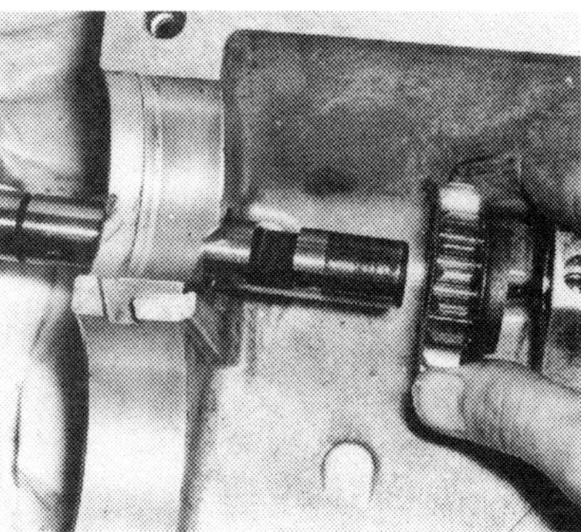
13.10 Assembling reverse gear and idler shaft

13.11 Fitting bronze thrust washer to reverse idler shaft

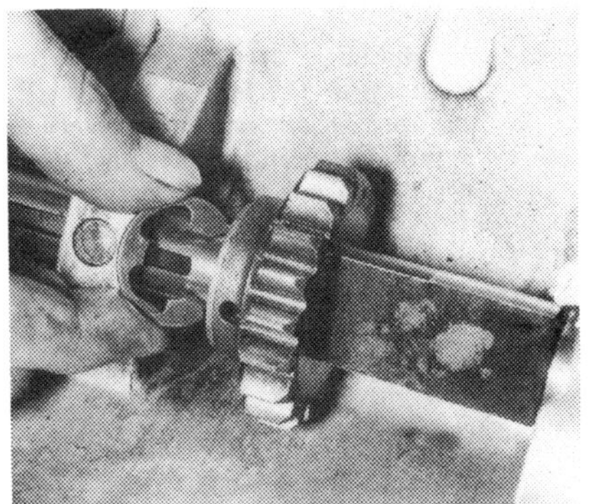
13.12 Fitting reverse idler shaft circlip

13.14A First motion shaft to layshaft roll pin

13.14B Fitting the layshaft to the gearbox

13.15A Lowering mainshaft into gearbox

13.15B Mainshaft roller bearing circlip and housing recess

13.16 Applying gasket cement to gearbox mating flanges

13.17A Mating the two halves of the gearbox housing

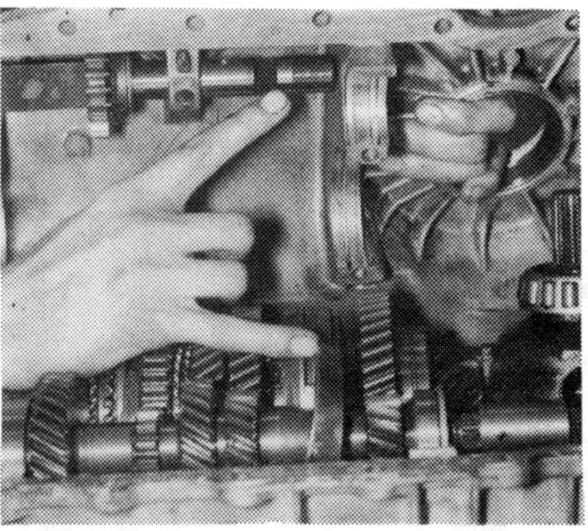
13.17B Mating of reverse swivel lever with reverse idler shaft

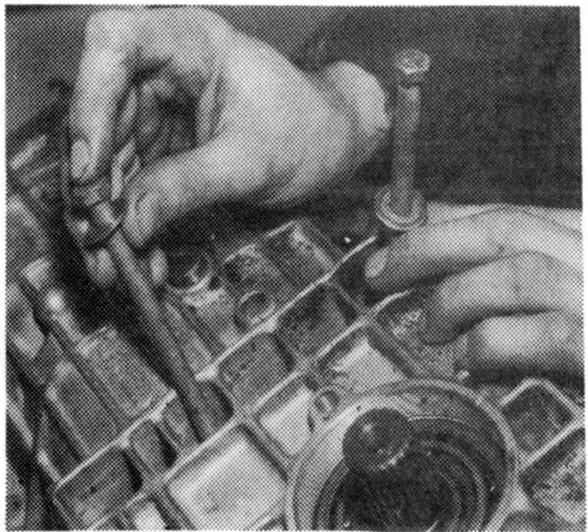
13.18 Inserting gearbox bolts

13 Fit the differential into the left hand half of the gearbox housing.
14 Pin the layshaft to the first motion shaft and fit the assembly to the gearbox (photo).
15 Fit the mainshaft/pinion drive shaft assembly and lock peg (photo). Note the roller bearing circlip (photo).
16 Apply recommended gasket cement to the mating edges of the two halves of the gearbox housing (photo).
17 Locate the right hand housing onto the left ensuring that the end of the reverse swivel lever fits into the slot on the reverse gear shaft (photos).
18 Insert all the securing bolts but do not tighten them (photo).
19 Fit the first motion shaft adjusting shims and spacer (photo).
20 Smear a new front housing paper gasket with jointing compound and stick it to the front face of the gearbox front housing (photo).
21 Offer up the front housing to the gearbox and engage the internal control lever in the selector shaft slots (photo).
22 Insert the front housing bolts only finger tight.
23 Tighten the half housing bolts to a torque of 15 lbf ft (2.1 kgf m) for 0.276 in (7 mm) diameter bolts or 20 lbf ft (2.8 kgf m) for 0.315 in (8 mm) diameter bolts. See Fig 11.B.8.
24 Tighten the front housing bolts.
25 At this stage, the crownwheel and pinion backlash must be checked. The backlash is adjusted by unscrewing nut located on the differential housing side and screwing in nut located on the crownwheel side, by an equivalent amount or by altering the side cover shim packs as fitted (photo).
26 Check the amount of backlash initially by hand. To do this, gently rotate the first motion shaft (input shaft) in both directions and feel the backlash between the pinion and crownwheel teeth. Where this is excessive, unscrew nut (1) and screw in nut (2) in order to reduce the backlash to reasonable proportions before final checking with a dial gauge. With shim type adjustment, reduce the shim pack thickness on one side and increase it on the other. (Fig 11.B. 13A.).
27 Fit a dial gauge to the gearbox housing so that its plunger is at right angles to one of the crownwheel teeth and as near to the outer diameter of the crownwheel as possible.
28 With shim type adjustment, fit the cover plate to the crownwheel side including the paper gasket and shims. Gradually tighten the securing bolts in rotation and check the backlash reading. This should be between 0.005 and 0.010 in (0.12 and 0.25 mm). If the correct backlash reading is obtained before the bolts are fully tightened then the shim pack on the crownwheel side is too thick and some of the shims must be transferred to the shim pack on the differential side. If the backlash reading is too small when the side cover bolts are fully tightened, then shims must be transferred from the differential side to the crownwheel side. When backlash is correct, apply gasket cement to the paper gaskets and tighten the side cover bolts to 15 lbf ft (2.1 kgf m).
29 Where adjustment is by means of nuts then these should be screwed in or out (each by an equivalent amount) as required. Lock the nuts, once the correct backlash has been obtained by the locking plates and bolts.
30 Check the condition of the oil seals in the clutch bellhousing and renew if necessary as described in Chapter 5.
31 Fit a new bellhousing to gearbox paper washer and smear it on both sides with gasket cement (photo).
32 Bolt the clutch bellhousing to the gearbox taking great care not to damage the oil seal lips as it passes over the first motion shaft splines. Taping the splines will prevent damage.
33 Do not fill the gearbox/transmission unit with oil until it is installed in the car as described in Section 2.

14 Steering Column Gearchange Control - Adjustment

1 Periodically due to wear or after dismantling, the column gearchange may require adjustment.

Model R1150 (up to 1968)

2 Engage 2nd gear by moving the steering column gearshift lever.
3 Check that the operating lever on the exterior of the gearbox is in the 2nd speed position.
4 Loosen the two clamp bolts which retain the two parts of the gearshift control tube together.
5 Operate the gearshift steering column control several times to free fully the two sections of the tube.
6 Check that the gearbox mounted control lever is still in second speed position.
7 Move the steering column control towards you and down (up against the reverse gear stop).
8 Move the hand control vertically so that the control centre line is below. The centre line passing horizontally through the steering wheel by the following amounts (LHD 13/16 in 30 mm) RHD 17/32 in (64 mm).
9 Pull the cross shaft in the direction of arrow 1 until the internal lever comes into contact with the reverse idler shaft. Now press the shaft in the opposite direction (2) until a clearance exists between the internal lever and reverse idler shaft of between 1/32 and 3/64 in (0.5 to 1 mm). This clearance (b) obviously cannot be seen but it may be determined by measuring the movement externally at the end face of the cross shaft. When the correct clearance is established, retain the shaft in this position.
10 Check that both column and gearbox levers are still in their correct position and tighten the control tube clamp bolts.
11 Test drive the car and check for correct gear selection.

Models R1150 (1968 onwards) R1151 and R1152

1 Select 4th gear on the steering column control and check that the gearbox external control lever is in 4th speed position.
2 Loosen the tube clamp bolts and operate the steering column control several times to free the control tube.
3 Check that the gearbox external lever is still in 4th speed position.
4 Lift the steering column control vertically until its centre line is $1\,{}^{13}/_{16}$ in (46 mm) below a horizontal line passing through the steering wheel hub.
5 Move the hand control either up or down in line with the steering column until the roll pin is centrally visible through the hole in the hand control which is arrowed in the figure.
6 Hold the hand control in this position and check that the gearbox external lever is still in 4th speed position.
7 Tighten the control tube clamp bolts and then road test the car for correct gear selection.

15 Steering Column Gearchange Control - Removal, Servicing and Refitting

1 Disconnect the battery.
2 Pull off the steering wheel embellisher and unscrew and remove the steering wheel retaining nut.
3 Ensure that the front wheels are in the straight ahead position and note the position of the steering wheel spoke so that the steering wheel may be refitted in its original position on the column splines.
4 Using a suitable puller, draw off the steering wheel. Protect the wheel and spokes from contact with the puller during this operation or the plastic covering may be damaged.
5 Remove the covers from the combination lighting switch.
6 Mark the position of the lighting switch bracket relative to the steering column so that it may be replaced in its original location.
7 Remove the lighting switch bracket bolt.
8 Unscrew and remove the ball joint locknut on the gear control rod. In order to carry out this operation, the gearchange

13.19A Fitting first motion shaft adjusting washers

13.19B Fitting first motion shaft spacer

13.20 Offering up the gearbox front housing

13.21 Engaging control lever with selector shaft slots (front housing)

13.25 Method of rotating differential nuts

13.27 Using a dial gauge to check the crownwheel to pinion backlash

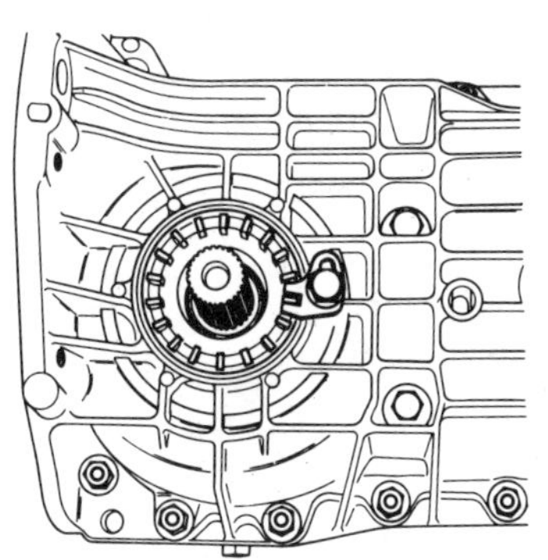
13.29 Differential bearing nut locking plate and bolt

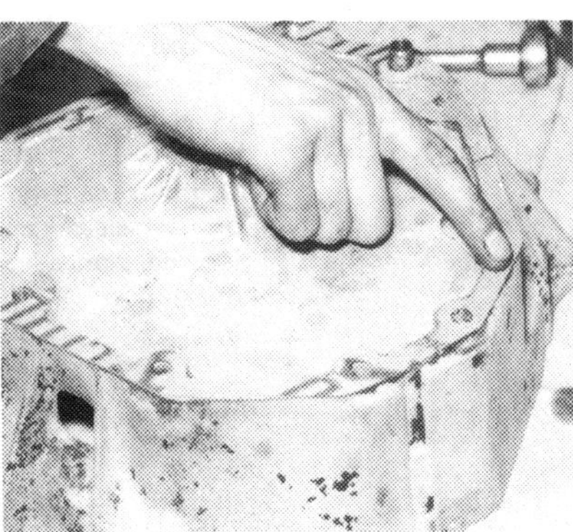
13.31 Locating bell housing to gearbox paper gasket

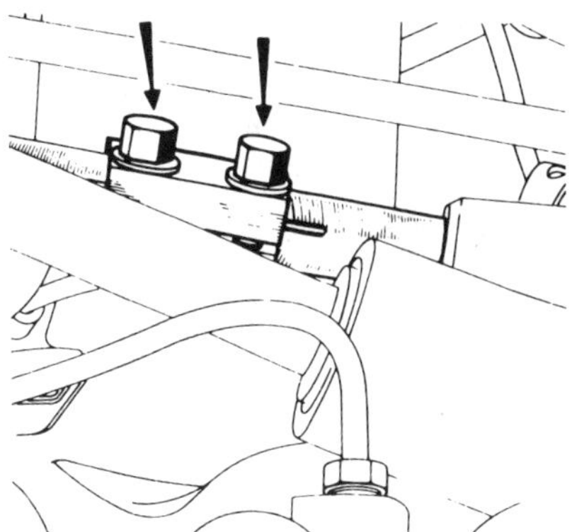
14.4 gearshift control tube clamp bolts

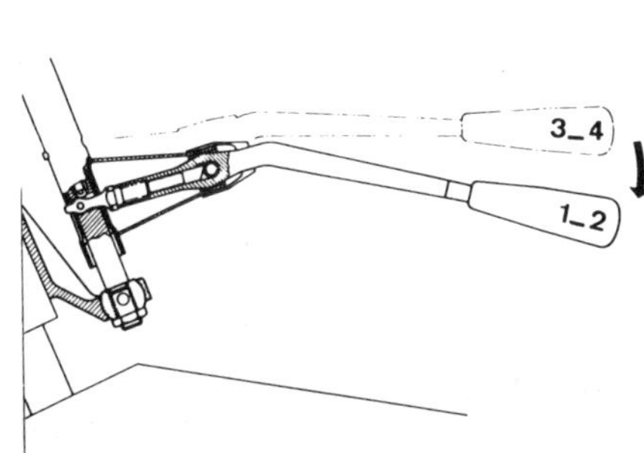

14.7 Gearshift control lever position prior to adjustment

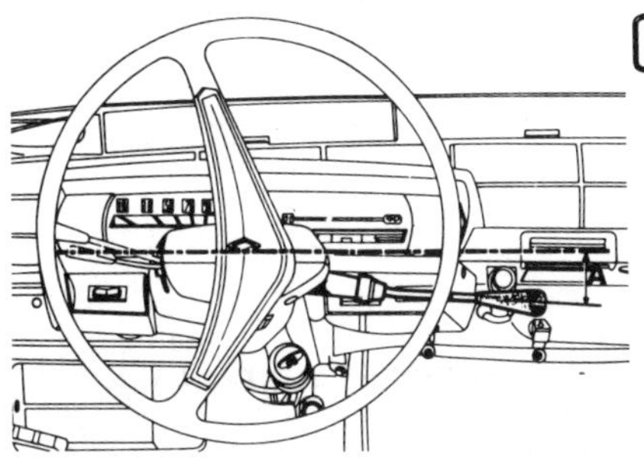
14.8 Diagram for hand control lever positioning prior to adjustment (models R1150 1968 onwards R1151 and R1152)

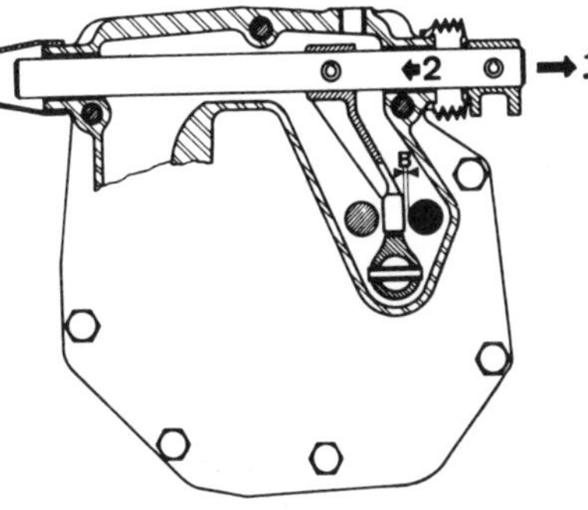

14.9 Front housing cross shaft clearance diagram

rod should be held in position by passing a rod or drift through the hole provided in the rod as shown.

9 Unlock and unscrew the ball joint, at the same time gradually pulling the lighting switch bracket towards you.

10 Unscrew the clamp securing screws which secure both ends of the gear control tube.

11 Pull back the lighting switch bracket in order to free the gear control rod and then swing the switch round the column. Lay the gear control rod and lever assembly to one side and free it from its clamp.

12 Remove the retaining clip which secures the link to the external gearbox lever and the gear control to housing bolts. Remove the gear control mechanism.

13 The column/tube/lever assembly, if worn, must be renewed as an assembly. Two designs are used, for model R1150 up to 1968 and for R1150 1968 onward and R1151 and R1152.

14 The roll pins and rubber cover may be renewed provided new roll pins are used and their slots are parallel with the steering column centre line.

15 The gear control mechanism at the gearbox may be dismantled and end play removed by using a thicker washer at 4. Washers are available in thicknesses of 0.004, 0.006, 0.008 in (0.10, 0.15, 0.20 mm).

16 Fit new roll pins after dismantling and ensure that their slots are at right angles to the pivot pin centre line.

17 Tighten bolts (6) to 10 lbf ft (1.4 kgf m).

18 To remove end play in the hinge, fit a thicker washer at 7. Washers are available in 0.004 and 0.008 in (0.10 and 0.20 mm) thicknesses. References are to Fig 6.5.

19 Do not grease the bushes (8) and do not tighten bolt (9) until the gearchange assembly is installed.

20 Refitting is a reversal of removal but check that the alignment marks made for the lighting switch are correctly located. The distance between the switch bracket and the underside of the steering wheel (A) should be 63/64 in (25 mm).

21 Grease the ball joint and tighten it until all end play has been removed.

22 Tighten the ball joint locknut to 10 lb ft (14.9 kg m) for 5/32 in (4 mm) nuts and 15 lbf ft (2.1 kgf m) for 9/32 in (7 mm) thick nuts. Hold the gearchange rod still with a drift or rod while tightening.

23 Tighten the pivot pin bolt to 20 lbf ft (2.8 kgf m).

24 Finally adjust the gearchange control as described in the preceding section.

16 Gearbox - Fault Finding

Faults in the gearbox can range from small noises and minor deficiencies in engagement of gears and operation of synchromesh, to serious faults consisting of loud whines, serious vibrations or inability to engage or remain in one or more gears. For serious faults there is no alternative other than removing the gearbox and either overhauling it completely or fitting another. For minor faults, other than those which can be detected in the change mechanism rather than the gearbox, it is more a question of how long can the fault be tolerated before taking action. Once something starts to wear to a degree which is noticeable, things usually start to deteriorate rapidly. Unfortunately, the amount of trouble to rectify a minor fault will be the same as for a major one - removal and dismantling of the gearbox. One may save something on spare parts but even this is problematical as it is not until the gearbox is stripped that many faults can be diagnosed accurately. Some faults can go on for thousands of miles without further deterioration to the whole unit - a worn synchro cone for example. Failure of the mainshaft bearing could, however, completely ruin the whole assembly in a few hundreds of miles.

The following list is intended as a guide to aid decisions on WHEN to take action.

FAULT	CAUSE
Ineffective synchromesh on one or more gears. Jumps out of one or more gears.	Worn synchro cones. Worn blocker bars. Worn selector forks. Weak detent springs. Worn gear engagement dogs. Worn selector hub fork grooves. Selector fork loose on rail (rare).
Noisy - rough - whining, vibration.	Worn bearings and / or laygear thrust washers (initially) resulting in extended wear generally due to play and backlash.
Noisy and difficult engagement of gear.	Clutch not disengaging properly.
Difficult selecting forward or reverse gears and moving change lever out of gear.	Worn change lever linkage, particularly on steering column controls. General wear on remote control.

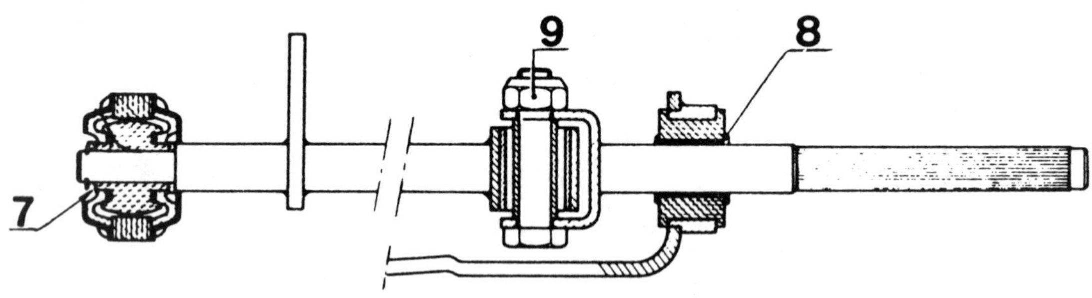

FIG.6.5 GEARSHIFT CONTROL HINGE MECHANISM

7 Washer *8 Bushes* *9 Bolt*

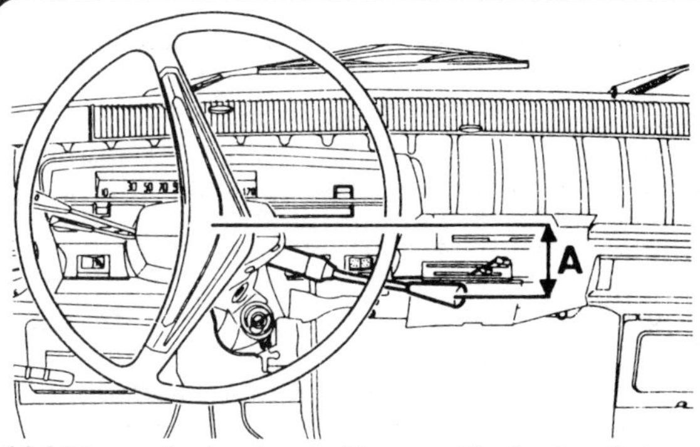

14.4 Diagram for hand control lever positioning to adjustment (models R1150, 1968 onwards R1151 and R1152)

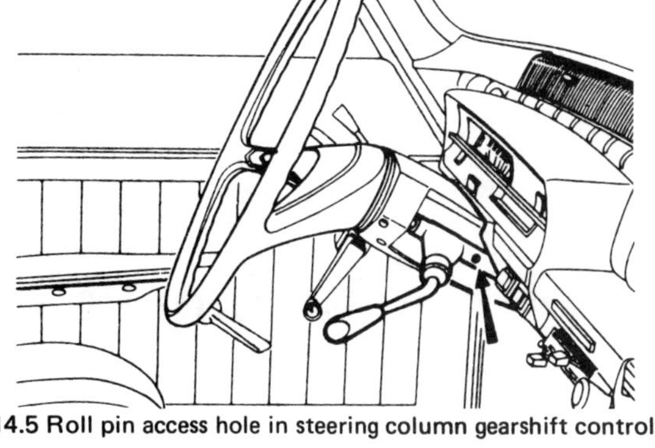

14.5 Roll pin access hole in steering column gearshift control

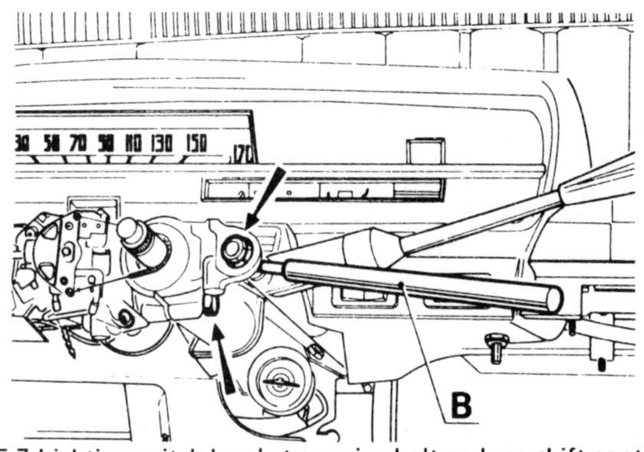

15.7 Lighting switch bracket securing bolt and gearshift control rod ball joint locknut. B is temporary restraining rod

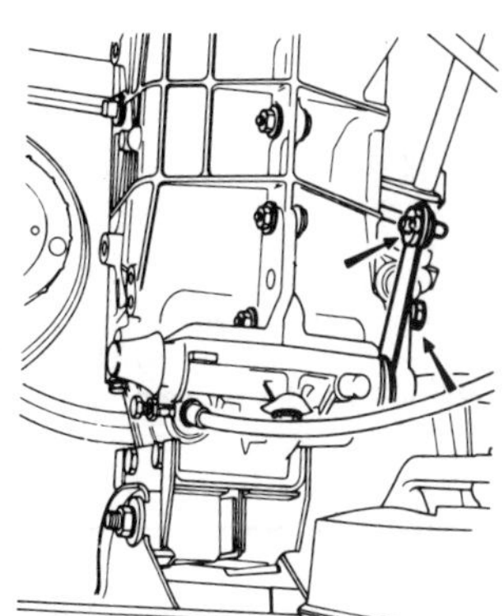

15.12 Gearbox control link to lever clip and control to gearbox housing bolts

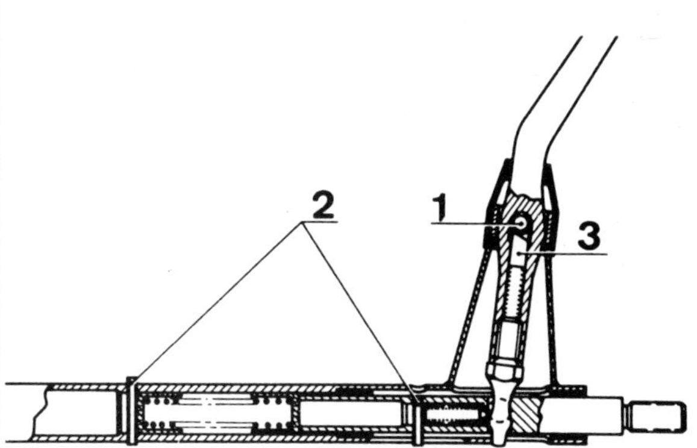

15.13A Gearshift hand control assembly (R1150 up to 1968). 1 Roll pin. 2 Roll pin. 3 Plunger and spring

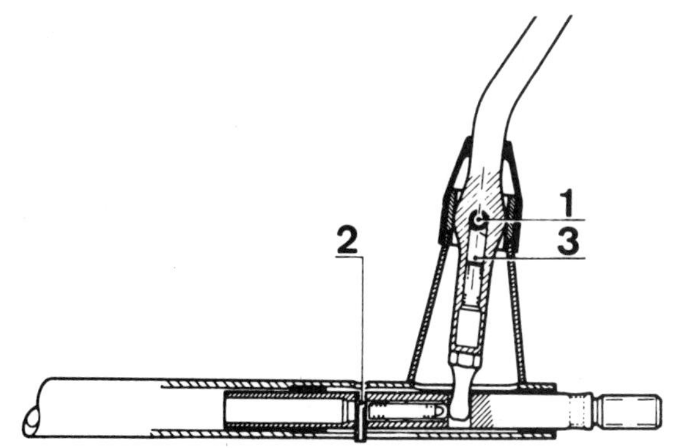

15.13B Gearshift hand control assembly (R1150, 1968 on. R1151 and R1152) 1 Roll pin. 2 Roll pin. 3 Plunger and spring

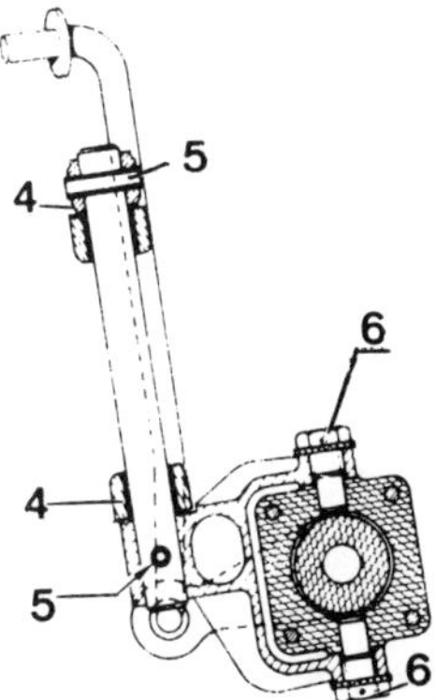

15.15 Gearshift control mechanism at gearbox housing. 4 Washer 5 Roll pins. 6 Bolts

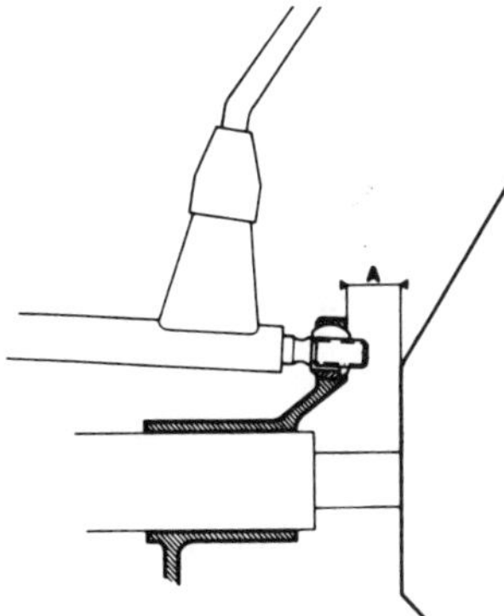

15.20 Gearshift control hand lever ball joint and positioning diagram

Chapter 7 Automatic gearbox

For modifications, and information applicable to later models, see Supplement at end of manual

Contents

Specifications

Torque convertor type	R9 - 240	
Maximum convertor torque ratio	2.2 : 2.3	
Oil capacity	5 pints (2.8 litres)	
Gearbox type	139 - 10	
Gears	3 forward 1 reverse	
	GEARS	**TOTAL**
Gear ratios		
First	2.33 : 1	9.052 : 1
Second	1.44 : 1	5.606 : 1
Third	1 : 1	3.879 : 1
Reverse	2 : 1	7.759 : 1
Rear axle crownwheel and pinion	9 x 34	
Total oil capacity (gearbox/transmission/convertor)	11 pints (6 litres)	

Torque wrench settings

	lbf ft	kgf m
Half housing bolts - 7mm dia.	15 - 18	2.1 – 2.5
8 mm dia.	20 - 25	2.8 – 3.4
Convertor drive plate to crankshaft flange	32 - 36	4.2 – 5.0
Convertor securing bolts	18	2.5
Front cover securing bolts - 7 mm dia.	5	0.7
5 mm dia.	2.5	0.34
Lower cover plate securing bolts	5	0.7
Bottom sump securing bolts	4	0.6

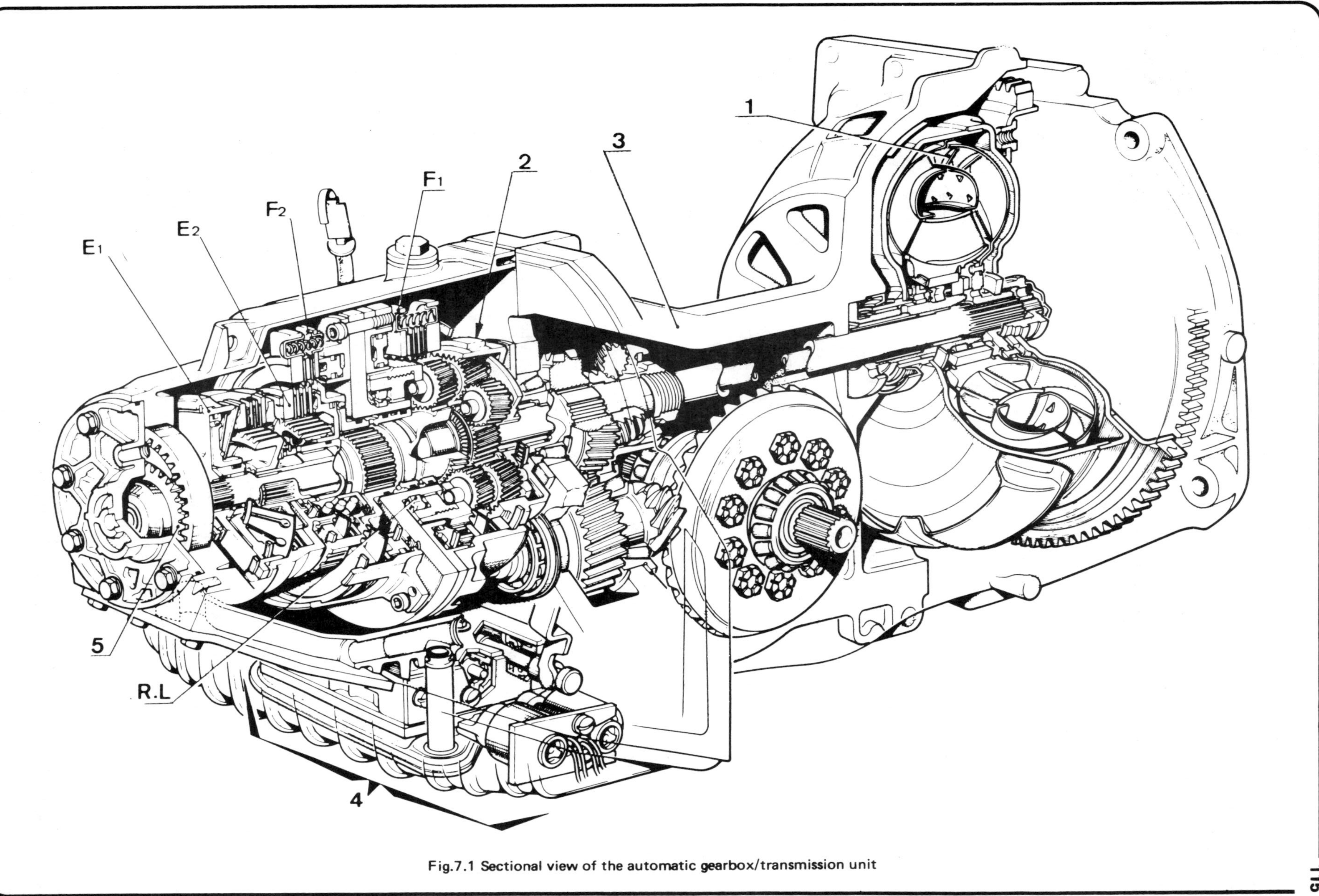

Fig.7.1 Sectional view of the automatic gearbox/transmission unit

1 General Description

1 R1153 and R1154 models are fitted with a type 139 (A139 - later identification) automatic transmission unit. The design of the unit gives fully automatic gear changing without the use of a clutch pedal, but over-riding selection is still left with the driver.

2 Major assemblies within the unit are the torque convertor, the gearbox with epicyclic gear train and the necessary hydraulic and electronic controls, the differential housing.

3 A sectional view of the automatic gearbox/transmission unit is shown in Fig 7.1.

4 The convertor (1) comprises the impeller, turbine and stator.

5 The epicyclic gear train receives its drive from the convertor and this power is transmitted through varying ratios to the crownwheel and pinion final drive.

6 These ratios are obtained through the medium of internal components: clutches E1 and E2, brakes F1 and F2 and a free-wheel RL.

7 The differential housing encloses the two reduction gears, crownwheel and pinion and the differential.

8 Actuation of the automatic transmission or manual selection of gears is effected by using the steering column control which has six positions marked - P (Park - R (Reverse) - N (Neutral - A (Drive) - 2 (Second gear hold) - 1 (low gear hold).

9 The major groups of operating control components and cover manual, hydraulic, vacuum and electrical assemblies. All are shown in Fig 7.2.

2 Operating Principle

1 The mechanical content of the gearbox comprises the torque convertor, the epicyclic gear train controlled by clutches and brakes, the power train and the differential.

2 The three forward gears and one reverse gear are obtained by action of two clutches (E1 and E2) and two brakes (F1 and F2) and the free wheel on the differential parts of the gear train (P1, P2, S1, S2 and C) all as shown in the figure. Engagement permutations between the components are shown in the following table.

Selector lever position	Components engaged E1	E2	F2	F1	R.L.	Box ratio
P						
R		*		*		2
N						
1	*				*	2.33
A 2	*		*			1.44
3	*	*				1
1	*				*	2.33
2 2	*		*			1.44
1	*			*		2.33

3 The torque convertor is located within the differential housing and comprises the impeller, turbine wheel and stator. (Fig.)

4 The torque convertor fulfills a dual function, acting as an automatic clutch and providing a torque increase during initial power take off.

5 Pressurised oil supply is supplied to the torque convertor by the gearbox oil pump.

6 The epicyclic gear train comprises the components featured in the figure.

7 The clutch is of multi-disc type and transmits the turbine shaft torque to the sun wheel (P1).

8 The bearing (19) and bellhousing (20) are integral with the turbine shaft. The Hub (21) when rotating becomes integral with the sun wheel shaft (P1) by means of splines.

9 Piston (22) is operated by oil pressure and transmits pressure to the pressure plate through a diaphragm. When the system is pressurised, the discs of the clutch are released and shaft (P1) is free.

10 The clutch (E2) is similar to clutch E1 as shown in Fig. 2.2. It can be seen that hub (24) is integral with the turbine shaft. The bellhousing is connected to sunwheel (P2) by splines. The piston (26) is operated by oil pressure and by compressing the pressure plate, clamps the clutch discs. The coil spring (28) returns the piston to the 'no drive' position. From the foregoing it can be seen that clutch E2 transmits turbine shaft torque to the sunwheel P2 through the medium of the E1 clutch interconnecting bellhousing. The ball valve (27) ensures rapid de-pressurisation of the clutches.

11 The brake assembly (F2) locks the P2 sunwheel and makes it integral with the gearbox case. It can be seen that piston (34) actuates by oil pressure and the brake discs are pressed together to lock P2. When the oil pressure is released, the coil springs (33) return the piston to the 'no drive' position.

12 The brake assembly (F2) locks the planet wheel carrier by locking it integrally with the gearbox case. It can be seen that the F1 brake assembly is fixed on bearing 36 integral with the gearbox case. The thrust plates (39) and (37) and the three flat steel discs are integral with the gearbox case while the four lined discs fitted between the plates are integral (when rotating) with the planet wheel carrier (40). The piston (41) when oil pressure actuated, compresses and locks the plates and discs. The coil springs (38) return the piston to the 'no drive' position.

13 The planet wheel carrier may also be locked by the free wheel RL but in one direction only.

14 With 1st gear in operation, sections P1 - RL - C are in use and give a gear ratio of 2.33 : 1. The clutch E1 locks up the turbine wheel to the sunwheel P1. The latter drives the ring gear (C) through the two sets of planet wheels. A torque reaction set up in the reverse direction to ring gear rotation acts upon the planet wheel carrier which, in turn is locked by freewheel (RL). Where 'low gear hold' has been selected by the hand control then brake F1 is actuated as the torque reaction element and provides engine braking when slowing down or descending an incline. References are to Fig 7.3.

15 With second gear in operation, sections P1 - F2 - C are in use, and give a gear ratio of 1.44 : 1. Clutch E1 remains locked to drive sunwheel P1. Brake F2 is locked to immobilise sunwheel P2. The sunwheel P1 drives the ring gear through the two sets of planet wheels. The planet wheel carrier revolves round the sunwheel P2. Where 'second gear hold' has been selected by the hand control, the component engagement is identical to that for automatic second gear selection. References are to Fig 7.4.

16 With third gear in operation, sections P1 - P2 - C are in use, and give a gear ratio of 1 : 1 (direct drive). Clutch E1 remains locked to drive sunwheel P1. Clutch E2 is locked to drive sunwheel P2. A self-locking effect is obtained and the epicyclic gear train assembly turns as one with the ring gear. References are to Fig 7.5.

17 With reverse gear in operation, sections P2 - F1 - C are in use and give a gear ratio of 2 : 1. Clutch E2 is locked to drive sunwheel P2. Brake F1 is locked to immobilise the planet wheel carrier. Sunwheel P2 drives the ring gear by one set of planet wheels and so reverses the drive. References are to Fig 7.6.

18 The differential housing is designed in two halves, one end of the unit being connected to the engine and the other to the gearbox. The gearbox drive shaft receives its torque from the epicyclic gear train. The drive shaft helical gear meshes with a second gear which is integral with the final drive pinion.

19 The crownwheel and pinion transmit the drive to the road wheels by means of a conventional differential assembly.

20 The drive shaft, differential pre-load and pinion protrusion are all capable of adjustment as fully described in the preceding chapter for manually operated gearbox/transmission units.

21 To achieve the foregoing gear selection modes, ancillary components are used. These include the oil pump, oil pressure regulator, hydraulic distributor, solenoid ball valves, governor and electronic computer. A 'kick-down' facility is provided for over-riding automatic changing up and thus giving rapid acceler-

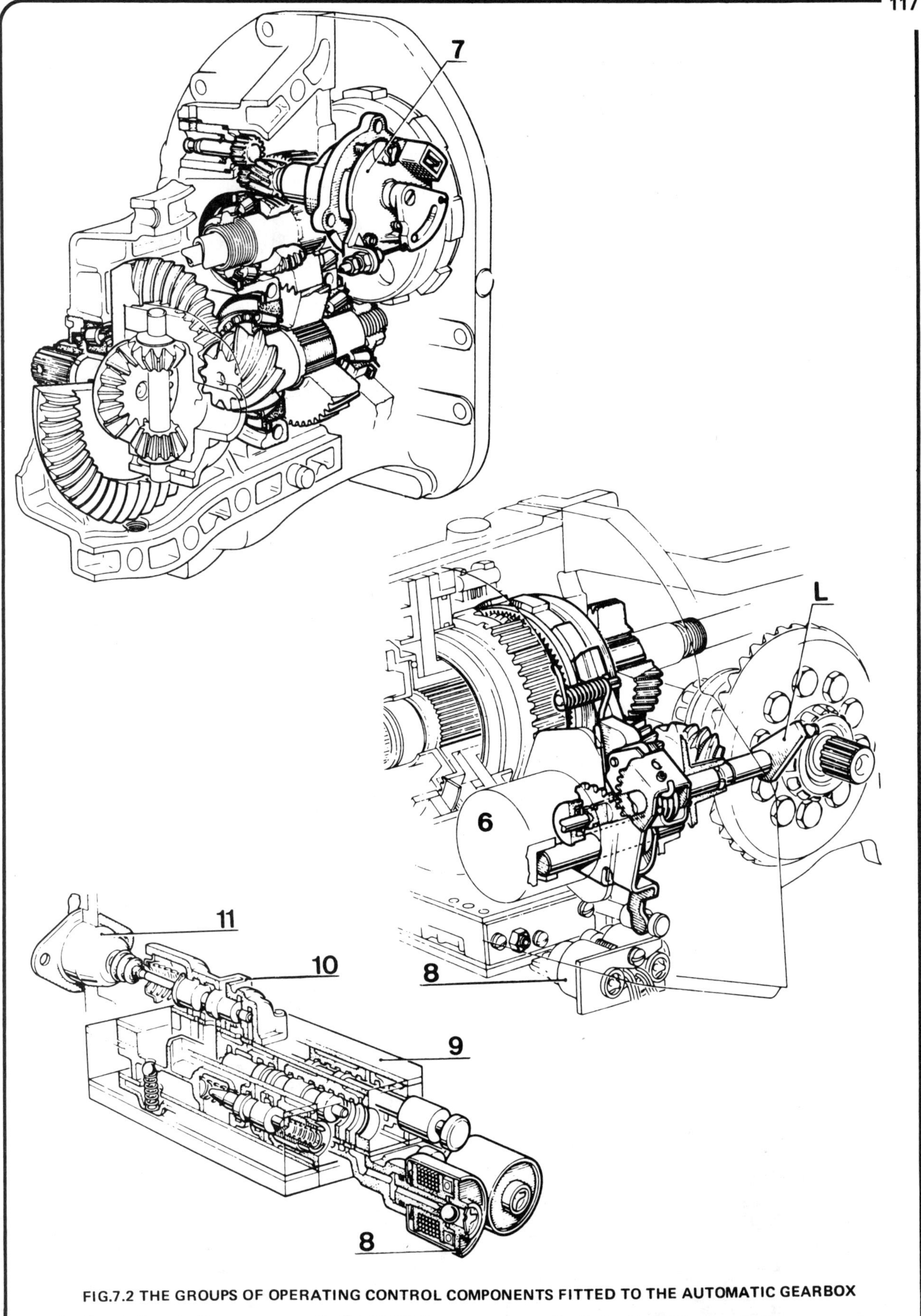

FIG.7.2 THE GROUPS OF OPERATING CONTROL COMPONENTS FITTED TO THE AUTOMATIC GEARBOX

L Gearshaft control lever
6 Electronic computer unit
7 The governor
8 Solenoid operated ball valves
9 Hydraulic distributor
10 Pressure regulator
11 Vacuum capsule

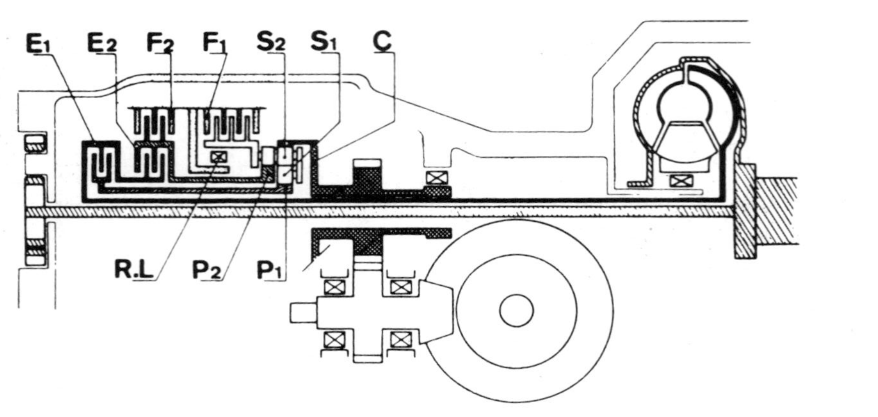

2.2 Cross sectional view of the epicyclic gear train: EI and E2 clutches. FI and F2 brakes. SI and S2 three single and three double planet wheels. C ring gear.

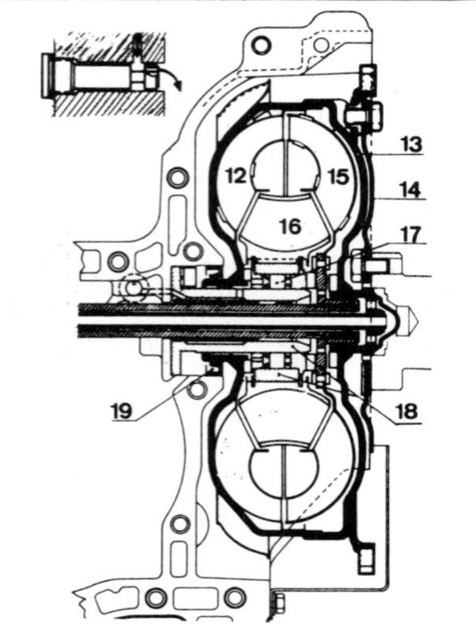

2.3 Sectional view of the torque converter: 12 Impeller. 13 impeller casing. 14 Driving plate. 15 Turbine wheel. 16 Stator. 17 Free wheel. 18 hub. 19 Rotating seal.

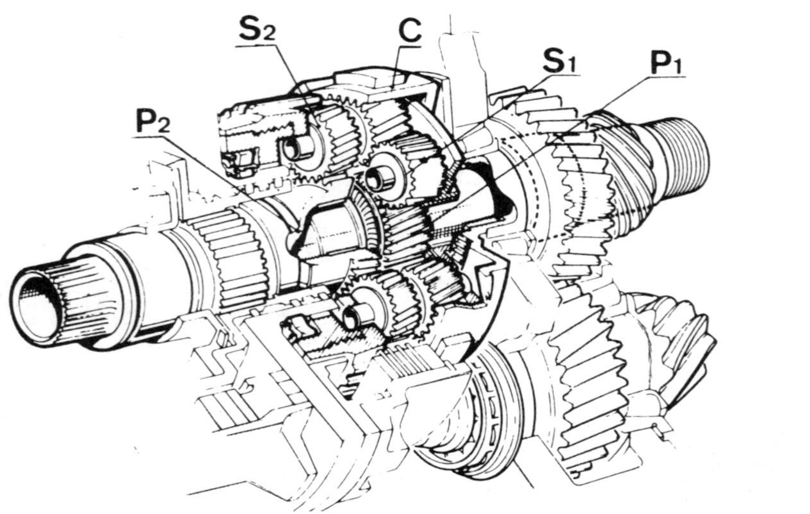

2.6 Components of the epicyclic gear train: PI and P2 sunwheels. SI and S2 planet wheels C ring gear

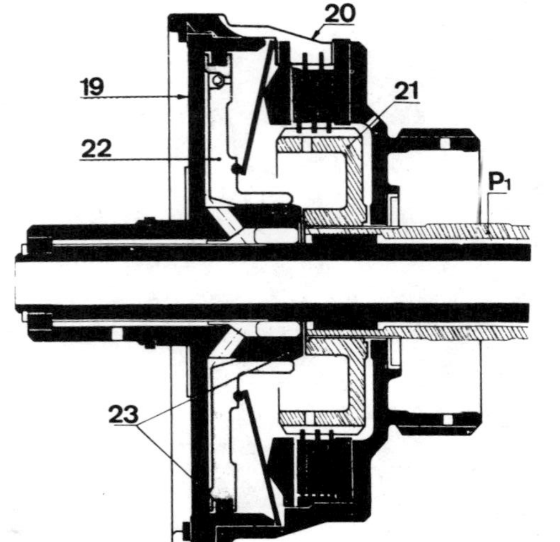

2.8 Cross sectional view of multi-disc clutch (EI): PI Sun wheel. 19 Bearing. 20 Bellhousing. 21 Hub. 22 Piston. 23 Seals

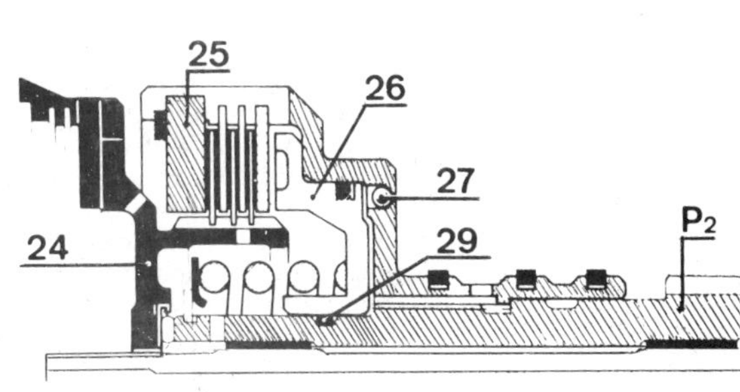

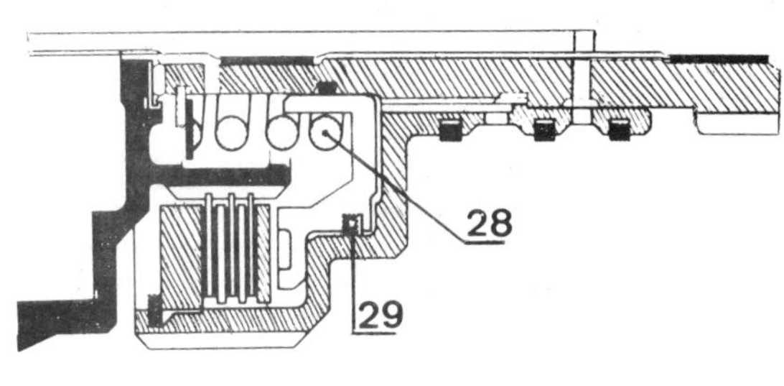

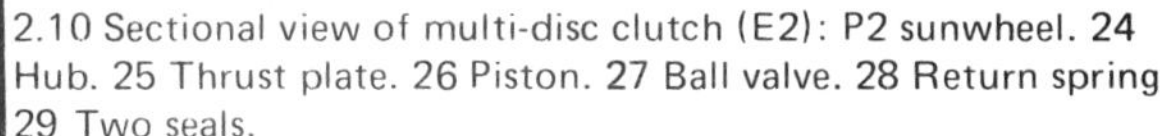

2.10 Sectional view of multi-disc clutch (E2): P2 sunwheel. 24 Hub. 25 Thrust plate. 26 Piston. 27 Ball valve. 28 Return spring. 29 Two seals.

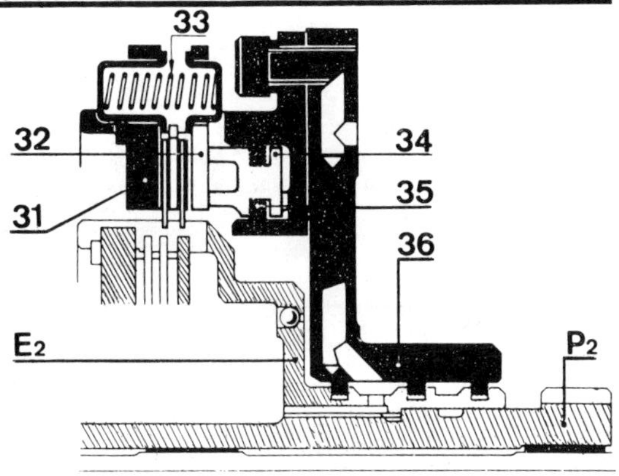

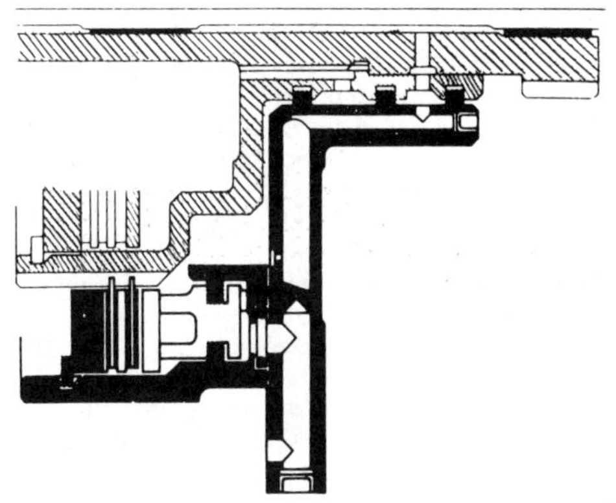

2.11. Sectional view of brake assembly (F2): P2 Sunwheel E2 Clutch. 31 Thrust plate. 32 Thrust plate. 33 Return spring. 34 Piston. 35 Seals. 36 Integral bearing.

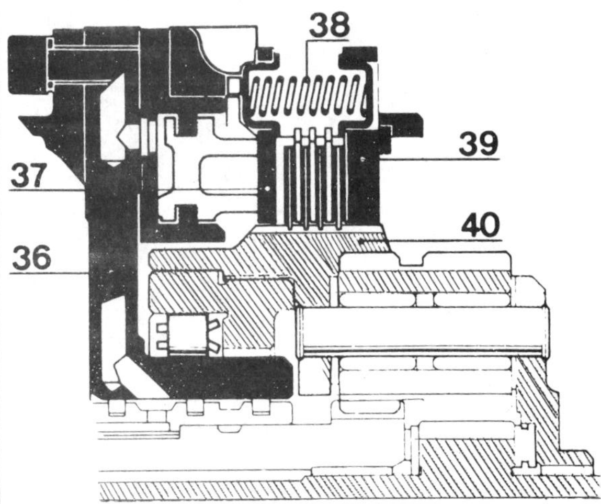

2.12 Sectional view of brake assembly (FI): 36 Integral bearing. 37 Thrust plate. 38 Return spring. 39 Thrust plate. 40 Planet wheel carrier.

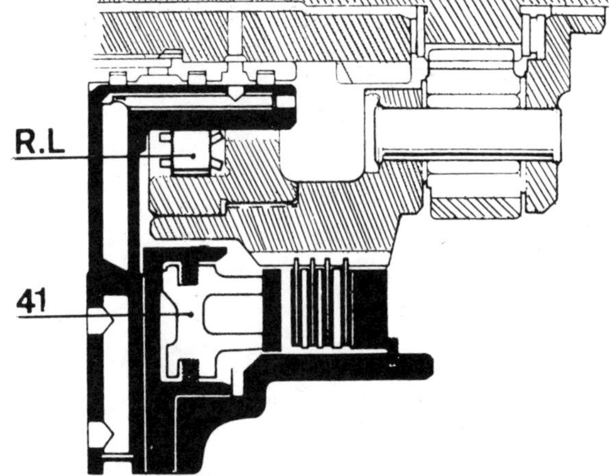

2.13 Sectional view of planet wheel carrier and freewheel: RL freewheel. 41 Piston.

ation.

22 Vital adjustments are described later in this Chapter but servicing of the gearbox internal components is not recommended and in the event of an internal fault the gearbox should be removed (Section 17) and exchanged for a factory replacement unit.

3 Lubrication - Maintenance

1 The oil used in the automatic gearbox/transmission unit provides the requirements of gearbox, convertor and final drive and must therefore be of specified grade and maintained at the correct level.

2 When checking oil level, position the vehicle on flat ground and place the hand control in 'P'. Start the engine and run it for two minutes to allow the convertor to fill up.

3 Allow the engine to tick over and, with the lever still in 'P', check the oil level on the dipstick.

4 Dependent on whether the car has just finished a run and the engine/gearbox is thoroughly hot or whether it has been started from cold, check as follows.

COLD - Minimum 1 or Maximum 2.

HOT - Minimum 2 or Maximum 3.

Do not allow the oil level to drop below the minimum mark and never overfill as this may cause overheating.

5 Oil changing is recommended at 9000 miles (15 000 km) intervals after the first two services to a new vehicle. Drain the oil hot by removing the two drain plugs and filler plug. Allow the oil to drain completely before refilling with approximately 11 pints (6 litres) of the correct grade of oil. This is special oil specified for this Renault transmission unit only. Use no other.

4 The Governor - Setting

1 When the governor or operating cable have been removed or renewed, then the following setting procedure must be carried out. Removal and replacement of the carburettor, accelerator control, cylinder head and rocker box will also necessitate checking of the governor control cable setting.

2 Adjust the cable stop (G) so that its threaded length is positioned equally either side of its retaining bracket.

3 Attach the control cable to the control segment (S).

4 Attach the other end of the operating cable to the cam at the side of the carburettor.

5 Press the accelerator right down and stretch the cable taut by removing the outer cable from its connection at (C). Now tighten the inner cable connection to the carburettor cam. There should not be any play in the inner cable run at this stage. Refit the outer cable at (C).

6 Release the accelerator pedal and then screw in the outer cable stop (G) about one turn and check the free travel at the end of the cable travel. When cable adjustment is correct, there should be free play between segment (S) and the pointer (1)within the scale cut-out, of 0.12 to 0.020 in (0.3 to 0.5 mm). When adjustment is correct, tighten the locknut (E).

5 Kick-down Switch - Adjustment

1 When the accelerator pedal reaches the limit of its normal travel, additional foot pressure will operate the kick-down switch which will have the action of changing the automatic gearbox to the next low ratio provided that the road speed is not above the maximum pre-set level at which the lower gear ratio can be engaged. The lower gear will only be held for as long as the speed does not exceed the maximum permitted revs for this ratio or the accelerator pedal is released in which case the gear will return to its original (higher) ratio.

2 It is imperative to maintain correct adjustment of the kick down switch and this should be carried out as follows:

3 First check the serviceability of the kick down switch by connecting a 12 volt test bulb between the switch and the

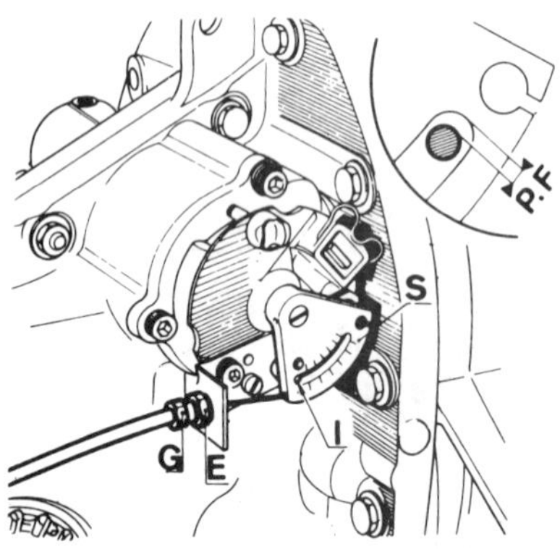

4.2 Governor and operating cable: G Outer cable stop. E Locknut. 1 Pointer. S Segment dimension. PF is free play.

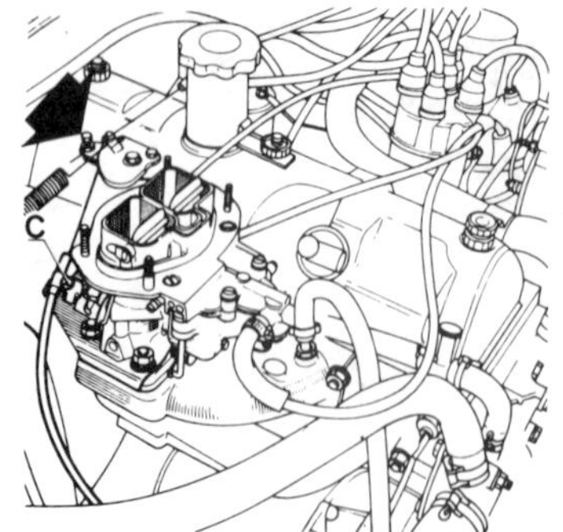

4.4 Governor operating cable cam attached to carburettor

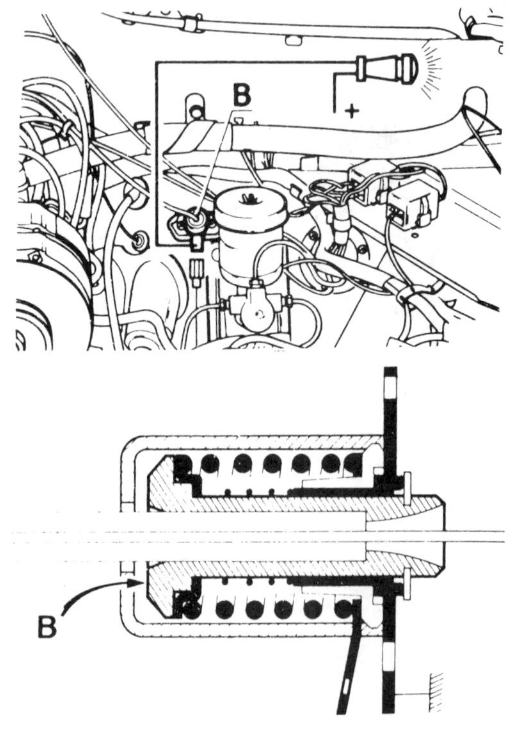

5.3. Kickdown switch testing and spring pad movement (B)

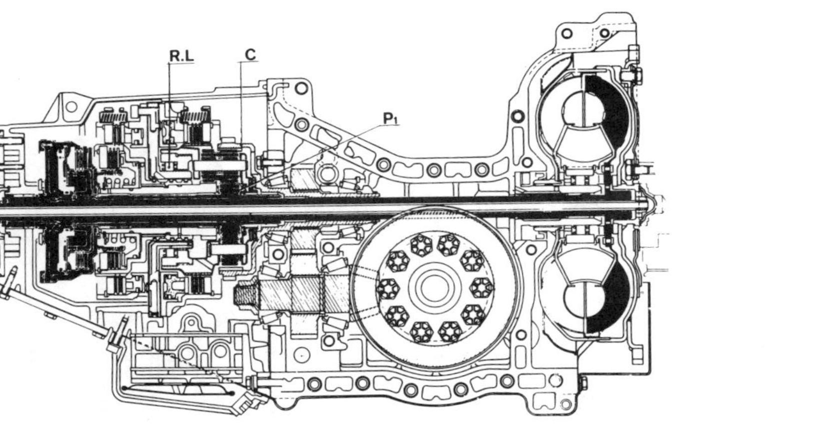

FIG.7.3 COMPONENT LOCATION WITH FIRST GEAR SELECTED

RL *Freewheel*
C *Ring gear*
Pl *Sun wheel*

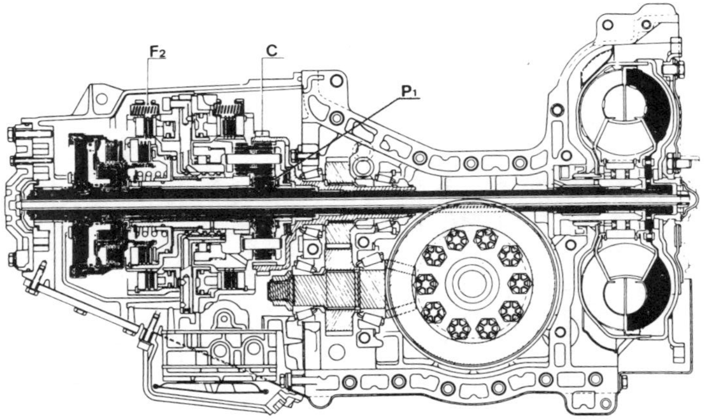

FIG.7.4 COMPONENT LOCATION WITH SECOND GEAR SELECTED

F2 *Brake*
C *Ring gear*
Pl *Sun wheel*

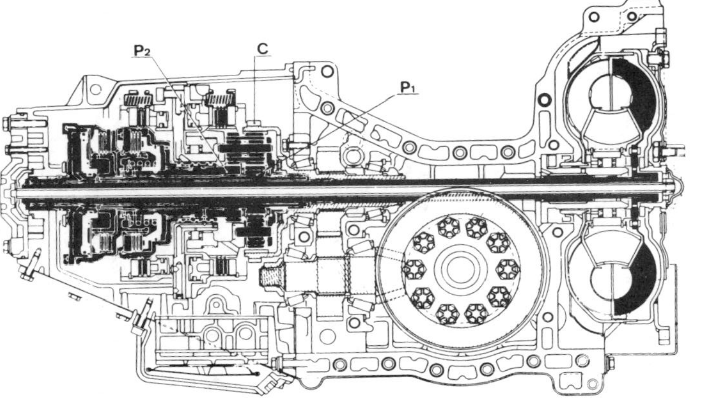

FIG.7.5 COMPONENT LOCATION WITH TOP GEAR SELECTED

P2 *Sun wheel*
C *Ring gear*
Pl *Sun wheel*

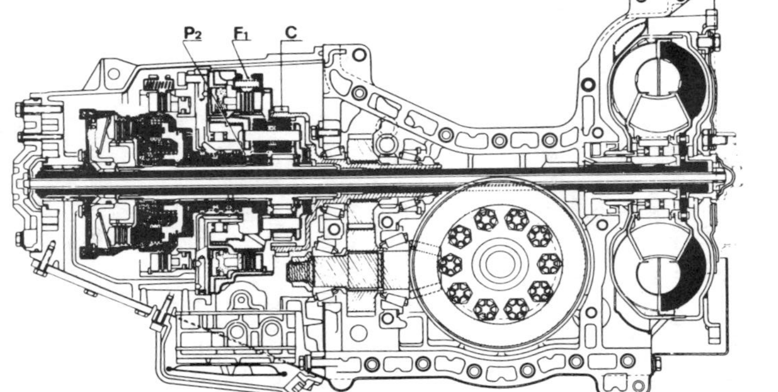

FIG.7.6 COMPONENT LOCATION WITH REVERSE GEAR SELECTED

P2 *Sun wheel*
Fl *Brake*
C *Ring gear*

battery + terminal. When the accelerator pedal is fully depressed, the test bulb will light proving the switch is in order.
4 Ensure that the choke is fully off (released) and that the accelerator cable has a little play when fully depressed to provide 1/8 to 5/32 in (3 to 4 mm) movement of the spring pad of the kick-down switch (B in the sectional view). Where the adjustment is incorrect then carry out adjustment of the accelerator cable, the governor control cable and the kick-down switch simultaneously as their tolerances and adjustment are interdependent.

6 Gear Selector Control - Adjustment

1 Remove the lighting switch covers and disconnect the electronic computer unit connecting link and unscrew the starter switch.
2 Unscrew the two screws from the clamp which secures the two parts of the gearchange control tube.
3 Engage the selector quadrant in the PARK position, pressing it down onto the bottom peg.
4 Unscrew the locking bolt (V) from the lighting switch cover support.
5 Remove the locknut from the gear selector rod ball joint and then fit a spacer, similar to the one illustrated to hold the gear selector lever in such a position that the measurements shown are as follows: X (bottom of steering wheel hub to ball joint bracket) - 63/64 in (25 mm) Y (centre of lever roll pin to upper surface of steering wheel) $8^3/_{16}$ in (208 mm). When measuring these dimensions, the lever should be set at 55° above the horizontal.
6 Hold the hand control lever in the correct position and checking that the selector quadrant is resting on the bottom peg (starter switch unscrewed) set the clamp so that A (edge of tube to end of bridge clamp) measures 25/32 in (20 mm). Tighten the clamp bolts to 15 lbf ft (2.1 kgf m). See Fig. 6.2.
7 Tighten the selector lever balljoint locknut.
8 Adjust the selector drum if necessary to maintain a distance of $11^9/_{16}$ in (294 mm) from the upper part of the control tube, with the hand control lever in A (Drive). Adjust the selector cable so that the selector indicator agrees with the gear position actually engaged. This may be achieved by turning the selector drum without altering its distance from the top end of the control tube. Movement of the selector drum is carried out by loosening the lockscrew. When adjustment is complete, check that the selector drum does not touch the starter switch or choke control when in positions P or I.
9 Where the lower part of the gear selector control requires adjustment then for LHD vehicles place the hand lever in A (Drive). Align the engagement shaft (L) with the A position on the segment scale.
10 Unscrew the nut (E) and press the link arm onto the engagement shaft and lever ball joints (L and M). Arrange the centre of ball joint (M) so that dimension (Z) measured from the side of the gearbox housing measures 1½ in (38 mm). Tighten locknut (E). Disconnect the link arm from lever (M) and check that the alignment of the lever has not altered during tightening of the nut. (Figs.
11 For RHD vehicles, the hand control is positioned on the opposite side of the steering column and the selector quadrant markings are reversed. When positioning the hand control in 'PARK' prior to adjustment, the hand control lever should be at an angle of 33° below the horizontal, otherwise the adjustment procedure outlined for LHD vehicles applies.
12 To adjust the bottom part of the gearshift control on RHD vehicles, set the quadrant in A (Drive) and set the electronic computer unit lever in position A as shown in Fig. 6.10A.
13 Unscrew screw V. Connect the control lever M to the gearbox engagement shaft with link arm B. Screw the ball joint so that its centre is a distance (Z) from the gearbox housing gasket face Z = $1^{25}/_{32}$ in (45.5 mm). Tighten screw V.

7 Starter Inhibitor Switch - Adjustment

1 Place the hand lever in A (Drive).
2 Unscrew the starter switch locknut (E).
3 Screw up or unscrew the switch to obtain a free movement of 0.12 in (0.3 mm) between lever (M) and the face of the switch, measuring with feeler gauges as shown.
4 Tighten locknut (E).

8 Operations with the Gearbox in Position in the Vehicle

1 The following can be carried out with the gearbox/transmission unit in position in the car and are fully described in the following sections.

Renewing the governor
Renewing the electronic computer unit
Renewing the vacuum capsule
Renewing the differential sunwheel oil seals
Renewing the oil pump cover gasket
Renewing the speedometer drive gear
Rectifying lower housing oil leak
Renewing the lower cover plate gasket

9 Governor - Removal and Replacement

1 Disconnect the governor control cable and feed wires.
2 Using a 5 mm Allen key, unscrew the three governor securing socket screws, and withdraw the unit as shown in the figure.
3 Fit a new gasket smeared with jointing compound when refitting the governor. Should difficulty be experienced in sliding the governor unit into position, turn the speedometer gear gently at the same time exerting slight pressure on the governor unit.
4 When the unit is correctly located, set the governor control cable as described in Section 4.

10 Electronic Computer Unit - Removal and Replacement

1 Disconnect the electrical feed wires and unscrew the securing screws from the unit. Withdraw the unit.
2 To fit the unit, turn the centre shaft clockwise as far as possible as shown in the figure.
3 Place the steering column gearshift lever into 1 (low hold position.
4 Offer up the electronic computer unit (fitted with new spacers) and screw in the securing screws finger tight.
5 Turn the computer unit and lever (L) as one assembly in an anti-clockwise direction (arrowed in the figure) without using any force. When it will rotate no further, tighten the securing screws just enough to retain the unit without compressing the plastic distance pieces.
6 Reconnect the feed wires.

11 Vacuum Capsule - Removal and Replacement

1 Disconnect the flexible hose and unscrew the two securing bolts. Withdraw the capsule.
2 When fitting a new unit, smear the oil seal with gasket cement and finally check and top up the gearbox/transmission oil level to make up for any loss of oil which may have occurred during removal of the vacuum capsule.

12 Differential Sunwheel Oil Seals - Renewal

1 Drain the gearbox.
2 Disconnect the brake caliper, the upper suspension ball joint and the steering arm ball joint as described in later Chapters of this manual.

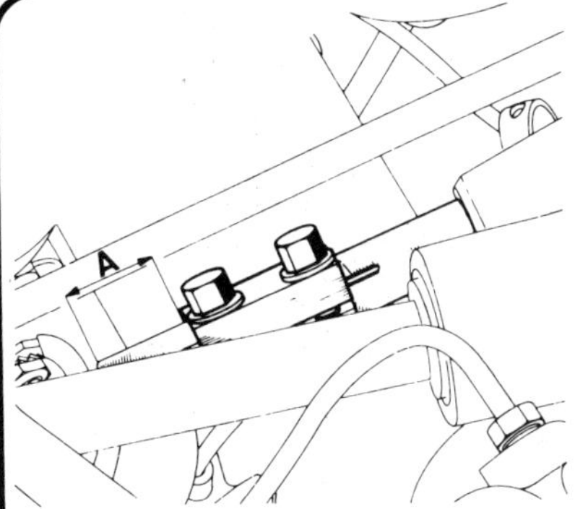

6.2 Gearshaft control tube clamp

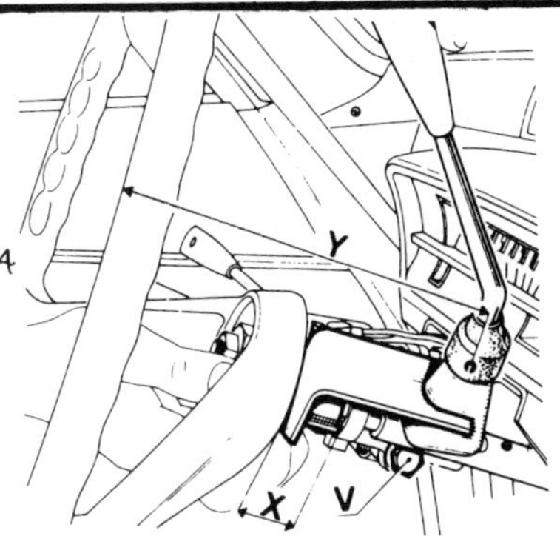

6.4 Hand gearshift lever positioning prior to adjustment

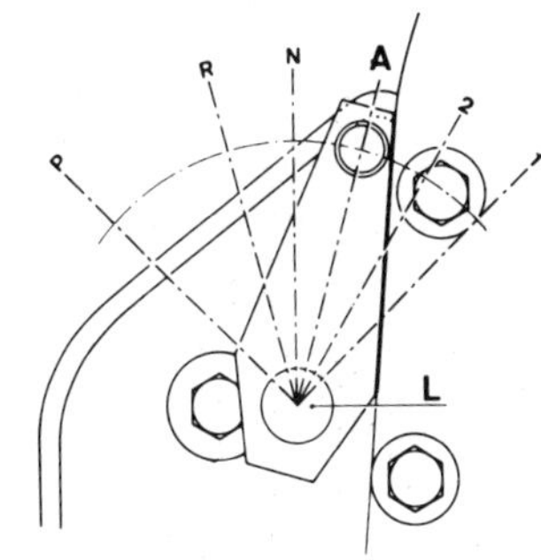

6.10A Gear selection engagement shaft positioning diagram prior to adjustment

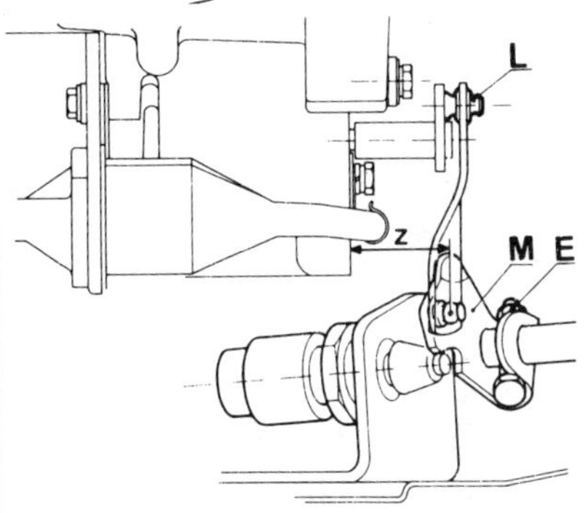

6.10B Link arm, engagement shaft and lever ball joint positioning diagram prior to final adjustment

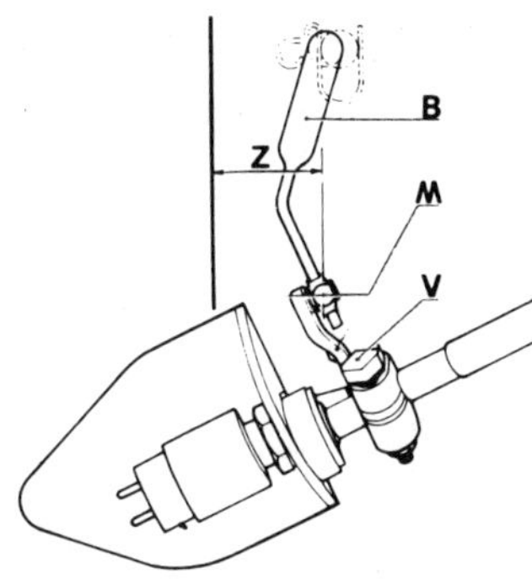

6.13 Link arm to ball joint positioning diagram

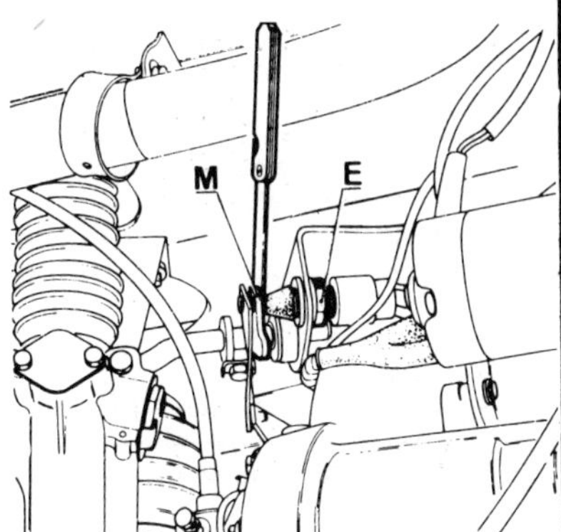

7.2 Starter inhibitor switch adjustment M lever. E locknut

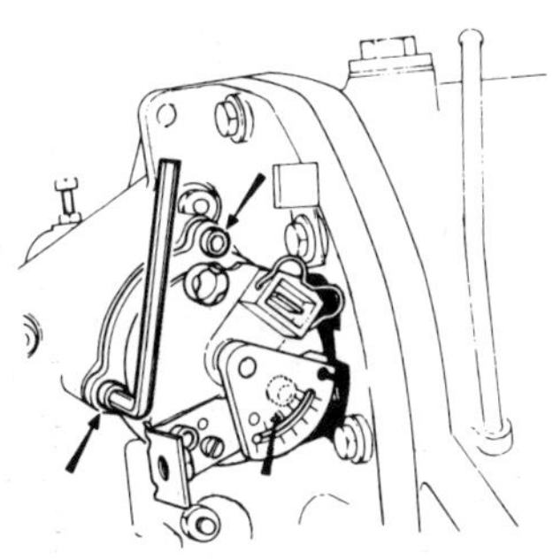

9.2 Unscrewing the governor retaining socket screws

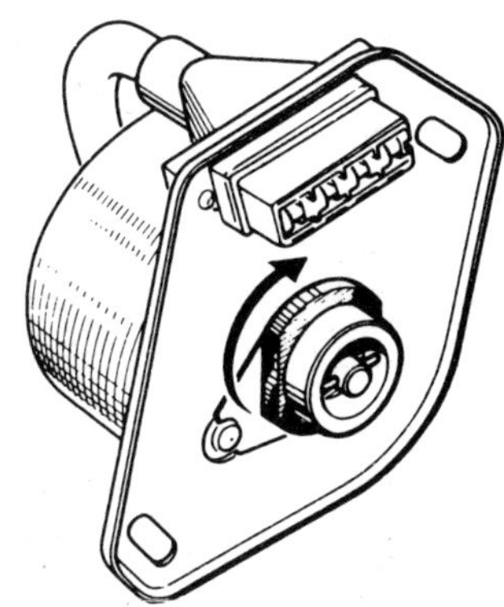

10.2 The electronic computer unit

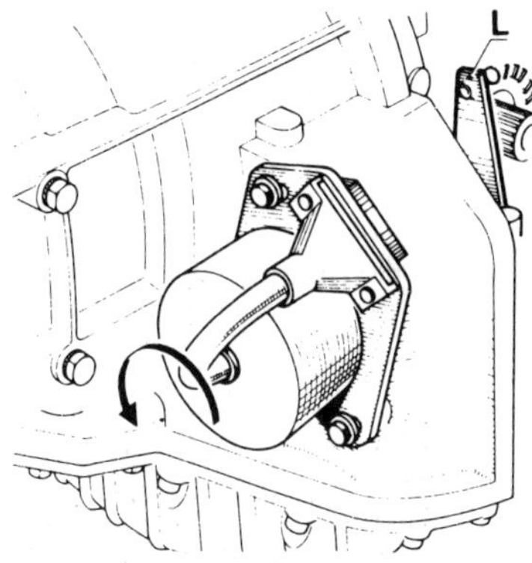

10.5 Rear view of computer unit

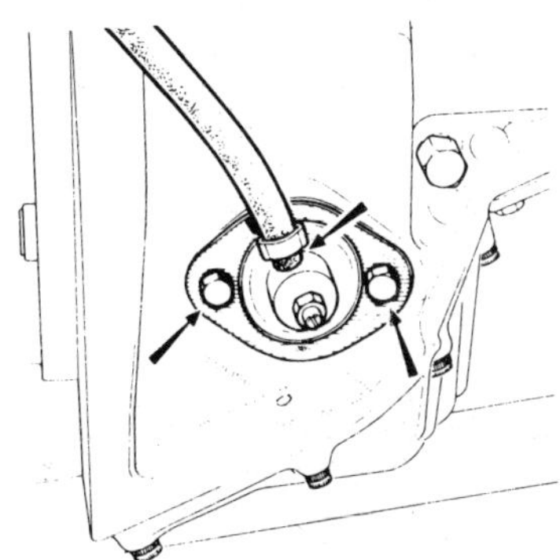

11.1 Vacuum capsule retaining screws and flexible hose

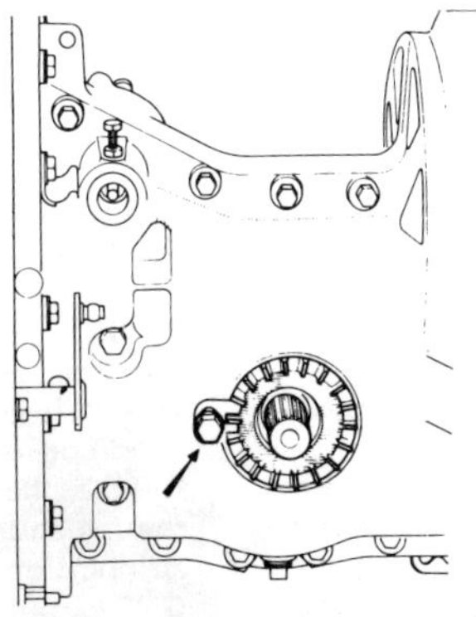

12.5A Differential adjusting nut lock tab and bolt

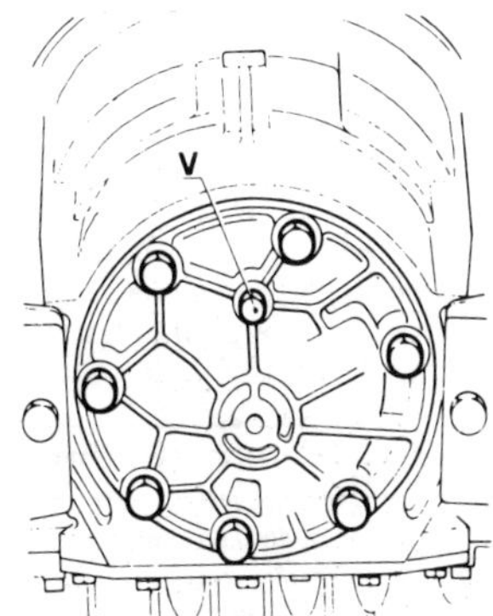

13.4 Oil pump cover gasket bolts. V is smaller inner retaining bolt

3 Remove the driveshaft from the sunwheel as described in Chapter 1 and fit the driveshaft joint restraining clip.
4 Dot punch the position of the differential bearing adjusting nut in relation to the gearbox casing.
5 Unscrew and remove the nut locking tab, unscrew the bearing adjustment nuts and renew the oil sealing 'O' rings and the lip type seals. The latter should be gently tapped in using a piece of tube of $2^1/_{16}$ in (52 mm) outside diameter as a drift. (Fig.)

13 Oil Pump Cover Gasket - Renewal

1 Clamp the radiator to expansion bottle tube and then disconnect it from the bottle.
2 Unscrew and remove the radiator securing bolts and swing the radiator up and support it in position over the engine.
3 Drain the oil from the gearbox.
4 Remove the seven peripheral bolts and the smaller inner bolt from the cover.
5 Lift off the cover and remove the old seal.
6 Clean the seal seating surfaces and fit a new seal which has been lightly greased.
7 Tighten the bolts on reassembly to 5 lbf ft (0.7 kgf m) except for bolt (V) which should be tightened to 2.5 lbf ft (0.34 kgf m) only.

14 Speedometer Drive Oil Seals - Renewal

1 Unscrew the locknut which holds the speedometer cable securing bolt.
2 Unscrew the bolt and detach the speedometer cable.
3 Withdraw the aluminium sleeve together with the speedometer drive gear.
4 Remove the internal and external oil seals from the aluminium sleeve and fit new ones.
5 Refit the aluminium sleeve by drifting it into position using a 0.553 in (14 mm) outside diameter tube.
6 Fit the speedometer drive gear into the sleeve and then locate the complete assembly in the gearbox. It may be necessary to turn the gear slightly to facilitate this operation.

15 Bottom Sump Gasket - Renewal

1 Drain the gearbox by removing the two drain plugs.
2 Remove the lower housing securing bolts in diametrically opposite sequence, a turn or two at a time working from the centre bolts towards each end.
3 Fit a new gasket dry and tighten the securing bolts to 4 lbf ft (0.55 kgf m).
4 Refill the gearbox.

16 Operations with the Gearbox/Transmission Removed from the Vehicle

1 The following operations can only be carried out after the gearbox has been removed from the vehicle.
Renewing the lower cover plate gasket
Removing and refitting the torque converter
Renewing the torque convertor oil seal.
2 These operations are fully described later in this Chapter.

17 Gearbox/Transmission - Removal and Replacement

1 This section describes removal of the gearbox/transmission leaving the engine in position in the vehicle. Removal of the engine/automatic gearbox/transmission as a combined unit is fully described in Chapter 1.
2 Jack up the front of the car and support it securely on blocks or axle stands. Remove the two front road wheels.
3 Drain the gearbox (two plugs) and remove the torque convertor cover (two bolts).
4 Disconnect the torque convertor by removing the three securing bolts. These are only accessible by using a universally jointed socket drive inserted between the crossmember and engine sump.
5 Disconnect the battery.
6 Remove the bonnet retaining strap and prop the bonnet lid in its maximum vertical position.
7 Remove the fixing clip on the expansion bottle.
8 Remove the centre bolt from the camshaft pulley and withdraw the pulley.
9 Disconnect the two leads from the radiator temperature sender unit and the cooling fan motor leads.
10 Remove the tie bar which connects the two front wing side bulkheads.
11 Remove the radiator fixing bolts and lift the radiator up and over to rest on the engine and then stand the expansion bottle on the wing.
12 Disconnect the speedometer cable (T) the gearshift control arm (V) the governor cable (G) the electronic computer unit plug (C) at the engine bulkhead, the gearbox earthing strap (X) and the vacuum capsule pipe (D).
13 Disconnect the drive shafts and steering column and remove the steering gear as described in Chapter 1 or for manual gearbox removal in Chapter 6.
14 Remove the brake calipers (Chapter 11) and remove the left and right hand upper ball joints.
15 Remove the gearbox mounting pad nuts and the radiator centre support.
16 Unscrew and remove the bolts which secure the gearbox/transmission unit to the engine.
17 Using suitable slings and a hoist, lift the unit slightly and ease it away from its front support. Now lower the unit so that it rests on the front crossmember.
18 At this stage, fit a clip to avoid displacement of the torque convertor.
19 Hoist the gearbox/transmission unit up and out at an angle from the engine compartment, taking care not to damage the centralising ball on the convertor or the gearbox external ancillary units and controls.
20 Refitting is a reversal of removal but the following points must be observed.
21 Ensure that the centralising dowels are in place on the engine.
22 Lower the gearbox into the engine compartment so that it rests on the front crossmember.
23 Remove the convertor retaining clip and then offer up the gearbox to the engine. The triangular driving plate (attached to the crankshaft flange) to which the convertor is bolted has one sharp angled machined apex which is identified by a white paint spot on the engine side. The convertor has a matching white spot on one of its threaded securing bosses and these two spots must be together when bolting the convertor to the driving plate.
24 Fit the securing bolts and use new wave washers. Tighten the bolts evenly and in rotation to ensure perfect centralisation of the convertor, to a torque setting of 18 lbf ft (2.5 kgf m). The use of a universally jointed socket drive, as specified for removal, will be required for tightening these bolts.

18 Torque Convertor Oil Seal - Renewal

1 Remove the gearbox/transmission unit as described in the preceding Section.
2 Carefully pull the convertor from the drive shaft. Check the condition of the convertor centralising ball, the oil seal bearing surface, the white metal convertor sleeve, the starter ring gear, the fan and the convertor threaded securing bosses for cracks or stripping of the threads. Renew as appropriate.
3 Pick out the oil seal, noting carefully the depth to which it is fitted within its recess.
4 Fit the new oil seal with a tubular drift and lubricate the seal bearing surfaces.

14.1 Speedo cable securing bolt

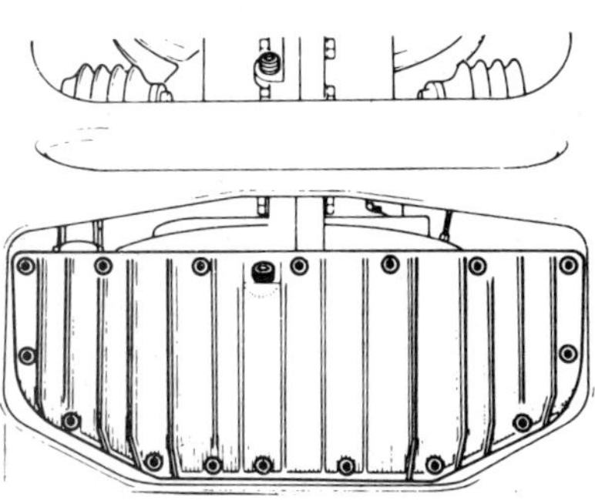
15.2 Bottom sump securing bolts

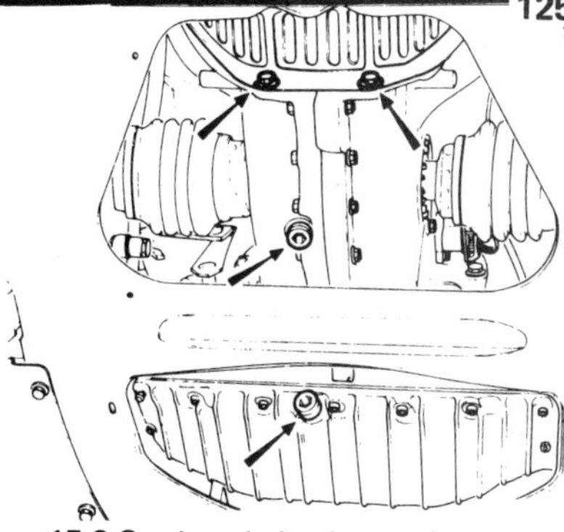
17.3 Gearbox drain plugs and torque convertor cover bolts

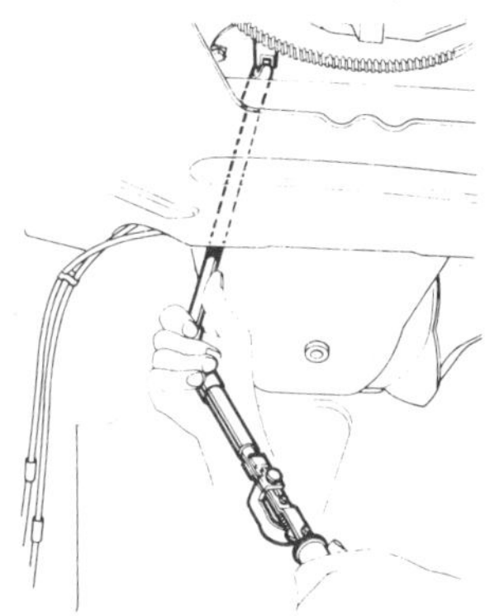
17.4 Unscrewing the torque convertor securing bolts

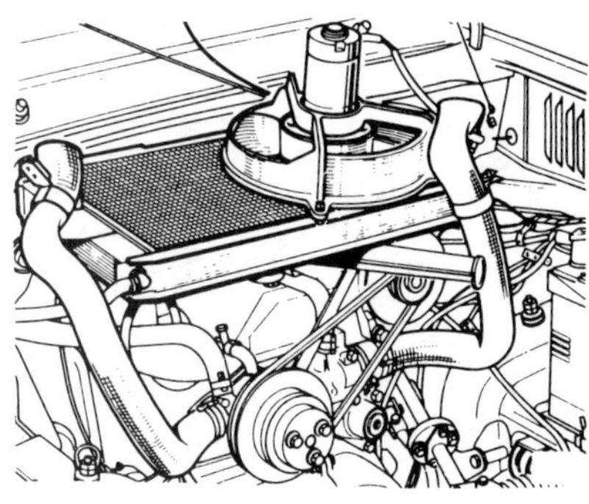
17.11 Location of radiator prior to removal of the gearbox

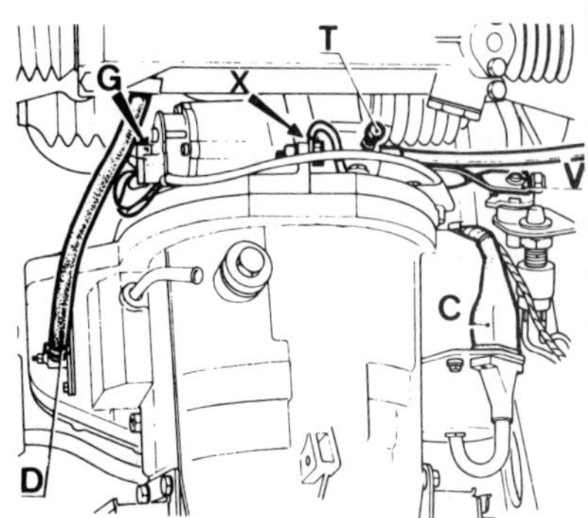

17.12 Disconnection points prior to removal of the gearbox: T Speedometer cable. G Governor cable. X earthing strap D vacuum capsule pipe. V gearshift control arm

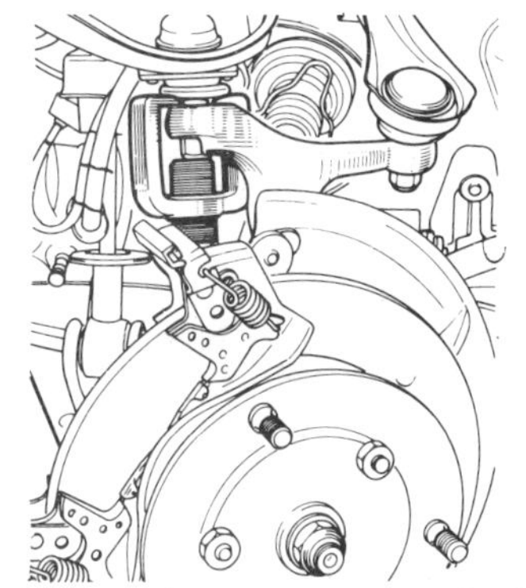
17.14 Removing an upper suspension ball joint

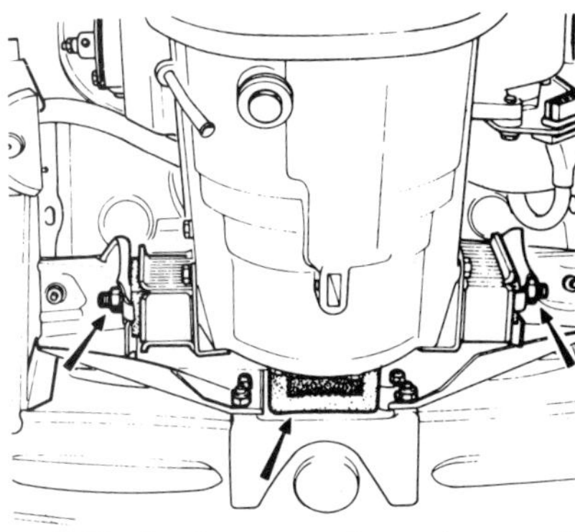
17.15. Gearbox mounting pad nuts and radiator centre support

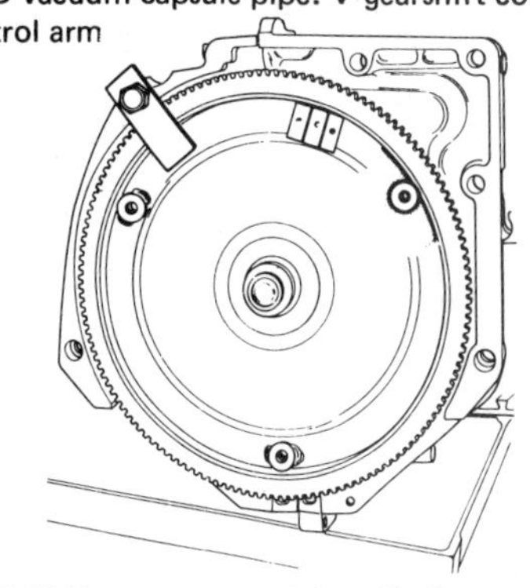
17.18 Temporary retaining clip for torque convertor during removal of the gearbox

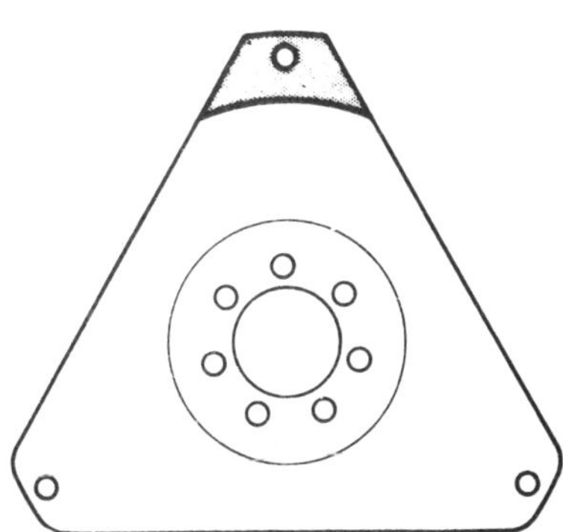
17.23 Crankshaft flange mounted, convertor driving plate

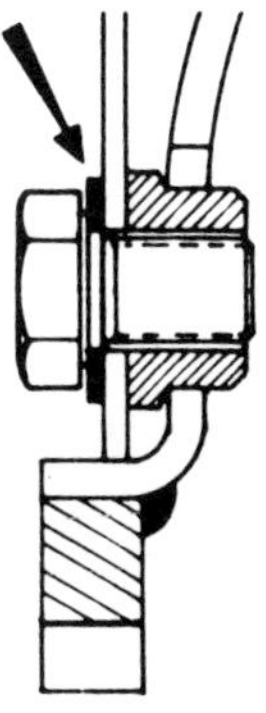
17.24 Convertor to driving plate securing bolt and washer

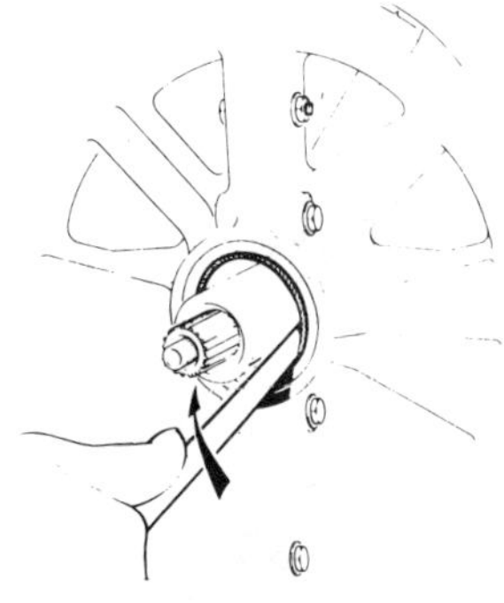
18.3 Torque convertor oil seal removal

5 Refit the torque convertor and the gearbox/transmission unit as previously described in the preceding Section.

19 Lower Cover Plate Gasket - Renewal

1 Remove the gearbox as described in Section 17.
2 Unscrew and remove the cover plate securing screws.
3 Fit a new gasket (dry) to scrupulously clean mating surfaces.
4 Tighten the securing bolts to 5 lbf ft (0.7 kgf m) evenly working from the centre outwards.
5 Top up the gearbox to the correct level to make up for any loss of oil during cover removal.

20 Gearchange Control Mechanism - Removal and Replacement

1 In the event of wear occuring in the components of the gearchange control mechanism which cannot be rectified by adjustment as described in Section 6, then the mechanism must be removed and dismantled and all faulty parts renewed.
2 Disconnect the battery and remove the steering wheel moulding which covers the securing nut.
3 Remove the steering wheel nut and mark the wheel hub in relation to the end of the splined shaft in order to ensure exact replacement. An extractor will almost certainly be required to pull the steering wheel from the shaft.
4 Remove the two steering column half covers.
5 Mark the position of the lighting switch bracket in relation to the steering column.
6 Remove the bracket securing bolt and unscrew the locknut from the gearchange control rod ball joint.
7 Unlock and unscrew the balljoint, at the same time gradually pulling back the lighting switch bracket.
8 Unlock and remove the two control tube clamp bolts.
9 Push back the lighting switch bracket and lift it from the control rod by swivelling it round the steering column.
10 Remove the selector drum control cable and remove the tube/lever assembly.
11 Disconnect the two wires (F) from the starter switch and the arm (V) at the control lever end.
12 Unscrew the two bracket securing nuts and then remove the control from the upper bracket.
13 The hand lever and tube assembly is similar to that for manual gearshift described in Chapter 6 to which reference should be made.
14 When dismantling the gearchange control at the gearbox end to renew faulty or worn parts, note that the quadrant (4) is retained by a roll pin and its notched side is towards the universal joint (5).
15 After reassembling and refitting any part of the gearchange control mechanism, refer to Section 6 and carry out all the checks and adjustments described.

21 Electrical Connections and Wiring

1 The electrical circuit is shown in diagrammatic form in the figure (Fig 7.7).
2 The governor plug connections are shown in the figure.
3 The junction box connections are shown in the figure.
4 The electronic computer unit plug connections are shown in the figure.
5 The kick-down switch connection is shown in the figure.
6 The location of the circuit fuses is shown in the figure.
7 There are certain knacks to disconnecting some of the electrical connections and plugs. To remove the terminals from the governor plug push a rod through which will raise the retaining tab and enable the wire to be released.
8 Junction box plugs are removed by pressing in both side catches simultaneously. Replacement of a female terminal is carried out by releasing the wire in a similar manner to that described for the governor plug.
9 To renew terminals on the male plug of the electronic computer unit, first remove the unit and drill out the rivets from the plug. When refitting the plug do not overspread the tubular rivets.
10 To renew a terminal on the electronic computer female plug, pull back the protecting cover.

22 Gear Position Indicator - Cable Renewal

1 The position of the steering column gearshift lever and the operational mode of the automatic gearbox are indicated by the cable operated index inset in the instrument panel.
2 Disconnect the battery.
3 Remove the instrument panel cowl.
4 Disconnect the gearchange selector cable from the drum.
5 Disconnect the speedometer cable.
6 Remove the three instrument panel securing screws. Disconnect the wires and remove the instrument panel.
7 Unscrew the two instrument panel glass securing screws and slide the glass out.
8 Remove the gearshift position indicator plate by lifting up the four rubber plugs.
9 Remove the cable securing plate at the end of the cable and detach it from the sleeve and the instrument panel.
10 To fit the new cable, tighten the securing plate and solder the cable into position.
11 Adjust the cable and drum as described in paragraph 8 Section 6.

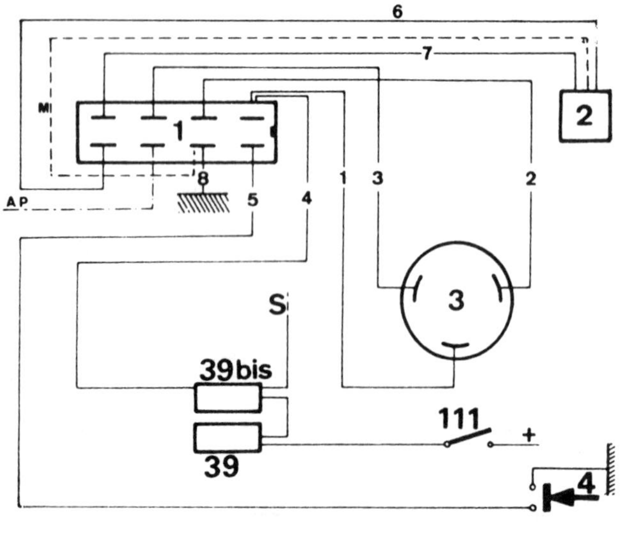

FIG.7.7 ELECTRICAL CIRCUIT OF AUTOMATIC GEARBOX

1	*Junction box for the electronic computer unit, seen from wiring side*
2	*Governor*
3	*Sealed junction box*
36b	*Fuse box (transmission fusebox : 5A)*
111	*Neiman ignition switch*
4	*Kick-down switch*
S	*Starter solenoid*

1	*Red*	*+ feed after ignition switch*
2	*Blue*	*Solenoid ball valve 1*
3	*White*	*Solenoid ball valve 2*
4	*Red*	*Fuse to junction box*
5	*Green*	*Kick-down switch*
6	*Pink*	*Governor to junction box*
7	*Pink*	*Governor to junction box*
8	*Grey*	*Earth (ground)*
AP		*Anti-pollution (USA model)*
M		*Governor earth (ground)*

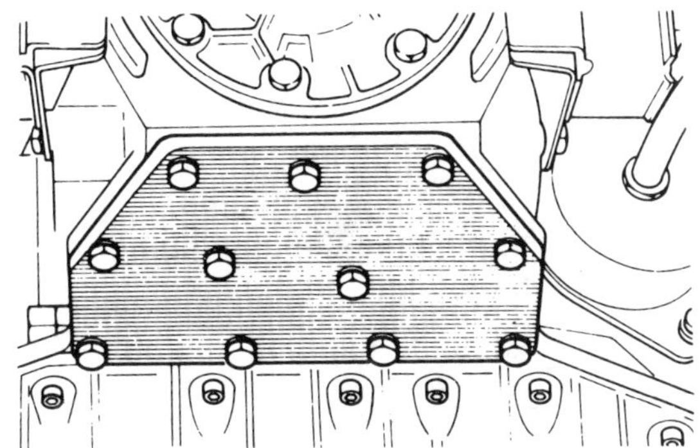

19.2 The cover plate and securing screws

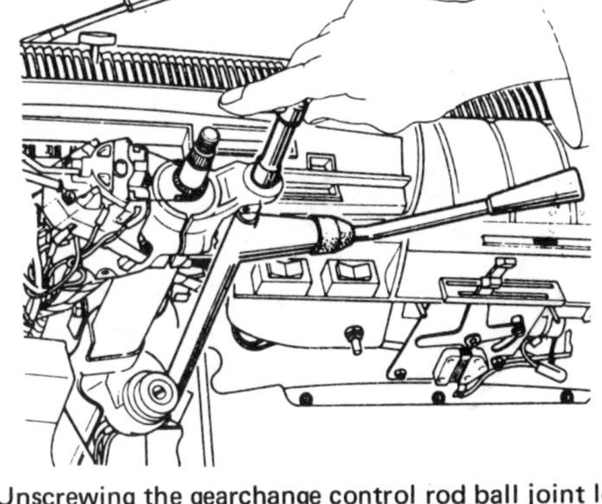

20.6 Unscrewing the gearchange control rod ball joint locknut

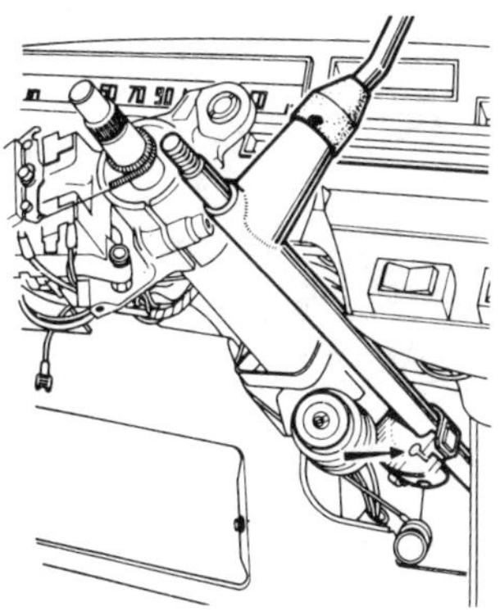

20.9 Removing the lighting switch bracket from the steering column

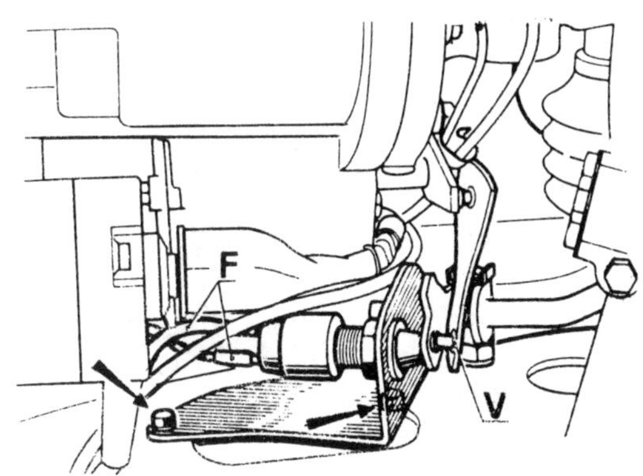

20.11 Location of the starter switch wires (F) and the control lever arm (V)

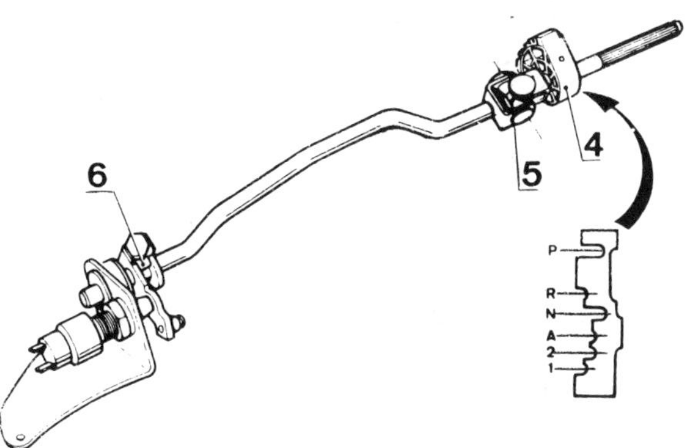

20.14 Gearchange control components at the gearbox end: 4 Quadrant. 5 Universal joint. 6 Arm.

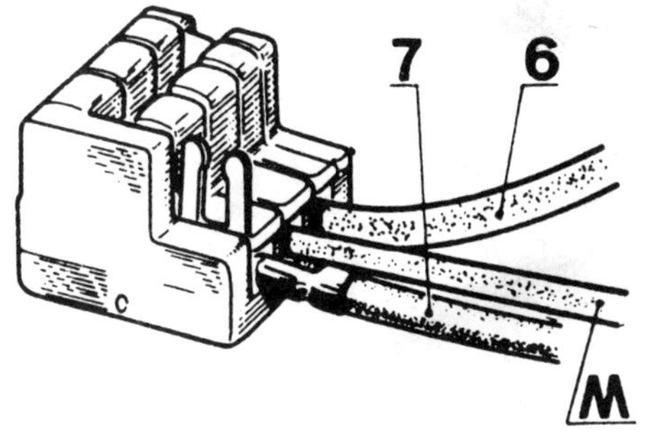

21.2 Governor plug connections: 6 Yellow Governor to junction box. 7 Yellow Governor to junction box. M Earth wire.

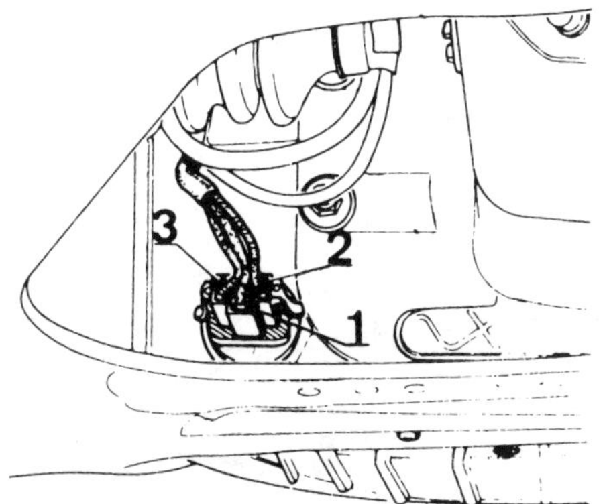

21.3 Junction box connections: 1 Red + feed after ignition switch. 2 Blue Solenoid ball valve 1. 3 White Solenoid ball valve 2.

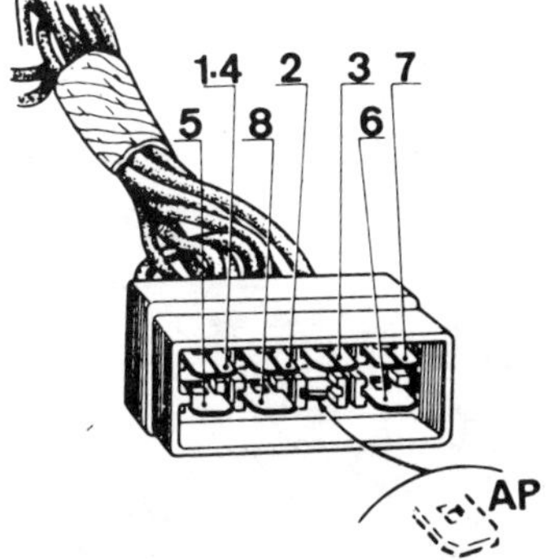

21.4 Electronic computer plug connections: 1 Red + feed after ignition switch. 2 Blue Solenoid ball valve 1. 3 White Solenoid ball valve 2. 4 Red Fuse box to junction box. 5 Green Kick-down switch. 6 Pink Governor to junction box. 7 Pink Governor to junction box. 8-M Grey Earth (ground). AP Anti-pollution (USA model)

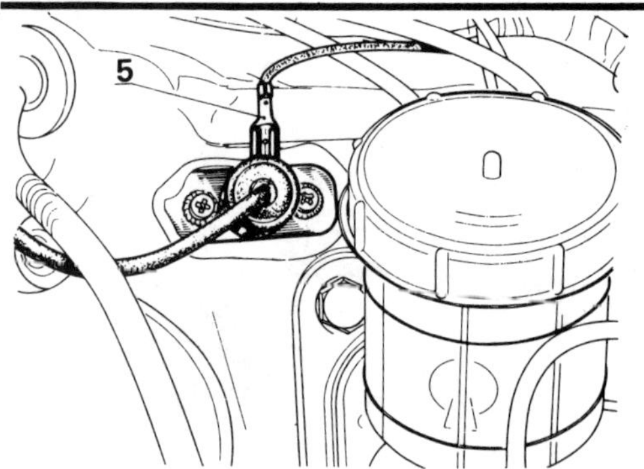

21.5 Kick-down switch connection. 5 Green

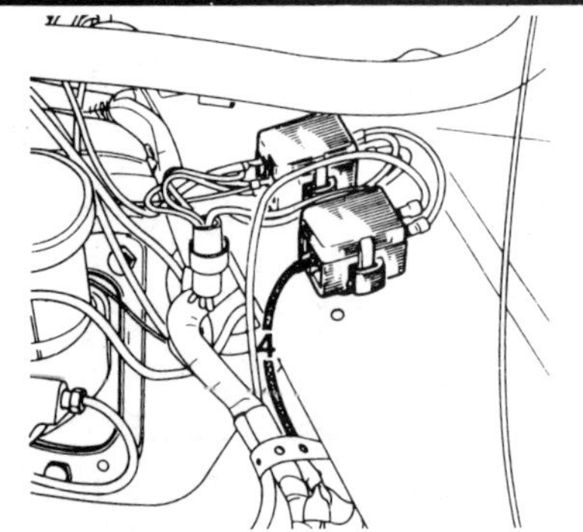

21.6 Location of the automatic gearbox circuit fuses. 4 Red fuse to junction box

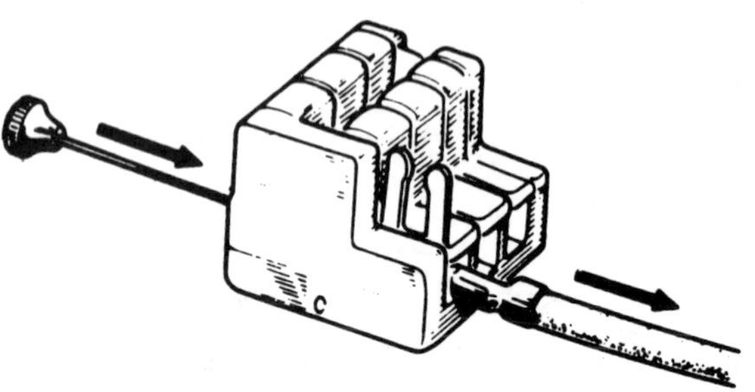

21.7 Releasing a cable from the governor plug

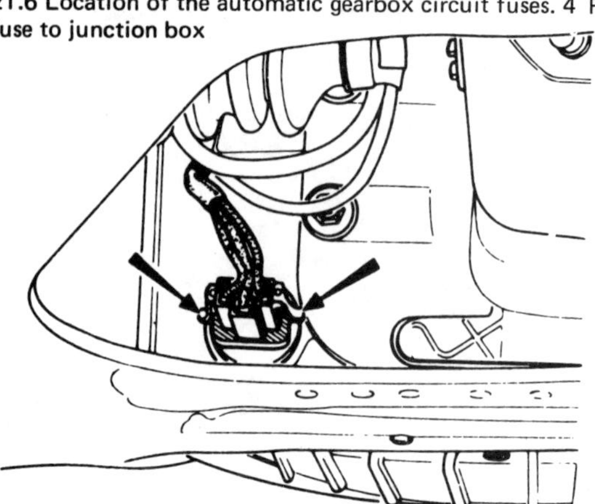

21.8 Pressure points to release a junction box plug

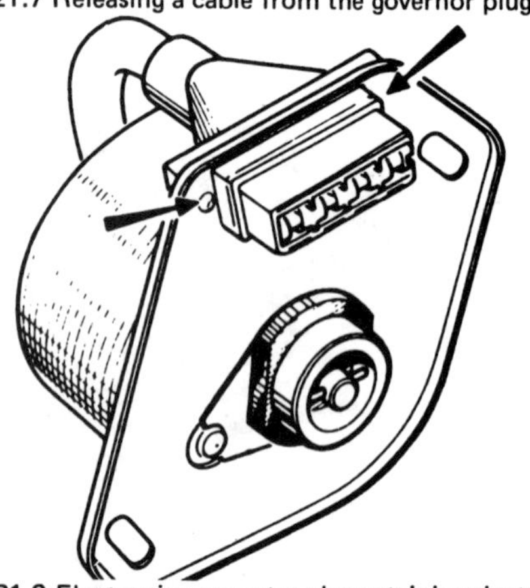

21.9 Electronic computer plug retaining rivets

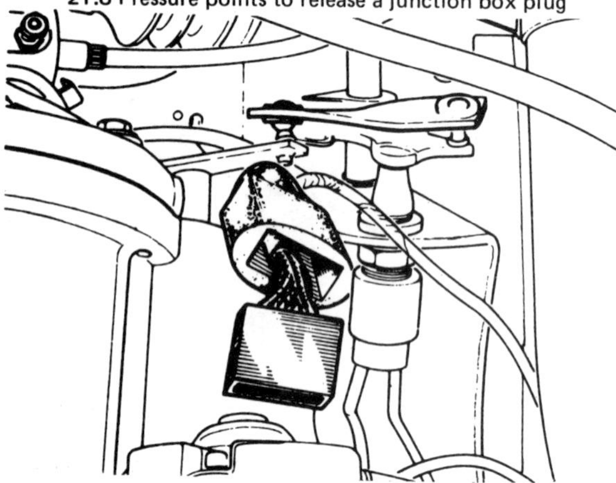

21.10 Female computer unit plug and protective cover

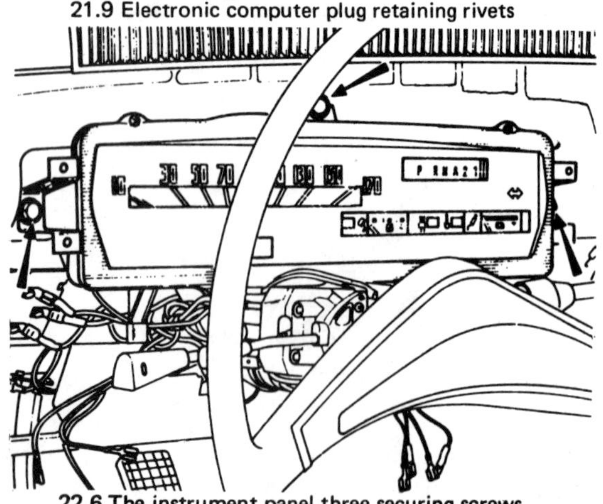

22.6 The instrument panel three securing screws

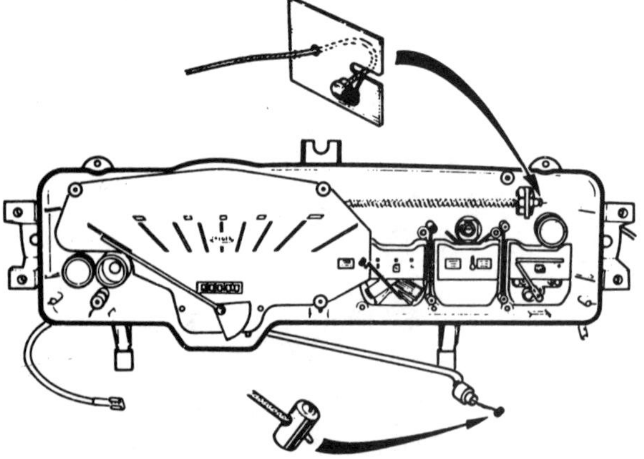

22.9 Components of the gearshift position indicator

Automatic gearbox - fault finding

The table below gives certain possible faults and a reason check number.

Operating faults		Check number
CREEP	In N	8. 9. 10. 27.
	Excessive in A	2. 3. 26.
SLIP	Moving off in A & R	1. 11. 26.
	Moving off in A only	31.
	During gear changing	4. 11. 12. 17. 18.
SNATCH	On starting off	2. 3.
	During gear changing	4. 11. 12. 17. 18.
INCORRECT MOMENTS OF GEAR CHANGE		
	Climbing and downhill at speed	5. 7. 13. 14. 16. 17.
	Only at kick-down	3. 5. 7. 14. 15.
STALLING ENGINE		2. 3.
UNEVEN TICKOVER		3. 12.
NO DRIVE		
	In A — 1st gear "Hold" — R	20. 21. 22. 23. 24. 25.
	In A — 1st gear "Hold"	27.
	In R — and 3rd gear automatic	17. 28.
	In R — and 1st gear "Hold"	17. 29.
NO	1st gear automatic	7. 14. 16. 31.
	2nd gear automatic	7. 14. 16. 17. 30.
	3rd gear automatic	7. 13. 14. 16. 17.
	2nd gear "Hold"	14.
	1st gear "Hold"	14.
REMAINS		
	In 1st gear automatic	7.13. 14. 17.
	In 3rd gear	6. 7. 14. 16. 17.
SOME RATIOS UNOBTAINABLE, SELECTOR LEVER FAULTY		8. 9. 10. 20.
PARK POSITION NOT WORKING		9. 32.
STARTER NOT WORKING		7. 9. 10. 19. 20.

REASON CHECK NUMBER

Checks and setting	Replacement unit required	Gearbox overhaul required
1 Oil level	12 Vacuum capsule	21 Oil pump
2 Faulty slow running (or choke)	13 Governor	22 Oil pump drive shaft
	14 Electronic computer unit	23 Turbine shaft
3 Accelerator control	15 Kick-down switch	24 Axle
4 Governor control cable	16 Solenoid ball valves	25 Convertor driving plate
5 Kick-down switch (adjustment)	17 Hydraulic distributor	26 Convertor
6 Fuse	18 Pressure regulator valve	27 E 1 — clutch
7 Wiring and terminals	19 Starter switch	28 E 2 — clutch
8 Electronic computer unit setting	20 Gear change control	29 F 1 — brake
9 Gear change control setting		30 F 2 — brake
10 Adjusting the indicator		31 Gear train free wheel
11 Pressure setting		32 Parking latch mechanism

Chapter 8 Front suspension, drive shafts and hubs

For modifications, and information applicable to later models, see Supplement at end of manual

Contents

Specifications

Suspension type ... Wishbone links, torsion bars, double acting hydraulic dampers and anti-roll bar.

Torsion bars ... length 403/4 in (1.035 in)
diameter (normal) 0.685 in (17.4 mm)
(heavy duty) 0.716 in (18.2 mm)

Number of splines
- anchor housing end ... 23
- suspension arm end ... 24

Drive Shaft joints

	Wheel end	Transmission end
Model R1150	Steel or cast 'BED'	Bendix - Weiss with rubber bellows or metal cover. Spider.
Models R1151 R1152 R1153	Cast 'BED'	Bendix - Weiss with rubber bellows.

Ball joints

Upper (prior to 1969)	Gemmer or Bendix
after 1969	Ehrenreich
Lower (prior to 1969)	Gemmer or Ehrenreich
after 1969	Ehrenreich

Damper type ... Allinquant or De Carbon

Anti-roll Bar ... diameter 0.748 in (19 mm)

Steering angles

King pin inclination (not adjustable)	13° to 15°
Camber angle	0° .15' to 1° positive
Castor angle	1° 40' to 3° 40' (vehicle empty)

Torque wrench settings

	lbf ft	kgf m
Stub axle nut	115	15.9
Damper lower mounting bolt	30	4.1
Lower ball joint nut	35	4.8
Upper ball joint nut	25	3.4
Suspension arm retaining bolts	30	4.1
Steering arm ball joint nut	25	3.4
Hub to disc bolts	45	6.2

Fig.8.1 Layout of the front suspension

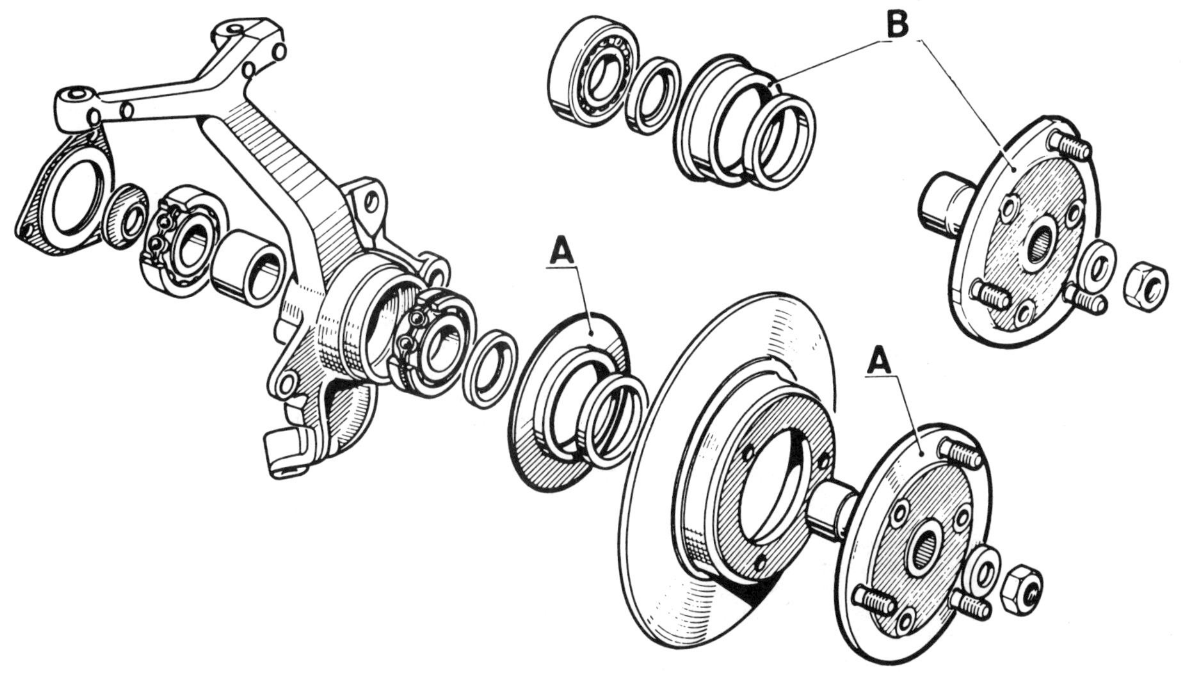

FIG.8.2 THE TWO TYPES OF FRONT HUB ASSEMBLIES

A Circular *B Triangular*

1 General Description

1 The front suspension is of independent type and incorporates double wishbones, torsion bars and hydraulically operated dampers. An anti-roll bar is also fitted as an essential part of the system.
2 Drive from the combined gearbox/transmission unit is transmitted through drive shafts to the two front road wheels. The drive shafts are fitted with constant velocity joints at both ends and these may be of differing type according to the date of vehicle manufacture.
3 The wheel hubs run on inner and outer ballraces and the hubs may be of circular or triangular shape according to date of manufacture. The design of road wheels is dependent upon the type of hub fitted and are not therefore interchangeable.

2 Front Hubs - Removal

1 The front hub/disc assembly may be one of two different designs. The circular type hub is fitted to models R1150 (fabrication No. 160852 onwards) R1151, R1152 and R1153 and the triangular type hub is fitted to models R1150 (fabrication Nos. 1 to 160851). Removal of both types of hub is similar.
2 Jack up the front of the car and remove the road wheel. Chock the rear wheels. Obtain a long steel lever, similar to a tyre lever but longer and stronger.
3 Place this lever between two of the three wheel studs and then place a socket on the stub axle nut.
4 As you press down on the socket extension to undo the nut (considerable force is needed) press down on toe lever in the opposite direction to counterbalance the rotation of the hub. When the nut is loose, remove it.
5 Unscrew and remove the three securing screws from the brake backplate.
6 Remove the brake caliper unit and its bracket as described in Chapter 11.
7 Now unscrew and remove the previously loosened stub axle nut.
8 Using a suitable three legged extractor which will engage beneath the three wheel nuts pull off the hub/disc assembly. Take care not to damage the threaded end of the stub axle during the process. Catch the bearing spacer as the hub is withdrawn.
9 The outer ballrace may be withdrawn with a conventional bearing extractor. The new bearing should be drifted into position using a piece of tube to bear upon its centre track. Ensure that the sealed side of the bearing is towards the hub. (Figs).
10 Before the inner bearing can be removed, the three suspension ball joints must be disconnected. See Section 3, paragraph 7 before commencing. Unscrew each of the ball joint nuts then use an extractor or a pair of forked wedges.
11 Remove the stub axle and then unscrew the three bearing closure plate securing screws.
12 Press out the inner bearing by using two pieces of tube of different diameters.
13 Fit the new inner bearing with its sealed end towards the closure plate. Seal the closure plate with jointing compound before fitting.
14 Refitting is a reversal of removal but line the inside of the hub with high melting point grease before assembly to the stub axle.
15 Remember to fit the distance piece on the hub splines. The hub must be drawn into position on the stub axle using a tool similar to the one shown. On no account must the hub be drifted into position or damage to the drive shafts, their joints, or the differential unit, may result.
16 Tighten the stub axle nut to 115 lbf ft (15.9 kgf m). This is a high tightening torque and the car will have to be lowered to the ground with road wheel replaced and handbrake applied in order to achieve it.

3 Drive Shafts - Identification, Removal and Refitting

Note: *When refitting the drive shaft to the hub, it may be necessary to use the Renault tool AV 236.*

1 Model R1150 vehicles may be fitted with either a steel or cast 'BED' type coupling at the road wheel end of the drive shaft and a 'Bendix - Weiss' type joint at the differential end of the drive shaft having a metal cover or rubber bellows. A 'Spider' type joint may be encountered as an alternative at the differential end.
2 Models R1151, R1152 and R1153 are fitted with the cast 'BED' type coupling at the road wheel end of the drive shaft and a 'Bendix - Weiss' type joint at the differential end.
3 The couplings at the road wheel ends of the drive shafts may be of different types (steel or cast) but the joints at the differential end must be of the same type, identical each side.
4 The 'BED' type joints are not capable of servicing and in the event of wear occurring then the drive shaft must be renewed as an assembly. The 'Bendix - Weiss' and 'Spider' type joints may be serviced and repair kits are available, (Sections 4 and 5).
5 Remove the stub axle nut and washer and remove the brake caliper.
6 Drive out the roll pins from the shafts at the gearbox end, using a suitable drift.
7 With 'Bendix - Weiss' type joints, a restraining clip must be fitted at this stage to prevent dislocation of the joint. Clips similar to (L) as illustrated are supplied with new drive shafts but a similar tool may be made up using worm drive clips and a length or two of thin rod.
8 Disconnect the steering arm and suspension upper ball joints.
9 Pull the drive shaft carefully from its connection with the differential sun wheel and tape the oil seal bearing surface of the shaft to protect it.
10 Using a three legged type extractor push out the drive shaft/stub axle assembly from the hub
11 Refitting is a reversal of dismantling but remember to remove the joint restraining clips once the shaft is fitted, and use two new roll pins and seal them. Finally when refitting is complete, top up the gearbox/transmission.

4 Bendix - Weiss Type Joint - Servicing

1 Servicing of this type of joint is limited to renewal of the rubber bellows. A repair kit is available comprising new bellows, two wormdrive clips and a charge of lubricant.
2 Remove the two crimped clips (1).
3 Pull off the bellows and then mark the position of the two joint yokes relative to each other.
4 Separate the coupling and mark each rubber ball with masking tape (1, 2, 3, 4) so that it will be returned to its original position. Each ball is sized individually for its respective recess.
5 Clean all components and check for wear or damage which if apparent, will necessitate exchange of the complete shaft assembly for a reconditioned unit.
6 Reassembly commences by gripping the shaft in a vice as closely as possible to the joint.
7 Position a piece of rubber tube (0.393 in 10 mm) diameter (2) in the jaws of the shaft yoke jaws (3).
8 Arrange the four rubber balls as shown.
9 Fit the upper yoke (4). Withdraw the rubber tube at the same time pushing the upper yoke downwards to locate the balls.
10 Tape together several lengths of rod (at one end) to provide a guide for fitting the new rubber bellows.
11 Refitting is basically a reversal of dismantling but remember to remove the joint restraining clips once the shaft is fitted, and use two new roll pins and seal them. Finally when refitting is complete, top up the gearbox/transmission.
12 Fit the new worm drive clip (supplied) complete with its two half shells and tighten the clip until the ends of the shells make contact with each other. Pull back the lip of the bellows and pour in the charge of lubricant supplied. A rod should be used to prise the lip of the bellows as it will also serve to allow air to

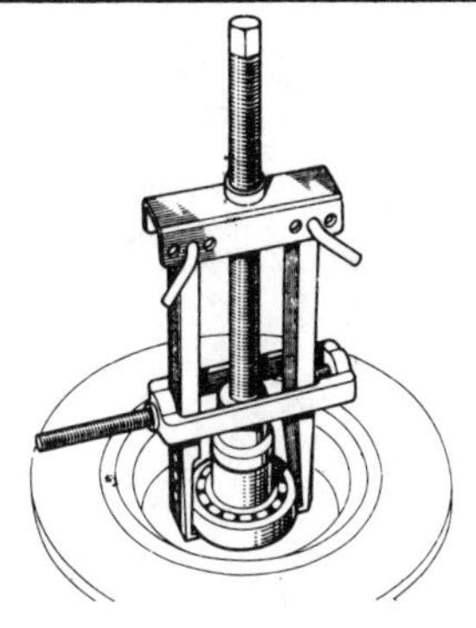

2.9A Extracting the outer hub bearing

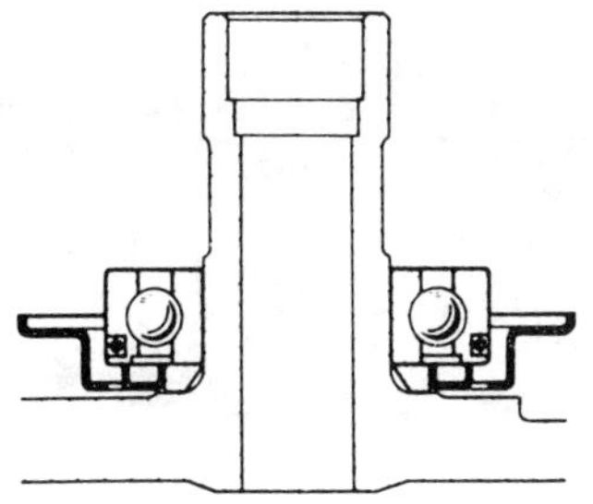

2.9B Correct orientation of the hub bearing

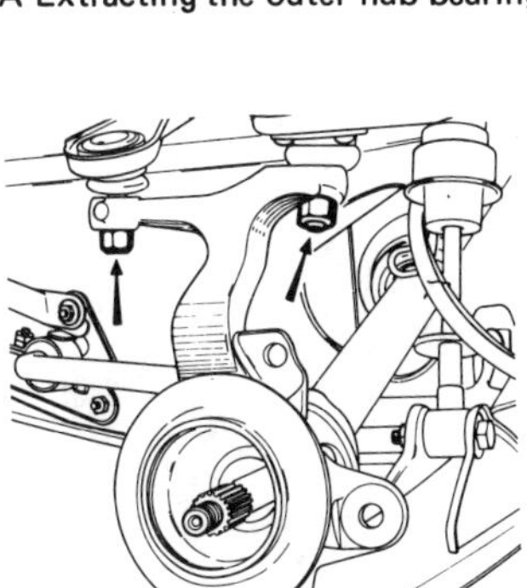

2.10A The three suspension ball joint nuts (one side only)

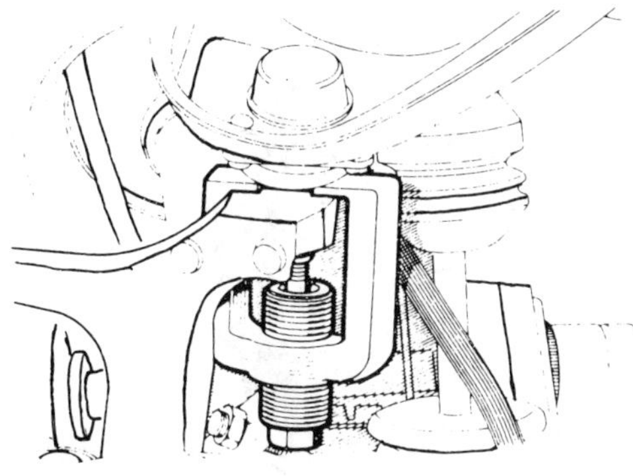

2.10B Using a ball joint extractor on the upper connection

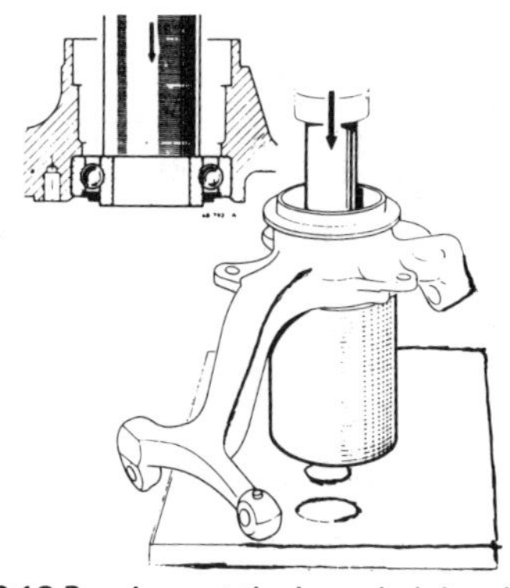

2.12 Pressing out the inner hub bearing

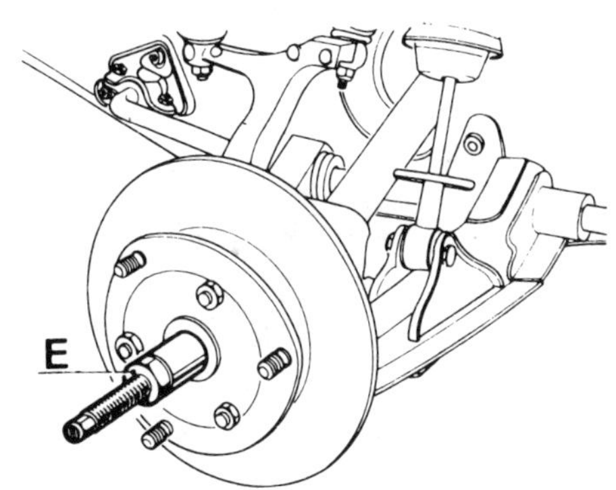

2.15 Fitting the hub/disc assembly to the stub axle using tool AV 236.

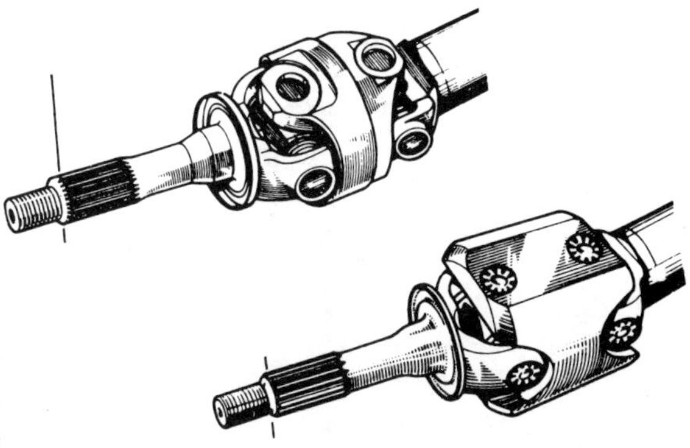

3.1A The two different types of drive shaft joints (road wheel end)

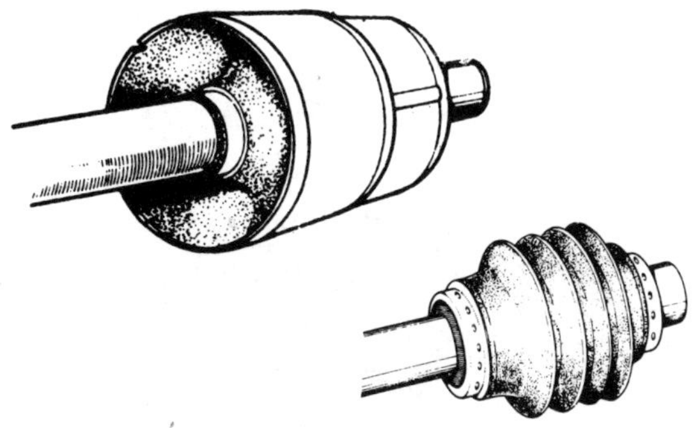

3.1B Bendix-Weiss drive shaft joints

3.1C Spider type drive shaft joint

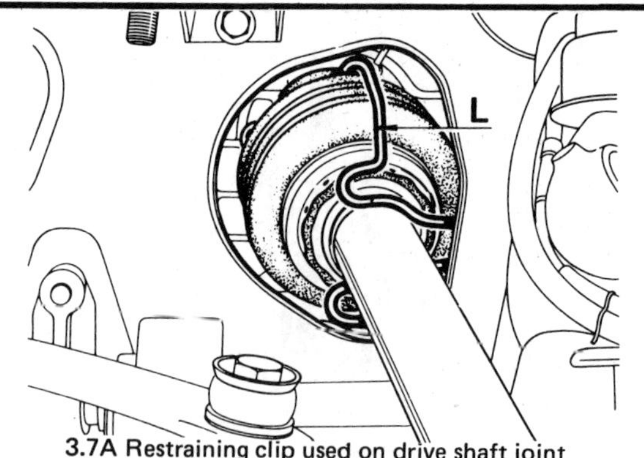

3.7A Restraining clip used on drive shaft joint

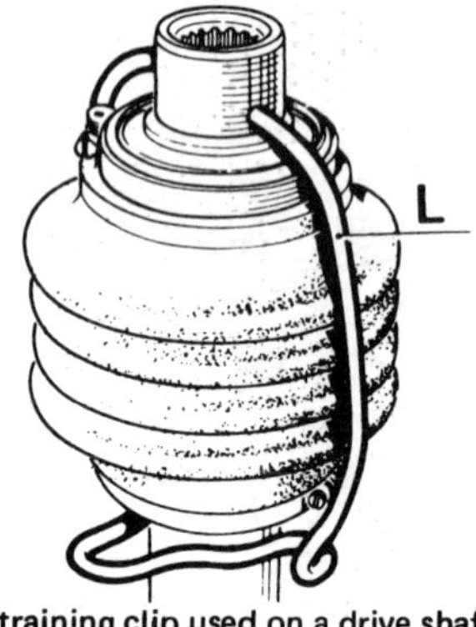

3.7B Restraining clip used on a drive shaft joint

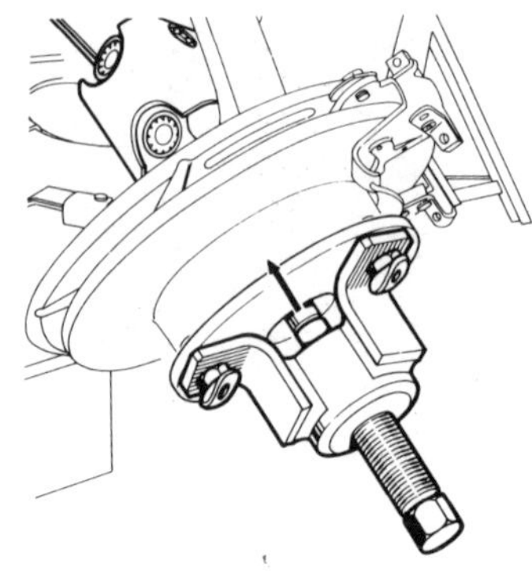

3.10 Pushing out the drive shaft/stub axle from the hub

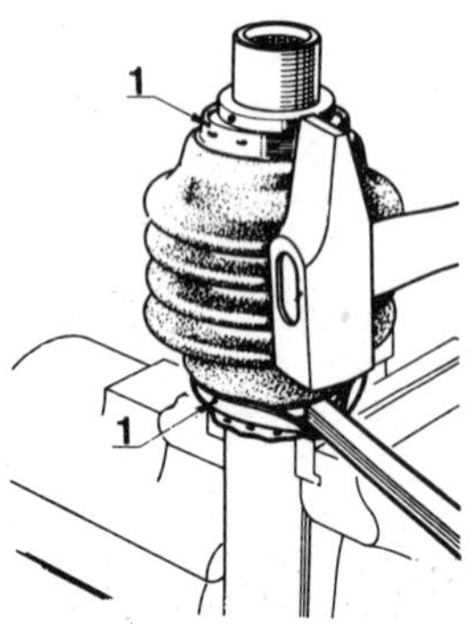

4.2 Removing a crimped retaining clip from a drive shaft joint bellows

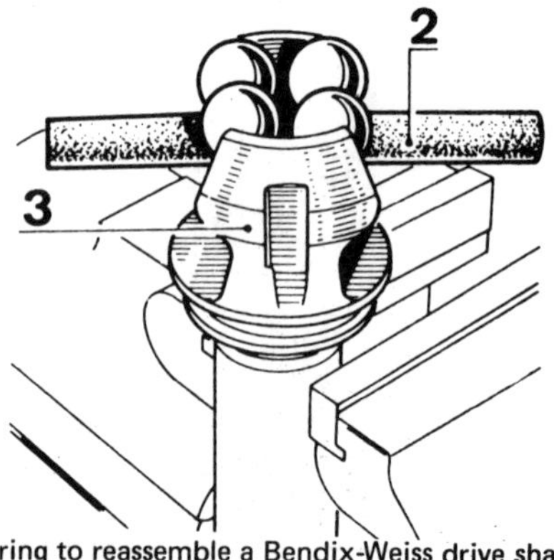

4.6 Preparing to reassemble a Bendix-Weiss drive shaft joint 2 temporary rubber tube. 3 Yoke.

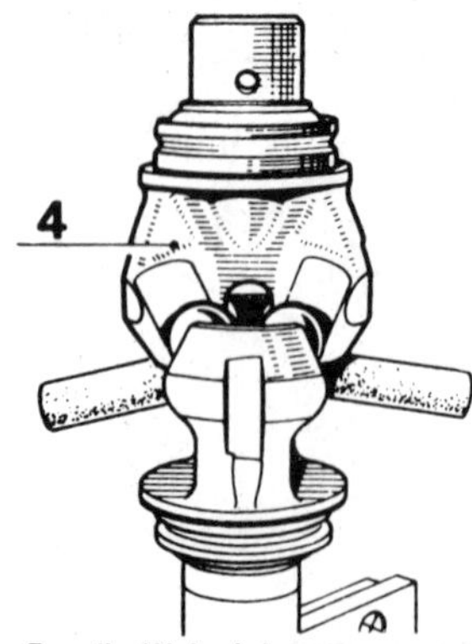

4.9 Pressing the Bendix-Weiss joint components into engagement. 4 Upper yoke.

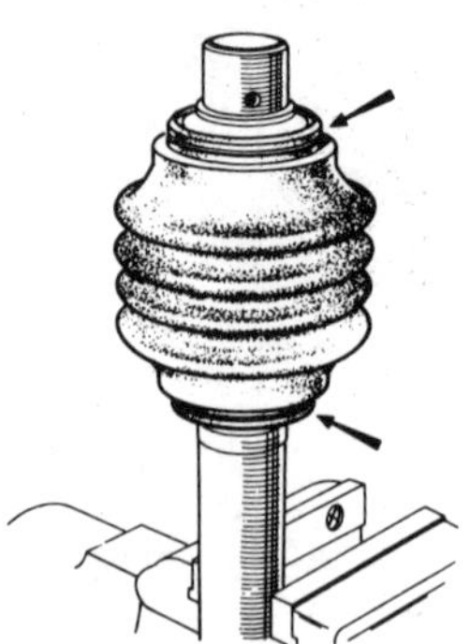

4.11 Drive shaft joint bellows lips correctly located

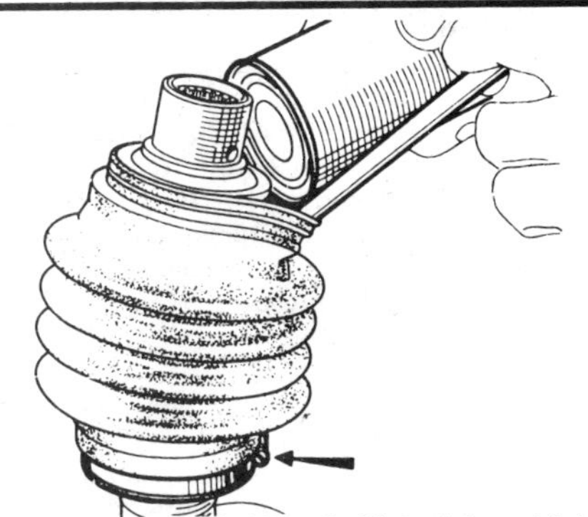

4.12 Charging a reassembled Bendix-Weiss joint with lubricant

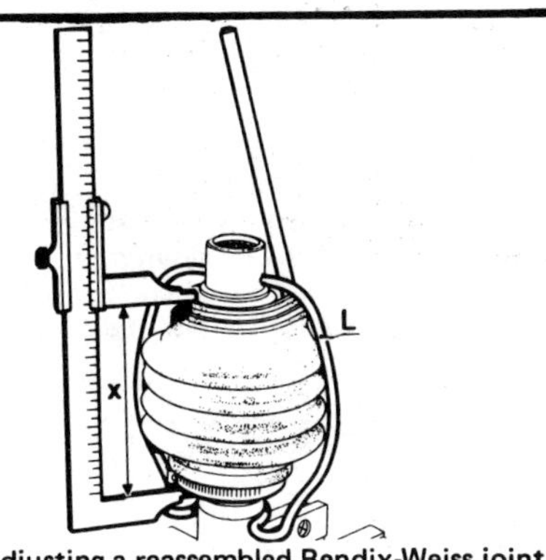

4.13 Adjusting a reassembled Bendix-Weiss joint

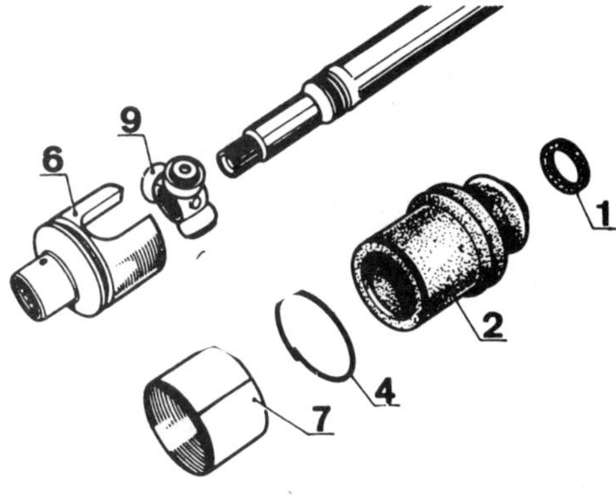

5.1 Components of a Spider type drive shaft joint. 1 Ring. 2 Bellows. 4 Circlips. 6 Yoke. 7 Cover. 9 Spider.

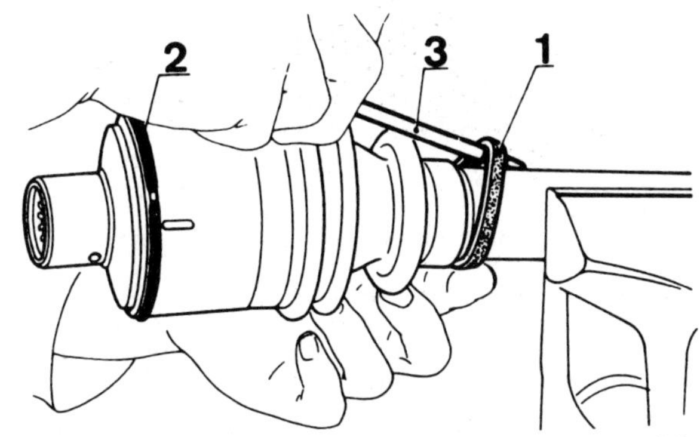

5.2 Dismantling a Spider type joint. 1 Rubber ring. 2 Clip. 3 Removal tool.

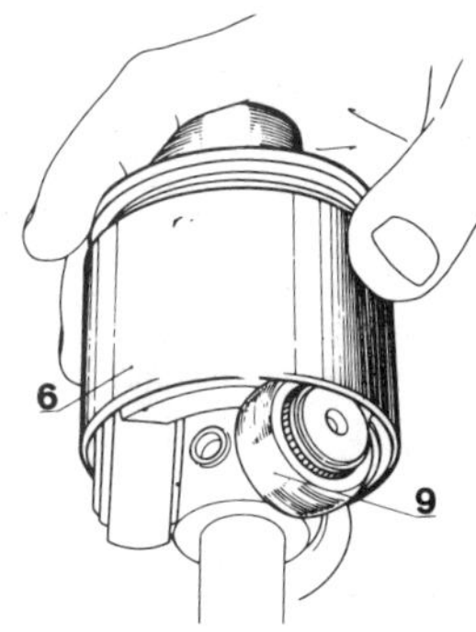

5.4 Pulling the Spider joint apart. 6 Yoke. 9 Needle roller cages.

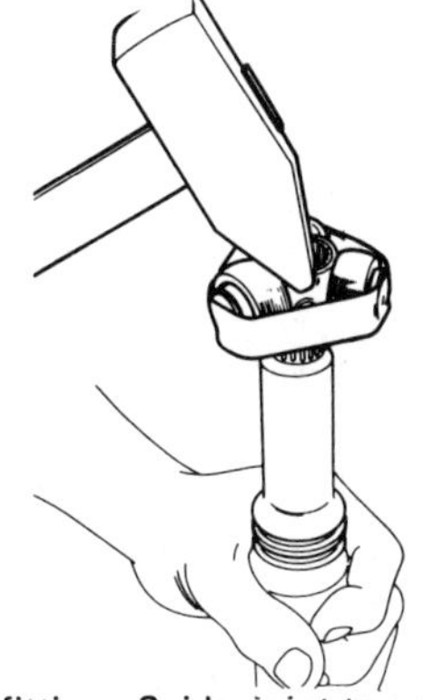

5.7 Refitting a Spider joint to a drive shaft

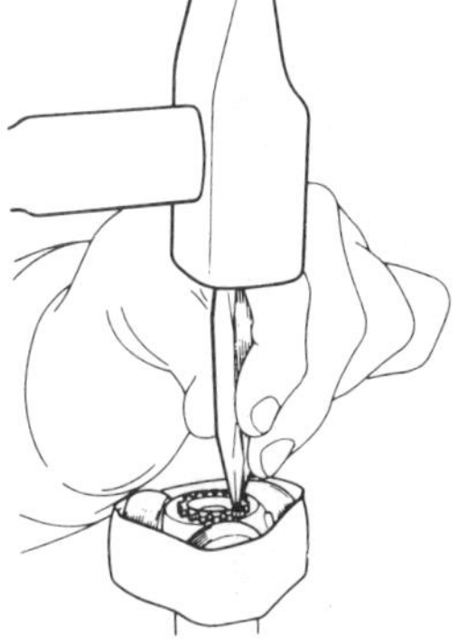

5.8 Locking a Spider joint by staking

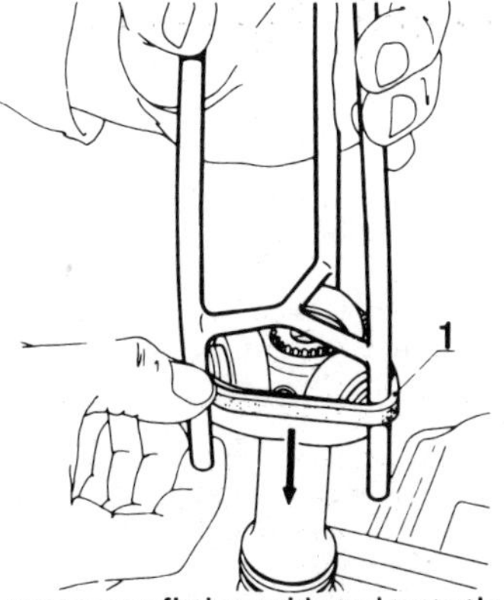

5.9A Using a temporary fitting guide to locate the Spider joint Rubber ring (1)

escape during the next operation.

13 At this stage fit the joint restraining clip (L) and compress the joint and then tighten the restraining clip to ensure a machine face to machine face measurement (X) of $4^7/_{16}$ in (113 mm). Fit the remaining wormdrive clip and half shells. Leave the joint restraining clip in position until the drive shaft is refitted to the car.

5 'Spider' Type Joint - Servicing

1 This type of drive shaft joint is capable of more extensive servicing than the type described in the preceding Section. Repair kits are available as three separate items (i) bellows kit (ii) yoke kit (iii) spider assembly kit.

2 Place the drive shaft horizontally in a vice, and prise off the ring (1) and clip (2) using a smooth pointed rod (3).

3 Cut the rubber bellows lengthwise and remove them.

4 Pull the yoke (6) from the spider. Do not allow the roller cages (9) to fall from their respective trunnions as they are matched to them individually. Wind masking tape round them to retain them.

5 Clean the grease fromthe joint components by wiping with a rag, never wash the parts in a solvent.

6 Check all components for wear or scoring and renew as necessary.

7 Remove the spider from the drive shaft by pressing it off. Refit the new spider (head chamfer towards shaft) by using a plastic or copper faced mallet. Drive it on until the chamfer just touches the shoulder on the shaft.

8 Using a fine punch, peen the splines at three equal points to a circle to lock the spider hub.

9 Make up a tripod type of guide from rods and slide on the ring (1) and the new bellows taking care to locate the bellows lips in the driveshaft grooves.

10 Apply the three sachets supplied with the repair kit, one into the bellows, two into the yoke. Remove the retaining tape from the roller bearing cages and smear the ends of the trunnions with grease.

11 Position the yoke opposite to the spider. Slide the bellows over the yoke, using a rod as shown to facilitate the operation. (Figs).

12 Fit the new circlip (4) supplied.

13 Use a rod (3) to permit any trapped air to escape and then compress or expand the joint to provide a measurement (A) of 5¾ in (146 mm) between the ends of the rubber bellows when correctly located in their grooves. Remove the rod and locate the rubber ring over the bellows.

6 Torsion Bars - Identification, Removal, Refitting

1 The torsion bars fitted to the left and right hand sides of the vehicle have different internal pre-load characteristics and must not be interchanged.

2 Place the car over a pit or raise it securely on jacks or blocks and support the side from which the torsion bar is to be removed on stands or blocks.

3 Remove the torsion bar cover plate and then from inside the vehicle, unlock bolt (1) and turn the cam (2) towards the outside of the car in order to return the cam to zero.

4 A splined tool will now be required (SUS.234) or one may be made up from an old torsion bar, to engage in the anchor housing socket to counterbalance the torsional effect of the bar. (Fig).

5 Remove the setscrews (4).

6 From beneath the car remove bolts (5) and (6).

7 At the torsion bar anchor housing end, make an alignment mark on the torsion bar splines (with chalk or grease pencil) to coincide with the mark on the anchor housing.

8 Release the tension and tool from the torsion bar and remove the anchor housing. Now check whether the mark just made on the torsion bar splines is in alignment with the punch mark on the end of bar or if offset, in which direction and by how many splines. Make a note of this for refitting purposes.

9 At the suspension arm end of the torsion bar, pull the bar forward through the splined socket but do not disengage it. Make an alignment mark on the torsion bar splines in a similar manner to that described in the preceding paragraph, and withdraw the torsion bar from the suspension arm.

10 Before refitting, smear the ends of the torsion bar with recommended grease.

11 Fit the torsion bar to the suspension arm with the marks made prior to dismantling, correctly aligned.

12 Fit the anchor housing to the other end of the torsion bar with the marks made prior to dismantling in alignment. Remember to offset the splines in the correct direction if they were originally set in this way.

13 Offer up the anchor housing so that the stud (1) slides into hole (2). Fit on the washer and nut, finger tight only.

14 Using the special tool or one made up from an old torsion bar, wind up the anchor housing against the torsion bar tension so that the anchor housing can be bolted to the crossmember (two setscrews inside car, one bolt below).

15 Remove the splined tool, check that the cover plate gasket is in good order and refit the cover plate.

16 A check should be made on the underbody height and adjust ment carried out if necessary as described in Section 7.

7 Underbody Height - Adjustment

1 The maintenance of the correct vehicle body height, overall and from side to side is dependent upon the correct setting of the torsion bars.

2 Underbody height measurement must only be carried out with the vehicle unladen but with a full fuel tank, correctly inflated tyres and standing on level ground.

3 The measurements H1 and H2 must be taken between the ground and the lower surface of the side members in line with the road wheel centres. See Fig.8.4

4 The correct underbody heights, according to vehicle type are listed below the figure and a tolerance is permissible, when taking measurements of between +3/8 and 5/8 in (10 - 15 mm). Variations in height are also specified where the vehicle is to be operated on poor road conditions.

5 Whenever underbody height adjustment is carried out, the brake limiter valve will also require adjustment as described in Chapter 11.

6 Two methods of adjusting the underbody height are employed, initially by cams and where the range of cam adjustment is insufficient (as set) by offsetting the bar and socket splines (differential spline method).

7 Refer to Fig. 6.3., unlock screw (1) and rotate the cam (2) towards the centre line of the vehicle to increase the underbody height or vica versa.

8 It will normally be essential to adjust the rear torsion bars in conjunction with the front. Release the locknut from the bolt (1) and turn the bolt/cam assembly in the direction of the arrow to increase the underbody height or vica versa. Retighten the locknut after adjustment is complete.

9 The differential spline method of adjusting underbody height is based upon the fact that there are a different number of splines on the opposite ends of the torsion bars (front 23 and 24, rear 28 and 30). A front or rear torsion bar is fitted to the vehicle by offsetting its splined ends in both the anchor housing and suspension arm by an equal number of splines and in the same direction. By offsetting the torsion bar one spline in either direction at each of its ends, this will have the effect of either raising or lowering the body by: FRONT 1/8 in (3 mm) for normal road surface settings and 5/32 in (4 mm) for poor road surface settings, REAR 15/64 in (6 mm).

10 Always adjust the front and rear torsion bar differential spline settings as pairs, left and right in order to maintain equal torsion loads.

11 Removal of the anchor housing, and torsion bars to adjust the front spline differential is described in the preceding Section.

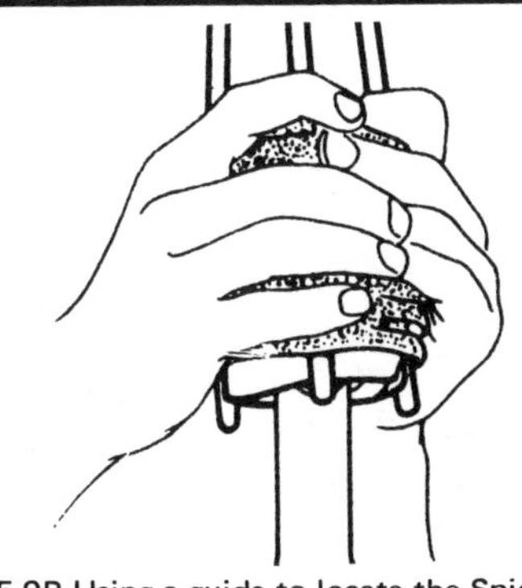

5.9B Using a guide to locate the Spider joint bellows

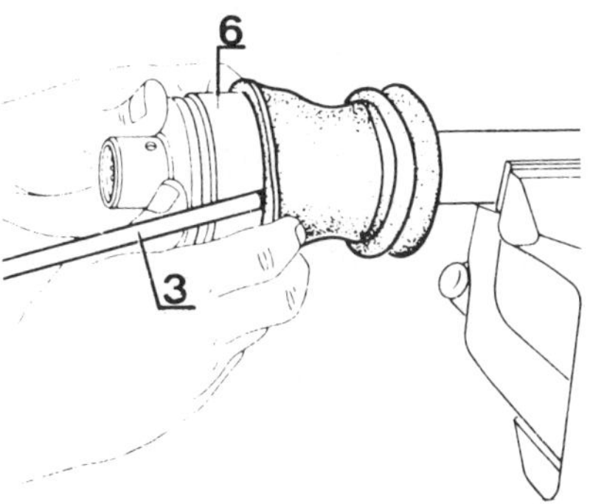

5.11 Using a rod as a guide to fit the Spider joint bellows. 3 tool. 6 cover

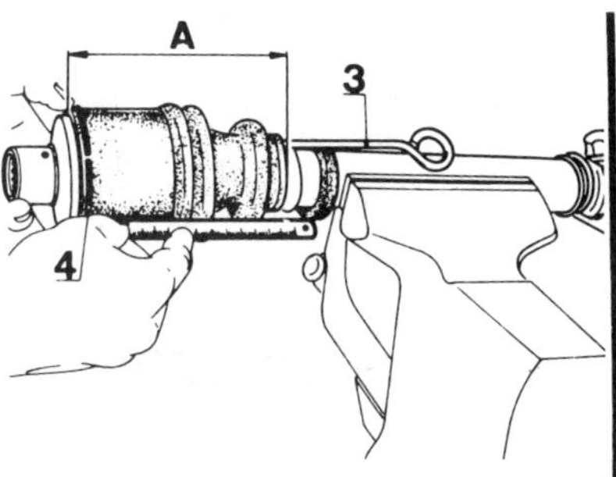

5.12 Adjusting the Spider joint after reassembly. (3) rod to release trapped air (4) circlip (A) 5¾ in (146 mm)

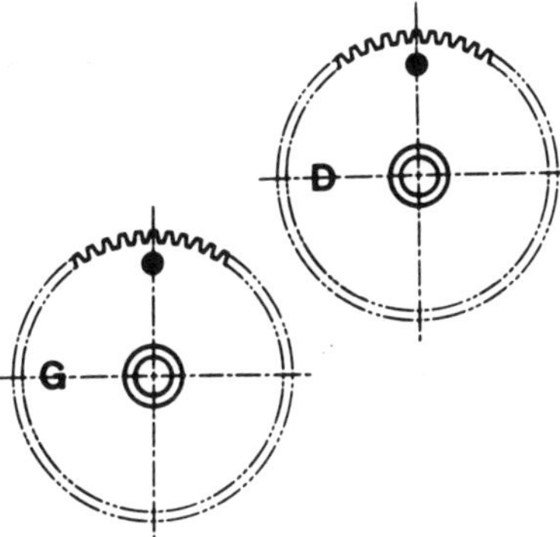

6.1A Front torsion bar identification marks (early vehicles)

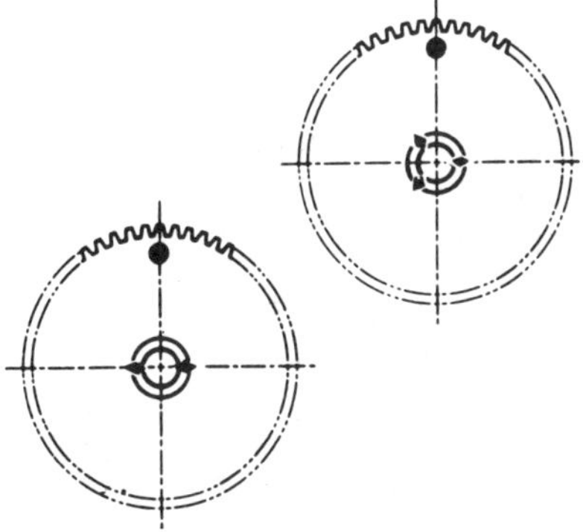

6.1B Front torsion bar identification marks (later vehicles)

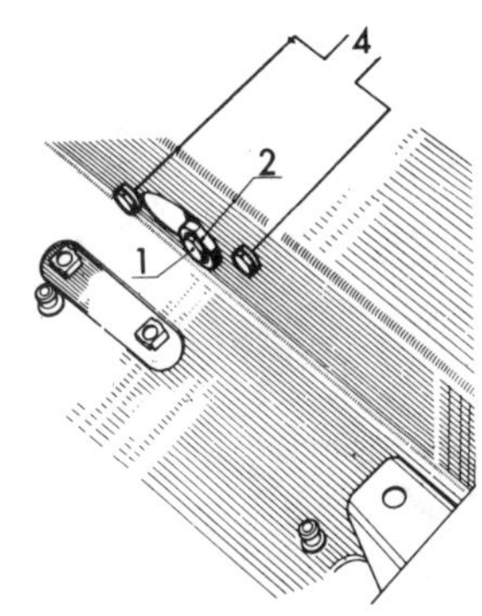

6.3 Torsion bar anchor housing bolts. 1 Lockbolt. 2 Cam. 4 Housing securing bolts.

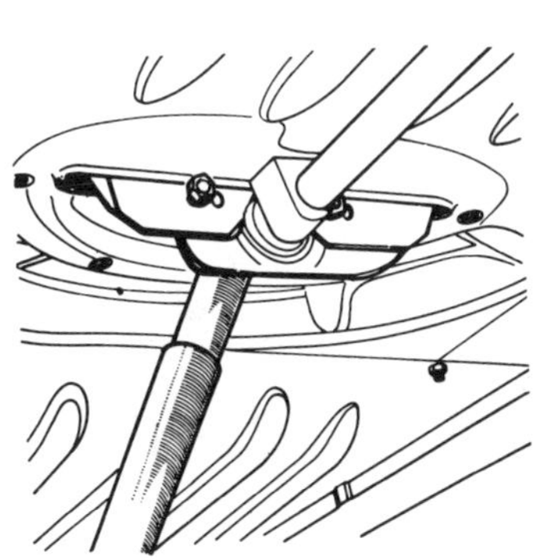

6.4 Counter balancing the torsion bar with a tool

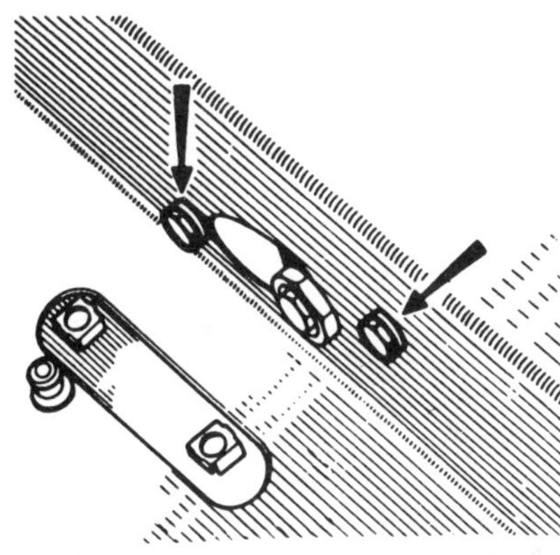

6.6 Torsion bar anchor housing bracket bolts

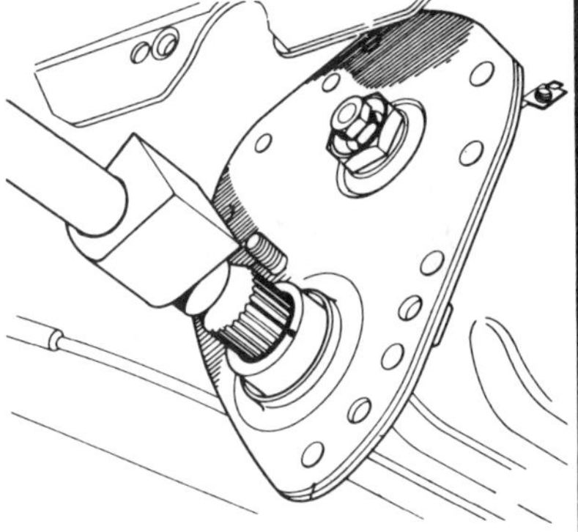

6.7 Torsion bar and anchor housing rocket alignment marks

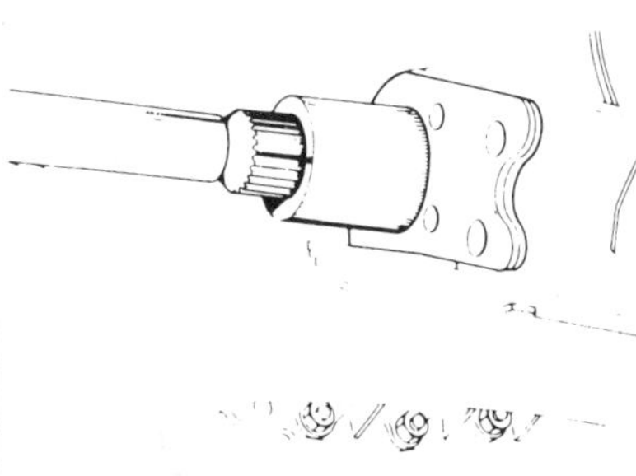

6.9 Torsion bar and suspension arm socket alignment marks

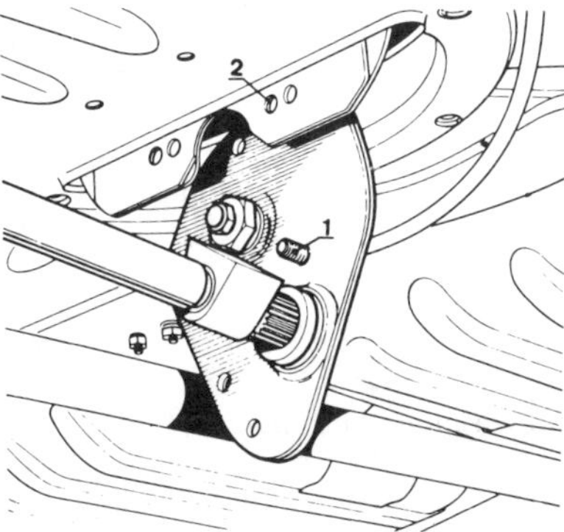

6.13 Locating the anchor housing. (1) stud (2) stud hole

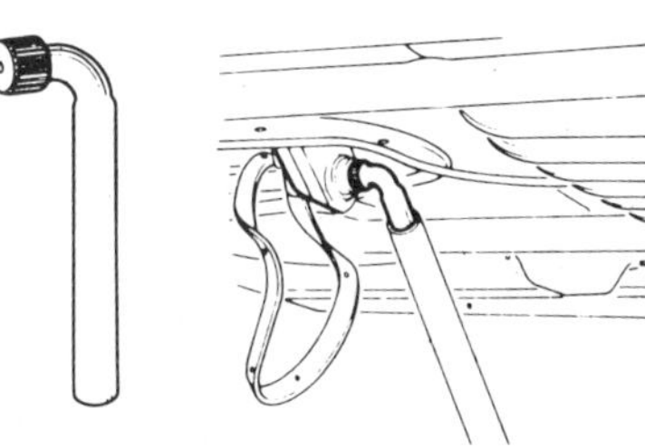

6.14 Winding up the torsion bar anchor housing

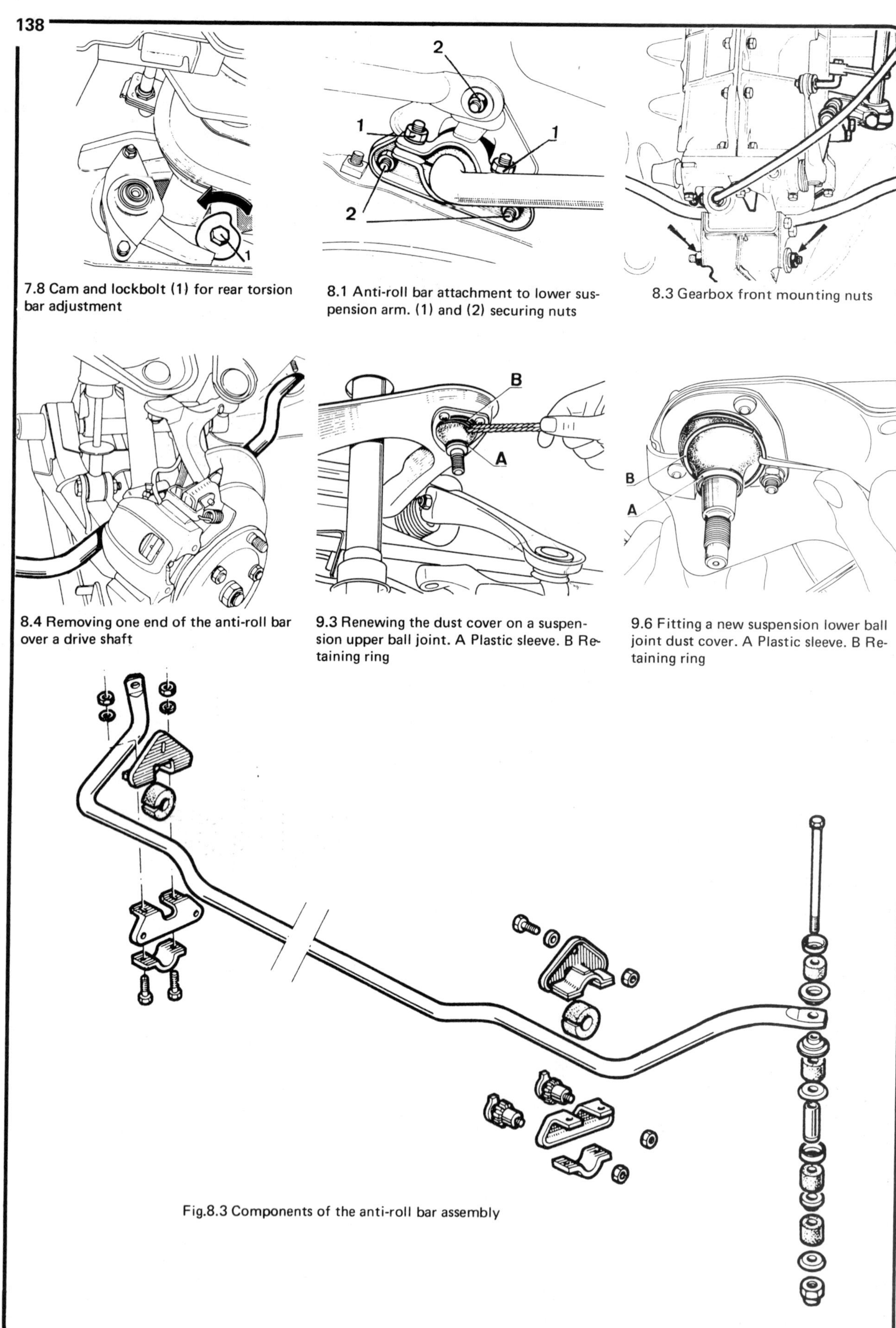

7.8 Cam and lockbolt (1) for rear torsion bar adjustment

8.1 Anti-roll bar attachment to lower suspension arm. (1) and (2) securing nuts

8.3 Gearbox front mounting nuts

8.4 Removing one end of the anti-roll bar over a drive shaft

9.3 Renewing the dust cover on a suspension upper ball joint. A Plastic sleeve. B Retaining ring

9.6 Fitting a new suspension lower ball joint dust cover. A Plastic sleeve. B Retaining ring

Fig.8.3 Components of the anti-roll bar assembly

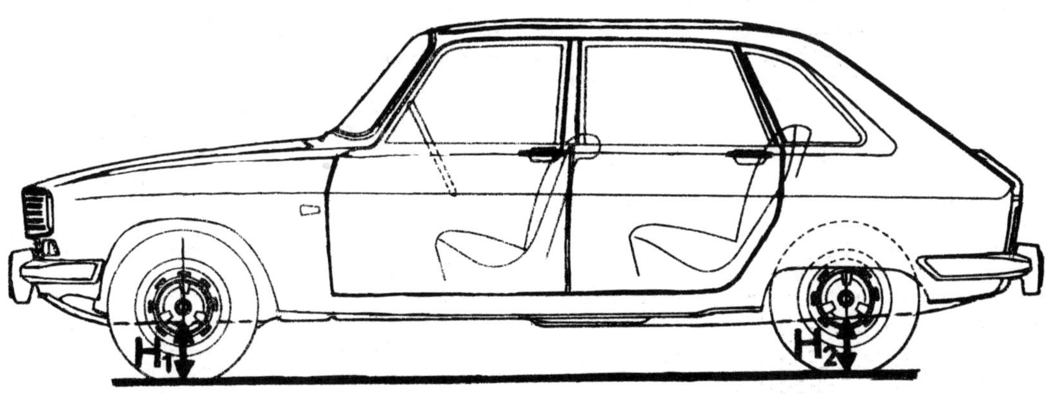

FIG.8.4 MEASUREMENT DIAGRAM FOR UNDERBODY HEIGHT

Normal Roads

Vehicle type	Tyre fitment	Front bar diameter	Rear bar diameter	Front H 1	Rear H 2
R1150	*145 x 14 Radial*	*17.4 mm (0.685 in)*	*21.6 mm (0.850 in)*	*200 mm (7 7/8 in)*	*260 mm (10 1/4 in)*
R1150 R1153	*145 x 14 Radial*	*17.4 mm (0.685 in)*	*22.5 mm (0.886 in)*	*200 mm (7 7/8 in)*	*260 mm (10 1/4 in)*
R1150 R1152	*155 x 14 Radial*	*17.4 mm (0.685 in)*	*22.5 mm (0.886 in)*	*210 mm (8 5/16 in)*	*270 mm (10 11/16 in)*
R1151	*155 x 14 Radial*	*17.4 mm (0.685 in)*	*22.5 mm (0.886 in)*	*195 mm (7 11/16 in)*	*255 mm (10 1/16 in)*

Vehicle type	Tyre fitment	Front bar diameter	Rear bar diameter	Front H 1	Rear H 2	Special versions
R1150 R1153	*155 x 14 Radial*	*18.2 mm (0.717 in)*	*22.5 mm (0.886 in)*	*210 mm (8 5/16 in)*	*270 mm (10 11/16 in)*	*241–242–246–250–801*
R1150	*155 x 14 Radial*	*18.2 mm (0.717 in)*	*22.5 mm (0.886 in)*	*225 mm (8 7/8 in)*	*285 mm (11 1/4 in)*	
R1150	*145 x 14 Radial*	*18.2 mm (0.717 in)*	*22.5 mm (0.886 in)*	*220 mm (8 11/16 in)*	*280 mm (11 1/16 in)*	
R1151	*155 x 14 Radial*	*18.2 mm (0.717 in)*	*22.5 mm (0.886 in)*	*220 mm (8 11/16 in)*	*280 mm (11 1/16 in)*	
R1151	*155 x 14 Radial*	*18.2 mm (0.717 in)*	*22.5 mm (0.886 in)*	*195 mm (7 11/16 in)*	*255 mm 10 1/16 in)*	*205–241–242–246–250–801*
R1152	*155 x 14 Radial*	*18.2 mm (0.717 in)*	*22.5 mm (0.886 in)*	*210 mm (8 5/16 in)*	*270 mm (10 11/16 in)*	*240*

Special versions

Vehicle type	Tyre fitment	Front bar diameter	Rear bar diameter	Front H 1	Rear H 2
R1150 R1153	*155 x 14 Radial*	*18.2 mm (0.717 in)*	*22.5 mm (0.886 in)*	*225 mm (18 7/8 in)*	*305 mm (12 in)*
R1151	*155 x 14 Radial*	*18.2 mm (0.717 in)*	*22.5 mm (0.886 in)*	*220 mm (18 11/16 in)*	*300 mm (11 13/16 in)*

For rear torsion bars, refer to the next Chapter.

8 Anti-Roll Bar - Removal, Servicing, Refitting

1 Detach the anti-roll bar at each of its ends from the lower suspension arms. Split the mounting bush by removing the nuts (1) and then remove the bush housing nuts (2)
2 Remove the right hand front road wheel.
3 Remove the two nuts and washers from the gearbox/transmission front mounting and then jack up the gearbox until it just touches the steering crossmember.
4 Push the anti-roll bar out towards the right hand side so that its end passes over the drive shaft;
5 The rubber half bushes should be renewed if they show signs of perishing or have deteriorated due to the presence of oil. When locating the new rubber bushes ensure that their slots are in alignment with those of the retaining housing;
6 Refitting is a reversal of removal but note particularly the sequence of components (Fig 8.3).

9 Suspension Ball Joints - Dust Cover Renewal

1 It is essential to regularly inspect the condition of the ball joint rubber dust covers. Any split in them will allow lubricant to leak out and dust to enter, both of which will cause rapid wear in the joint.
2 To renew the dust cover on an upper ball joint, jack up the car, remove the road wheel, unscrew the balljoint nut and disconnect the joint by means of an extractor or forked wedges.
3 Remove the worn dust cover and wipe the joint clean. Half fill the new dust cover with heavy type grease and then fit the plastic sleeve A to it. Slide the dust cover into position and then using a piece of cord, as shown, locate the retaining ring (B). (Fig).
4 Reconnect the ball joint stud to the stub axle carrier, refit the nut and tighten to 25 lbf ft (3.4 kgf m).
5 The lower ball joint should be disconnected after removal of the drive shaft as described in Section 3.
6 Removal and refitting the dust cover is similar to the procedure described for the upper ball joint.
7 Reconnect the ball joint stud and tighten the ball joint nut to 35 lbf ft (4.8 kgf m). Check the front wheel track as described in Chapter 10.

10 Suspension Upper Ball Joint - Renewal

1 Disconnect the ball joint as described in the preceding Section, also the steering arm ball joint.
2 Drill out the retaining rivets.
3 Fit the new ball joint using the bolts supplied and with 1969 model vehicles only, fit the support plate inside the suspension arm. Note the position of the bolt heads, on the dust cover side of the arm.
4 Reconnect the ball joint and tighten the nut to 25 lbf ft (3.4 kgf m). Check the steering geometry (Section 15) the track adjustment and the steering box shimming both described in Chapter 10.

11 Suspension Lower Ball Joint - Renewal

1 Jack up the car on the side concerned.
2 Remove the brake caliper (Chapter 11).
3 Disconnect the steering arm ball joint and the upper suspension ball joint but leave them in position in their eyes with their stud nuts screwed on a few threads.
4 Remove the drive shaft (Section 3).
5 Disconnect the lower ball joint using an extractor or forked wedges.
6 Drill out the ball joint securing rivets.
7 Fit the new ball joint, using the bolts supplied. Ensure that the bolt heads are on the dust cover side.
8 Reconnection is a reversal of disconnection but tighten the ball joint nut to 35 lbf ft (4.8 kgf m) and top up the oil level in the gearbox after the drive shaft has been refitted.
9 Check the castor angle (Section 15) the steering box shimming and the track.

12 Upper Suspension Arm - Removal and Refitting

1 Jack up the vehicle on the appropriate side.
2 Jack up the lower suspension arm to counteract the action of the torsion bar.
3 Disconnect the damper top mounting, disconnect the upper ball joint and unscrew and remove the two suspension arm securing nuts.
4 Where the suspension arm swivel bushes are worn, the complete suspension arm assembly must be renewed.
5 Refitting is a reversal of removal but the castor angle, track and steering box height must be checked on completion.

13 Lower Suspension Arm - Removal and Refitting

1 Jack up the appropriate side of the vehicle.
2 Remove the drive shaft connecting roll pins from the transmission sunwheel, Section 3.
3 Remove the torsion bar, Section 6.
4 Remove the damper bottom mounting pin and the anti-roll bar connecting bolt.
5 Disconnect the lower ball joint.
6 Unscrew the lower suspension arm securing bolts and pull the suspension arm outwards away from the chassis taking care not to let the drive shaft drop from engagement with the transmission sunwheels.
7 Using a suitable three legged puller, press the drive shaft stub axle sufficiently far from the hub disc assembly to permit the lower suspension arm to be freed from the stub axle carrier.
8 Refitting is a reversal of removal but ensure that any castor angle shims are replaced behind the suspension arm swivel bar.
9 Check the underbody height (Section 7), the brake limiter valve (Chapter 11) the steering box shimming and the track.

14 Dampers - Testing and Renewal

1 The front dampers are of double acting hydraulic telescopic type.
2 A wide variety of models has been fitted according to the anticipated road usage and the suspension rating. It is strongly recommended that only a damper similar to the original is fitted as a replacement.
3 Removal of a damper must not be carried out with a road wheel hanging free and the car jacked up, but only removed when the weight of the vehicle is on the suspension.
4 Remove the upper mounting locknut and retaining nut, noting carefully the positioning of the rubber buffers and cups. (Figs).
5 Compress the damper rod to withdraw the upper mounting from the body frame and then remove the bottom fixing bolt and remove the damper.
6 The dampers cannot be serviced and must be renewed as an assembly if they show signs of fluid leakage, or they do not offer any resistance when extended and contracted in a vertical attitude, rapidly, ten or twelve times in succession.
7 Refitting a damper is a reversal of removal but grease the bottom fixing bolt before inserting and do not overcompress the upper mounting rubbers.

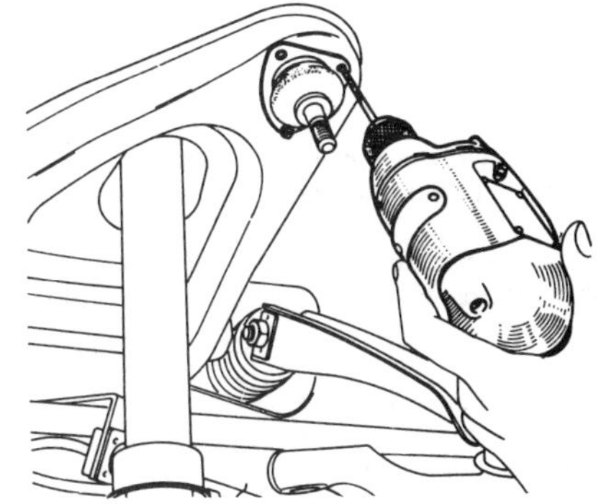

10.2 Drilling out the retaining rivets on an upper ball joint

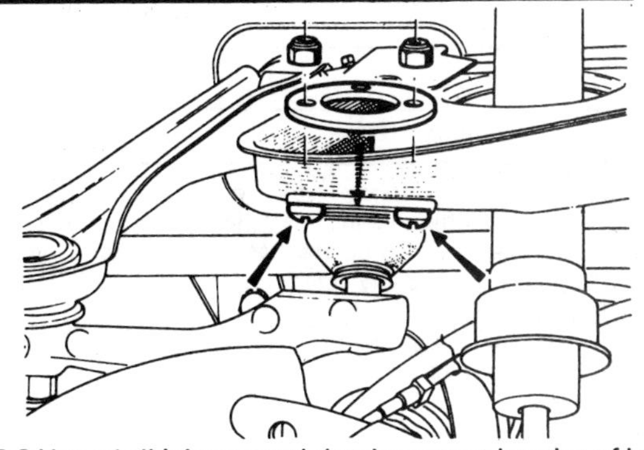

10.3 Upper ball joint renewal showing correct location of bolt heads and support plate (1969 models only).

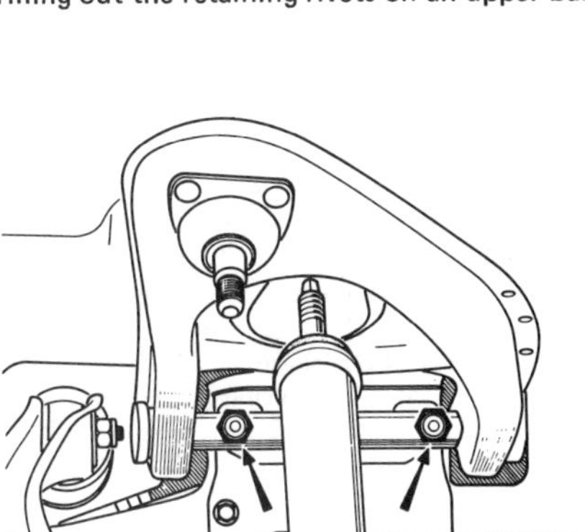

12.3 Damper upper attachment and upper suspension arm securing nuts

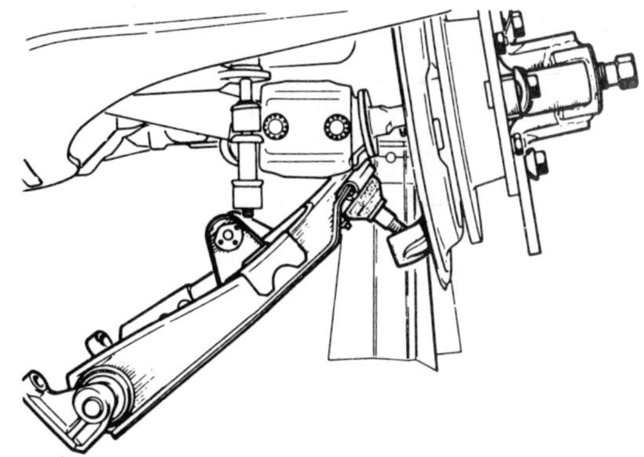

13.7 Pressing the stub axle from the hub assembly to free the suspension lower arm

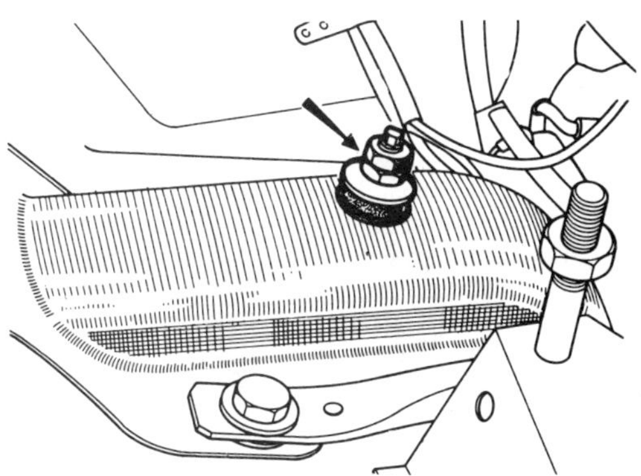

14.4A Damper upper mounting

14.4B Damper upper mounting bushes and cups

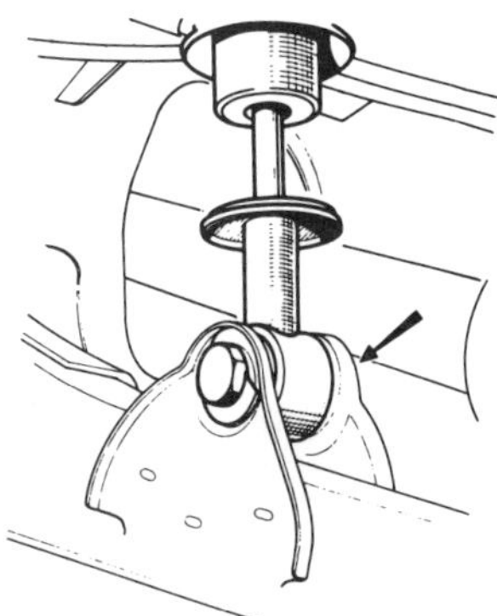

14.5 Damper bottom fixing bolt

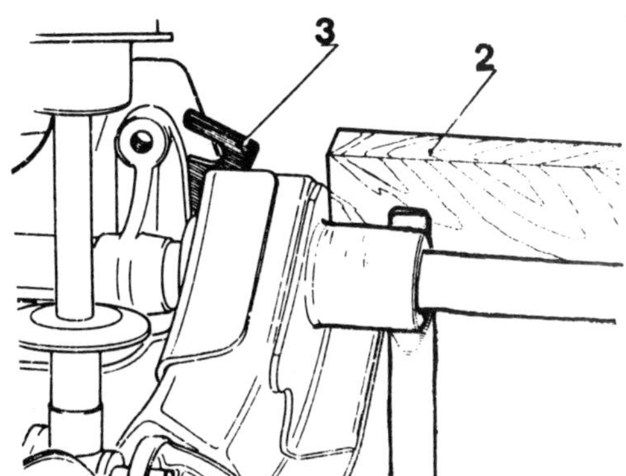

15.8 Lower suspension arm bracket. 2 Wooden block as lever. 3 Shim.

15 Suspension Geometry

1 The term 'steering geometry' refers to the layout and certain specified angles of the steering mechanism and components. These are designed to provide the best possible handling and steering characteristics and any deterioration in them will require immediate investigation.

2 Before checking the geometry of the front axle and suspension, test or check the following:

Tyre pressures
Buckled road wheels
Play in the ball joints
End float in the hub bearings
The efficiency of the dampers
The condition of the suspension rubber bushes
Underbody height
Wheel balance

3 The three angles to be considered are:

Camber which is the angle of inclination from the vertical (when viewed from the front of the car) of the front road wheel centre lines. Positive camber is the angle in degrees that the wheels are inclined outwards at the top. If they are inclined inwards then the camber is negative.

4 Castor is the angle between the steering axis and the vertical when viewed from the side of the car. The angle is positive when the axis is inclined rearwards at the top.

5 The king pin inclination is the angle between the vertical and a line drawn between the upper and lower ball joint centres and about which the wheel pivots for directional control of the vehicle.

6 The camber and castor angles are capable of adjustment by the fitting of shims but the king pin inclination cannot be altered.

7 It is preferable to have all steering angles checked on modern service station equipment but a reasonably accurate measurement of the camber angle can be carried out by using a plumb line held against a line marked vertically on a piece of board held edge on to the top and bottom road wheel rims. The angle of deviation of the fixed line from the plumb line is the camber angle. The correct angle is between 0° 15' and 1o positive. Adjustment can be carried out to obtain the correct setting by inserting or removing shims between the upper suspension arm and the wing cowl side.

8 The correct castor angle is 1° 40' to 3° 40' positive and may be adjusted if necessary by inserting or removing shims behind the lower suspension arm brackets. To carry out this operation, do not remove the securing bolts but only unscrew them sufficiently far to enable the shims to be inserted after prising the bracket away from the body frame.

9 After adjustment of the steering angles, check the steering box shimming and the track adjustment as described in Chapter 10.

16 Fault Finding

Cause	Trouble	Remedy
Symptom WHEEL WOBBLE AND VIBRATION		
General wear or damage	Worn hub bearings	Renew
	Loose wheel bolts	Tighten
	Worn suspension arm bushes	Renew
	Drive shafts bent or out of balance	Renew
	Drive shaft couplings worn	Repair or renew according to type
	Front road wheels out of balance	Balance statically and dynamically.
Symptom POOR ROADHOLDING AND CORNERING		
General wear or damage	Dampers unserviceable	Renew
	Torsion bars and underbody height incorrectly adjusted	Adjust by cam or differential spline method.
Symptom SENSITIVE TO ROAD CAMBER		
General wear or damage	Wear in upper or lower suspension arm ball joints	Renew
	Wear in hub bearings	Renew

Chapter 9 Rear suspension and hubs

Contents

Specifications

Suspension type ... Independent by two parallel torsion bars and hydraulic double acting dampers

Torsion bars

Vehicle type	Tyres Fitted	Rear bar diameter	
R1150	145 x 14 Radial	21.6 mm 0.0850 in	See also underbody height adjustment tables, Chapter 8.
R1150 R1153	145 x 14 Radial	22.5 mm 0.886 in	
R1150	155 x 14 Radial	22.5 mm 0.886 in	
R1151	155 x 14 Radial	22.5 mm 0.886 in	

Suspension arms ... Welded steel pressings

Hinge bearings

at roadwheel end ... early models - rubber bushes
later models - needle roller

at chassis centre ... 'fluid bloc' flexible type

R1150 Vehicle No 1 to No 39 644 inclusive	R1150 Vehicle No 39 645 to No 221 330 inclusive	R1150 from Vehicle No 221 331 - R1151 - R1152 - R1153
Rear bearings fitted with rubber bushes	Rear bearings fitted with needle roller sleeves	Rear bearings fitted with needle roller sleeves
Stub axle diameter: 17 mm (.670")	Stub axle diameter: 17 mm (.670")	Stub axle diameter: 20 mm (.788")

Track	4 ft 27/8 in (1.292 m)
Total toe-in	0 to 5/32 in (0.to 4 mm)
Right hand wheelbase	8 ft 821/64 in (2.656 m)
Left hand wheelbase	8 ft 11 in (2.717 m)

Dampers

Type ... Hydraulic double acting telescopic.

Torque wrench settings

	lbf ft	kgf m
Suspension arm external bearing nuts	32	4.4
Suspension arm internal bearing nuts	20	2.8
Anti-roll bearing nuts	7	0.97

1 General Description

1 The rear suspension layout comprises torsion bars located at right angles to the centre line of the vehicle, double acting hydraulic dampers and an anti-roll bar.
2 The road wheels are independently sprung and the hubs run on inner and outer ball races. Drum brakes are fitted. Suspension arms swivel on either rubber or needle bearings.

2 Rear Hub - Adjustment

1 The rear hub/drum assembly varies in dimensional detail according to year of manufacture and model.
2 After dismantling and reassembly, the hub bearings must be adjusted.
3 Jack up the vehicle and remove the road wheel. Chock the front wheels.
4 Check that the handbrake is fully off and that the shoes are not binding.
5 Knock off the grease cap and remove the split pin from the stub axle.
6 Detach the nut locking cover.
7 Using a torque wrench, tighten the stub axle nut to 25 lbf ft (3.4 kgf m) and rotate the drum during the operation.
8 Unscrew the nut a quarter of a turn and check the hub for endfloat by pushing and pulling the assembly. When correctly adjusted, there should be between 0.002 and 0.004 inch end play (0.06 to 0.09 mm). Adjust the nut until a feeler of suitable thickness can be interposed between the rear face of the nut and the front face of the thrust washer and when inserted will take up the required end play and prevent any movement of the hub/drum assembly on the stub axle.
9 When adjustment is correct, carefully fit the nut locking cover without disturbing the nut. This cover may be removed and turned until one of its slots is in exact alignment with the stub axle split pin hole. Fit a new split pin.
10 Fill the grease cap ¾ full with high melting point grease and tap it into position.
11 Refit the roadwheel and lower the vehicle.

3 Rear Hub and Bearings - Removal and Refitting

1 Carry out the operations described in paragraphs 1 to 6 of the preceding Section.
2 Using a suitable extractor remove the brake drum. (Fig).
3 Extract the outer bearing and thrust washer as the brake drum is withdrawn. Drift out the outer track ring.
4 Extract the oil seal and press out the inner bearing track rings from the hub/drum assembly.
5 Using a bearing extractor, withdraw the inner taper roller bearing and thrust washer from the stub axle, (Fig).
6 Renew hub bearings as supplied (taper roller and track ring), never try to fit a new roller assembly to an old track ring, as the bearing components are matched in manufacture.
7 Fit a new bearing thrust washer to the stub axle by first heating the washer and holding it in its correct location until it cools down.
8 Fit the new inner taper roller bearing by using a piece of tube as a distance piece and tightening the stub axle nut (Fig).
9 Press in new inner and outer track rings to the hub/drum assembly and tap a new oil seal into position.
10 Line the inside of the hub/drum assembly between the two track rings with wheel bearing grease and locate the assembly on the stub axle.
11 Fit the outer taper bearing to the stub axle and then fit the thrust washer.
12 Fit the stub axle nut and adjust the rear hub as described in the preceding Section.

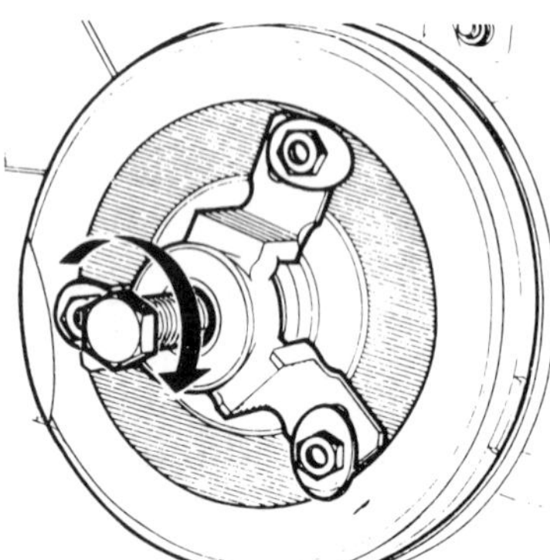
3.2 Using an extractor to remove a rear brake drum

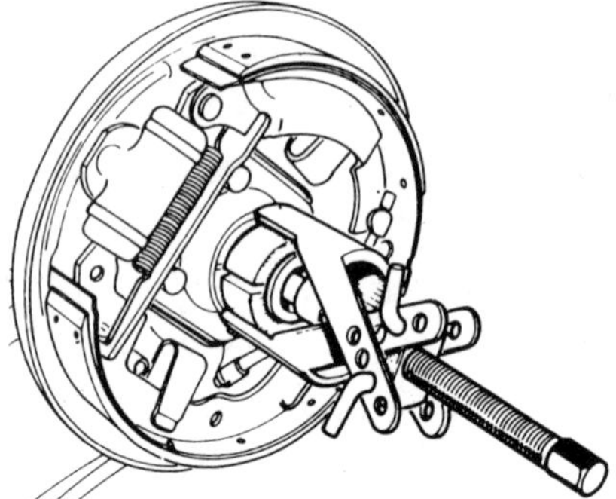
3.5 Removing the inner roller bearing from a rear stub axle

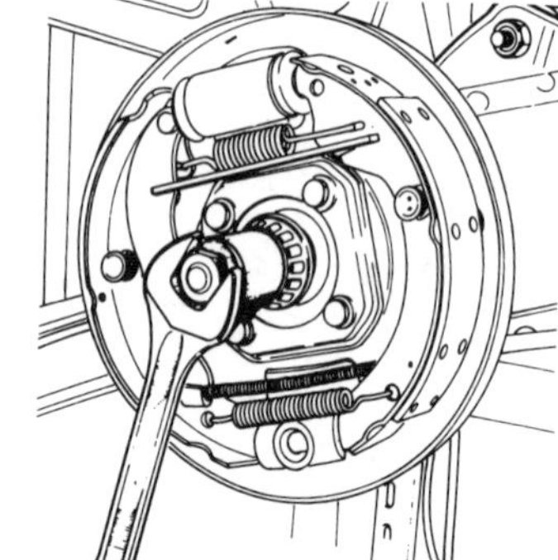
3.8 Fitting a new inner roller bearing to a rear stub axle

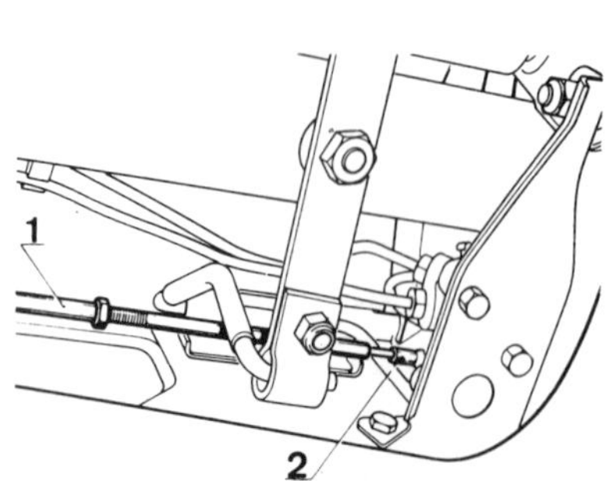

4.4 Handbrake cable attachment. 1 Screwed sleeve. 2 Cover

4.5 Handbrake cable securing clamp (3)

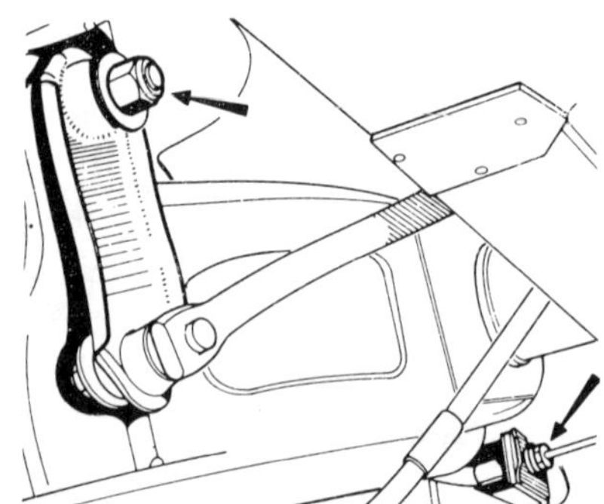
4.6 Rear hydraulic brake pipe union and damper lower mounting

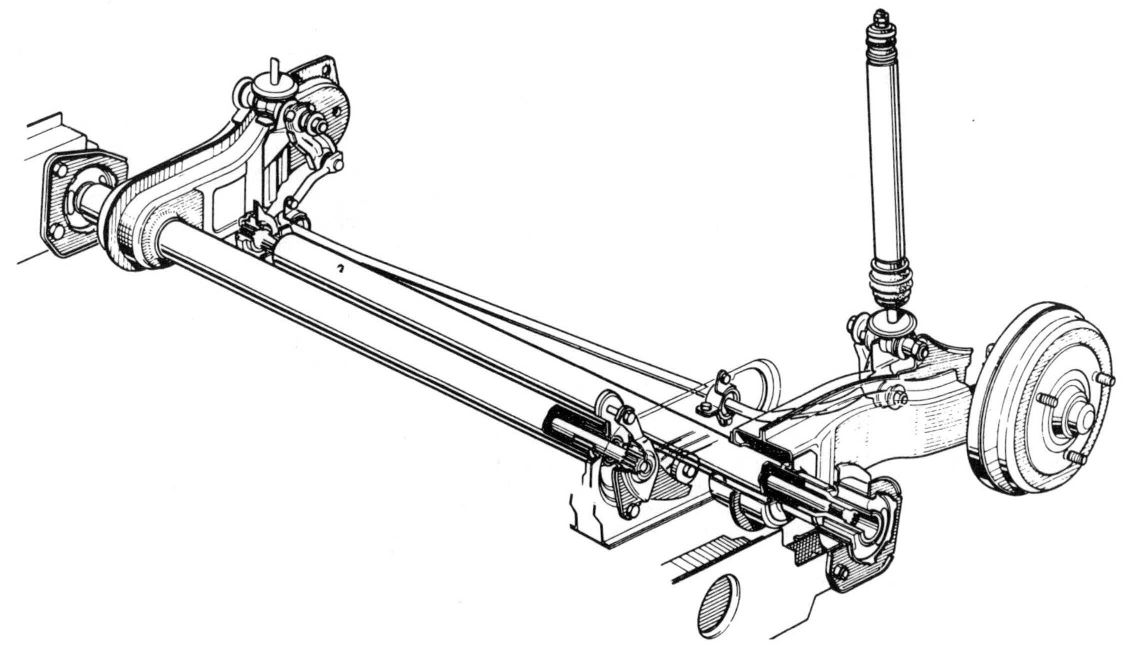

FIG.9.1. LAYOUT OF THE REAR SUSPENSION

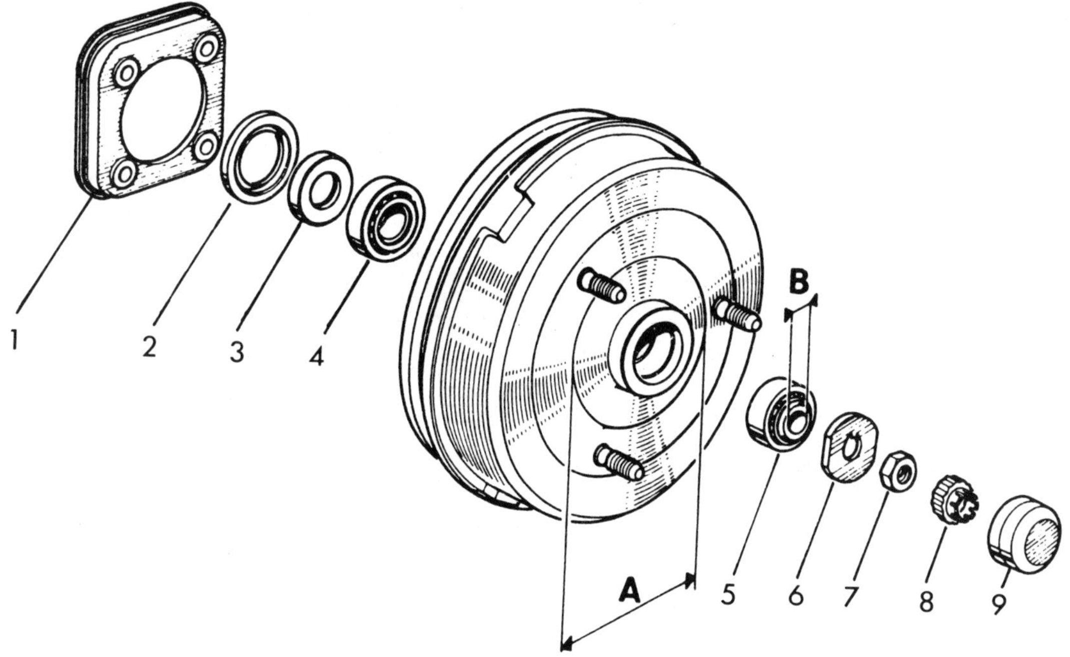

FIG.9.2 THE REAR HUB/DRUM ASSEMBLY

1 Axle tube flange
2 Oil seal
3 Thrust washer
4 Inner roller bearing
5 Outer roller bearing
6 Thrust washer
7 Stub axle nut
8 Nut locking cover
9 Grease cap

	R1150 From vehicle No. 1 to vehicle No. 160 880 inclusive	R1150 From vehicle No. 160 881 to No. 221 330 inclusive	R1150 From vehicle No. 221 331 R1151–R1152–R1153 from vehicle No. 1.
Wheel location diameter A	126 mm (4 15/16 in)	118 mm (4 5/8 in)	118 mm (4 5/8 in)
Outer bearing B	internal diameter 17 mm (0.670 in)	internal diameter 17 mm (0.670 in)	internal diameter 20 mm (0.788 in)

4 Suspension Arm - Removal and Refitting

1 The left hand suspension arm must be removed before the right hand one can be removed through the body frame side member.
2 The method of suspension arm removal is similar whether rubber or needle bearing type swivels are fitted.
3 Jack up the car and remove the road wheel.
4 Disconnect the handbrake cable and push back the cover (Fig).
5 Remove the other end of the handbrake cable from its securing clamp (Fig).
6 Disconnect the hydraulic brake pipe at the union on the chassis and plug the pipe to prevent loss of fluid (Fig).
7 Detach the damper lower mounting taking the load from the suspension arm by supporting it with a jack.
8 Unscrew the lock bolt from the underbody height adjustment cam.
9 Remove the two inner bearing securing bolts the exhaust silencer bolts, and the brake pressure limiter valve adjuster screw.
10 Rotate the torsion bar adjuster cam to zero, remove the anchor housing bolts, the anti-roll bearing bolts and pull the anti-roll bar to the rear as far as possible. (Fig).
11 Remove the outer bearing securing nuts from the suspension arm and then apply pressure with a lever so that the two securing bolts can be withdrawn (Fig).
12 Free the inner suspension arm bearing by pulling it towards the rear, turning it through 90°, again pulling it as far as it will go and removing it (Fig).
13 Removal of the right hand suspension arm is carried out in a similar manner to that just described for left hand arms but the inner bearing must be straightened before it can be removed in a rearward direction.
14 Refitting must start with the right hand suspension arm. Pass the suspension arm, complete with torsion bar through the aperture in the bodyframe. Fit the outer bearing and use a lever to align the fixing holes.
15 Fit the anchor housing to the torsion bar, noting the alignment procedure as described in Section 7.
16 Attach the outer bearing to the side member.
17 Using a hook (E) made up from a piece of rod, secure the suspension arm to the plate (G) so that the arm lies at an angle of about 45° to the horizontal (Fig).
18 For vehicles whose rear suspension arms are 3.15/16 inch (100 mm) thick and are mounted on needle roller bearings, a guide should be made up in accordance with the figure.
19 For vehicles whose rear suspension arms are 4 inch (101.5 mm) thick and mounted on needle roller bearings, then tool T.AR.386–01 must be borrowed/hired from a Renault dealer. In both cases the tool/guide should be positioned as shown in Fig.4.17. and the suspension arm pushed and pulled so that it will fit freely (without binding) into the forked part of the tool.
20 Anchor the torsion bar, remove the hook and guide.
21 Pass the left hand suspension arm complete with torsion bar through the body frame aperture. As it slides into position, ensure that the inner bearing goes between the right hand arm tube and the car floor.
22 Carry out the fitting procedure in a manner similar to that already described for the right hand suspension arm

23 Fit the anti-roll bar bearings and attach the anti-roll bar to the suspension arms. Reconnect the dampers to the suspension arms.

24 Fit the exhaust silencer bolts, reconnect the hydraulic brake pipe and reconnect the brake limiter valve spring blade screw.

25 Adjust the underbody height (if necessary) as described in Section 8.

26 Adjust the handbrake, the brake limiter valve and then bleed the brakes, all as described in Chapter 11.

5 Suspension Arm Bearings - Types and Renewal

1 The bearings at the wheel end of the suspension arm may be of needle roller or rubber bush type. The rubber type cannot be renewed and in the event of wear, then the complete suspension arm must be renewed as an assembly but the replacement will be fitted with needle type bearings.
2 The suspension arm inner bearings are of flexible type (fluid bloc) and are renewable.
3 To renew a needle bearing at the wheel end, remove the suspension arm as described in the preceding Section.
4 Remove the bearing from arm, detach the plastic plug, remove the 'O' ring seal. (Fig).
5 Renew the complete needle bearing assembly.
6 Refitting is a reversal of removal but smear the needle roller sleeve with recommended grease before fitting.
7 The suspension arm inner bearings comprise an outer sleeve and the flexible bearing (Fig).
8 The inner flexible bearing may be renewed by simply removing and inserting.
9 If the outer sleeve is worn however, saw it lengthwise with a hacksaw blade and twist it from its tubular location with a pair of pliers. (Fig).
10 Press the new outer sleeve into position so that it just touches the shoulder of the tube recess and it should project 5/64 to 5/32 inch (2 to 4 mm).
11 The flexible bearing should be greased before inserting it into the outer sleeve.

6 Rear Wheel Tracking - Checking

1 Provided that the wheel and suspension bearings are in good condition and that suspension reassembly has been carried out correctly after dismantling, then the correct tracking of the rear wheels should be automatic.
2 Should abnormal or uneven tyre wear be apparent then the track should be checked preferably by a service station having the appropriate equipment.
3 Simple forked tools may be made up to check the out of true tolerance of the rear suspension based on the Renault service tool shown in the two figures for twist and parallelism between the stub axle and the hinge mounting. Note that the washer (R) if made to the outside diameter dimension of the hinge tube will obviate any need for offset in length of plane of the fork ends. It may be wiser to take the car to a Renault agent to have this done.

7 Torsion Bars - Identification, Removal and Refitting

1 The left and right hand torsion bars are not interchangeable and are identified on their end faces as illustrated.
2 Neither torsion bar can be removed unless both suspension arms are first disconnected at their chassis attachment points as described in Section 4.
3 Mark the torsion bars as follows before disconnecting the suspension arms. Slide the anchor housing along the torsion bar splines just sufficiently far (without disconnecting the engagement of the splines) to make spline alignment marks on both components with a grease pencil.
4 By counting the number of splines between the punch mark on both components and the new alignment marks, the amount of offset and in which direction can be noted.

5 Carry out similar alignment marking at the suspension arm end of the torsion bar. This is a rather difficult operation as the end of the torsion bar is recessed some distance down the suspension arm splined housing. A needle engaging with the torsion bar end face dot punch mark can be used as a guide to project the spline alignment onto the rim of the arm housing. (Fig)
6 Disconnect the suspension arms so that they will move freely

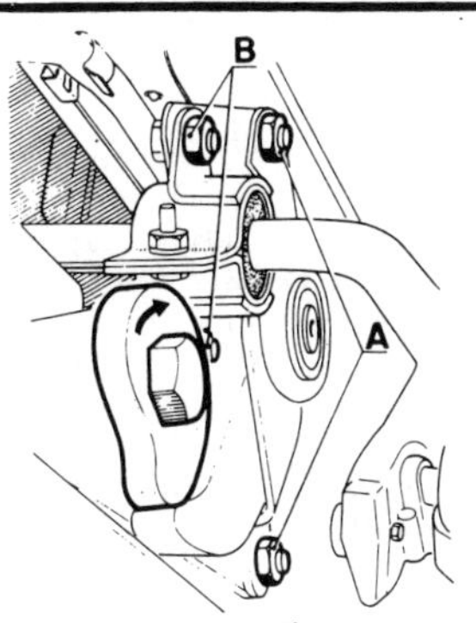

4.10 Rear torsion bar adjuster cam. A anchor housing bolts. B anti-roll bar bearing bolts

4.11 Levering a rear suspension arm to enable the outer bearing securing bolts to be withdrawn

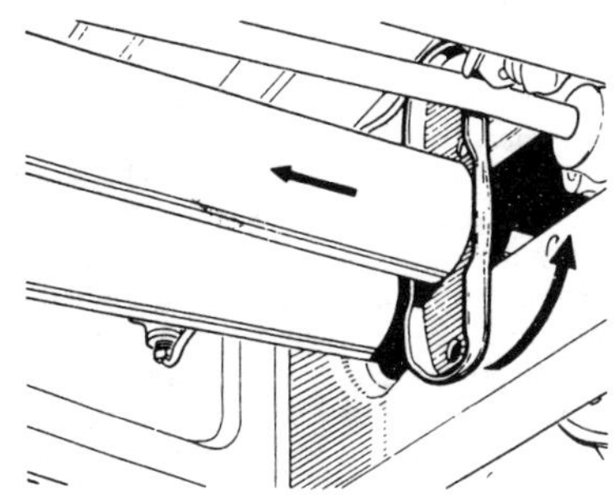

4.12 Removing a left hand suspension arm

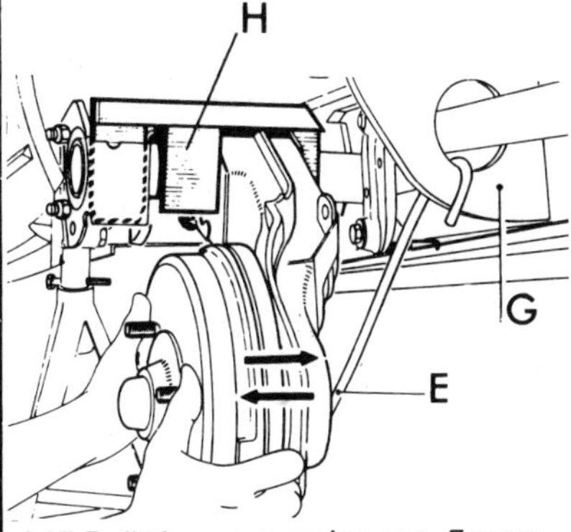

4.17 Refitting a suspension arm. E temporary hook. G body frame plate. H guide tool

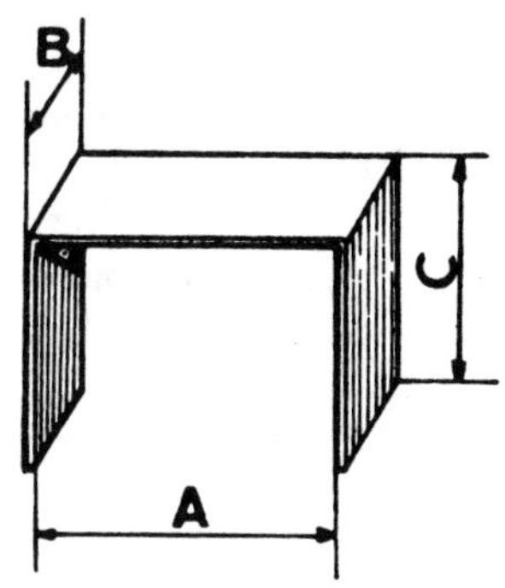

4.18 Guide tool for refitting suspension arm. A 3 15/16 in (100 mm). B 1 9/16 in (40 mm). C 2 3/4 in (70 mm). Metal gauge 0.24 in (6 - 10 mm)

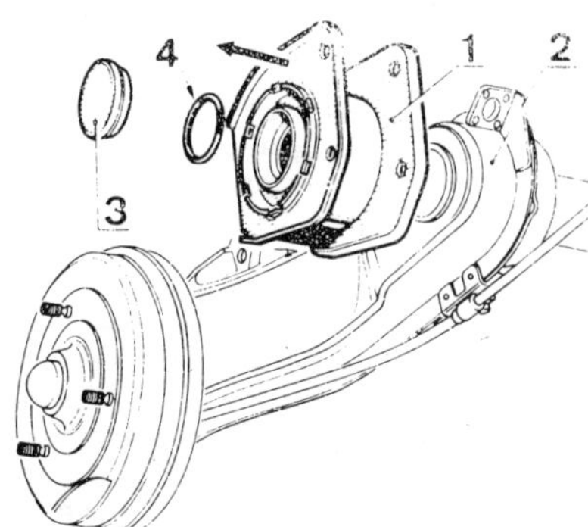

5.4 The suspension arm outer bearing. 1 Bearing housing. 2 Suspension arm. 3 Plastic plug. 4 'O' ring seal.

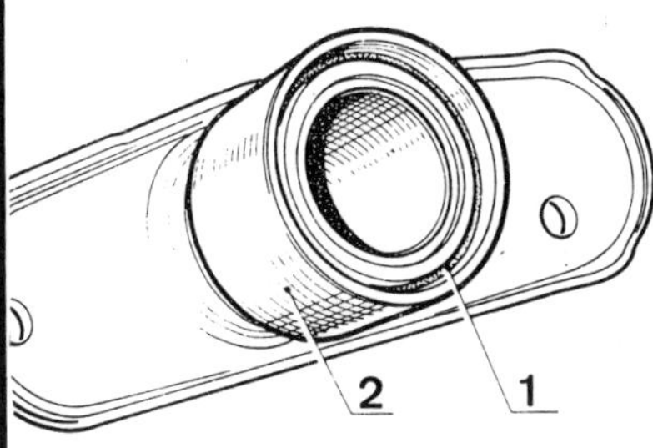

5.7 Suspension arm inner bearing. 1 Flexible bearing. 2 Outer sleeve

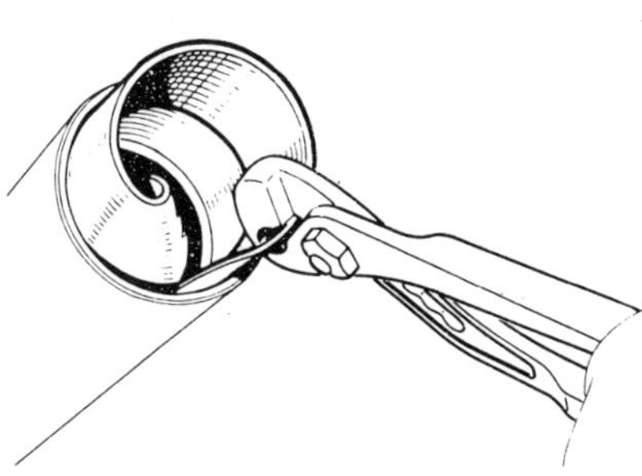

5.9 Removing the outer sleeve of an inner bearing

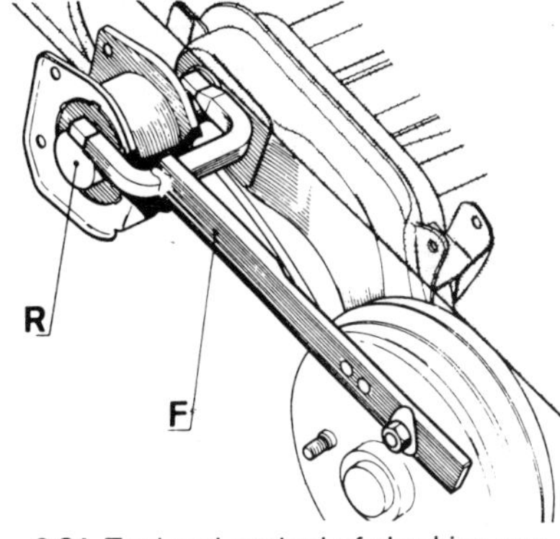

6.3A Tool and method of checking rear stub axle for twist

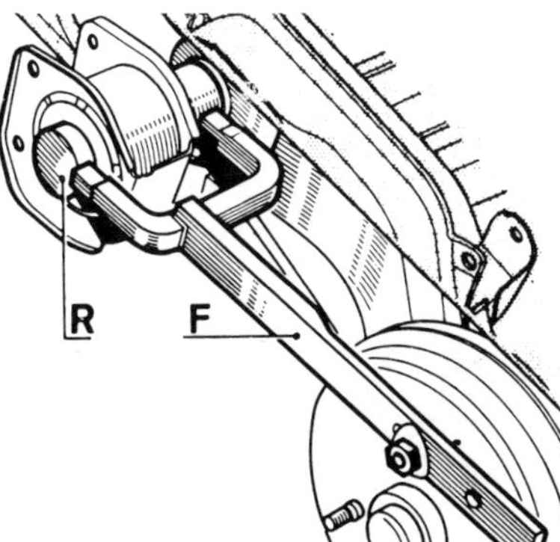

6.3B. Tool and method of checking rear stub axle for parallelism

7.1A Torsion bar identification marks (early)

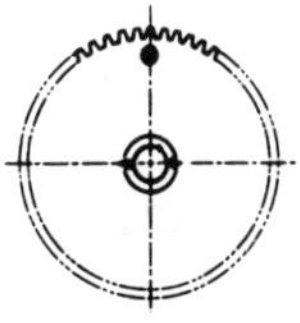

7.1B Torsion bar identification marks (later)

in the body frame side members and permit withdrawal of the torsion bars. (Fig).

7 In case the identification marks on the torsion bars are not clear, it is wise to tape and mark them on withdrawal in respect of left and right hand.

8 To refit the torsion bars, slide them into engagement with the suspension arms (larger diameter end of bar to arm). Push the bar through the suspension arm until it is flush with the face of the splined socket of the arm.

9 Turn the torsion bar so that alignment marks made on dismantling will provide the original spline offset and engage the torsion bar splines with the suspension arm splines.

10 Fit the anchor housing to the other end of the torsion bar again ensuring that the alignment marks made on dismantling will return the spline offset to the original position. When fitting the anchor housing, do not let the other end of the torsion bar be pushed from the suspension arm splines but use a wooden block to retain it.

11 Adjust the underbody height as fully described in Chapter 8, Section 7, initially by the cam provided and if necessary by the differential spline method.

8 Underbody Height - Adjustment

1 Whenever major dismantling operations have been carried out to the rear suspension then the underbody height should be checked. Adjustment of the rear torsion bars will usually be undertaken in conjunction with similar adjustment of the front bars and the necessary procedure and height specification tables relative to vehicle model and suspension type are given in Chapter 8, Section 7.

9 Anti-Roll Bar - Removal, Servicing, Refitting

1 From each anti-roll bar end bearing, remove screw followed by the two bearing to chassis securing bolts. (Fig).

2 Disconnect the brake limiter valve by unscrewing the nut. (Fig).

3 Disconnect the anti-roll bar at both ends and remove it. The attachment components (one side) are shown in the figure.

4 Renewal of the silentbloc bearing rubber bushes should be made where they show signs of compression or deterioration. When refitting, ensure that the slot in the rubber bush is in line with the bearing housing joint.

5 Refitting is a reversal of removal and dismantling but adjust the brake limiter valve as described in Chapter 11.

10 Dampers - Removal, Testing, Refitting

1 The damper is secured at the top by rubber mountings and locknuts and washers. There are alternative fittings.

2 The damper bottom mounting is by means of rubber bushes and a retaining bolt on which the damper swivels.

3 Do not remove a rear damper with the road wheel and suspension arm hanging free.

4 The rubber mounting bushes may be renewed but other than these, the damper is not capable of repair and must be renewed as a unit should a fault develop.

5 Testing a damper should be carried out as described in Chapter 8, Section 14.

6 Refitting is a reversal of removal but do not overtighten the upper securing nut.

11 Wheel Loading - Checking

1 It is possible to find that after suspension reassembly and all other adjustments are completed, that the torsion bars are still slightly out of balance and give rise to different reactions on two wheels fitted to the same axle.

2 Where this is the case, the vehicle should be checked for individual wheel loading. This must be carried out by a Renault agent if any degree of success is desired!

12 Fault Finding

Cause	Trouble	Remedy
Symptom WHEEL WOBBLE AND VIBRATION		
General wear or damage	Damper rubber bushes worn	Renew
	Loose damper mountings	Tighten
	Suspension arm bushes worn	Dismantle and renew
Symptom UNEVEN TYRE WEAR		
Incorrect assembly or accident damage	Rear stub axles twisted or out of alignment	Check and renew
	Hubs incorrectly adjusted for end-float	Adjust
Symptom POOR ROADHOLDING AND CORNERING		
Incorrect adjustment after dismantling and reassembly	Torsion bars incorrectly adjusted	Check underbody height dimensions
	Dampers unserviceable	Renew

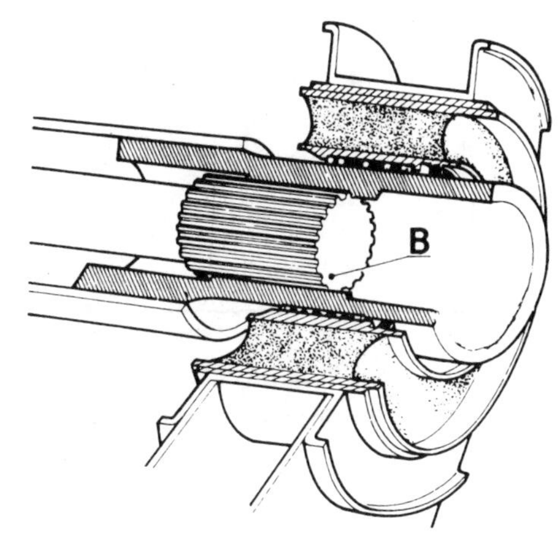

7.5 Torsion bar at suspension arm end. B is dot punch mark

7.6 Withdrawing a rear torsion bar

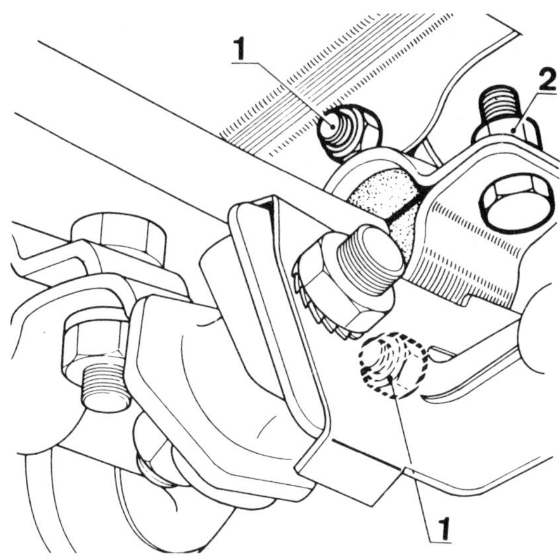

9.1 Anti-roll bar bearing attachment to body frame. 1 securing bolt to body frame. 2 bearing securing bolt

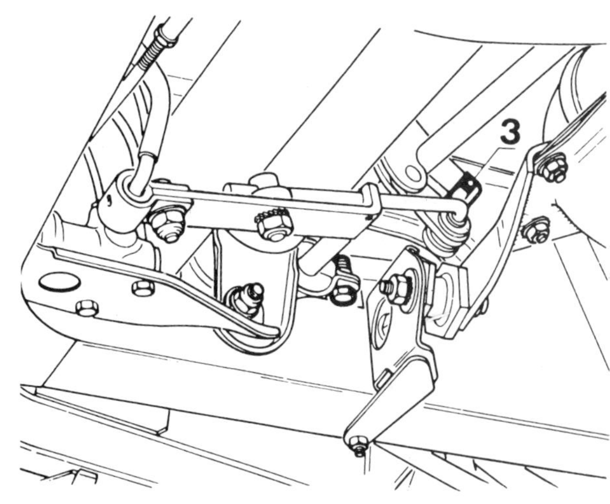

9.2 Brake limiter valve securing nut (3)

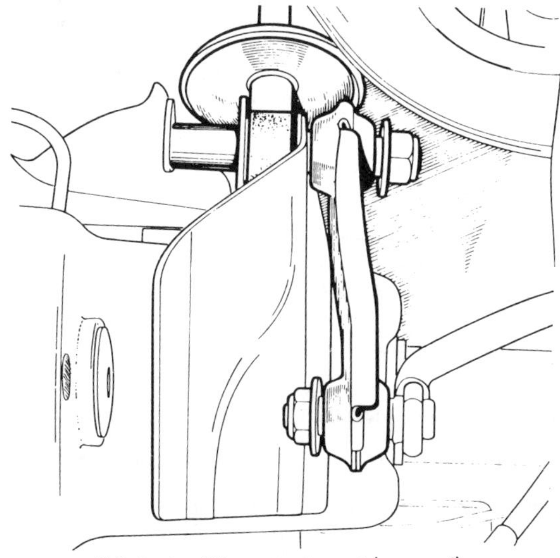

9.3 Anti-roll bar attachment (one end)

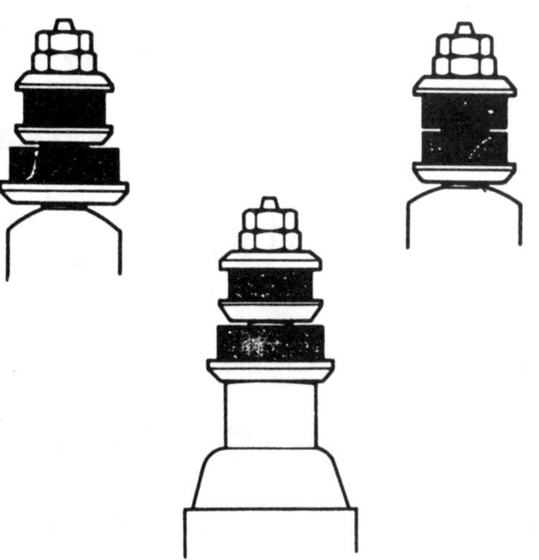

10.1 Alternative top mountings for rear dampers

Chapter 10 Steering

Contents

Specifications

Type ... Rack and pinion
Tubular column with solid internal shaft divided at upper end by universal joint and at lower end by flexible coupling.

Reduction Ratio	23 : 1
Toe-in or toe-out (see table Section 1)	0 to 1/8 in (0 to 3 mm)
Track	44 27/32 in (1.342 m)

Torque wrench settings

	lbf ft	kgf m
Steering wheel retaining nut	30	4.1
Steering shaft nut	25	2.4
Rack and pinion housing bolt to crossmember	15	2.1
Steering arm ball joint	25	2.4
Flexible coupling bolt	10	1.4
Metal universal joint nut	25	2.4

1 General Description

1 The steering gear is of rack and pinion type and may vary in detail according to the vehicle model and date of manufacture.
2 The steering column is of divided type, connected by one rigid and one flexible joint in the interest of safety in the event of a front end collision.
3 A two spoked wheel is fitted to the steering column by splined hub.
4 Motion from the rack is transmitted to the road wheels through the rack end fittings and short pressed steel arms connected by ball joints to the arms of the stub axle carrier.
5 The steering rack and pinion assembly cannot be serviced or repaired and in the event of wear or damage then the unit must be exchanged for a factory reconditioned one.

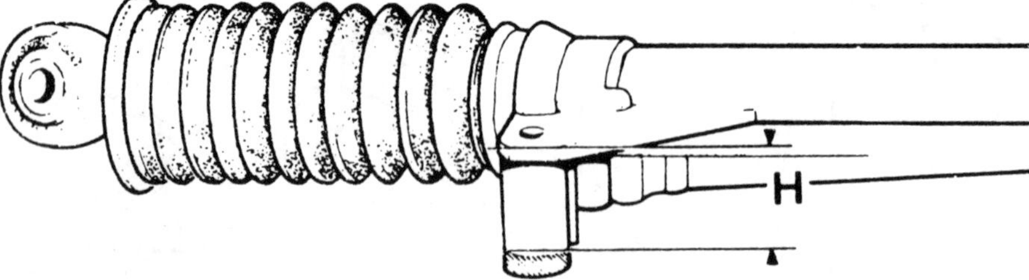

FIG.10.1 STEERING BOX HEIGHT DIFFERENCES ACCORDING TO MODEL AND DATE OF MANUFACTURE

Vehicle type	R1150 to 209884		R1150 from 209885		R1150, 1152, 1153, 1151 from 1968	
Method of fixing sleeve	*Fixed on side opposite rack pinion*		*Floating on side opposite to rack pinion*		*Floating on side opposite to rack pinion*	
Steering box height H	*42 mm*	*1 21/32 in*	*42 mm*	*1 21/32 in*	*37 mm*	*1 15/32 in*
Track setting	*0 - 3 mm*	*toe-in*	*0 - 3 mm*	*toe-in*	*0 - 3 mm*	*toe-out*

2 Steering Gear - Removal and Refitting

1 Disconnect the battery, remove the spare wheel from the engine compartment and jack up the front of the car and remove the two road wheels.
2 Using an extractor or a pair of forked wedges, disconnect the right hand balljoint. (Fig)
3 Withdraw the hinge pin from its location joining the rack and fitting to the steering arm on the left hand side.
4 Remove the two securing bolts from the steering column flexible coupling (arrowed) in the figure.
5 Remove the four bolts which secure the steering rack and pinion mechanism to the crossmember.
6 Turn the steering wheel so that the road wheels are at full right lock and disconnect the end fitting from the steering arm on the right hand side.
7 Remove the steering assembly by drawing it forward and at the same time turning it. Carefully retain any hook-ended shims which may be located beneath the securing bolt pillars. (Fig)
8 Refitting is a reversal of removal but the following points must be carefully noted.
9 If the original steering assembly (and crossmember if removed) are being refitted, replace the original shims found on dismantling.
10 If a new steering box is being fitted and the type is identical to the original (see height specification, Section 1) then refit the original shims.
11 If a steering box of different type is being fitted or any doubt exists regarding the original shims, then shims of 0.079 in (2 mm) thickness must be positioned, one under each steering box mounting pillar.
12 Whenever dismantling or refitting of the steering assembly has been carried out then the following checks must be made.

The steering centre point (Section 5).
The steering rack and pinion height setting.
The tracking of the front road wheels. (Section 6).

13 Note that left and right hand steering arms are not interchangeable. The straight part of the arm must face forward. (Fig. 2.13).
14 Grease the end fitting to steering arm hinge pin and ensure that it is in a perfectly horizontal plane otherwise the balljoints will not be able to operate over their full arc of travel. Should the end fitting require rotating slightly to enable the hinge pin to lie horizontally, then loosen the locknut (2) and turn the end fitting (3). Retighten the locknut. (Fig)

3 Steering Column - Removal and Refitting

1 Disconnect the battery.
2 Turn the ignition key to position 2 (steering column unlocked).
3 Remove the embellisher from the steering wheel spokes (2 screws from behind the spokes). Unscrew the column nut.
4 Using an extractor and taking care not to damage the plastic surfaces of the wheel pull the steering wheel from the retaining splines.
5 Remove the lighting switch housing and disconnect the return spring on the flasher switch. Remove the lighting switch securing bolts and free it from the steering column. Mark the clamp position in relation to the steering column tube. (Fig).
6 Remove the bolt which secures the gearshift control clamp. Disconnect the gearshift control balljoint by freeing the clamp on the steering column.
7 Free the glove compartment from the fascia panel and mark the electrical wiring with masking tape for exact replacement and then disconnect the terminals from the steering lock, the

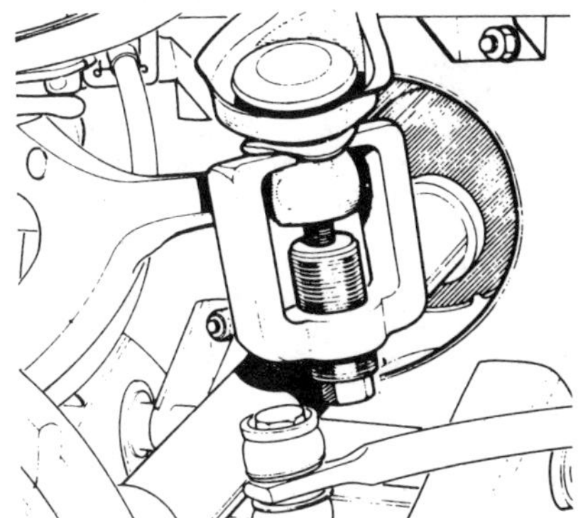
2.2 Disconnecting the right hand steering arm ball joint

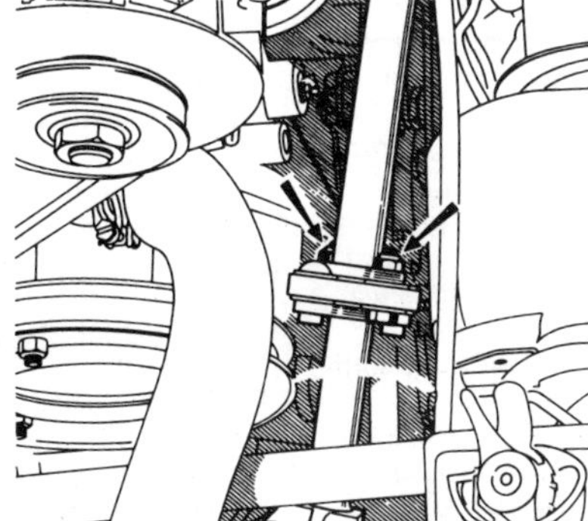
2.4 Location of the two steering column flexible coupling bolts

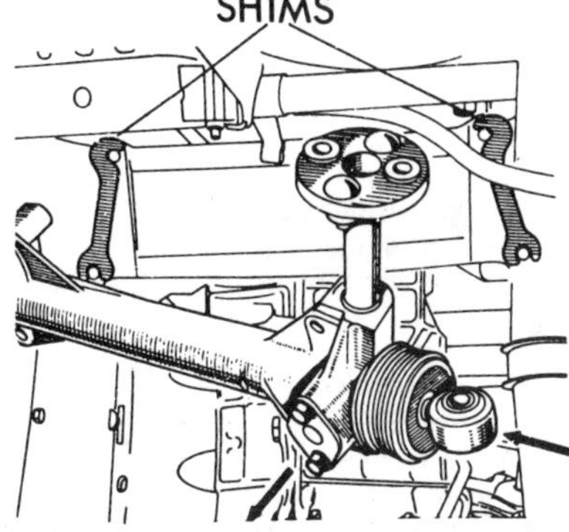

2.7. Method of removal of the steering assembly, note shims

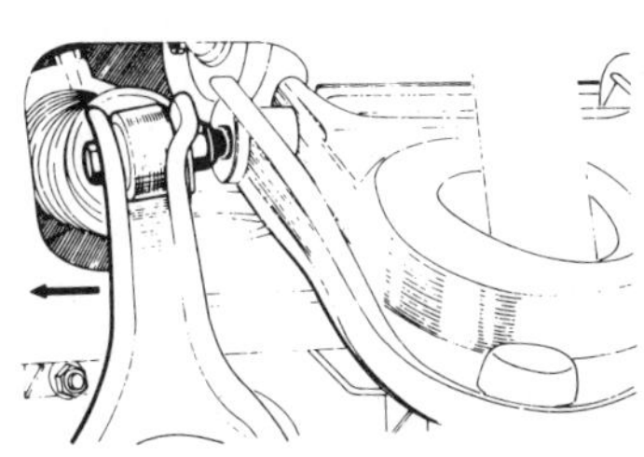
2.13 Correct method of fitting left and right hand steering arms (straight edge facing forward)

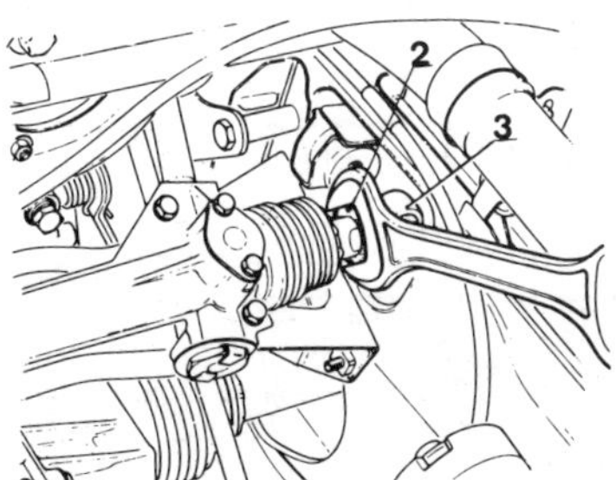

2.14 Rack end fitting to steering arm connections. 2 Locknut. 3 End fitting

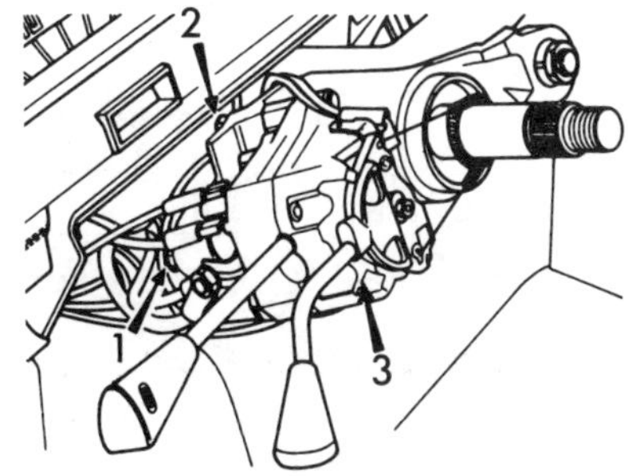

3.5 Lighting and flasher switch details. 1 and 2 lighting switch securing bolts. 3 flasher switch return spring.

stop light switch. Disconnect the clutch and brake pedal return springs. Remove the pedal shaft clip and remove the foot pedals. Free the outer cable from its stop on the pedal assembly bracket. (Fig).

8 Remove the steering column universal joint pin at the foot pedal assembly end. Disconnect the steering column top fixing by first disconnecting the speedometer cable to gain access to the securing pin.

9 On all vehicles remove the brake master cylinder securing bolts (B) and on cars fitted with a servo system, remove the additional bolts (A). (Fig. 3.9).

10 As an alternative to removing the pin from the steering column universal joint (A or B) the bolts may be removed from the column to pinion flange flexible coupling. In either case, the steering column assembly may now be withdrawn into the interior of the car. (Fig).

11 Refitting is a reversal of removal but the following points must be observed.

Seal the column lower clamp with sealing compound.

Do not tighten the column upper clamp until assembly is complete.

Set the steering centre point (Section 5) and connect the universal joint, having first greased the retaining pins. These pins (A and B in Fig. 3.10) must be tightened in the following manner: Pin A, steering rack in straight ahead position, tighten to 25 lbf ft (2.4 kgf m). Pin B, steering turned one quarter turn to the right, tighten to 25 lbf ft (2.4 kgf m).

12 When reassembly is complete, check the clutch free movement (Chapter 5) the gearshift control operation (Chapter 6) the brake master cylinder operating rod clearance (Chapter 11) and the satisfactory operation of the brake light switch and all electrical accessories operated by the combination lighting switch.

4 Steering Column Shaft Bushes - Renewal

1 If rocking of the steering column shaft is apparent, then the upper and lower bushes are worn and must be renewed.

2 Remove the steering column as described in the preceding Section and take out the brake pedal cross shaft.

3 To extract the lower bush, tap lightly on the splined (steering wheel) end of the steering shaft. Protect the end of the shaft against the hammer blows with a plastic or hardwood block. (Fig. 4.3).

4 The bottom split bush will be ejected together with the split collar. Withdraw the shaft downwards.

5 Remove the retaining circlip from the sleeve located at the steering wheel end of the column. Drive out the top bush by using a length of rod 1 1/32 in (26 mm) inserted from the bottom end of the steering column.

6 Refitting of the bushes commences by tapping in the one at the top of the steering column using a suitable tubular drift and then fitting the retaining circlip.

7 Ensure that the bush is hard up against the depression in the steering column.

8 Insert the steering shaft through the bottom end of the column.

9 Fit the bottom bush and collar halves and tap them into position using an angled drift and working evenly round until they locate against the depression in the column. Apply some grease to all these components before assembling.

5 Steering Centre Point - Checking and Adjusting

1 After dismantling and reassembling the steering gear, as a preliminary to checking the track of the front road wheels and to position the spokes of the steering wheel in the horizontal plane, the steering centre point must be established.

2 Align the mark on the steering column with the web cast on the rack and pinion assembly housing. Check measurement with Fig.10.3.

3 With the steering column retained in this position the two spokes of the steering wheel should form equal angles with the horizontal.

4 Where this is not the case, remove the steering wheel securing nut, pull off the wheel, using a suitable extractor and rotate the wheel a number of splines to correct the position. Do not tighten the retaining nut until you have checked that the steering column mark is still in alignment with the web of the housing.

6 Track - Adjustment

1 The thickness of the shims located beneath the mounting pillars of the steering housing have an effect upon the amount of toe-in or toe-out of the front road wheels which is a precise tolerance as given in Specifications according to the vehicle model and steering box fitted.

2 The total toe-in and toe-out must be correct and the measurement must be equally distributed (each front road wheel toe-in or toe-out must be equal that of the one opposite).

3 Where no shims are fitted beneath the steering box mounting pillars and yet the correct tracking cannot be obtained, then the camber will require adjustment by adding or removing shims from behind the suspension arm mounting swivels.

4 Distribution of toe-in or toe-out is adjusted by loosening the steering rack end fitting locknuts and rotating the end fittings, Fig 2.14.

5 All adjustments to track and steering angles must be undertaken with the front suspension under compression and in view of the special gauges and tools required, this is obviously a job for the Renault dealer.

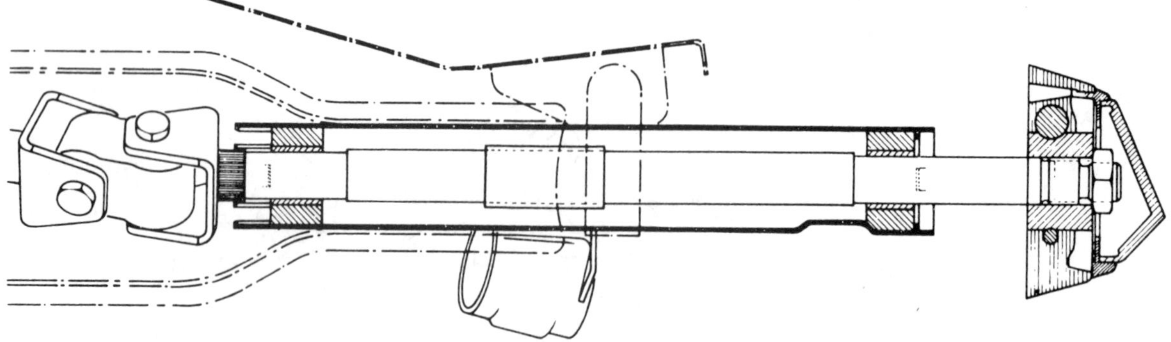

Fig.10.2 Sectional view of the steering column/shaft assembly

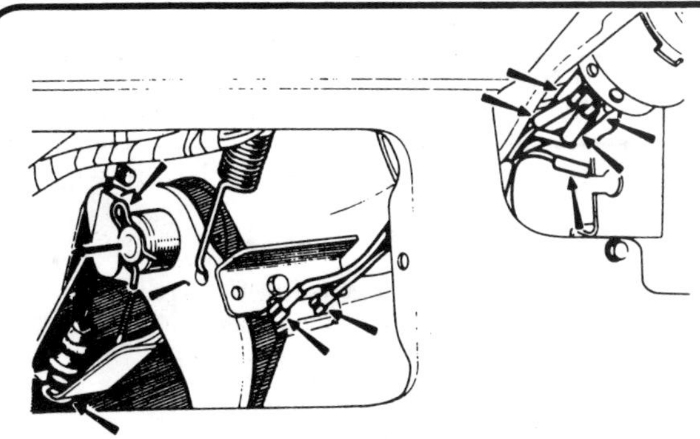
3.7 Foot pedal details and stop light and steering lock electrical terminals

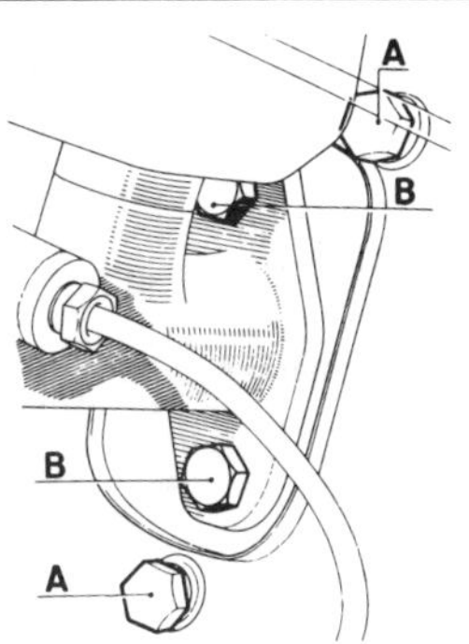

3.9 Brake master cylinder securing bolts (B). Additional bolts (A) for cars fitted with servo unit

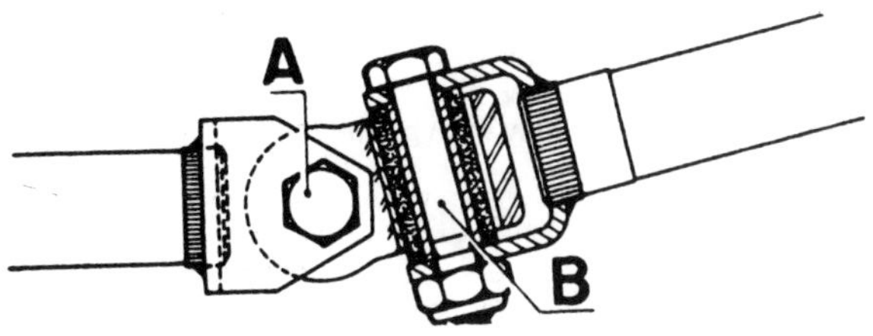

3.10 Steering column upper (metal) universal joint

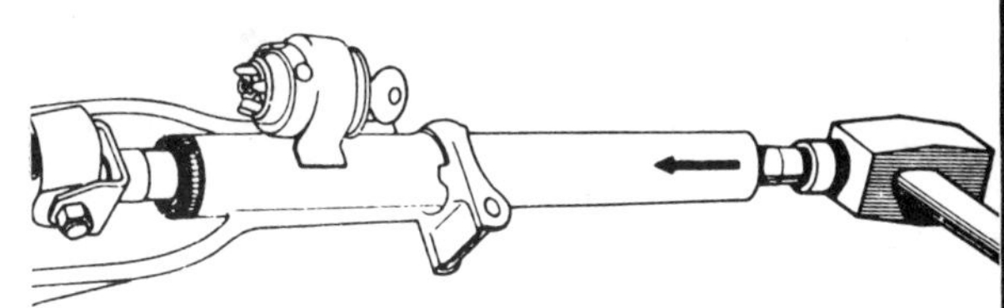
4.3 Extracting the steering column lower bush

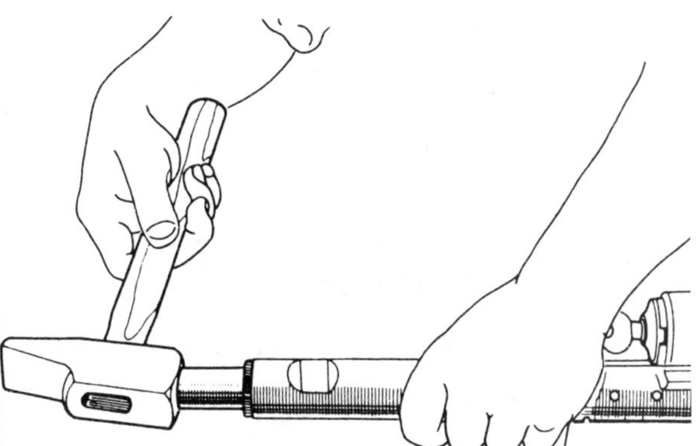
4.6 Refitting the steering column upper bush

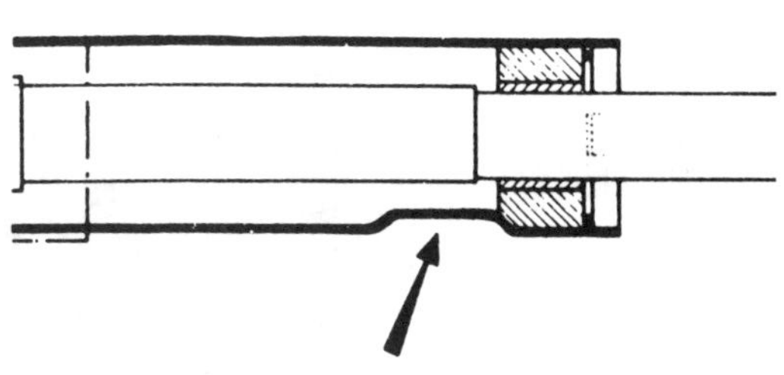
4.7 Correct location of the steering column upper bush

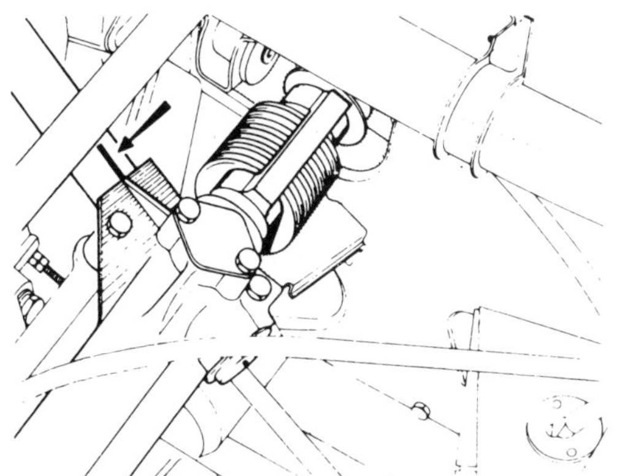
5.2 Steering centre point alignment marks

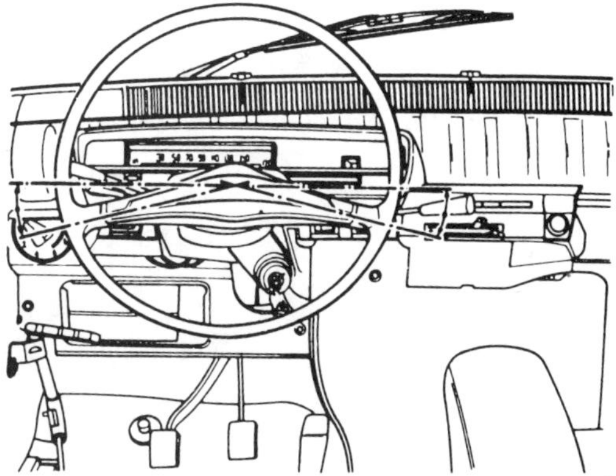
5.3 Correct positioning of the steering wheel with the steering centred.

Cause	Trouble	Remedy
Symptom HEAVY STEERING		
General wear, corrosion or damage	Corroded or seized ball joints	Renew
	Incorrect suspension geometry and track	Check all steering angles and adjust.
Symptom WHEEL WOBBLE		
General wear, damage or lack of servicing	Wear in rack and pinion and ball joints	Renew assemblies.
	Incorrect steering geometry	Check and adjust
Symptom LOST MOTION		
General wear	Worn flexible coupling bolt holes	Renew
	Worn steering column universal joint	Renew
	Loose steering wheel	Tighten
	Worn ball joints	Renew
	Worn rack and pinion mechanism	Renew as an assembly

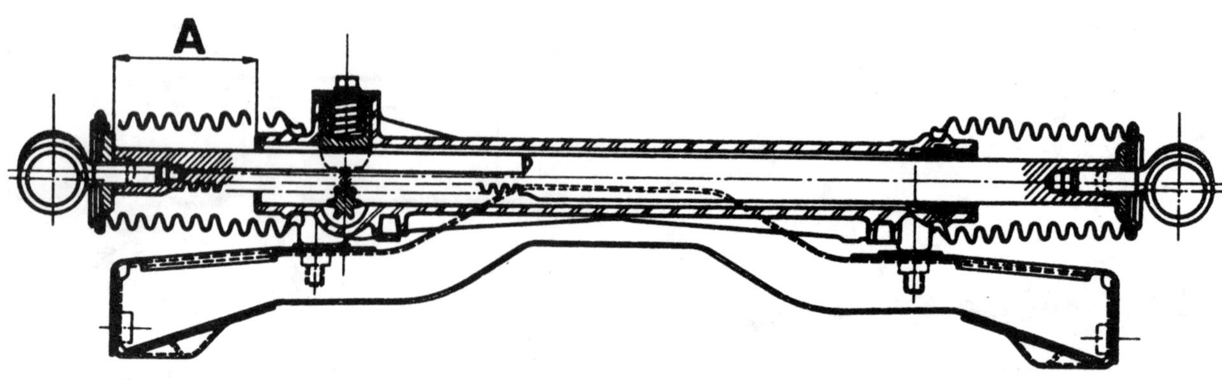

Fig.10.3. Cross-sectioned view of the steering rack. At steering centre point. A = 78 mm (3.1/16 inch)

Chapter 11 Brakes

For modifications, and information applicable to later models, see Supplement at end of manual

Contents

Specifications

System	Hydraulically operated, four wheel. Discs at front, drums at rear. Mechanically operated handbrake on rear wheels only.
Makes and applications	
Bendix type 11	Model R1150 (prior to 1969)
Bendix type 111 AS or Girling	Model R1150 (1969 onwards)
Bendix type 111 AS	Models R1151, R1152, R1153 (inc. USA)
Supplementary equipment and applications	
Servo (Master Vac) unit	Models R1151 and R1152 and R1153
Pressure drop indicator	Models R1152 and R1153
Tandem master cylinder	Models R1152 and R1153
Master cylinder	
Bendix type 111 AS	fitted to R1151 and R1153 models
Diameter	0.689 in (17.5 mm) stroke 1 9/16 in (40 mm)
Bendix type 111 AS	fitted to R1152 and R1153 (USA)
Diameter	0.749 in (19 mm) stroke 1 3/16 in (30 mm)
All other models:	
Diameter	0.812 in (20.6 mm) stroke 1 7/32 in (31 mm)
Front discs	
Caliper piston	(Girling)
Diameter	1 29/32 in (48.08 mm)
Caliper piston	(all other models)
Diameter	1 57/64 in (48 mm)
Disc diameter	
Bendix type 11	9 7/8 in (250 mm)
Bendix type 111 AS	10 in (254 mm)
Girling	10 9/16 in (268 mm)
Disc thickness	
Bendix type 11	2 3/64 in (9 mm)
Bendix type 111 AS	0.472 in (12 mm)
Girling	0.410 in (10.4 mm)

Width of braking area on disc surface	
Bendix type 11	1 9/16 in (40 mm)
Bendix type 111 AS	1 11/16 in (48 mm)
Girling	2 3/32 in (53.5 mm)
Disc pad thickness (including backing)	
Bendix type 11	15/32 in (12 mm)
Bendix type 111 AS	0.630 in (16 mm)
Girling	0.552 in (14 mm)
Rear brakes (all models)	
Wheel cylinder diameter	7/8 in (22 mm) except Bendix type 11 with normal fulcrum point 3/4 in (19 mm)
Drum diameter	9 in (228.5 mm)
Friction lining width	1 9/16 in (40 mm)
Friction lining thickness	0.197 in (5 mm)
Brake limiter valve cut-off pressure	415–485 lb in^2
Caliper shim thicknesses (except Girling)	0.02 in (0.5 mm) 0.039 in (1 mm) 0.059 in (1.5 mm) 0.079 in (2 mm) 0.099 in (2.5 mm)

Torque wrench settings

	lbf ft	kgf m
Rigid pipe unions	10	1.4
Flexible hoses	15	2.1
Bleed screws	5 - 7	0.7 – 1.0
Girling caliper direct to stub axle carrier	25	3.4

1 General Description

1 The braking system is of four wheel hydraulic type with disc brakes on the front and drum brakes on the rear wheels.
2 A mechanically operated handbrake operates on the rear wheels only.
3 Actuation of the braking system is by means of a foot-operated pedal working through a master cylinder and combined fluid reservoir.
4 A brake pressure limiter valve is fitted in the system to prevent locking of the wheels and to adjust the braking effort between the front and rear wheels and is adjustable in conjunction with the weight and suspension characteristics of the vehicle.
5 Certain additional equipment is fitted in conjunction with the braking system. Servo assistance is fitted to vehicles, models R1151 and R1153 which have Bendix type 111 AS brakes also to models R1151 and R1153 and special versions marketed in the USA. The latter (USA models) are also fitted with a hydraulic pressure drop indicator and a tandem master cylinder. Some Bendix type disc brakes are fitted with a pad wear indicator warning lamp device.
6 Various types of brakes are fitted as detailed in Specifications according to vehicle model and date of manufacture.
7 Visual identification of the front disc brakes fitted to a particular vehicle may be made from Fig 11.1
8 The rear brake assemblies are identified in Fig 11.2. .
9 The front brakes are self-adjusting, the rear brakes have back-plate adjusters.

2 Disc Brake Pads - Inspection, Removal, Refitting

1 The front disc friction pads must be checked visually at regular intervals and renewed if their friction material thickness is worn down to 1/8 in (3.2 mm). The pads on both front wheels must be changed at the same time with friction material of the same grade.
2 Jack up the car and remove the road wheel and then free the brake caliper from the bracket and then pull out the pads (from the side on 111 AS types, upwards on type 11). If necessary, disconnect the pad wear warning wire. Detach the pad thrust springs and check their flexing.
3 Pull the rubber dust cover from its housing and wipe the end of the piston clean with methylated spirit applied with a non-fluffy piece of cloth.
4 Fit a block of wood within the caliper jaws so that when the brake pedal is depressed, the piston will only emerge by 3/8 in (9.5 mm) before impringing upon the block.
5 Depress the brake pedal to eject the piston by the required amount and then apply 'Spagraph' grease to the piston skirt. Push the piston back into the caliper by means of the wooden block held square to the piston face.
6 Clean the rubber dust cover in methylated spirit and refit it.
7 Renew any faulty components and then slide the new brake pads into position in the caliper.
8 With type 111 AS brakes, fit the long springs (D) on the outside and the short spring (B) on the inside
9 With type 11 brakes fit the pad thrust springs to the caliper bracket (2) going to the outside and (1) to the inside
10 With both types, refit the caliper to the bracket and if previously removed, reconnect the pad wear warning wire.
11 Refit the road wheel and lower the jack.
12 With Girling type brakes, remove clips A and B
13 Pull out both pins and remove the friction pads. Refitting is a reversal of dismantling.
14 An alternative method of checking friction disc pad wear on Bendix type 11 brakes may be carried out without the necessity of removing the road wheel.
15 Measure the extent to which the brake pad (1) on the piston side of the caliper is recessed without reference to the caliper bracket (2).
16 The recess dimension should not exceed 13/64 in (5 mm) otherwise renew the pads.

3 Rear Brake Linings - Renewal

1 The rear brake linings should be renewed when the surface of the friction linings is worn down almost to the level of the rivet heads. It is not desirable to repeatedly remove the drums for purposes of inspection, as a puller is required and the bearings will need adjustment on refitting.

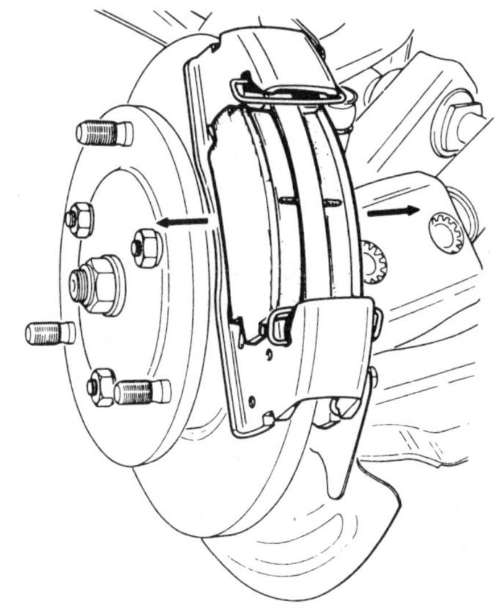

2.2 Direction of disc brake pad removal on Bendix III as type brakes

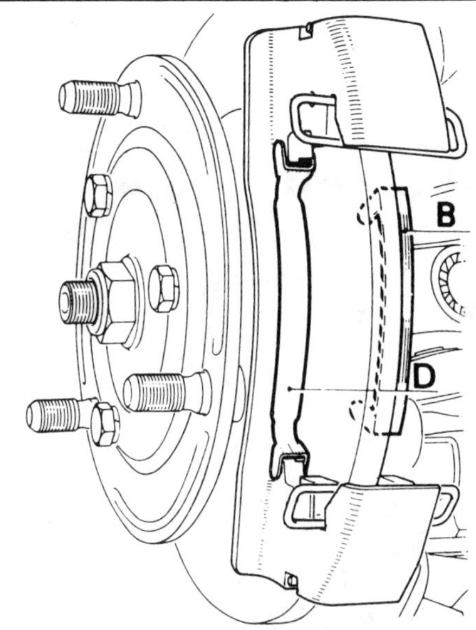

2.8 Correct location of Bendix type III AS disc pad springs. D long spring to the outside. B short spring to the inside

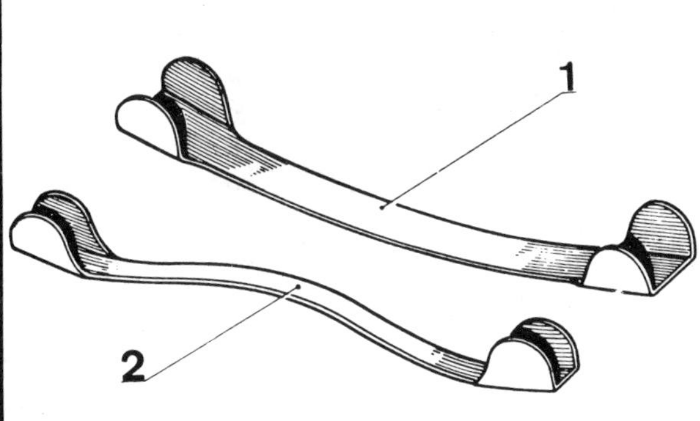

2.9 Bendix type II disc pad thrust springs. 2 locates on the outside. 1 locates on the inside

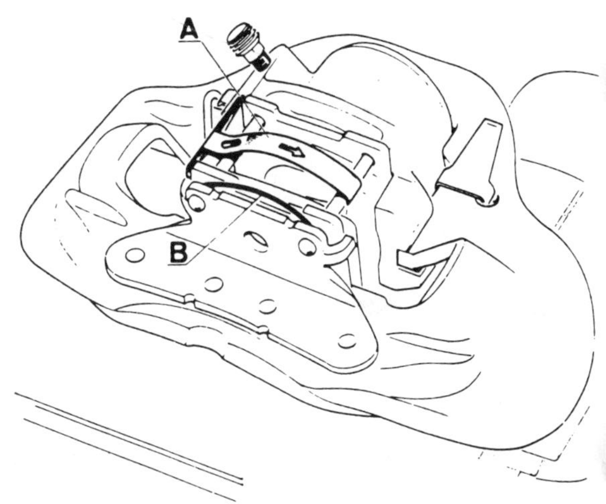

2.12 Girling type disc brake clip (A) and spring (B)

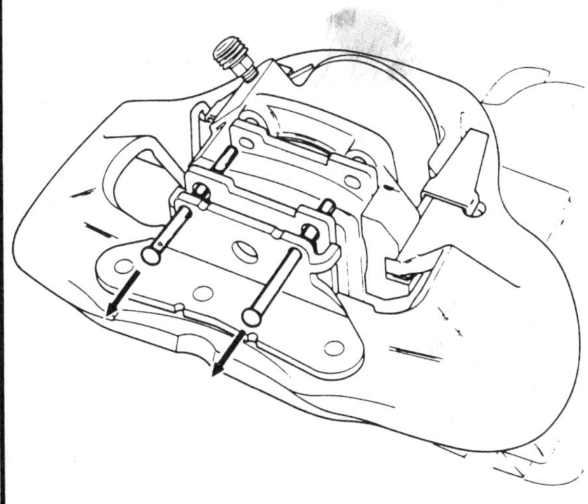

2.13 Removing disc pad retaining pins on Girling brakes

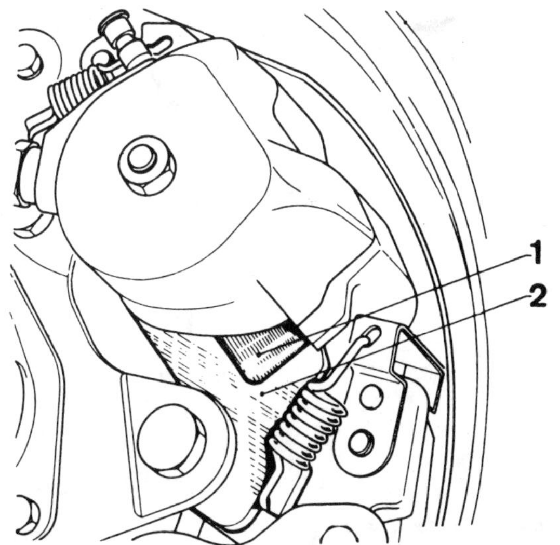

2.15 Checking disc pad thickness on Bendix type II. 1 Disc pad. 2 Caliper bracket

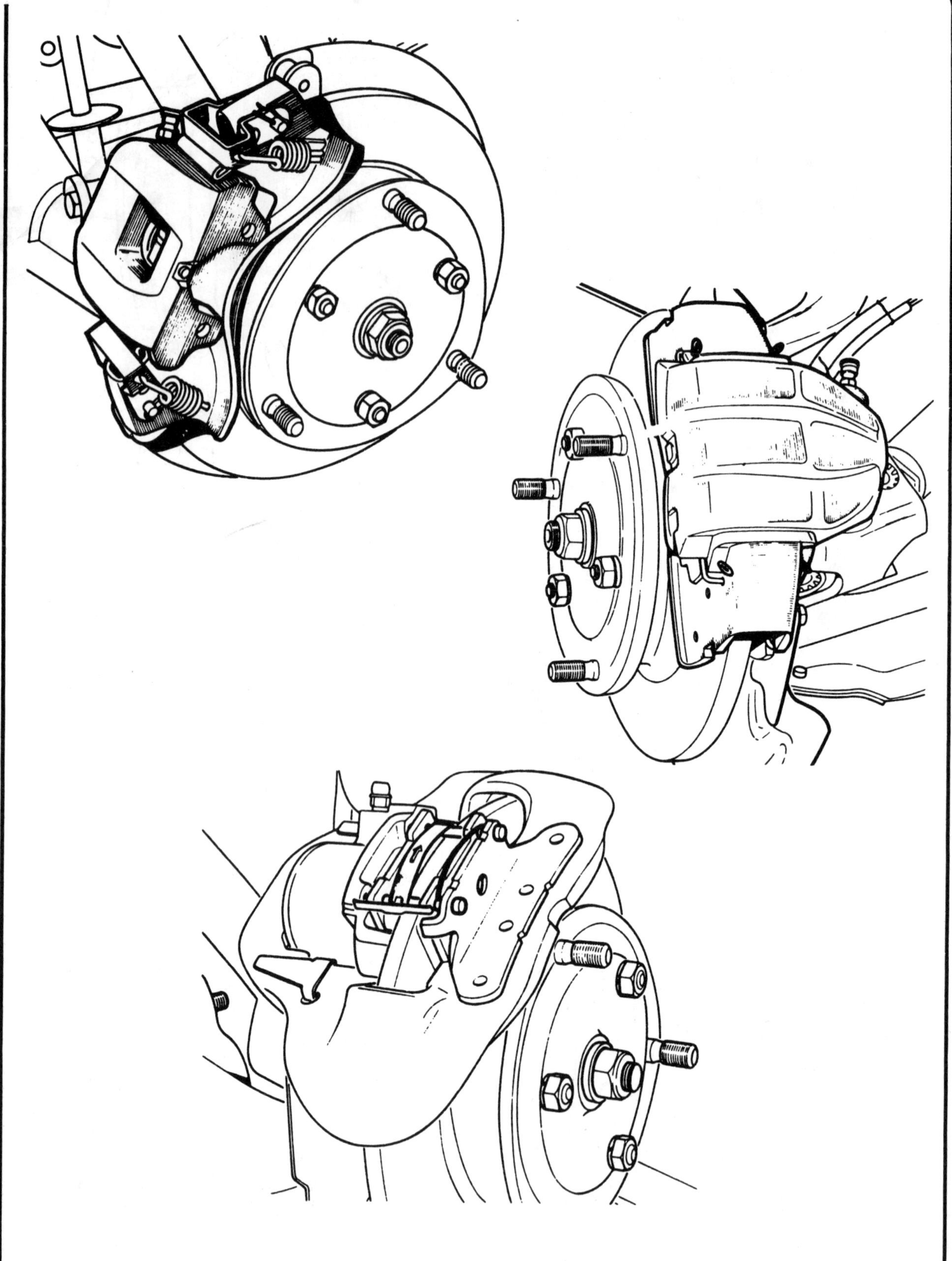

FIG.11.1 FRONT DISC BRAKE IDENTIFICATION

Top left - Bendix type II *Top right - Bendix type III AS* *Bottom - Girling*

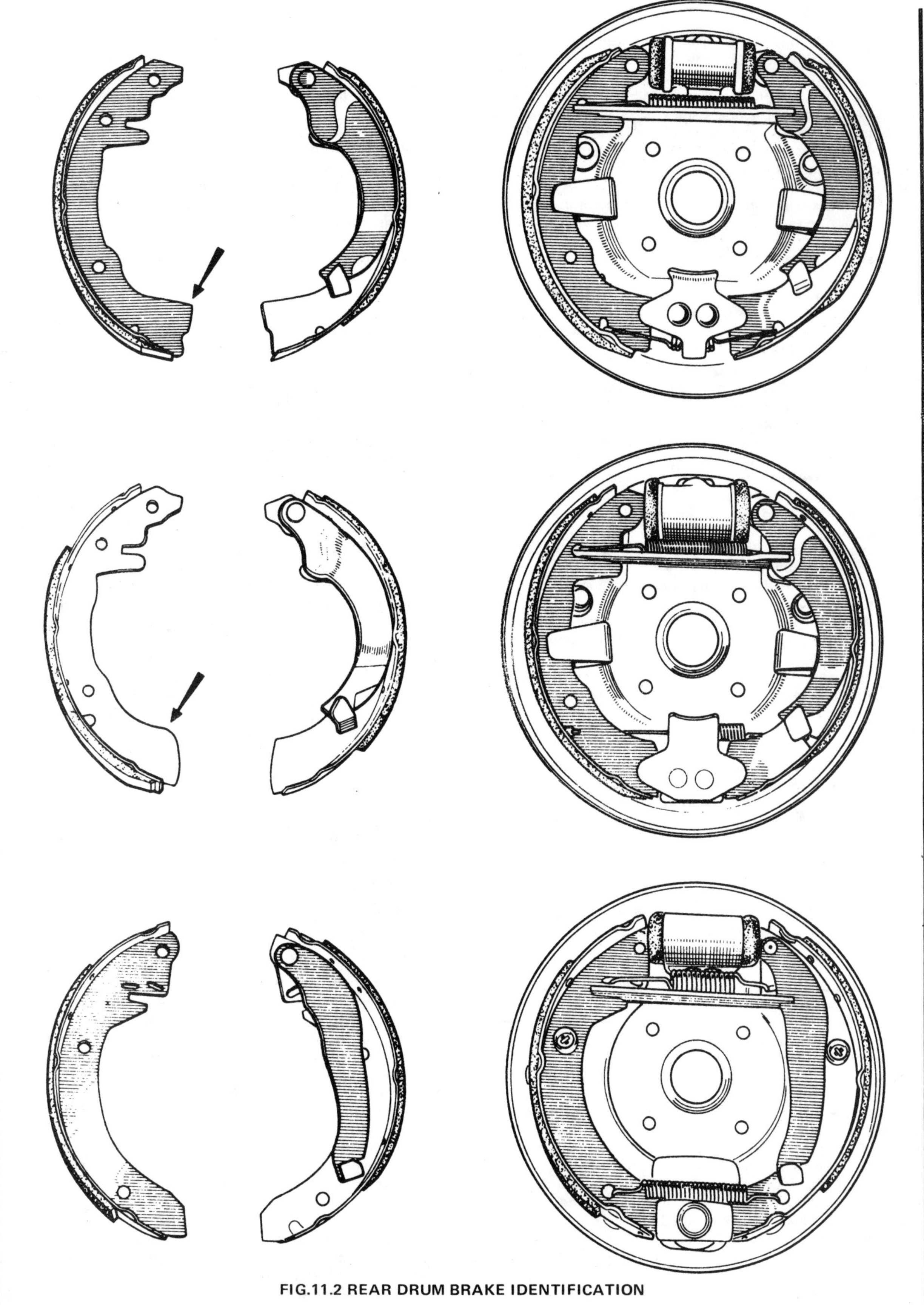

FIG.11.2 REAR DRUM BRAKE IDENTIFICATION

Top - Bendix normal fulcrum *Centre - Bendix lowered fulcrum* *Bottom - Girling*

A rough guide to wear may be obtained from the rate of wear of the front friction pads. When they require renewal, check the rear linings.

2 Observe strict cleanliness when handling the friction lining surfaces. A few oily fingermarks may be removed immediately by rubbing with a fuel soaked rag. Where there is evidence of grease saturation however, renew the shoes and remedy the cause which will probably be due to an excess of grease in the hub cavity.

3 Always make a sketch of the shoe web holes in which the return springs engage before dismantling so that they can be refitted in their original locations. Note carefully the 'handing' of the pairs of shoes in respect of leading and trailing edges, this is most important.

4 Always renew all four rear brake shoes at one and the same time. Renew shoes on an exchange basis and do not be tempted to renew the linings yourself, they are not ground to contour and seldom prove satisfactory.

5 Knock off or twist out of its seating, the hub grease cap.

6 Jack up the vehicle and remove the road wheel.

7 Remove the split pin, the nut lock cap, the nut and thrust washer from the stub axle. Slacken the adjuster right off.

8 Extract the brake drum by using a suitable three legged puller.

9 With the brake shoes now exposed, detach the upper shoe return spring, using a pair of pliers.

10 Disconnect the hand brake cable from its attachment at the brake back plate.

11 Remove the shoe steady springs (A) and pull back the shoes in order to remove rod (B). (Fig).

12 Remove the shoes from the backplate, still connected by the lower return spring.

13 Lay the two new shoes on the bench, correctly orientated in respect of leading and trailing edges and fit the lower return spring.

14 Fit the shoes (connected by their lower return spring) into position on the backplate.

15 Fit the upper shoe return spring, using pliers and then refit all other components removed on dismantling.

16 Cover the clips (A) with jointing compound where their surfaces are visible on the outside face of the backplate.

17 With Girling type brakes, renew the shoe retaining clips and spring rods whenever the brake shoes are renewed.

18 Refit the brake drum and adjust the hub bearings as described in Chapter 9. Reconnect the handbrake cable.

19 Adjust the brakes as described in the following Section.

20 Fit the road wheel and lower the jack.

21 Do not operate the brake foot pedal at any time when the brake drum is removed or the wheel cylinder pistons will be ejected and the system will have to be topped up with fluid and bled.

4 Rear Brakes - Adjustment

1 Jack up each of the rear road wheels in turn, chock the front wheels and ensure that the handbrake is fully off.

2 With Bendix brakes, turn the adjusters (C) and (T) in the direction of the arrows. (Fig).

3 Use a close fitting, open ended or special brake spanner and turn the adjusters until, rotating the wheel, the linings of the shoes just make contact with the drum. Free the adjusters just sufficiently to prevent them scraping the drum.

4 With Girling type brakes, turn the adjuster (D) in a clockwise direction and follow the procedure described in the preceding paragraph for Bendix type brakes. (Fig).

5 Lower the car and remove the jack.

5 Handbrake - Adjustment

1 Adjustment of the handbrake should not be required unless the cable has stretched or components of the rear braking assembly have been dismantled or reassembled.

2 Check the brake foot pedal free movement and adjust if necessary as described in Section 7.

3 Jack up the rear of the vehicle and release the handbrake fully.

4 Loosen the nuts (3) and turn the sleeve (1) until the shoes make contact with the drums. (Fig).

5 Turn the sleeve just sufficiently in the opposite direction to permit the wheels to turn freely. Tighten the locknuts.

6 Where handbrake travel is still excessive after the foregoing adjustment has been carried out then screw in the threaded adjuster on the clevis (2) as a secondary method of decreasing the handbrake travel. (Fig).

7 Lower the jack and remove it.

6 Brake Pressure Limiter Valve - Inspection and Adjustment

1 Correct adjustment of the brake pressure limiter valve is essential to safe and efficient braking. Before checking can be carried out, the vehicle must be placed on a level surface with a full fuel tank and a person sitting in the driver's seat.

2 A pressure gauge is essential (400–500 lb in^2 range) and must incorporate a bleed valve. A suitable instrument can be made up with a tee piece and utilising one of the proprietory type automatic brake bleeding nipples.

3 Connect the pressure gauge in place of one of the rear brake cylinder bleed nipples.

4 Bleed the system through the gauge bleed valve in a manner similar to that described in Section 17 but it will not be necessary to bleed other than from the gauge nipple.

5 Check that the rod is securely clamped to the anti-roll bar.

6 Check the cut-off pressure specified on the limiter link. Where this is not shown, use a cut off pressure of between 415 and 485 lb in^2.

7 Apply the footbrake pedal several times in succession and check the reading on the pressure gauge. Where necessary, loosen the nut and adjust the position of the link until the pressure reading on subsequent pedal applications lies within the range specified.

8 Remove the gauge, refit the original bleed nipple, bleed the brakes (Section 17) and top up the master cylinder reservoir.

9 The brake pressure limiter valve cannot be serviced and in the event of failure or leakage, renew the complete unit.

10 New valves are of different external shape from earlier models and it is possible when fitting the new units to connect the fluid lines incorrectly. The pipes from the rear wheel cylinders must connect with ports (1) and (2) which are at 90° to each other and the line from the master cylinder to port (3) on the inclined face of the limiter valve. (Fig).

7 Master Cylinder - Removal and Refitting

1 Ideally, before removal of the master cylinder, the brake fluid should be drained from the reservoir. The fluid may be syphoned out or one of the unions disconnected and the foot brake pedal depressed until the fluid is expelled from both the master cylinder and the reservoir.

2 Disconnect all the fluid pipe unions from the master cylinder. (Fig).

3 On models fitted with a pressure drop indicator, unscrew the securing plug and carefully move the indicator aside. (Fig).

4 Unscrew the master cylinder securing bolts (two) or if servo fitted (four).

5 Cap the ends of the fluid lines (rubber bleed nipple rubber covers are ideal) to prevent the ingress of dirt.

6 As the master cylinder is withdrawn, the pedal operating rod will be left attached to the foot pedal.

7 To refit the master cylinder, engage the operating rod with the piston assembly and bolt the master cylinder into its location.

8 Reconnect the unions, refill the reservoir and bleed the

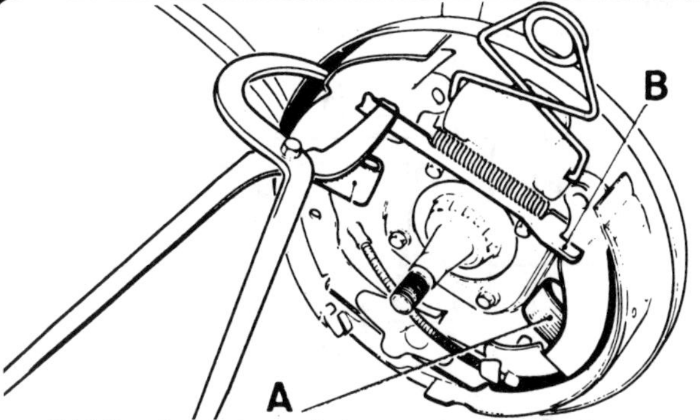

3.11 Rear brake shoes. A shoe steady spring. B Rod

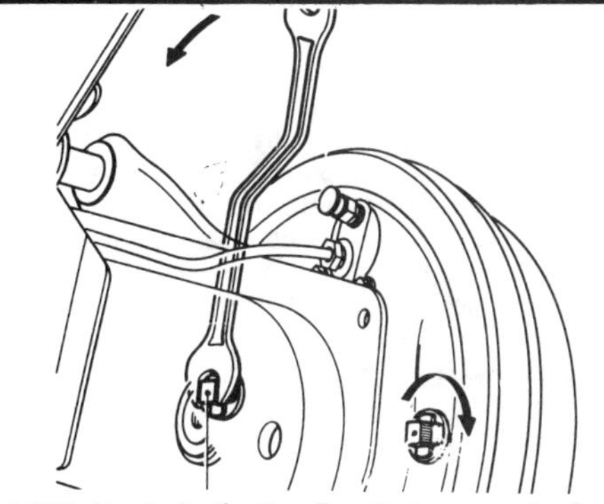
4.2 Method of adjusting Bendix type rear brakes

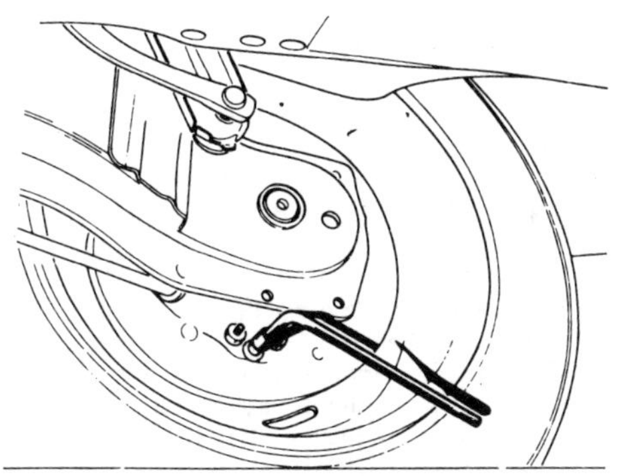
4.4 Method of adjusting Girling type rear brakes

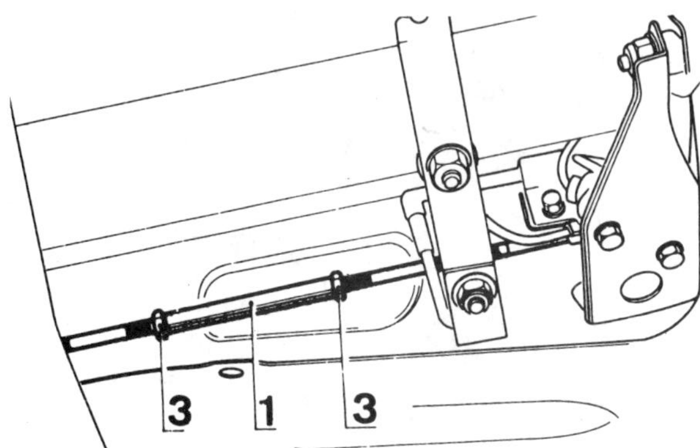

5.4 Handbrake adjuster sleeve (1) and locknuts (3)

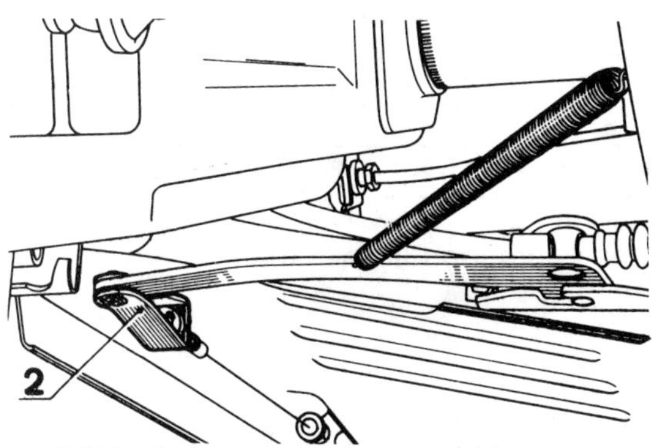

5.6 Handbrake secondary adjustment (2) clevis

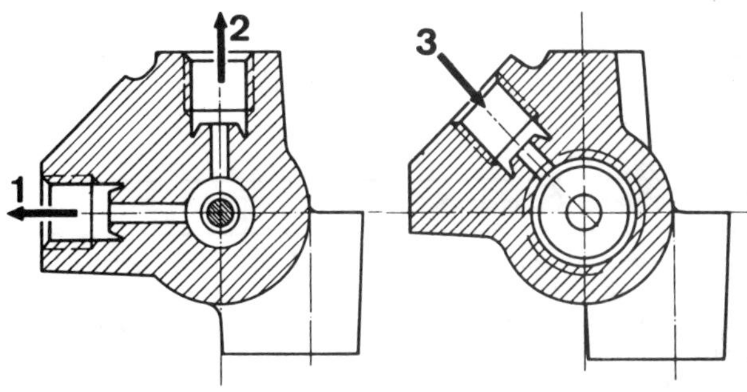

6.10 Hydraulic brake pipe attachment points to brake pressure limiter valve body. 1 and 2 from rear wheel cylinder. 3 from master cylinder

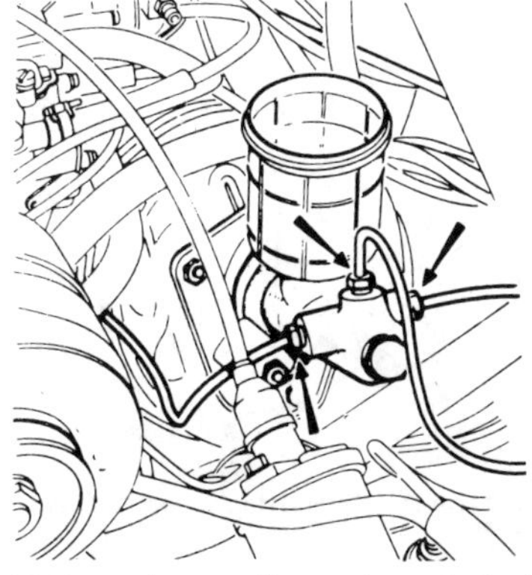
7.2 Rigid pipe unions on the master cylinder body

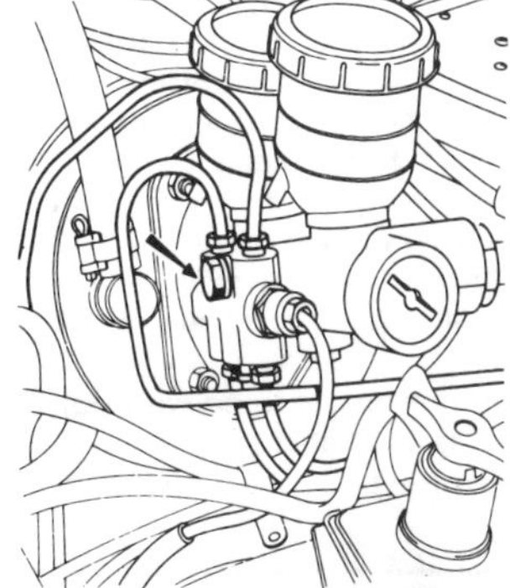
7.3 Bolt which secures brake pressure limiter valve to master cylinder.

system as described in Section 17.

9 Check the free movement of the master cylinder operating rod. This should be 1/64 in (0.5 mm) and is adjusted by slackening the locknut (E) and rotating the rod (1). (Fig).

10 The clearance must obviously be measured at the foot pedal arm or the free movement 'felt'. Where a servo unit is fitted, then the free movement is adjusted on the servo unit itself.

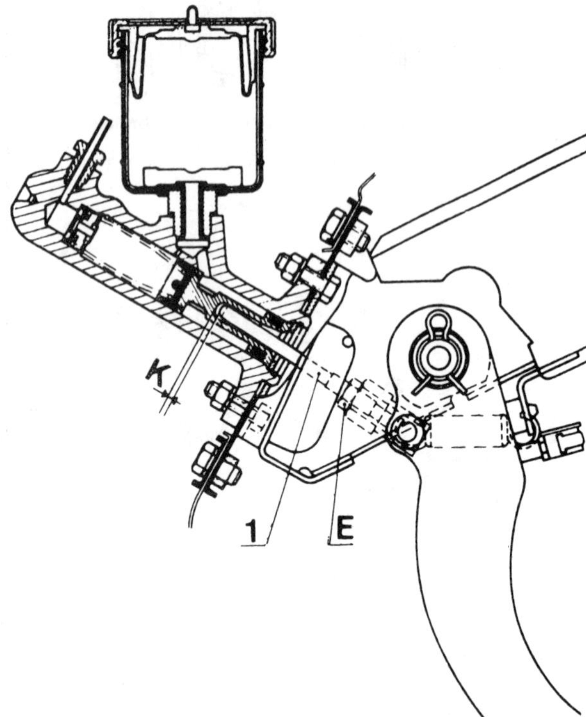

7.9 Sectional view of master cylinder showing operating push-rod and brake pedal. 1 Push-rod. E Locknut. K Free movement

8 Single Master Cylinder - Servicing

1 Observe absolute cleanliness during all operations to hydraulic units. Wash components in clean brake fluid or methylated spirit only and renew all seals as a matter of course from the repair kits available.

2 Remove the circlip (1) and stop washer (2). Fig 11.3.

3 Withdraw the piston assembly (3) by either knocking the master cylinder body on a piece of wood or applying air pressure from a tyre pump at one of the ports whilst keeping the others covered with the fingers.

4 Remove the copper washer (4) the rubber sealing cup (5) the return spring (6) and the valve assembly (7).

5 Examine the surfaces of the piston and cylinder bore for scoring and 'bright' areas of wear. If any are visible, renew the complete unit on an exchange basis.

6 Reassembly is a reversal of dismantling but fit the seals using the fingers to manipulate them and lubricate all the components with clean brake fluid. Note the exact sequence of component fitting with particular referemce to the chamfers and lips of the seals.

7 Where the fluid reservoir is fitted with a diaphragm type cap, it should be shaped as illustrated.

8 If the diaphragm is worn, renew it with one of newer design.

9 Tandem Master Cylinder - Description and Servicing

1 This type of master cylinder operates the front and rear brakes as two separate circuits. This is a valuable safety factor

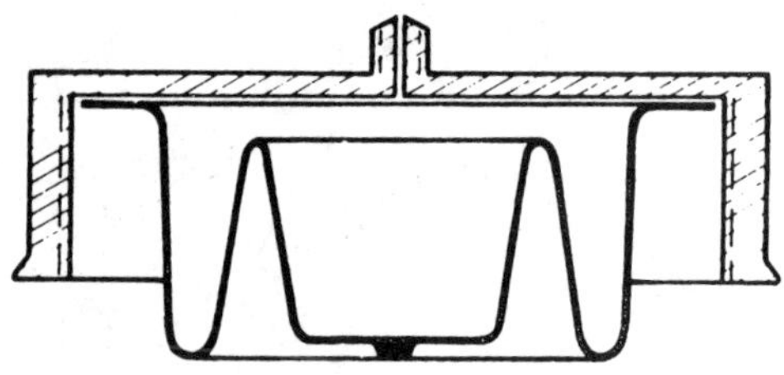

8.7 Fitting diagram for reservoir cap diaphragm

for in the event of a fault 50% braking effort will still be available.

2 A primary (P) and a secondary (S) piston assembly are employed as shown in Fig 11.4..

3 To dismantle the unit, secure the housing in a vice, protecting the jaws with wooden strips.

4 Unscrew and remove both fluid reservoirs.

5 Using a length of wooden dowelling, actuate the pistons (movement of about 3/16 in 4.8 mm) so that the stop screw (1) may be removed.

6 Unscrew and remove the plug (5) using a right angled blade, remove the copper washer (6).

7 Withdraw the secondary piston (S) together with the spring (7). An exploded view of the unit is shown in Fig 11.5.

8 Push out the primary piston (P) using a piece of wood to prevent scoring the bore.

9 Remove the circlip (8) and withdraw the stop washer (9).

10 Unscrew the pressure drop indicator valve union.

11 Wash all components in clean brake fluid or methylated spirit and renew all seals. Reassembly, after having checked for scoring or wear to the piston or cylinder bore surfaces. Where these are apparent, renew the complete assembly on an exchange basis. The end plug (5) should be tightened to 75 lbf ft (10.4 kgf m).

10 Caliper (Bendix type 11) - Removal and Refitting

1 Jack up the car and remove the road wheel.

2 Remove the pins (13) which secure the swing clamps (14). (Fig).

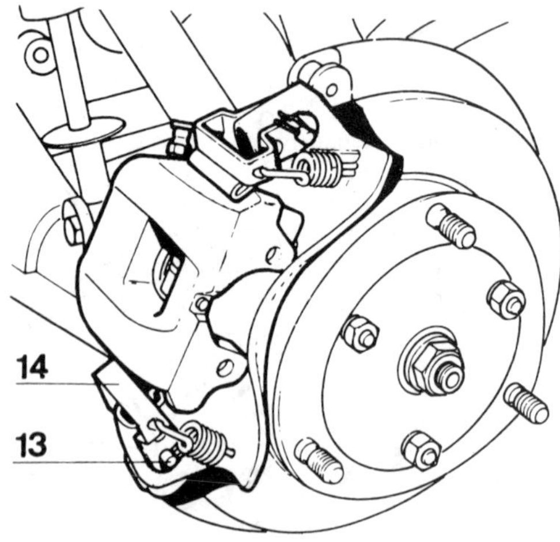

10.2 Bendix type II caliper attachment. 13 securing pins. 14 swing clamps

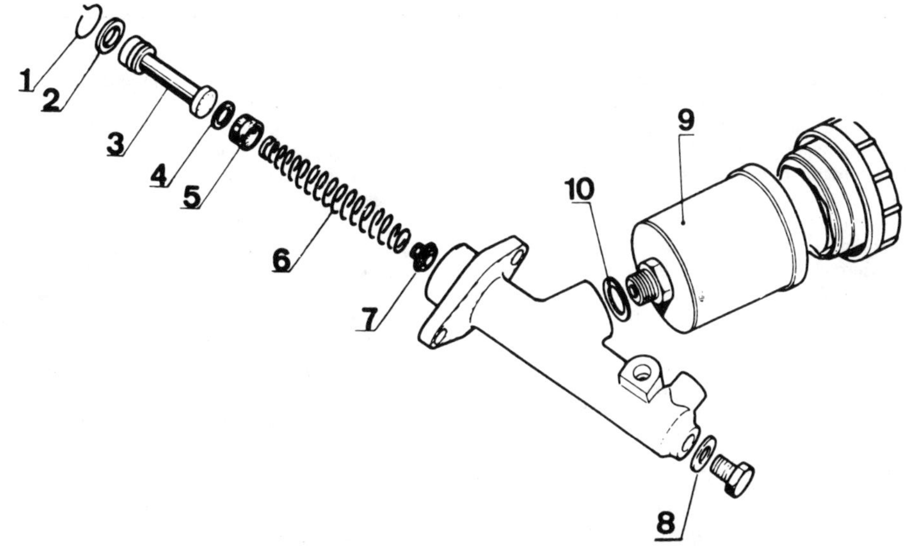

FIG.11.3 EXPLODED VIEW OF THE SINGLE TYPE MASTER CYLINDER

1 Circlip
2 Stop washer
3 Piston assembly
4 Copper washer
5 Seal
6 Piston return spring
7 Valve assembly
8 Plug washer
9 Reservoir body
10 Sealing washer

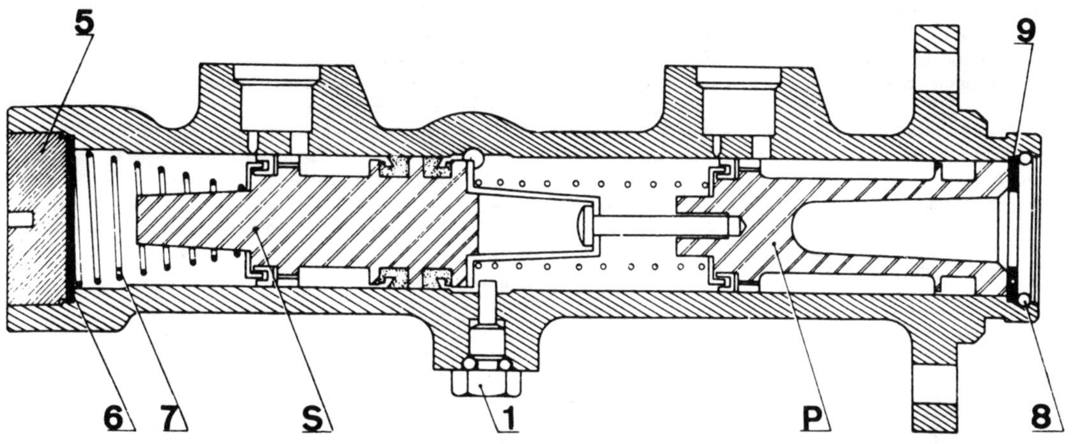

FIG.11.4 SECTIONAL VIEW OF THE TANDEM TYPE MASTER CYLINDER

P Primary piston assembly
S Secondary piston assembly
1 Stop screw
5 Plug
6 Copper washer
7 Spring
8 Circlip
9 Stop washer

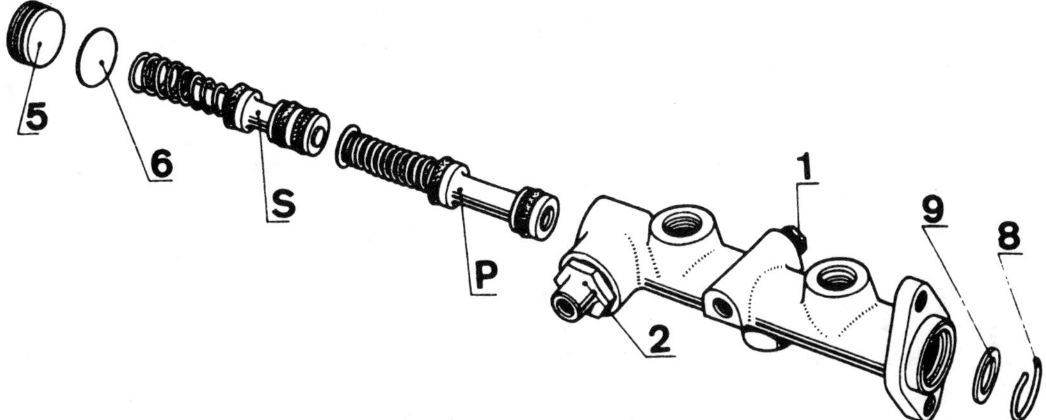

FIG.11.5 EXPLODED VIEW OF THE TANDEM MASTER CYLINDER

P Primary piston assembly
S Secondary piston assembly
1 Stop screw
2 Residual pressure valve
5 Plug
6 Copper washer
7 Spring
8 Circlip
9 Stop washer

3 Tilt the clamps and withdraw the caliper by pulling it rearwards with the flexible hydraulic hose still attached.
4 Remove the friction pads.
5 At the support bracket, unscrew the union (D) remove the clip (C) and lift the caliper away. (Fig).
6 Plug the fluid line and do not touch the brake pedal until reassembly is completed.
7 Unscrew the flexible hose (B) from the support bracket and then unscrew the flexible hose from the caliper. Keep the hose straight during the unscrewing operation and retain the copper sealing washer (see Section 26).
8 Refitting is a reversal of removal but fill the caliper with clean fluid before connecting the hoses as this will save time during the bleeding operation.
9 Bleed the brakes (Section 17) refit the road wheel and lower the jack.

11 Caliper (Bendix Type 111 AS) - Removal and Refitting

1 Jack up the vehicle and remove the road wheel.
2 Remove the pins (A). (Fig).
3 Slide the key (B) sideways and free the caliper from its bracket. (Fig).
4 Disconnect the pad wear warning wire (if fitted).
5 Unscrew the rigid to flexible pipeline union and remove the retaining clip from the flexible hose bracket and free the caliper. Plug the fluid line and do not operate the brake pedal.
6 Unscrew the flexible hose from the caliper.
7 Carry out the operations described in paragraph 8 of the preceding Section.
8 Refitting will be facilitated if one end of the caliper is slipped between the spring and the bearing surface for the key on the caliper bracket,(Fig)..
9 Locate the other end of the caliper by compressing both springs.
10 Fit the first key then slip a screwdriver in the slot for the second key, lever in a downward direction and slide in the second key. (Fig).
11 Fit the four retaining pins (flat section facing caliper bracket) and reconnect the pad wear warning light.
12 Bleed the brakes (Section 17) fit the road wheel and lower the jack.

12 Caliper (Girling) - Removal and Refitting.

1 Disconnect the rigid to flexible hydraulic pipe union and plug the end of the metal pipe.
2 Remove the clip which secures the flexible brake hose to the support bracket.
3 Loosen the flexible brake hose connection to the caliper unit but do not twist the hose (1). (Fig).
4 Unscrew the two securing bolts (2) which hold the caliper to the stub axle carrier. Withdraw the caliper and unscrew and remove the flexible hose and retain the copper sealing washer.
5 Withdraw the friction pads as described in Section 2, paragraphs 12 and 13.
6 Free the floating caliper bracket by sliding it in the direction illustrated.
7 Refitting is a reversal of removal but see Section 25 for the correct fitting of flexible brake hoses and bleed the hydraulic system as described in Section 17.

13 Calipers (all types) - Servicing

1 Having removed the caliper unit from the car as described in the preceding Sections, thoroughly clean the exterior of the unit with methylated spirit.
2 Withdraw the cover (3), unscrew the nut (2) whilst holding the shaft (6) with a screwdriver engaged in its slotted end.

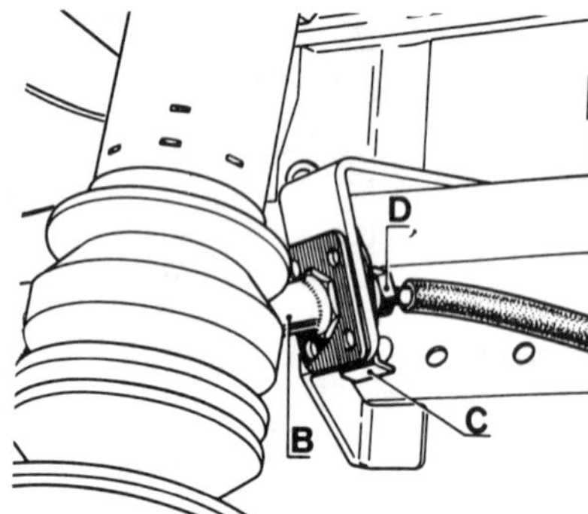

10.5 Fluid line connection to Bendix type II caliper. B flexible hose. C Clip. D union.

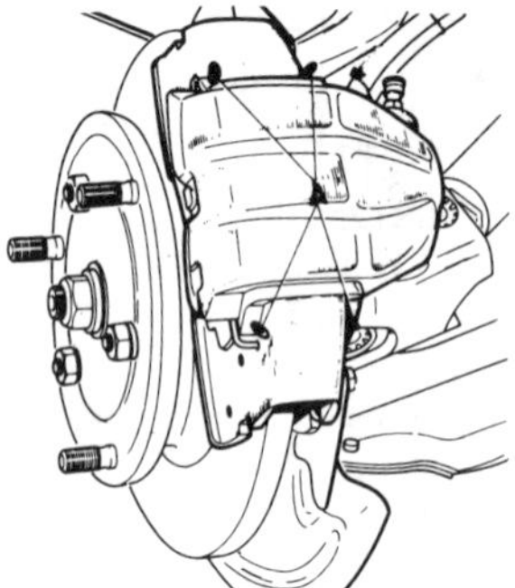
11.2 Bendix type III AS caliper attachment pins (A)

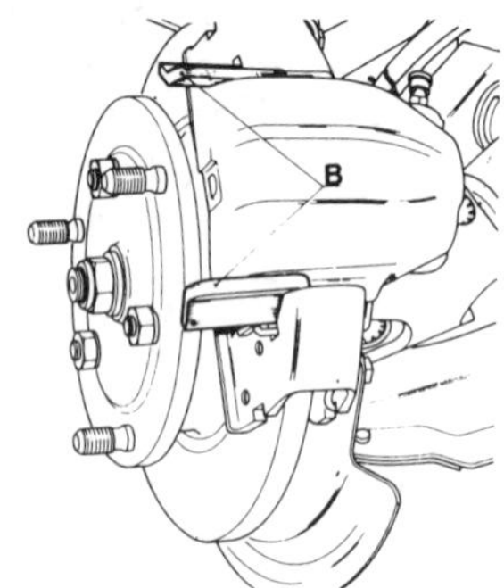

11.3 Bendix type III AS caliper keys (B)

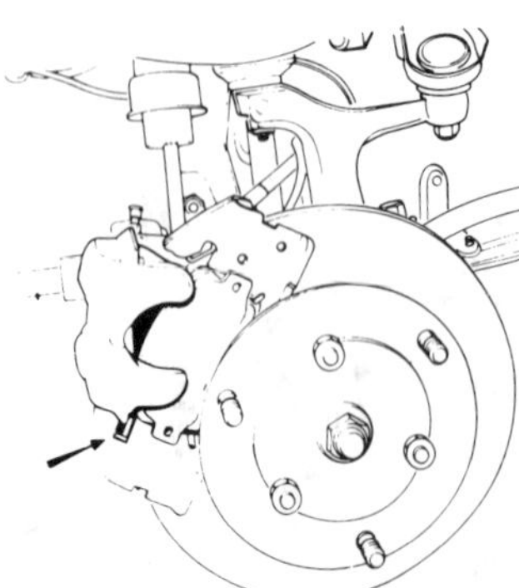
11.8 Method of refitting Bendix III AS caliper

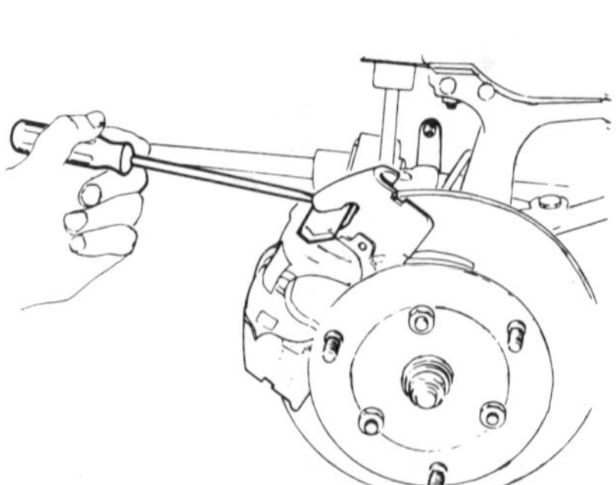
11.10 Levering a Bendix III AS caliper downwards prior to inserting the second key

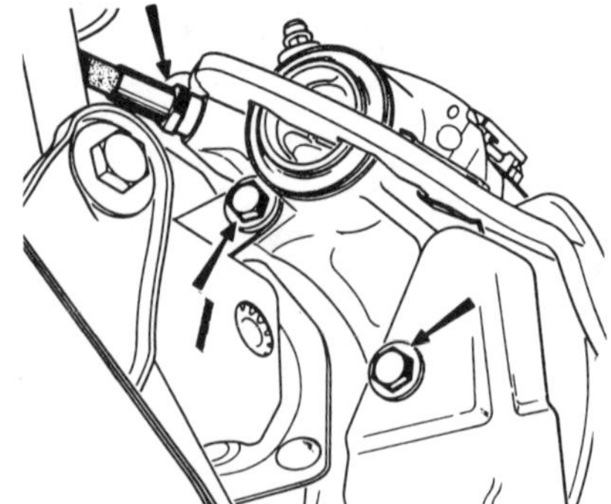
12.3 Flexible hose attachment and two bracket to stub axle carrier bolts on a Girling caliper

3 Push out the piston (4) and then prise out the 'O' ring seal (5) (some models are fitted with square section seals) using a plastic or smooth edged strip as illustrated.

4 Do not attempt to dismantle the wear take-up mechanism inside the piston.

5 Thoroughly clean all components in methylated spirit or clean brake fluid and examine the surface of the piston for scoring or bright marks indicating wear. If these are visible then the piston assembly must be renewed. Check the caliper unit and cylinder for corrosion (particularly in the seal groove) and for wear and renew if necessary.

6 Fit a new seal into the cylinder bore groove, using the fingers only for manipulation and lubricating generously with brake fluid.

7 Assemble the piston and cylinder unit by hand pressure only. Hold the piston (4) fitted with a new seal (7) in a vertical position so that the shaft thread is uppermost. (Fig).

8 Push the piston gently into the cylinder bore with thumb pressure, refit the nut to the piston shaft and tighten it to 10 lb ft (14.9 kg m).

9 Ensure that the mark (P) located on the piston face is located as near as possible to the bleed nipple. (Fig).

10 Smear the outside of the piston with recommended grease and fit a new dust cover (E) to Bendix type calipers. (Fig).

11 With Girling type calipers, the dust covers are retained in position by a plastic snap ring. (Figs).

12 Girling caliper pistons are ejected by applying pressure from a tyre pump at the flexible brake hose orifice. Renew all rubber seals and assemble the internal components exactly as illustrated.

14 Front Brake Disc - Removal and Refitting

1 Brake discs should be renewed if severe scoring or rusting has occurred or where disc thicknesses have been reduced by wear to below the following minimum permissible dimensions.

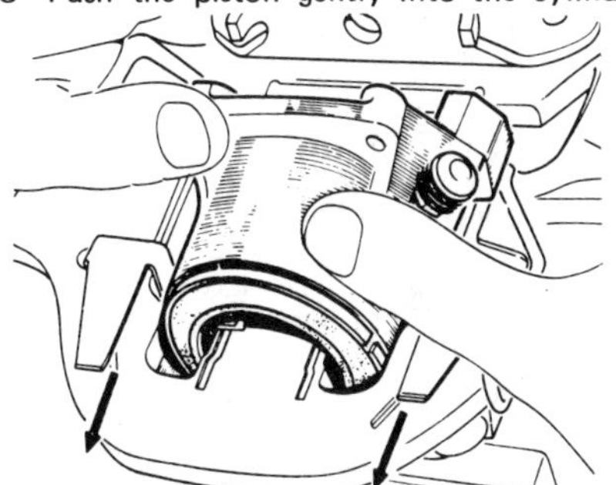

12.6 Freeing the floating caliper bracket on a Girling caliper

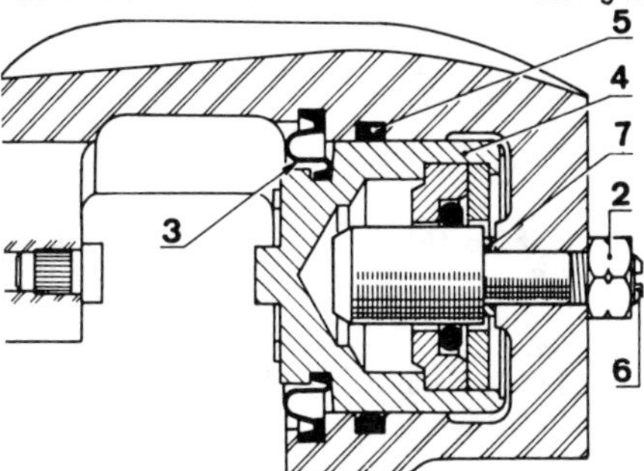

13.2 Cross sectional view of Bendix type calipers. 2 nut. 3 dust cover. 4 piston. 5 seal. 6 shaft. 7 seal

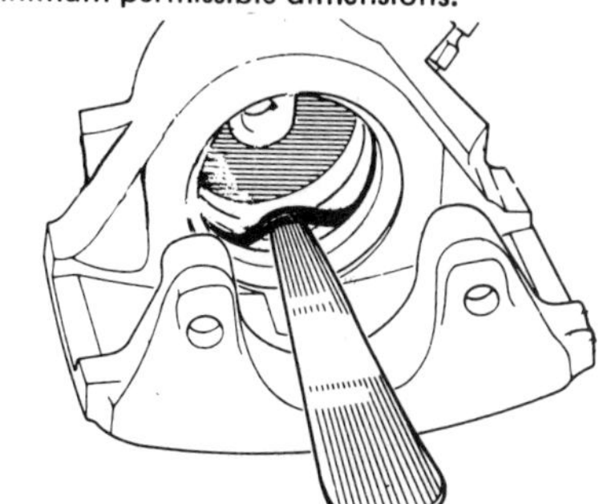

13.3 Removing a caliper piston seal

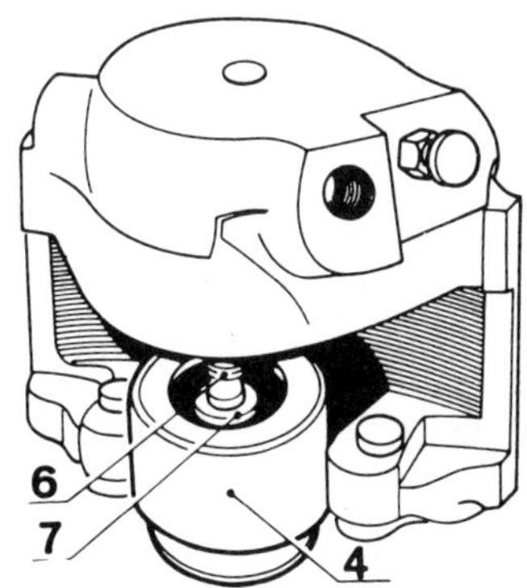

13.7 Reassembling a Bendix type caliper

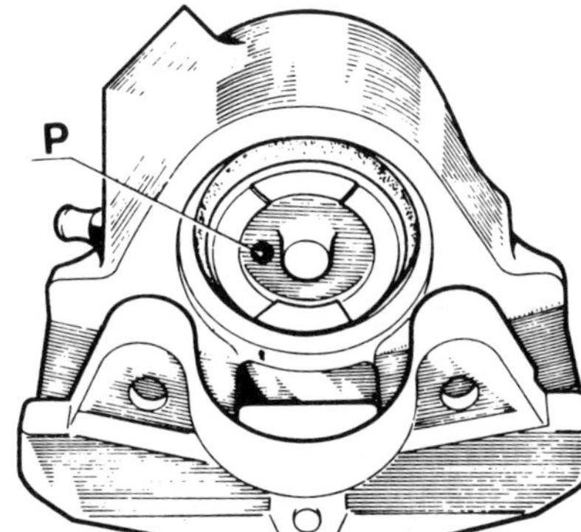

13.9 Mark to show correct orientation of piston in a Bendix caliper

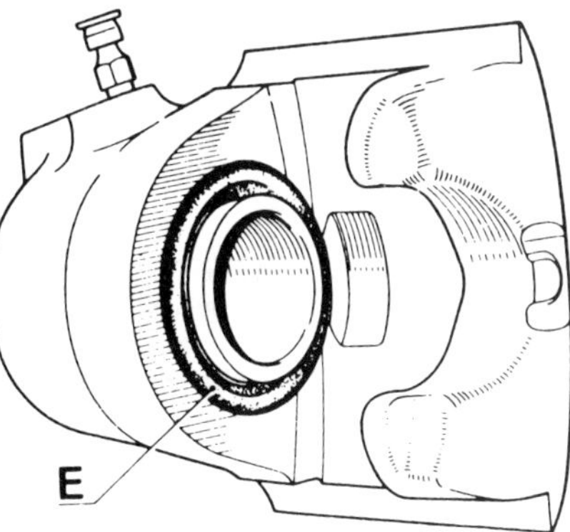

13.10 Location of dust cover on Bendix type caliper

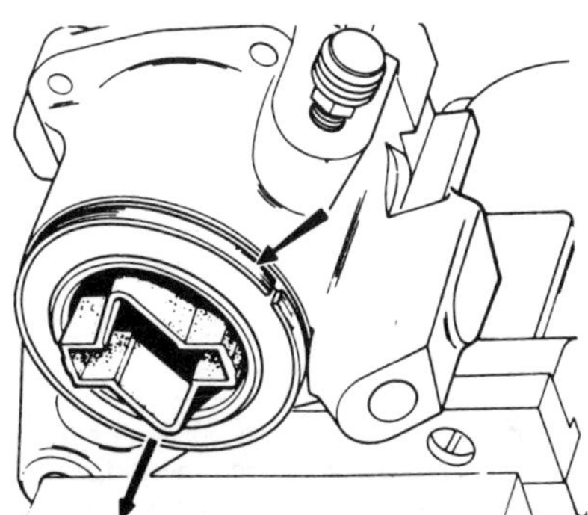

13.11A Girling caliper showing plastic piston guide and dust cover snap rings

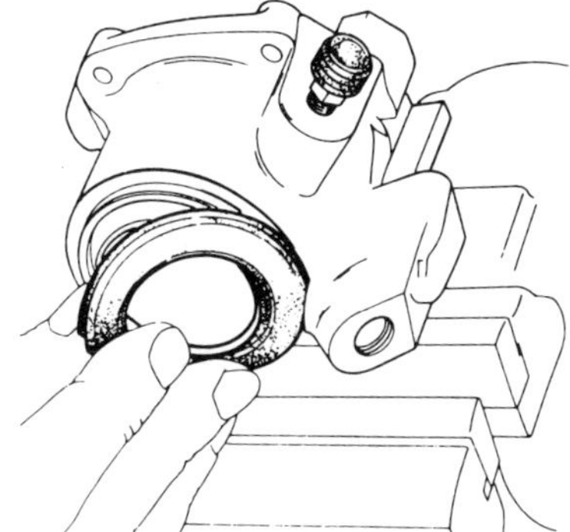

13.11B Removing the rubber dust covers (two) from a Girling caliper

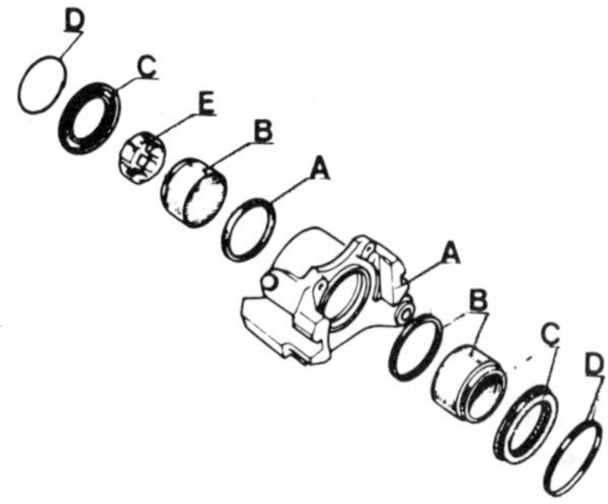

13.12 Exploded view of a Girling type caliper unit. A seals. B pistons. C dust covers. D snap rings

2 Model R1150 (pre 1969) 0.315 in (8 mm).
3 All models (1969 onwards) 0.434 in (11 mm).
4 Model R1150 (fitted with Girling brakes 0.374 in (9.5 mm).
5 Should the disc have become distorted or have a run-out beyond the specified tolerance, then again the disc should be renewed.
6 Withdraw the hub/disc assembly as described in Chapter 8. The hydraulic circuit need not be disconnected if the caliper is detached and swung to one side as illustrated.
7 Separate the disc from the hub and then fit a new disc and refit the hub/disc assembly in the reverse order to removal.

15 Caliper - Shimming

1 With Bendix type calipers, shims (A) are positioned between the caliper bracket and its support. (Fig).
2 Normally the shims originally fitted should be replaced but where the caliper or disc have been renewed then the clearances (a) and (b) must be checked. (Fig).
3 For Bendix 11 type brakes the clearances must be 3/32 in. (2.5 mm).
4 For Bendix 111 AS type brakes, only clearance (a) should be 1/8 in (3 mm).
5 Where the clearances are incorrect, adjust the shims (A) for thickness to rectify. (Fig).
6 The shims are available in thicknesses: 0.02 - 0.039 - 0.059 - 0.079 and 0.099 in (0.5 - 1.0 - 1.5 - 2.0 and 2.5 mm).
7 Girling calipers are not fitted with shims but are bolted directly to the stub axle carrier and tightened to a torque of 25 lbf ft (3.4 kgf m).

16 Rear Wheel Cylinder - Removal, Servicing, Refitting

1 Jack up the vehicle and remove the road wheel, check that the handbrake is fully off. Turn the shoe adjuster to zero.
2 Remove the brake drum as described in Section 3.
3 Detach the brake shoe upper return spring and pull the shoes aside at their upper ends but do not remove them from their backplate location.
4 Disconnect the hydraulic pipe union (1) on the wheel cylinder housing and plug the pipe to prevent loss of brake fluid. Do not operate the foot pedal until reassembly is complete. (Fig. 16.4).
5 Unscrew and remove the two wheel cylinder securing bolts (2) and remove the cylinder.
6 Check the shoe linings for brake fluid contamination and renew the shoes if necessary.
7 Dismantle the wheel cylinder by removing the dust covers (1) ejecting the pistons (2) by knocking the cylinder on a piece of wood or applying a tyre pump to the pipeline orifice, and removing the seals (3) and the spring (4). (Fig).
8 Wash the components in clean brake fluid or methylated spirit and examine the piston and bore surfaces for scoring or 'bright' wear marks. If these are apparent, renew the complete wheel cylinder on an exchange basis.
9 Renew the seals from the repair kit supplied and reassemble, using the fingers for manipulation and clean brake fluid for lubrication. Ensure that the components are fitted in the sequence shown and pay particular attention to the orientation of seal lips and chamfers.(Fig 16.7).
10 Refit the cylinder to the backplate. reconnect the shoe upper return spring, refit the brake drum and connect the hydraulic pipe to the cylinder housing.
11 Bleed the brakes as described in the next Section and then adjust the brake shoes as described in Section 4.
12 Refit the road wheel and lower the jack.

17 Hydraulic System - Bleeding

1 The system should need bleeding only when some part of the system has been dismantled which would allow air into the fluid circuit; or if the reservoir level has been allowed to drop so far that air has entered the master cylinder.

In order to minimise fluid loss from the hydraulic system and entry of air whenever a component of the system is removed or dismantled, it is helpful to remove the master cylinder reservoir cap and place a piece of ploythene sheeting over the top of the reservoir and screw on the cap. This operation will have the effect of sealing the air hole in the reservoir cap and create a partial vacuum in the reservoir and prevent fluid from running out of the disconnected pipe union.
2 Ensure that a supply of clean non-aerated fluid of the correct specification is to hand in order to replenish the reservoir during the bleeding process. It is advisable, if not essential, to have someone available to help, as one person has to pump the brake pedal while the other attends to each wheel. The reservoir level has also to be continuously watched and replenished. Fluid bled out should not be re-used. A clean glass jar and a 9-12 inch (220-310 mm) length of 1/8 inch (3.2 mm) internal diameter rubber tube that will fit tightly over the bleed nipples is also required.
3 Bleed the front brakes first as these hold the largest quantity of fluid in the system.
4 Make sure the bleed nipple is clean and put a small quantity of fluid in the bottom of the jar. Fit the tube onto the nipple and place the other end in the jar under the surface of the liquid. Keep it under the surface throughout the bleeding operation.
5 Unscrew the bleed screw ½ turn and get the assistant to depress and release the brake pedal in short sharp bursts when you direct him. Short sharp jabs are better than long slow ones because they will force any air bubbles along the line ahead of the fluid rather than pump the fluid past them. It is not essential to remove all the air the first time. If the whole system is being bled, attend to each wheel for three or four complete pedal strokes and then repeat the process. On the second time around operate the pedal sharply in the same way until no more bubbles are apparent. The bleed screw should be tightened and closed with the brake pedal fully depressed which ensures that no aerated fluid can get back into the system. Do not forget to keep the reservoir topped up throughout.
6 When all four wheels have been satisfactorily bled depress the foot pedal which should offer a firmer resistance with no trace of 'sponginess'. The pedal should not continue to go down under sustained pressure. If it does there is a leak or the master cylinder seals are worn out.
7 It is recommended that the brakes are bled in the sequence shown in Fig.11.6

18 Handbrake Control Lever - Removal and Refitting

1 Release the handbrake fully.
2 Disconnect the clevis from the lever.
3 Remove the left hand glove compartment, the securing screws (4) from under the wing, the screws (5) and (6). (Fig.)
4 Position pin (7) in line with hole (8) and then drift out the pin. (Fig).
5 Slide the sleeve (9) along the rod and free the cable clamp (10). Take out the end stop (11) and clip (12) and withdraw the control lever.
6 Refitting is a reversal of removal but seal the under wing bolts with sealing compound after tightening.

19 Handbrake Cables - Renewal

1 Where the cables have stretched beyond the scope of adjustment or are frayed in any way then they must be renewed.
2 Remove the hand control lever and separate the cable from it as described in the preceding Section.
3 Disconnect the clevis on the primary cable and remove the sleeve which connects the primary and secondary cables.
4 Free the cables from their bracket and cable cover clamp.

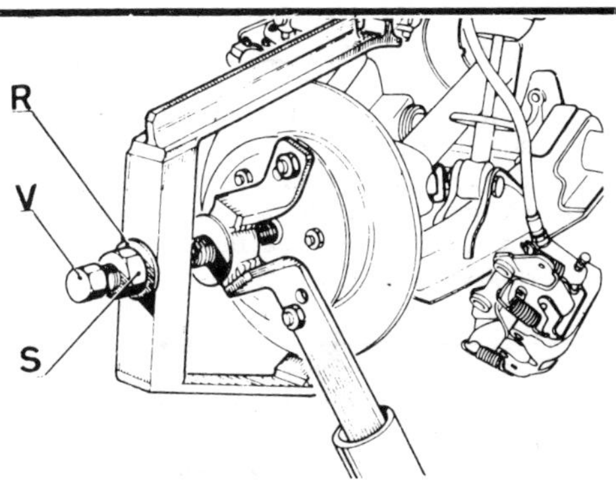

14.6 Removing a hub/disc assembly

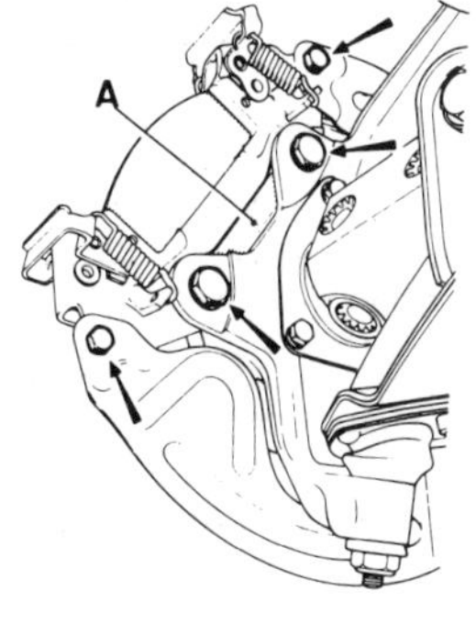

15.1 Caliper unit showing securing bolts and shim (A)

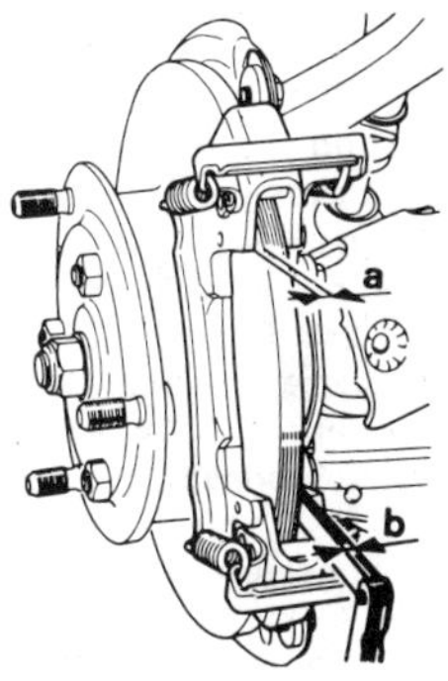

15.2 Disc running clearances. For (a) and (b) dimensions see text

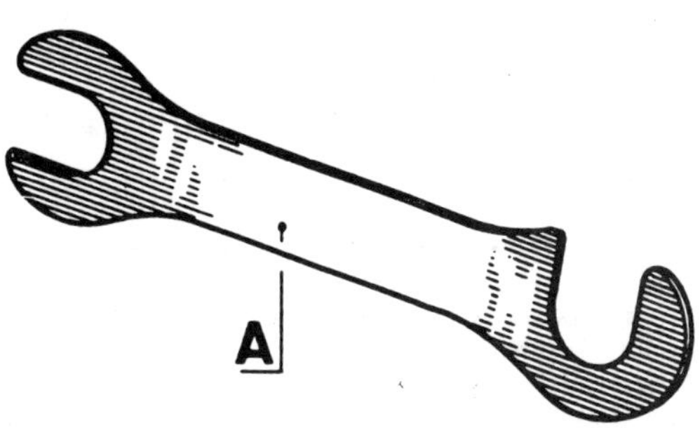

15.5 A shim used in fitting Bendix type calipers

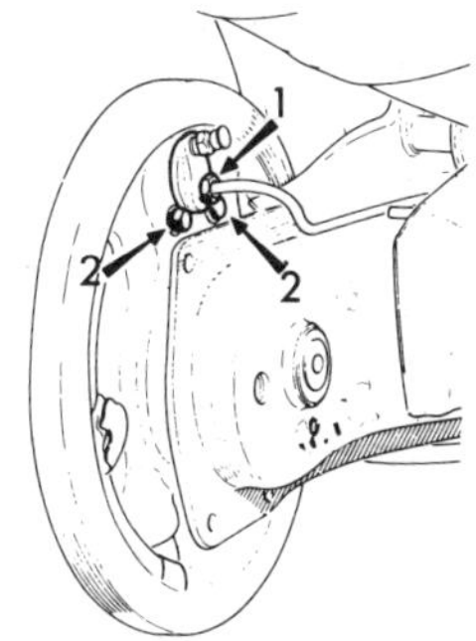

16.4 Rear wheel cylinder securing bolts and pipe union

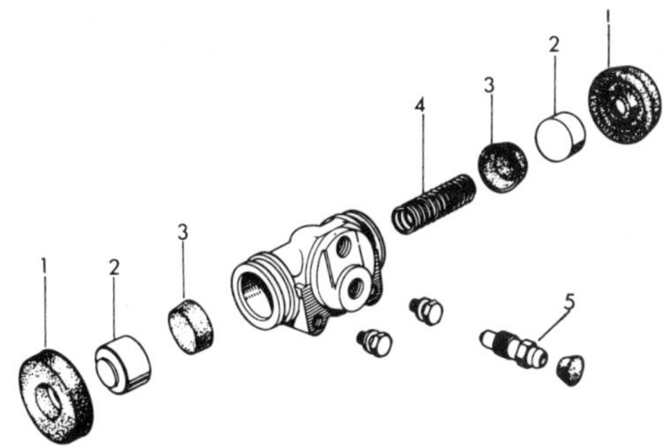

16.7 Exploded view of a rear wheel brake cylinder. 1 Dust covers. 2 Pistons. 3 Seals. 4 Return spring. 5 Bleed nipple.

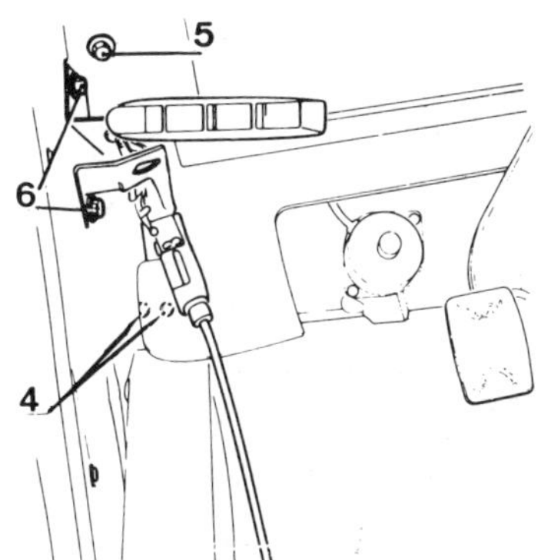

18.3 Disconnecting the handbrake control. 4 glove compartment securing screws. 5 and 6 handbrake securing screws

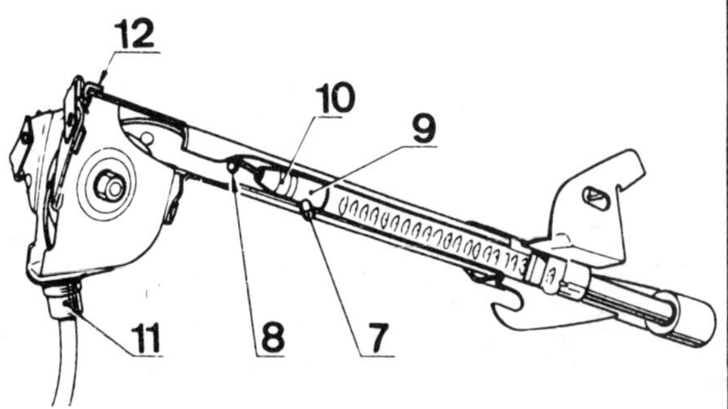

18.4 Method of attachment of handbrake control lever to cable 7 pin. 8 hole. 9 sleeve. 10 cable clamp. 11 end stop. 12 clip

5 Remove the brake drums as described in Section 3.
6 Free the end of the cable from lever (2) and push back the cable cover from its stop on the brake backplate. (Fig).
7 Fitting the new cables is a reversal of their removal but apply sealing compound at the point on the brake backplate where they pass through and adjust the handbrake as described in Section 5.

20 Servo (Master Vac) Unit - Description and Testing

1 The brake servo unit operates from vacuum pressure supplied from the engine manifold. It is emphasised that it is servo assistance and in the event of the unit failing then normal hydraulic braking will still be available by foot pressure.
2 Leaks in, or failure of, the servo unit may be detected by a sudden increase in the brake pedal pressure required to retard or stop the vehicle. Uneven running or stalling of the engine may also indicate leaks in the servo system.
3 Before carrying out any servicing of the unit, check for split or perished vacuum hose connections.

21 Servo (Master Vac) - Removal and Refitting

1 Disconnect the battery.
2 Using a syphon or syringe, drain the brake fluid from the reservoir, as illustrated.
3 Unscrew the hydraulic pipe unions (R) on the master cylinder.
4 With model R1152 vehicles, detach the pressure drop indicator from the master cylinder.
5 Disconnect the vacuum hose (D) from the servo unit non-return valve connection (2) (Fig 11.7).
6 Disconnect the master cylinder operating push rod from the brake pedal arm.
7 Unscrew and remove the securing bolts, two located each side of the brake pedal.
8 Withdraw the servo and master cylinder assembly and then separate the two units by removing the two securing bolts.
9 Refitting is a reversal of removal but bleed the system after assembly is complete.

22 Servo (Master - Vac) - Servicing

1 Servicing operations must be limited to the following components: the air filter, the non-return valve and the diaphragm seal. Where failure or incorrect operation of the servo unit emanates from components other than those specified then the complete unit should be renewed on an exchange basis.
2 Every 9000 miles (15 000 km) clean or change the air filter element. For this operation it is not necessary to remove the servo unit but simply to disconnect the operating rod fork and unscrew the locknut (E) (Fig).
3 Unscrew the forked end (C), remove the spring and withdraw the air filter element. Clean the filter with compressed air or renew according to its condition.
4 Fit the components in reverse order to removal and adjust the dimension D to 1 5/8 in (42 mm) which is essential to provide the correct pedal free movement.
5 To renew the non-return valve, leave the servo unit in position in the vehicle. Disconnect the vacuum inlet hose from the servo unit.
6 Pull and twist the non-return valve out of engagement with its rubber sealing washer.
7 Renew the valve and sealing washer if required. Refitting will be eased if both components are first lubricated with clean brake fluid.
8 Renewal of the diaphragm seal will require removal of the servo unit as described in the preceding Section.
9 Do not attempt to pull out the rod as the disc may fall inside

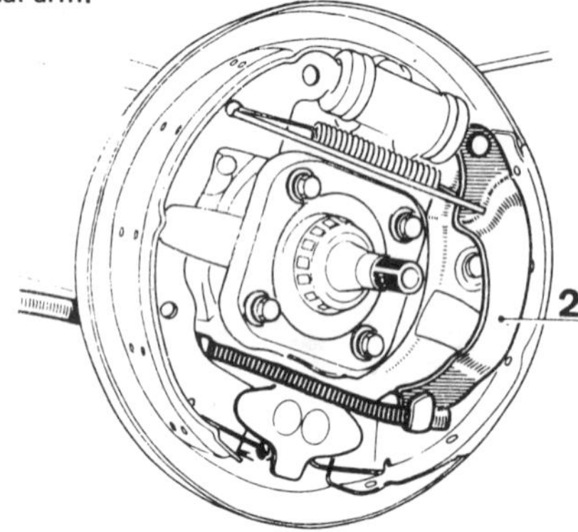

19.6 Rear brake assembly showing handbrake operating lever (2)

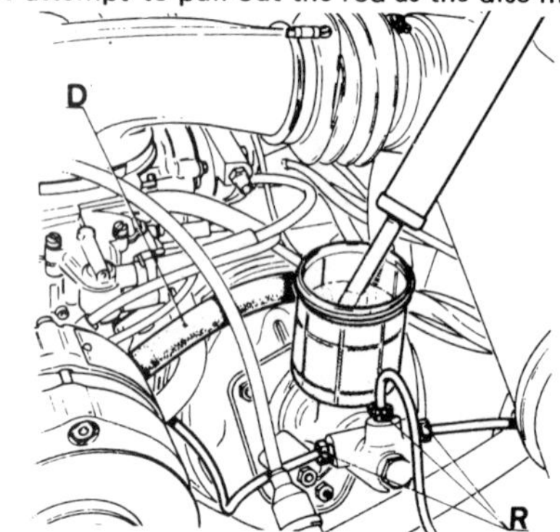

21.2 Using a syringe to empty a brake fluid reservoir. D vacuum hose for servo. R hydraulic pipe unions

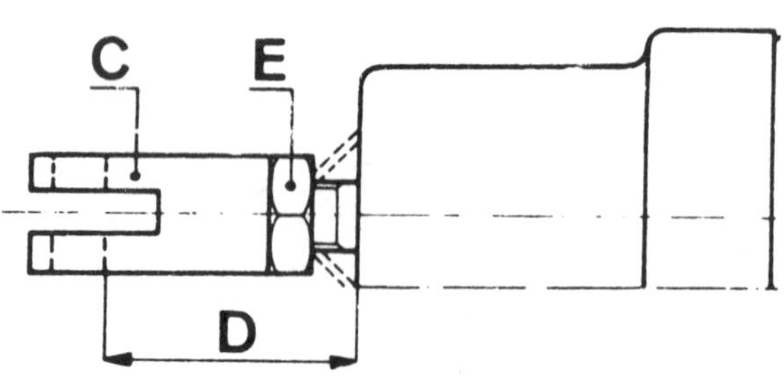

22.2 Gaining access to servoair filter. C operating rod fork. E Locknut. D Dimension to ensure correct pedal free movement (see text)

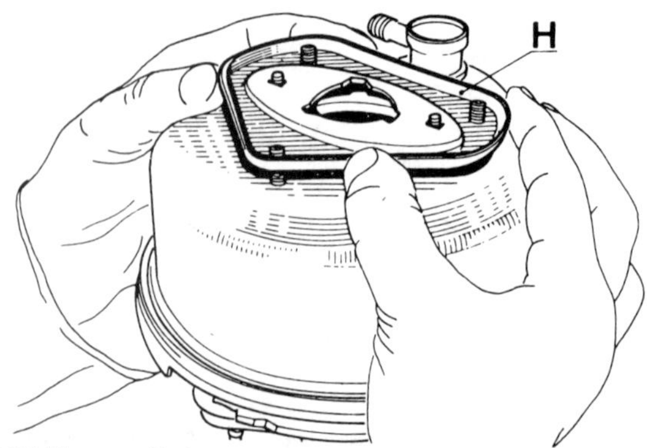

22.10 Master cylinder mounting flange correctly located on servo vacuum chamber

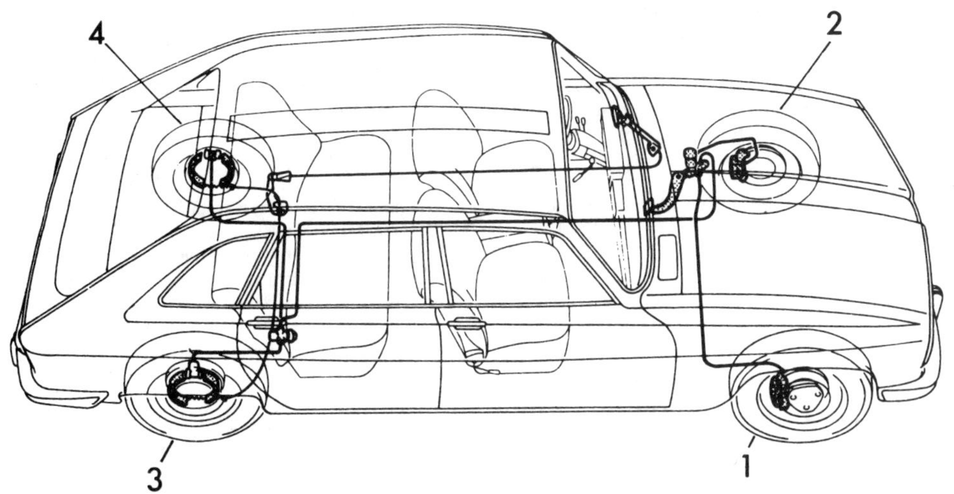

Fig.11.6 Brake bleeding sequence diagram

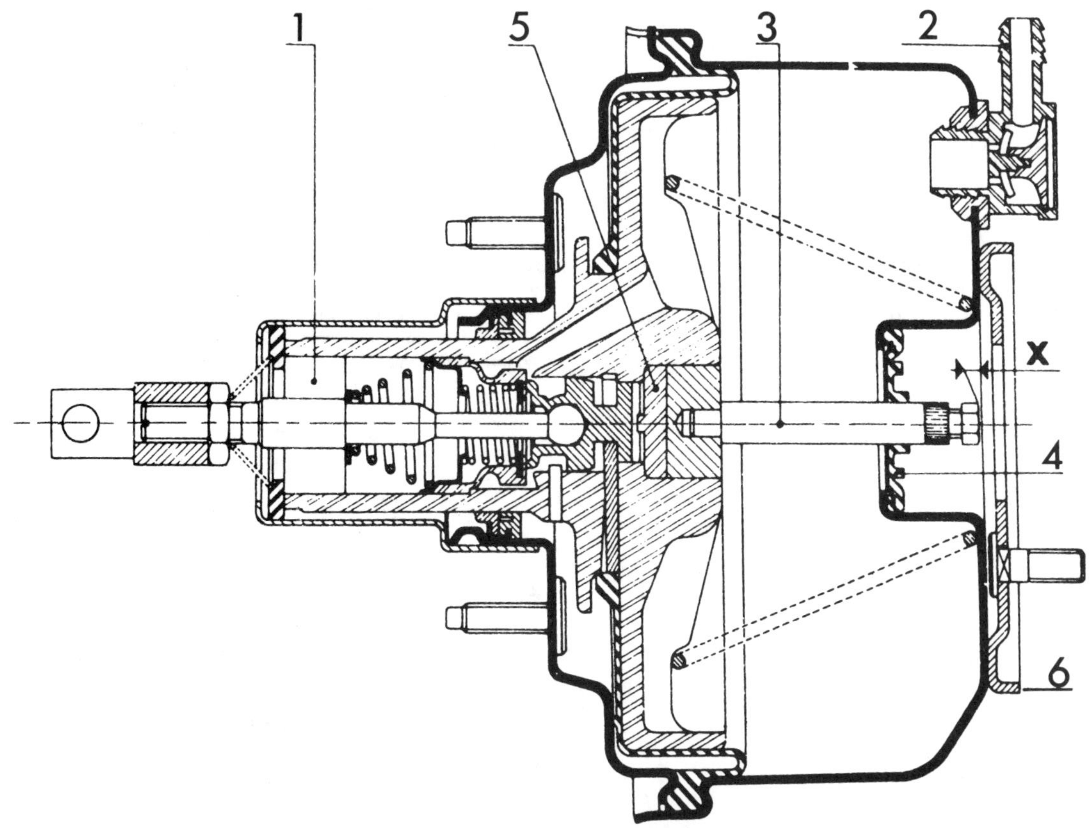

FIG.11.7 SECTIONAL VIEW OF SERVO UNIT

1 Air filter
2 Non-return valve
3 Push rod
4 Diaphragm seal
5 Disc
6 Master cylinder mounting
X flange clearance

the vacuum chamber.
10 Commence dismantling by taking off the flange (H) (Fig).
11 Tape the grooved part of the push rod as a protective measure during removal and refitting of the seal.
12 Fit the diaphragm seal by locating it in the chamber (after first greasing the push rod) and guiding it into position with a piece of 1½ in (40 mm) outside diameter tube. (Fig).
13 Fit the flange the correct way round so that it does not foul the non-return valve.
14 Fit the flat washer, the master cylinder and the securing nuts but do not tighten them fully until the flange is centralised.
15 Rotate the push rod nut (3) to provide a measurement between the push rod end face and the servo unit to master cylinder mating faces of between 0.228 and 0.236 in (6 mm) dimension X (Fig 11.7).

23 Pressure Drop Indicator - Description and Faults

1 This component is fitted in conjunction with tandem type master cylinders to indicate any difference in hydraulic pressure between the two independent braking circuits.
2 A sectional view of the pressure drop indicator is illustrated.
3 The operating principle is that where the two circuit hydraulic pressures are equal, then the piston (3) is in balance. Any variation in pressure between one circuit and the other will cause the piston to move and complete an electrical circuit to give a warning through an indicator lamp on the fascia panel.
4 The warning lamp will illuminate for one of the following reasons:
System requires bleeding.
Leakage (externaly) from some part of the hydraulic system.
Operating fault within the tandem master cylinder.
5 Fault diagnosis should be made and rectified immediately.

24 Pressure Drop Indicator - Removal and Refitting

1 Drain the fluid reservoir or seal the cap (see Section 17) and disconnect the hydraulic pipe unions from the pressure indicator housing.
2 Disconnect the switch electric lead, unscrew the retaining plug bolt and withdraw the switch.
3 The pressure indicator switch cannot be serviced and must be renewed as an assembly.
4 Refitting is a reversal of removal but position the switch on the tandem master cylinder as shown and bleed the system as described in Section 17.

25 Brake Pedal - Removal and Refitting

1 Remove the spring clip (1) and free the spring (2) from the clutch pedal. (Fig).
2 Remove the split pin and clevis pin from the brake master cylinder operating rod to pedal connection.
3 Withdraw the clutch pedal from the pedal cross shaft then use a bronze drift to move the cross shaft to the right sufficiently far so that the brake pedal can be removed. (Fig).
4 Refitting is a reversal of removal but smear the cross shaft with grease and adjust the brake and clutch pedal clearances if necessary as described in Chapter 5 and Section 7 of this Chapter respectively.

26 Flexible Brake Hoses - Inspection, Removal, Refitting

1 At regular intervals examine all flexible brake hoses for deterioration. Bend each hose at an acute angle and examine the surface for signs of perishing (tiny cracks) or stickiness. Check for leakage of brake fluid and rubbing or chafing as a result of incorrect fitting. Renew as necessary.
2 Always remove a flexible hose by (i) unscrewing the union which couples the rigid line to it (ii) detaching the flexible pipe from the support bracket and (iii) unscrewing the flexible hose from the caliper unit. Keep the flexible hose straight and do not kink it during the unscrewing operations.
3 Retain the copper sealing washer used at the caliper unit and plug the rigid pipe to prevent loss of fluid.
4 Fit a flexible hose to the caliper unit using a new copper sealing washer, if obtainable, and then locate its end in the clip and bracket. If necessary, in order to align the anti-rotation notches or in order to prevent the flexible hose rubbing against a suspension component, the hose may be turned two or three notches in the direction arrowed, according to which side (left or right) it is being fitted. (Fig). 1.59).
5 Fit the hose retaining clamp to the support bracket and remove the plug from the rigid brake pipe and reconnect the union.
6 Check that the flexible hose is not rubbed during all positions of the steering between left and right lock. Bleed the hydraulic system as described in Section 17.

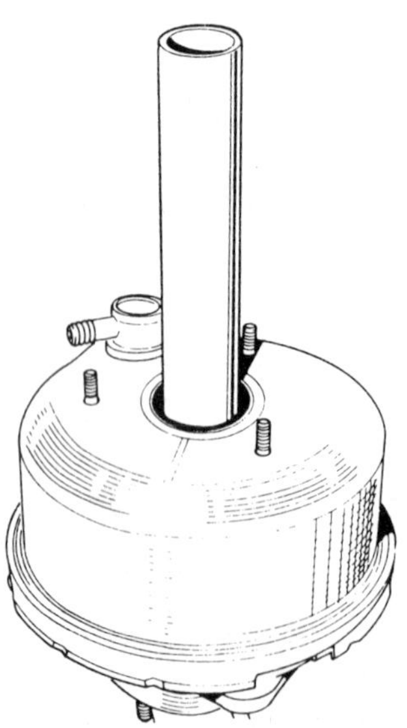

22.12 Using a tubular guide to fit a servo unit diaphragm seal

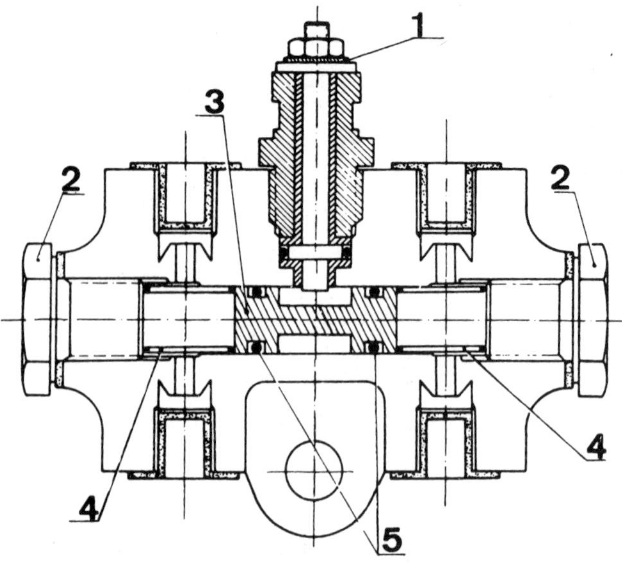

23.2 Sectional view of the pressure drop indicator. 1 electrical terminal. 2 end sealing plugs. 3 pistons. 4 springs. 5 seals.

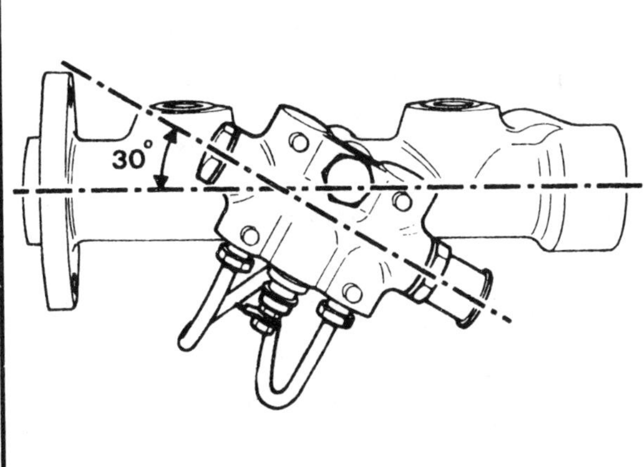

24.4. Correct positioning of pressure drop indicator on Tandem master cylinder

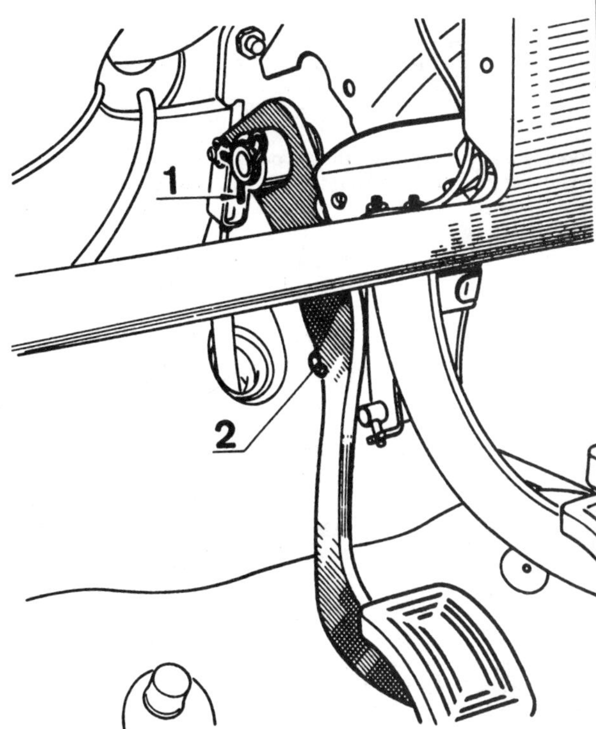

25.1 Clutch pedal attachment. 1 pedal to shaft securing clip. 2 return spring

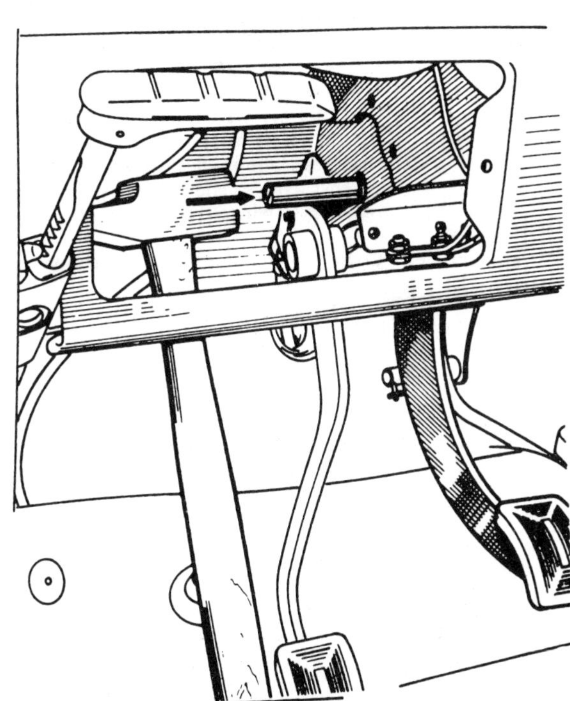

25.3 Drifting the pedal cross shaft to enable the brake pedal to be removed

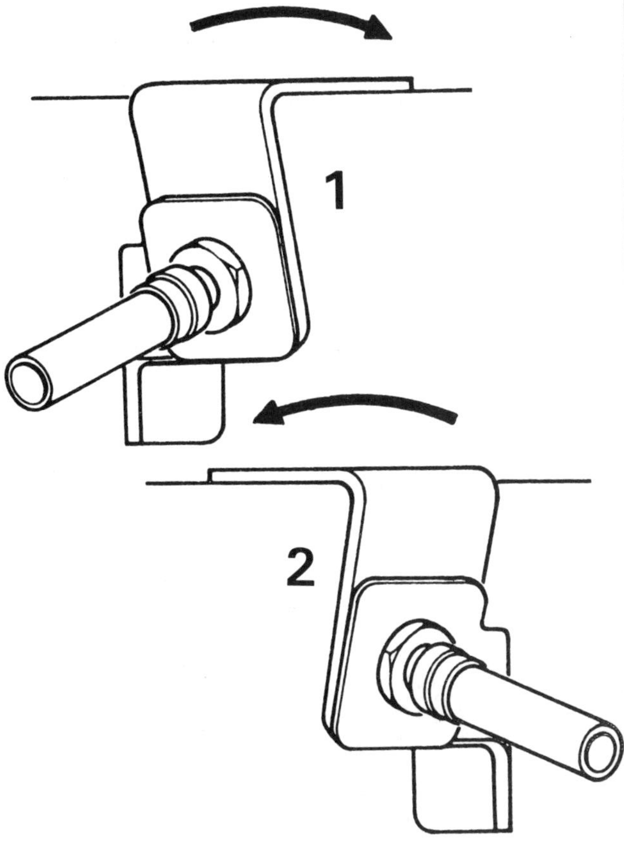

26.4 Fitting diagram for flexible brake hoses. 1 Front left hand. 2 Front right hand

Symptom	Reason	Remedy
Pedal travels a long way before the brakes operate	Seized adjuster on rear shoes or requires adjustment	Check and repair rear brake adjusters.
	Disc pads or linings excessively worn	Inspect and renew as necessary.
Stopping ability poor, even though pedal pressure is firm	Linings, pads, discs or drums badly worn or scored	Dismantle, inspect, and renew as required.
	One or more caliper piston or rear wheel cylinder seized, resulting in some pads/shoes not pressing against discs/drums	Dismantle and inspect cylinders and repair or renew as necessary.
	Brake pads or linings contaminated with oil	Renew pads or linings and repair source of oil contamination.
	Wrong type of pads or linings fitted (too hard)	Verify type of material which is correct for the car and fit it.
	Brake pads or shoes incorrectly assembled	Check for correct assembly.
	Servo unit (where fitted) not functioning	Check and repair as necessary.
Car veers to one side when brakes are applied	Brake pads on one side are contaminated with oil.	Renew pads and repair source of oil contamination.
	Hydraulic pistons in calipers are partially or wholly seized on one side	Inspect caliper pistons for correct movement and repair as necessary.
	A mixture of pad materials used between sides	Standardize on types of pads fitted.
	Unequal wear between sides caused by partially seized hydraulic pistons in brake calipers	Check pistons and renew pads and discs as required.
Pedal feels spongy when the brakes are applied	Air is present in the hydraulic system	Bleed the hydraulic system and check for any signs of leakage.
Pedal feels springy when the brakes are applied	Rear brake linings not bedded into the drums (after fitting new ones).	Allow time for new linings to bed in.
	Master cylinder, brake caliper or drum backplate mounting bolts loose	Tighten mounting bolts as necessary.
	Severe wear in rear drums causing distortion when brakes are applied	Renew drums and linings.
Pedal travels right down with little or no resistance and brakes are virtually non-operative	Leak in hydraulic system resulting in lack of pressure for operation of wheel cylinders.	Examine the whole of the hydraulic system and locate and repair the source of the leak(s). Test after repairing each and every leak source.
	If no signs of leakage are apparent the master cylinder internal seals are failing to sustain pressure	Overhaul the master cylinder, if indications are that seals have failed for reasons other than wear, all the wheel cylinder seals should be checked also and the system completely replenished with the correct fluid.
Binding, juddering, overheating	One, or a combination of causes given in the foregoing sections.	Complete and systematic inspection of the whole braking system.
	Reservoir air vent blocked	Probe and clear.

Chapter 12 Electrical system

For modifications, and information applicable to later models, see Supplement at end of manual

Contents

For additional information on instrument panels, refer to Chapter 14

Specifications

System ...	12 volt, negative earth	
Battery ...	R1150 - R1151 - R1153	R1152
	9 plate 40 A/h	11 plate 45 A/h

Alternator	R1150 (1966 - 67)	R1150 (1968 - 69) and all other models
Make ...	SEV/MOTOROLA	SEV/MOTOROLA
Type ...	A 12/30	A 14/30
Nominal voltage ...	12 volts	
Nominal current flow ...	30 amps at 3000 rev/min	
Field coil resistance ...	5.2 (± 0.2)ohms at 25°C (77°F)	
Speed ratio (engine to alternator) ...	2.12:1	

Regulator	R1150 (1966 - 67)	R1150 (1968 - 69) and all other models
Make ...	SEV/MOTOROLA	DUCELLIER OR SEV
Type ...	E144 (electronic)	Reed type
Setting ...	14.40 volts (± 0.15) at 25°C (77°F)	13.8 to 14.8 volts

Starter	R1150 (1966 - 68)		R1150 (1969) and all other models			
Make ...	Paris-Rhone		Ducellier		Paris-Rhone	
Type ...	D8/E49	D10/E43	C183	D8/E71	D8/E84	D10/E48
Locked pinion Torque ...	8 lb/ft (11.9kg/m)	13 lb/ft (19.3kg/m)	9 lb/ft (13.4kg/m)	8 lb/ft (13.4kg/m)	8 lb/ft (11.9kg/m)	13 lb/ft (19.3kg/m)
Locked pinion current flow ...	355A	400A	375A	355A	355A	400A

Windscreen Wiper	R1150 (1969)	R1150 (1967 - 68)	R1150 (2 speed) R1151 – R1152 – R1153
Make ...	Bosch	SEV or Bosch	Bosch
Type ...	WS 1500 RIF	SEV 116012 Bosch WS 1500 R3F	WS 1500 R4F

Bulbs

Headlamps (Cibie' rectangular)	40/45 watts
Front flashers, rear flashers	21 watts
Parking lamps, number plate and luggage boot lamps	5 watts
Flasher side repeater lamp	4 watts
Side parking lamp	2 watts
Rear and stop lamps	6/21 watts
Vehicle interior lamp	7 watts
Oil pressure warning lamp	4 watts
Water temperature warning lamp	4 watts
Instrument panel and other indicator lamps	2 watts
Glove compartment	4 watts

1 General Description

1 The electrical system is of 12 volt type and comprises a battery (negative earth), an alternator and voltage regulator to keep the battery charged and supply the electrical requirements of the vehicle.
2 The alternator is driven by a vee belt from the camshaft pulley.
3 Electrical ancillary components are of conventional type and include a starter motor, distributor and ignition accessories and all necessary wiring harness.
4 On specified models, the sun roof, the windows, the screen washers and the heated rear window are all electrically operated and are described in later Sections of this Chapter.

2 Battery - Removal and Replacement

1 The battery is positioned on a tray in the front of the engine compartment forward of the nearside suspension.
2 Disconnect the earthed negative lead and then the positive lead by slackening the retaining nuts and bolts or, by unscrewing the retaining screws if these are fitted.
3 Remove the battery clamp and carefully lift the battery off its tray. Hold the battery vertical to ensure that no electrolyte is spilled.
4 Replacement is a direct reversal of this procedure.

NOTE: Replace the positive lead and the earth (negative) lead, smearing the terminals with petroleum jelly (vaseline) to prevent corrosion. NEVER use an ordinary grease as applied to other parts of the car.

5 In order to prevent damage to the alternator rectifying diodes, the following precautions must be observed whenever servicing of the electrical system or components is being undertaken.

Always switch off the engine before disconnecting the battery. Never disconnect the battery terminals until the engine has been switched off and has come to rest.

Never run the engine with either the alternator leads or the vehicles own battery leads disconnected. When charging the battery from a mains charger, always remove the battery from the car. Avoid short circuits.

3 Battery - Maintenance and Inspection

1 Normal weekly battery maintenance consists of checking the electrolyte level of each cell to ensure that the separators are covered by ¼ in. of electrolyte. If the level has fallen top up the battery using distilled water only. Do not overfill. If a battery is overfilled or any electrolyte spilled, immediately wipe away the excess as electrolyte attacks and corrodes any metal it comes into contact with very rapidly.
2 As well as keeping the terminals clean and covered with petroleum jelly, the top of the battery, and especially the top of the cells, should be kept clean and dry. This helps prevent corrosion and ensures that the battery does not become partially discharged by leakage through dampness and dirt.
3 Once every three months remove the battery and inspect the battery securing bolts, the battery clamp plate, tray, and battery leads for corrosion (white fluffy deposits on the metal which are brittle to touch). If any corrosion is found, clean off the deposits with ammonia and paint over the clean metal with an anti-rust/anti-acid paint.
4 At the same time inspect the battery case for cracks. If a crack is found, clean and plug it with one of the proprietary compounds marketed by firms such as Holts for this purpose. If leakage through the crack has been excessive then it will be necessary to refill the appropriate cell with fresh electrolyte as detailed later. Cracks are frequently caused to the top of the battery cases by pouring in distilled water in the middle of winter AFTER instead of BEFORE a run. This gives the water no chance to mix with the electrolyte and so the former freezes and splits the battery case.
5 If topping up the batteries becomes excessive and the cases have been inspected for cracks that could cause leakage, but none are found, the batteries are being over-charged and the voltage regulator will have to be checked and reset.
6 With the batteries on the bench at the three monthly interval check, measure their specific gravity with a hydrometer to determine the state of charge and condition of the electrolyte. There should be very little variation between the different cells and if a variation in excess of 0.025 is present it will be due to either:-

a) Loss of electrolyte from the battery at some time caused by spillage or a leak resulting in a drop in the specific gravity of the electrolyte, when the deficiency was replaced with distilled water instead of fresh electrolyte.
b) An internal short circuit caused by buckling of the plates or a similar malady pointing to the likelihood of total battery failure in the near future.

7 The specific gravity of the electrolyte for fully charged conditions at the electrolyte temperature indicated, is listed in Table A. The specific gravity of a fully discharged battery, at different temperatures of the electrolyte is given in Table B.

TABLE A

Specific Gravity - Battery Fully Charged

1.268 at 100°F or 38°C electrolyte temperature
1.272 at 90°F or 32°C electrolyte temperature
1.276 at 80°F or 27°C electrolyte temperature
1.280 at 70°F or 21°C electrolyte temperature
1.284 at 60°F or 16°C electrolyte temperature
1.288 at 50°F or 10°C electrolyte temperature
1.292 at 40°F or 4°C electrolyte temperature
1.296 at 30°F or -1.5°C electrolyte temperature

TABLE B

Specific Gravity - Battery Fully Discharged

1.098 at 100°F or 38°C electrolyte temperature
1.102 at 90°F or 32°C electrolyte temperature

1.106 at 80°F or 27°C electrolyte temperature
1.110 at 70°F or 21°C electrolyte temperature
1.114 at 60°F or 16°C electrolyte temperature
1.118 at 50°F or 10°C electrolyte temperature
1.122 at 40°F or 4°C electrolyte temperature
1.126 at 30°F or -1.5°C electrolyte temperature

4 Electrolyte Replenishment

1 If the battery is in a fully charged state and one of the cells maintains a specific gravity reading which is 0.025 or more lower than the others, and a check of each cell has been made with a voltage meter to check for short circuits (a four to seven second test should give a steady reading of between 1.2 to 1.8 volts), then it is likely that electrolyte has been lost from the cell with the low reading at some time.

2 Top up the cell with a solution of 1 part sulphuric acid to 2.5 parts of water. If the cell is already fully topped up draw some electrolyte out of it with a pipette. The total capacity of each cell is ¾ pint.

3 When mixing the sulphuric acid and water NEVER ADD WATER TO SULPHURIC ACID - always pour the acid slowly onto the water in a glass container. IF WATER IS ADDED TO SULPHURIC ACID IT WILL EXPLODE.

4 Continue to top up the cell with the freshly made electrolyte and then recharge the battery and check the hydrometer readings.

5 Battery Charging

1 In winter time when heavy demand is placed upon the battery, such as when starting from cold, and much electrical equipment is continually in use, it is a good idea to occasionally have the battery fully charged from an external source at the rate of 3.5 to 4 amps.

2 Continue to charge the battery at this rate until no further rise in specific gravity is noted over a four hour period.

3 Alternatively, a trickle charger charging at the rate of 1.5 amps can be safely used overnight.

4 Specially rapid 'boost' charges which are claimed to restore the power of the battery in 1 to 2 hours are most dangerous as they can cause serious damage to the battery plates through over-heating.

5 While charging the battery note that the temperature of the electrolyte should never exceed 100oF.

6 Always remove the battery from the vehicle for charging, otherwise damage to the alternator may occur.

6 Alternator - General Description and Maintenance

1 All models are fitted with an alternator. The R.1150 (1966 - 67) has a SEV/MOTOROLA type Á 12/30 and all other models and years of manufacture are fitted with type A 14/30, this alternator has an additional support at the rear of its body.

2 Voltage regulators are fitted in conjunction with types of alternator and are described in Section 30.

3 Maintenance consists of keeping the outside of the body clean and checking the security of the connections.

4 No lubrication is required as the bearings are grease sealed.

5 The drive belt tension must be maintained at all times and is accomplished by loosening the bolts A and B and prising the alternator away from the engine.

6 Retighten the bolts when adjustment is correct which is evident when the belt can be pushed or pulled a total deflection of ¼ in (6.4 mm) at the mid point of its top run.

7 Alternator - Removal and Refitting

1 Loosen the alternator mounting bracket bolts and strap, push the unit towards the engine until the driving belt may be slipped off the pulley. Do not use a lever or screwdriver to force the belt over the pulley run or the belt will be damaged.

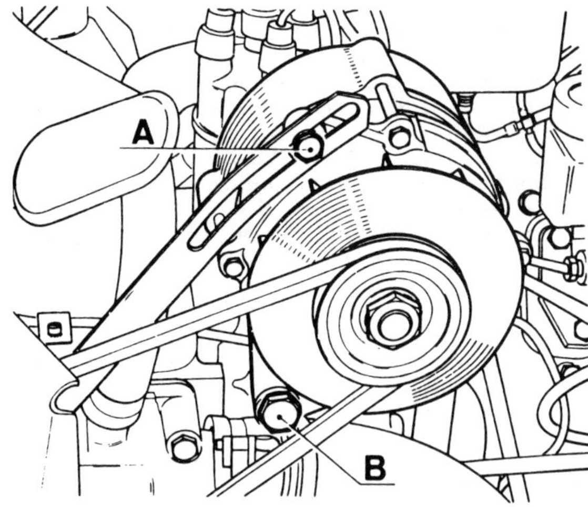

Fig.12.1 Alternator adjustment (A) and mounting bolt (B)

2 Disconnect the battery and the three alternator leads.

3 Remove the bolts A and B and on later type alternators, the rear mounting bolt as well.

4 Lift the alternator from its location.

8 Alternator - Servicing

1 No attempt should be made to dismantle or repair the alternator. It should be removed as described in the preceding Section and checked by a competent auto electrician. If faulty it should be exchanged on a factory replacement basis.

9 Starter Motor - General Description

1 One of two types of pre-engaged starter motor may be fitted according to vehicle model and date of manufacture (See Specifications).

2 The starter motor solenoid is actuated through movement of the key in the steering column mounted multi-position switch.

10 Starter Motor - Testing

1 If the starter motor does not operate when the ignition key is turned, carry out the following check list before removing the motor from its location in the vehicle.

2 Check the state of charge of the battery and the security of the battery terminals.

3 Check the security of the starter motor and solenoid electrical leads.

4 In the case of automatic vehicles, check that the gear selection lever is in P or A. If so and the starter does not operate, check that the lever and cable adjustment is correct.

5 The starter motor is of pre-engaged type and any failure of the drive gear will mean that the pinion and screwed armature shaft must be cleaned as described in Section 14 and any defective parts renewed.

6 Disconnect the lead from the distributor LT terminal in order to prevent the engine from firing, and then connect a 0 - 20v voltmeter between the starter terminal and earth. Operate the starter switch to crank the engine and note the voltmeter reading. A minimum reading of 4.5 volts indicates satisfactory cable and switch connections. Very slow cranking at this voltage indicates a fault in the starter motor.

7 Now connect the voltmeter between the battery and the starter motor terminal. Operate the starter motor and observe whether the voltage drop with the engine turning exceeds 6 volts. If the drop is greater than that specified, then excessive resistance in the starter circuit is indicated.

11 Starter Motor - Removal and Refitting

1 Disconnect the battery earth (negative) terminal.
2 Disconnect the starter motor electrical leads.
3 Unscrew and remove the three starter securing bolts (tab or plain type washers may be fitted below the bolt heads). Lift the starter motor up and out of its clutch bell housing location. (Remove the exhaust manifold on right hand drive vehicles).
4 With R1151 models the starter motor shield and the dipstick guide tube must be removed before the starter can be withdrawn. (Fig.)
5 With R1152 models the exhaust pipe shield and pipe clip must also be removed. (Fig).
6 Refitting the starter is a reversal of removal but engage the starter drive teeth carefully with the flywheel ring gear and ensure that the latter are not worn or chipped otherwise exchange the flywheel assembly as described in Chapter 1.

12 Starter Motor - Dismantling and Reassembly

1 Remove the rear protective shield and the rear bearing securing nuts.
2 Lift out the bush, the solenoid connecting fork shaft which is secured by a circlip.
3 Withdraw the starter motor body, the solenoid and the armature.
4 Servicing of the brushes and the drive gear is fully described in Sections 13 and 14 respectively.
5 Test the field coils for continuity by connecting a test bulb in circuit with the starter terminal and each brush in turn. Where a break in the field coil wiring is indicated, exchange the complete starter motor for a reconditioned unit as removal of the field coils is beyond the scope of the home mechanic.
6 Wipe the armature clean with a dry non-fluffy cloth.
7 If the segments of the commutator have worn level with the insulators, then the insulators should be undercut to a depth of 0.020 in (0.51 mm). The best method of doing this is to grind a hacksaw blade down so that it will not widen the groove between the copper segments as it is drawn back and forth to cut away the insulating material.
8 The commutator should be free from pits and burning. Slight discoloration may be removed by rotating the commutator while fine glass paper is wrapped round it. Never use emery cloth for this purpose.
9 Finally clean the commutator surface with a fuel moistened cloth.
10 The starter motors fitted to this range of vehicles are similar in general but vary in detail design. The various types used are shown in exploded form in Figs. 12.2, 12.3, 12.4, 12.5, and 12.6. For application see Specifications.

13 Starter Motor - Brush Renewal

1 On starter motors fitted with a cover band, this may be slid back to examine the state of the brushes. With other types, remove the rear plate to gain access to the brushes and holders. Do not strain the brush wire connected to the yoke.
2 Should the carbon brushes have worn down to nearly their specified length, 7/16 in (11.1 mm) they must be renewed).
3 Prise back the brush springs and remove both the brushes from their holders.
4 Unsolder each of the brush lead connections and solder the new brushes into position. (Figs).
5 Ensure that the brushes are a sliding fit in their respective holders. Should they stick, then clean the holders with fuel and if really necessary, smooth the surfaces of the brushes with a fine file.

14 Starter Motor Drive - Servicing

1 Periodically, remove the starter motor from its clutch bell housing location and wash the drive gear end in paraffin. Allow the drive gear to dry naturally, after shaking off the surplus, do not lubricate with oil.
2 If wear is apparent on components of the starter drive then with Ducellier model 6183 starters, the complete starter motor will have to be exchanged on a factory reconditioned basis. With all other models, the pinion-free wheel assembly may be renewed in the following manner.
3 Using a suitable length of tube, push the pinion-free wheel assembly stop back towards the pinion.
4 Remove the snap ring and withdraw the stop and pinion-free wheel assembly.
5 When refitting, use a new snap ring and push the stop back over it. With Paris - Rhone D8E49 and D10E43 starters, always use a new stop when refitting the components.
6 With Ducellier starter motors (other than model 6183) line up the splines so that the pinion and armature notches will mate, notch in armature to recess in pinion.
7 When the pinion stop has been released after fitting and covers the snap ring, then it should be secured over at various points of its edge in order to secure the snap ring.

15 Starter Motor Solenoid - Removal, Refitting, Adjustment

1 The starter motor solenoid is removed after unscrewing and withdrawing the securing bolts and the solenoid to pinion connecting fork retaining shaft.
2 Fitting the new solenoid is a reversal of removal but pinion end stop clearance must be checked and adjusted.
3 Disconnect the feed wire (1) and temporarily attach two leads from the battery.
4 With the solenoid energised, the pinion will be thrown forward and there should be a clearance (H) between the pinion end face (2) and the stop (3) of between 0.020 and 0.099 in (0.5 and 2.5 mm).
5 Where the clearance is incorrect, remove the solenoid and screw the fork (4) in or out as necessary.

16 Fuses and Relays

1 The fuse box may contain two or six fuses according to vehicle model and electrical accessories fitted.
2 Model R1150 (1966) has a fuse box similar to the one shown.
3 Models R1150 (1967 - 1968 - 1969) have a fuse box as shown.
4 Model R1151 has a fuse box as shown in the figure.
5 Model R1152 has a fuse box as shown in the figure.
6 Relays are located within the engine compartment and are fitted in accordance with the electrical component and accessory specification of a particular vehicle model.

17 Flasher unit

1 The flasher operating unit is located to the rear of the facia panel and is shown according to type in Fig 12.7.
2 Failure of one of the vehicle flashers may not necessarily indicate failure of the flasher unit and a check for a blown bulb or poor earth should be made before proceding with a test of the flasher unit itself.
3 Switch together the terminals marked + and COM and operate the flasher switch. If the indicator lamps now light then

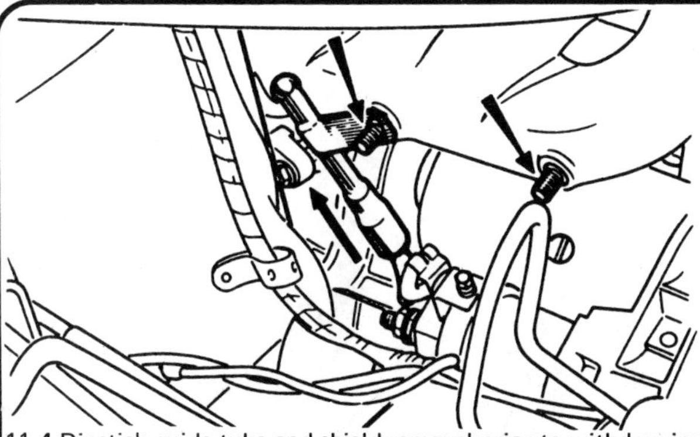
11.4 Dipstick guide tube and shield removal prior to withdrawing starter motor on model R1151.

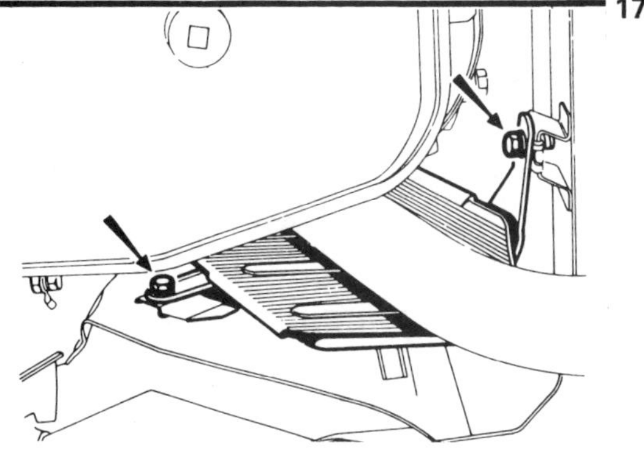
11.5 Exhaust pipe clip and shield removal prior to withdrawing starter motor on model R1152

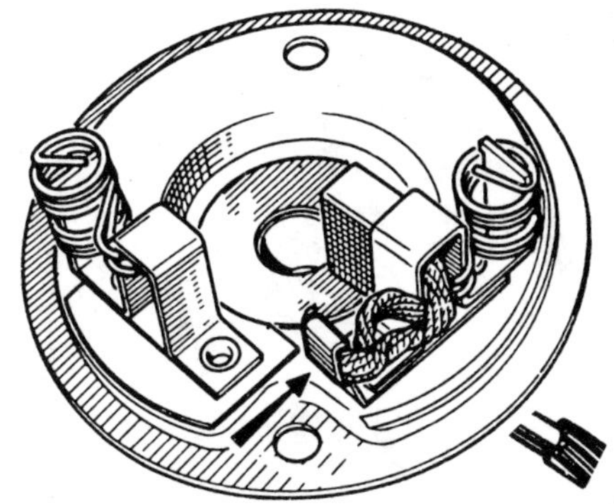
13.4A Starter motor brush lead attachment to end cover

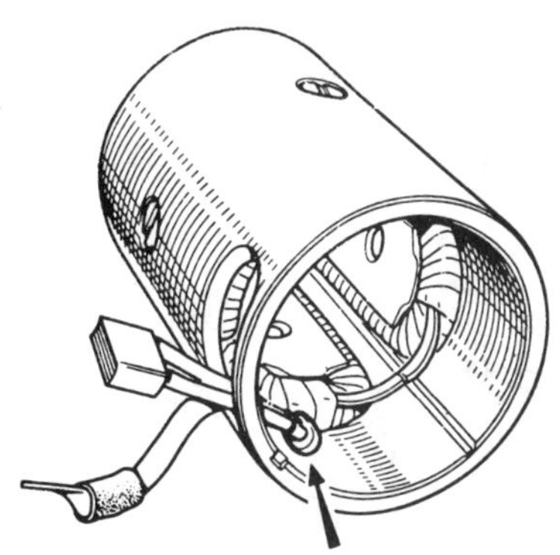
13.4B Starter motor brush lead attachment to field coils

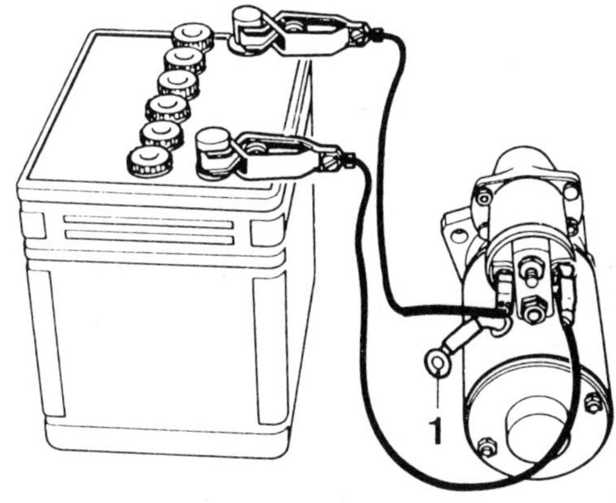

15.3 Method of energising a starter solenoid to check end play

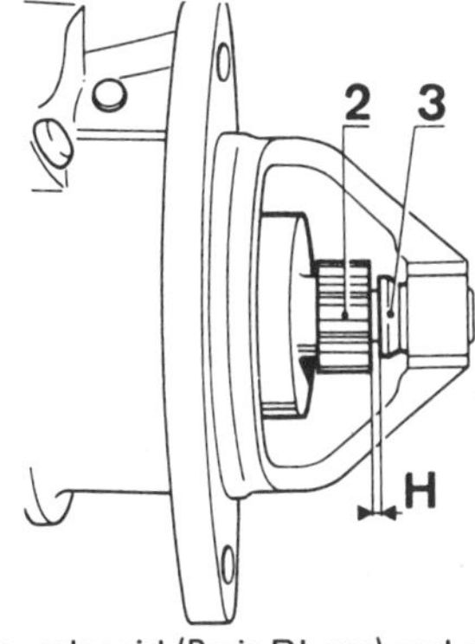

15.4 Starter motor solenoid (Paris-Rhone) end play. 2 pinion. 3 stop. H correct end play (0.020 to 0.099 in – 0.5 to 2.5mm)

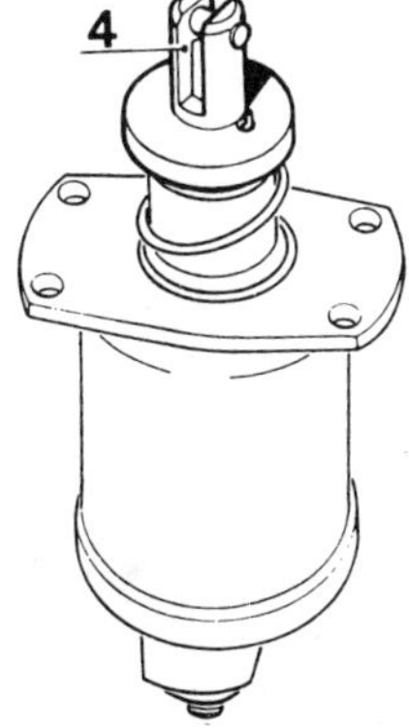

15.5 Starter motor solenoid fork (4)

18.1 Instrument panel (R1150). 1 Trim. 2 Embellisher securing screws. 3 Embellisher

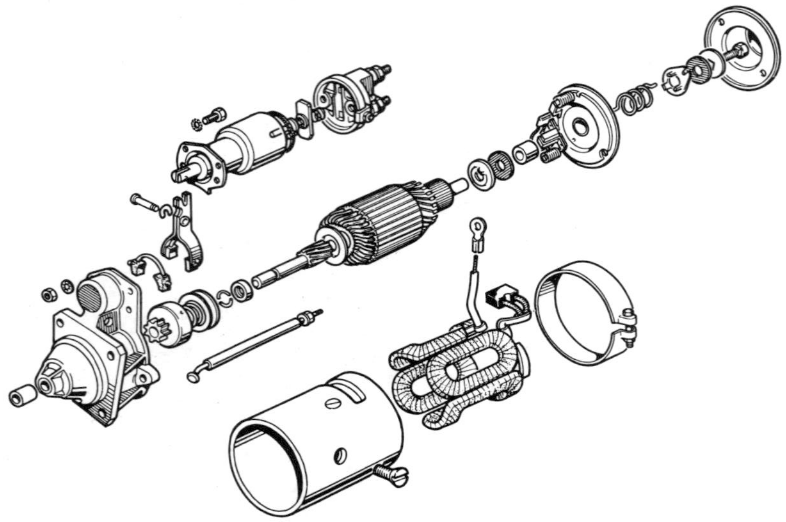

Fig.12.2 Exploded view of Paris-Rhone D8E49 starter motor

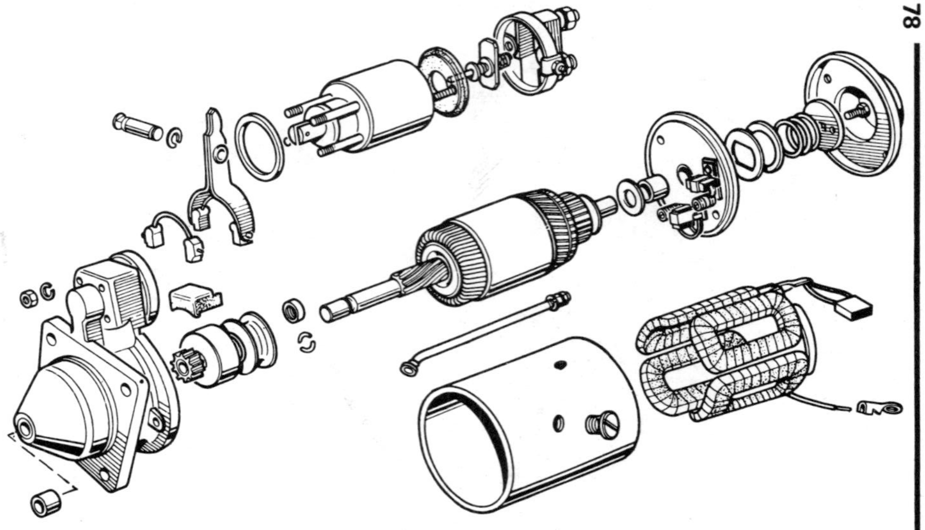

Fig.12.3 Exploded view of Paris-Rhone D10/E43 starter motor

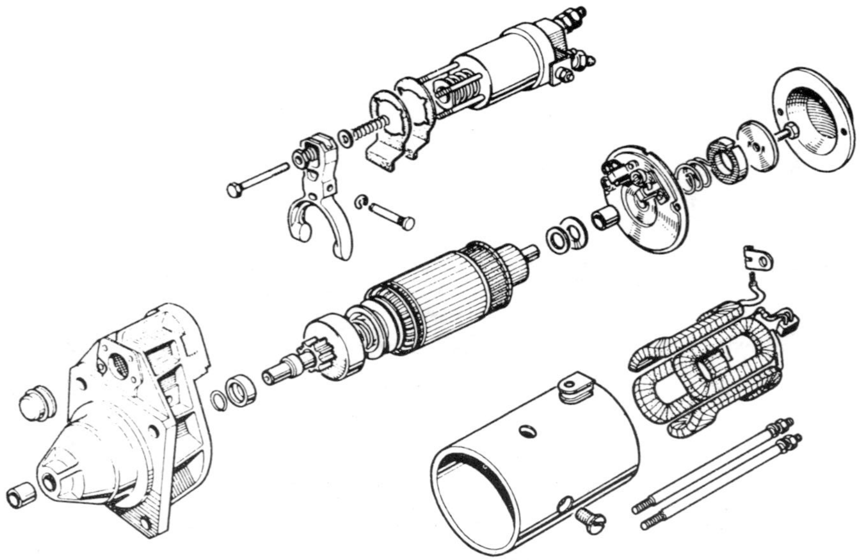

Fig.12.4 Exploded view of Ducellier 6/183 starter motor

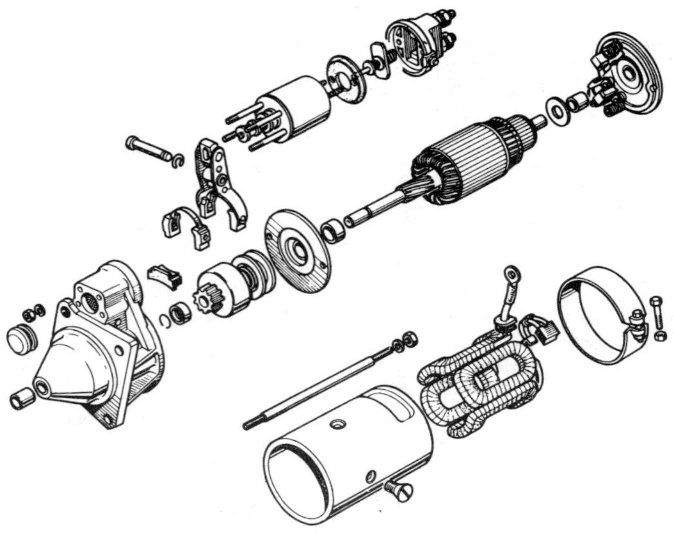

Fig.12.5 Exploded view of Paris-Rhone D8/E71 and D8/E84 starter motors

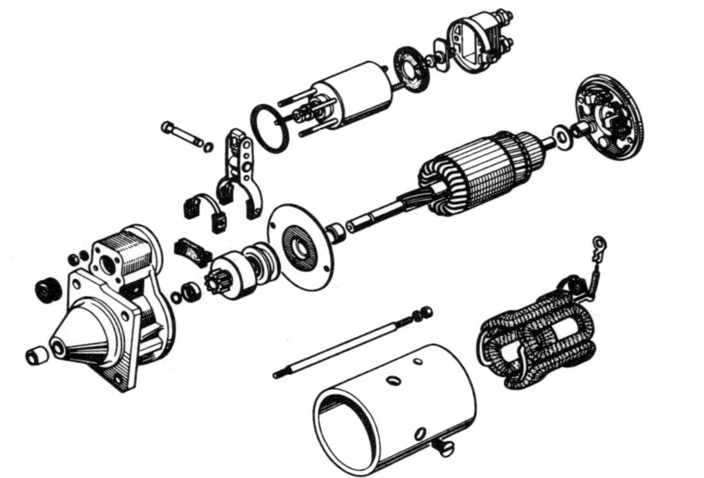

Fig.12.6 Exploded view of Paris-Rhone D10/E48 starter motor

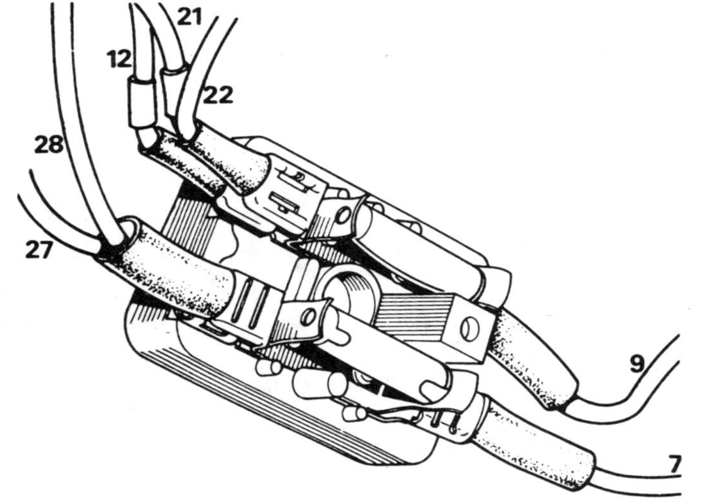

16.3 Fuse box (R1150 - 1967 to 1969). 4 Regulator +. 7 Fuse + from ignition switch. 9 Fuse + direct. 12 Feed to cigar lighter, luggage boot lamp. 16 Feed to heater switch. 21 Feed to wiper switch. 27 Feed to instrument panel. 28 Feed to heater.

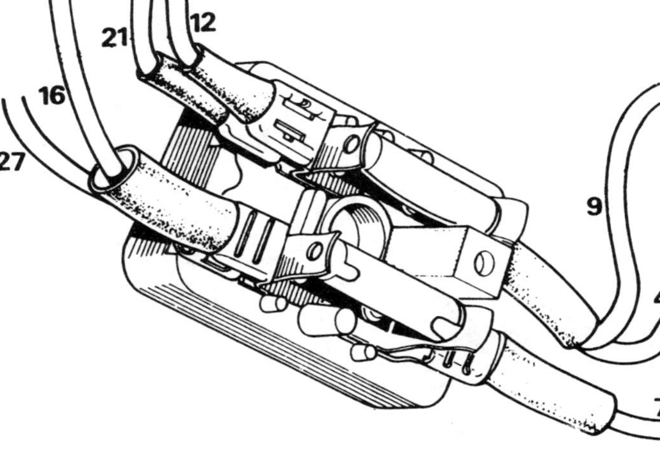

16.2 Fuse box (R1150 - 1966). 4 Regulator +. 7 Fuse + from ignition switch. 9 Fuse + direct. 12 Feed to cigar lighter, luggage boot lamp. 16 Feed to heater switch. 21 Feed to wiper switch. 27 Feed to instrument panel. 28 Feed to heater.

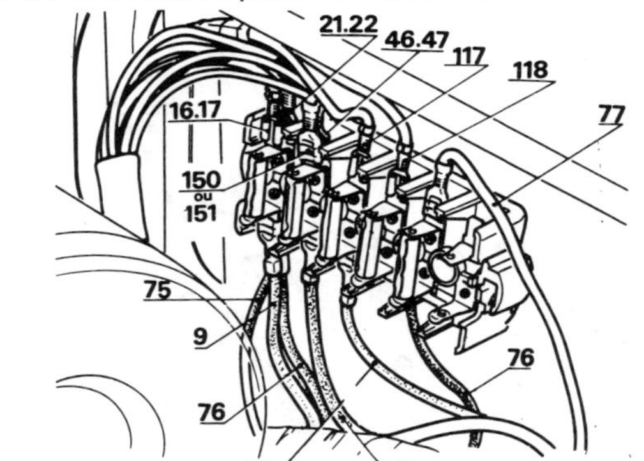

16.4 Fuse box (R1151). 7 Fuse + after ignition switch. 9 Fuse + direct. 16 Feed to windscreen wiper switch. 17 Feed to pedal—operated windscreen washers. 21 Feed to cigar lighter. 22 Feed to stop light switch. 46 Feed to stop light switch. 47 Feed to rear screen switch and reverse lights. 75 Quartz iodine headlights direct +. 76 Sunroof fuse. 77 Feed to sunroof relay. 116 Feed to window winder fuse. 117 Feed to left hand door change-over switch. 118 Feed to right hand change-over switch. 150 Electric window relay field (without sunroof). 151 Electric window relay field (with sunroof)

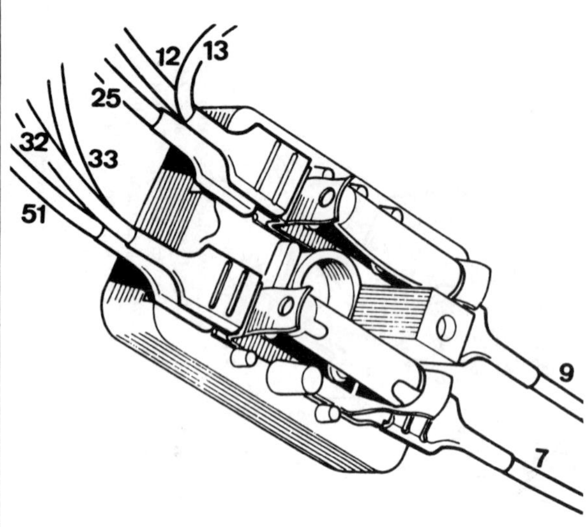

16.5 Fuse box (R1152). 7 Fuse + after ignition switch. 9 Fuse + direct. 12 Feed to cigar lighter and interior light. 13 Feed to luggage compartment light. 25 Feed to windscreen wiper switch. 32 Feed to instrument panel. 33 Feed to heater. 51 Feed to reverse light switch

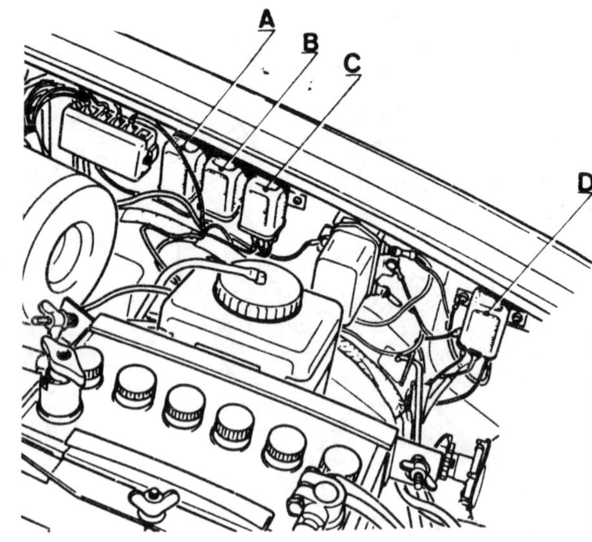

16.6 Location of relays. A Windscreen wiper. B Sliding roof. C Quartz iodine headlamps. D Radiator cooling fan motor

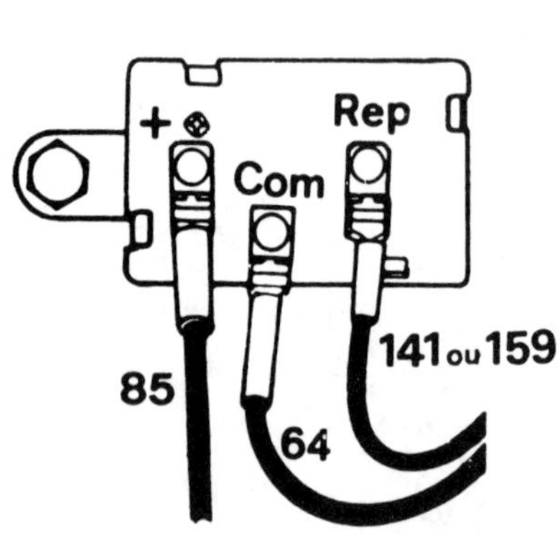

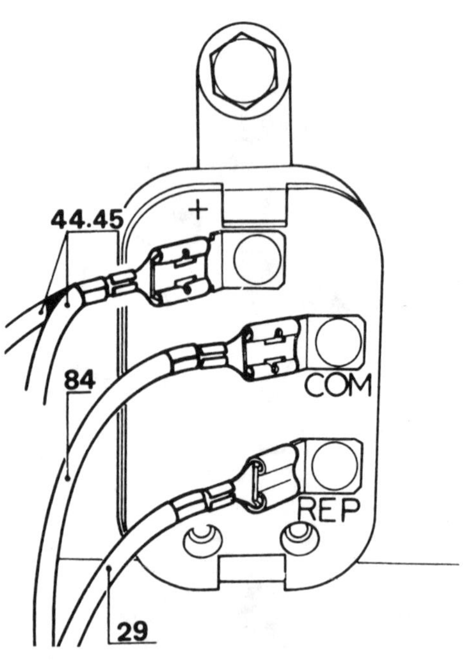

FIG.12.7 FLASHER (INDICATOR) UNITS

A fitted to R1150/R1152 — *B fitted to R1151*

64 Feed to flasher change over switch
85 Feed to flasher unit
159 Flasher tell-tale

29 Flasher tell-tale
44 Feed to heater
45 Feed to flasher unit
84 Feed to flasher change-over switch

the flasher unit is defective and must be renewed.

18 Instrument Panel (R1150) - Removal, Dismantling, Refitting

1 Remove the two half shells of the combination lighting switch and the trim (1). (Fig).
2 Unscrew and remove the two screws (2) which hold the embellisher (3) in position.
3 Pull out the two switches, mark the leads for replacement and disconnect them. Unscrew the four screws which secure the cowl.
4 Unscrew and remove the three bolts (7,8 and 9) which secure the instrument panel in position. (Fig).
5 Disconnect the speedometer cable and remove the panel sufficiently far to enable the wires (marked for identification) to be disconnected.
6 The instrument panel may be dismantled and the speedometer removed by removing the two screws from the glass securing bracket and withdrawing the glass from underneath.
7 Remove the four rubber plugs which secure the inscription plate and the two speedometer retaining screws. (Fig).
8 Refitting is a reversal of removal and dismantling.

19 Instrument Panel (R1151) - Removal, Dismantling, Refitting

1 The location of switches on the facia panel is to the left and right of the four centre dials.
2 To withdraw the instrument panel, remove all the switches (mark the leads for replacement) and the two half shells from the combination lighting switch.
3 Insert a screwdriver through the switch openings and remove the two instrument cowling securing screws.
4 Pull the cowl forward, disconnect the instrument panel lighting rheostat and withdraw the cowl.

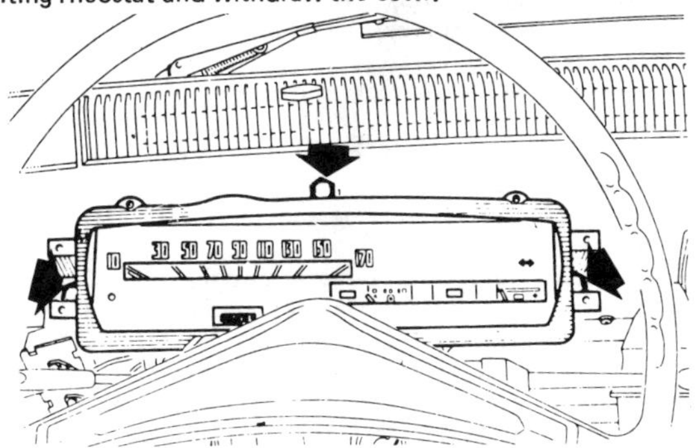

18.4 Instrument panel (R1150) securing screws

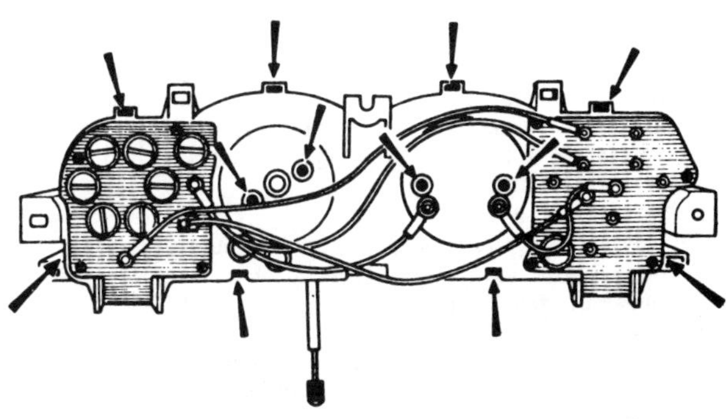

19.6 Clips and tabs securing speedo, and rev. counter heads in position (R1151)

5 Unscrew the instrument panel securing screws, disconnect the speedometer cable and the two junction boxes.
6 The speedometer or revolution counter heads may be removed by lifting off two clips and pressing on the tabs (arrowed) to remove the glass. (Fig).
7 Remove the two securing screws from each instrument and disconnect the revolution counter leads.
8 Refitting is a reversal of removal and dismantling.

20 Instrument Panel (R1152) - Removal, Dismantling, Refitting

1 Remove the two embellishers (1) the air distributor (2) the steering wheel (Chapter 10) and the facia embellisher. (Fig).
2 Remove the half shells from the combination lighting switch. Remove the facia panel moulding then disconnect the electrical leads.
3 Withdraw the instrument panel and repeat the operations described in paragraphs 5, 6 and 7 of Section 18.

21 Instrument Panel (R1153, R1154 and R1155) - Removal, Dismantling, Refitting

1 Refer to Chapter 14.

22 Combination Lighting Switch - Removal and Refitting

1 Remove the two half shells from the switch.
2 Remove the glove compartment.
3 Disconnect the electrical leads from the switch terminals.
4 Remove the flasher control return spring (1) the three screws (2) which secure the screw to its bracket. (Fig).
5 Refitting is a reversal of removal and disconnection but according to model refer to the relevant lead connection dia-

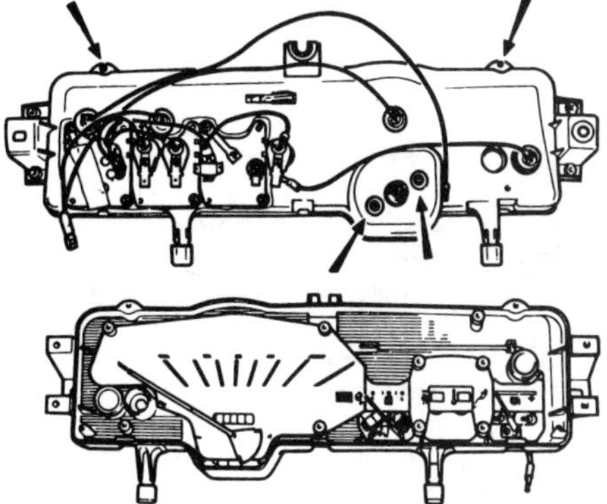

18.7 Instrument panel (R1150) inscription plate plugs and speedo. screws.

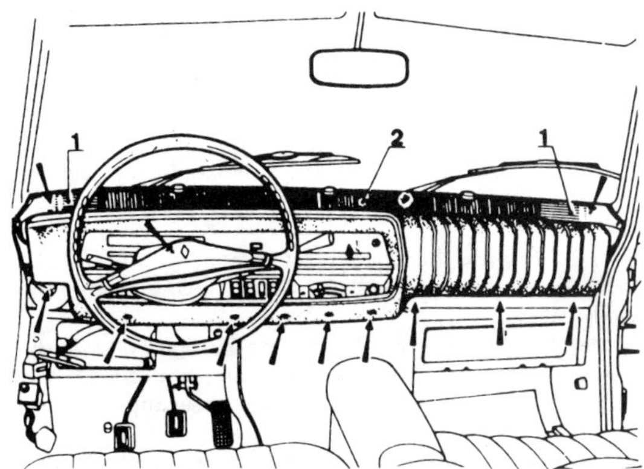

20.1 Instrument panel (R1152). 1 Embellishers. 2 Air distributors

gram. Model R.1150, Fig 12.8, Model R.1151, Fig 12.9, Model R.1152, Fig 12.10.

23 Heated Rear Window - Operation and Fault Diagnosis

1 The heated rear window has its filament supplied with electrical current through the connection made by two pairs of contacts (two fixed, two moving).
2 Should the rear window fail to heat up, then check the current supply to the switch, the security of the contacts and the junctions between the supply terminals on the window and the feed wires.
3 The switch leads and terminals are shown in the figure.

24 Electrically Operated Sliding Roof - Servicing

1 Where an electrically operated sliding roof is fitted, no routine maintenance is called for. In the event of a failure in the operating mechanism, the roof may be operated manually by removing the plug (A) and turning the operating motor spindle with a screwdriver. (Fig.)
2 Before dismantling the operating mechanism subsequent to failure, check the following items: the fuse, the thermal cut-out switch, the connections and current supply to the switch, the track and the motor.
3 Where motor failure is evident, run the roof back sufficiently far to gain access to the screws.
4 Disconnect the battery.
5 Unscrew the motor embellisher fixing screws and withdraw the motor rearwards.
6 Disconnect the motor leads, unscrew the guide bearing securing screws and pull back the bearings.
7 Unscrew the motor securing screws, raise the sliding roof slightly and remove the motor.
8 Disconnect the motor drive shaft by punching out the drive shaft pin. Renew the motor on an exchange basis as it is not designed for repair.
9 Refitting is a reversal of removal but the sliding roof must be adjusted quite square for correct closure by moving the tracks as necessary.
10 If essential, the track and pick-up shoes can be withdrawn after complete removal of the sliding roof. This is accomplished by pulling the roof forward and carrying out the operations described in paragraphs 3 to 6 of this Section. Then from inside the car, raise the front of the sun roof and lay it aside. Remove the packing pieces (15) as a precaution against the rear rubber seal coming unstuck. (Fig).
11 Remove the track by pulling it from its location with pliers or a hook. (Fig).
12 Check that the electrical contact surfaces are in good condition, if not, renew them.
13 Check the condition of the pick-up shoe pads, ensure that the return spring operates correctly and that the two shoes are quite parallel. (Fig).
14 Should the drive belt have stretched or broken, then remove the embellisher and the four motor securing screws and turn the motor until the belt can be slipped off the driving flanges.
15 To refit the sliding roof, insert a pliable piece of cardboard on the current feed track ensuring that the packing pieces are removed.
16 The pads may now be fitted into position.
17 Clean the lead ramps (18) and lightly grease them, but not the tracks. (Fig).
18 Locate the sliding roof by inclining it slightly towards the rear. Fit the roof into position keeping the edges exactly parallel to the frame. Hook the retaining springs under the roof also the pads onto the centre track.
19 Packing pieces (15) are available in different thicknesses to ensure surface alignment. (Fig).
20 Remove the slide fingers (23).
21 Unscrew the retaining screw (24). (Fig).
22 Move the slide finger forward to free the lug (25) from its slot (26). (Fig).
23 Do not unstick the rubber sealing during the foregoing operations.
24 To ensure satisfactory operation of the sliding roof, check the condition of the side components, the correct fitting of the racks and anti-rattle spacers.
25 Tighten the nuts (13) with the sliding roof positioned 5 7/8 in (150 mm) from the front end of the roof opening. (Fig).
26 Place the pinions on the racks, push the guide bearings (14) against the side components to act as guides and then pull the bearings back by about 1/16 in (1.5 mm). Refit the cover plate (12).

25 Electric Window Winder Mechanism - Removal and Refitting

1 To remove the window winder stabiliser, detach the door interior trim as described in the next Chapter, Section 7
2 Disconnect the electrical leads and remove the junction box. (Fig).
3 Align the roller arm (23) with the upper assembly (24) and remove the three nuts (25). Push the assembly inwards to free it, Fig 12.11.
4 Take out the lower window counter balance and free the roller (26). (Fig).
5 Temporarily refit the window and retain it in its upper position with some stripes of adhesive tape.
6 Tilt the counter balance in the direction of the arrow and remove it through the door frame aperture.
7 When reassembling the winder mechanism, check that the operating arms A and B are in line. (Fig).
8 If they are not in line, connect two leads from the car battery and check the direction of operation as the motor turns. If the action is contrary, reverse the electrical leads to the motor.
9 Should the winder motor prove defective, unscrew the two securing screws and withdraw the motor shaft from the bonded rubber bearing.
10 The window winder motor is of sealed type and must be renewed as a unit.
11 The winder reduction gear may be removed by withdrawing the three securing screws. (Fig).
12 The gear cannot be repaired and must be renewed as an assembly.
13 Refitting is a reversal of removal but the following adjustments can be made to improve the action of the electrically operated winder mechanism if necessary.
14 Adjust the alignment of the window by moving the support clamp nut which is accessible through the door aperture.
15 Adjust the stop so that the top edge of the window glass is level with the upper edge of the door panel, with the window fully dropped.

26 Windscreen Wiper Motor - Removal and Refitting

1 The wiper motor may be removed with or without its mounting plate. Remove the wiper arms from their spindles.
2 To remove the wiper motor complete with plate, prise the air inlet grille from its location using a screwdriver and block of wood.
3 Disengage the air grille operating rod securing clip and remove the rod eye circlip and disconnect the rod. (Fig).
4 Remove the scuttle crossmember securing screws and the retaining nuts from the wiper arm shaft housings. Lift out the crossmember.
5 Unscrew the three bolts which secure the wiper motor mounting plate in position and remove the complete motor/plate/linkage assembly. The motor may be detached after withdrawl of the operating shaft centre screw. (Fig).
6 If attention is not to be given to the drive links or wiper arm operating shafts, then the motor may be removed leaving the shaft support plate together with linkage in position, by with-

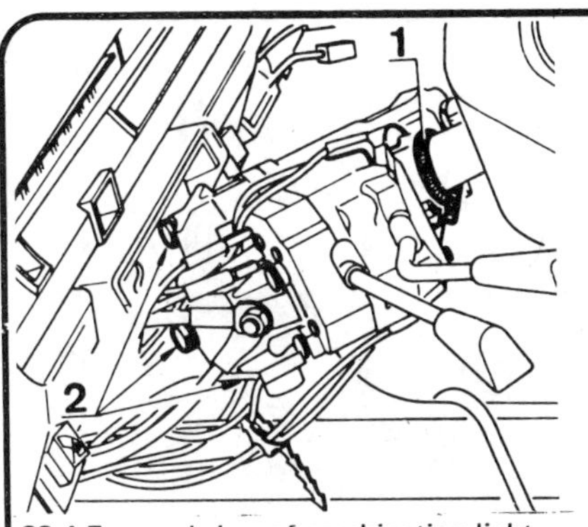

22.4 Exposed view of combination lightting switch. 1 Flasher control return spring 2 Switch securing screws

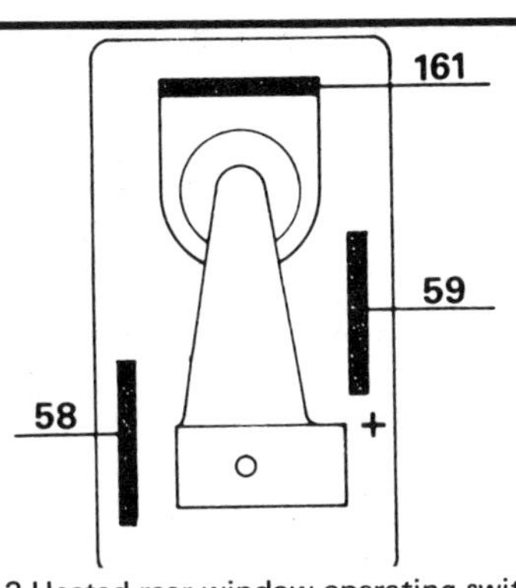

23.3 Heated rear window operating switch connections. 58 To element. 59 Feed to switch. 161 Indicator lamp (earth)

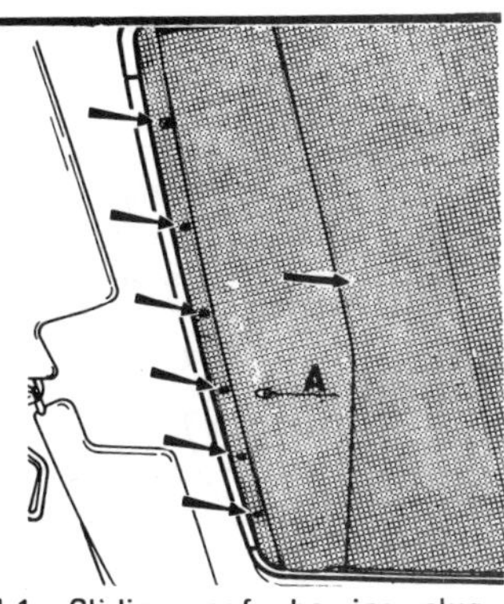

24.1. Sliding roof showing plug (A) removable for access to motor spindle for hand cranking

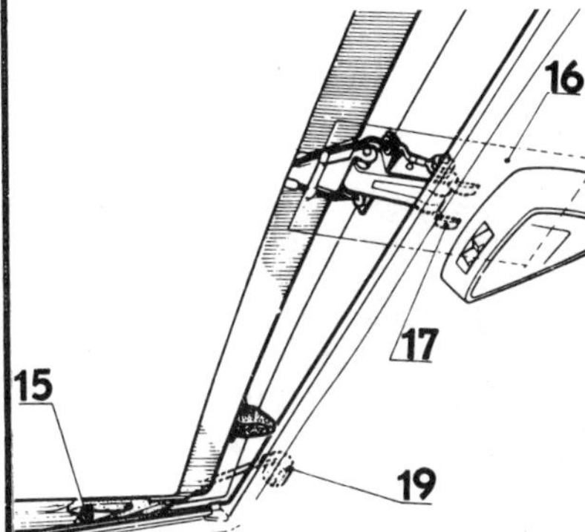

24.10 Location of sliding roof packing pieces (15) track (16) pads (17) springs (19)

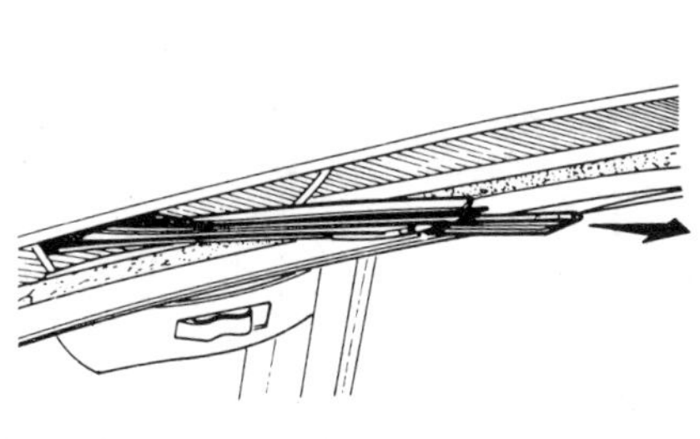
24.11 Removing a sliding roof track

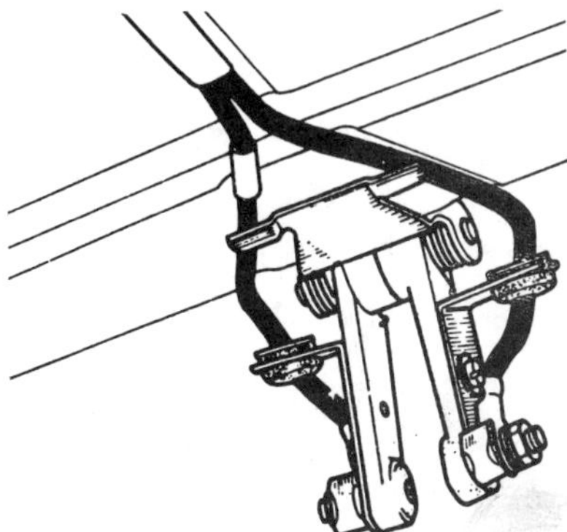
24.13 Sliding roof pick up shoes and pads

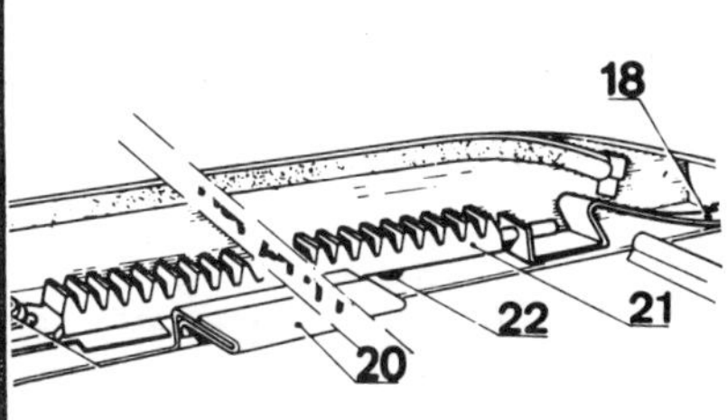

24.17 Components of the sliding roof gear 18 Ramp. 20 Side member. 21 Rack. 22 anti-rattle spacers

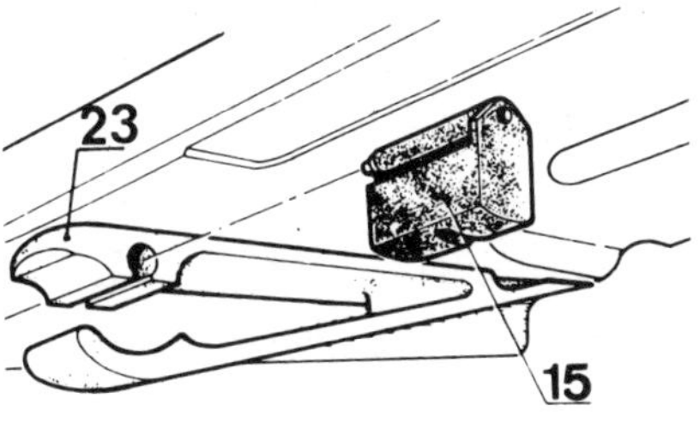

24.19 Location of packing pieces (15) and slide fingers (23) fitted to sliding roof

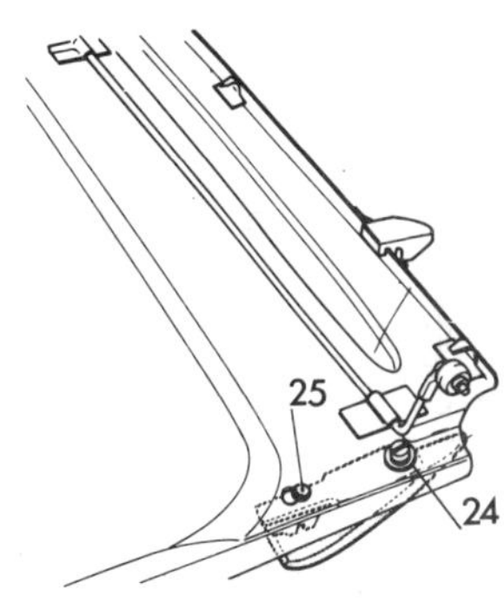

24.21 Part of the sliding roof mechanism 24 Retaining screw. 25 Lug

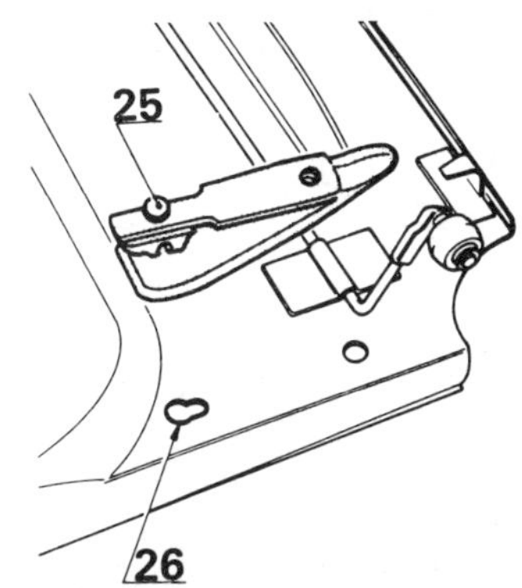

24.22 Removing a sliding roof slide finger (25) from its slot (26)

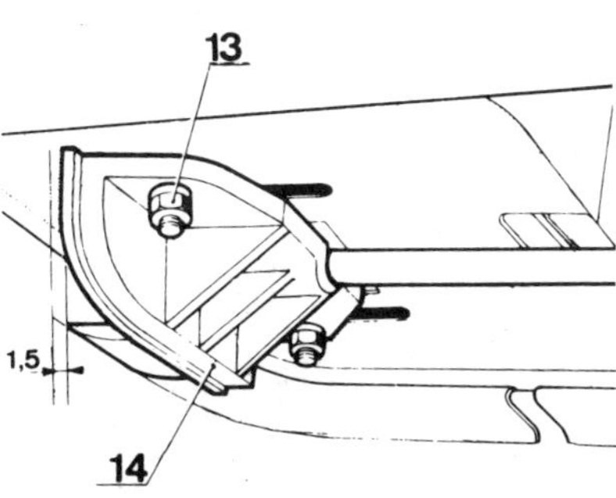

24.25 Sliding roof guide bearing (14) and securing nut (13)

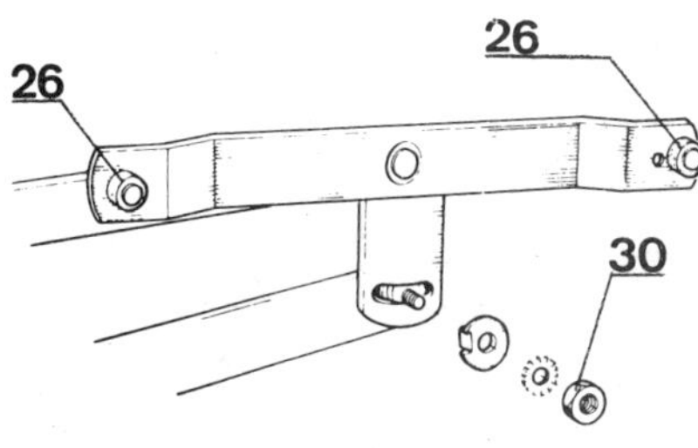

25. 4 Electrically operated window winder, details of roller mechanism. 26 Rollers 30 Clamping nut

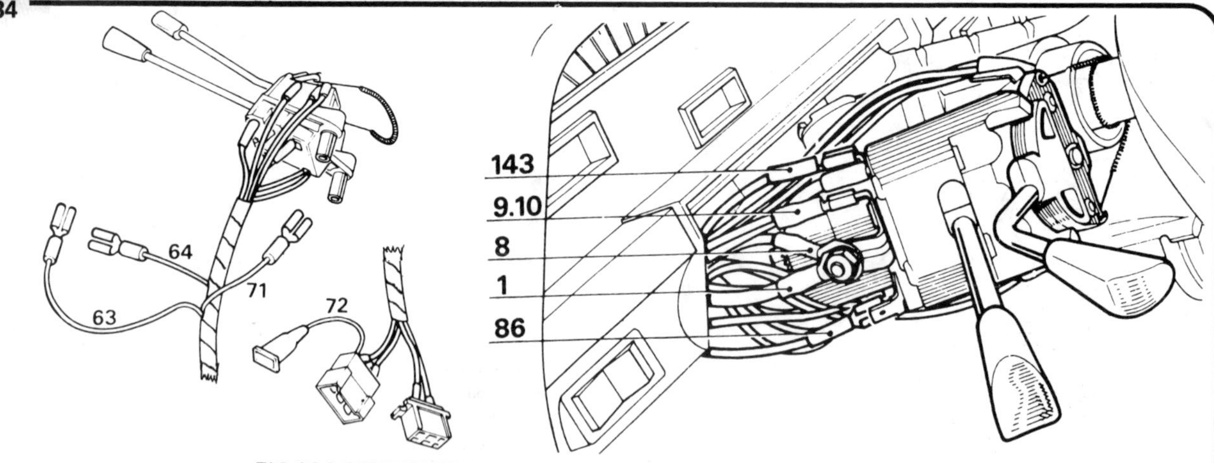

FIG.12.8 COMBINATION LIGHTING SWITCH CONNECTIONS (R1150)

1 Main feed
8 Neiman type ignition switch
9 Fuse direct +
10 Feed to parking lamp
63 Return from stop lamps
64 Feed to flasher switch
71 Brake warning lamp
72 Handbrake indicator lamp
86 Feed to panel light rheostat
143 Headlamp main beam indicator

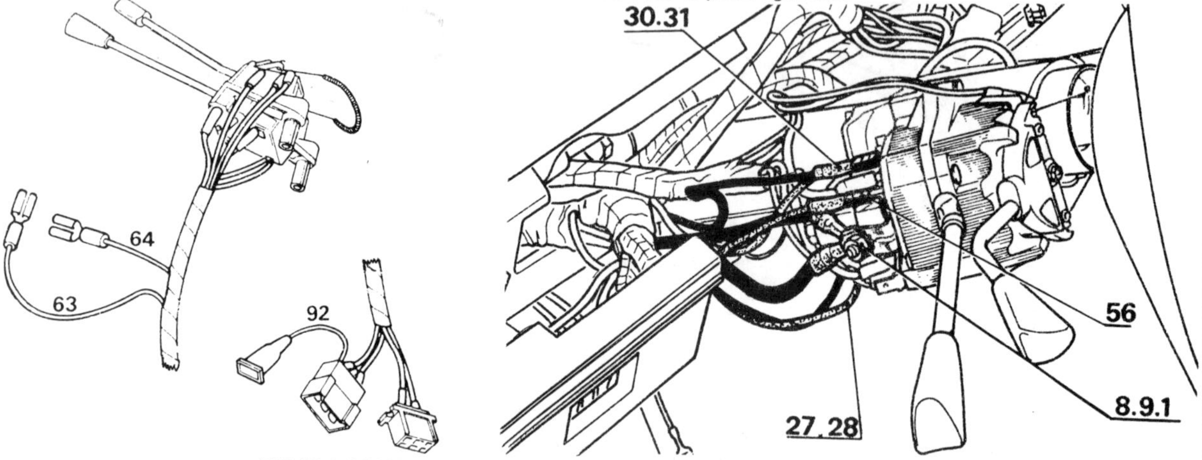

FIG.12.9 COMBINATION LIGHTING SWITCH CONNECTIONS (R1151)

1 Main feed
8 Neiman type ignition switch
9 Fuse direct +
27 Cigar lighter lamp
28 Feed to panel light rheostat
30 Headlamp main beam indicator lamp
31 Feed to quartz iodine headlamps
56 Feed to parking lamps
63 Return from stop lamp
64 Feed to flasher switch
92 Handbrake indicator lamp

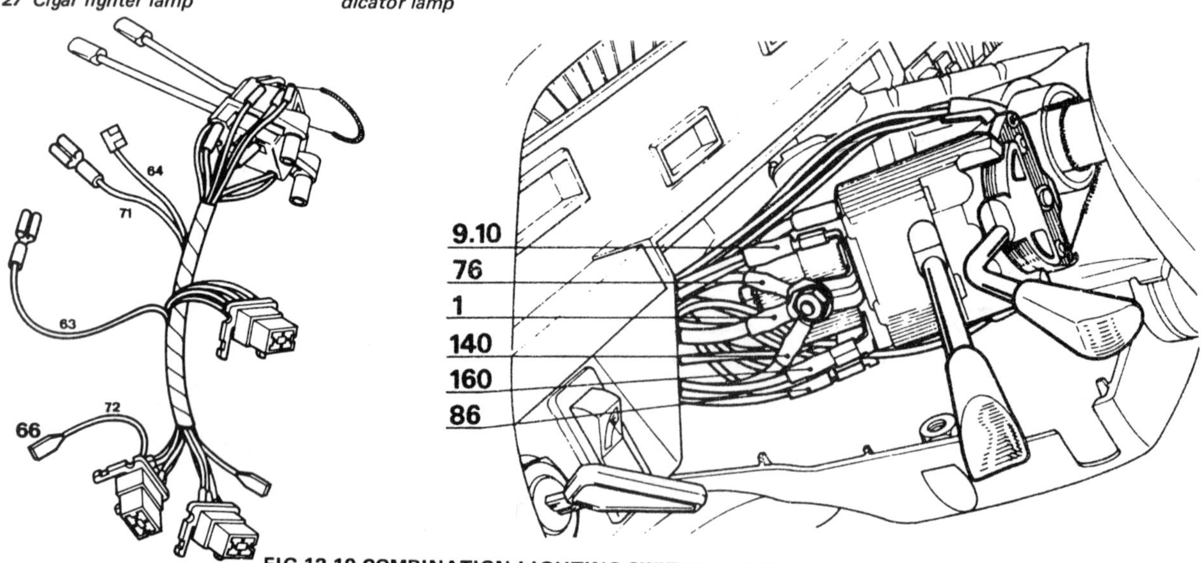

FIG.12.10 COMBINATION LIGHTING SWITCH CONNECTIONS (R1152)

1 Main feed
9 Fuse direct +
10 Feed to parking lamp
63 Return from stop lamp
64 Feed to flasher switch
66 Feed to rear lamps
71 Disc pad wear warning lamp
72 Handbrake indicator lamp
76 Feed to fuse
86 Feed to panel lighting
140 Feed to ignition switch
160 Headlamp main beam lamp

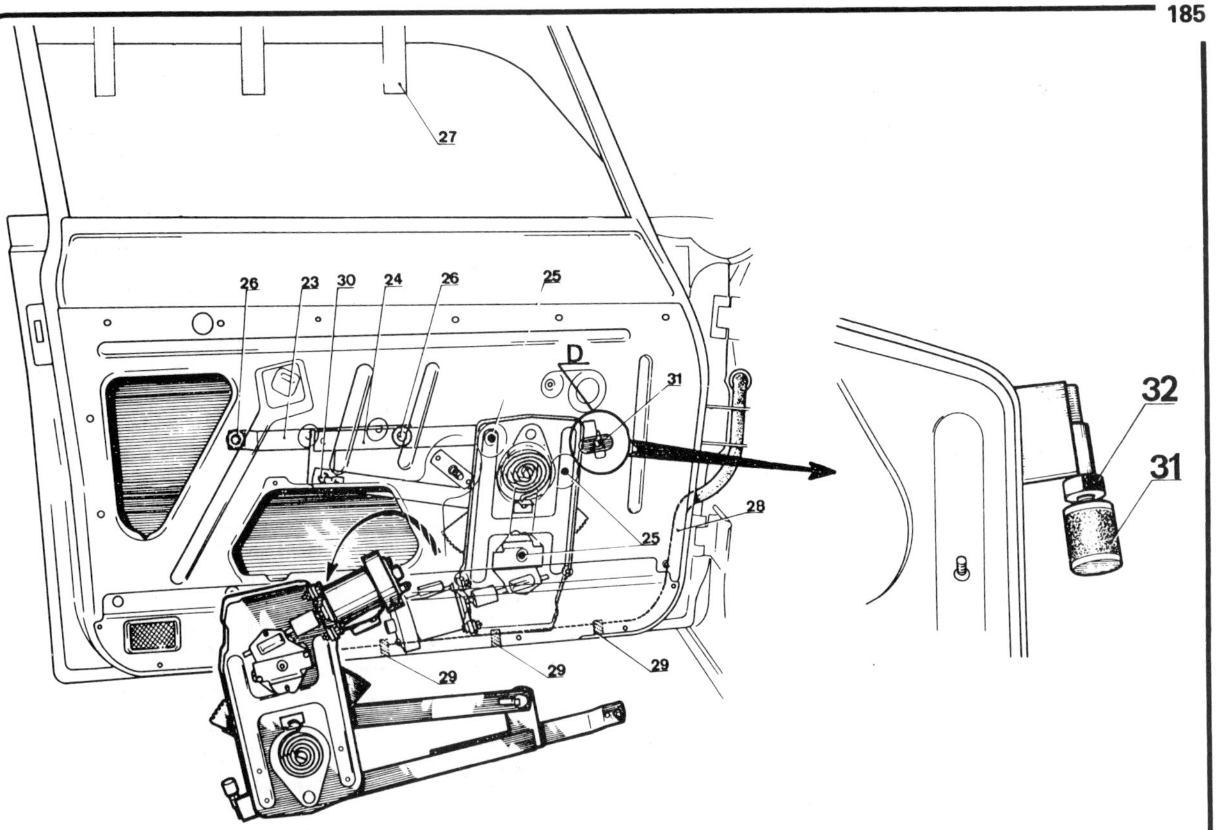

FIG.12.11 DETAILS OF LOCATION AND REMOVAL OF ELECTRIC WINDOW WINDER

23 Roller arm
24 Upper mechanism
25 Securing studs
26 Slide and roller
27 Supporting tape
28 Door frame
29 Clips
30 Clamp nut
31 Stop
32 Lock nut

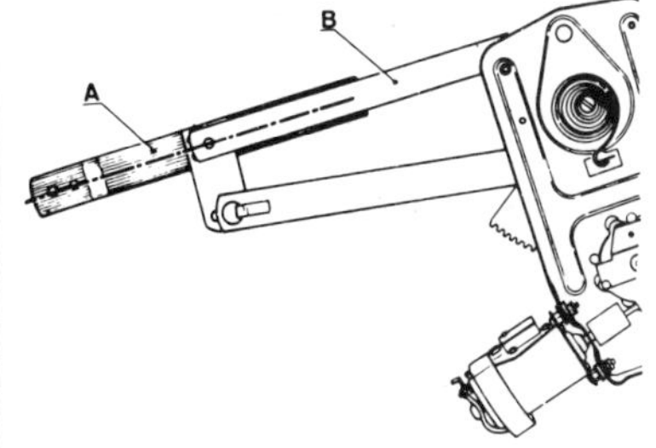

25.7 Correct alignment of window winder operating arms

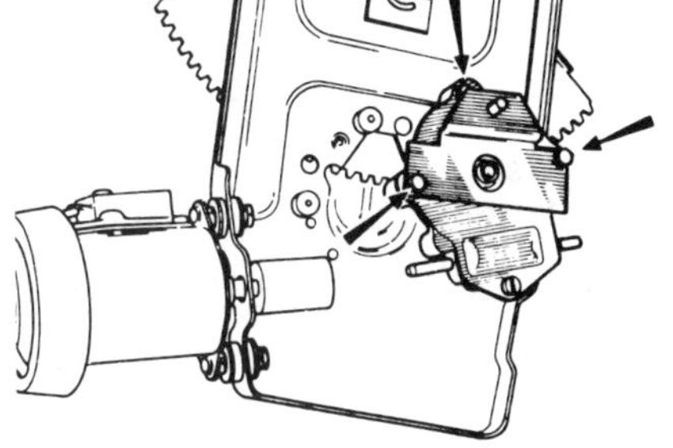

25.11 Window winder mechanism securing screws

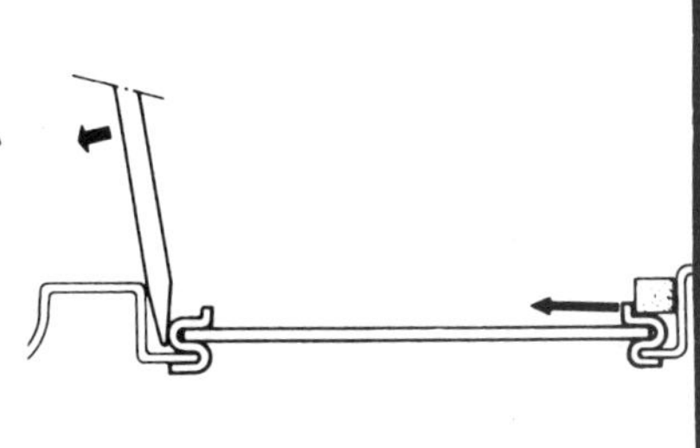

26.2 Prising the air inlet grille from its location

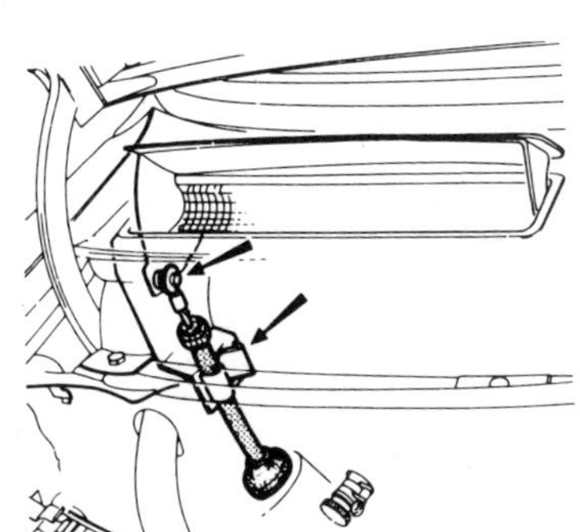

26.3 Air grille operating rod clip and connecting pin

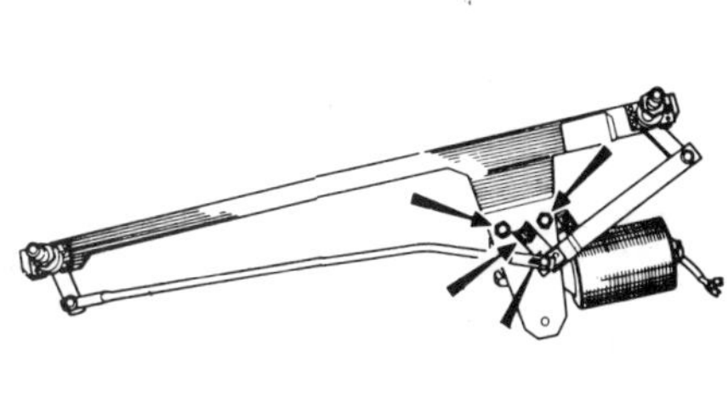

26.5 Wiper motor, support bar and linkage removed together as a unit

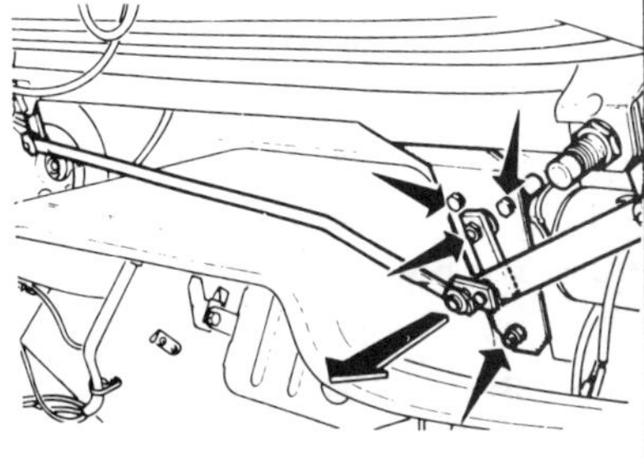

26.6 Points of disconnection to remove wiper, leaving linkage and support bar in position

drawing the motor securing bolts. (Fig).

7 Refitting is a reversal of removal but the linkage must be adjusted as described in the next Section.

27 Wiper Linkage - Adjustment

1 Ensure that the wiper motor is switched off and in the 'park' position. Adjust the linkage so that the links A and B take up the positions shown in the figure.

28 Windscreen Wiper Motor - Servicing

1 Various types of single and two speed wiper motors are fitted according to vehicle model and date of manufacture as listed in Specifications.

2 Exploded views of the wiper motors are shown in the figures.

3 With wiper motors type Bosch WS 1500 RIF and SEV 116012 the armature is removed by withdrawing the two long body screws (A) and removing the body and access to the drive gear and pick-up shoes is gained by removing the five screws (B). (Fig).

4 With wiper motors type Bosch WS 1500 RF3 (single speed) and WS 1500 RF4 (two speed) access to the armature is by means of withdrawing screws (A) and to the gear and pick-up shoes by withdrawing screws (B). (Fig).

5 Servicing should be limited to renewal of worn or damaged components. The brushes can be renewed by unsoldering the old ones and resoldering the new ones. RIF and SEV models are shown in the figure.

6 Check that the brushes are not sticking in their holders when refitting.

7 Brushes fitted to RF3 and RF4 wiper motors are not renewable and when worn, the complete wiper motor unit must be exchanged for a factory reconditioned assembly.

29 Wiper Arm Shaft Bearing - Renewal

1 Remove the wiper arms.

2 Remove the scuttle crossmember as described in Section 26.

3 Disconnect the coupling link (1) and remove the two shaft bearing securing screws (2). (Fig).

4 Scratch off the dab of paint on the shaft end.

5 Drift out the shaft carefully and renew any of the components, as necessary, which are shown in the figure. (Fig 12.15).

6 Reassemble in the sequence shown and grease the shaft and bearing body. Push the splined end fitting (4) onto the shaft until it locates against the bottom of the chamfer.

30 Voltage Regulators

1 A voltage regulator is fitted in conjunction with the alternator. This may be either a reed or electronic type. A SEV/Motorola type E144 electronic regulator is fitted to R1150 vehicles (1966 - 1967). (Fig).

2 A Ducellier or SEV reed type regulator is fitted to R1150 vehicles (1968 - 1969) and to R1151, R1152 and R1153 models. (Fig).

3 In the event of malfunction of either type of regulator it should be renewed as a unit as it is not designed to be repaired.

31 Headlamps - Removal and Refitting

1 Rectangular type headlamps are fitted to vehicle models R1150, R1151 and R1153. The lamp units may be removed after detachment of the three piece radiator grille. (Fig).

2 Place the headlamp adjuster lever in the raised position and remove the four rim support securing screws and withdraw the headlamp unit. (Fig).

3 Twin sealed beam headlamps are fitted to model R1152 vehicles.

4 Remove the three moulding retaining screws and withdraw the moulding. (Fig).

5 Prise each of the retaining circlips upwards and remove the beam unit in a forward direction.

6 If the sealed beam unit is to be renewed then the sealing ring must be separated into its two half sections by the removeval of the three securing screws. (Fig).

7 Where quartz-iodine type headlamps are installed, remove them by disconnecting the electrical lead and unscrewing the securing nut. (Fig).

8 Refitting of all types of headlamps is a reversal of removal but adjustment must then be carried out as described in the next Section.

32 Headlamps - Adjustment

1 With all types of headlamp unit, it is preferable to have the beams adjusted using modern optical setting equipment at a service station.

2 An alternative method is to position the car on a level surface with the tyres correctly inflated, 25 ft (7.6 m) from a wall or screen. Make two marks on the wall directly in front of and at the same height as the lamp centres. Check that the lamp unit level control lever is in the fully depressed position and the lamp beams are undipped.

3 Cover each lamp in turn and adjust the headlamp so that its concentrated light pattern is centred upon the marks made on the wall.

4 Adjustment of rectangular type lamp is made by means of screws A and B as shown in Fig.31.1.

5 Adjustment of circular twin sealed beam type lamps is made by means of screws A and B as shown in Fig.31.4.

6 Adjustment of quartz-iodine type lamps is carried out by slackening the securing nut and moving the unit on its ball joint. (Fig).

33 Rear and Parking Lamps - Bulb Replacement

1 The front parking lamp is combined with the front flasher. The lamp cover is held in place by two screws, which should be removed for access to the bulbs.

2 Rear lamp and brake stop light double filament bulbs are accessible after removal of the three casing screws.

3 The rear number plate lights are retained by two screws to a support. Unscrew them a few turns to lower the bottom part of the support and to allow the screw heads to press through the support. The bulbs may now be renewed.

4 The dual flasher repeater and side parking lights have their covers secured by two screws. When refitting, remember that the red section of the cover faces towards the rear of the car.

5 The specified bulb types and capacities are listed in Specifications.

34 Ancillary Switches - Description and Connections

1 The switches and lead connections are illustrated in this Section to facilitate their location, identification and correct connection to the wiring circuit where the components have to be removed and replaced due to failure or malfunction.

2 The sliding sun roof is controlled by the switch shown in the figure.

3 A thermal cut-out switch is also incorporated in the sliding roof control gear.

4 The foot brake stop light switch can be one of two types (Figs).

5 A foot operated dipper switch fitted to model R1152.

6 Two types of cigar lighter were fitted (Figs).

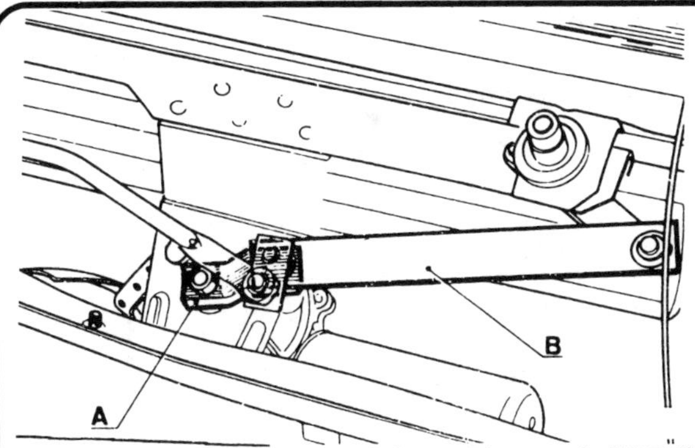

27.1 Correct alignment of wiper linkage with motor in 'PARK' position

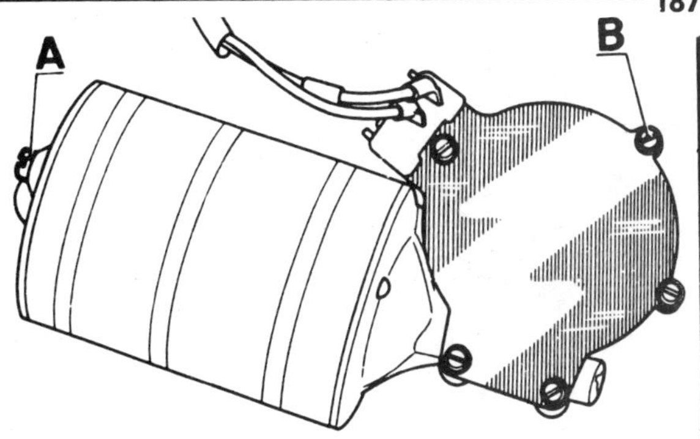

28.3 Bosch WS 1500 RIF and SEV 116012 wiper motors. A body securing tie bolts. B gear drive and pick up shoe cover screws.

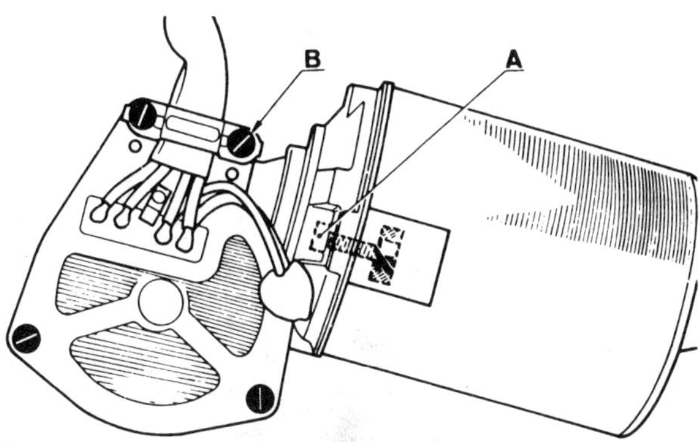

28.4 Bosch WS 1500 RF3 and RF4 wiper motors. A body securing screws. B drive gear cover securing screws

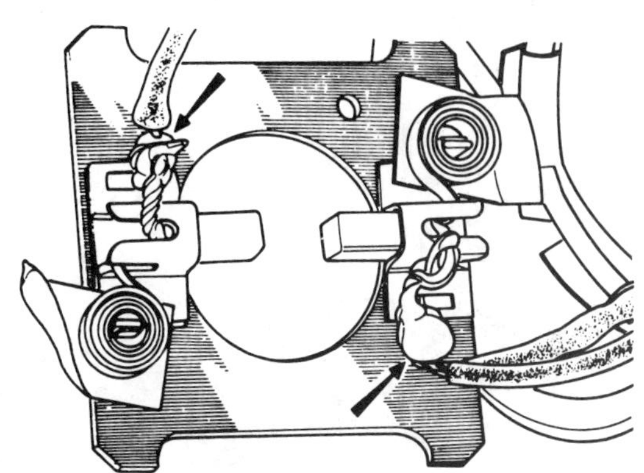
28.5 Method of soldering wiper motor brushes in RIF and SEV types

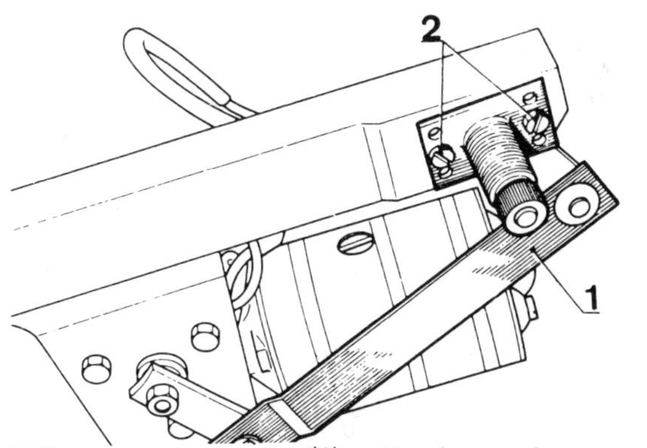

29.3 Wiper motor coupling link (1) and bearing securing screws (2)

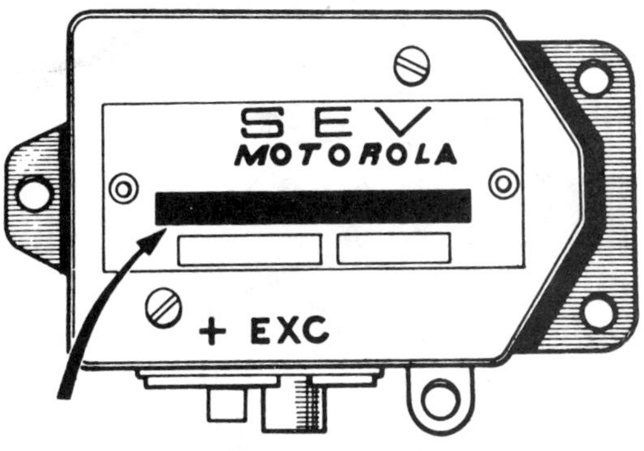

30.1 Type SEV/MOTOROLA E144 regulator

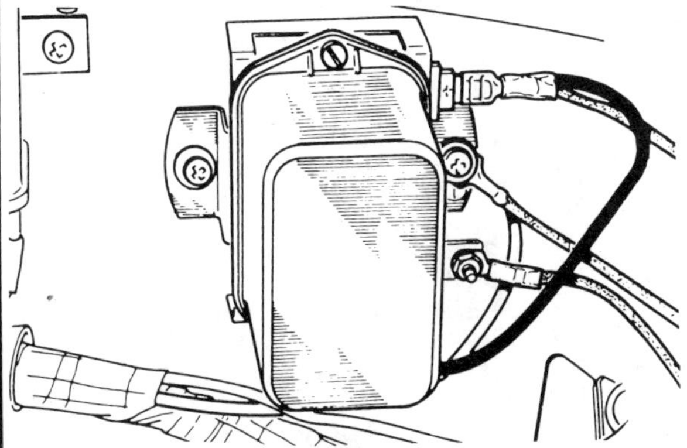
30.2 Ducellier or SEV type regulator

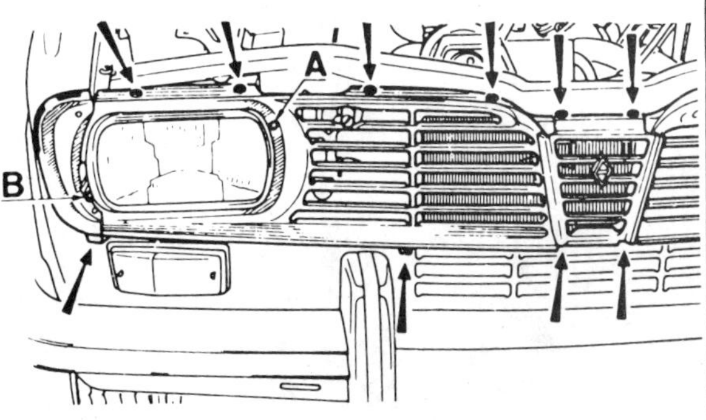

31.1 Radiator grille securing screws. A lateral adjustment screw. B beam height adjustment.

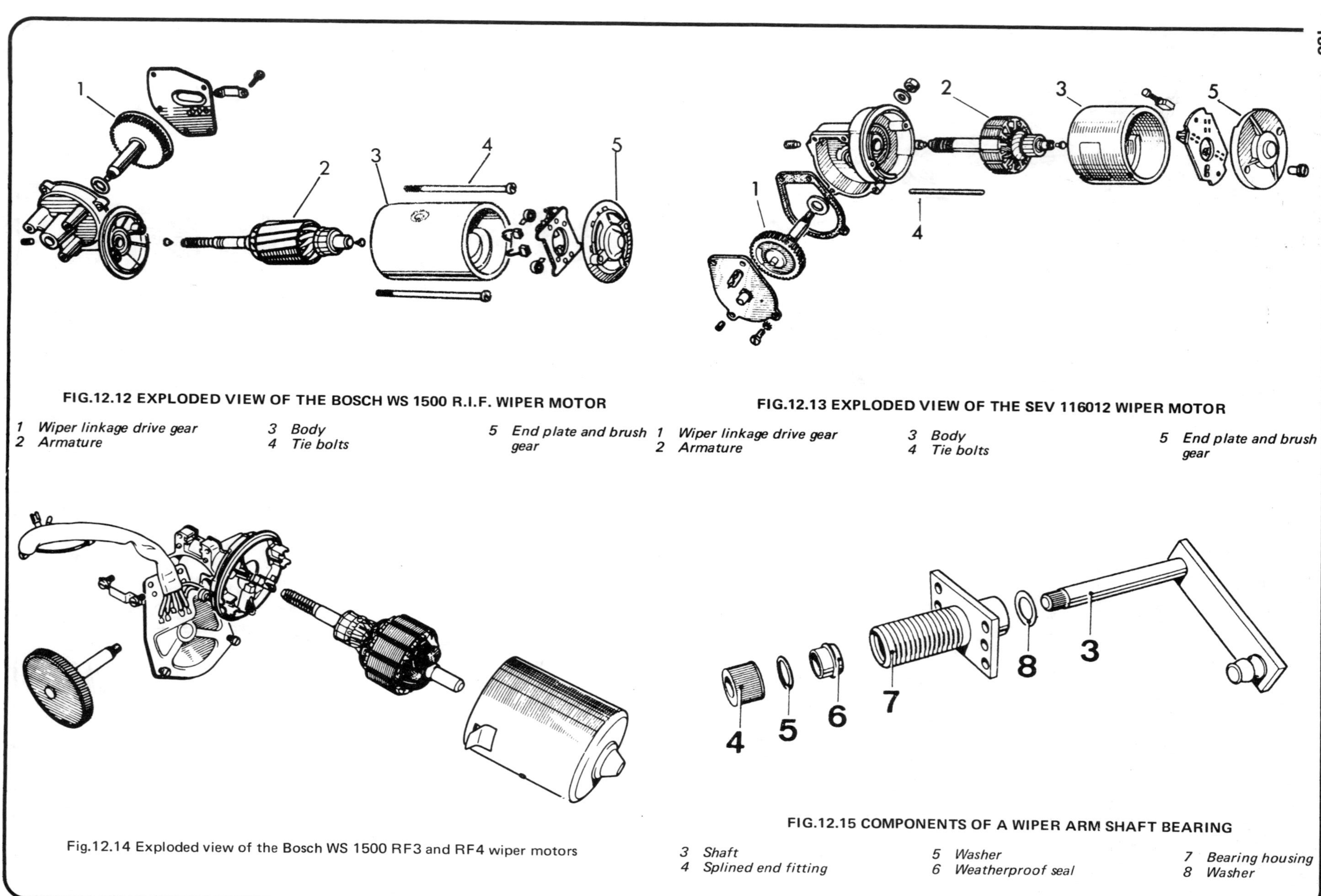

FIG.12.12 EXPLODED VIEW OF THE BOSCH WS 1500 R.I.F. WIPER MOTOR

1 Wiper linkage drive gear 2 Armature 3 Body 4 Tie bolts 5 End plate and brush gear

FIG.12.13 EXPLODED VIEW OF THE SEV 116012 WIPER MOTOR

1 Wiper linkage drive gear 2 Armature 3 Body 4 Tie bolts 5 End plate and brush gear

Fig.12.14 Exploded view of the Bosch WS 1500 RF3 and RF4 wiper motors

FIG.12.15 COMPONENTS OF A WIPER ARM SHAFT BEARING

3 Shaft 4 Splined end fitting 5 Washer 6 Weatherproof seal 7 Bearing housing 8 Washer

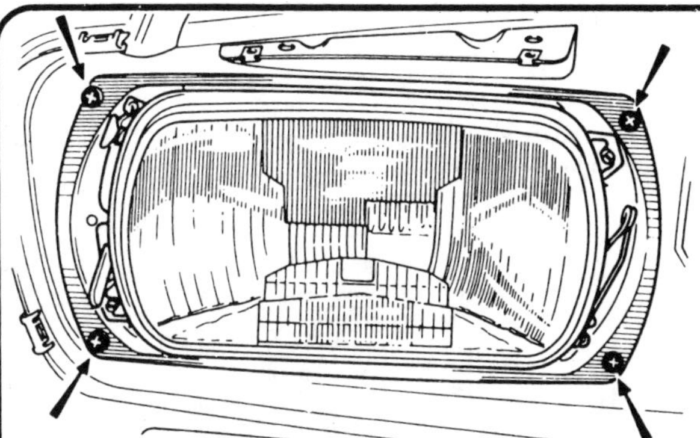

31.2 Headlamp unit securing screws

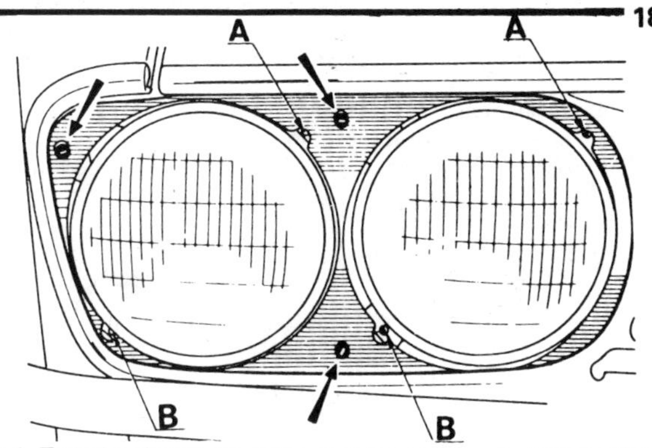

31.4. Twin headlamp moulding securing screws. A lateral adjustment screw. B beam height adjustment screw

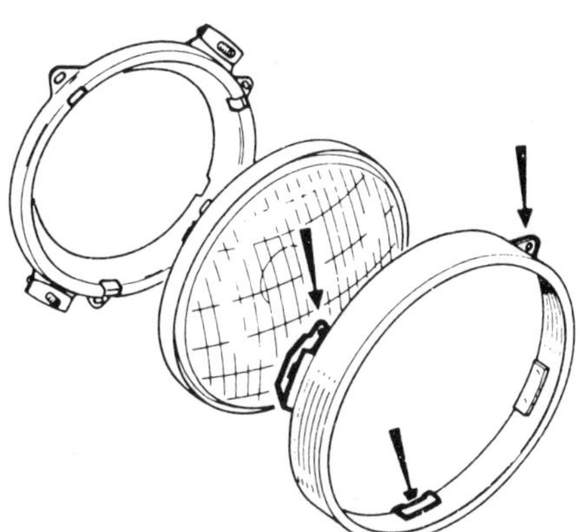

31.6 Components of a sealed beam type headlamp unit

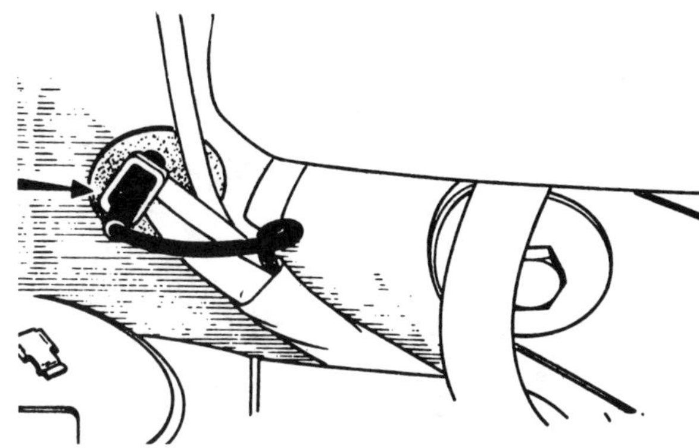

31.7 Quartz iodine type headlamp lead and securing nut

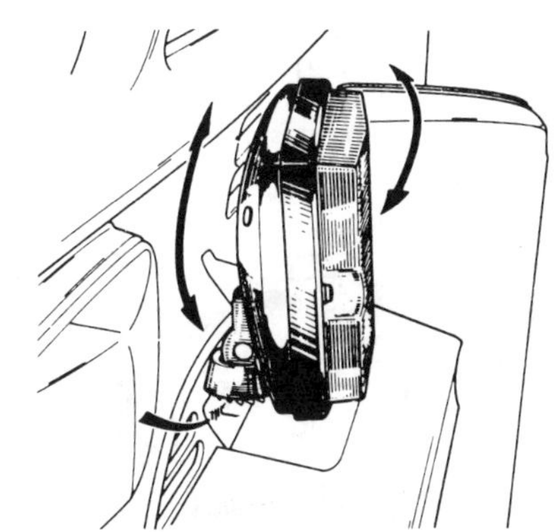

32.6 Quartz iodine type headlamp adjustment

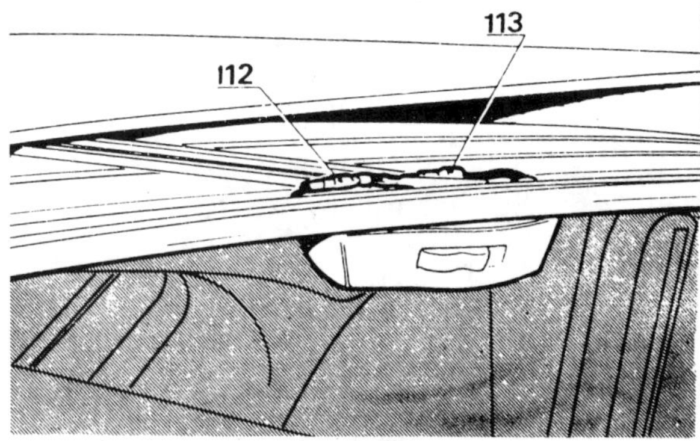

34.2 Sliding roof control switch. 112 motor +. 113 return from motor

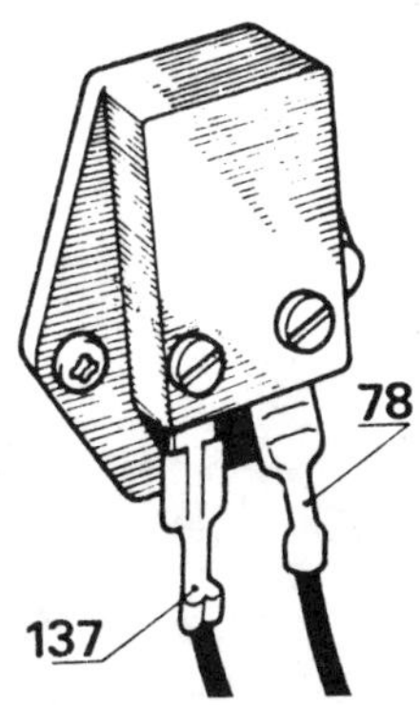

34.3 Sun roof thermal cut-out switch (R1151). 78 Feed to cut-out switch. 137 feed to operating switch

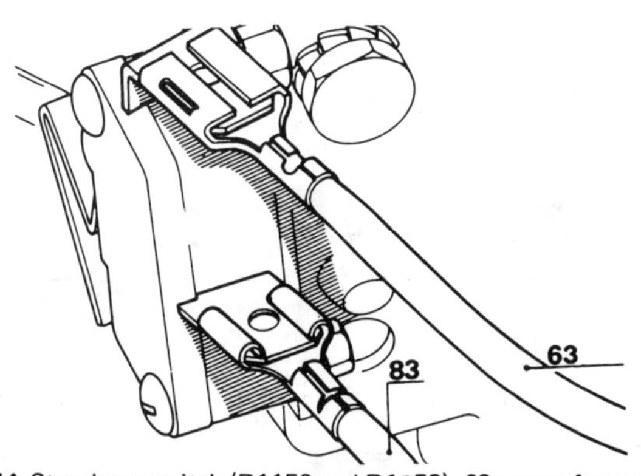

34.4A Stop lamp switch (R1150 and R1152). 63 return from stop lamp. 83 feed to switch

7 The vehicle interior light details are shown in the figure.
8 The map reading light is shown in the figure.
9 The reverse lamp switch is shown fitted to the gearbox in the figure.
10 The windscreen washer pump (model R1151) connections are shown in the figure.

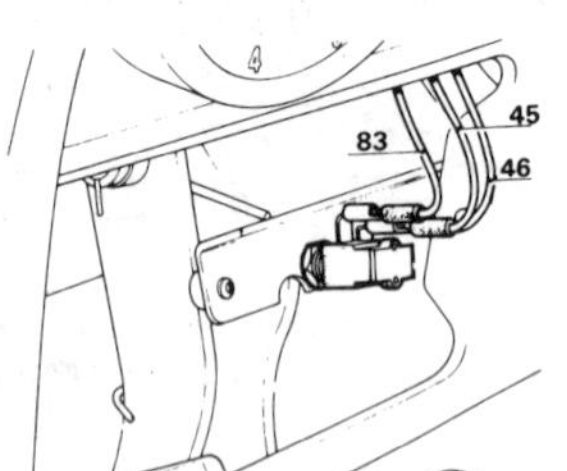

34.4B Stop lamp switch (R1151). 45 feed to flasher. 46 feed to stop lamp switch. 83 return from stop lamp.

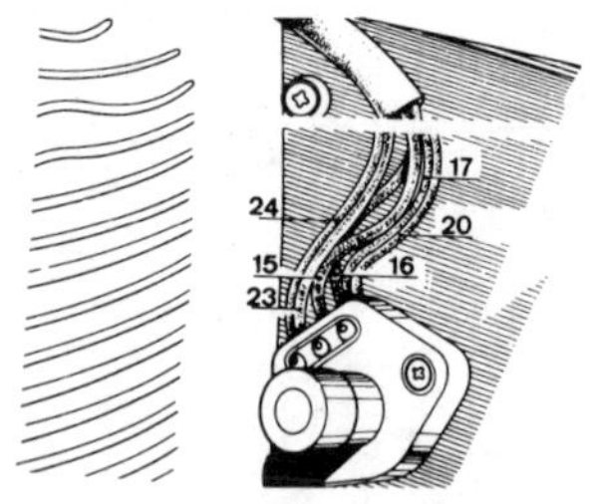

34.5 Foot operated headlamp dipper switch (R1152). 15 feed to switch. 16 headlamp main beam indicator. 17 feed to left hand headlamps. 20 feed to right hand headlamps. 23 left hand dipped beam. 24 right hand dipped beam

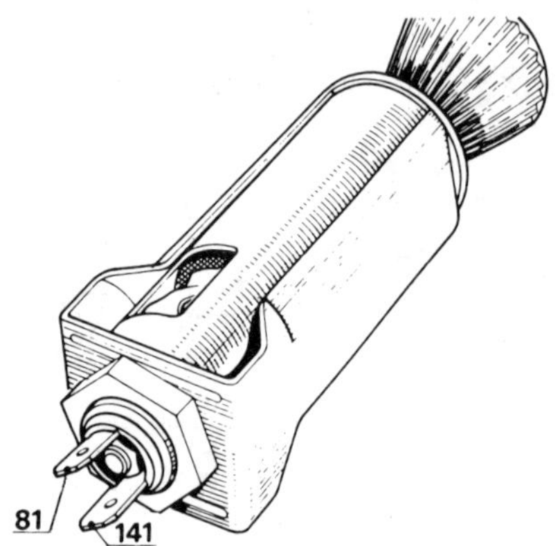

34.6A. Cigar lighter (R1150 and R1152) 81 feed. 141 feed to glove compartment lamp

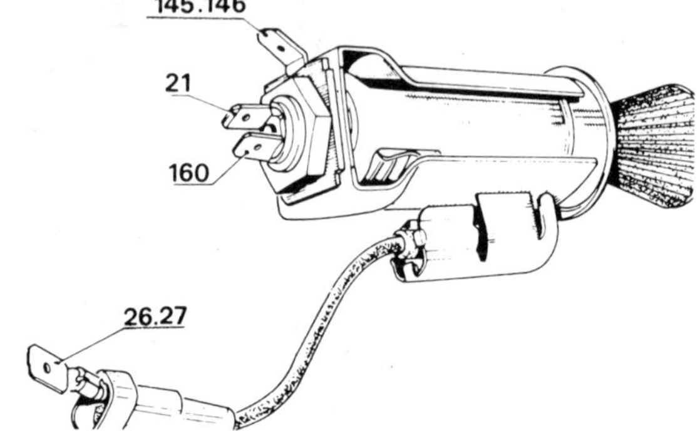

34.6B Cigar lighter (R1151). 21 feed to lighter. 26/27 ash tray and cigar lighter lamps. 145/146 earth (cigar lighter and ash tray) 160 feed to glove compartment lamp

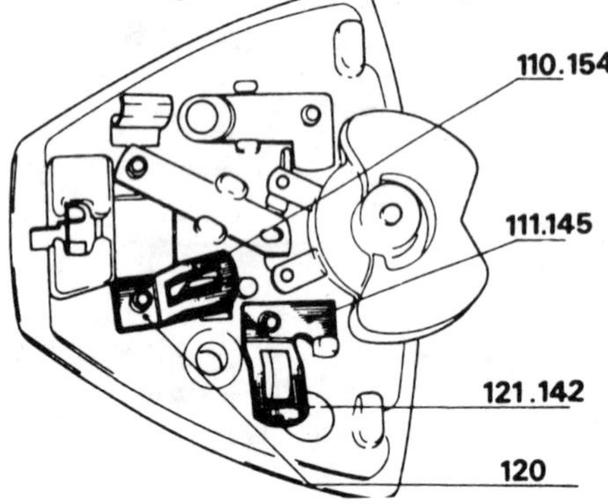

34.7 Vehicle interior lamp switch (R1150 and R1151). 110 feed 154 feed to map reading lamp. 111 left hand door pillar (earth). 145 right hand door pillar (earth). (R1152). 120 feed. 121/142 left or right door pillar earth

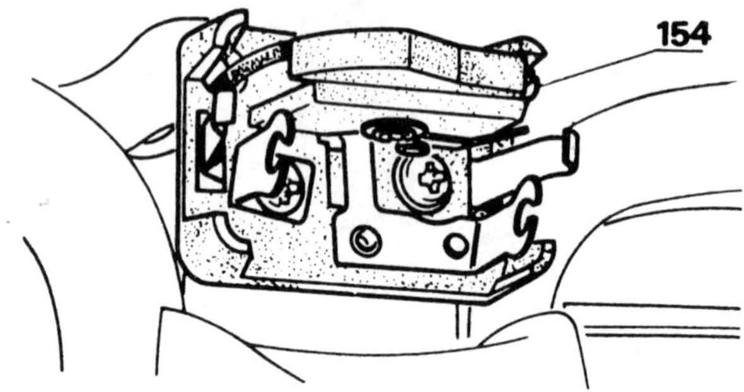

34.8 Map reading lamp (R1151). 154 feed wire

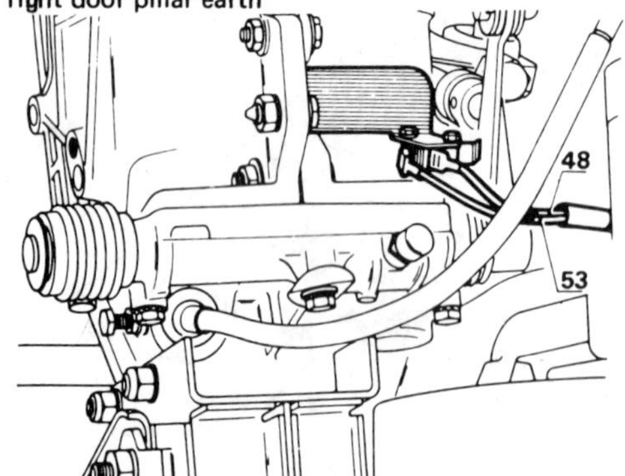

34.9 Gearbox reverse lamp switch (R1151 and R1152). 48 feed to switch. 53 feed to lamps

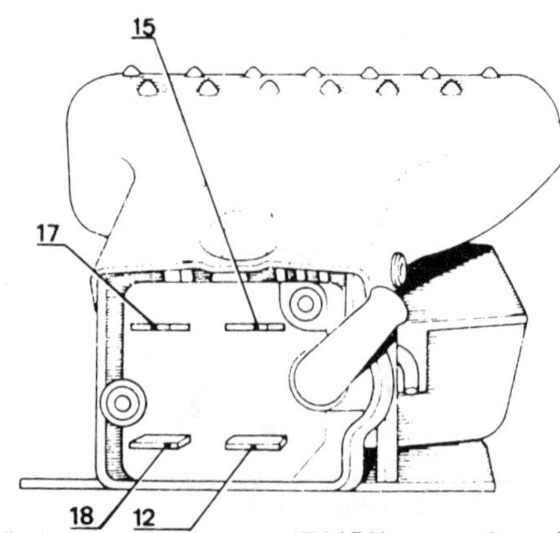

34.10 Windscreen washer pump (R1151) connections. 12 wiper slow speed. 15 wiper fast speed. 17 feed to washer. 18 slow speed

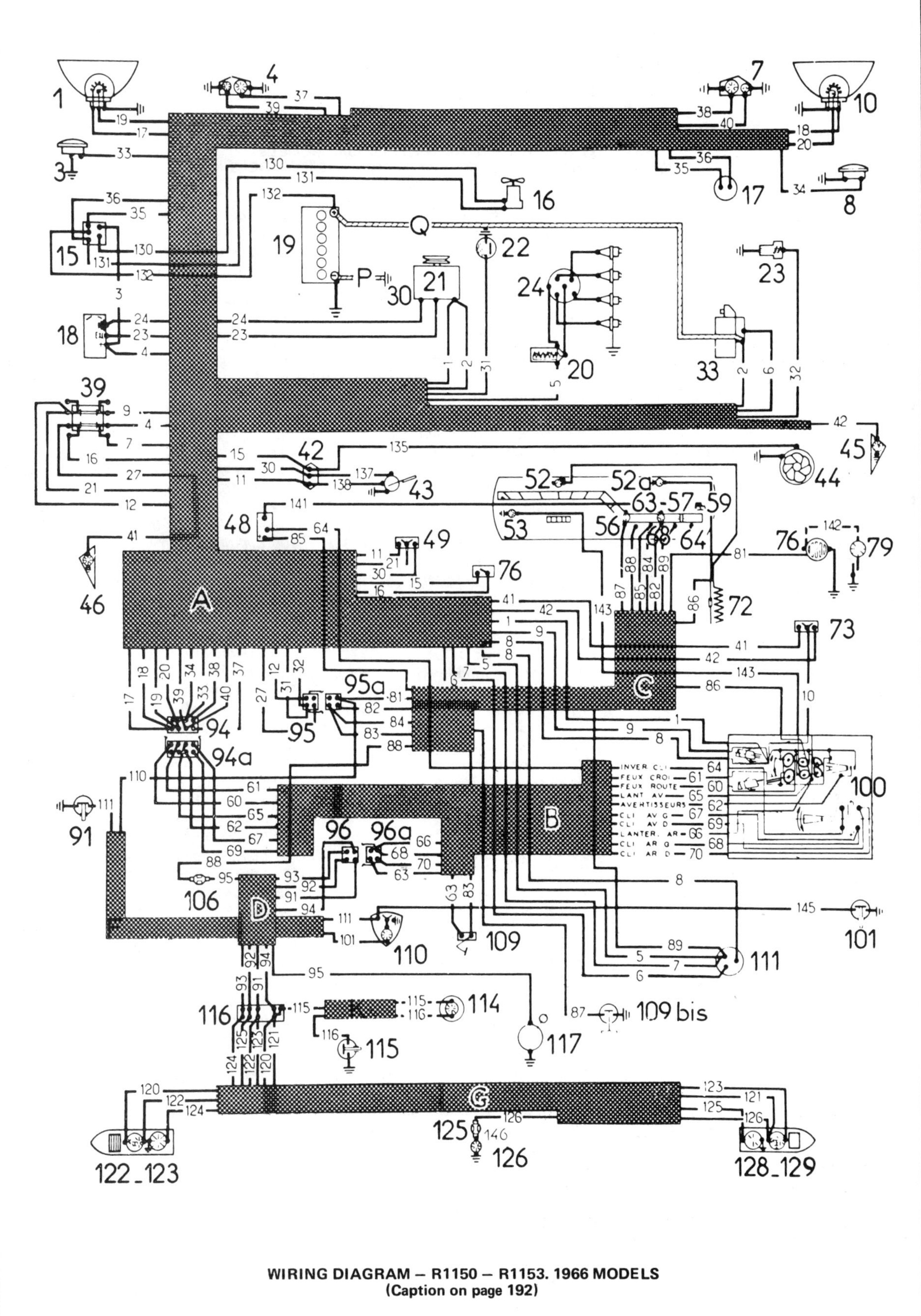

WIRING DIAGRAM – R1150 – R1153. 1966 MODELS
(Caption on page 192)

WIRING DIAGRAM – R1150 – R1153. 1966 MODELS
WIRING DIAGRAM – R1150 – R1153. 1967 - 1968 MODELS

1 Left-hand headlight
2 Left-hand inner headlight (R1152)
3 Left-hand horn
4 Left-hand sidelight and flasher
5 Left-hand QI lamp (R1151)
6 Right-hand QI lamp (R1151)
7 Right-hand sidelight and flasher
8 Right-hand horn
9 Right-hand inner headlight (R1152)
10 Right-hand headlight
11 Reverse light switch (R1151), (R1152)
12 Left-hand headlight wires connection (R1152)
12bis Right-hand headlight wires connection (R1152)
13 Left-hand QI lamp junction (R1151)
14 Right-hand QI lamp junction (R1151)
15 Cooling fan relay
16 Cooling fan
17 Temperature switch (Mosta)
18 Regulator
19 Battery
20 Coil
21 Alternator
22 Oil pressure switch
23 Thermal resistance (R1151) or thermal switch
24 Distributor
25 QI lamps relay (R1151)
26 Sunroof relay
27 Window winder relay (R1151)
28 Solenoid flap valve relay (R1152)
29 Brake warning light switch (R1152)
30 Battery earth (ground)
31 Tachometer detector (R1152)
32 Idling speed damper
33 Starter motor,
34 Right-hand front brake pad junction
35 Right-hand front brake pad
36 Solenoid flap valve (R1152)
37 Left-hand front brake pad junction
38 Left-hand front brake pad
39 Main fuse box
40 Window winder fuse box (R1151)
41 Sunroof fuse box
42 Cowl side junction box
43 Windscreen wiper
44 Heater/ventilator
45 Right-hand parking light
46 Left-hand parking light
47 Foot-operated dipswitch (R1152)
48 Flasher unit
49 Windscreen wiper switch
50 QI lamp switch (R1151)
51 Rear screen demister switch
52 Instrument panel lighting
52a Instrument panel lighting
53 Headlight main beam warning light
54 Brake warning light (R1152)
55 Handbrake and brake pad wear warning light
56 Choke warning light
57 Oil pressure and water temperature warning light
58 QI lamp warning light (R1151)
59 Flasher warning light
60 Rear screen demister warning light
61 Tachometer
62 Speedometer
63 Fuel level indicator
64 Voltmeter
65 Water temperature gauge (R1151)
66 Instrument panel left-hand group connection (R1151)
67 Instrument panel right-hand group connection (R1151)
68 Instrument panel + terminal
69 Sunroof switch
70 Left-hand window winder switch (R1151)
71 Right-hand window winder switch (R1151)
72 Instrument panel rheostat
73 Parking light switch
74 Sunroof thermal cut-out
75 Instrument panel and sunroof earth (ground)
76 Cigar lighter
77 Ashtray illumination
78 Cigar lighter illumination
79 Glove compartment light
80 Heater rheostat
81 Brake pressure warning light switch (R1152)
82 Windscreen washer pedal
83 Feed wire connection (R1151)
84 Brake warning light connection
85 Right-hand window winder earth (ground) (R1151)
86 Right-hand window winder (R1151)
87 Right-hand window winder junction (R1151)
88 Left-hand window winder (R1151)
89 Left-hand window winder junction (R1151)
90 Left-hand window winder earth (ground)
91 Left-hand door pillar switch
92 Handbrake switch
93 Handbrake wires junction clip
94, 94a Group junction
95, 95a Group junction
96, 96a Group junction
96b, 96c Group junction
97, 97a Group junction
98 Fuel level indicator junction clip (R1152)
99 Brake pressure warning light switch earth (ground) (R1152)
100 Lighting switch
101 Right-hand door pillar switch
102 'Hazard' warning light fuse (R1152)
103 'Hazard' warning light control unit (R1152)
104 'Hazard' warning light switch (R1152)
105 'Hazard' warning light junction clip (R1152)
106 Fuel level indicator junction clip
107 Sunroof motor
108 Sunroof track
109 Stoplight switch
109bis Choke switch
110 Interior light
111 Ignition/starter switch
112 Neiman switch illumination (R1151)
113 Map reading light
114 Luggage compartment light
115 Luggage compartment light switch
116 Rear harness junction box
117 Fuel level indicator
118 Reverse light junction
119 Rear screen demister + switch
120 Rear screen heater
121 Rear screen demister switch
122 Left-hand rear and stoplights
123 Left-hand rear flasher
124 Left-hand reverse light (R1151 – R1152)
125 Rear light junction clip
126 Number plate light
127 Right-hand reverse light (R1151–R1152)
128 Right-hand rear flasher
129 Right-hand rear and stop lights

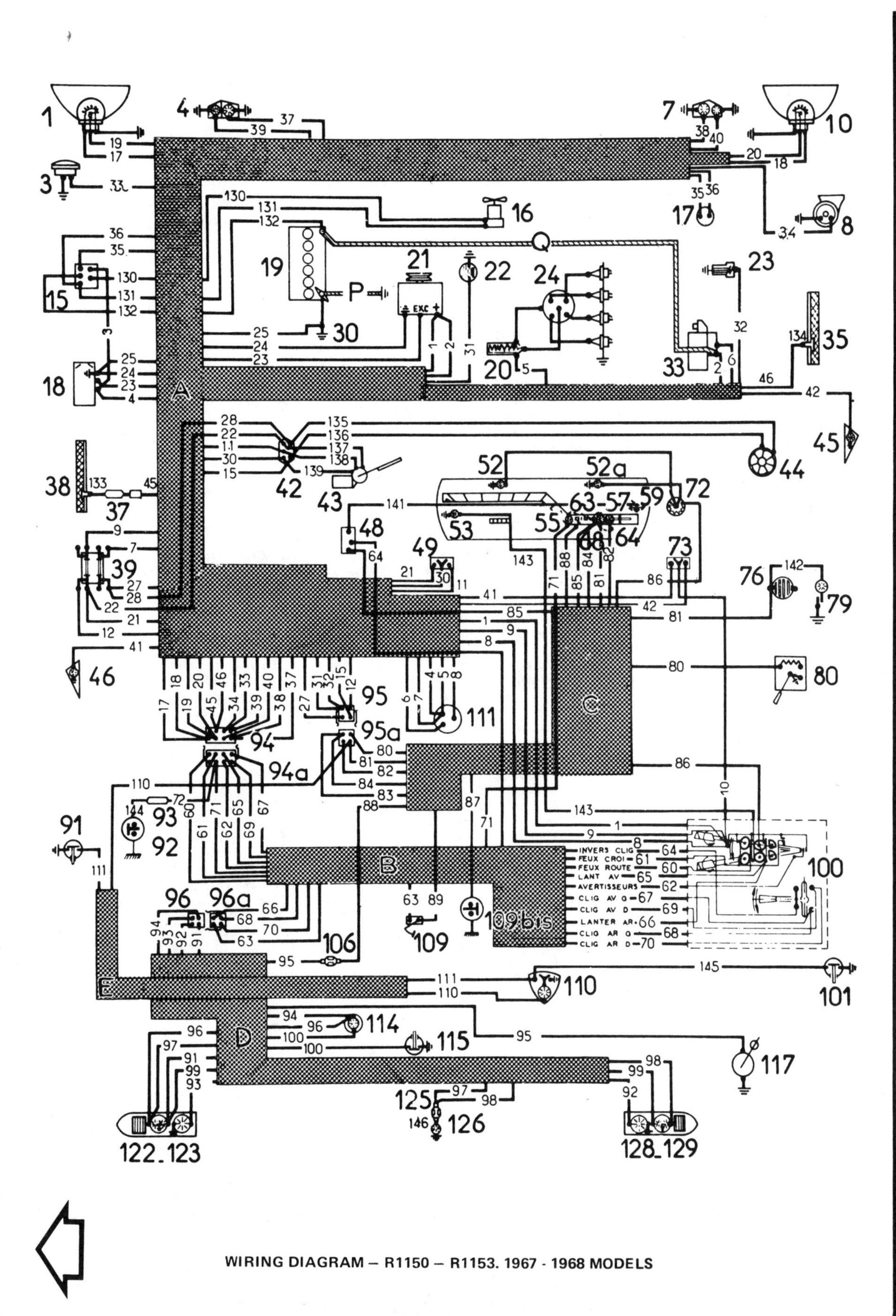

WIRING DIAGRAM – R1150 – R1153. 1967 - 1968 MODELS

WIRING DIAGRAM – R1151

1 LH front sidelight and direction indicator
2 LH front headlight
4 LH horn
5 LH Q.I. driving light
6 RH Q.I. driving light
7 RH horn
9 RH front headlight
10 RH front sidelight and direction indicator
14 Reversing light switch or dummy switch
15 Cooling fan motor
16 Temperature switch (mosta)
18 Cooling fan motor relay
19 Battery
20 Ignition coil
22 Alternator
23 Temperature or temperature sender switch
26 Junction plate
27 Regulator
28 Q.I. driving lights relay
29 Sunroof relay
30 Window winder relay
31 Fusebox
32 Stoplight switch
34 Distributor
35 Oil pressure sender switch
37 Starter
38 LH parking light
40 Brake warning light wire junction
41 RH parking light
42 Earth (ground)
43 LH front brake pad
44 LH front brake pad junction terminal
45 Scuttle junction plate
46 Windscreen wiper
47 Heater fan
48 RH front brake pad junction terminal
49 RH front brake pad
50 LH door pillar switch
52 Flasher unit
53 Headlight tell-tale
55 Instrument panel lighting
56 Brake pad wear warning light
57 Fuel contents gauge
58 Choke 'on' warning light
59 Oil pressure and water temperature warning light
60 Voltmeter
60a Instrument panel + terminal
61 Direction indicator tell-tale
62 Water temperature gauge
64 Heated rear screen switch
65 Windscreen wiper switch
66 Heated rear screen tell-tale
67 Q.I. driving lights tell-tale
68 Revolution counter
69 Speedometer
70 Sunroof switch
71 RH window winder switch
71a LH window winder switch
72 Clock
72a Clock illumination
73 Instrument panel lighting rheostat
74 Heater fan motor rheostat
75 RH door pillar switch
76 Parking lights switch
77 Sunroof switch or blanking plate
82 Heated rear screen switch and tell-tale
84 Junction block - combination lighting-direction indicator switch to front harness
85 Junction block - combination lighting direction indicator switch to rear harness
86 Combination lighting-direction indicator switch
87 Junction block - instrument panel harness
88 Junction block - front harness to rear harness
89 Flasher unit fuse
90 Junction block-instrument panel (after ignition switch)
91 Junction block - instrument panel (+ direct)
92 Instrument panel junction (LH)
93 Instrument panel junction (RH)
94 LH window winder
95 Ignition-starter switch illumination
96 Neiman
97 Choke 'on' position
98 Handbrake 'on' switch
99 Thermal overload switch
100 Earth (ground) on glove compartment
101 Cigar lighter
103 Ashtray illumination
104 Cigar lighter illumination
105 RH window winder earth (ground)
106 RH window winder
107 Luggage compartment light
108 Luggage compartment light switch
109 Windscreen washer pedal
110 Sunroof
111 Interior light
111a Map reading light
112 Fuel tank
115 Heated rear screen switch
116 Feed to heated rear screen
117 Heated rear screen switch
119 Reversing lamp wire junction
120 LH rear direction indicator
121 LH stop light and rear light
122 Feed to LH reversing light
123 Licence plate light junction terminal
124 Licence plate light
125 Feed to RH reversing lamp
126 RH rear stop light and rear light
127 RH rear direction indicator

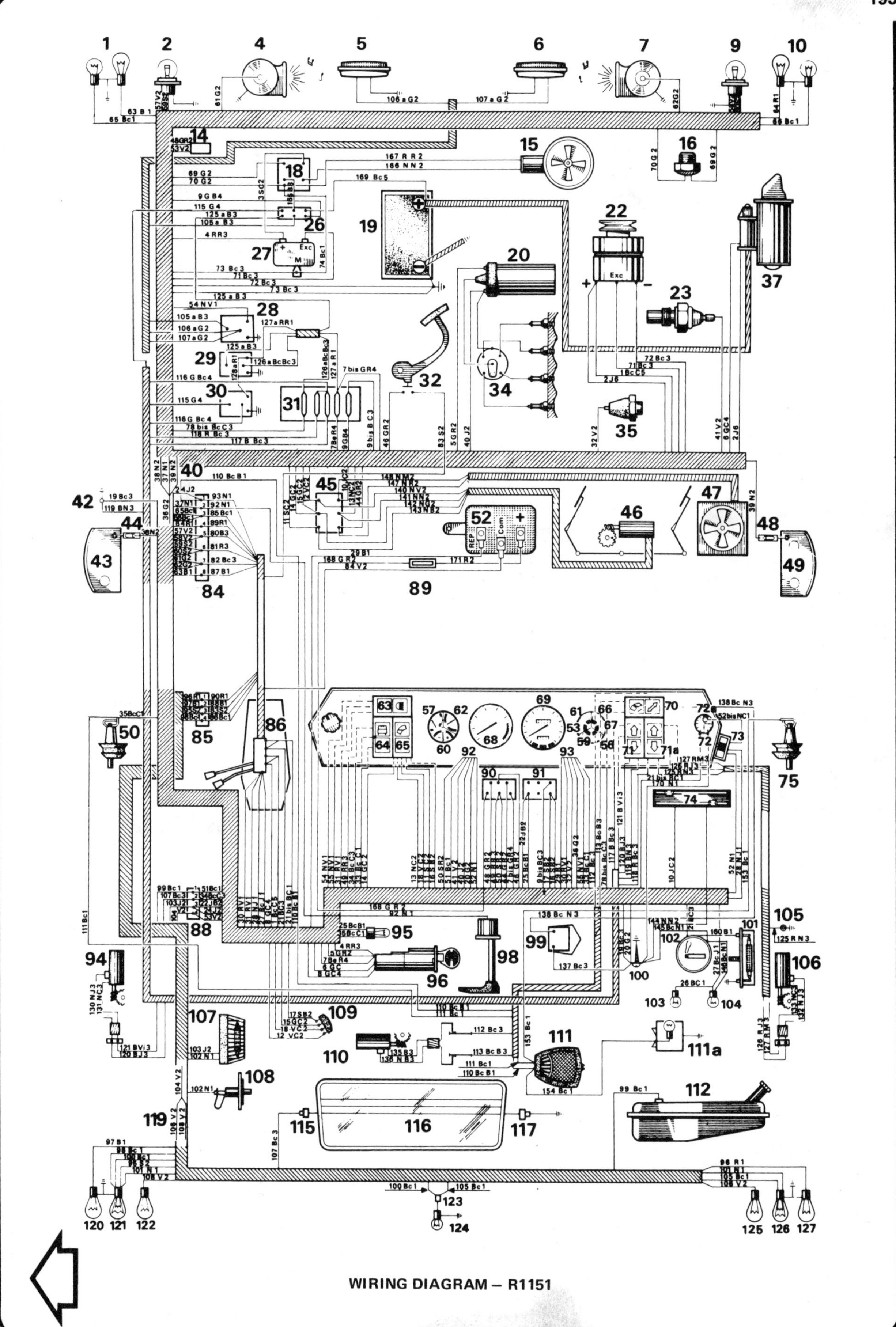

WIRING DIAGRAM – R1151

WIRING DIAGRAM – R1152

1 *LH front sidelight and direction indicator*
2 *LH front headlight*
4 *LH horn*
7 *RH horn*
9 *RH front headlight*
10 *RH front sidelight and direction indicator*
14 *Reversing lamp switch*
15 *Cooling fan motor*
16 *Temperature switch (mosia)*
18 *Cooling fan motor relay*
19 *Battery*
20 *Ignition coil*
22 *Alternator*
23 *Temperature or temperature sender switch*
27 *Regulator*
29 *Junction terminals*
31 *Fusebox*
32 *Stoplight switch*
34 *Distributor*
35 *Oil pressure sender switch*
37 *Starter*
38 *LH parking light*
40 *Brake warning light wire junction*
41 *RH parking light*
43 *LH front pad*
44 *LH front brake pad junction terminal*
45 *Scuttle junction plate*
46 *Windscreen wiper*
47 *Heater fan*
48 *RH front brake pad junction terminal*
49 *RH front brake pad*
50 *LH door pillar switch*
52 *Flasher unit*
53 *Headlight tell-tale*
55 *Instrument panel lighting*
56 *Brake pad wear and handbrake 'on' warning light*
57 *Fuel contents gauge*
58 *Choke 'on' warning light*
59 *Oil pressure and water temperature warning light*
60 *Voltmeter*
60a *Instrument panel + terminal*
61 *Direction indicator tell-tale*
65 *Windscreen wiper switch*
73 *Instrument panel lighting rheostat*
74 *Heater fan motor rheostat*
75 *RH door pillar switch*
77 *Sunroof switch or blanking plate*
84 *Junction block - combination lighting - direction indicator switch to front harness*
85 *Junction block - combination lighting direction indicator switch to rear harness*
86 *Combination lighting-direction indicator switch*
87 *Junction block - instrument panel harness to front harness*
88 *Junction block - front harness to rear harness*
89 *Flasher unit fuse*
96 *Neiman*
97 *Choke 'on' position*
98 *Handbrake 'on' switch*
101 *Cigar lighter*
107 *Luggage compartment light*
108 *Luggage compartment light switch*
111 *Interior light*
112 *Fuel tank*
116 *Feed to heated rear screen*
119 *Reversing lamp wire junction*
120 *LH rear direction indicator*
121 *LH stoplight and rear light*
122 *Feed to LH reversing lamp*
123 *Licence plate light junction terminal*
124 *Licence plate light*
125 *Feed to RH reversing lamp*
126 *RH rear stop light and rear light*
127 *RH rear direction indicator*

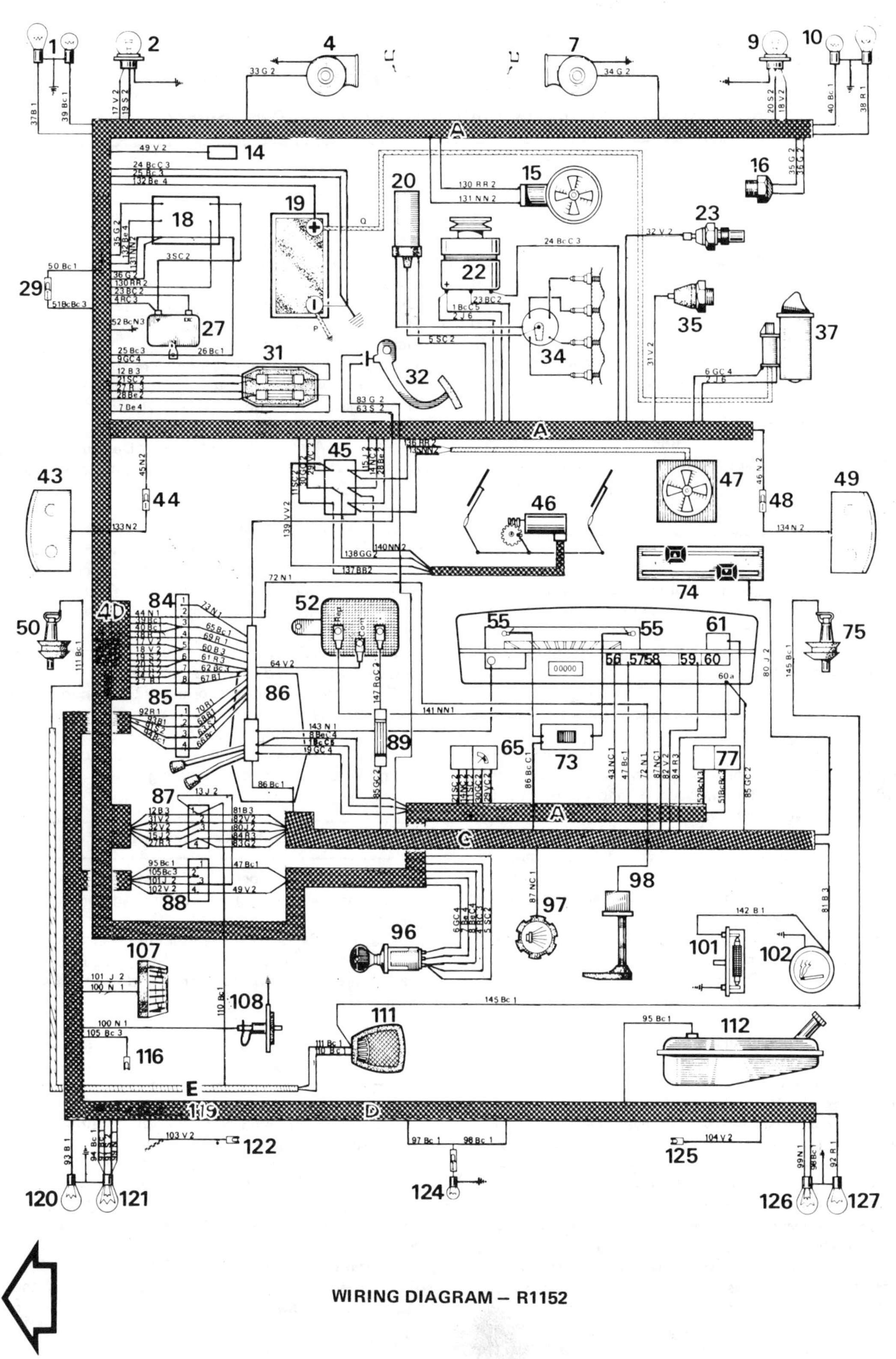

WIRING DIAGRAM – R1152

Chapter 13 Bodywork and underframe

For modifications, and information applicable to later models, see Supplement at end of manual

Contents

1 General Description

1 The body and underframe is an all steel, welded fabrication of unitary construction. Detachable components are a feature; front wings and door lower panels are renewable as separate components which should provide a measure of economy in the event of body repairs being required.

2 Maintenance - Bodywork and Underframe

1 The condition of your car's bodywork is of considerable importance as it is on this that the second-hand value of the car will mainly depend. It is very much more difficult to repair neglected bodywork than to renew mechanical assemblies. The hidden portions of the body, such as the wheel arches and the underframe and the engine compartment are equally important, though obviously not requiring such frequent attention as the immediately visible paintwork.
2 Once a year or every 9000 miles (15 000 km), it is a sound scheme to visit your local main agent and have the underside of the body steam cleaned. This will take about 1½ hours. All traces of dirt and oil will be removed and the underside can then be inspected carefully for rust, damaged hydraulic pipes, frayed electrical wiring and similar maladies. The car should be greased on completion of this job.
3 At the same time the engine compartment should be cleaned in the same manner. If steam cleaning facilities are not available then brush 'Gunk' or a similar cleanser over the whole engine and engine compartment with a stiff paint brush, working it well in where there is an accumulation of oil and dirt. Do not paint the ignition system but protect it with oily rags when the Gunk is washed off. As the Gunk is washed away it will take with it all traces of oil and dirt, leaving the engine looking clean and bright.
4 The wheel arches should be given particular attention as undersealing can easily come away here and stones and dirt thrown up from the road wheels can soon cause the paint to chip and flake, and so allow rust to set in. If rust is found clean down the bare metal with wet and dry paper, paint on an anti-corrosive coating such as Kurust, or if preferred, red lead, and renew the paintwork and undercoating.
5 The bodywork should be washed once a week or when dirty. Thoroughly wet the car to soften the dirt and then wash the car down with a soft sponge and plently of clean water. If the surplus dirt is not washed off very gently, in time it will wear the paint down as surely as wet and dry paper. It is best to use a hose if this is available. Give the car a final washdown and then dry with a soft chamois leather to prevent the formation of spots.
6 Spots of tar and grease thrown up from the road can be removed with a rag dampened with petrol.
7 Once every six months, or every three months if wished, give the bodywork and chromium trim a thoroughly good wax polish. If a chromium cleaner is used to remove rust on any of the cars plated parts remember that the cleaner also removes part of the chromium so use sparingly.

3 Maintenance - Upholstery and Carpets

1 Remove the carpets and thoroughly vacuum clean the interior of the car every three months or more frequently if necessary.
2 Beat out the carpets and vacuum clean them if they are very dirty. If the headlining or upholstery is soiled apply an upholstery cleaner with a damp sponge and wipe off with a clean dry cloth.

4 Minor Body Repairs

1 At some time during your ownership of your car it is likely that it will be bumped or scraped in a mild way, causing some slight damage to the body.
2 Major damage must be repaired by your local Renault agent, but there is no reason why you cannot successfully beat out, repair, and respray minor damage yourself. The essential items which the owner should gather together to ensure a really professional job are:-
a) A plastic filler such as Holts 'Cataloy'.
b) Paint whose colour matches exactly that of the bodywork either in a can for application by a spray gun, or in an aerosol can.
c) Fine cutting paste.
d) Medium and fine grade wet and dry paper.
3 Never use a metal hammer to knock out small dents as the blows tend to scratch and distort the metal. Knock out the dent

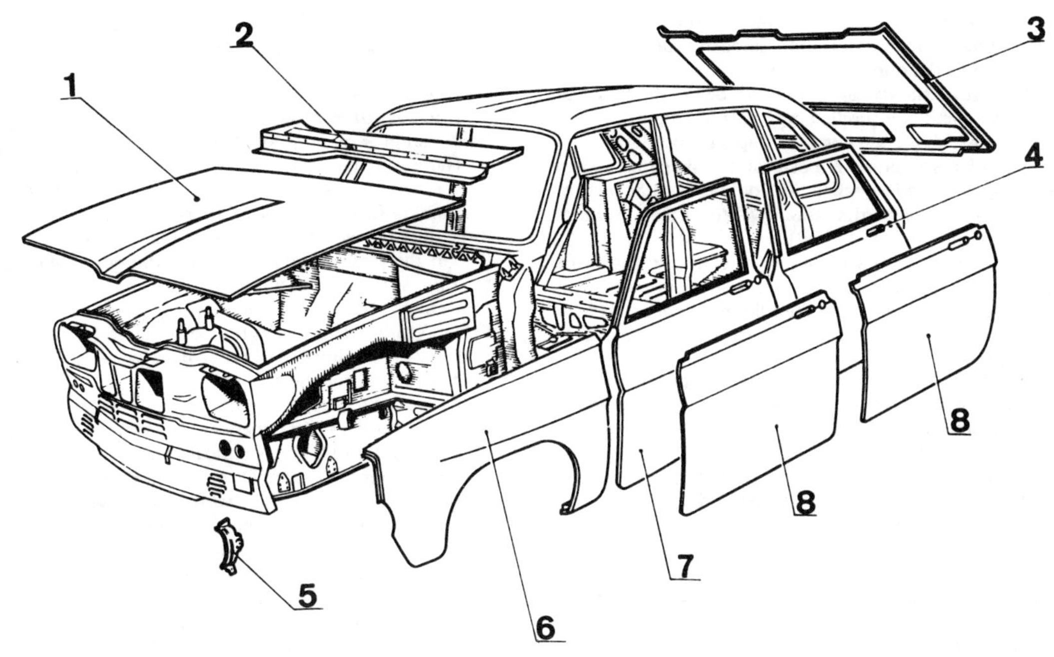

FIG.13.1 THE DETACHABLE COMPONENTS OF THE BODY

1 Bonnet (hood)
2 Scuttle grille
3 Tailgate
4 Rear door
5 Wing flange
6 Front wing
7 Front door
8 Door panels

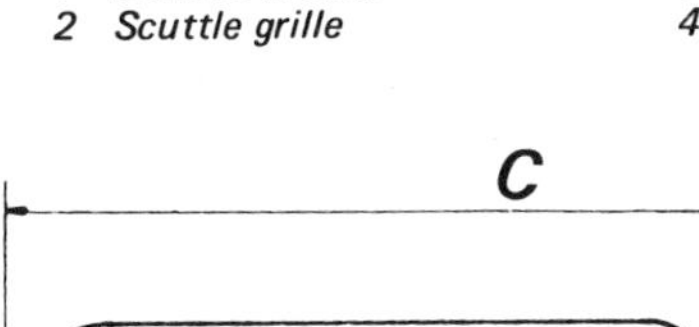

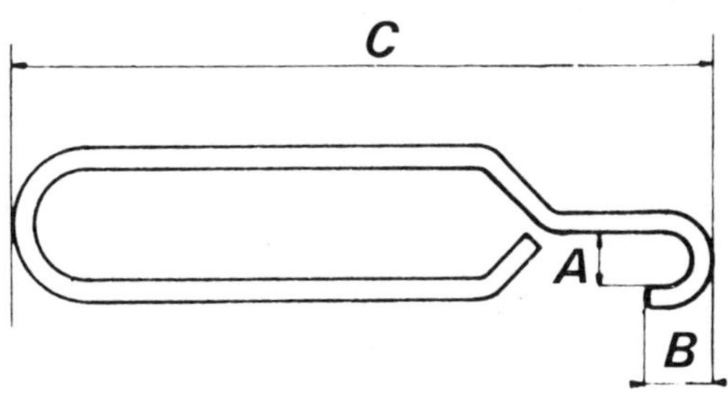

7.1 Diagram of hook required to release window winder handle.
A 10mm (3/8in) B 15mm (5/8in) C 150mm (5 7/8in)

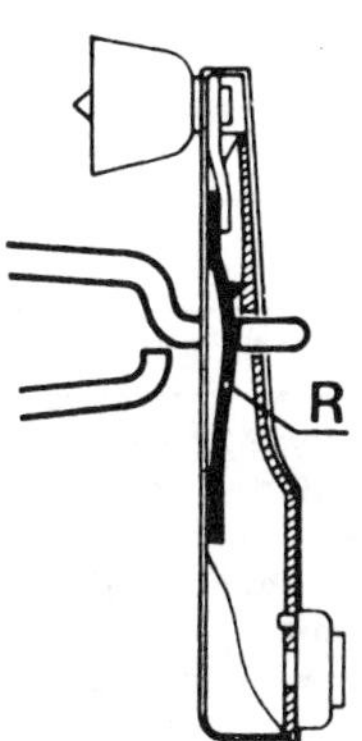

7.2A Using a hook to depress the winder handle securing spring (R)

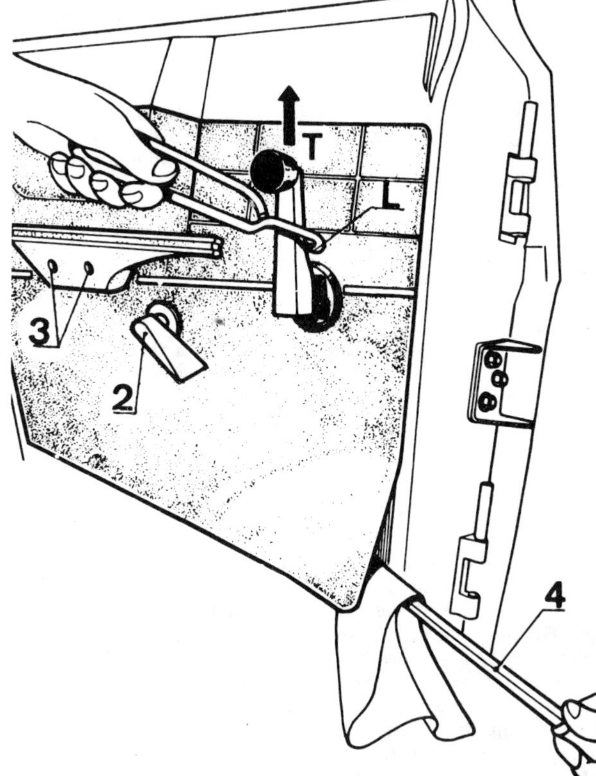

7.2B Removing the interior trim from a front door. 2 interior door handle. 3 arm rest securing screws. 4 screwdriver for trim removal. L winder spring clip access hole. T direction of removal of winder handle trim

with a mallet or rawhide hammer and press on the underside of the dented surface a metal dolly or smooth wooden block roughly contoured to the normal shape of the damaged area.
4 After the worst of the damaged area has been knocked out, rub down the dent and surrounding area with medium wet and dry paper and thoroughly clean away all traces of dirt.
5 The plastic filler comprises a paste and a hardener which must be thoroughly mixed together. Mix only a small portion at a time as the paste sets hard within five to fifteen minutes depending on the amount of hardener used.
6 Smooth on the filler with a knife or stiff plastic to the shape of the damaged portion and allow to thoroughly dry - a process which takes about six hours. After the filler has dried it is likely that it will have contracted slightly so spread on a second layer of filler if necessarv.
7 Smooth down the filler with fine wet and dry paper wrapped round a suitable block of wood and continue until the whole area is perfectly smooth and it is impossible to feel where the filler joins the rest of the paintwork.
8 Spray on from an aerosol can, or with a spray gun, an anti-rust undercoat, smooth down with wet and dry paper, and then spray on two coats of the final finishing using a circular motion.
9 When thoroughly dry polish the whole area with a fine cutting paste to smooth the resprayed area into the remainder of the wing and to remove the small particles of spray paint which will have settled round the area.
10 This will leave the wing looking perfect with not a trace of the previous unsightly dent.

5 Major Body Repairs

1 Because the body is built on the monocoque principle and is integral with the underframe, major damage must be repaired by competent mechanics with the necessary welding and hydraulic straightening equipment.
2 If the damage has been serious it is vital that the body is checked for correct alignment, as otherwise the handling of the car will suffer and many other faults such as excessive tyre wear and wear in the transmission and steering may occur. Renault produce a special alignment jig and to ensure that all is correct a repaired car should always be checked on this jig.

6 Maintenance - Hinges and Locks

Once every six months or 9000 miles (15 000 km), the door, bonnet and boot hinges should be oiled with a few drops of engine oil from an oil can. The door striker plates can be given a thin smear of grease to reduce wear and ensure free movement.

7 Front Door - Removal and Refitting

1 Remove the window winder handle. To do this, make up a hook based upon the diagram. (Fig).
2 Engage the hook at the rear of the handle and depress the spring (R), push downwards slightly and then pull upwards in the direction (T) to remove the trim piece. (Fig).
3 Remove the arm rest (two screws) and the interior door handle (one screw below plate or a roll pin).
4 Remove the door interior trim panel by prising it from its retaining clips, using a screwdriver.
5 Unstick the moisture proof sealing panel.
6 Using a cranked rod with right-angled ends of different lengths (so that the hinge pins may be removed progressively) press out the pins and remove the door.
7 Refitting the door is a reversal of removal.

8 Front Door Window Winders and Glass - Removal and Refitting

1 Removal of electrically operated window winder gear is fully described in Section 25 of Chapter 12.
2 Removal of manually operated winder mechanism is carried out be first removing the door trim as described in the preceding Section, raising the glass to its fullest extent and removing the three nuts (5) which secure the winder handle plate. (Fig).
3 Tip the plate downwards inside the door cavity to disengage the rollers from the channel (7).
4 Remove the winder mechanism, lower the glass, turn it so that the forward edge is at the bottom and lift it out.
5 Remove the inner and outer glass wiper strips and withdraw the two sliding channels.
6 Where new glass is being fitted, press the bottom rubber moulding and metal channel onto the glass so that the dimensions A and B are as indicated in the figure.
7 Fit the window channel in the window frame, starting at an upper corner. Fit the wiper strips, using new clips.
8 Position the glass so that its pointed corner is facing downwards and locate it in the door frame window channel. Turn the glass so that as the winder mechanism is offered into position, the rollers engage in the window bottom channels.
9 Fit the winder plate nuts (loosely) and test the operation of the window winder two or three times, tighten the nuts. Refit the door interior trim.

9 Front Door Locks - Removal and Refitting

1 Remove the interior handles and door trim as described in Section 7.
2 Remove the rod which is connected to the interior door handle and the clip from the door frame. Unscrew the three lock retaining screws from the edge of the door frame, remove the remote control mechanism and the plate.
3 Remove the lock by following the sequence shown in the figure.
4 Refitting commences by fitting the inner plate and passing it round behind the window channel to enable lever (L) to rest on the lug (M). (Fig).
5 Fit the lock and the plate together.
6 Fit the remote control to the inside door handle lever (18) and in turn to the plate which is secured by two screws (9). (Fig).
7 Fit the clip (G) and after checking the lock operation, tighten the screws (9). (Fig).
8 On certain vehicles the front door locks can be actuated by the interior lever. To remove this type of lock, detach the housing (1). (Fig).
9 Press in the push botton (3) so to free the peg (4) and permit the latch to be tipped and removed. Remove the plate by passing it round behind the window channel.

10 Rear Door - Removal and Refitting

1 Support the door by placing a jack or blocks under its bottom edge. Mark round the hinge outlines to ease replacement.
2 Unscrew and remove the hinge screws from the door pillar.
3 Using an angled rod, similar to the one illustrated, press the hinge pin from its location.
4 Disconnect the door restraining pin from its clip and remove the door from the car.
5 Refitting is a reversal of removal. Position the upper hinge in its original marked location and close the door carefully. If necessary make minor adjustments to the hinge positions and door lock striker plate.

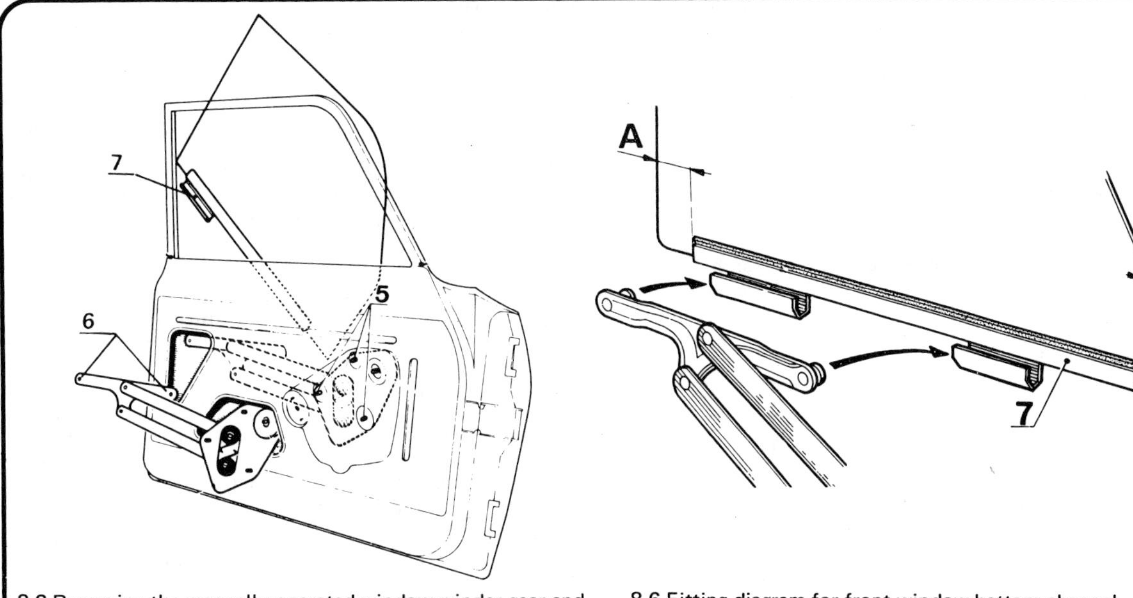

8.2 Removing the manually operated window winder gear and glass from a front door. 5 winder mechanism mounting plate screws. 6 rollers. 7 bottom channel

8.6 Fitting diagram for front window bottom channel. A 4 11/32 in (110 mm). B 1 11/32 in (34 mm). 7 bottom channel

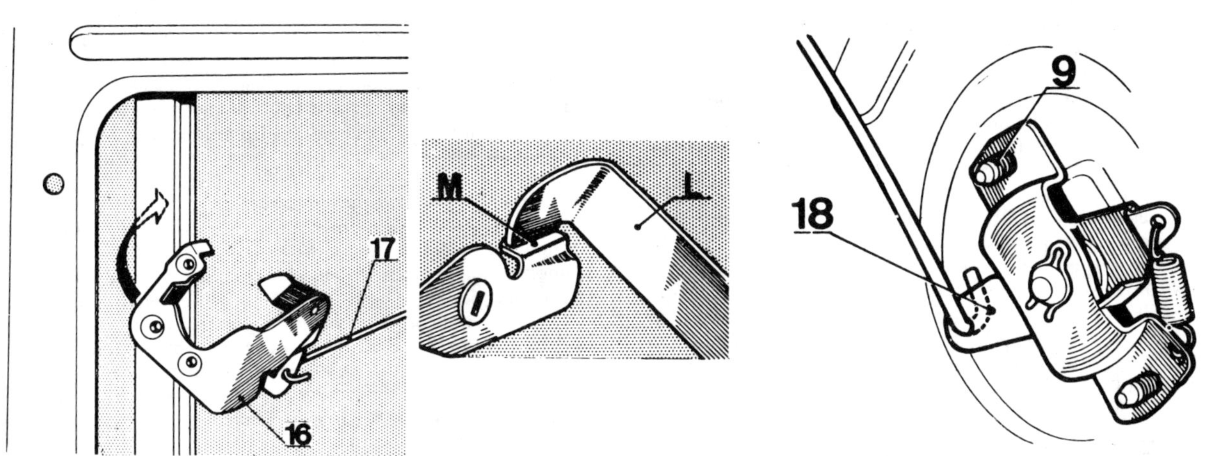

9.4 Method of refitting a front door lock. L lever. M lug. 16 inner plate. 17 connecting rod

9.6 Door interior remote control lever assembly. 9 securing screws. 18 lever

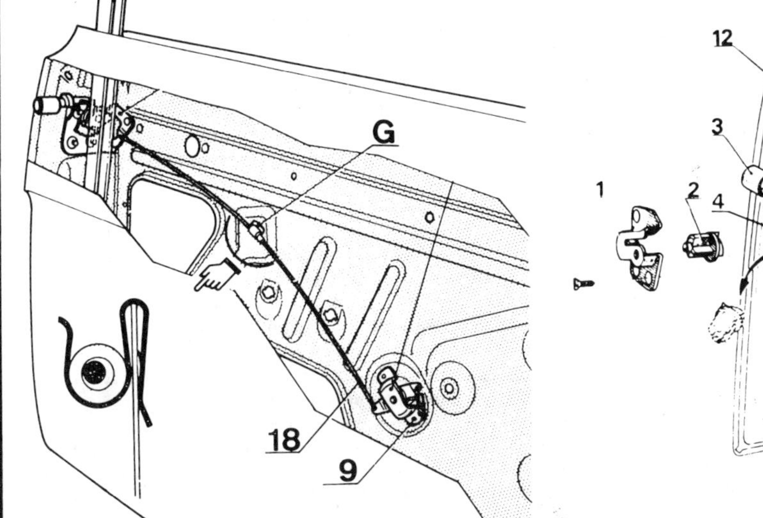

9.7 Components of the front door remote control mechanism. 9 securing screws. 18 connecting rod. G locating clip

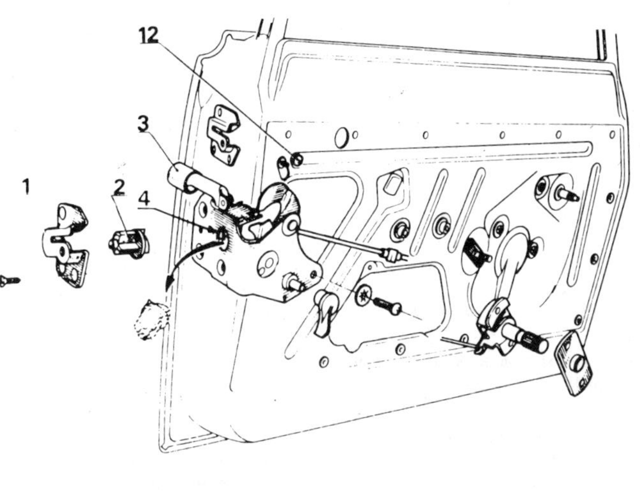

9.8 Exploded view of front door lock with interior control. 1 housing. 2 latch. 3 push button. 4 peg. 12 plate securing hole

11 Rear Door Window Winder and Glass - Removal and Refitting

1 Refer to Section 7 of this Chapter and remove the arm rest, the interior door handle, the ash tray, the window winder handle, the trim panel and sealing panel.
2 Wind the window to its fully closed position and unhook the winder return spring.
3 Wind the window to its fully open position, remove the clips and free the winder mechanism from the bottom of the window.
4 Unscrew and remove the three securing screws from the winder mechanism and withdraw it through the lower aperture in the door frame.
5 Remove the two screws which hold the rear channel, also the screw on the door frame.
6 Free the surround rubber channel by drawing it upwards complete with the polished aluminium frame.
7 Pull the glass upwards and tilt it to remove.
8 Commence refitting by pressing the rubber (2) and metal (1) channels onto the lower edge of the glass, ensuring that the attachment bracket hole centre is positioned as indicated. (Fig).
9 Fit the rubber surround (3) into the top and side of the door frame (A). (Fig).
10 Fit the wiper strip (C) by means of clips.
11 Locate the glass by inserting it into the door cavity with its front edge pointing downward and then turning it.
12 Fit the rubber surround (4) into the rear channel (5). (Fig).
13 Pinch the glass wiper strips and fit the upright channel in the door frame, secure its bottom end (6) but do not tighten it.
14 Fit the aluminium moulding and the rear channel and moulding but do not tighten them.
15 Through the door frame aperture fit the winder mechanism (8) followed by the foam pad (9) and anti-rattle rubber sleeve in the spring (10). (Fig).
16 Remove the pin (11) loosen the two securing screws (12). Leave the nuts in position without tightening them. Fit the winder arm pin in the hole in the window bottom channel lug and secure it with clip (13). Lubricate the winder mechanism and operate it several times to check its action. The dimensions A and A should be equal, adjust the channels as required to achieve this and then tighten the screws (6) (14) and (12). Refit handles and trim.

12 Rear Door Locks - Removal and Refitting

1 On vehicles manufactured prior to 1969, the door locks are removed and refitted in a manner similar to that described for front door locks in Section 9.
2 The lock operates when lever (34) is pressed inwards to cause lever (35) to move and actuate link (36). (Fig).
3 The action of the link prevents the lock (37) from moving downwards when the exterior push-button is depressed.
4 A child proof lock is also fitted to this type of vehicle which prevents the interior door lock control operating due to the movement of lug (38) locking the link (39). (Fig).
5 On vehicles manufactured after 1969, the remote door lock control is of plunger type. (Fig).
6 The plunger (1) is removed simply by unscrewing the knob.
7 To remove the lock mechanism, wind the window fully up and remove the securing screws (12) and the nut (3) with the push button fully depressed. Free the clips (4) and (5) and remove the three screws (6).
8 Remove the lock plate by sliding it downwards between the door frame and the window channel.
9 Refitting commences by fitting the lock plate inside the door frame edge ensuring that both the remote controls and the relay (7) are attached between the door frame and the channel.
10 Fit the lock (8) in position and offer up the plate having the lever (9) upwards so that it is above the lug (10).
11 Secure the lock/plate assembly and check for correct operation.
12 Fit the inner door handle assembly (2) connecting it to the operating rod. Fit the relay (7) and clips (4) and (5).
13 Where components of the door lock mechanism are broken or worn, renew them, it is seldom satisfactory to attempt to repair them.
14 Where an external cylinder type lock is also fitted to the rear doors, then it may be removed in a similar way to that described in Section 9 for front doors except that the plunger rod (1) and ashtray must be removed. (Fig).

13 Bonnet and Lock - Removal and Refitting

1 The bonnet (hood) may be removed in one of two ways. The hinge arm securing screws (1) may be removed or the hinge pin circlip (2) removed. The latter can only be withdrawn after removal of the scuttle grille, see Section 26 Chapter 12. (Fig).
2 The bonnet lock may be renewed by removing the front panel attachments (1) punching out the roll pin (2) and removing the barrel. (Fig).

3 Refitting a new lock is a reversal of removal and engagement of the locking sprag is assured by adjustment of the elongated hole (3).

14 Front Wing - Removal and Refitting

1 Each front wing is attached by ten self-tapping screws and one screw with 'captive' nut.
2 Remove the beading (1) the flasher repeater (2) the front panel and embellisher (3) the two bumper blade securing screws (4) and (5) and the two screws (6) from under the wing. (Fig).
3 Remove the screw (7) from inside the engine compartment the four screws (8) and the three screws (9) accessible from under the wing and finally the screw (10).
4 Refitting is a reversal of removal but place a strip of sealing compound at (c) before locating the wing. When refitting is complete, apply underseal to the undersurface and ensure that the joints and screw heads are adequately covered against water penetration and corrosion.
5 On vehicles fitted with electrically operated window winder mechanism, a slot must be cut with metal shears and the metal bent away to permit the winder cable to be extracted. (Fig).
6 When refitting the wing, drill a hole 53/64 in (21 mm) in the position illustrated.
7 Cut a slot to the hole and bend the metal away to allow the cable to pass. When refitting is complete, seal the cable entry hole and fill the slot with suitable sealing compound.

15 Tailgate and Lock - Removal and Refitting

1 Components of the tailgate are shown in the figure.
2 Removal is carried out by unscrewing the screws which attach the counterbalance arms to the frame (3). (Fig).
3 Remove the hinge arm securing screws (4) from the tailgate. (Fig).
4 Refitting is a reversal of removal.
5 The tailgate lock is removed by taking out the two screws (1) from inside the tailgate frame. (Fig).
6 Push out the roll pin (2) and lift out the lock barrel.
7 Refitting is a reversal of removal and any final adjustment may be made by means of the elongated holes (3).

16 Bumpers - Removal and Refitting

1 The front bumpers are removed by unscrewing the two screws (8) removing the tie bar nuts (9), the overrider reinforcement retaining nuts and the bumper iron screws (11). (Fig).
2 Removal of the rear bumper assembly is achieved by removing from inside the luggage boot, the distance piece screws (2) the securing nuts (8) and the overrider reinforcement screws (9). (Fig).

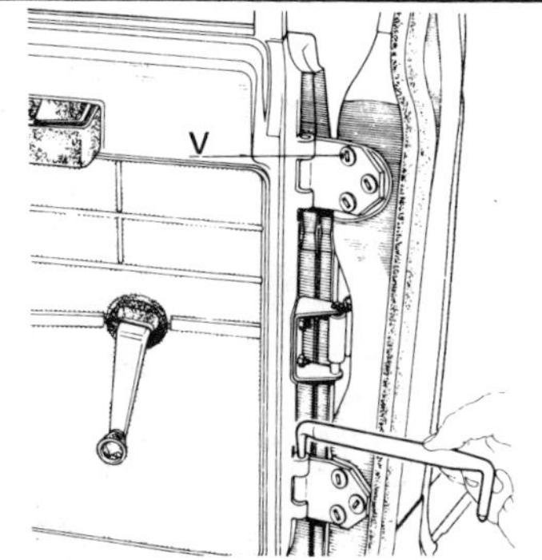

10.3. Pressing out a rear door hinge pin. V hinge retaining screws

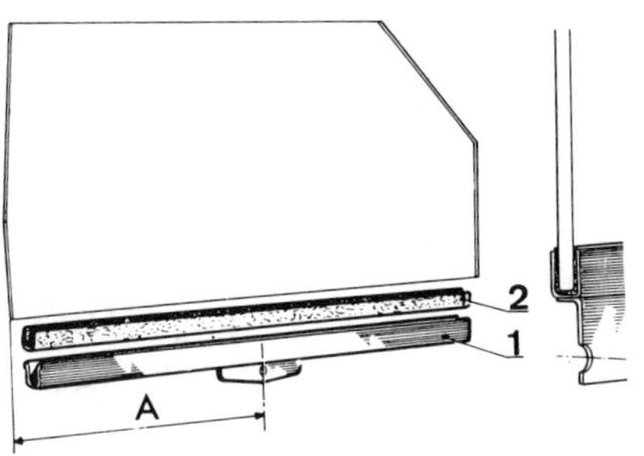

11.8 Rear door window glass components 1 metal channel. 2 rubber channeling. A 8.3 in (317 mm)

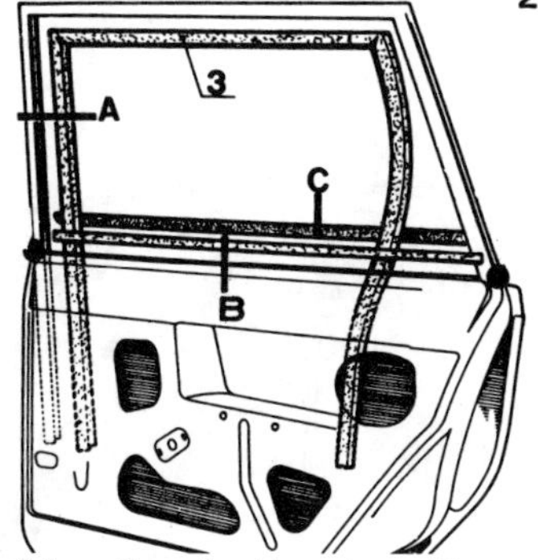

11.9 Location of rubber channel in rear door frame. 3 rubber surround. B and C wiper strips

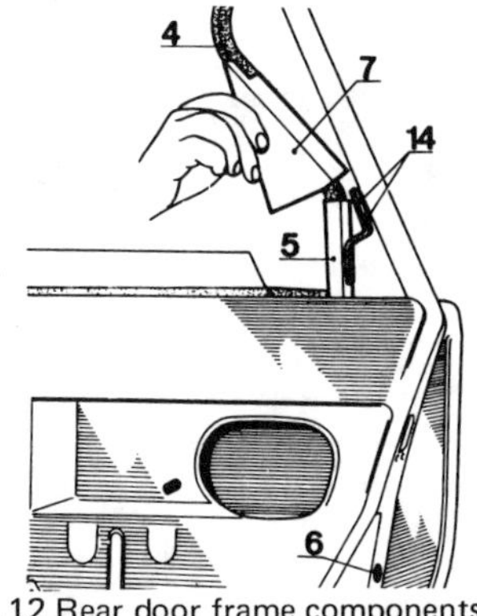

11.12 Rear door frame components. 4 rubber channel. 5 metal channel. 6 channel securing screw. 7 aluminium moulding. 14 bracket

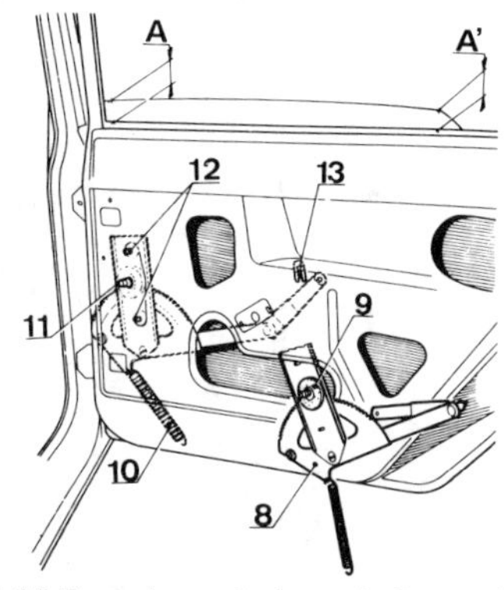

11.15 Rear door window winder mechanism (manually operated). 8 winder mechanism. 9 foam pad. 10 rubber sleeve and spring. 11 pin. 12 securing screws. 13 safety clip. A/A1 equal measurements

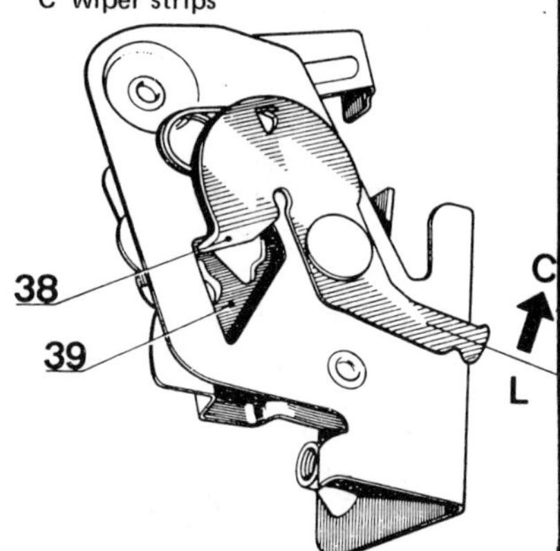

12.4 Detail of rear door childproof lock (pre 1969). 38 lug. 39 link. C locked. L unlocked

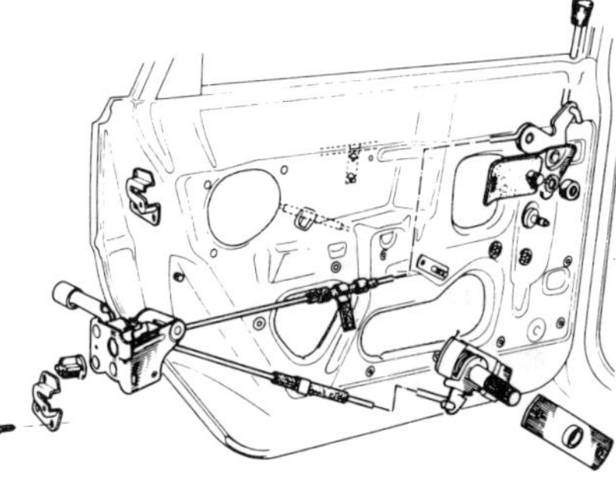

12.14 Components of cylinder type lock fitted to a rear door

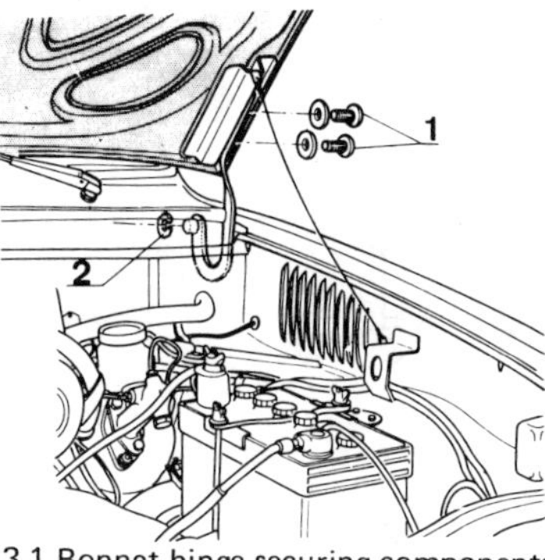

13.1 Bonnet hinge securing components

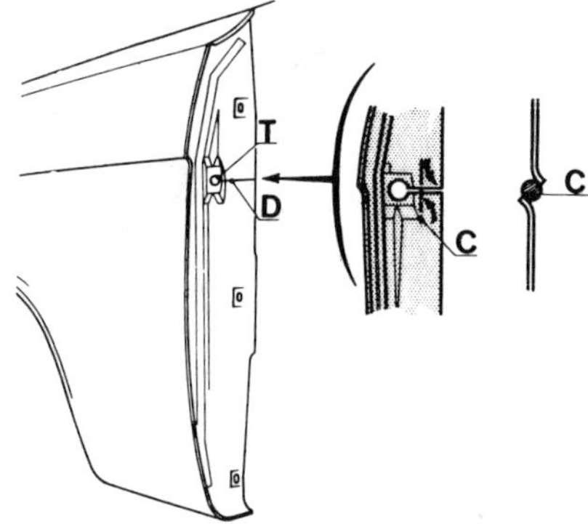

14.5. Cutting diagram to permit cable extraction when removing front wing from vehicle fitted with electric window winder. C cable. D slot. T hole for cable.

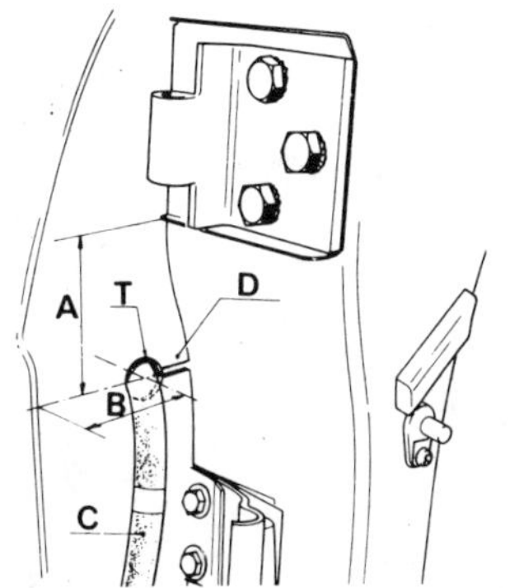

14.6 Cutting diagram to permit cable entry when fitting new front wing to vehicle fitted with electric window winders. A 2 9/16 in (65 mm). B 2 3/16 in (55 mm). C cable D slot. T hole

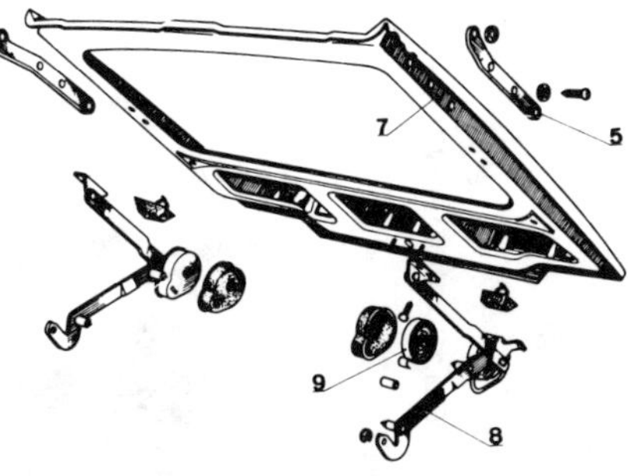

15.1 Components of the tailgate. 5 side arms. 7 tailgate frame. 8 counter balance arms. 9 compensating springs

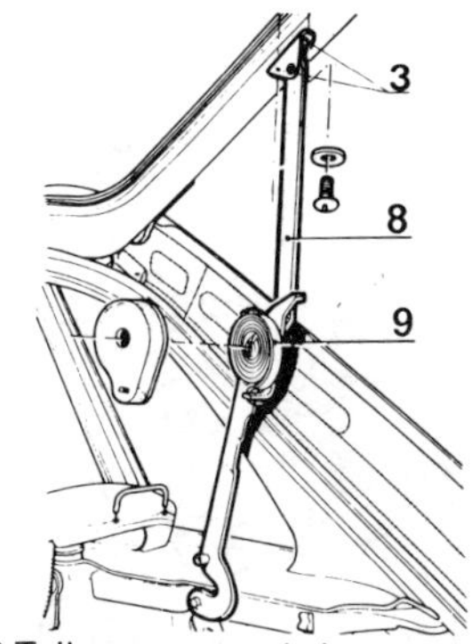

15.2 Tailgate counter balance arm. 3 securing screws. 8 counter balance arm. 9 compensating spring

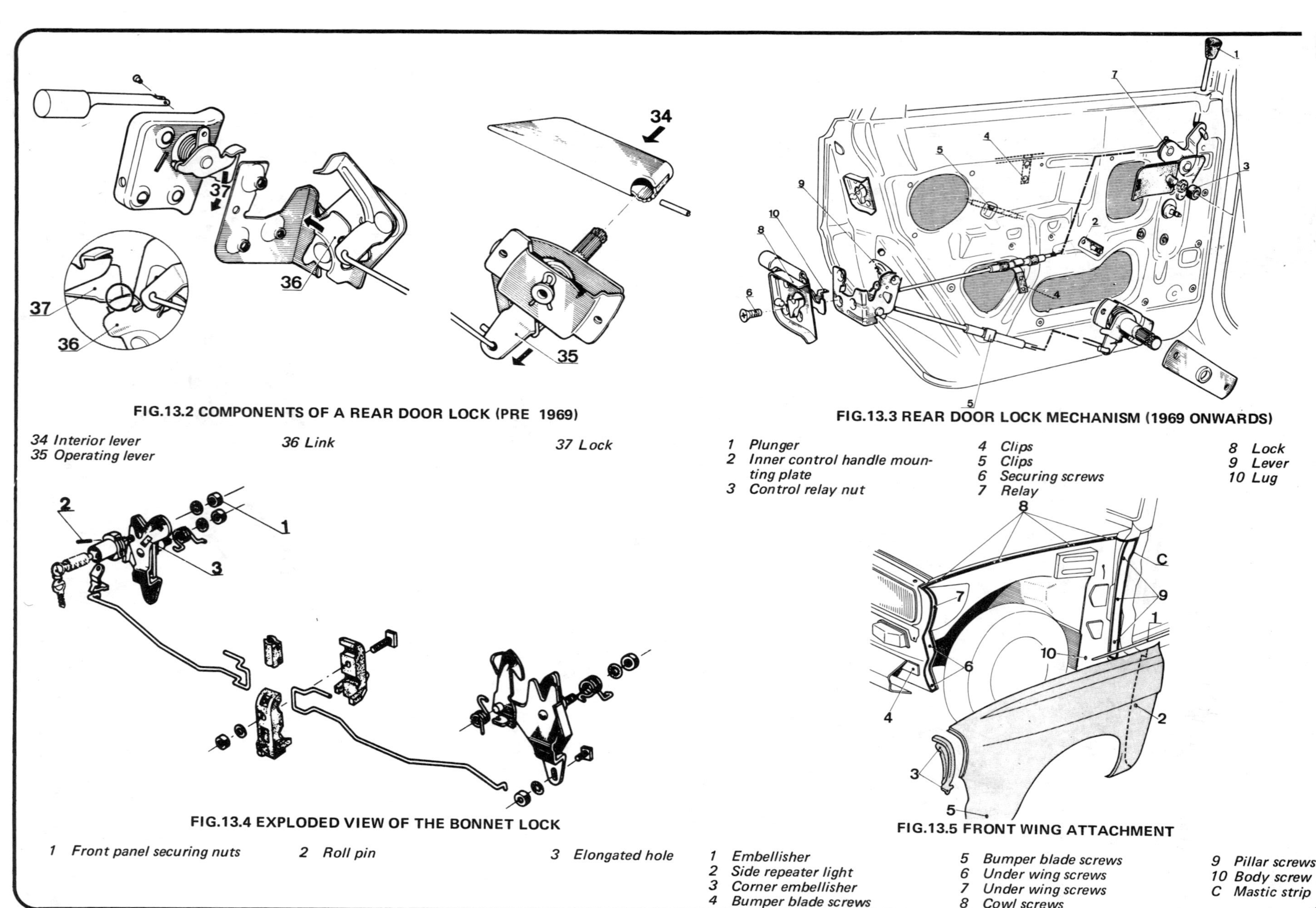

FIG.13.2 COMPONENTS OF A REAR DOOR LOCK (PRE 1969)

34 Interior lever
35 Operating lever
36 Link
37 Lock

FIG.13.3 REAR DOOR LOCK MECHANISM (1969 ONWARDS)

1 Plunger
2 Inner control handle mounting plate
3 Control relay nut
4 Clips
5 Clips
6 Securing screws
7 Relay
8 Lock
9 Lever
10 Lug

FIG.13.4 EXPLODED VIEW OF THE BONNET LOCK

1 Front panel securing nuts
2 Roll pin
3 Elongated hole

FIG.13.5 FRONT WING ATTACHMENT

1 Embellisher
2 Side repeater light
3 Corner embellisher
4 Bumper blade screws
5 Bumper blade screws
6 Under wing screws
7 Under wing screws
8 Cowl screws
9 Pillar screws
10 Body screw
C Mastic strip

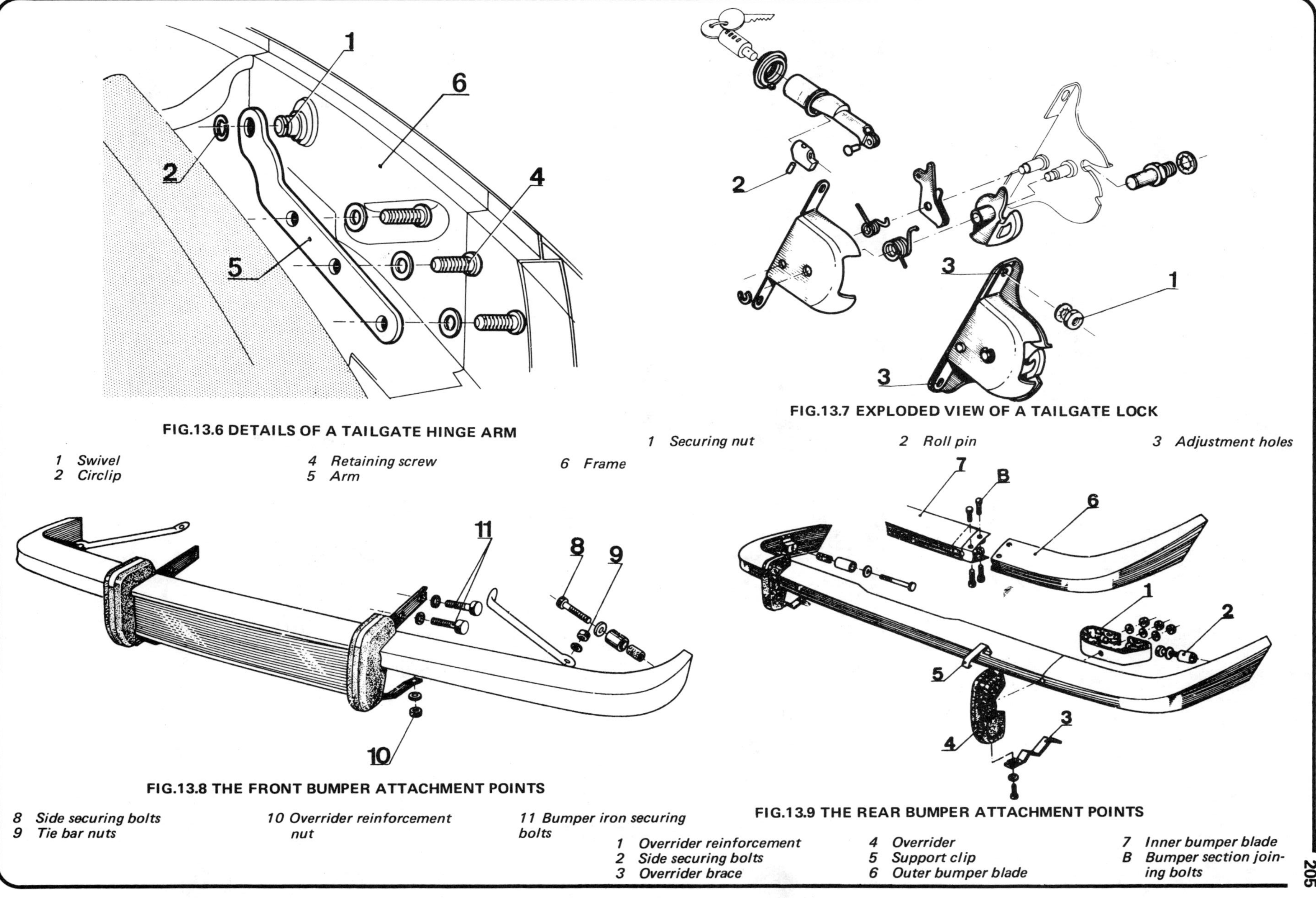

FIG.13.6 DETAILS OF A TAILGATE HINGE ARM

1 Swivel
2 Circlip
4 Retaining screw
5 Arm
6 Frame

FIG.13.7 EXPLODED VIEW OF A TAILGATE LOCK

1 Securing nut
2 Roll pin
3 Adjustment holes

FIG.13.8 THE FRONT BUMPER ATTACHMENT POINTS

8 Side securing bolts
9 Tie bar nuts
10 Overrider reinforcement nut
11 Bumper iron securing bolts

FIG.13.9 THE REAR BUMPER ATTACHMENT POINTS

1 Overrider reinforcement
2 Side securing bolts
3 Overrider brace
4 Overrider
5 Support clip
6 Outer bumper blade
7 Inner bumper blade
B Bumper section joining bolts

This sequence of photographs deals with the repair of the dent and paintwork damage shown in this photo. The procedure will be similar for the repair of a hole. It should be noted that the procedures given here are simplified – more explicit instructions will be found in the text

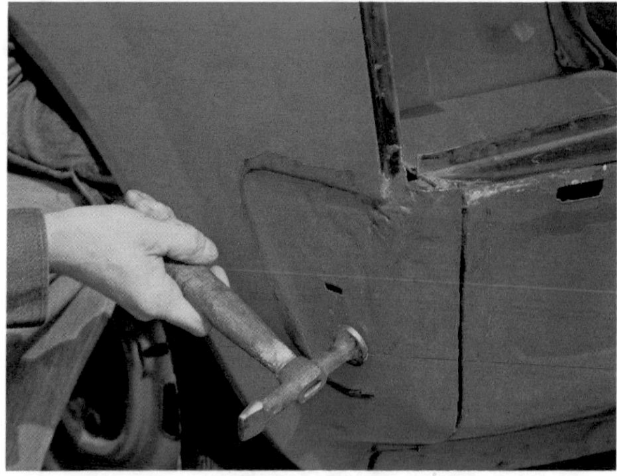

In the case of a dent the first job – after removing surrounding trim – is to hammer out the dent where access is possible. This will minimise filling. Here, the large dent having been hammered out, the damaged area is being made slightly concave

Now all paint must be removed from the damaged area, by rubbing with coarse abrasive paper. Alternatively, a wire brush or abrasive pad can be used in a power drill. Where the repair area meets good paintwork, the edge of the paintwork should be 'feathered', using a finer grade of abrasive paper

In the case of a hole caused by rusting, all damaged sheet-metal should be cut away before proceeding to this stage. Here, the damaged area is being treated with rust remover and inhibitor before being filled

Mix the body filler according to its manufacturer's instructions. In the case of corrosion damage, it will be necessary to block off any large holes before filling – this can be done with aluminium or plastic mesh, or aluminium tape. Make sure the area is absolutely clean before ...

... applying the filler. Filler should be applied with a flexible applicator, as shown, for best results; the wooden spatula being used for confined areas. Apply thin layers of filler at 20-minute intervals, until the surface of the filler is slightly proud of the surrounding bodywork

Initial shaping can be done with a Surform plane or Dreadnought file. Then, using progressively finer grades of wet-and-dry paper, wrapped around a sanding block, and copious amounts of clean water, rub down the filler until really smooth and flat. Again, feather the edges of adjoining paintwork

The whole repair area can now be sprayed or brush-painted with primer. If spraying, ensure adjoining areas are protected from over-spray. Note that at least one inch of the surrounding sound paintwork should be coated with primer. Primer has a 'thick' consistency, so will find small imperfections

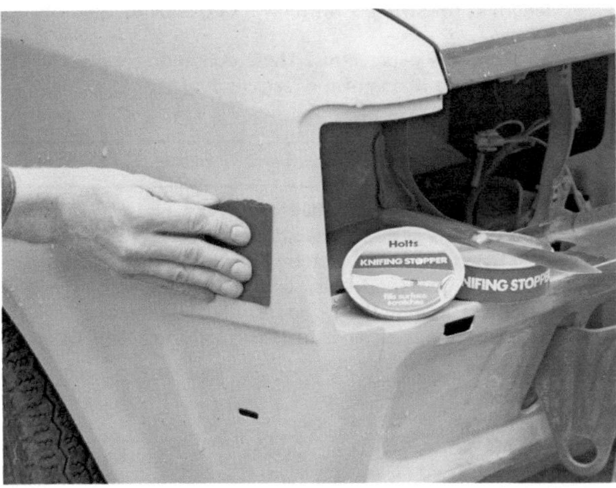

Again, using plenty of water, rub down the primer with a fine grade wet-and-dry paper (400 grade is probably best) until it is really smooth and well blended into the surrounding paintwork. Any remaining imperfections can now be filled by carefully applied knifing stopper paste

When the stopper has hardened, rub down the repair area again before applying the final coat of primer. Before rubbing down this last coat of primer, ensure the repair area is blemish-free – use more stopper if necessary. To ensure that the surface of the primer is really smooth use some finishing compound

The top coat can now be applied. When working out of doors, pick a dry, warm and wind-free day. Ensure surrounding areas are protected from over-spray. Agitate the aerosol thoroughly, then spray the centre of the repair area, working outwards with a circular motion. Apply the paint as several thin coats

After a period of about two weeks, which the paint needs to harden fully, the surface of the repaired area can be 'cut' with a mild cutting compound prior to wax polishing. When carrying out bodywork repairs, remember that the quality of the finished job is proportional to the time and effort expended

3 The inner and outer blade sections of the rear bumper are held together by spot welds. Either section may be renewed independently by chiselling the sections apart and refitting with nuts and bolts.
4 Refitting of the complete rear bumper bar assembly is a reversal of removal but adjust the bumper irons if necessary to obtain the correct bumper angle when it is fitted to the rear apron.

17 Windscreen and Rear Window - Removal and Replacement

1 Removal of either the windscreen or rear window will be required for one of two reasons; the glass shattering or deterioration of the rubber surround causing water leaks into the interior of the vehicle. Remove the wiper arms.
2 Where the glass has shattered, the easiest way to remove the screen is to stick a sheet of self-adhesive paper or plastic sheeting to each side and push it from the inside outwards. Seal the air intake grille on the scuttle and the air ducts and radio speaker slots on the facia panel to prevent glass crystals from falling into them during the removal operation. Protect the surface of the bonnet with a blanket to prevent scratching.
3 Where the glass is to be removed in order to renew the rubber surround, make up two pads of cloth and with the aid of an assistant press the two top corners of the screen from the inside outwards and at the same time pulling the rubber surround from the upper corners. Remove the rubber surround as soon as the screen is withdrawn and clean the edges of both the glass and the body screen frame.
4 Commence refitting by positioning the rubber surround round the edge of the windscreen glass. Place the assembly flat down on a bench or table.
5 Lay a length of string or thin cord (F) in the channel in the inner side of the rubber surround. (Fig).
6 The string should be about 1/8 in (3 mm) diameter and the ends should overlap at the bottom edge by 4½ in (114.3 mm) and leave a few inches to grip with the hands.
7 Place a bead of sealing mastic in the lower two corners of the screen frame.
8 Locate the lower edge of the screen surround in the body frame so that the two ends of the spring hang inside the car, then pull both ends of the string while an assistant presses the glass and surround into position as the operation progresses.
9 The string will finally emerge from the top centre of the rubber surround and the screen and rubber surround lip should be in correct engagement with the screen frame.
10 Using either a sealing mastic gun or tube, insert the nozzle between the rubber surround lip and the outer surface of the screen frame and insert a thin even bead of sealer. Press the rubber surround hard to spread the sealer and to ensure correct location. Wipeaway any excess sealer with a paraffin moistened cloth.
11 The surround embellisher is fitted by first placing a length of string in the groove (R) and using a short piece of tubing as a hand hold. (Fig).
12 Offer up and insert the inner edge of the embellisher in the slot of the rubber surround and locate it progressively alòng its length as the string is withdrawn outwards to open the lips of the slot.
13 Refit the wiper arms. These operations apply equally to the removal and fitting of the rear window.

18 Quarter Light - Removal and Refitting

1 In the event of breakage of the glass in a quarter light, remove as suggested for windscreen in the preceding Section.
2 Fitting is carried out by first locating the rubber surround onto the glass and then use the string method as previously described, pulling the string from outside the car.
3 When the quarter light is correctly installed fit a small right

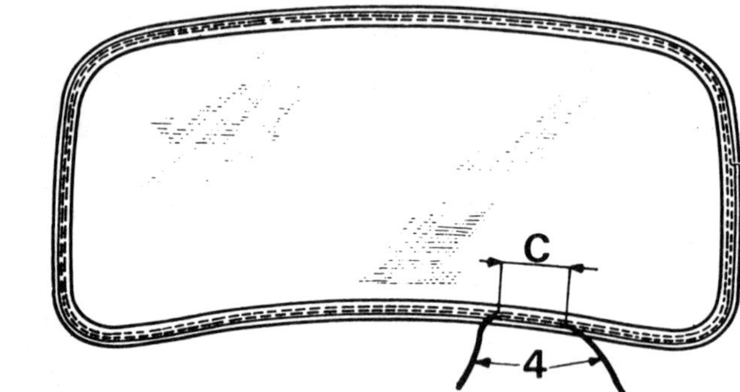

17.5 Location of windscreen surround fitting string (4). C overlap
F string or cord

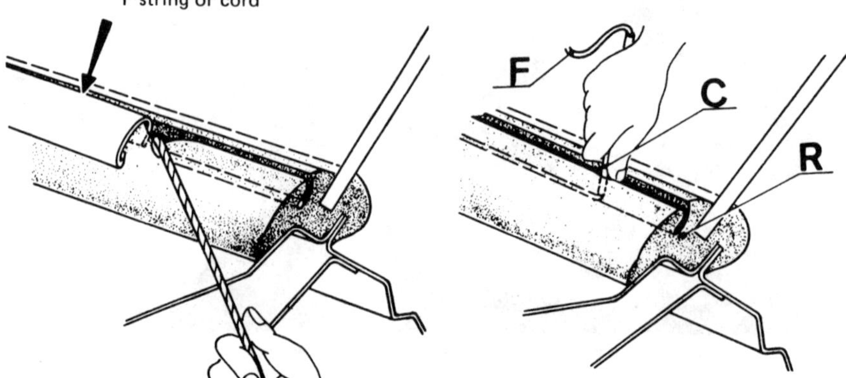

17.11 Method of fitting windscreen surround embellisher. C tube
F spring. R slot

18.3 Location of quarter light bracket (7)

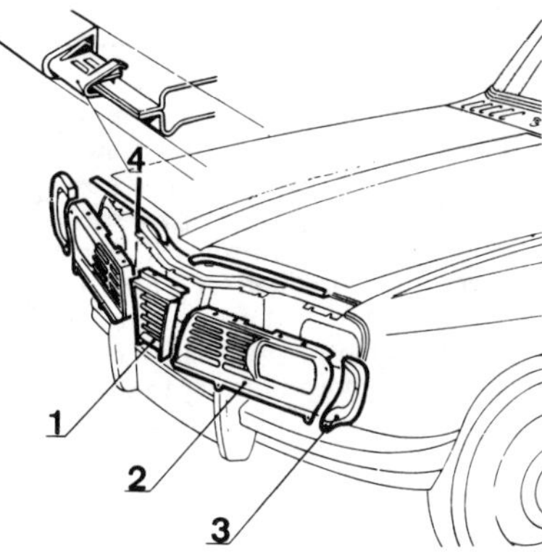

19.1 The radiator grille. 1 centre section. 2 side section. 3 end covers. 4 bending

angled bracket as shown in the figure.

4 Finally seal the rubber surround to the body with a narrow bead of sealing compound.

19 Radiator Grille - Removal and Refitting

1 The grille comprises a centre section (1) two sections with headlamp apertures (2) and two end covers (3). (Fig).

2 The assembly is secured by 16 self-tapping screws and it is also engaged with a clip at the bottom of the centre section.

3 The grille fitted to model R1152 cars manufactured for the USA market is secured by a combination of screws, clips and tabs as shown in the figure.

20 Heater - General Description

1 The car interior heater comprises a matrix (radiator) which is heated by water from the engine cooling system, a booster fan and a control valve for the regulation of the hot water flow from the engine.

2 Air is drawn from the exterior of the car and when the car is moving, the ram effect of the air will absorb the heat as it passes over the matrix and warm the car interior. The electrically operated fan will boost the air supply when the car is travelling slowly or is stationary.

3 Components of the water circuit of the heater are shown in Fig 13.13.

21 Heater Fan Motor - Removal and Refitting

1 Remove the scuttle crossmember as described in Chapter 12, Section 26.

2 From the now exposed heater motor, remove the three

FIG.13.10 RADIATOR GRILLE FITTED TO USA MODELS (R1152)

1 Retaining screws
2 Bendover tabs
3 Screws
4 Tag
5 Retaining screws
6 Retaining screws
7 Retaining screws

securing screws and disconnect the two electrical leads.
3 Withdraw the heater motor fan assembly from its location.
4 The fan may be detached from the motor by unscrewing the socket screws. The motor is secured to the support housing by three nuts and is mounted on rubber pads.
5 Refitting is a reversal of removal.

22 Heater Fan Motor - Dismantling, Servicing, Reassembly

1 Remove the two tie bolts, noting their differing lengths and their respective locations, Fig 13.11.
2 Free the brushes and remove the single bearing bracket (7) and the body (8).
3 Remove the circlip (10) and washer (11) the armature (9) the washer (13) the brush carrier and bearing plate (12).
4 Servicing the motor should be limited to renewing the brushes (by unsoldering the old ones and re-soldering the new) and cleaning the armature. In the event of wear or damage occuring outside these components, then the motor should be renewed as a complete unit.
5 Reassembly is a reversal of dismantling.

23 Heater Matrix and Control Valve - Removal and Refitting

1 Remove the scuttle crossmember as described in Chapter 12, Section 26.
2 Disconnect the heater hoses, remove the matrix securing clips and lift the matrix from its location.
3 From the heater control knob inside the car, hook off the embellisher. Remove the control handle by removing the securing screw which is now exposed.
4 Disconnect the heater hoses from the control valve
5 Pull the control valve forward so that its control rod is withdrawn, still attached, through the engine bulkhead.
6 Refitting is a reversal of removal for both the heater matrix and the control valve but the system will have to be topped up and bled as described in Chapter 2.

24 Heater Matrix and Control Valve - Servicing

1 If the heater matrix is leaking, it should be renewed as soldering is seldom satisfactory as a permanent repair.
2 Where the matrix is fully or partially blocked, try reverse flushing by attaching a cold water pressure hose and directing the flow in the reverse direction to normal. In severe cases, use a chemical cleaning or descaling agent but flush the matrix thoroughly after use.
3 The control valve should be renewed if it is tight or appears seized, no servicing can be carried out to this component.

25 Car Interior Air Circulation System - Description

1 The knob of the adjustable hot water control valve is mounted on a graduated scale. When the knob (A) is in the white sector (1 to 6) only the lower air stream is heated. (Fig).
2 When the knob is in the red sector then both the upper and lower airstreams are heated as they enter the car.
3 The progressive air flow control (B) opens the external ventilation flap during the first part of its movement. When the control reaches the centre of its travel the heater fan is switched on and the speed of the fan progressively increased by means of a rheostat as the handle is moved further to the left.
4 The lower air stream control is shown as (C) in the illustration.
5 The adjustable flap controls (D) control the direction of the upper air stream.
6 The most appropriate setting of the various controls is a matter of personal preference according to the prevailing

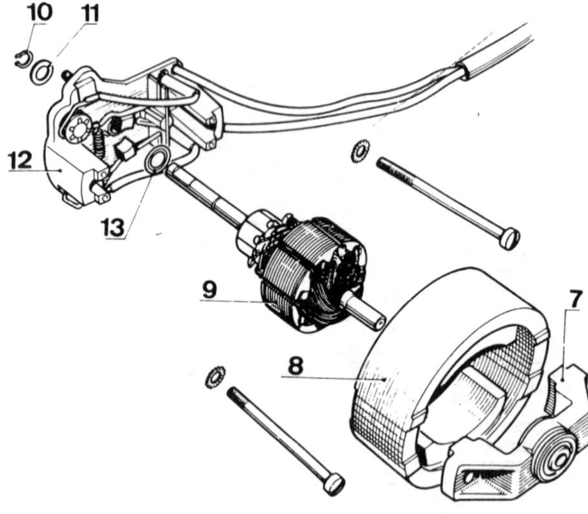

FIG.13.11 EXPLODED VIEW OF THE HEATER FAN MOTOR

7 Bearing bracket
8 Body
9 Armature
10 Circlip
11 Washer
12 Brush/bearing assembly
13 Washer

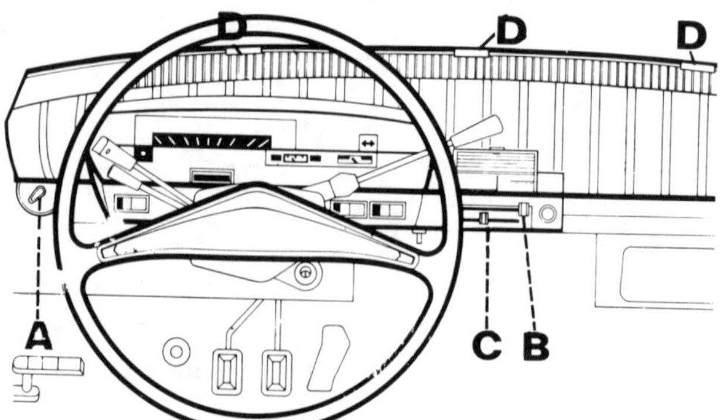

FIG.13.12 THE HEATING AND VENTILATING SYSTEM INTERIOR CONTROLS

A Water control valve knob
B Air flow control
C Lower air stream control
D Adjustable flap controls

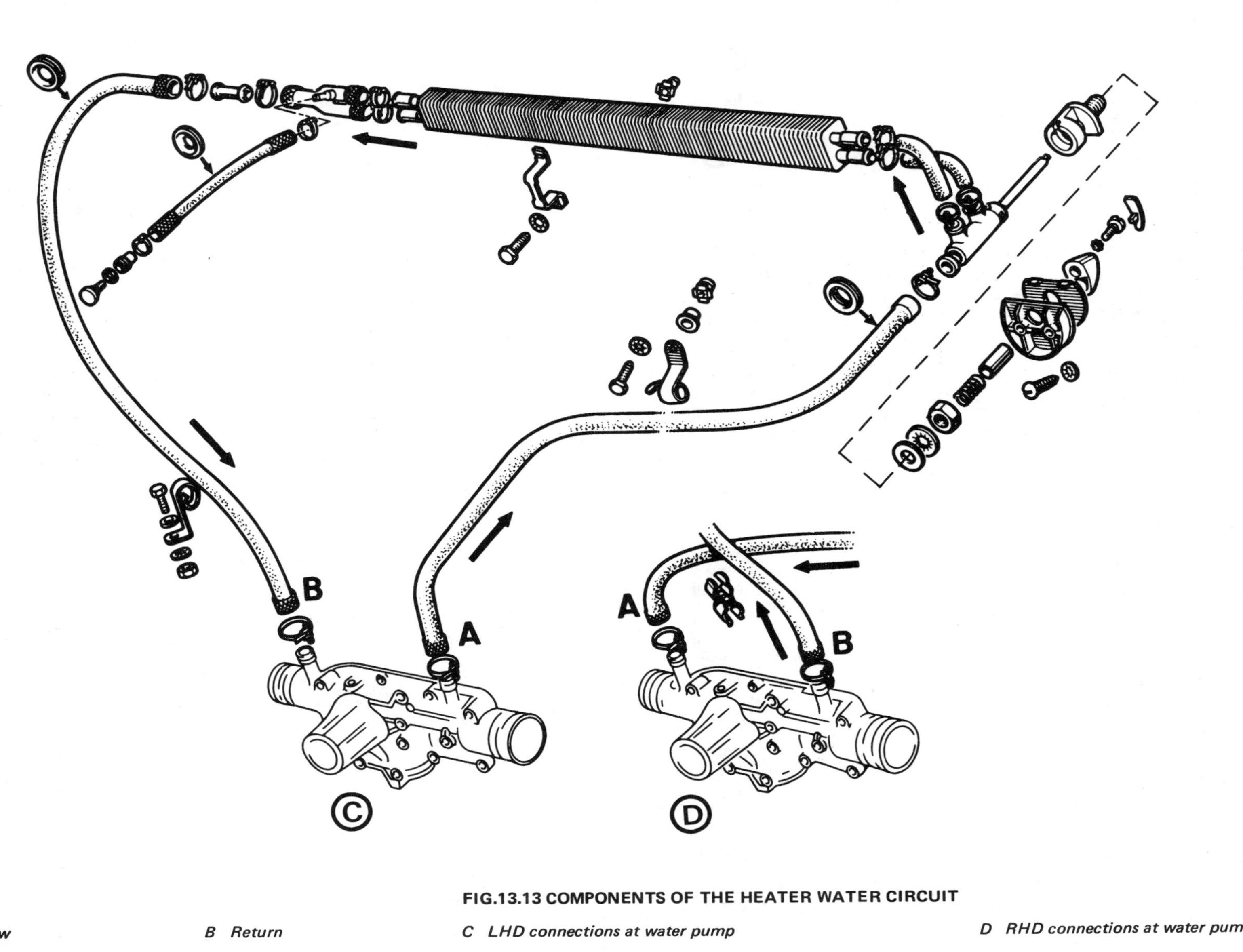

FIG.13.13 COMPONENTS OF THE HEATER WATER CIRCUIT

A Flow *B Return* *C LHD connections at water pump* *D RHD connections at water pump*

weather conditions.

7 When the outside temperature is very low the water control valve may be stiff to operate until the engine coolant warms up. This is a normal condition.

8 Metal channels are fitted under the carpets in vehicles designed to operate in cold climates, to provide a warm air flow to the rear passenger compartment. These are illustrated in the figure.

26 Air Circulation System - Dismantling and Reassembly

1 The control lever assembly is removed by detaching the cover plate and unscrewing the three panel screws. (Fig).

2 Unscrew the cable sleeve clip and remove the circlip and disconnect the electrical lead. (Fig).

3 Disconnect the air circulation flap control.

4 The two control levers are fitted one each side of the support plate to a common shaft (13) and held in position by a clip (14). (Fig).

5 Remove the clip and the shaft (15) on the flap and rheostat side, free the levers and retain the washers.

6 The rheostat is riveted to the support plate and they must be drilled out to renew the unit.

7 The air circulation flap is accessible after removal of the following components, the instrument panel cowl (Chapter 12, Section 18) the heater control panel, the instrument panel (Chapter 12, Section 19) and the left and right hand glove compartments.

8 The flap may now be removed by unscrewing the four securing screws (1) and the bridge pieces (2). (Fig).

9 Refitting is a reversal of removal and dismantling.

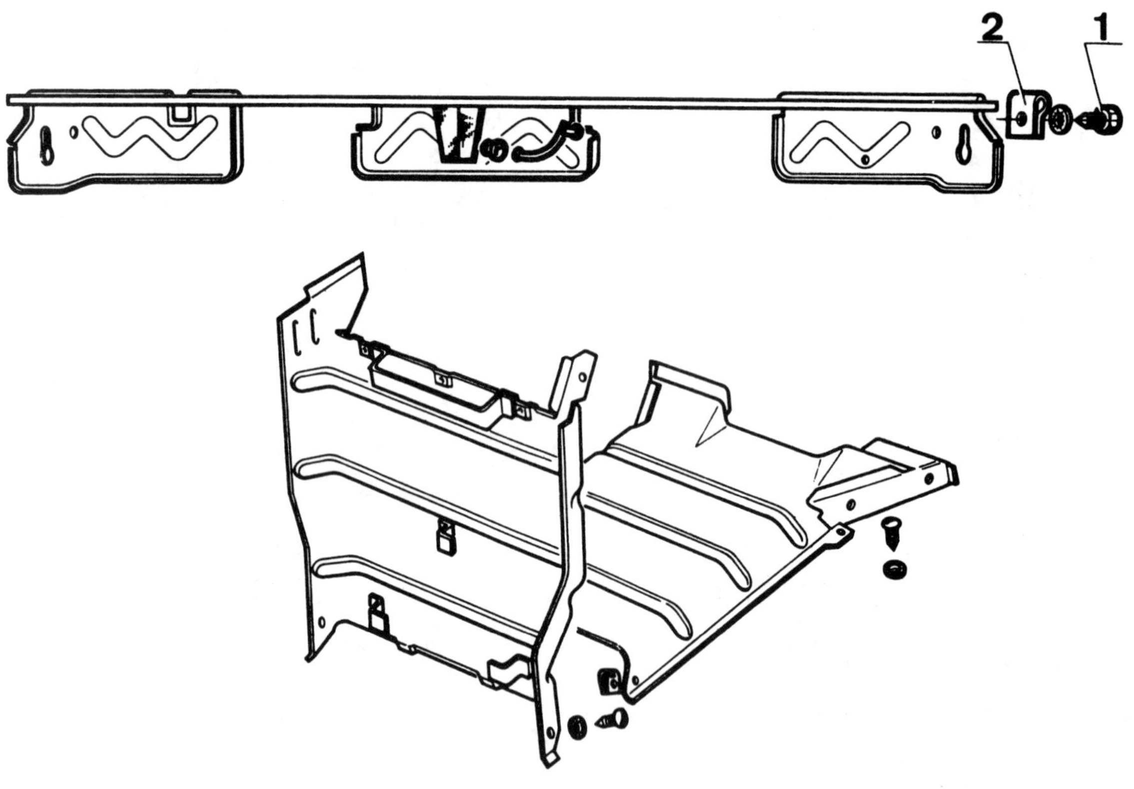

Fig.13.14 Air ducts to the rear compartment

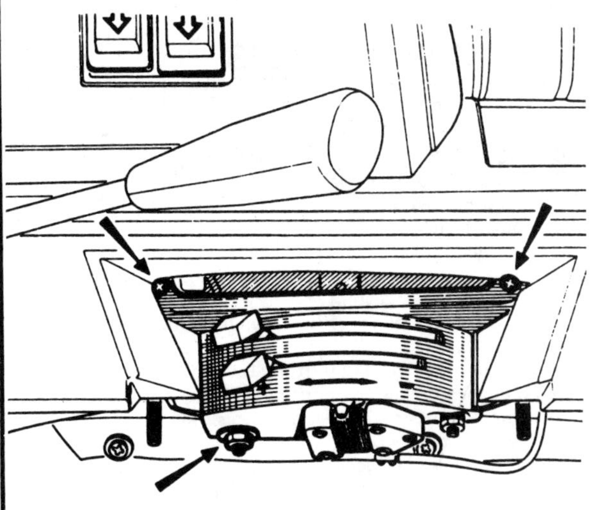

26.1 Air lever assembly securing screws

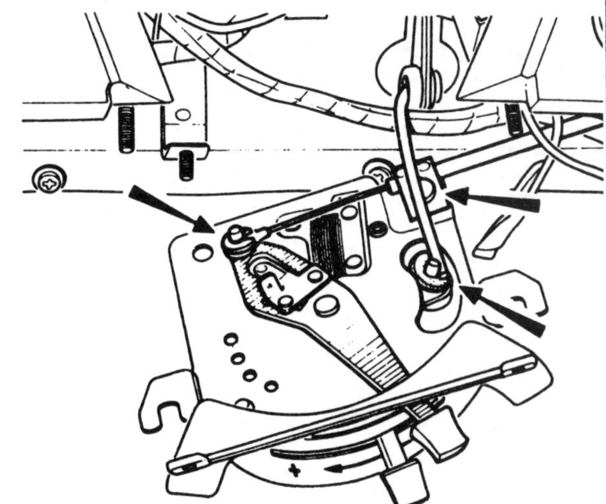

26.2 Cable connections to the lever assembly

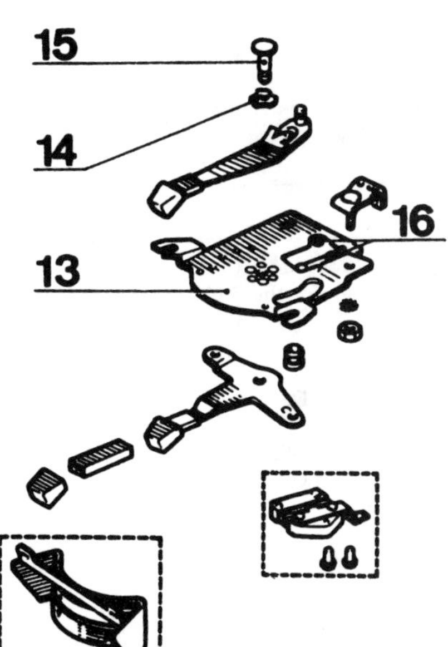

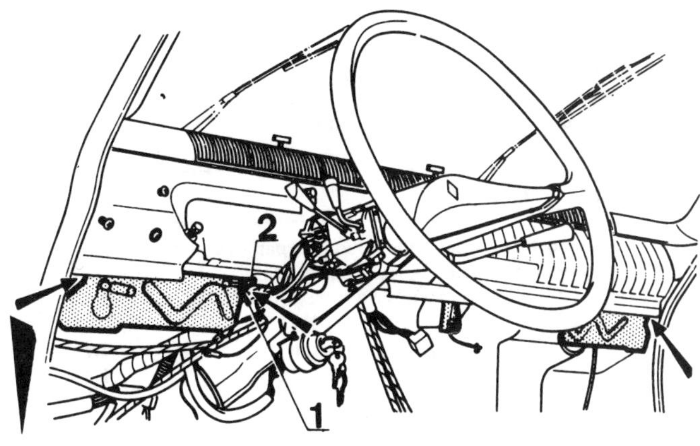

26.8 Air control flap removal. 1 securing screws. 2 bridge pieces

26.4 Components of the air control lever assembly. 13 support plate. 14 clip. 15 shaft. 16 rivets

Chapter 14 Supplement: Revisions and information on later models

Contents

1 Introduction

The following table shows the model types covered in this manual together with their Renault designations. This supplement identifies the R1155 model and introduces the R1156 and R1157; it also includes additional and updated information applicable to that given for the R1150 to R1154 models covered in Chapters 1 to 13.

Model	Designation	Market
16 DL or GL	R1150	UK and US
16TS	R1151	UK
16L or TL	R1152	UK and US
16TL automatic	R1153	UK and US
16TS automatic	R1154	UK
16 automatic	R1155	US
16TX manual and automatic	R1156	UK
16TL	R1157	–

2 Specifications

These Specifications are revisions of, or supplementary to, the Specifications at the beginning of each of the preceding Chapters.

The following information applies to the 1647cc engines type 841 and 843 and supplements the information given in Chapter 1. Apart from dimensional differences, the 841 engine is essentially the same as the 697 and 821 and the 843 is a larger version of the 807 but with the valves arranged in a double row. Differences in engine ancillary equipment are also detailed.

Vehicle type	Engine type and index	Cubic capacity	Bore	Stroke	Compression ratio
R1155	841-04	1647cc	3.110 in (79 mm)	3.307 in (84 mm)	7.5
R1156	843-01	1647cc	3.110 in (79 mm)	3.307 in (84 mm)	9.25
R1157	821-02	1565cc	3.032 in (77 mm)	3.307 in (84 mm)	8.6
R1157	821-03	1565cc	3.032 in (77 mm)	3.307 in (84 mm)	7.60 or 8.6

Engine

Type ...	841-04		843-01
Valve arrangement ...	Single line		Double line
Compression ratio ...	7.5:1		9.25:1
Valve timing	2 valve springs	1 valve spring	
Inlet valve opens (BTDC) ...	10°	18°	24°
Inlet valve closes (ABDC) ...	42°	54°	68°
Exhaust valve opens (BBDC) ...	46°	58°	68°
Exhaust valve closes (ATDC) ...	10°	18°	24°
Static ignition advance BTDC ...	$3^o \pm 1^o$		$4^o \pm 1^o$
Gudgeon pin length ...	2.716 in (69 mm)		
Gudgeon pin diameter:			
External ...	0.788 in (20 mm)		0.827 in (21 mm)
Bore ...	0.437 in (12 mm)		0.437 in (12 mm)

Cooling system

Thermostat	**Except R1156**	**R1156**
Type ...	Methylated spirit	Wax
Starts to open:		
Except hot countries ...	84^oC (183^oF)	83^oC (181^oF)
Hot countries ...	73^oC (164^oF)	75^oC (167^oF)
Fully open:		
Except hot countries ...	94^oC (201^oF)	93^oC (199^oF)
Hot countries ...	83^oC (181^oF)	85^oC (185^oF)
Valve maximum travel ...	0.25 in (6.5 mm)	0.25 in (6.5 mm)

Fuel system

Carburettor type (R1153 - US) ...	Solex 32 - 32 SEIA	
Carburettor mark ...	549	
	1st barrel	**2nd barrel**
Choke tube ...	24	24
Main jet ...	130	145
Air compensator jet ...	140 N3'	200 NH'
Idling jet ...	43	80
Needle valve ...	0.067 in (1.7 mm)	
Initial throttle opening ...	0.04 in (1 mm)	
Initial choke opening ...	0.137 in (3.5 mm)	
Accelerator pump jet ...	45	
Carburettor type (R1152 - US, R1153 - US and R1155) ...	Solex 26 - 32 DIDSA 8	
Carburettor marks:		
R1152 - US ...	478, 478-1, 478-2, 502 and 502-1	
R1153 - US ...	479, 479-1, 510 and 510-1	
R1155 ...	499	
	1st barrel	**2nd barrel**
Choke tube ...	23.5	26
Main jet:		
R1152 - US ...	120	155
R1153 - US ...	120	165
R1155 ...	122.5	155

Air compensator jet:		
R1152 - US	120	100 (Mk 478)
	–	110 (Mk 502)
R1153 - US	110	85
R1155	125	95
Idling jet:		
R1152 - US	65	90
R1153 - US	65	80
R1155	70	45
Needle valve	0.067 in (1.7 mm)	
Accelerator pump jet	35	
Diffusers:		
R1155	3.2	
Float weight:		
R1155	7.3 g	
Idling speed:		
Manual gearbox	650 ± 25 rpm	
Automatic transmission	625 ± 25 rpm (selector lever at A)	

Carburettor type (R1156)	Weber 32 DAR 7	
	1st barrel	**2nd barrel**
Choke tube	24	26
Main jet	135	135
Air compensator jet	170	145
Idling jet	52	45
Accelerator pump jet	60	
Needle valve	0.069 in (1.75 mm)	
Float weight	11 g	
Float level	0.275 in (7 mm)	
Initial throttle opening	0.047 in (1.2 mm)	
Pneumatic part-open setting	0.236 to 0.413 in (6 to 10.5 mm)	

Carburettor type (R1152 - UK, R1155 and R1157)	Solex 32 MIMAT	
Carburettor marks	633, 634 and 700	
	1st barrel	**2nd barrel**
Choke tube	24	25
Main jet:		
633	125	117.5
634 and 700	127.5	140
Air compensator jet:		
633	150	120
634 and 700	140	165
Idling jet:		
633	40	65
634	40	45
700	40	40
Emulsifier	X3	X2
Accelerator pump jet:		
634	45	–
633 and 700	40	–
Needle valve:	0.067 in (1.7 mm)	
Enrichment device:		
633	60	
634 and 700	50	
Deflooding device setting:		
633	0.256 in (6.5 mm)	
634	0.197 in (5 mm)	
700	0.138 in (3.5 mm)	
Float level	1.260 in (32 mm)	
Initial throttle opening (extreme cold):		
633	0.051 in (1.3 mm)	
634	0.043 in (1.1 mm)	
700	0.047 in (1.2 mm)	
Pneumatic part-open setting	0.090 in (2.3 mm)	
Butterfly angle	0.137 in (3.48 mm)	
1st barrel butterfly opening limit:		
700 only	0.374 in (9.5 mm)	
Exhaust gas content at idle	2 to 2.5%	
Idling speed:		
Manual gearbox	700 ± 25 rpm	
Automatic transmission	625 ± 25 rpm (selector lever at A)	

Ignition system

Distributor

Vehicle type	Engine	Compression ratio	Distributors	Static ignition timing °BTDC
R1150	697-01	8.6	4159, 4160, 4239, 4240	0 ± 1
R1150	697-02	7.6	4163, 4164, 4193, 4194	0 ± 1
R1151	807-01	8.6	4231, 4232, 4235, 4236, SEV 411 00 312	0 ± 1
R1151	807-01	8.6	4215, 4217	2 ± 1
R1151	807-02	7.6	4237, 4238	0 ± 1
R1151	807-03	8.6	4231, 4232, 4235, 4236, SEV 411 00 312	0 ± 1
R1151	807-03	7.6	4237, 4238	0 ± 1
R1151	807-04	8.6	4235, 4236	0 ± 1
R1152	821-02	8.6	4219, 4220, 4329, 4330	0 ± 1
R1152	821-03	7.6 or 8.6	4329, 4330	0 ± 1
R1153	821-01	7.6 or 8.6	4219, 4220, 4298, 4299	6 ± 1
R1153	821-04	8.6	4298, 4299	6 ± 1
R1153	821-04 US	8.6	4219, 4220	0 ± 1
R1154	807-05	8.6	4348, 4349	6 ± 1
R1154		8.6	4433, 4434	10 ± 1
R1154		7.6	4237, 4238*	6 ± 1
R1154	807-06	8.6	4348, 4349	6 ± 1
R1155	841-04	7.5	–	3 ± 1
R1156	843-01	9.25	4235, 4236	4 ± 1

Note information relating to R1152 vehicle type in Section 7 of this Supplement.

Dwell (cassette type points)

Angle	54 to 60°
Percentage	60 to 67%

Spark plugs

Model	Engine	AC	Champion	Renault Eyquem	Marchal	NGK
R1150	697-01	45XL	–	–	35HS	–
R1151	807-01, 807-02, 807-03, 807-04	44XL	N3	750L	35HSB	BP6ES
R1152	821-02, 821-03*	42XLS	N5	750L	–	BP6ES
R1153	821-01*, 821-04	42XLS	N5	750L	–	BP6ES
R1154	807-05, 807-06	44XL	N3	750L	35HSB	BP6ES
R1155	841-04	45XL	N5	–	–	–
R1156	843-01	42XLS	N7Y	755L	–	–

** For engines with a compression ratio of 7.6 to 1, use spark plugs AC 45XL or Champion N5*

Clutch

Model	Assembly	Clutch type
R1150, R1151, R1152	First	200 D 325 with withdrawal pad thrust plate
R1151, R1152	Second	200 DBR 325 without withdrawal pad thrust plate
R1156	–	200 DBR 375 without withdrawal pad thrust plate

Gearbox

Type ... ... BV 385

Operation ... ... Manual, five forward gears and reverse. Synchromesh on all forward gears.

Gear Ratios

1st	3.46:1
2nd	2.24:1
3rd	1.48:1
4th	1.04:1
5th	0.91:1
Reverse	3.08:1

Crownwheel

Number of teeth 31

Pinion

Number of teeth	8

Speedometer drive	6 x 12
Oil capacity	3 pints (Imp), 3.5 pints (US), 1.7 litres
Oil grade	See 'Recommended lubricants and fluids'

Braking system (R1156)

Type	Bendix 111AC

Front brakes

Wheel cylinder diameter	2.126 in (54 mm)
Disc diameter	10 in (254 mm)
Disc thickness	0.472 in (12 mm)
Minimum disc thickness	0.433 in (11 mm)
Pad minimum thickness	0.276 in (7 mm)

Rear brakes

Type	Girling automatic
Wheel cylinder diameter	0.937 in (23.8 mm)
Drum diameter	9 in (228.5 mm)
Maximum drum diameter	9.035 in (229.5 mm)
Lining width	1.575 in (40 mm)
Lining thickness	0.197 in (5 mm)

Master cylinder

Type	Tandem
Diameter	0.812 in (20.6 mm)
Stroke	1.181 in (30 mm)
Pressure drop indicator	Fitted to some models only
Brake servo diameter	6.889 in (175 mm)

Electrical system

Starter motor (R1155 and R1156)

Type	Paris-Rhone D8E84
Commutator diameter:	
Standard	1.614 in (41 mm)
Minimum	1.535 in (39 mm)
Insulation undercut depth	0.20 in (5 mm)
Brush length:	
Standard	0.551 in (14 mm)
Maximum	0.315 in (8 mm)

Alternator

Make	Type	Voltage	Current	Rotor resistance
SEV-motorola	26 607, 26 647, 34 837	12V	30/40A	5.2 ohms between slip rings
Paris-Rhone	A13R63	12V	30/40A	4.4 ohms between slip rings
	A13R123	12V	50A	4.4 ohms between slip rings

Voltage regulator

Type	Cutting in speed (rpm)	Checking voltage
26 607	900	14
26 647		
34 837		
A13R63	900	13.2
A13R123	1000	14

Headlamps

Number	4
Type	QI
Main beam	Centre pair and outer pair of lights on
Dipped beam	Outer pair of lights on

Bodywork

Underbody height setting dimensions

	Type of tyre	Type of vehicle	H1 (front)	H2 (rear)
Normal roads	145 x 14	R1150, R1152, R1153	7.874 in (200 mm)	10.236 in (260 mm)
Normal roads	155 x 14	R1150, R1152, R1153	8.267 in (210 mm)	10.630 in (270 mm)
Normal roads	155 x 14	R1151, R1154, R1156	7.677 in (195 mm)	10.039 in (255 mm)
Poor roads	145 x 14	R1150	8.661 in (220 mm)	11.023 in (280 mm)
Poor roads	155 x 14	R1150, R1152, R1153	8.267 in (210 mm) or 8.858 in (225 mm)	10.630 in (270 mm) or 11.220 in (285 mm)*
Poor roads	155 x 14	R1151, R1154, R1156	8.661 in (220 mm) or 7.677 in (195 mm)	11.023 in (280 mm) or 10.039 in (255 mm) *
Special versions	560 x 14	R1150, R1152, R1153	9.449 in (240 mm)	12.60 in (320 mm)
Special versions	155 x 14	R1150, R1152, R1153	8.858 in (225 mm)	12.008 in (305 mm)
Special versions	155 x 14	R1151, R1154	8.661 in (220 mm)	11.811 in (300 mm)

** For some versions*

3 Jacking and towing

Jacking

1 The jack supplied with the vehicle is not designed for service or repair operations, but purely for changing a wheel in the event of a puncture. A strong pillar or trolley type jack should be employed for maintenance and repair tasks requiring the vehicle to be raised.

2 To change a wheel, remove the spare wheel, jack and wheelbrace from their respective locations in the engine compartment. Apply the handbrake and place the vehicle in gear. Ideally, the vehicle should be parked on firm, level ground with the wheel diagonally opposite the one to be changed firmly chocked.

3 Slightly loosen the wheel nuts, pushing down on the centre of the wheelbrace to free them. Position the jack beneath the vehicle, inserting its head in the jacking point nearest to the defective wheel. If the ground is soft, prevent the jack from sinking by positioning a small plank of wood beneath its base. Extend the jack by hand until it is taking the weight of the car; bias the jack base slightly inboard.

4 Fit the wheelbrace to the jack and raise the car until the wheel is just clear of the ground. Remove the wheel nuts and then the wheel. Fit the serviceable wheel and tighten the wheel nuts as much as possible with the wheel clear of the ground. Lower the car and remove the jack. Finally tighten the wheel nuts and recheck them after running the car a few miles.

5 When using a pillar or trolley type jack, first obtain a strong length of wood and position it between the jack head and vehicle body so that it acts to spread the load and prevent the body from distorting.

6 At the front of the vehicle, position the jack directly beneath the sidemembers, in line with the wheel centres. At the side, position the jack directly beneath the body valance, beneath and parallel to the front door. At the rear, position the jack beneath the centre of the rear end panel.

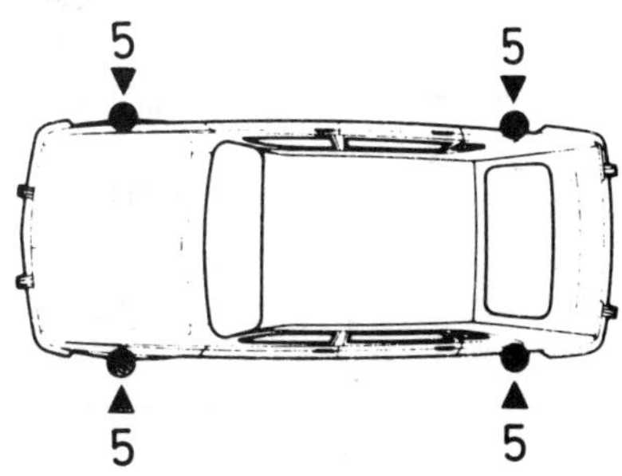

Fig. 14.1 Jacking and support points (Sec 3)

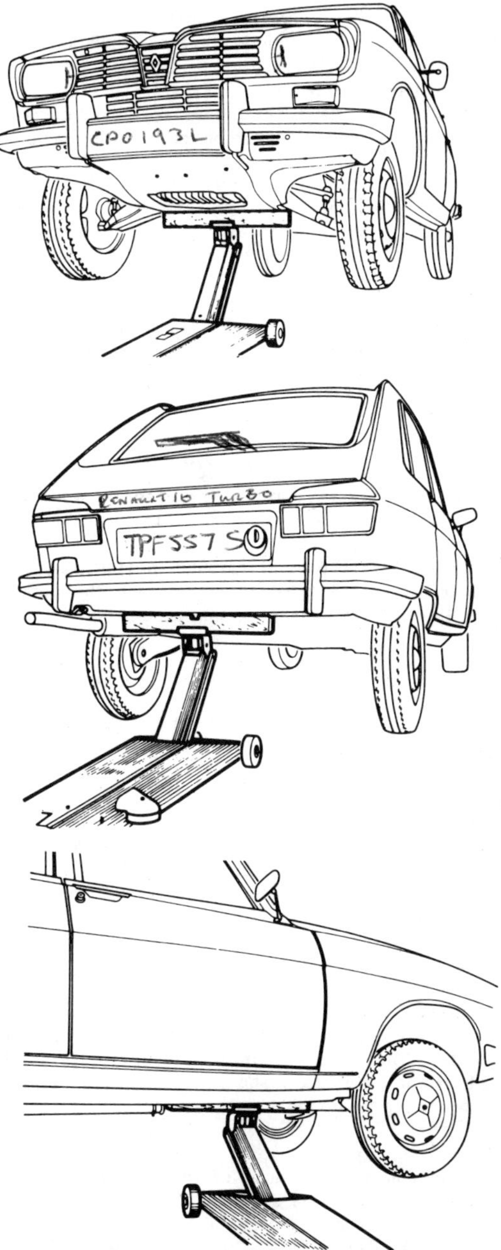

Fig. 14.2 Lifting positions when using trolley jack (Sec 3)

Towing

7 Ensure that the tow rope to be used is of sufficient length and has a high enough breaking strain. Never attach the rope to the lower suspension arms or to the driveshafts.

8 When towing a vehicle equipped with automatic transmission, it must be remembered that the transmission fluid pump is driven directly by the engine. The front wheels must therefore be raised clear of the ground when towing.

9 Under circumstances in which the maximum distance to be towed does not exceed 30 miles (50 km), the vehicle may be towed normally at a speed of 18 mph (30 km/h) or less, but an extra 4 pints (2 litres) of transmission fluid must be added to the transmission before commencing the journey. This additional oil must then be drained off on arrival at your destination.

4 Engine modifications and component interchangeability

Cylinder block - 697 engine (R1150)

1 Only the new type of cylinder block is available as a spare part, which means that liners must be fitted which match the locating diameters of 82.5 mm.

2 The two cylinder head fixing bolts at the timing gear end (Fig. 14.3) must be fitted as shown on the following table:

	1st Cylinder block H = 82 mm	
Side	Manifold	Distributor
Bolt	6.063 in (154 mm)	5.393 in (137 mm)
Washer	0.157 in (4 mm)	0.157 in (4 mm)
Spacer	–	–

	2nd Cylinder block H = 65 mm	
Side	Manifold	Distributor
Bolt	5.393 in (137 mm)	5.393 in (137 mm)
Washer	0.157 in (4 mm)	–
Spacer	–	0.945 in (24 mm)

Cylinder block - 843 engine (R1156)

3 On the 843 engine the depth of thread for the bolts securing the main bearing caps has been increased to accept longer fixing bolts.

4 This modification will be applied progressively to the cylinder blocks on all types of engine, and the dimensions shown in Fig. 14.4 will be as in the following table:

	L	A
697, 821, 807, 841 (1st assembly)	2.637 in (67 mm)	1.063 in (27 mm)
821, 807, 841 (2nd assembly) and 843	3.425 in (87 mm)	1.260 in (32 mm)

Crankshaft

5 There are differences in the end of the crankshaft with engines of different assemblies as shown in Fig. 14.5.

6 On 1st assembly engines, the timing sprocket on the nose of the crankshaft is secured by a distance piece, washer and bolt.

7 On 2nd assembly engines the sprocket is a shrink-fit onto the crankshaft and the sprocket must be heated in an oven before fitting.

8 On some 3rd assembly engines the nose of the crankshaft is long enough for a pulley and a sprocket to be fitted. When this crankshaft is fitted, a shrink-fit sprocket should be used and the bolt, washer and spacer should be discarded to eliminate the risk of fouling the timing cover.

Valves

9 The inlet and exhaust valves of the 807 and 843 engines are different, although the diameters of the heads and stems, and the seat taper angles, are the same.

10 Valves on the 843 engine having split cotters of KK pattern (Fig. 14.6) may be fitted to the 807 engine, but 807 engine valves may not be fitted to an 843 engine.

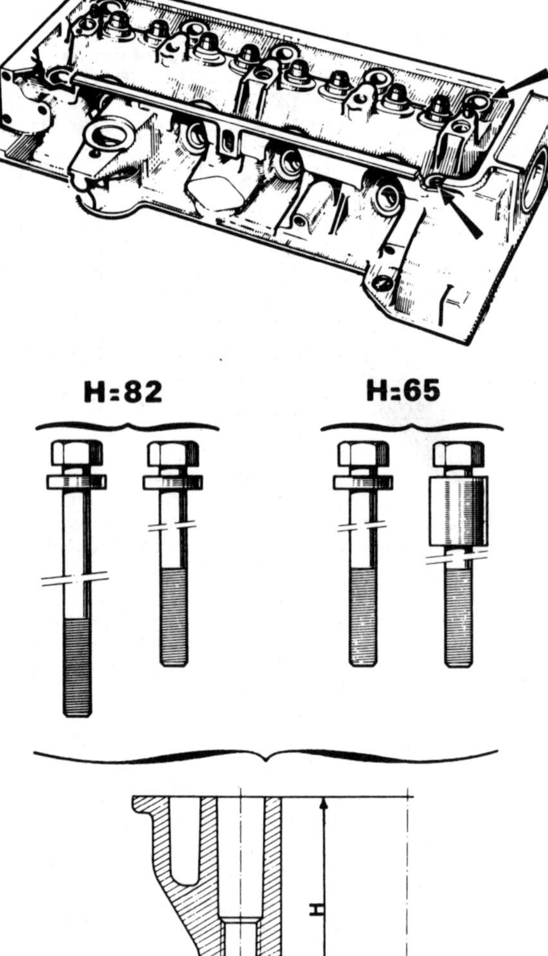

Fig. 14.3 Cylinder block modification – 697 engine (R1150) (Sec 4)

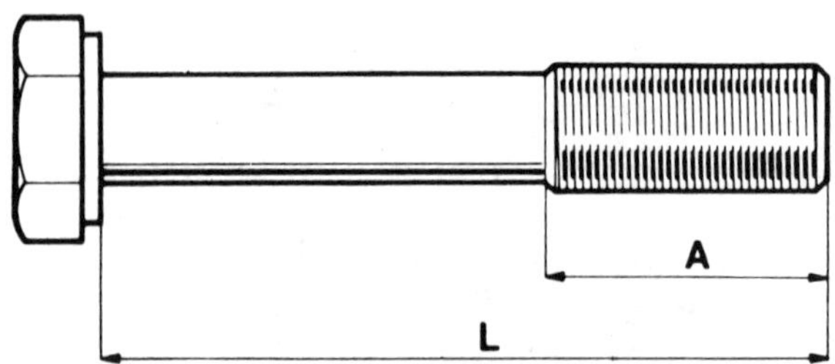

Fig. 14.4 Main bearing bolts – 843 engine (R1156) (see text) (Sec 4)

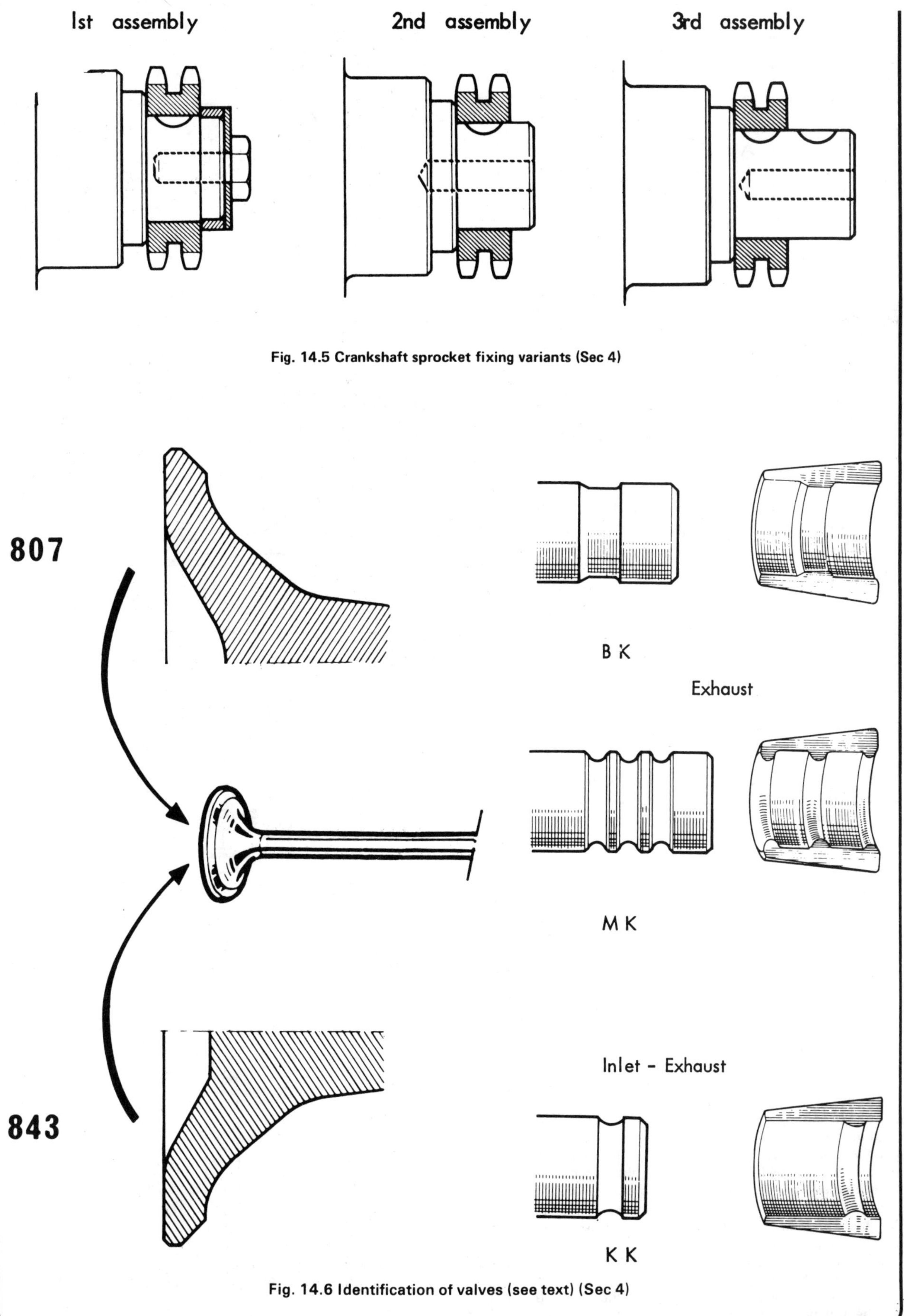

Fig. 14.5 Crankshaft sprocket fixing variants (Sec 4)

Fig. 14.6 Identification of valves (see text) (Sec 4)

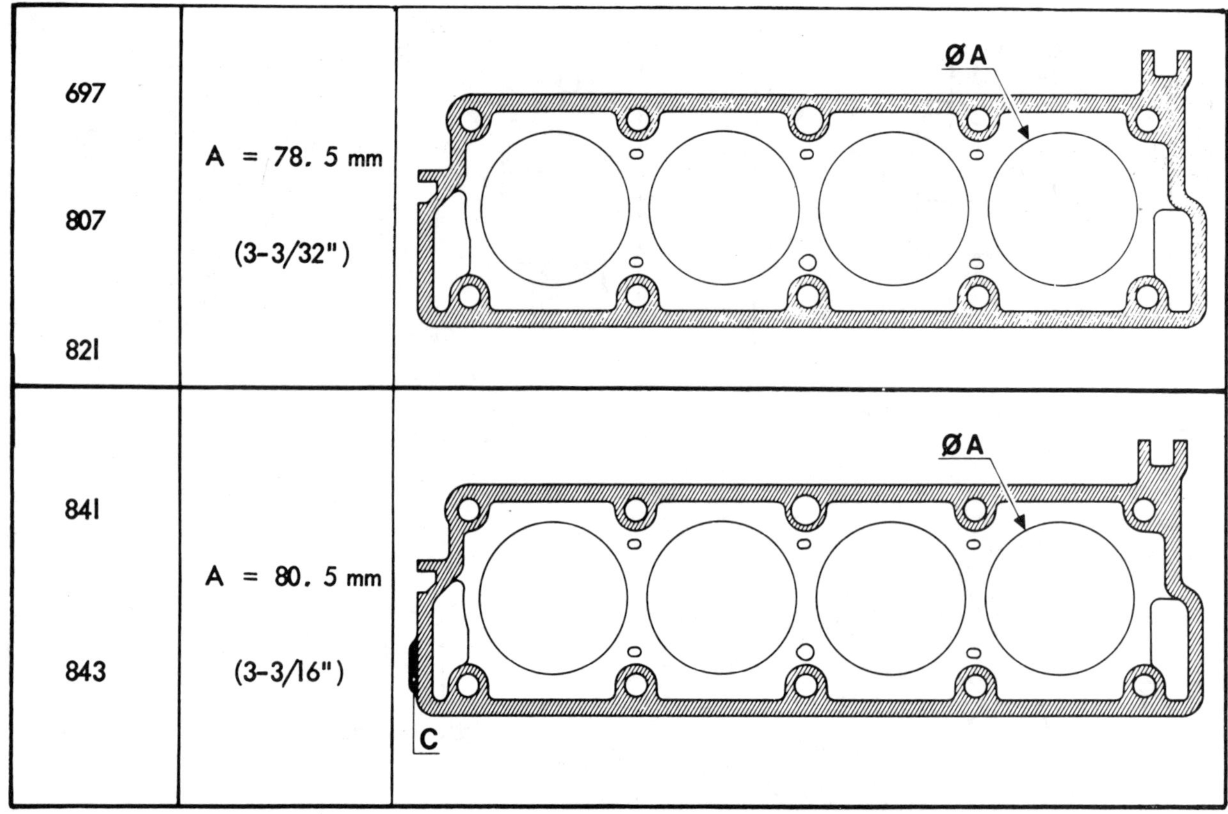

Fig. 14.7 Identification of cylinder head gaskets (see text) (Sec 4)

Cylinder head gaskets

11 The cylinder head gaskets used on the 687, 821 and 807 engines are different from those used on the 841 and 843 engines.

12 The different gaskets may be identified by the diameter of the hole A (Fig. 14.7). As an additional means of identification it should be noted that there is a tab (C) on the gasket of the 841 and 843 engines.

5 Cooling system

Water pump and thermostat - 843 engine (R1156)

1 The R1156 model is fitted with a wax thermostat (Fig. 14.8) and in no circumstances whatsoever may the spirit-type thermostat used on other models be used as a replacement.

2 The wax-type thermostat necessitates a different water pump as well as a different hose between the pump and the radiator. The differences are shown in Figs. 14.9 and 14.10.

Fan motor - dismantling and reassembly

3 Motors of various types and different manufacturers are used and the operations required for each particular motor are as given in the following paragraphs.

4 *SEV-Marchal, types MD and LD2:* Referring to Fig. 14.11, remove the two tie-bolts, noting that their lengths are not the same. Remove the bearing bracket and body, then the retaining clip and washer. Withdraw the armature, taking care not to lose the thrust washer. Reassembly is the reverse of the operations necessary for dismantling.

5 *SEV-Marchal, type LY:* Referring to Fig. 14.12, remove the two field coil fixing screws to free the field coil, then remove the four screws clamping the two halves of the motor frame. Lift off the top half of the motor frame, remove the armature and

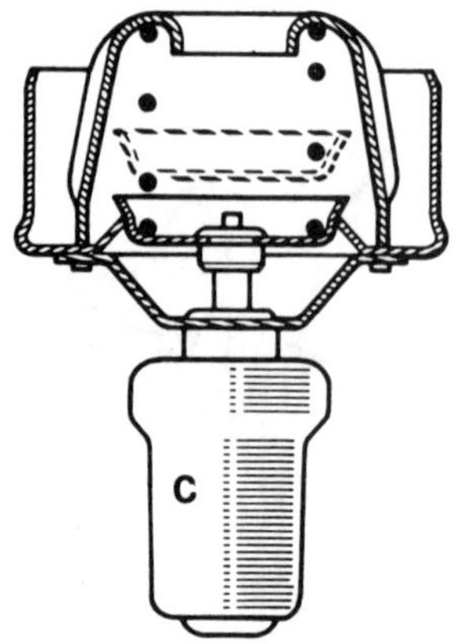

Fig. 14.8 Wax-type thermostat (Sec 5)

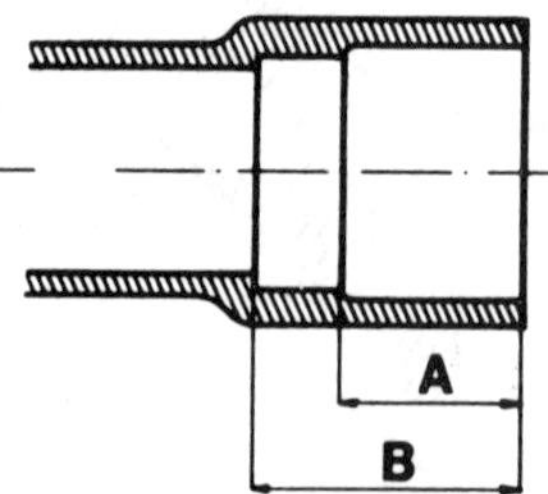

Fig. 14.9 Hose end for wax-type thermostat (Sec 5)

A = 1.063 in (27 mm) *B = 1.653 in (42 mm)*

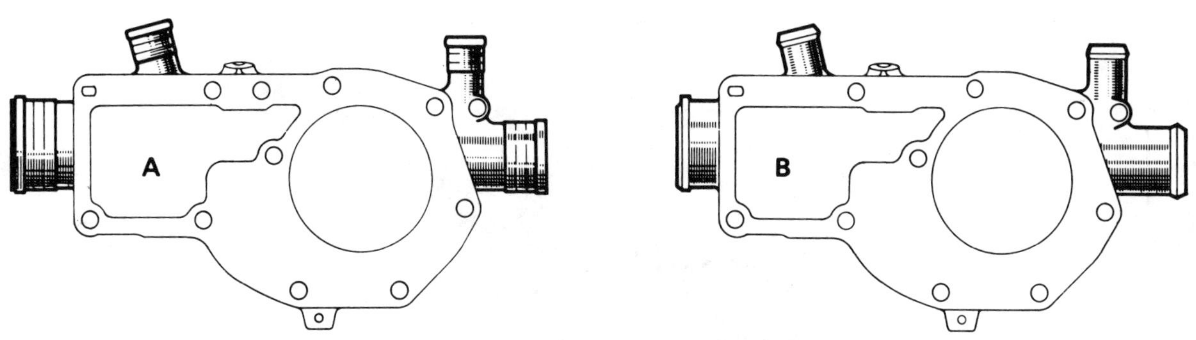

Fig. 14.10 Water pump and hose identification (Sec 5)

A Water pump for spirit-type thermostat *B Water pump for wax-type thermostat*

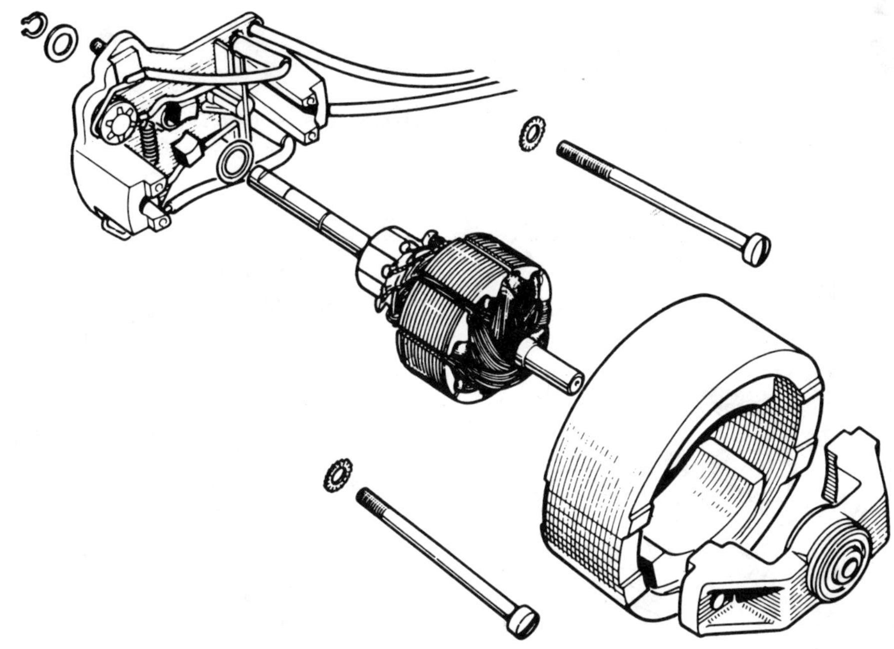

Fig. 14.11 SEV-Marchal motor-types MD and LD2 (exploded view) (Sec 5)

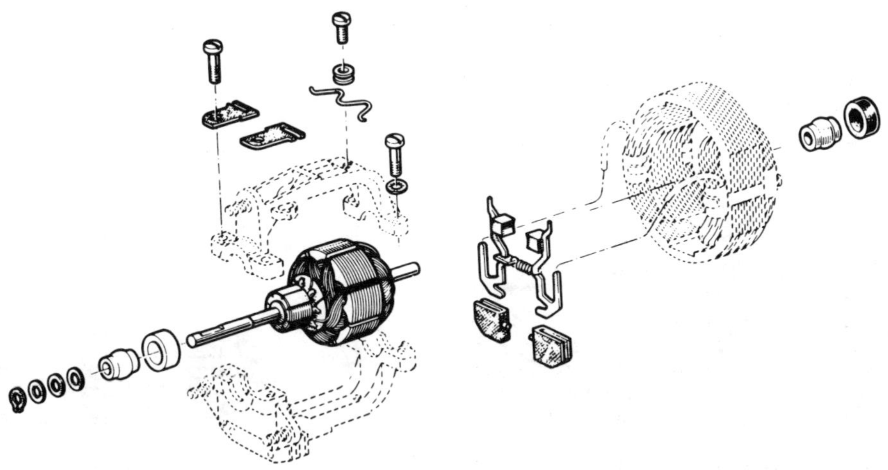

Fig. 14.12 SEV-Marchal motor-type LY (exploded view) (Sec 5)

Fig. 14.13 Rabotti motor (exploded view) (Sec 5)

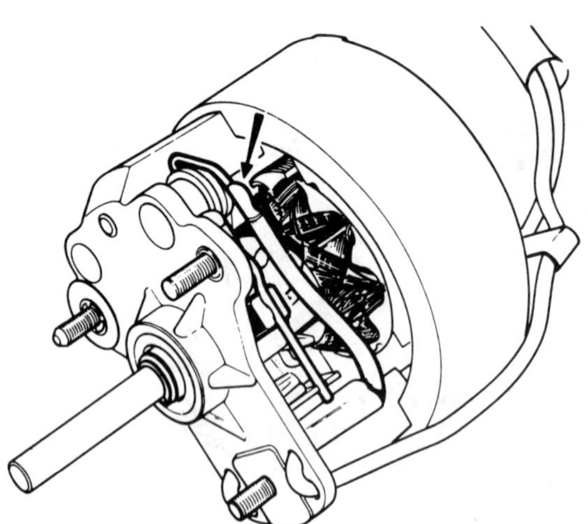

Fig. 14.14 SEV-Marchal – types MD and LD2 (Sec 5)

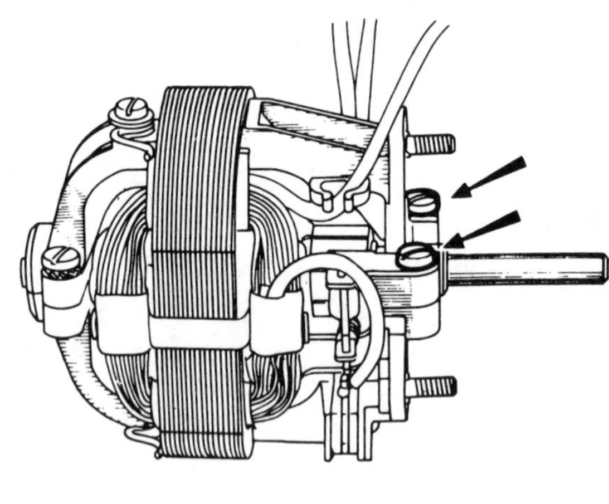

Fig. 14.15 SEV-Marchal – type LY (Sec 5)

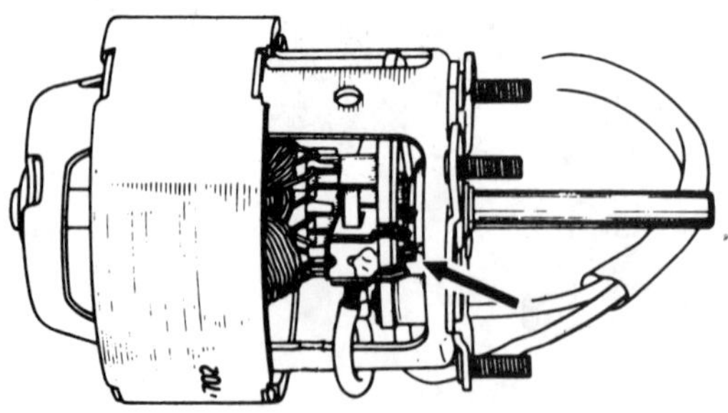

Fig. 14.16 SEV-Marchal – type 738 (Sec 5)

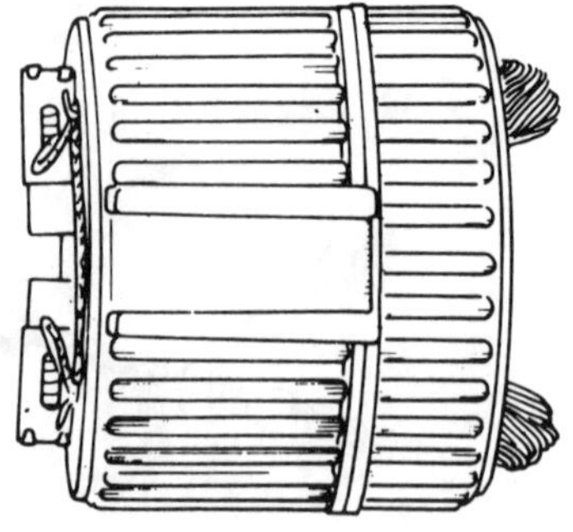

Fig. 14.17 Rabotti motor (Sec 5)

take the brushes out. Reassembly is a reversal of the operations necessary for dismantling.

6 *Rabotti motor:* Referring to Fig. 14.13, remove the two through-bolts and take off both end covers, leaving the armature free. If the packing washers are removed from the armature shaft, note their positions before removing them. Reassembly is a reversal of the operations necessary for dismantling.

Fan motor brush renewal

7 *SEV-Marchal, types LD2 and MD:* Unhook the brush retaining springs (arrowed Fig. 14.14) and free the brushes. Unsolder the brush connections, remove the old brushes and fit new ones. Before refitting the motor, clean the commutator with a piece of cotton rag, moistened with petrol.

8 *SEV-Marchal, type LY:* Remove the two screws (arrowed in Fig. 14.15) and lift off the brush guide plates. Unhook the brush retaining springs to free the brushes, then unsolder the brush connections and remove the old brushes. Clean the commutator with a piece of cotton rag moistened with petrol, then solder on the new brushes and refit the brush guide plates.

9 *SEV-Marchal, Type 738:* Bend back the brush carrier lugs (arrowed in Fig. 14.16) to free the brush carrier. Unsolder the brush connections and remove the old brushes, then clean the commutator with a piece of cotton rag, moistened with petrol. Fit the new brushes and solder their connections.

10 *Rabotti:* Remove the two motor through-bolts and pull off the cover at the commutator end. Unsolder the old brushes, withdraw them from their holders and fit the new brushes. Clean the commutator with a piece of cotton rag, moistened with petrol, before refitting the motor end cover.

6 Fuel system

Solex 32 MIMAT carburettor - R1152, R1155 and R1157 - idle speed adjustment

1 The following methods of adjustment both require removal of the tamperproof cap from the fuel screw. The manufacturers fit this cap to discourage (and to detect) adjustment by unqualified or unskilled operators. Before removing this cap, satisfy yourself that you are not breaking any local or national anti-pollution laws by doing so. If the vehicle is still under warranty, be aware that you may be in breach of warranty conditions. Fit a new cap on completion where this is required by law. With the cap removed, proceed as follows.

Adjustment with exhaust gas analyser

2 Run the engine until it reaches normal operating temperature. Fit the analyser equipment in accordance with the manufacturer's instructions. Turn the volume screw until the idle speed is approximately that specified. Now turn the fuel screw until the analyser reading is close to the specified gas content percentage. Repeat adjustment of both screws until idle speed and exhaust gas content are correct.

Adjustment without exhaust gas analyser

3 Run the engine until it reaches normal operating temperature. Turn the volume screw to obtain the highest specified idle speed for the type of vehicle. Now turn the fuel screw to obtain maximum engine speed. Repeat adjustment of both

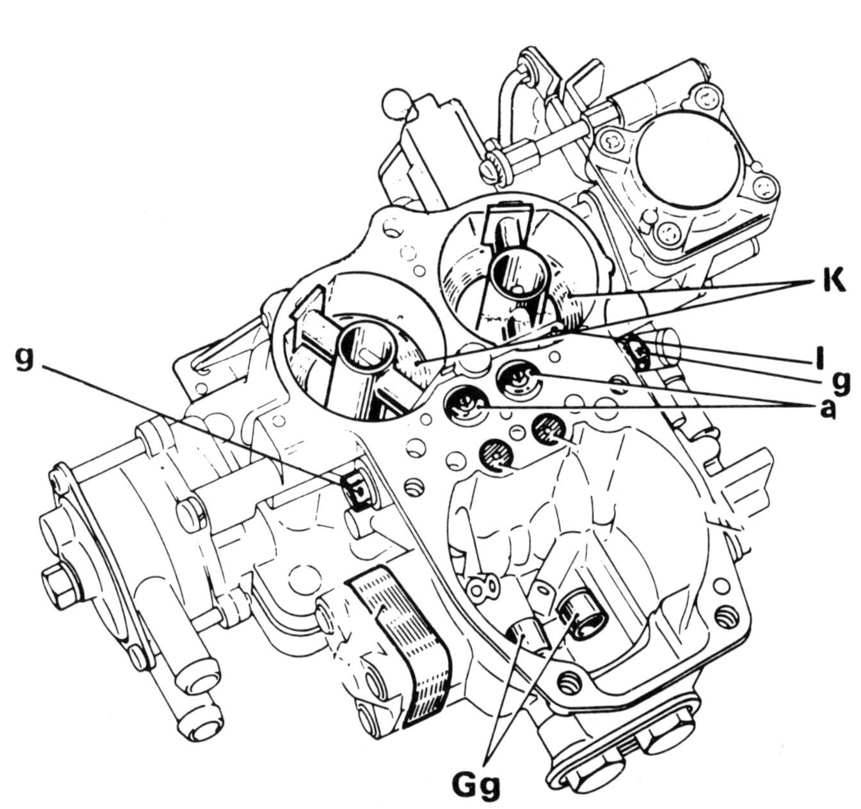

Fig. 14.18 Solex 32 MIMAT carburettor – jet location (Sec 6)

1 Accelerator pump jet *g Idling jet* *a Air compensator jet* *Gg Main jet* *K Venturi*

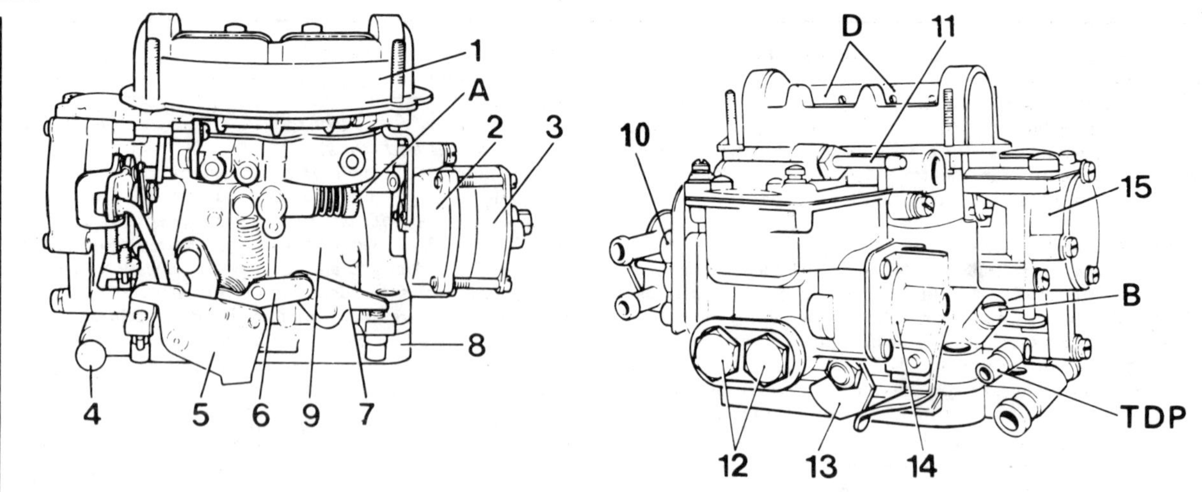

Fig. 14.19 Solex 32 MIMAT carburettor – component parts (Sec 6)

1 Float chamber top
2 Bimetal spring housing
3 Coolant body (automatic choke)
4 Coolant union (carburettor base heating)
5 Throttle lever
6 Intermediate lever
7 Throttle lever (2nd barrel)
8 Carburettor base heating flange
9 Float chamber body
10 Richness corrector
11 Fuel inlet union
12 Main jet access plugs
13 Accelerator pump cam
14 Accelerator pump
15 Choke flaps pneumatic part-open setting device
A Volume screw
B Fuel screw
D Choke flaps
TDP Vacuum take-off (distributor)

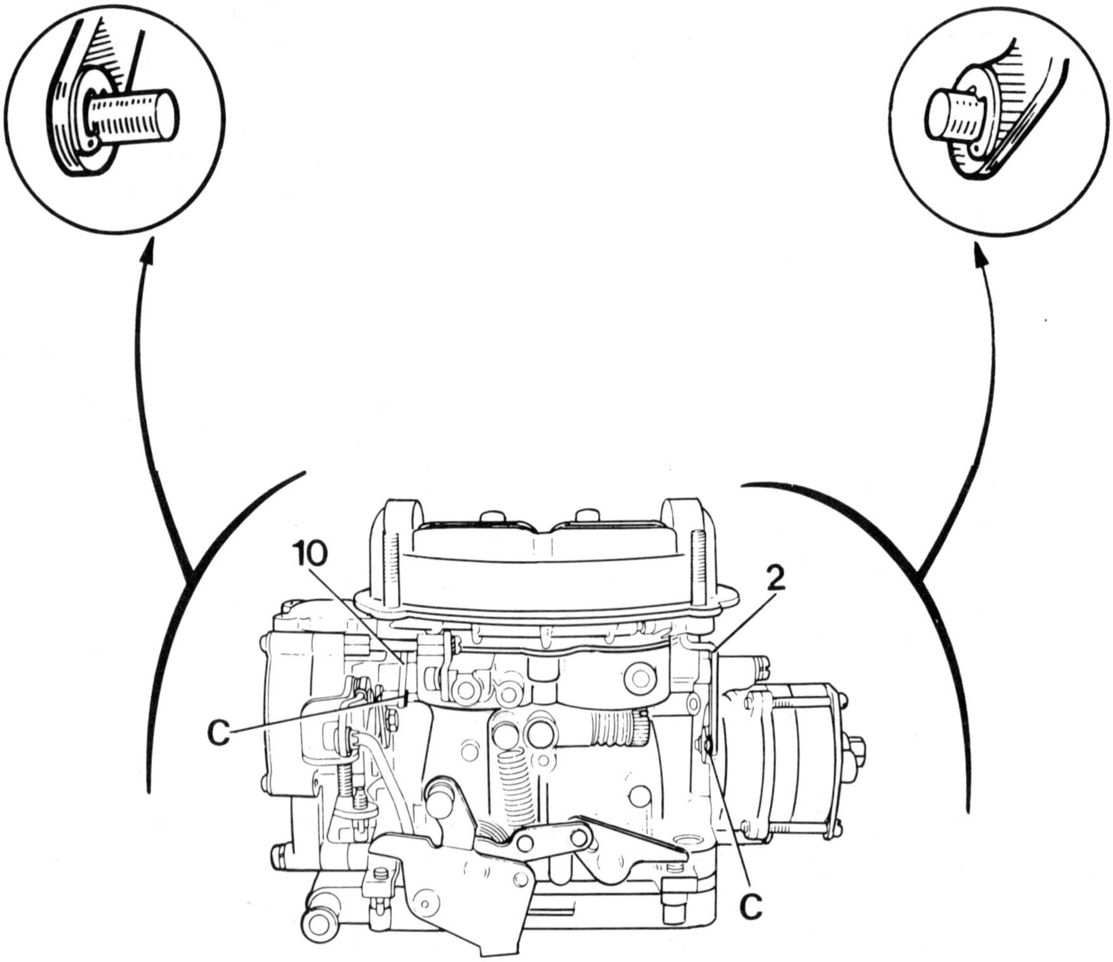

10
2
C
C

Fig. 14.20 Solex 32 MIMAT carburettor – float chamber removal (Sec 6)

C Arm retaining clips *2 and 10 Operating arms*

screws until the highest idle speed is obtained by final adjustment of the fuel screw.

4 Screw in the fuel screw to both weaken the mixture and reduce engine speed by 25 to 30 rev/min. Do this without upsetting the smooth running of the engine. The engine should now be running at the normal specified idle speed. If not, repeat the adjustment procedure.

Float level check

5 Remove the float chamber top securing screws. Refer to Fig. 14.20 and detach the clips from the arms shown. Remove the arm (2) from its spindle, slightly lift the float chamber top and remove the other arm from its spindle.

6 To check float level, invert the chamber top and hold it horizontal as shown in Fig. 14.21. With the gasket removed from the mating surface, the distance between the mating surface and the float periphery furthest from it must equal that specified. If necessary, adjust the float level by tightening the float valve seat to compress its washer. Do not exceed a torque loading of 12 lbf/ft (16 Nm).

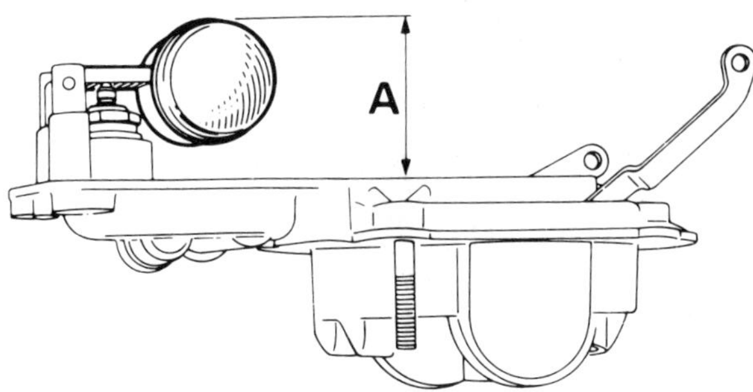

Fig. 14.21 Solex 32 MIMAT carburettor – float level check (Sec 6)

A Float level

Butterfly angle check

7 Before attempting this operation, obtain special tool nos. Mot. 522, Mot. 522 - 01 and Mot. 522 - 03. Remove the carburettor from the vehicle and detach its heating flange body with the bakelite spacer.

8 Refer to Fig. 14.22 and fit the special tool seating washer so that it is fully located in the carburettor. Fit the special tool so that its locking screw is in position A. Check that the automatic choke is fully off.

9 To determine the butterfly angle, first zero the clock gauge. Zero will then equal the lower side of the butterfly. Release the locking screw and rotate the knurled section of the tool through 180° until the locking screw is in position 3. Note the gauge reading, which should equal the butterfly angle specified.

10 If necessary, adjust the butterfly angle by turning the appropriate adjuster the required amount, see Fig. 14.23. Re-check the angle.

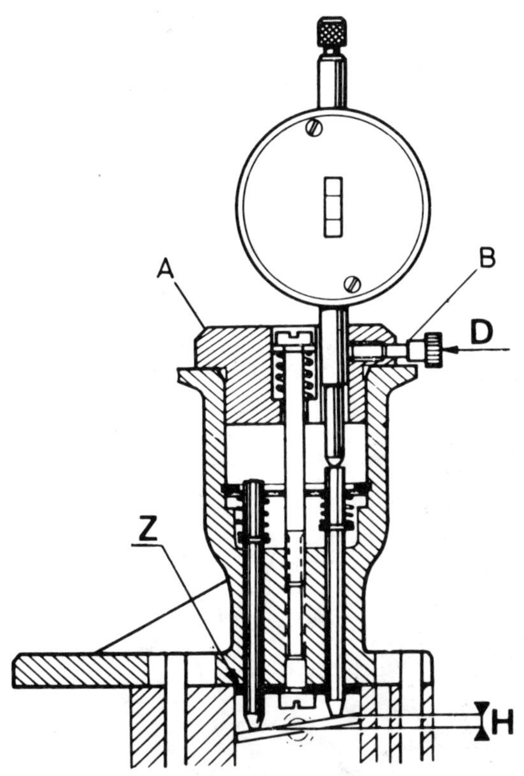

Fig. 14.22 Solex 32 MIMAT carburettor – butterfly angle check (Sec 6)

H Butterfly angle *D Locking screw*
Z Seating washer *A and B Screw positions*

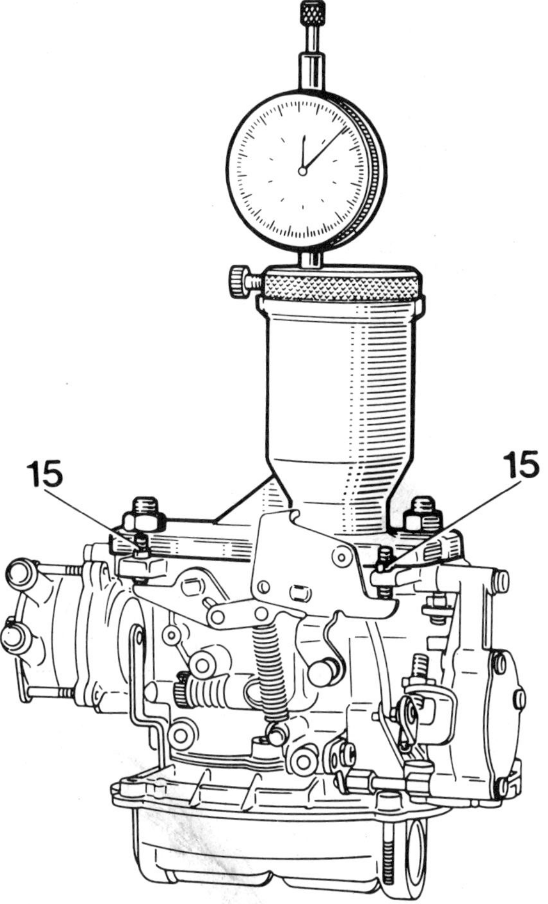

Fig. 14.23 Solex 32 MIMAT carburettor – butterfly angle adjustment (Sec 6)

15 Adjuster screws

Initial throttle opening check

11 Before attempting this operation, obtain a set of gauge rods from special tool set MS 532. Alternatively, manufacture a rod of the required diameter.

12 Position the choke mechanism. The initial opening cam largest radius must be facing downwards towards the carburettor base, that is in the 'extreme cold' position. Using the gauge rods, measure the first barrel initial throttle opening.
13 The measured opening should equal that specified for the carburettor mark. If necessary, adjust the opening by turning the screw shown in Fig. 14.24. Recheck the opening.

Pneumatic part-open setting adjustment

14 Position the choke mechanism; the initial opening cam largest radius facing downwards towards the carburettor base. Note the specified setting.
15 Refer to Fig. 14.25 and slowly turn the setting screw so that it just contacts the cam. Using a gauge rod, measure the choke flap opening on its smaller offset side. Now turn the setting screw again to make any necessary adjustment.

Flooding device adjustment

16 Position the choke mechanism; the initial opening cam largest radius facing downwards towards the carburettor base. Fully open the throttle.
17 Using a gauge rod, measure the choke flap opening on its smaller offset side. Refer to Fig. 14.25 and if necessary, bend the operating rod to make adjustment so that the opening equals that specified for the carburettor mark.

Fig. 14.24 Solex 32 MIMAT carburettor – initial throttle opening adjustment (Sec 6)

6 Adjuster screw

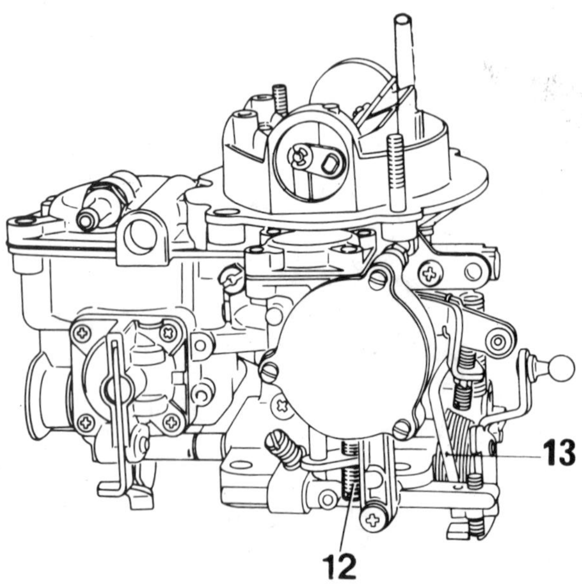

Fig. 14.25 Solex 32 MIMAT carburettor – pneumatic part-open setting and flooding device adjustments (Sec 6)

12 Setting screw *13 Operating rod*

7 Ignition system

Cassette type distributor - later R1152 vehicles

1 To improve efficiency of the ignition system, the distributor

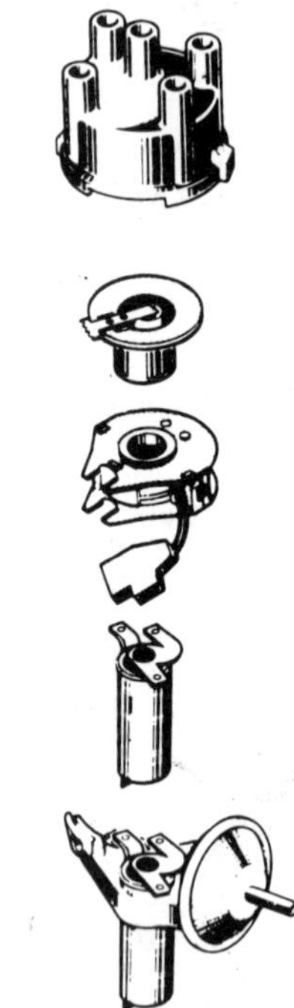

Fig. 14.26 Exploded view of cassette type distributor (later R1152 vehicles) (Sec 7)

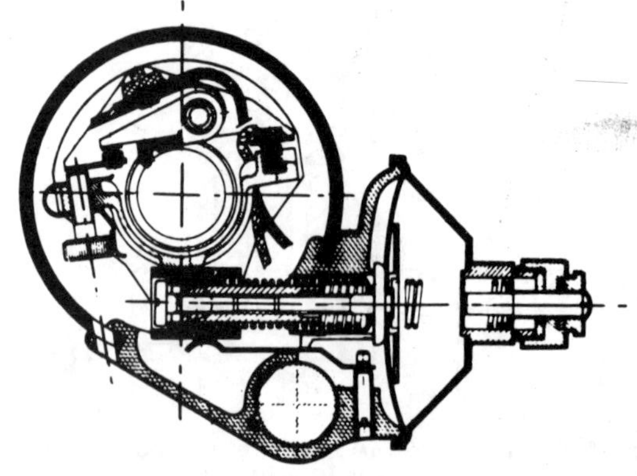

Fig. 14.27 Sectional view of cassette type distributor (later R1152 vehicles) (Sec 7)

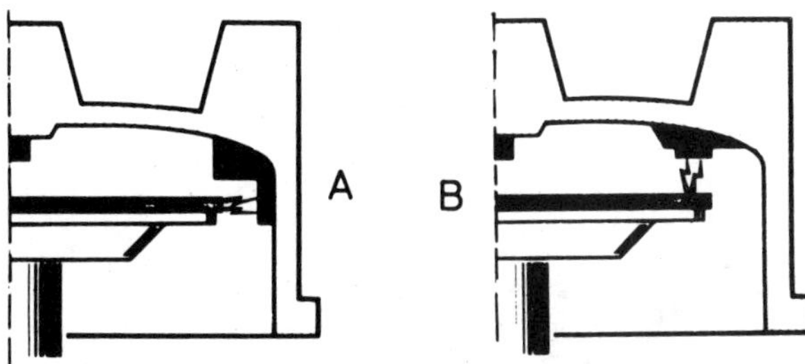

Fig. 14.28 Spark track comparison (Sec 7)

A Conventional distributor *B Cassette distributor*

fitted to later R1152 vehicles has a cassette arrangement fitted in place of the conventional contact breaker points. Reference to Fig. 14.28 shows that with the conventional arrangement, the spark passing between the rotor arm and the distributor cap jumps sideways which means that if there is any side play in the distributor spindle, the spark appearing at each spark plug will vary in strength. With the cassette, the spark jumps vertically thereby obviating any variation caused by spindle movement.

Contact breaker points (cassette type) - condition check

2 The condition of the contact breaker points within the cassette can be determined by measuring the voltage across them with the gap closed. If the voltage reading obtained exceeds 0.2 volts with the ignition on, then suspect a fault. Apart from points in bad condition, faults may include the low tension wire between the HT coil and distributor being defective, a defective earth between the distributor body and the engine or an internal fault in the distributor.

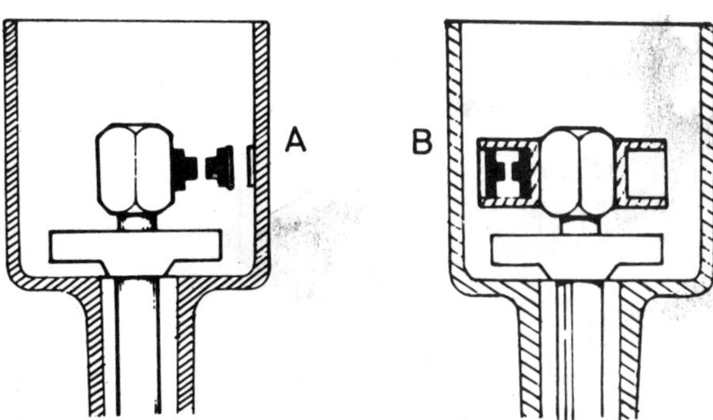

Fig. 14.29 Contact breaker assembly comparison (Sec 7)

A Conventional distributor *B Cassette distributor*

Contact breaker points (cassette type) - adjustment

3 There are two methods of checking and adjusting the gap between the contact breaker points. The most accurate method is by using a dwellmeter to determine the dwell angle, which is the angle through which the distributor cam turns between the instance of closure and opening of the contact breaker points during one ignition cycle. A reduction of the points gap will increase the dwell angle and vice versa.

4 With the dwellmeter attached to the ignition system in accordance with the manufacturer's instructions, measure the dwell angle. This angle must be as specified. Alternatively, if the correct type of meter is available, measure the dwell percentage, which must also be as specified. If necessary, refer to the relevant sub-Section for dwell adjustment.

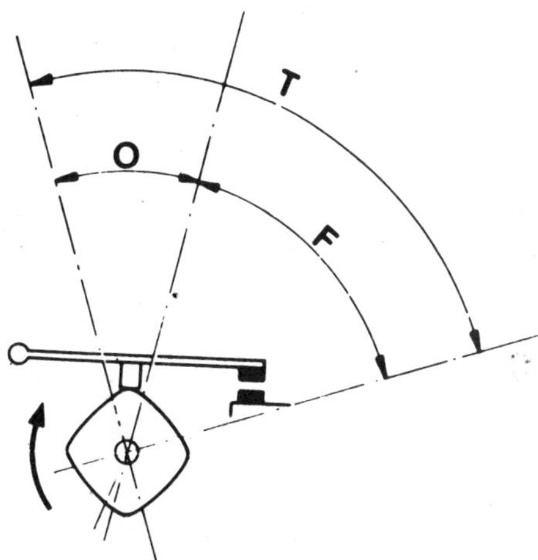

Fig. 14.30 Dwell angle identification (Sec 7)

T Total angle (90°) *F Dwell angle (57°)*
O Angle of opening (33°)

5 The second method of adjustment requires the manufacture of a special tool, that is a length of metal bar with a diameter of 0.667 in (16.96 mm). Insert this tool into the centre of the cassette in place of the drive spindle and then adjust the points gap to 0.016 in (0.40 mm) by using a feeler gauge.

Contact breaker points (cassette type) - changing

6 The contact breaker points form an integral part of the cassette. Figs. 14.31 and 14.32 show removal of the cassette from the distributor and disconnection of the cassette from the vacuum capsule.

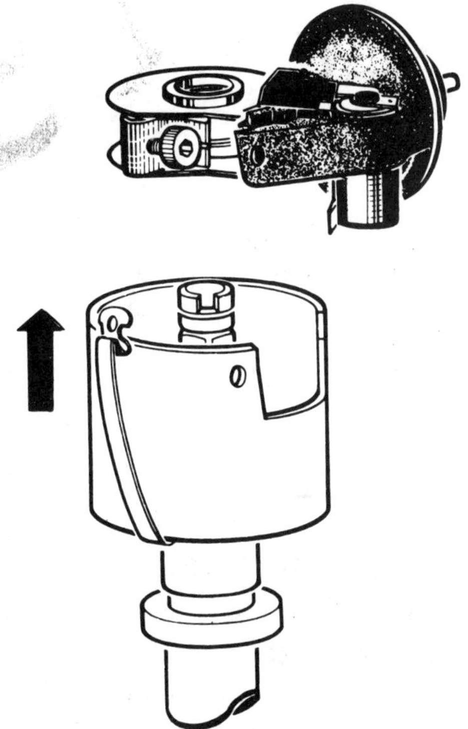

Fig. 14.31 Withdrawing the cassette from the distributor body (later R1152 vehicles) (Sec 7)

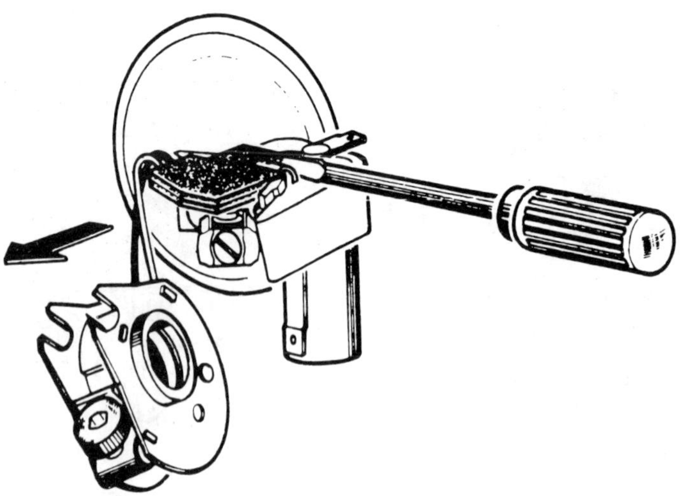

Fig. 14.32 Detaching the cassette electrical connector (later R1152 vehicles) (Sec 7)

7 New cassettes are preset by the manufacturer and require no further adjustment. Fig. 14.33 shows details of fitting the cassette. Take care when fitting the cassette over the cam, to make sure that the contact heel is not damaged by coming into contact with the apex of a cam. When refitting the rotor arm, ensure that it is fully home in the drive spindle and that the complete cassette/condenser assembly is fully home in the distributor body. Recheck all electrical connections after assembly. Reset the initial ignition timing.

Dwell angle and percentage adjustment (cassette type points)

8 Making this adjustment is simply a matter of inserting a 3 mm Allen key through the distributor body and into the adjuster

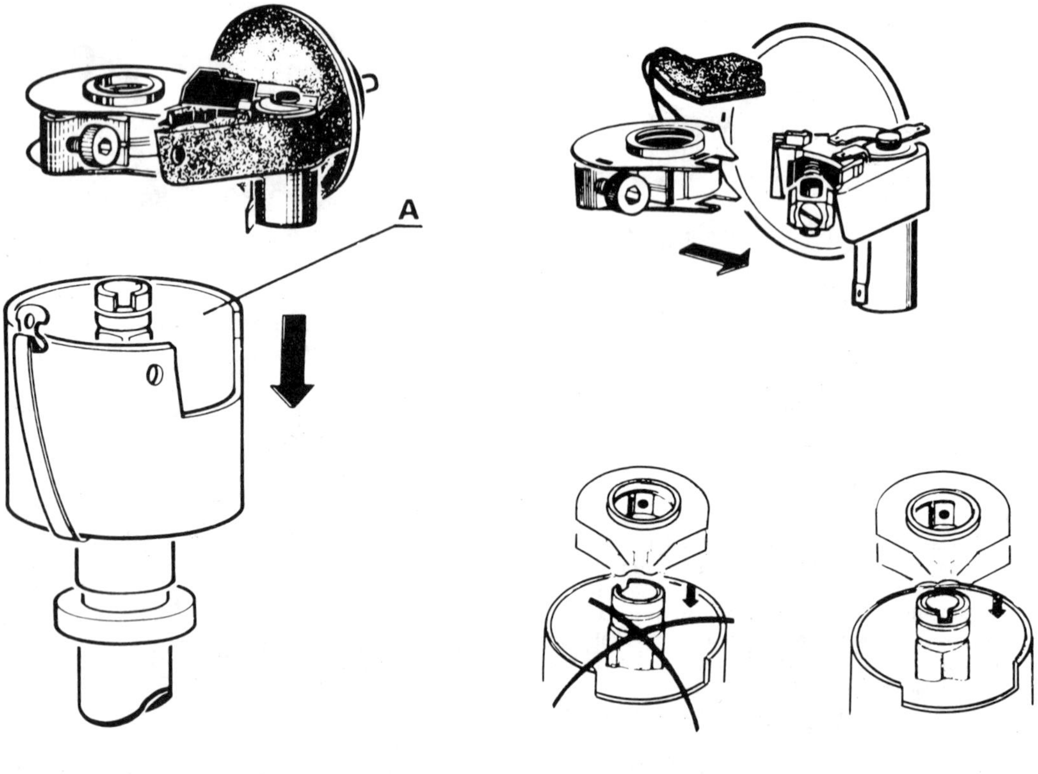

Fig. 14.33 Fitting a replacement cassette (later R1152 vehicles) (Sec 7)

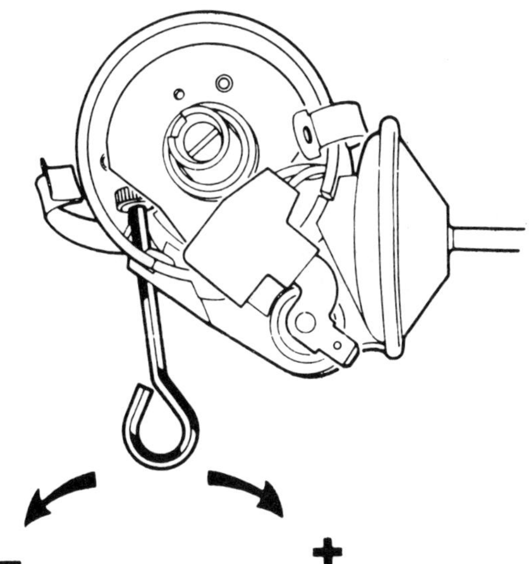

Fig. 14.34 Dwell angle and percentage adjustment (later R1152 vehicles) (Sec 7)

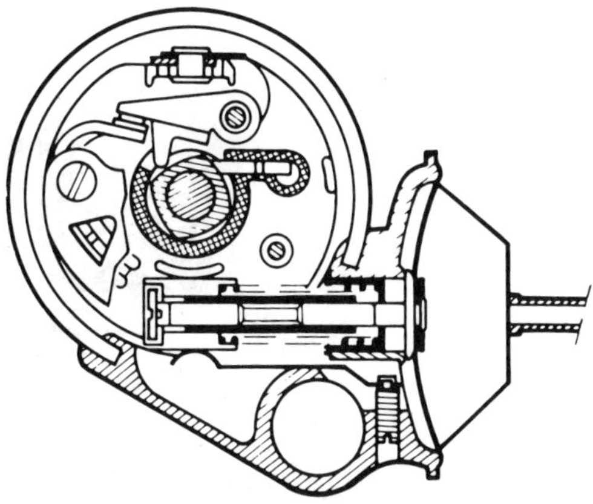

Fig. 14.36 Sectioned view of SEV-Marchal cassette type distributor (Sec 7)

screw (see Fig. 14.34) and then turning it either clockwise to increase dwell or anti-clockwise to decrease dwell. Dwell angle adjustment can be carried out with the engine idling.

SEV-Marchal cassette type distributor

9 By comparing the exploded views of both distributors, it will be seen that the Marchal distributor bears some resemblance to that type fitted to later R1152 vehicles. Changing the cassette is therefore a similar operation to that previously described, although the figures which accompany this text show the detail differences and points to note.

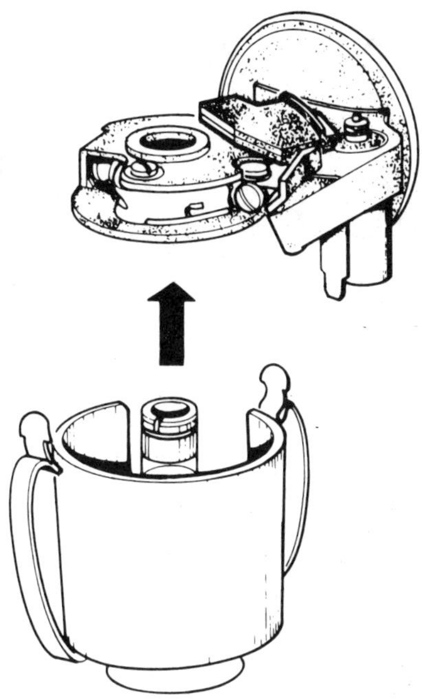

Fig. 14.37 Withdrawing the cassette from the distributor body (SEV-Marchal) (Sec 7)

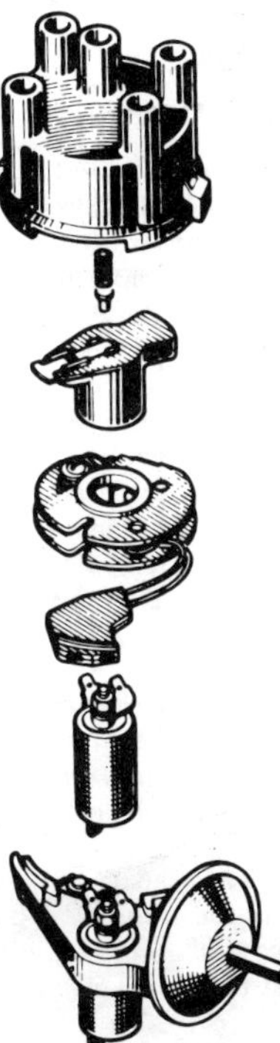

Fig. 14.35 Exploded view of SEV-Marchal cassette type distributor (Sec 7)

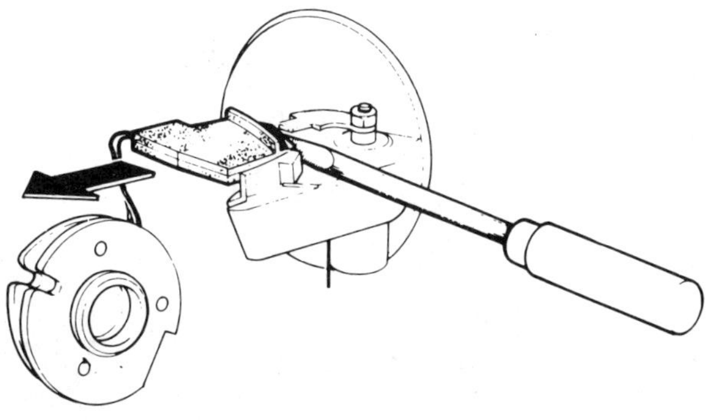

Fig. 14.38 Detaching the cassette electrical connector (SEV-Marchal) (Sec 7)

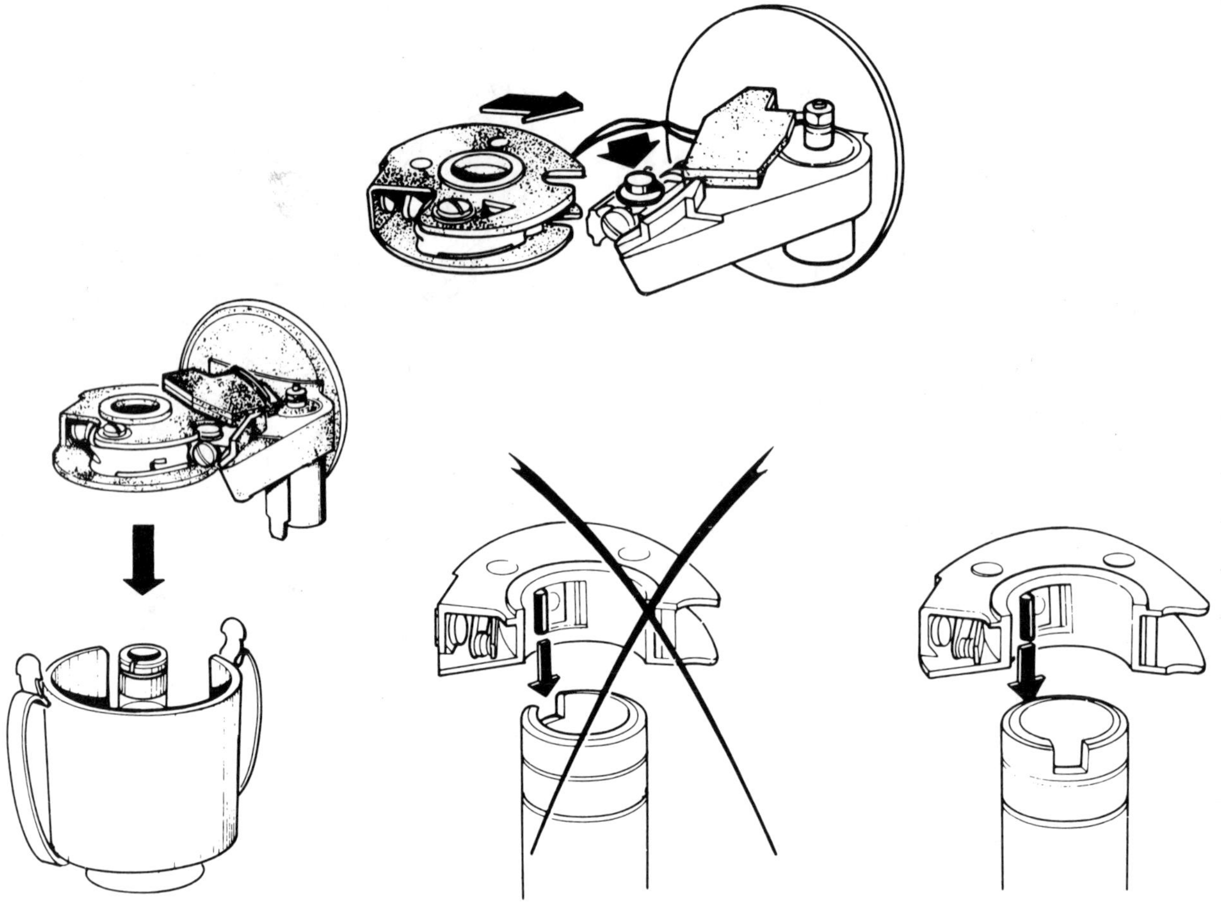

Fig. 14.39 Fitting a replacement cassette (SEV-Marchal) (Sec 7)

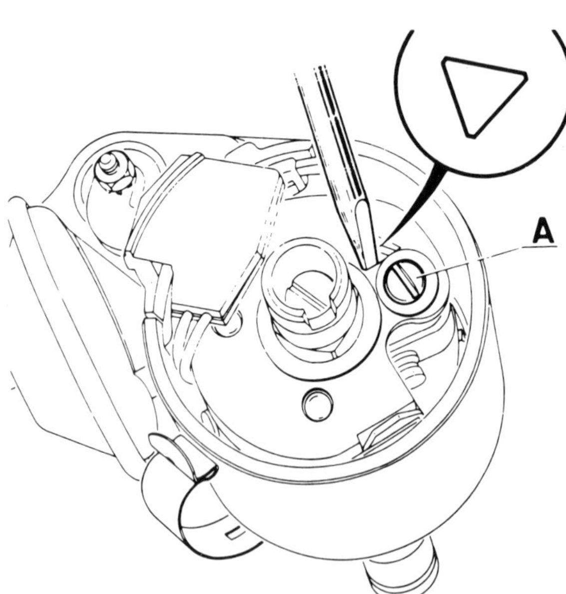

Fig. 14.40 Adjusting the contact breaker points (SEV-Marchal) (Sec 7)

10 Fig. 14.40 shows the method of contact breaker point adjustment. Do not loosen the screw A; simply insert the flat of a small screwdriver into the triangular cutout shown and turn the screwdriver to effect adjustment.

8 Clutch

1 Later models have a clutch assembly which does not have a withdrawal pad thrust plate; a sectional view of this type is shown in Fig. 14.41. The type of clutch is identified by a number stamped on the clutch plate face, and the differences between the two main types are shown in Fig. 14.42.

Withdrawal pad - changing

2 Unhook the springs on the withdrawal pad and fork (arrowed in Fig. 14.43), then remove the withdrawal pad.
3 Lubricate the withdrawal pad guide, the fork fingers and the area of the diaphragm with which the pad makes contact, using Molykote BR2 grease.
4 Fit the new withdrawal pad and spring, fitting the ends of the spring into the holes in the withdrawal pad carrier and fork.
5 After the gearbox and transmission has been refitted, it will be necessary to adjust the clutch clearance.

Clutch fork - changing

6 Remove the withdrawal pad and use a suitable extractor, or Renault tool EMB 384 to extract the two fork retaining pins. On this model of clutch the pins are splined and shouldered.

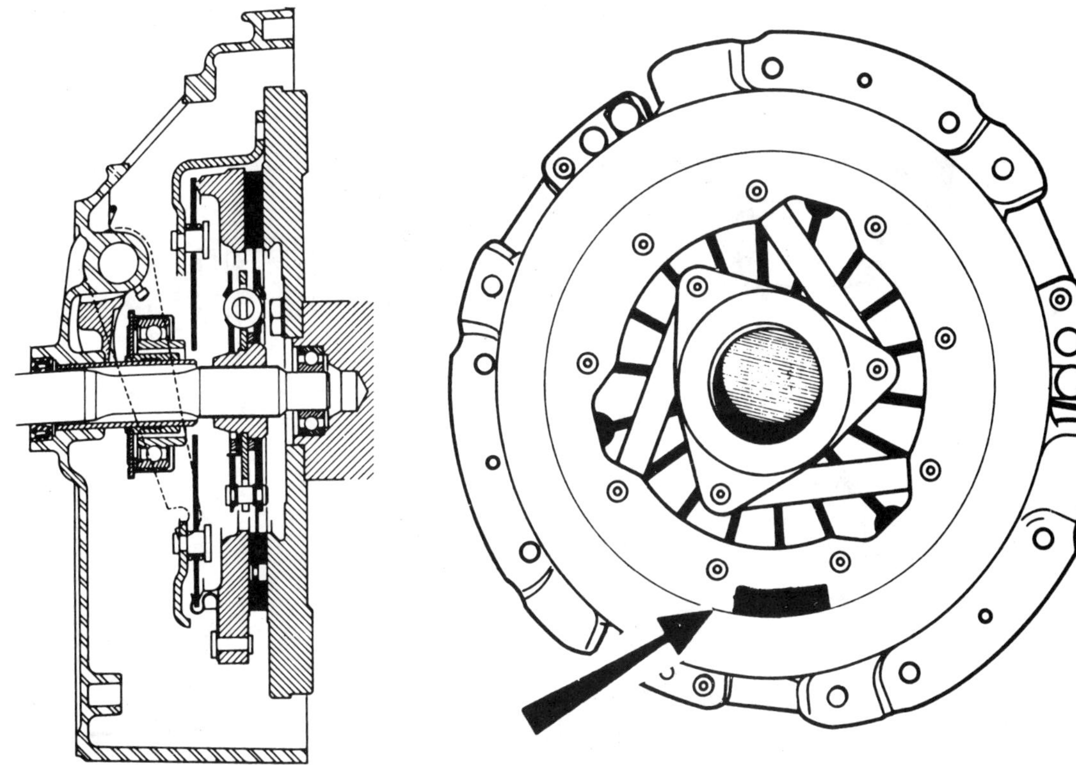

Fig. 14.41 Clutch assembly without thrust withdrawal plate (sectioned view) (Sec 8)

Fig. 14.42 Location of clutch type reference (arrowed) (Sec 8)

Fig. 14.43 Clutch pad retaining springs (arrowed) (Sec 8)

VEHICLE TYPE	MECHANISM	DISC	SHAFT	FLYWHEEL	WITHDRAWAL PAD
R. 1150 R. 1151 R. 1152 (1st assembly)	200 D 325 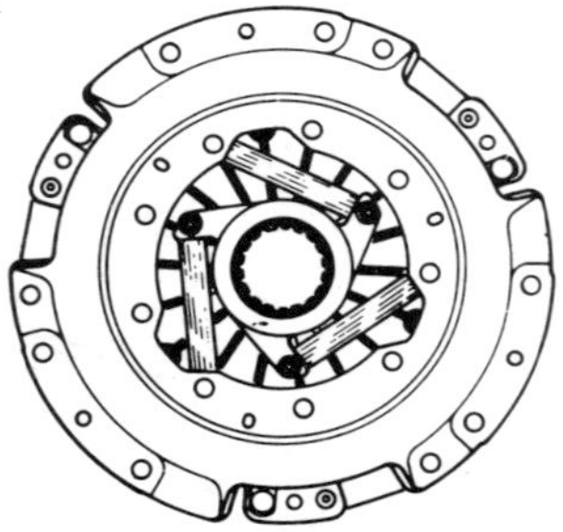	 E=7.7 mm (.304")	L=139.5 mm (5-1/2") A=249 mm (9-51/64") 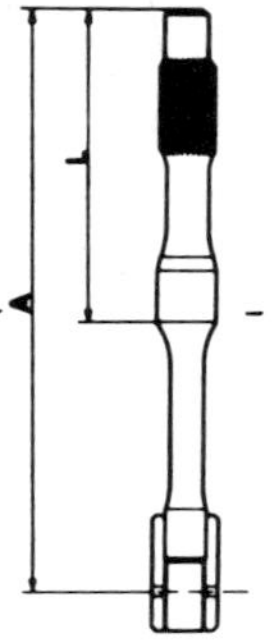	 C = 17.5 mm (.689")	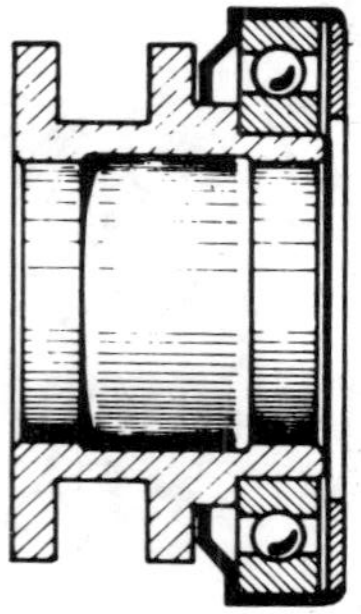
R. 1151 R. 1152 (2nd assembly) R 1156	200 DBR 325 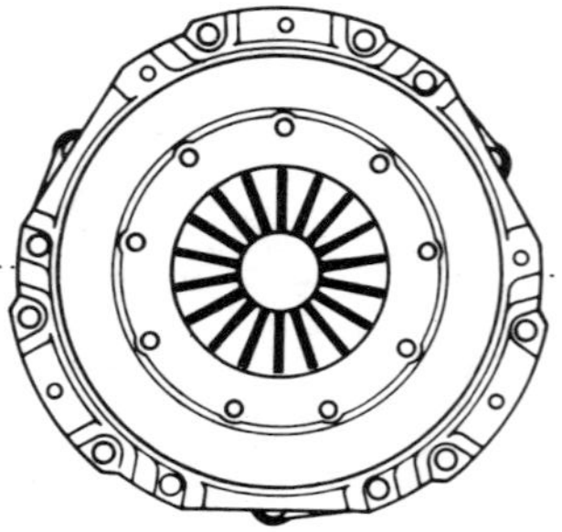 200 DBR 375	 E=7.7 mm (.304")	L=146.5 mm (5-25/32") A=249 mm (9-51/64")	 C = 17.5 mm (.689")	

Fig. 14.44 Clutch identification (Sec 8)

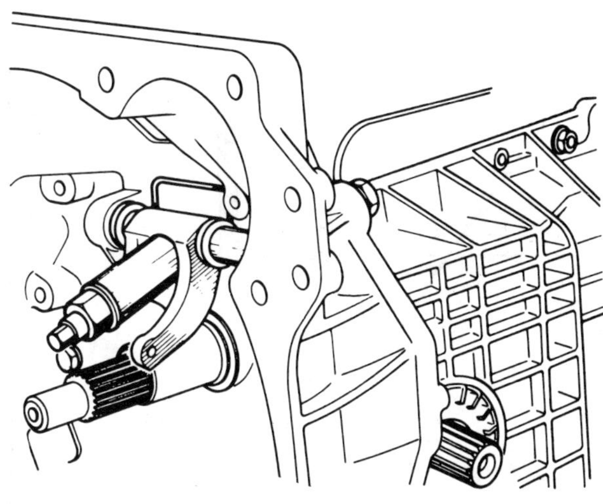

Fig. 14.45 Extracting the clutch fork pins (Sec 8)

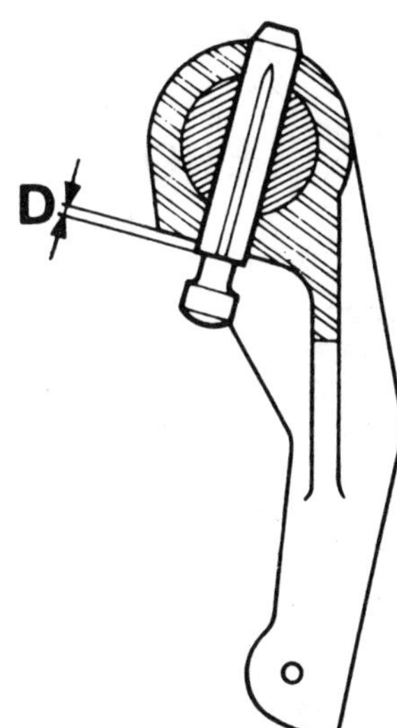

Fig. 14.46 Correct insertion of clutch fork pins (Sec 8)

D 0.04 in (1 mm)

7 After the pins have been removed, withdraw the fork shaft, and lift out the fork and spring.
8 Before refitting the fork, lubricate the fork shaft with Molykote BR2 grease.
9 Position the fork and spring, and then slide the shaft into place.
10 Line-up the holes in the fork and the shaft. Insert the pins and drive them in until dimension D (Fig. 14.46) is 0.04 in (1 mm).
11 After the gearbox and transmission have been refitted, it will be necessary to adjust the clutch clearance.

9 Manual gearbox

BV 385 type (five-speed) - dismantling and reassembly

1 When dismantling, adjusting and reassembling the five-speed BV 385 gearbox, follow the instructions given for the type 336 gearbox in Chapter 6, adding the following for the 5th gear assembly.

Dismantling

2 Select neutral and then remove the plug, spring and ball of the fifth speed locking mechanism (Fig. 14.50).
3 Remove the plug, plunger and locking ball between the 3rd speed shaft and the 4th/5th speed shaft.
4 Unscrew and remove the eight gearbox front housing bolts and lift the front housing off.
5 Lock the geartrain by selecting two speeds (5th, and either 3rd or 4th).
6 Unlock the nuts of the 5th speed gear synchro hub and the speedometer drive, and remove them.
7 Put mating marks on the 5th speed sliding gear and its hub.
8 Remove the circlip from the end of the reverse gear shaft and then take off the 5th speed synchro assembly, the 5th speed fork, 5th speed gear and the spacer plate.

Reassembly

9 When refitting the synchro springs, ensure that they are facing opposite ways and clip the bent end of each spring into the same slot.
10 Fit the circlip and ensure that it is fully home in its groove.
11 After reassembling and refitting the synchro hub, ensure that the synchro ring is hard against the synchro cone and that the pinion is hard up against the hub.
12 Check the clearance between the 5th speed synchro ring and the hub endface (dimension J in Fig. 14.54), which should be 0.008 in (0.2 mm).

BV 336 and 385 types - all 1978 vehicles

Fitting

13 Before fitting a new or service exchange gearbox to a vehicle equipped with air conditioning, check that both holes indicated in Fig. 14.55 are drilled to 0.354 in (9 mm) diameter. If necessary, carefully drill them to the correct diameter.

Differential ring nut sealing

14 Before obtaining replacement differential ring nut seals, check to determine if the seals have been modified to improve efficiency. Any modifications will have led to the gearbox having a new identification suffix number, see the following table.

Vehicle type	Suffix change
R1156 - no air conditioning	385 - 04 to 385 - 26
	385 - 08 to 385 - 30
	385 - 05 to 385 - 27
	385 - 20 to 385 - 32
R1156 - with air conditioning	385 - 06 to 385 - 28
	385 - 09 to 385 - 31
R1156 - Sweden	336 - 18 to 336 - 107
R1152	336 - 89 to 336 - 109
	336 - 00 to 336 - 100
	336 - 19 to 336 - 108
	336 - 05 to 336 - 103
	336 - 04 to 336 - 102
	336 - 09 to 336 - 104
	336 - 01 to 336 - 101
R1157	336 - 89 to 336 - 109
	336 - 96 to 336 - 110
	336 - 97 to 336 - 111

15 Reference to Fig. 14.56 will show the modified sealing arrangement with the O-ring on the nut outer periphery, the felt on the nut outer face and the lip type seal.
16 The gearbox casing now has a contact surface for the O-ring and each nut has a groove into which the O-ring fits. Fig. 14.57 shows the difference between modified and unmodified crownwheels and driveshafts. Under no circumstances should modified and unmodified components be interchanged.

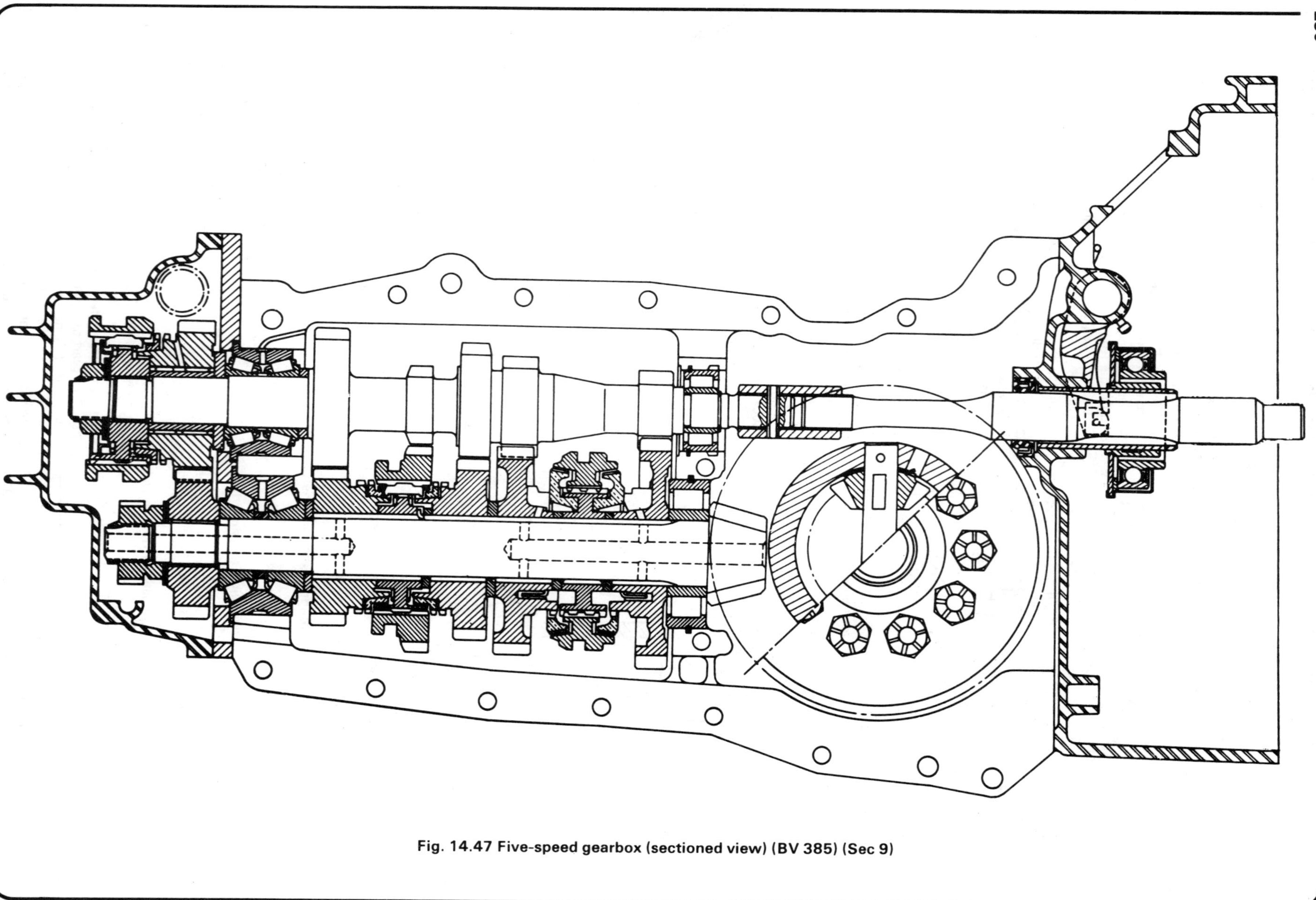

Fig. 14.47 Five-speed gearbox (sectioned view) (BV 385) (Sec 9)

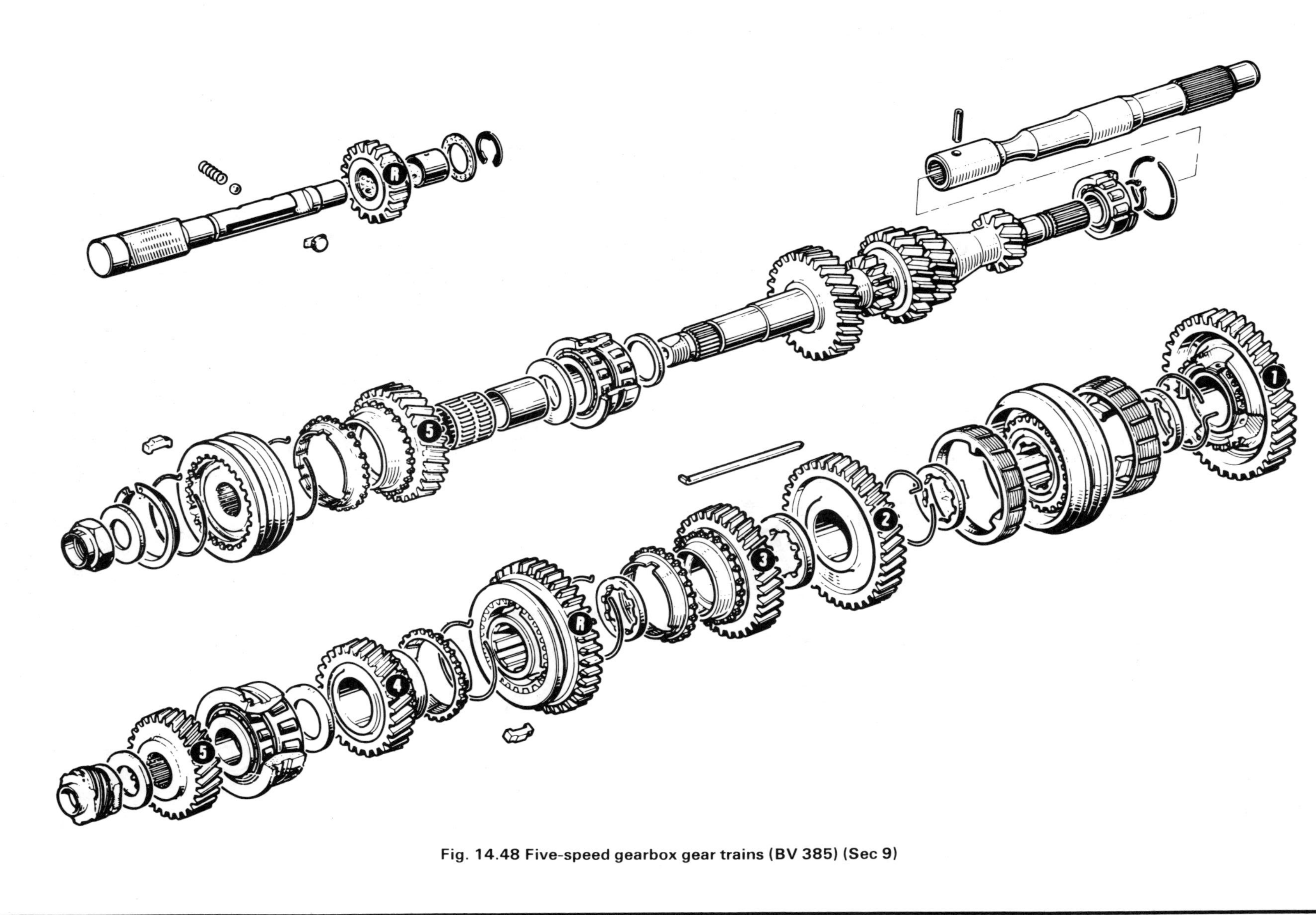

Fig. 14.48 Five-speed gearbox gear trains (BV 385) (Sec 9)

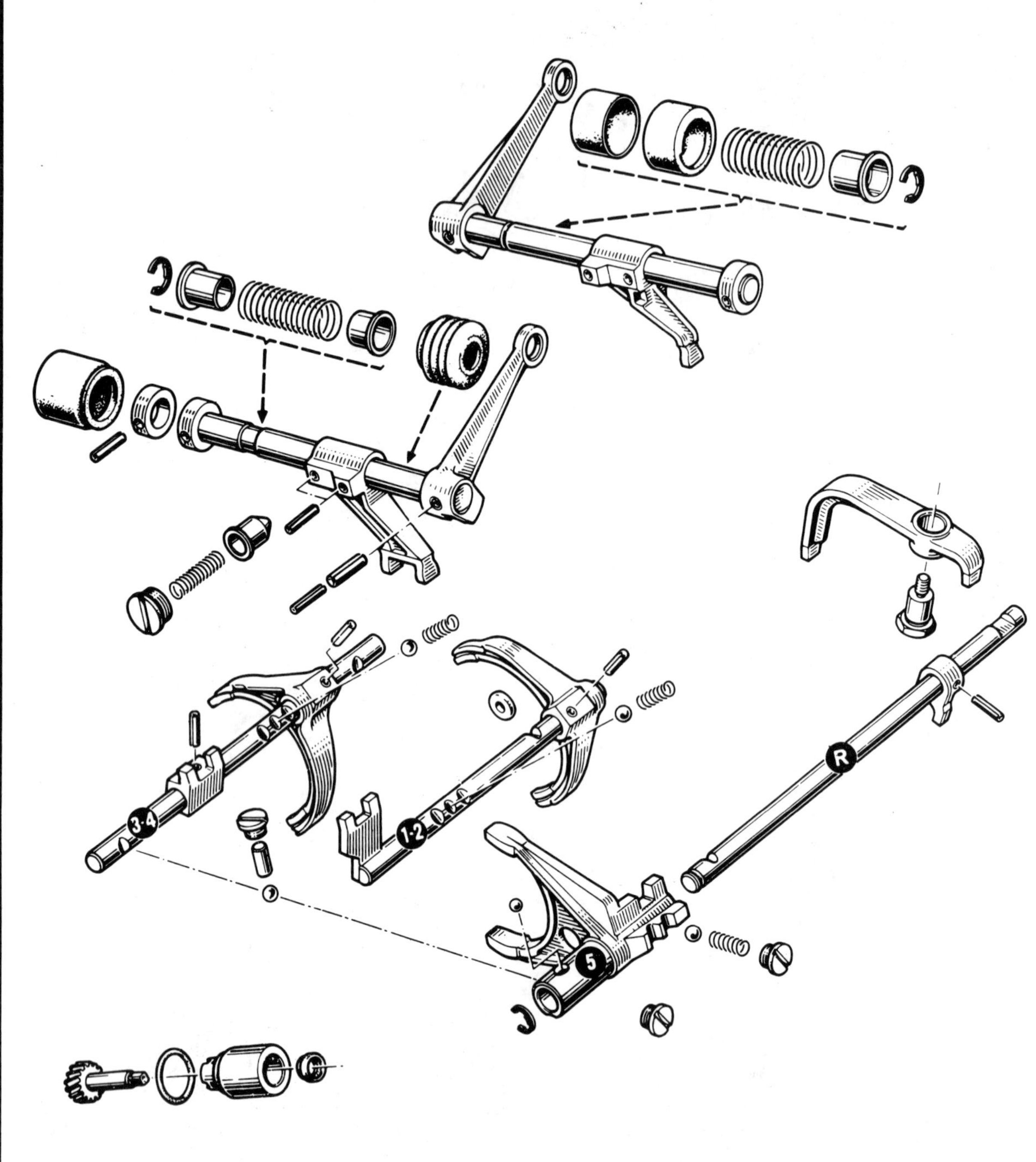

Fig. 14.49 Five-speed gearbox shift forks and rods (BV 385) (Sec 9)

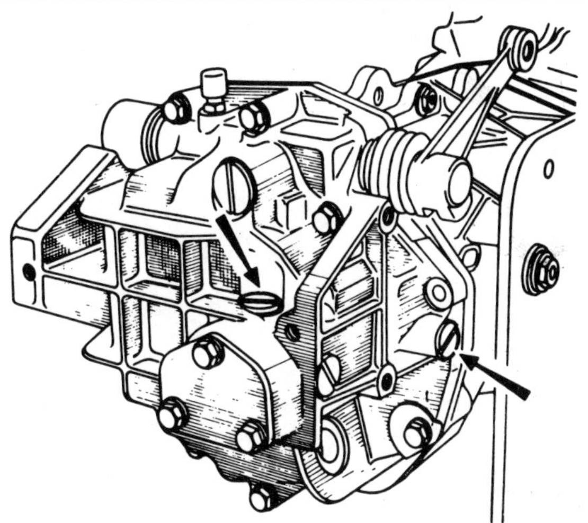

Fig. 14.50 Fifth speed locking plug (arrowed) (BV 385) (Sec 9)

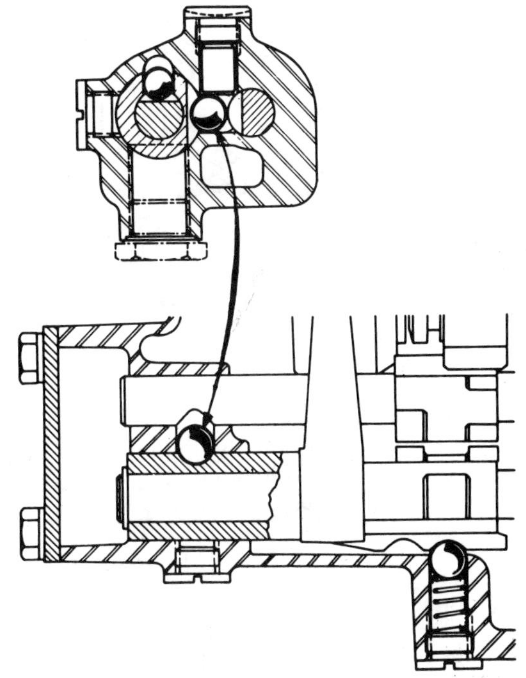

Fig. 14.51 Third and fourth/fifth-speed locking ball (sectioned view) (BV 385) (Sec 9)

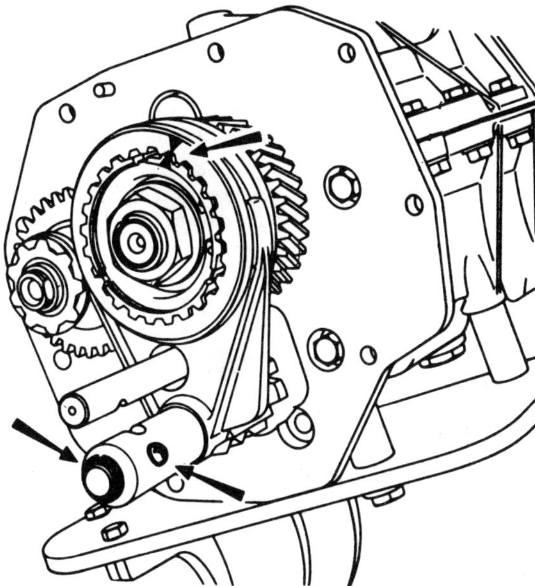

Fig. 14.52 Fifth speed synchro and reverse gear shaft (arrowed) (BV 385) (Sec 9)

Fig. 14.53 Correct positions of synchro springs (BV 385) (Sec 9)

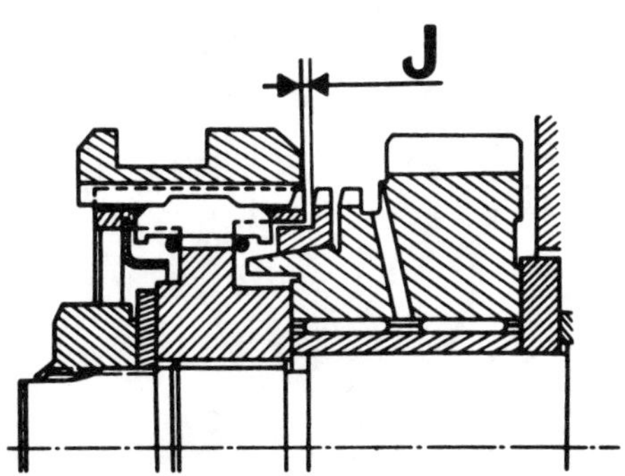

Fig. 14.54 Fifth speed synchro clearance (sectioned view) (BV 385) (Sec 9)

J 0.008 in (0.2 mm)

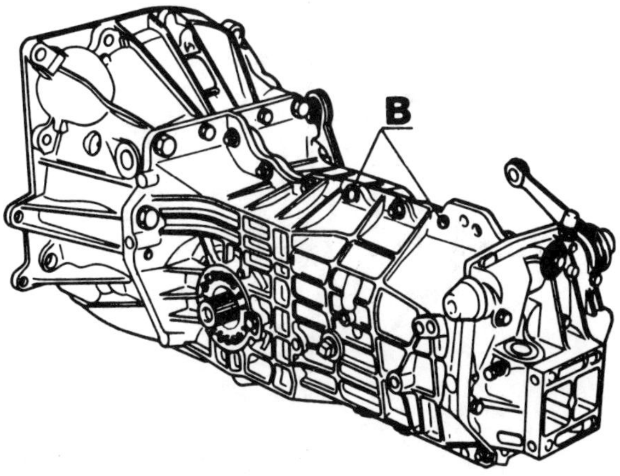

Fig. 14.55 Check hole dimensions before fitting gearbox (BV 336 and 385, 1978 vehicles) (Sec 9)

B Holes – 0.354 in (9 mm) diameter

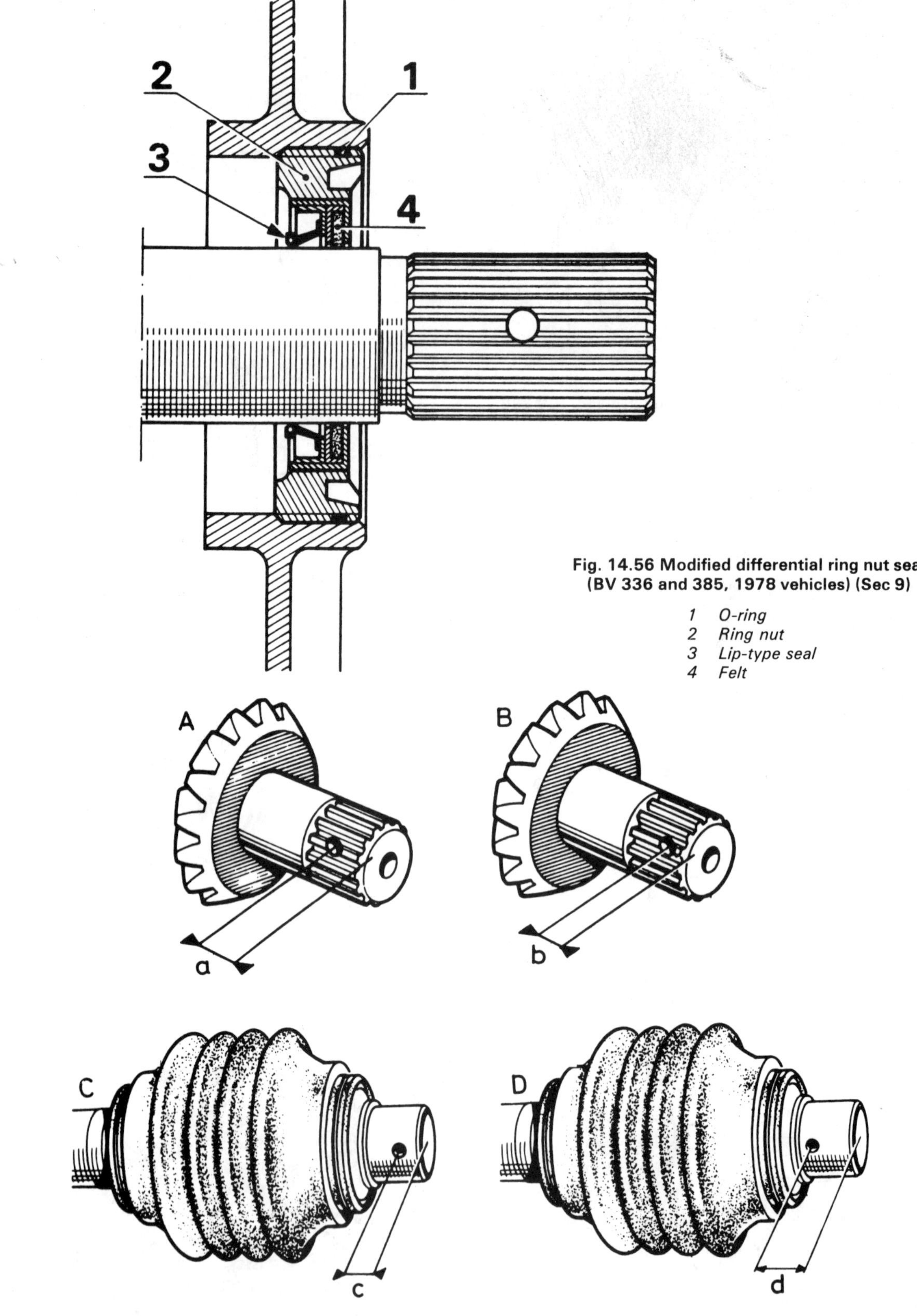

Fig. 14.56 Modified differential ring nut seal (BV 336 and 385, 1978 vehicles) (Sec 9)

1 O-ring
2 Ring nut
3 Lip-type seal
4 Felt

Fig. 14.57 Differences in sunwheel and driveshaft types (Sec 9)

A 1st pattern sunwheel
B 2nd pattern sunwheel (modified sealing)
C 1st pattern driveshaft
D 2nd pattern driveshaft (modified sealing)
a 0.78 in (20 mm)
b 0.63 in (16 mm)
c 0.75 in (19.25 mm)
d 0.91 in (23.25 mm)

BV336 and 385 types - later vehicles

Removal

17 **Warning:** *On vehicles fitted with air conditioning, under no circumstances disconnect the refrigeration circuit pipes to facilitate gearbox removal.*

18 The procedure given in paragraph 21, Section 2, Chapter 6, for disconnection of the driveshafts is not applicable to later vehicles because there is insufficient clearance to enable sideways movement of the gearbox. Instead, refer to the appropriate Chapters and carry out the following procedure.

19 Detach each front brake caliper from its mounting. Disconnect each steering arm at its rack end connection. Disconnect the suspension upper balljoints; using Renault tool T Av 476 if necessary. Tilt the stub axle carriers to allow withdrawal of the driveshafts from the crownwheels.

20 Remember to support the vehicle correctly before carrying out the above work. Refer to the Section on Jacking and Towing and do not take risks.

10 Automatic transmission

Oil cooler fitment

1 It is advisable to fit an oil cooler to any vehicle with automatic transmission which is to be used for towing. The following table gives the recommended maximum all-up weights which can be towed by a vehicle equipped with an oil cooler. Any attempt to tow loads greater than those recommended will result in damage to the transmission.

Vehicle type	Unbraked trailer		Braked trailer	
	No cooler	*Cooler fitted*	*No cooler*	*Cooler fitted*
R1153, R1154	992 lb (450 kg)	1102 lb (500 kg)	992 lb (450 kg)	2310 lb (1050 kg)
R1155, R1156	992 lb (450kg)	1102 lb (500 kg)	992 lb (450 kg)	2403 lb (1090 kg)

2 Oil cooler kits are available from your Renault dealer. There are two types: the first is supplied for vehicles without air conditioning and the second is supplied for vehicles with air conditioning although it will eventually supersede the first type. The component parts of each assembly are shown in Figs. 14.58 and 14.59.

3 If the second type of oil cooler is to be fitted and the vehicle type is R1153 or R1154, then locate the transmission identification plate (see the Section 'Vehicle Identification Numbers' at the front of this manual) and compare the number found with those in the following table:

-4139-00 Nos 1 to 5917
-4139-02 Nos 1 to 0580
-4139-10 Nos 1 to 7349
-4139-11 Nos 1 to 1225

4 If the transmission number is one of those listed, then it is necessary to obtain an additional valve and seal. Reference to Fig. 14.60 will show the **fitted** position of the plug which must be removed to allow fitting of the valve and seal.

5 With the battery disconnected, the transmission drained of oil and the spare wheel removed, refer to Fig. 14.61 and remove the two plugs from the transmission unit. Replace the lower plug with the union and the upper plug with the valve. With the valve pipe horizontal, tighten the valve body to a torque loading of 26 lbf ft (35 Nm).

6 Fig. 14.62 shows the fitted position of the radiator on the left-hand inner wing panel. Two 0.275 in (7 mm) holes must be drilled to allow insertion of the radiator fixing cage nuts.

7 Remove one of the top securing bolts from the transmission casing and fit the pipe support bracket (2). Route the pipe (3) from the radiator top connection to the transmission valve (C). Route the second pipe (4) from the radiator button connection to the transmission union. Push both pipes into their support bracket.

8 When connecting the pipes, check that they are pushed well onto the unions. Align the pipe clips as shown in Fig. 14.63 before tightening them. Where the vehicle has air conditioning, attach the pipes to the compressor bracket with the plastic clips provided.

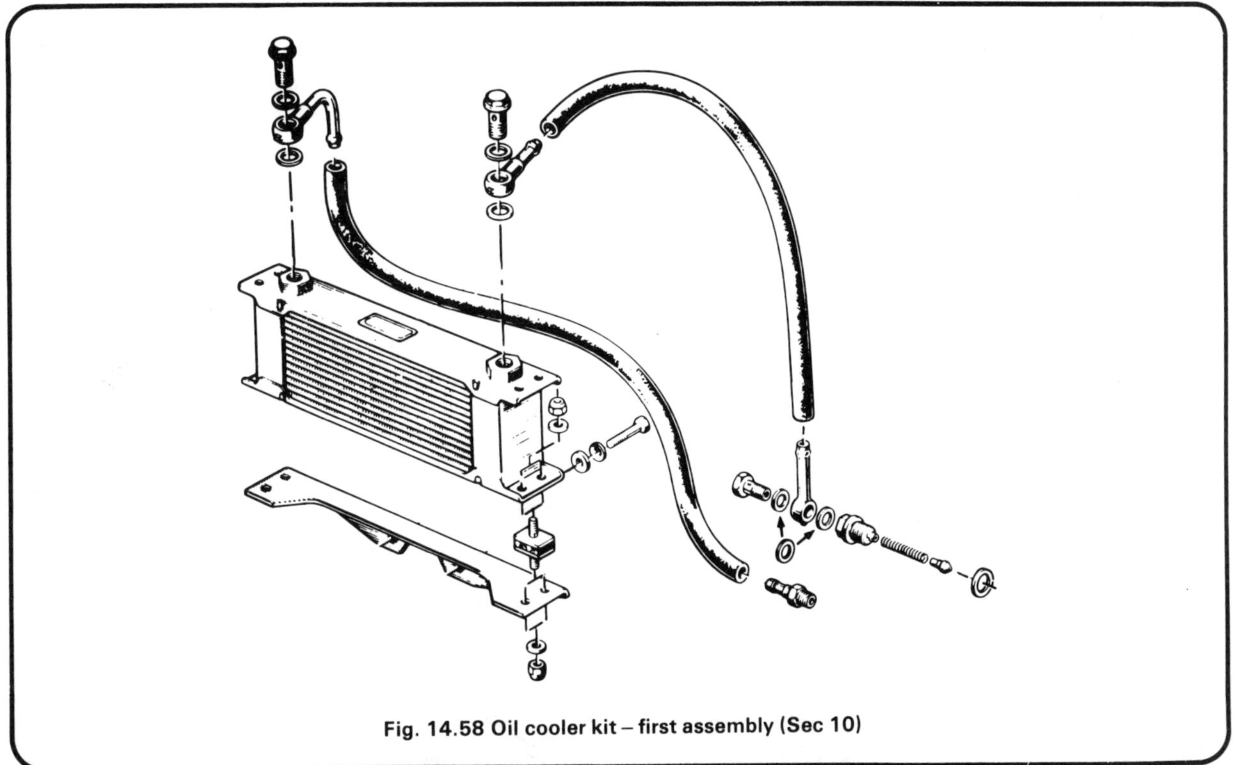

Fig. 14.58 Oil cooler kit – first assembly (Sec 10)

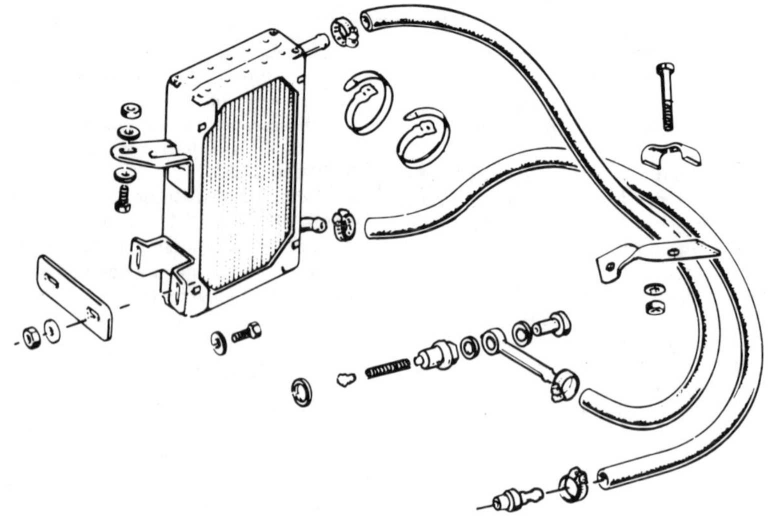

Fig. 14.59 Oil cooler kit – second assembly (Sec 10)

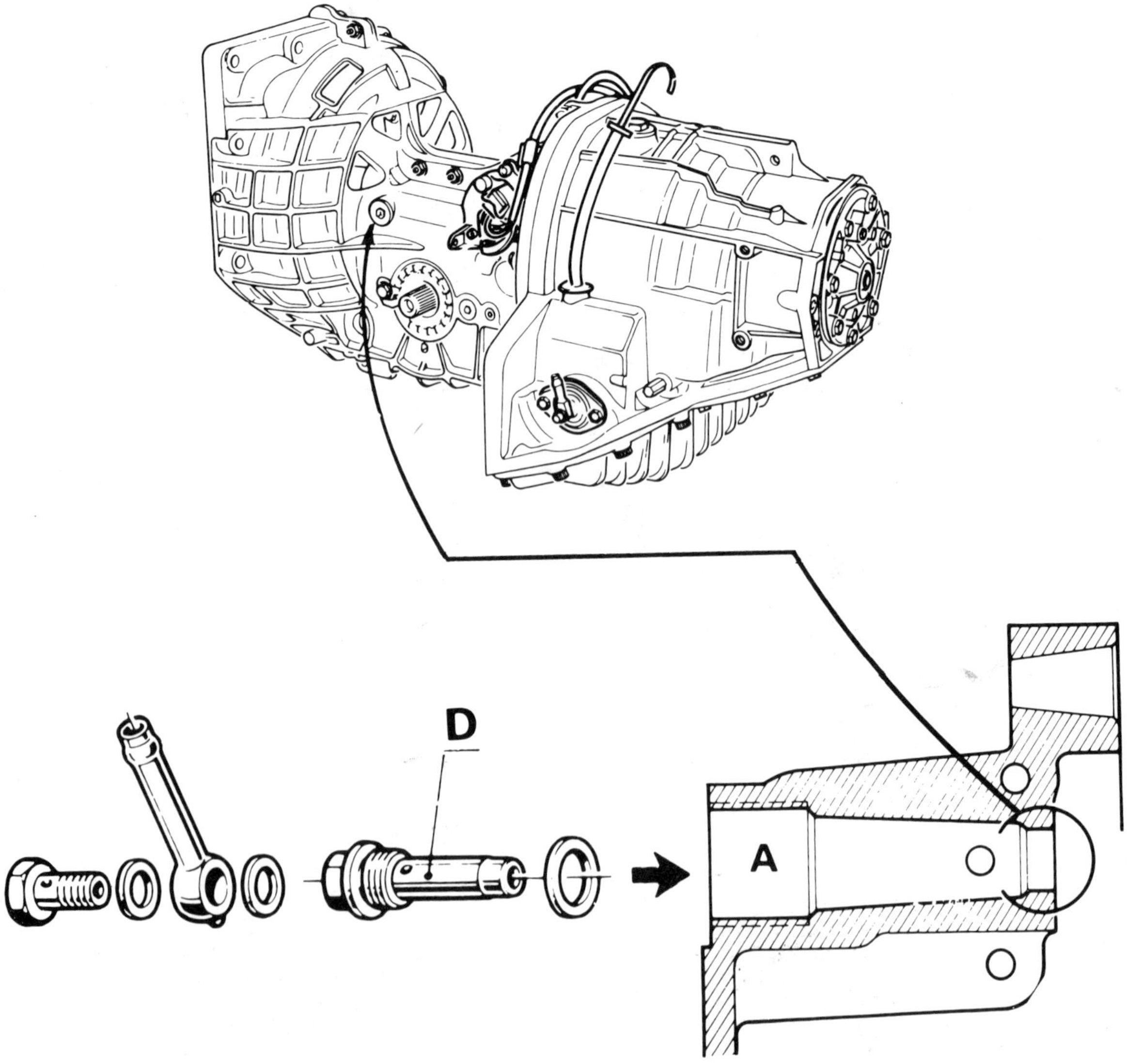

Fig. 14.60 Additional valve and seal arrangement – second assembly oil cooler (Sec 10)

A Plug *D Valve*

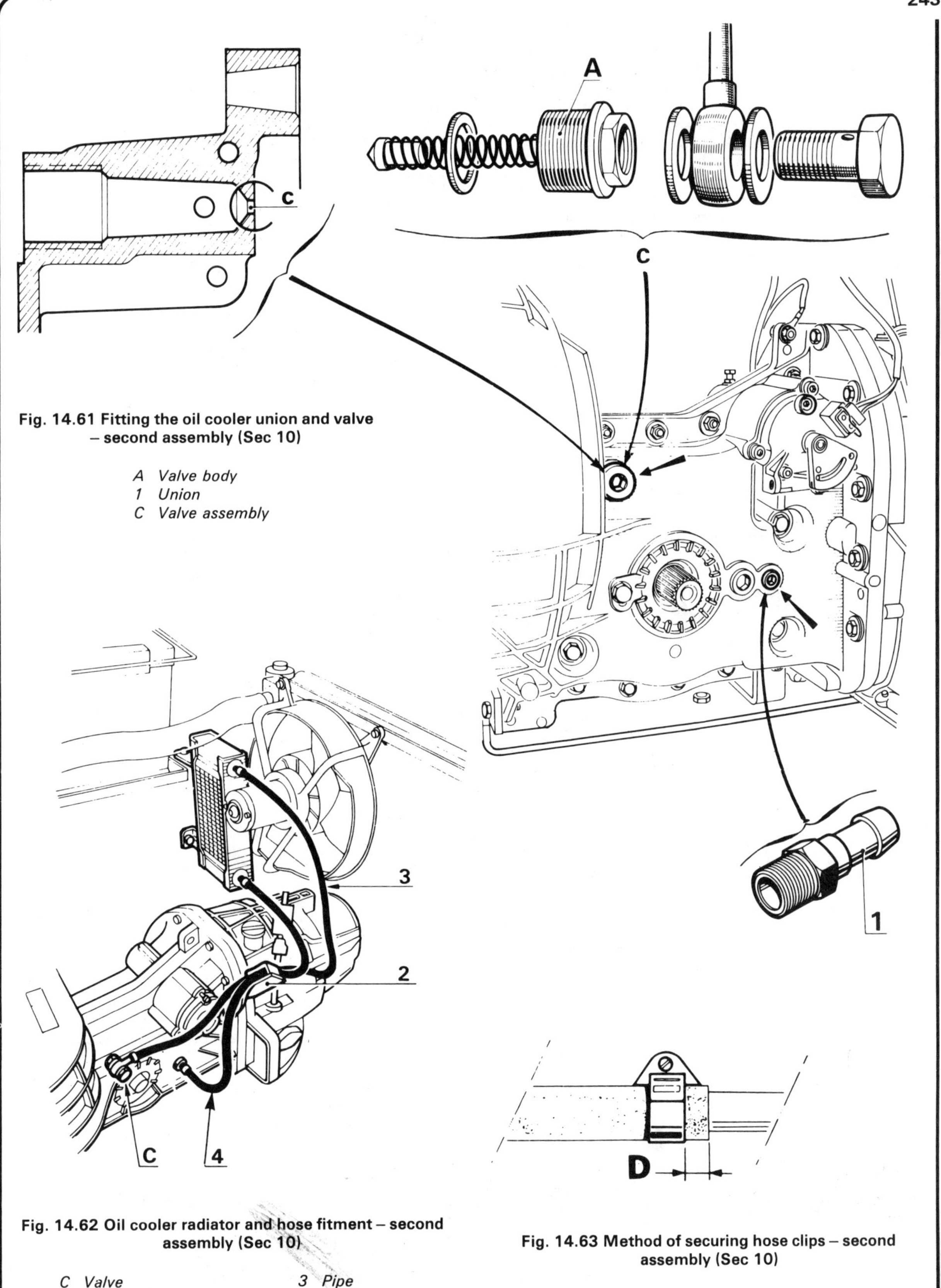

Fig. 14.61 Fitting the oil cooler union and valve – second assembly (Sec 10)

A Valve body
1 Union
C Valve assembly

Fig. 14.62 Oil cooler radiator and hose fitment – second assembly (Sec 10)

C Valve
2 Pipe support bracket
3 Pipe
4 Return pipe

Fig. 14.63 Method of securing hose clips – second assembly (Sec 10)

D 0.23 in (6 mm)

9 On completion of fitting the cooler, refer to Chapter 7, Section 3 and refill the transmission with the recommended fluid. Check for oil leaks.
10 Once fitted, the cooler should present few problems, but a check should be kept on the pipes and their connections for any signs of deterioration and leakage. Check that the pipes are not chafing on any adjacent component part.

Differential ring nut sealing

11 Full information on ring nut sealing modifications is contained in the preceding Section of this Chapter. These modifications have led to the introduction of new transmission identification suffix numbers, which are as follows:

Vehicle type	Suffix change
R1153 - RHD	4139 - 03 to 4139 - 05
R1155 - LHD	4139 - 04 to 4139 - 06
R1156 - LHD	4139 - 12 to 4139 - 16
R1156 - RHD	4139 - 13 to 4139 - 17

11 Driveshafts

Coupling interchangeability

1 There are a variety of types of coupling for both the gearbox end and the wheel end of the driveshafts. The original provision and permitted interchangeability of couplings is shown in Figs. 14.64 and 14.65.

Spider GE 86 couplings - suspension modification

2 The lower suspension arm used with the Spider GE 86 coupling is different from that used with any of the earlier types of drive shaft coupling; and the differences between the old and modified types are shown in Fig. 14.66.
3 All R1154, R1155 and R1156 vehicles have modified arms but under no circumstances must Spider GE 86 couplings be fitted to the wheel end of other models unless the vehicle has modified lower suspension arms.

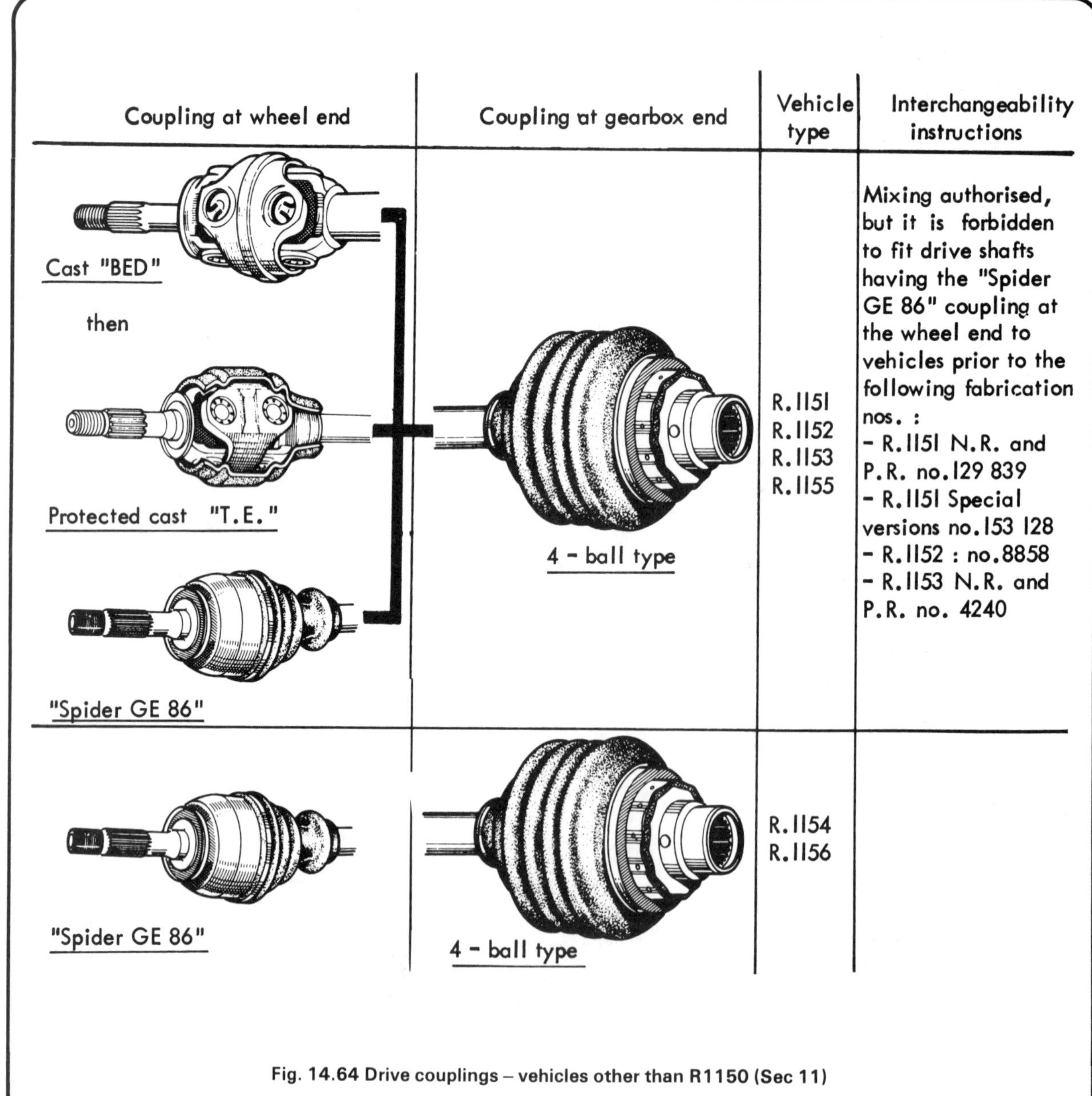

Fig. 14.64 Drive couplings – vehicles other than R1150 (Sec 11)

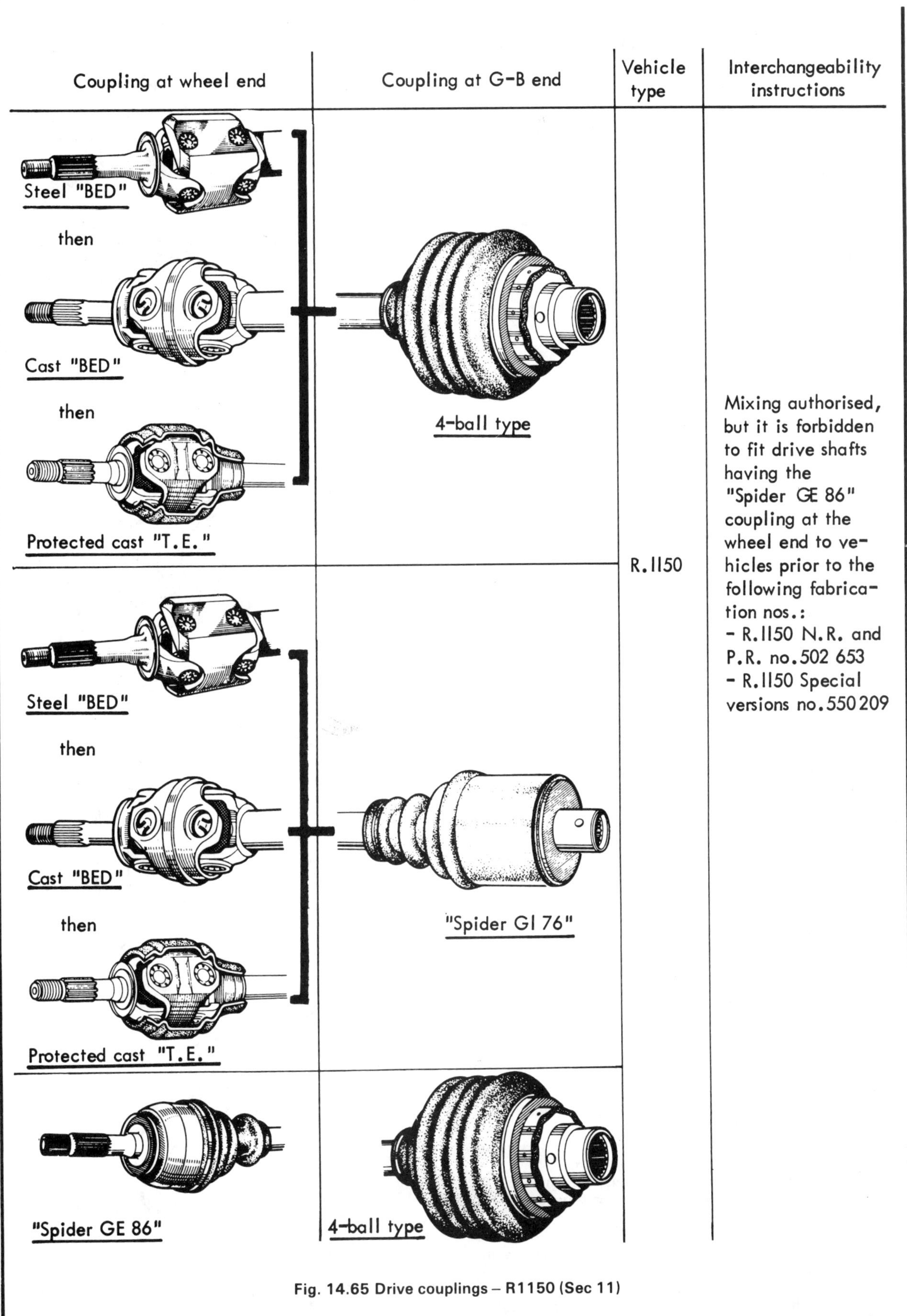

Fig. 14.65 Drive couplings – R1150 (Sec 11)

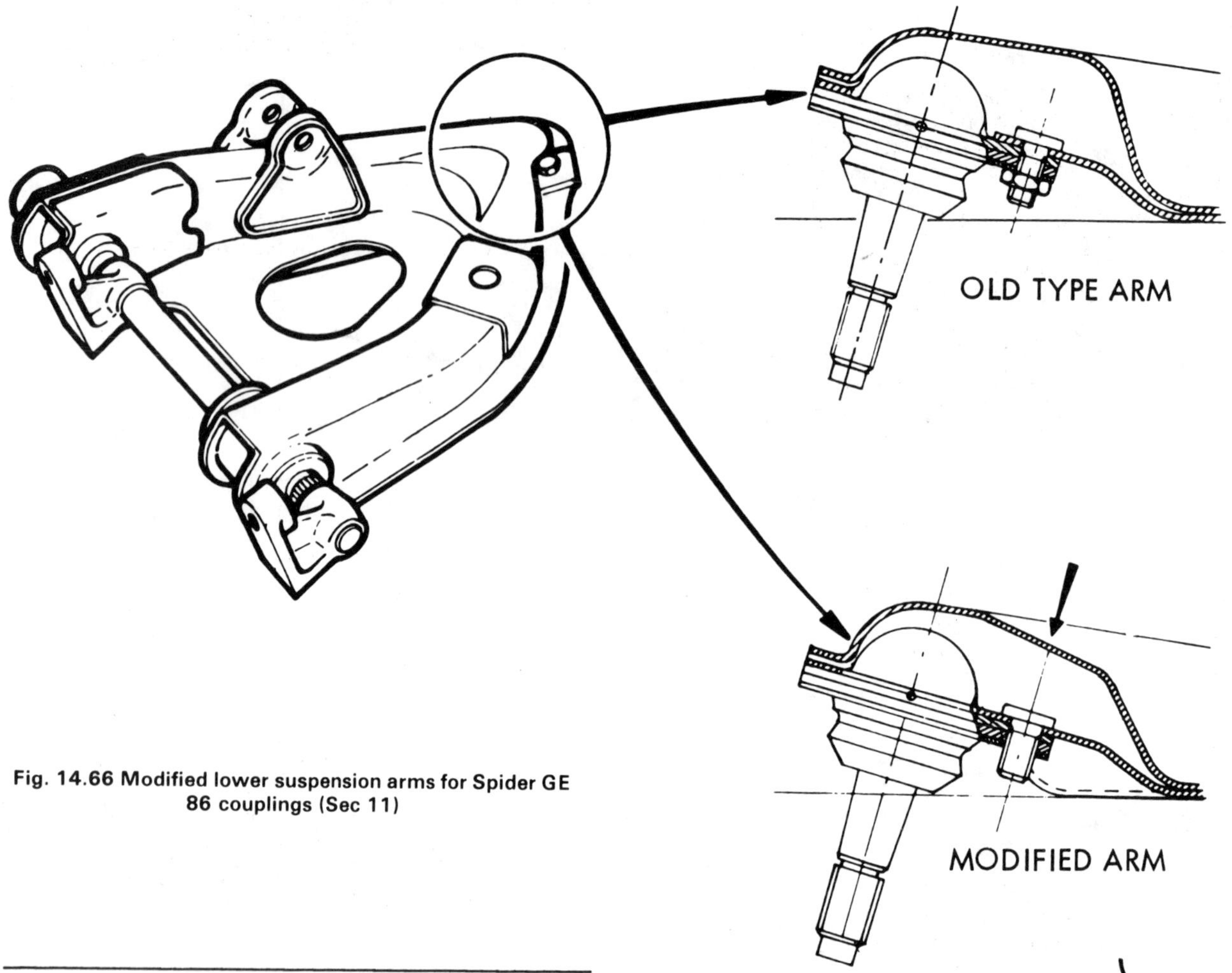

Fig. 14.66 Modified lower suspension arms for Spider GE 86 couplings (Sec 11)

12 Brakes

Rear shoes - removal and refitting (self-adjusting type)

1 Slacken off the handbrake secondary cables.

2 Remove the sealing plug from the brake backplate and use a screwdriver to push in the handbrake lever to free the stop lug resting in the shoe. This has the effect of reducing the length of the thrust link and backing-off the brake shoe.

3 Apart from these additional operations, the removal and refitting of the brake drums is the same as for manually adjusted brakes.

4 Unhook the tension spring (5) in Fig. 14.68 and remove it from the adjusting lever (C), and then remove the adjusting lever.

5 Unhook and remove the upper shoe return spring.

6 Press in the brake shoe retainers and turn each one to release it. Remove the cup, spring and pin from each retainer; then unscrew the ratchet adjuster to shorten link (B).

7 Cross the brake shoes over each other to release the tension on the bottom spring and remove the shoes by pulling them upwards (Fig. 14.70).

8 When refitting the shoes, first fit the bottom return spring to the two shoes, and cross the shoes over to fit them.

9 Before fitting the top return spring, adjust the length of the thrust link so that the brake drum can just be slipped over the shoes.

10 Position the adjusting lever parallel to the wheel cylinder so that the ratchet finger is 0.276 in (7 mm) below the centre-line of the adjusting lever.

11 Push the handbrake lever back against the shoe.

12 Check that the top and bottom return springs are hooked on correctly.

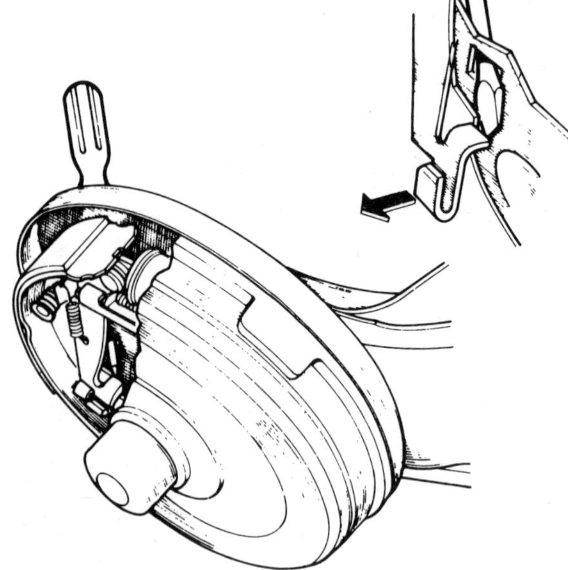

Fig. 14.67 Releasing self-adjusting rear brake shoes (Sec 12)

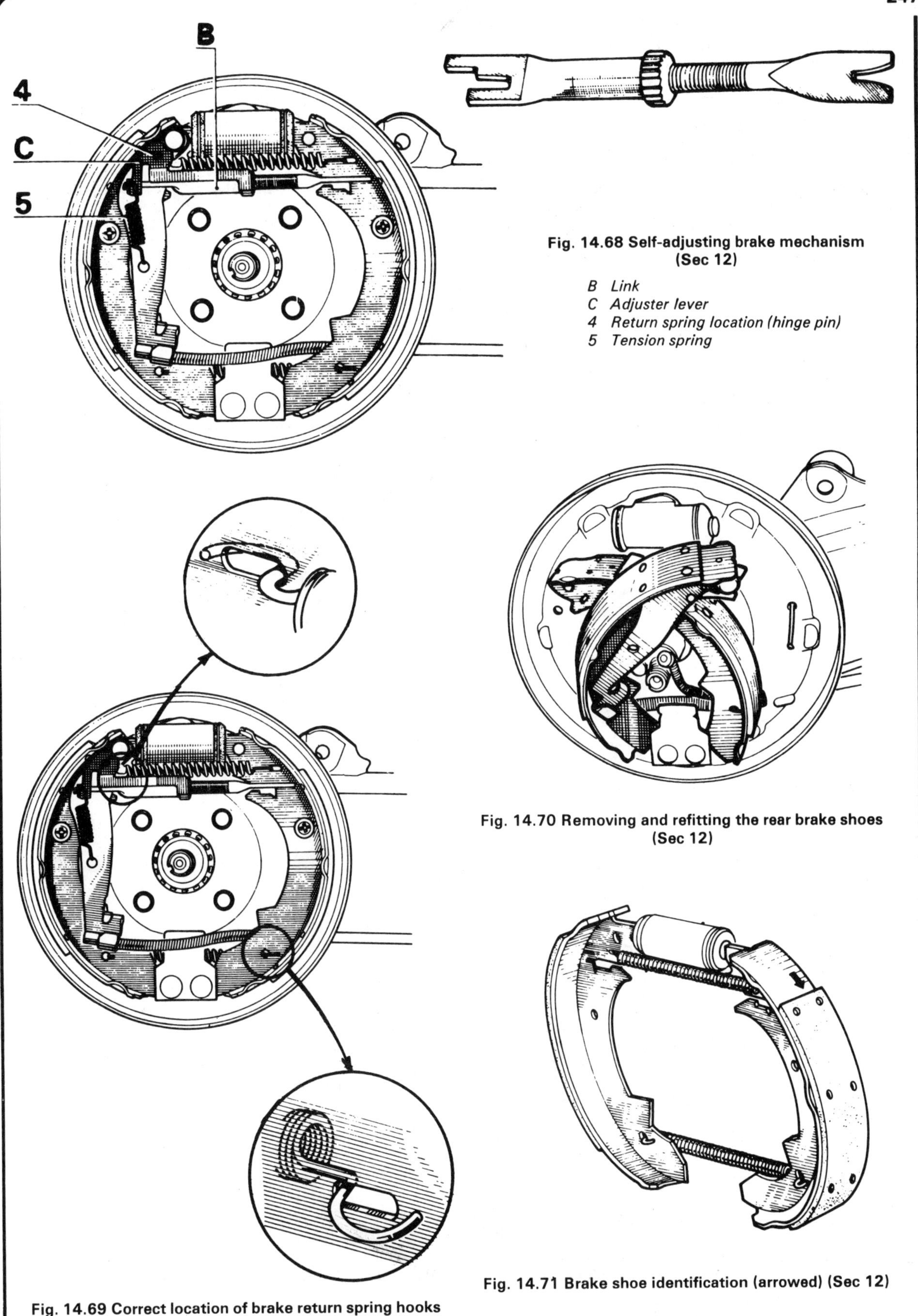

Fig. 14.68 Self-adjusting brake mechanism (Sec 12)

B Link
C Adjuster lever
4 Return spring location (hinge pin)
5 Tension spring

Fig. 14.70 Removing and refitting the rear brake shoes (Sec 12)

Fig. 14.71 Brake shoe identification (arrowed) (Sec 12)

Fig. 14.69 Correct location of brake return spring hooks (Sec 12)

Self-adjusting brakes - description and operation

13 The self-adjusting system consists of a thrust link (B) which consists of three pieces, but which is essentially a turnbuckle with a ratchet adjuster.

14 An adjusting lever (C) which is fixed to one shoe by a hinge pin (4) is also connected to the handbrake lever by a spring (5), which exerts a twisting action on the thrust link.

15 When the brake pedal is depressed, the wheel cylinder pistons travel outwards and push the shoes towards the drum. Under these conditions link (B) is no longer pressed against lever (C) and the lever moves on its hinge pin under the action of the spring.

16 This movement causes the ratchet adjuster to turn and increase the length of the thrust link.

17 If there is only a small clearance between the brake linings and the drum, the load exerted by the spring is insufficient to move the ratchet wheel adjuster and the length of the thrust link remains the same.

18 Operation of the handbrake has no effect upon the self-adjusting mechanism.

Identification of brake shoes and thrust link

19 The brake shoes of the self-adjusting brakes are *not* identical, and each one is marked with an arrow which *must point in the direction of forward rotation.*

20 The RH and LH thrust links are not interchangeable, and can be identified as follows:

	LH Brake	RH brake
Threaded pushrod	*LH thread*	*RH thread*
Adjusting thimble	*Flanged*	*Chamfered*

ICP bypass

21 Some models have an additional brake safety feature so that if there is a leak in a front wheel circuit, the pressure on the rear brakes is increased.

22 The hydraulic circuit has an additional circuit (C) in Fig. 14.72 which is connected downstream of the limiter so that it is unaffected by the limiter.

23 An additional valve in the rear brake circuit has a piston

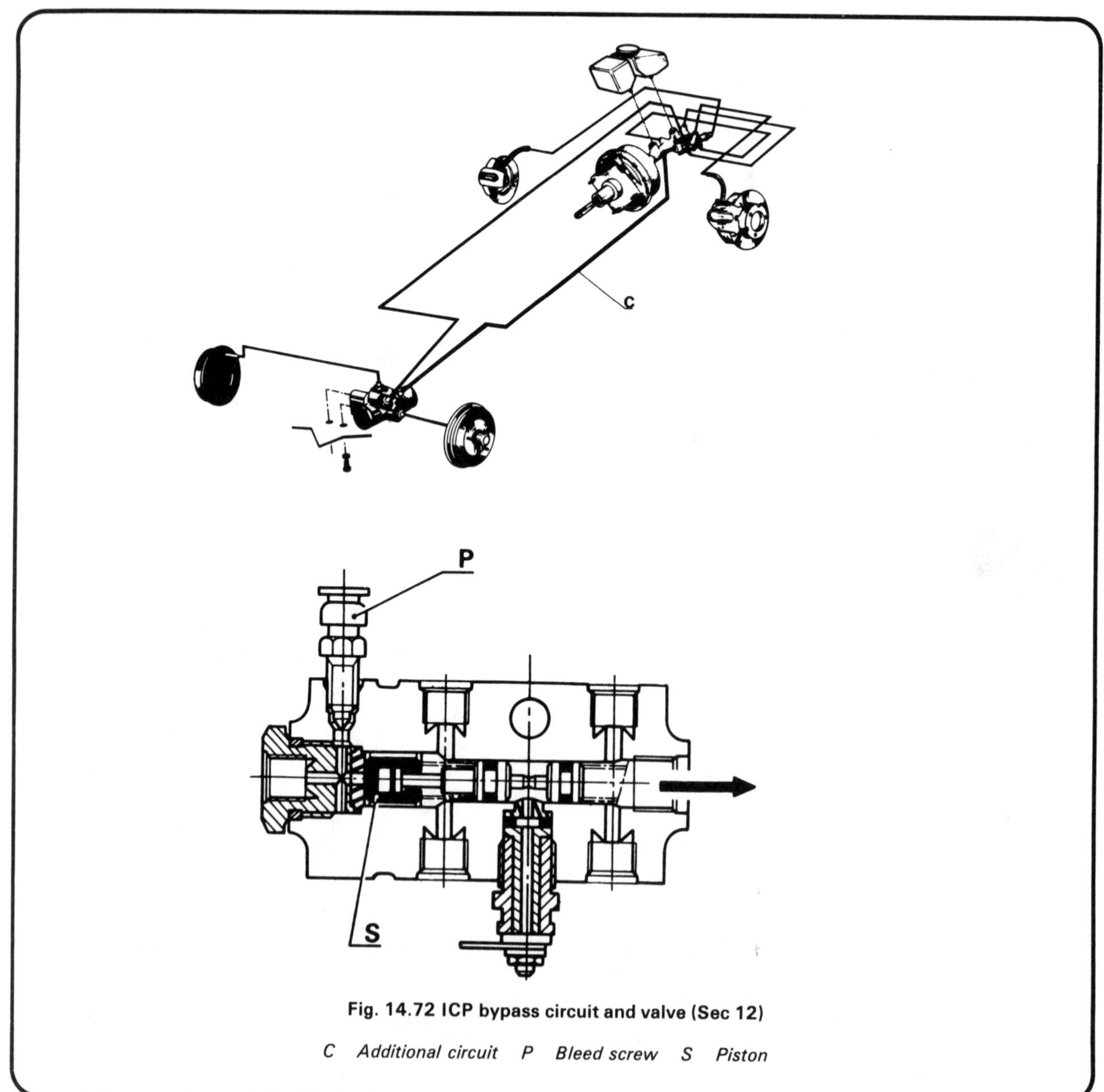

Fig. 14.72 ICP bypass circuit and valve (Sec 12)

C Additional circuit P Bleed screw S Piston

(S) which moves when the balance of pressure is disturbed. When the valve opens there is a direct feed from the master cylinder to the rear wheel cylinders.
24 The additional hydraulic circuit incorporates a bleed screw (P) and this circuit must be bled after all the four wheel cylinders on the vehicle have been bled.

Brake compensator - general

25 Brake compensators are only fitted to R1156 vehicles. The compensator is a valve to ensure that the pressure on the rear brakes is always lower than that on the front brakes.
26 The compensator does not limit the pressure on the rear brakes to any pre-determined figure, but reduces the pressure from the master cylinder to the rear brakes by an amount which varies with vehicle load.
27 The pressure distribution is controlled by a spring which is hooked to a clamp on the anti-roll bar.

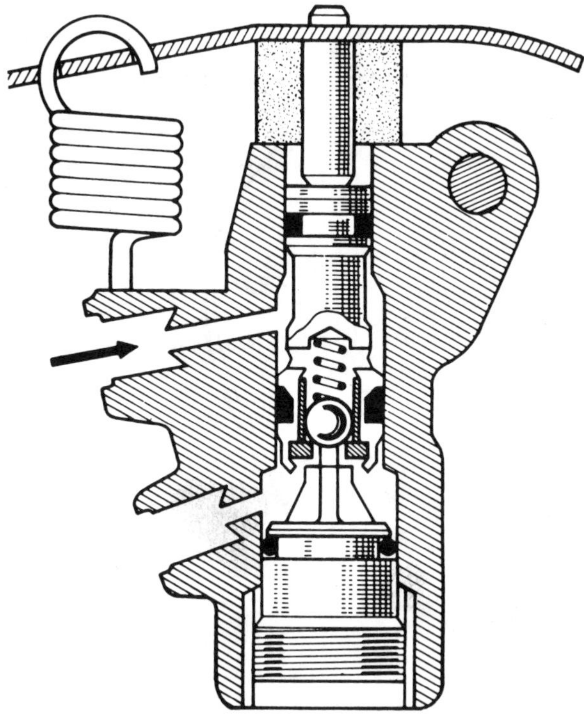

Fig. 14.73 Brake compensator (sectioned view) (Sec 12)

Brake compensator - removal and refitting

28 Unscrew the three brake unions and remove the pipes from the compensator.
29 Unhook the end of the spring from the clamp on the anti-roll bar.
30 Unscrew and remove the two bolts securing the compensator, and remove it.
31 When refitting the unit, first bolt it to its fixing bracket.
32 Connect the three pipes from the master cylinder to the compensator inlet (Fig. 14.74) and the four outlet pipes to the brake wheel cylinders.
33 With the compensating lever (2) in its rest position, the vehicle having a full fuel tank, the driver sitting in the car, the luggage compartment empty and the car having all four wheels on the ground, position the fixing sleeve.
34 Under the conditions of the previous paragraph, the sleeve should be fixed so that there is a clearance (dimension A) of 0.02 in (0.5 mm) between the sleeve and the compensator lever.
35 Bleed the braking system and then check the installation and operation of the compensator.

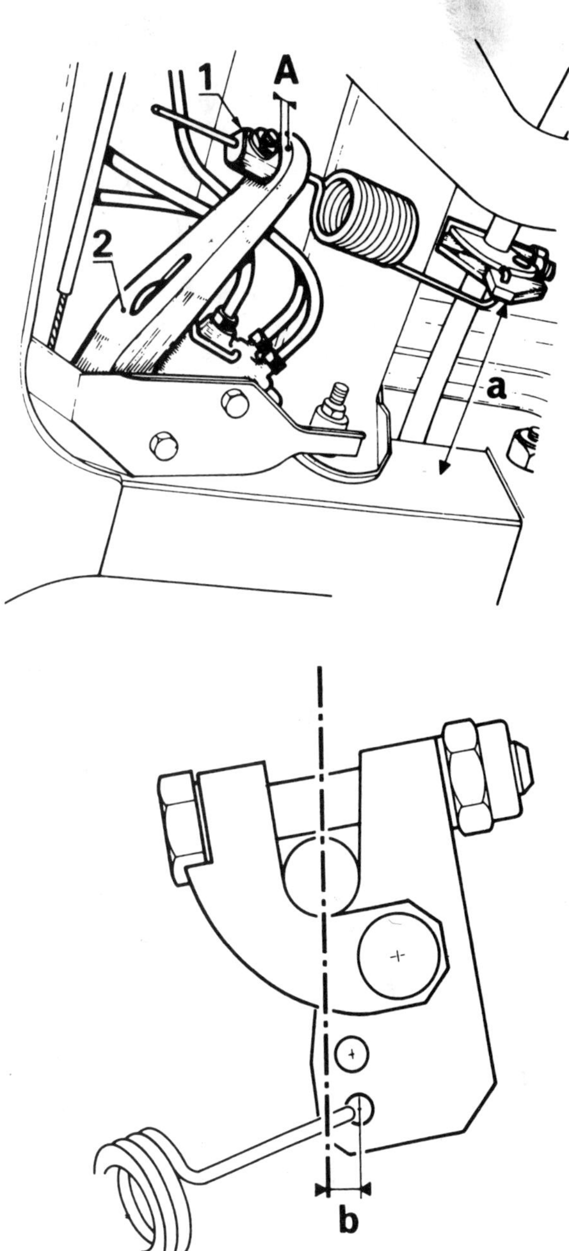

Fig. 14.74 Brake compensator installation (Sec 12)

1 Adjuster clamp bolt
2 Compensating lever
A 0.02 in (0.5 mm)
a 3.661 in (93 mm)
b 0.138 in (3.5 mm)

Adjusting and checking

36 The clamp must be fixed to the anti-roll bar so that it is at a distance (dimension a) of 3.661 in (93 mm) from the side-member.
37 The centre of the spring fixing hole in the clamp should be 0.138 in (3.5 mm) to the rear of a vertical centre-line through the centre of the anti-roll bar (dimension b).
38 With the two previous dimensions correct, the clearance (A) between the adjusting sleeve and the compensator lever should be 0.02 in (0.5 mm).

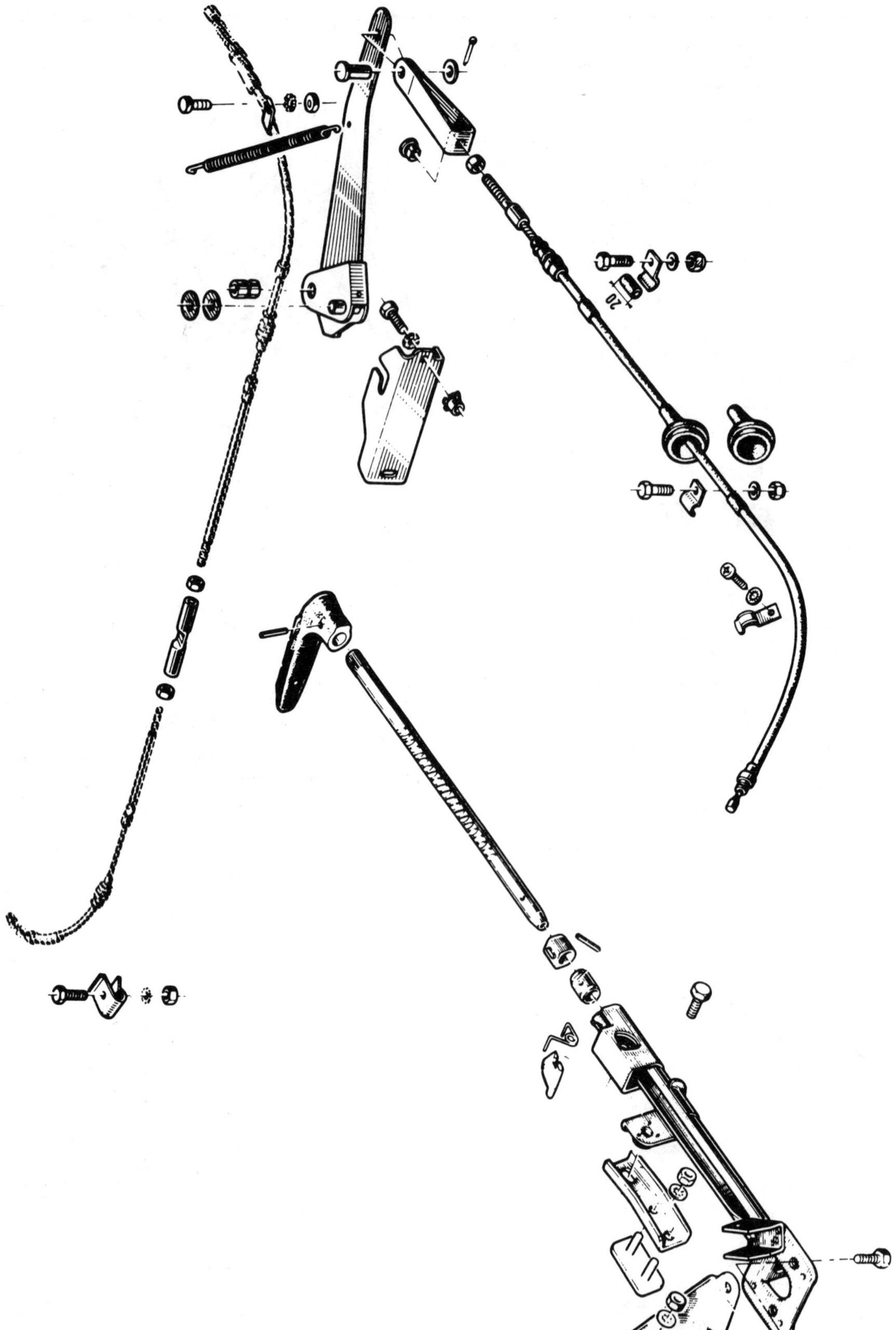

Fig. 14.75 Handbrake assembly – second pattern (Sec 12)

39 When the dimensional checks have been completed, connect a pressure gauge to one of the front brakes in place of a bleed nipple, and connect a second pressure gauge in place of a rear brake bleed nipple. Bleed the braking system and the pressure gauge connections.

40 Press the brake pedal gradually and when the pressure on the front gauge is registering 710 lbf/in^2, read the rear gauge, which should be registering in the range 400 to 455 lbf/in^2.

41 Increase the front brake pressure to 1140 lbf/in^2 and check that the rear brake pressure is 500 to 555 lbf/in^2.

42 If the rear brake pressures are not within the limits of pressure given, fit a new compensator.

Handbrake lever (second pattern)

43 Later models have a handbrake lever which has different fixings from the one used originally and although there are slight differences in the operations of removing and refitting, adjustment is the same for both patterns.

Removing and refitting

44 Release the handbrake and at the rear of the vehicle remove the split cotter and clevis pin from the swivel lever (Fig. 14.76).

45 Unscrew and remove the three bolts securing the handbrake lever assembly.

46 Line-up the pin (1) (Fig. 14.78) opposite the hole in the guide tube and punch out the pin, using a pin punch.

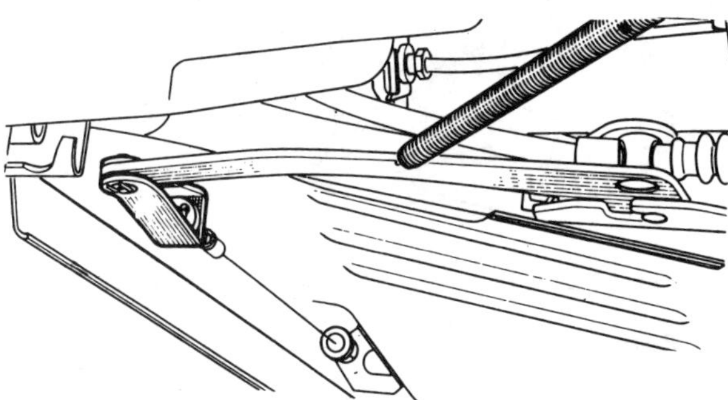

Fig. 14.76 Handbrake cable to swivel lever attachment – second pattern (Sec 12)

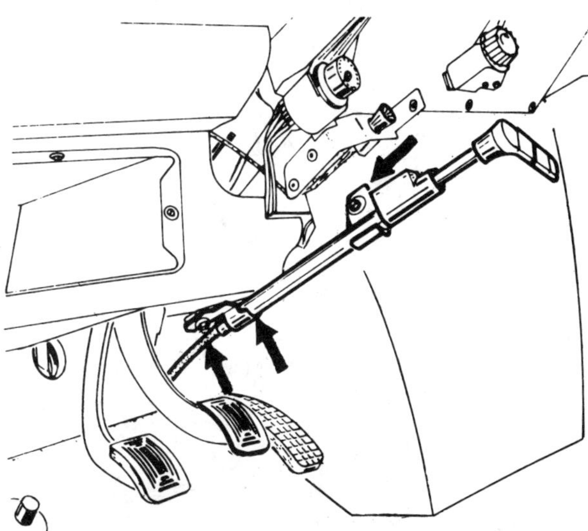

Fig. 14.77 Handbrake assembly securing bolts (arrowed) – second pattern (Sec 12)

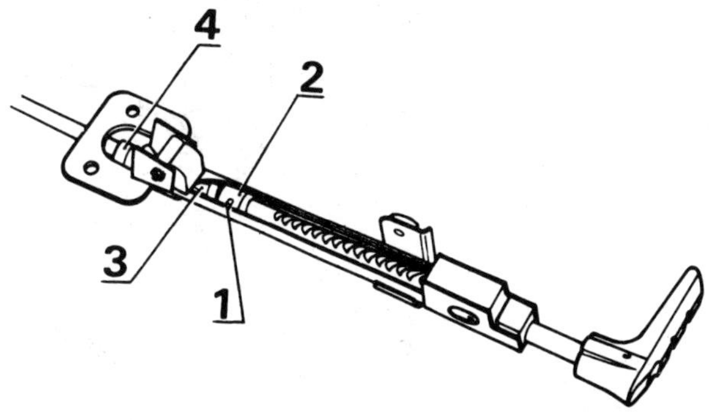

Fig. 14.78 Handbrake cable to lever attachment – second pattern (Sec 12)

1 Pin
2 Sleeve
3 Cable stop
4 Sleeves top

47 Slide the sleeve (2) along the rod, free the cable stop (3) and pull out the sleeve stop (4).

48 Refit the handbrake by reversing the operations necessary for removal.

49 Adjust the handbrake (Chapter 11).

50 Apply sealing compound to all external fixing bolts.

13 Electrical system

Headlamps (R1156) - removal and refitting

1 Disconnect the plugs from the light units.

2 Unhook the light unit retaining springs and withdraw the headlamp unit from the front of the car.

3 Refit the unit by reversing the operations and then check the beam alignment.

Headlamp bulb - removal and refitting

4 The headlamps are fitted with quartz-halogen (QI) bulbs and it is important that the bulb envelope is not touched with the fingers.

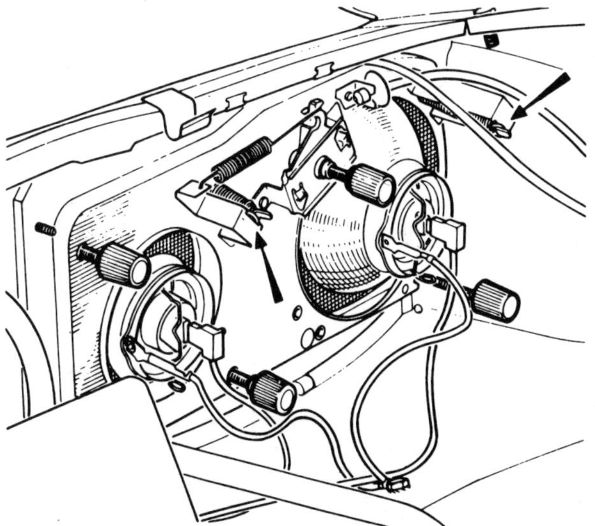

Fig. 14.79 Headlamp connections and fixings (R1156) (Sec 13)

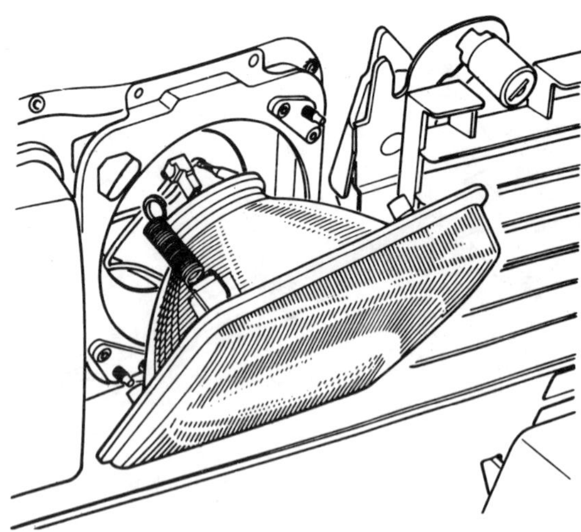

Fig. 14.80 Headlamp removal (R1156) (Sec 13)

5 Always hold the bulb either by the connecting terminal, or use a piece of soft paper.
6 Disconnect the plug connector from the bulb.
7 Unhook the end of the bulb retaining spring, swing back the spring and remove the bulb.
8 Fit a new bulb, being careful not to touch the bulb envelope with the fingers, clip the spring into place and refit the cable connector.
9 After fitting a new bulb, check the beam alignment as described later.

Headlamps with bulb rotator

10 On some vehicles the light unit is fitted with a bulb rotator which enables the setting of the dipped beam to be changed to suit the rule of the road (driving on the left, or driving on the right).
11 To make this change, remove the bulb as in bulb changing and slide the rotator on the bulb holder to the right, for driving on the left and to the left, for driving on the right.
12 Refit the bulb and check the beam alignment.

Headlamp alignment

13 It is recommended that the setting of the headlamp beams is checked with a proprietary beam-setting apparatus.
14 Temporary setting-up of the headlights can be achieved by using the knurled knobs on the headlamp mountings turning screw (A) Fig. 14.81 for adjustment of beam direction and screw (b) to alter the height of the beam.
15 Ensure that the headlamps are switched to the main beam position before making any adjustments to the alignment screws.

Instrument panels (later types)

Automatic transmission models

16 Before removing an instrument panel from any car with automatic transmission, the gear position indicator (selector repeater) cable must be detached at the point shown. After refitting, the cable must be adjusted as described in Chapter 7, Section 6, paragraph 8.

R1151, R1154 and R1156 - removal and refitting

17 Disconnect the battery earth lead.
18 Lift up the front of the cowl then, using a screwdriver, free the clips from the instrument panel.
19 Remove the circular ventilator after first pressing in the retaining tags behind the dashboard metal beading.
20 Mark the switch leads for identification, then remove the switches and detach the leads.
21 Remove the instrument panel moulding, then remove the three panel fixing screws and the speedometer cable.
22 Disconnect the two junction blocks then lift out the instrument panel.
23 Refitting is basically the reverse of the removal procedure, but it is necessary to stick the rubber in position when the circular ventilator is fitted.

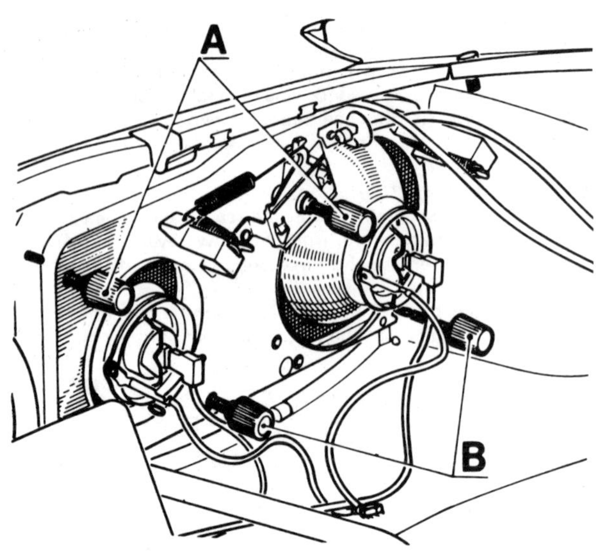

Fig. 14.81 Beam setting screws (R1156) (Sec 13)

A Beam direction adjustment B Beam height adjustment

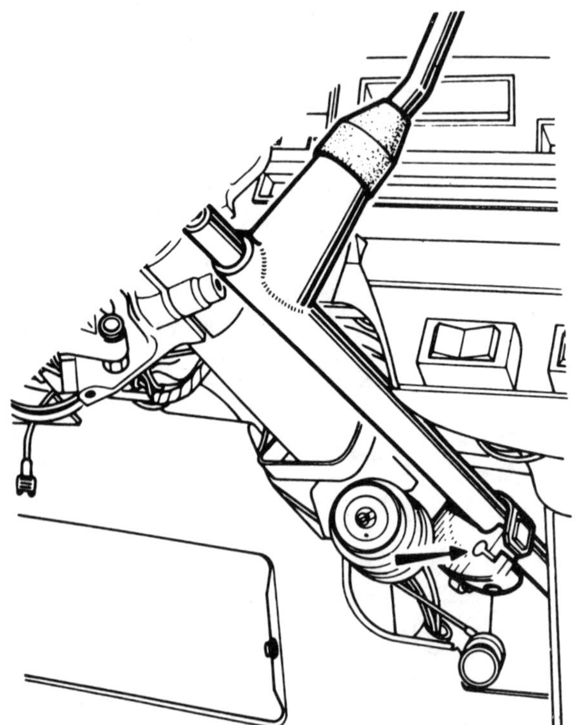

Fig. 14.82 Selector repeater cable connection (arrowed) on automatic transmission models (Sec 13)

Fig. 14.83 Prising free the instrument panel clips (R1151 and R1154) (Sec 13)

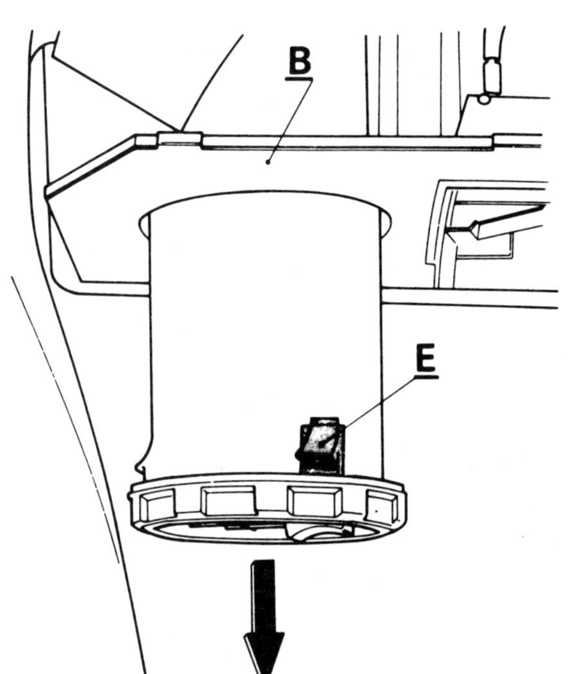

Fig. 14.84 Circular ventilator (Sec 13)

B Metal beading *E Retaining tag*

R1152 and R1153 (except USA and Canada) - removal and refitting

24 Disconnect the battery earth lead.

25 Remove the retaining screw and take off the right-hand veneer panel.

26 Remove the two retaining screws and take off the left-hand veneer panel.

27 Remove the five screws and take off the demister grille.

28 Remove the three retaining screws and detach the retaining bar.

29 Remove the cigar lighter and the recessed screw above it.

30 Remove the two dome nuts and the self-tapping screw beneath the instrument cowl, and take off the cover plate.

31 Remove the three nuts and take off the heater control panel.

32 Remove the sleeve stop and retaining pin, and take off the flap operating cable.

33 Remove the two screws on the windscreen lower frame and take out the ashtray.

34 Remove the instrument panel fixing bolts, and separate the two parts.

35 Refitting is basically the reverse of the removal procedure. Make sure that a washer is fitted on the screw shown as item 16 in Fig. 14.89, and that the heater lever moves freely after the flap cable has been attached; note that the cable eye should be facing upwards. Before finally tightening any nuts and screws, make sure that all components are correctly aligned.

R1152, R1153 and R1155 (USA and Canada) - removal and refitting

36 Disconnect the battery earth lead.

37 Remove the retaining screws at each side and detach the side veneer panels.

38 Remove the three retaining screws and take off the demister grille.

39 Remove the two screws at the top and nine at the bottom and take off the dashboard trim.

40 Remove the steering wheel as described in Chapter 10.

41 Release the trim panel by raising it slightly so that it disengages from the retaining lugs.

42 Remove the retaining screws and take off the instrument panel moulding.

43 Mark the switch leads for identification then disconnect them. Also disconnect the speedometer cable.

44 Remove the instrument panel.

45 Refitting is the reverse of the removal procedure.

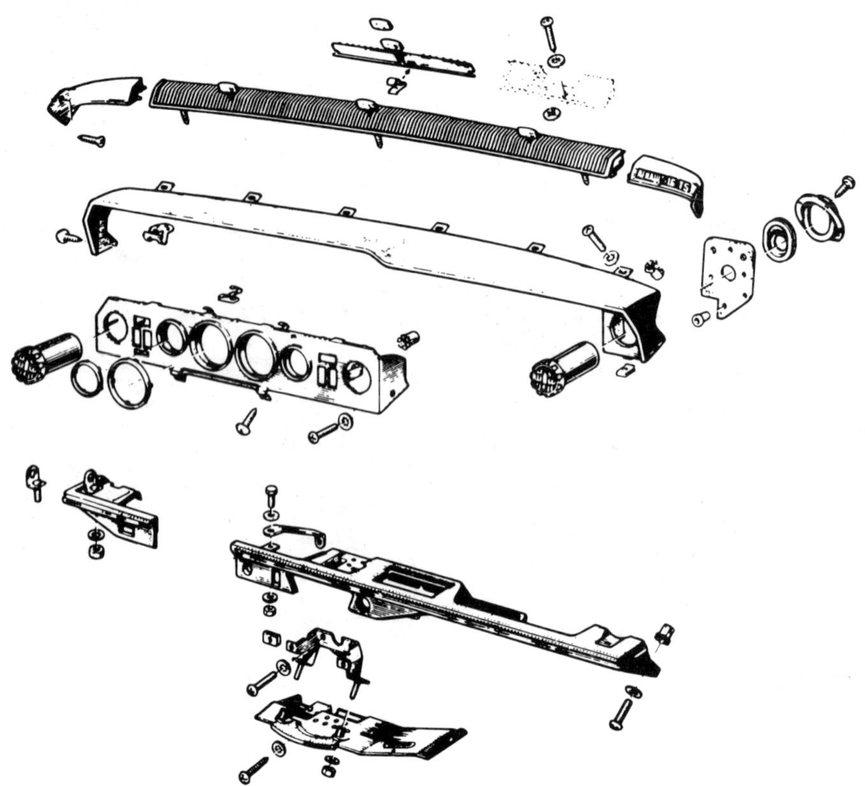

Fig. 14.85 Facia components (R1151 and R1154 -- except Sweden) (Sec 13)

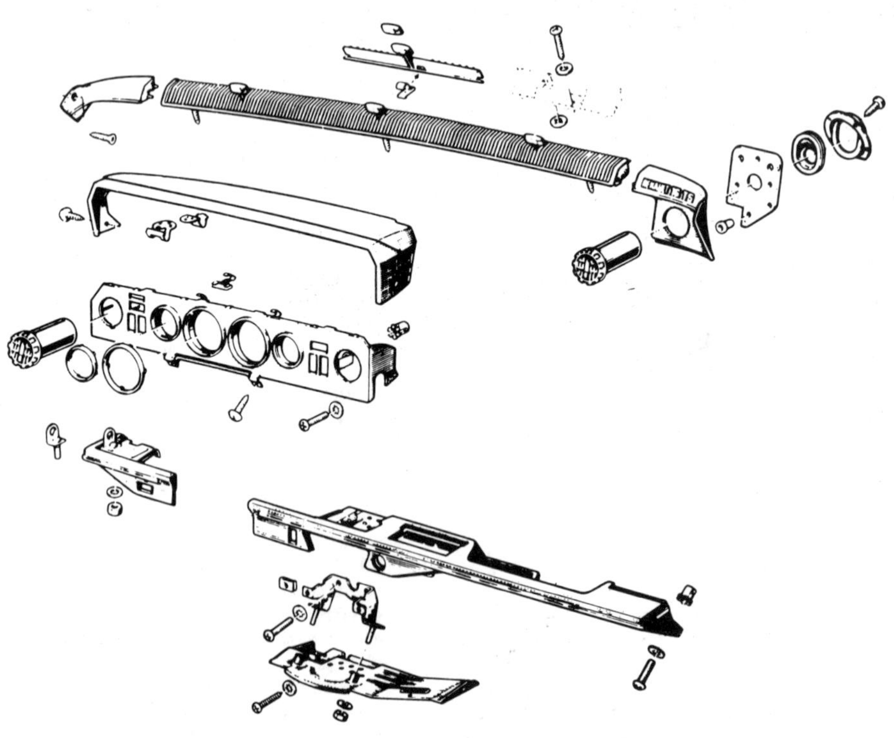

Fig. 14.86 Facia components (R1151 and R1154 – Sweden) (Sec 13)

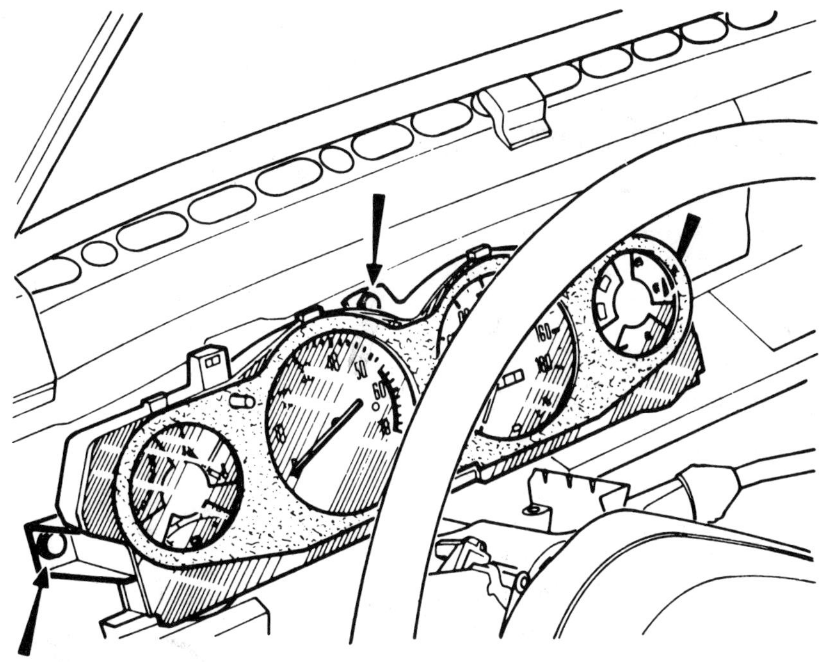

Fig. 14.87 Typical left-hand drive vehicle instrument layout (R1151, R1154 and R1156) (Sec 13)

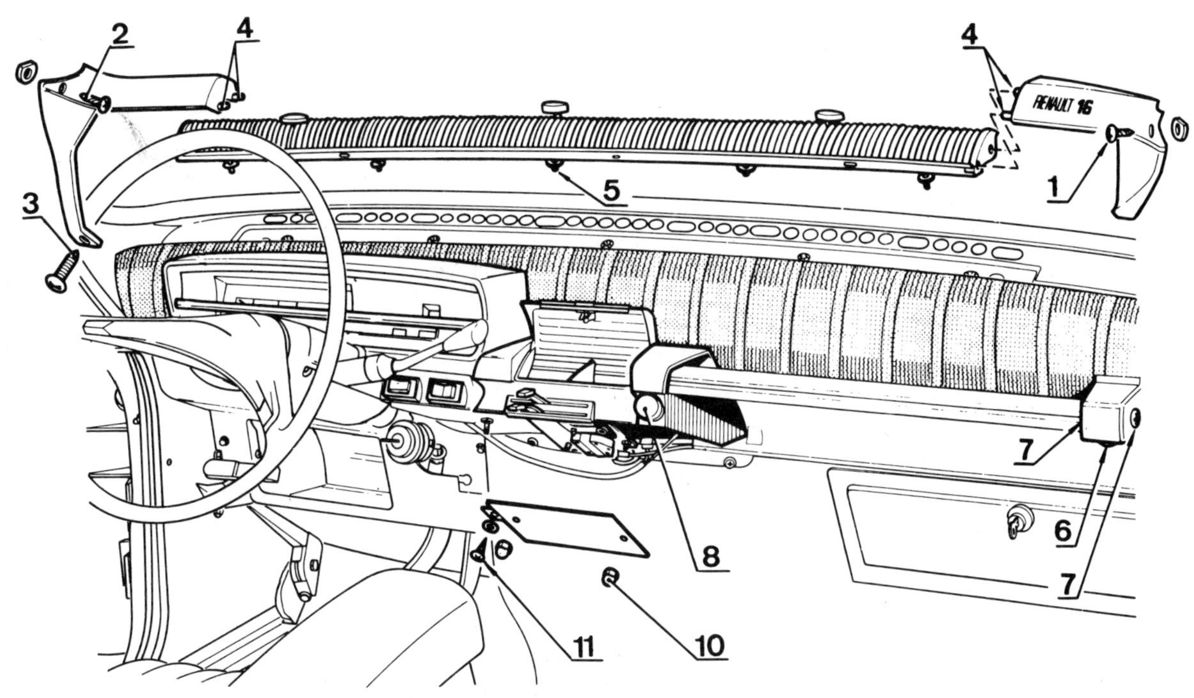

Fig. 14.88 First stage of instrument panel removal (R1151 and R1153) (Sec 13)

1	*Screw*	*5*	*Screws*	*8*	*Cigar lighter*
2	*Screw*	*6*	*Retaining bar screws*	*10*	*Dome nuts*
3	*Screw*	*7*	*Retaining bar screws*	*11*	*Self-tapping screw*
4	*Locating dowels*				

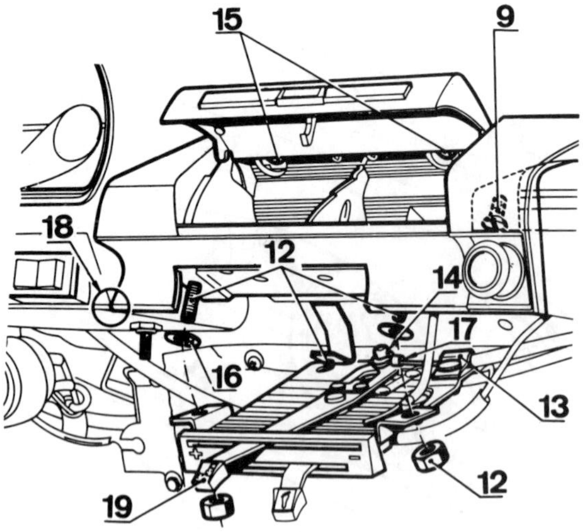

Fig. 14.89 Second stage of instrument panel removal (R1152 and R1153) (Sec 13)

9 Recessed screw
12 Heater control nuts and studs
13 Sleeve stop
14 Retaining pin
15 Screws
16 Washer
17 Eye
18 Checking point for alignment
19 Heater flap lever

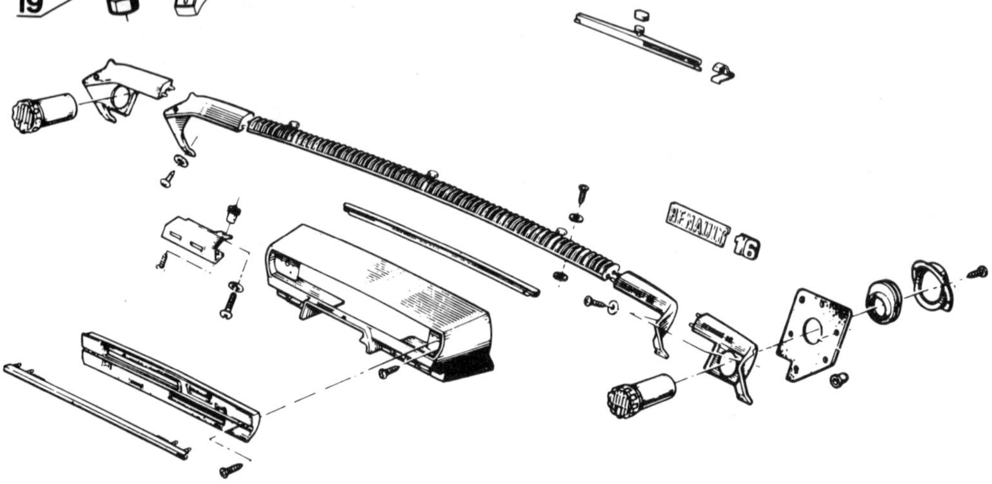

Fig. 14.90 Facia components (R1152 – second type) (Sec 13)

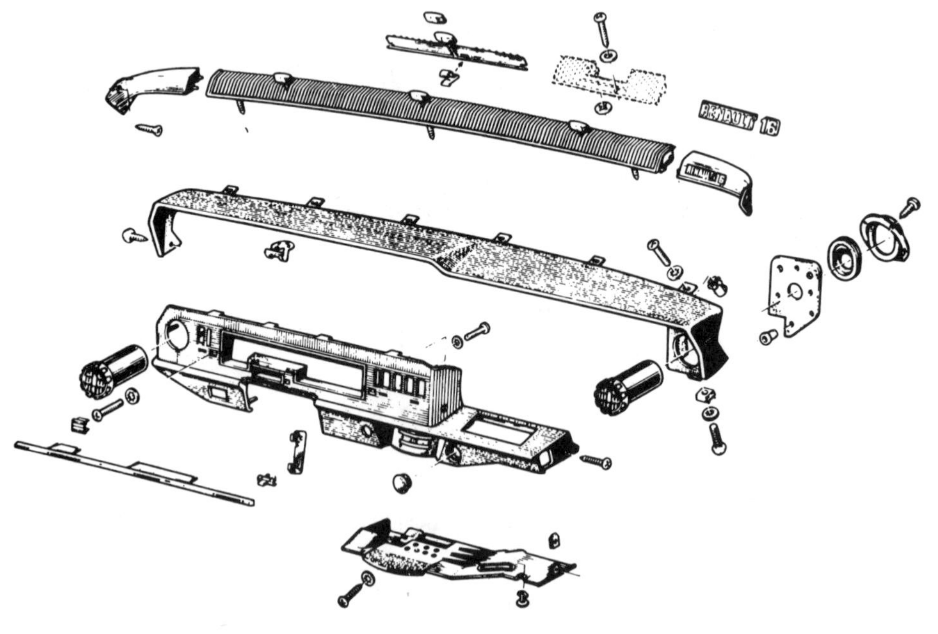

Fig. 14.91 Facia components (R1152 – third type) (Sec 13)

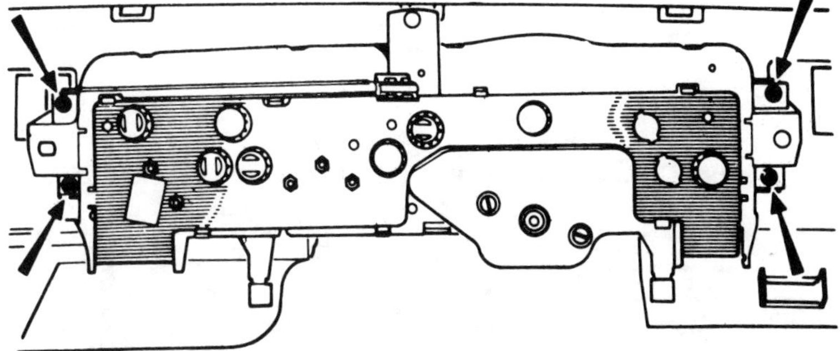

Fig. 14.92 Instrument panel attachment points (arrowed) – R1152 and R1153 (Sec 13)

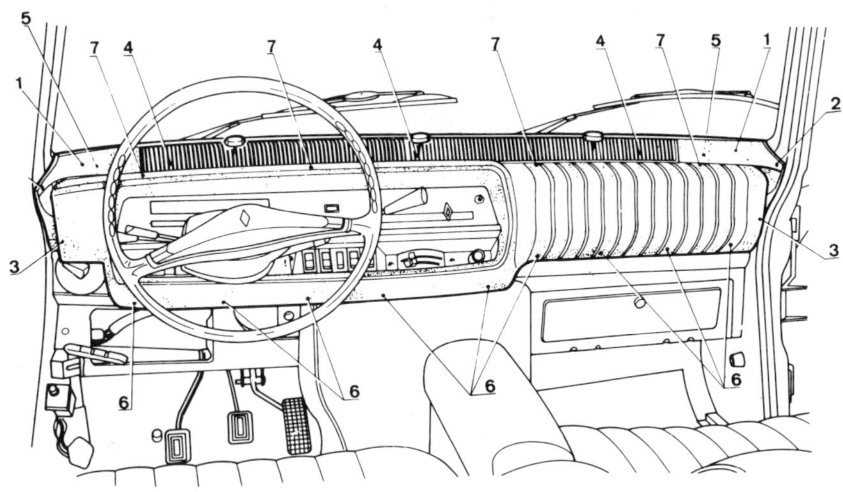

Fig. 14.93 Facia panel removal (R1152 – Sweden and USA) (Sec 13)

1 Side veneers
2 Attachment points
3 Attachment points
4 Demister grille screws
5 Trim screws
6 Trim screws
7 Retaining lugs

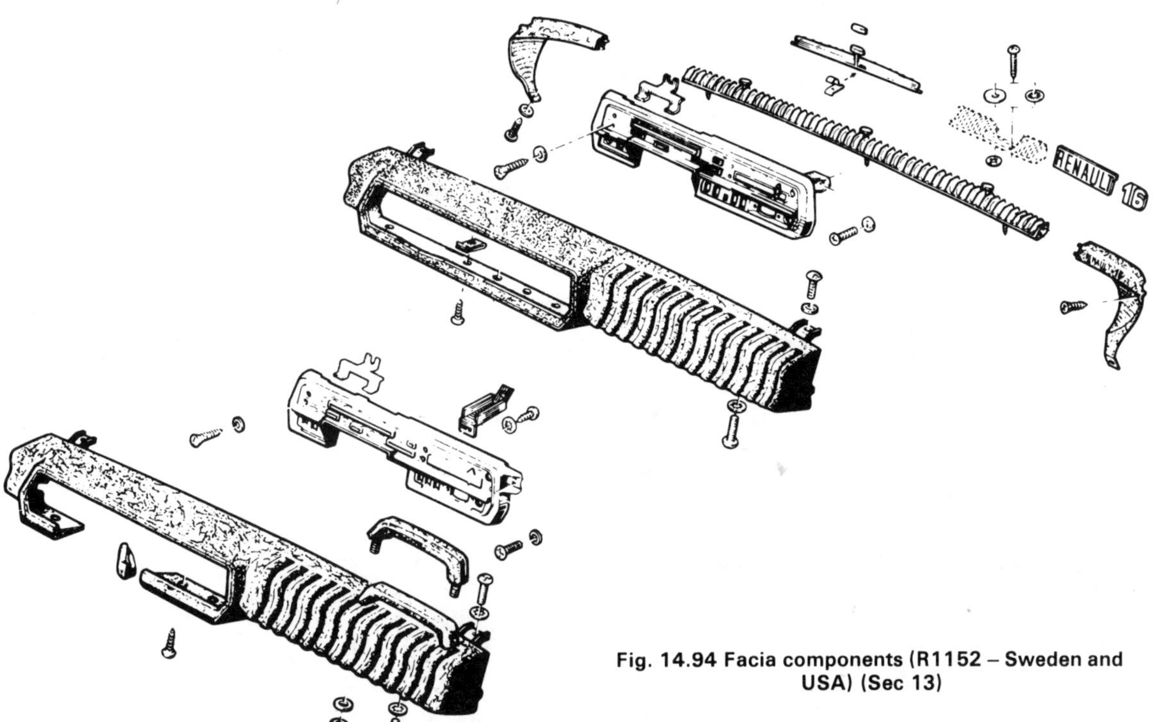

Fig. 14.94 Facia components (R1152 – Sweden and USA) (Sec 13)

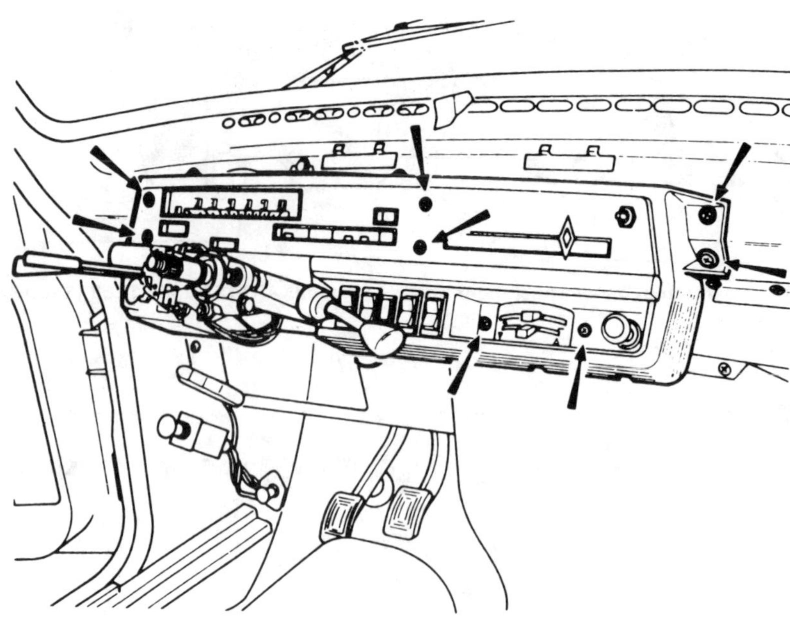

Fig. 14.95 Instrument panel attachment points (arrowed) – R1152 and R1153, USA and Canada (Sec 13)

Instrument panels (Jaeger types - R1150, R1152, R1153 and R1155)

46 The accompanying figures show the printed circuit and non-printed circuit types of Jaeger instrument panels which are fitted to the Renault 16. Figs. 14.96 and 14.97 complement Fig. 18.7 of Chapter 12 whereas Figs. 14.98 and 14.99 complement Fig. 14.92 of this Chapter.

47 On automatic transmission models, remove the instrument glass and the cable securing plate before withdrawing the selector repeater cable from its sleeve.

Fig. 14.96 Standard circuit type Jaegar instrument panel components (R1150, R1152, R1153 and R1155) (Sec 13)

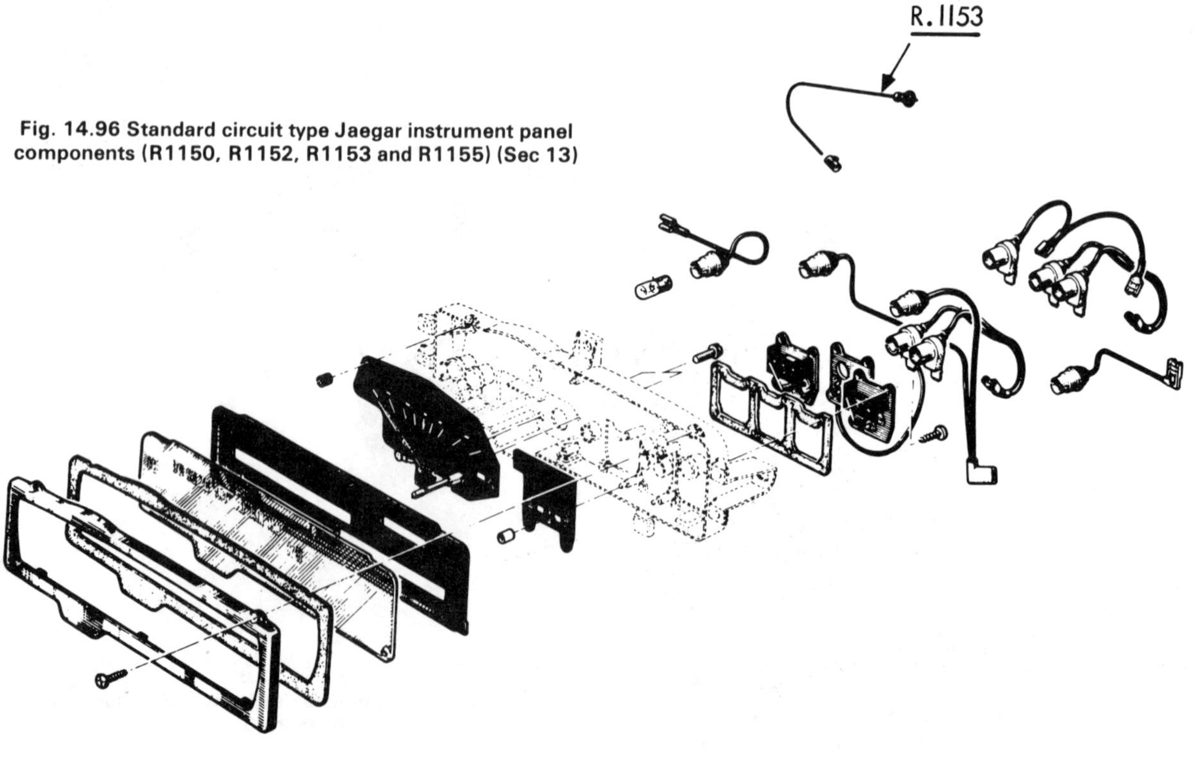

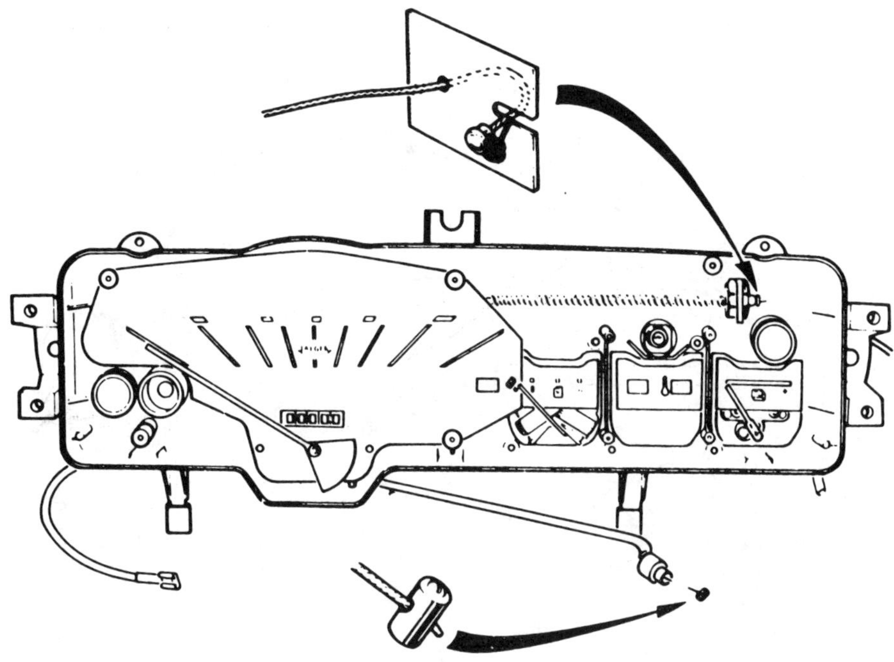

Fig. 14.97 Selector repeater cable attachment to standard circuit type Jaeger panel (Sec 13)

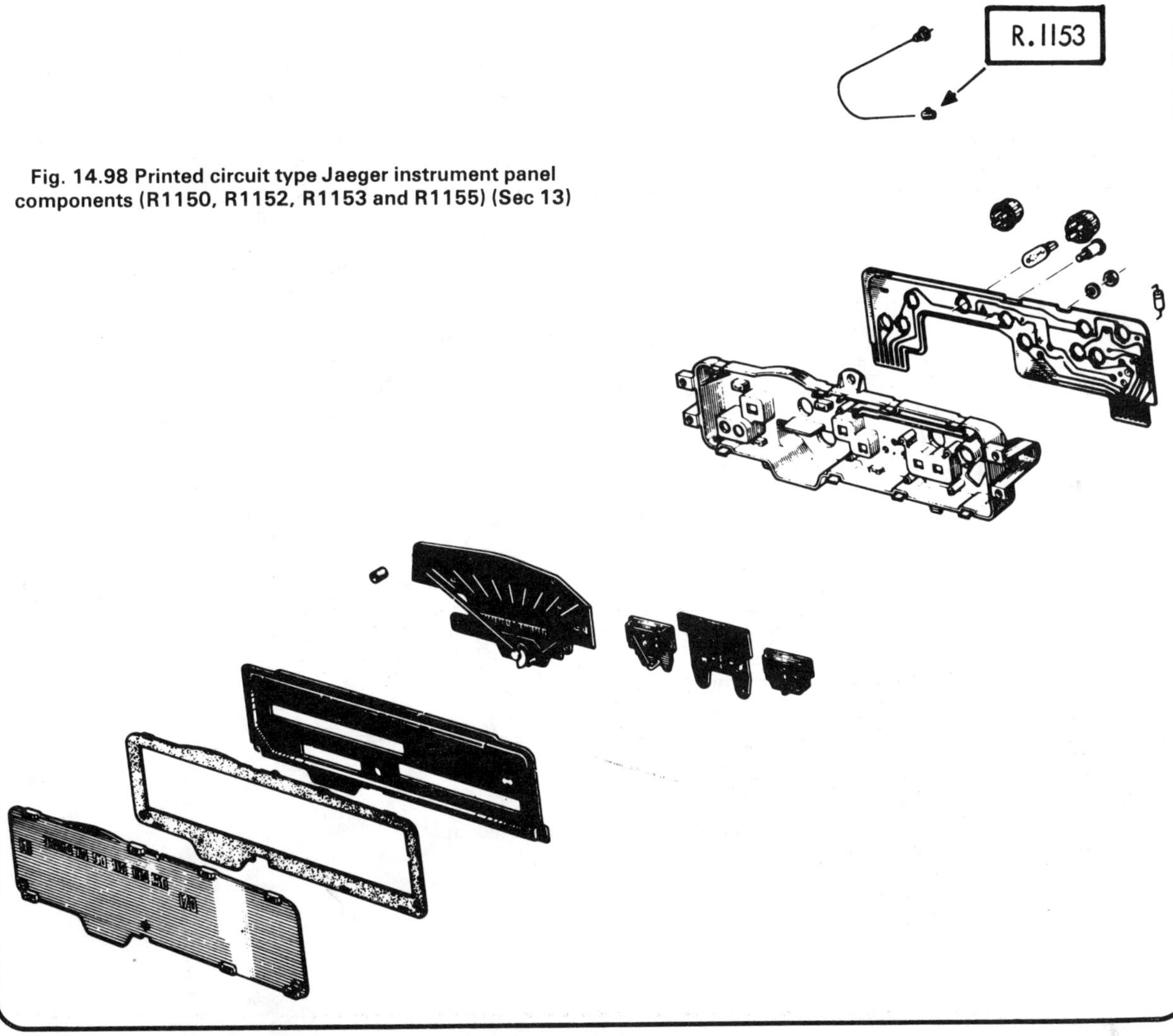

R.1153

Fig. 14.98 Printed circuit type Jaeger instrument panel components (R1150, R1152, R1153 and R1155) (Sec 13)

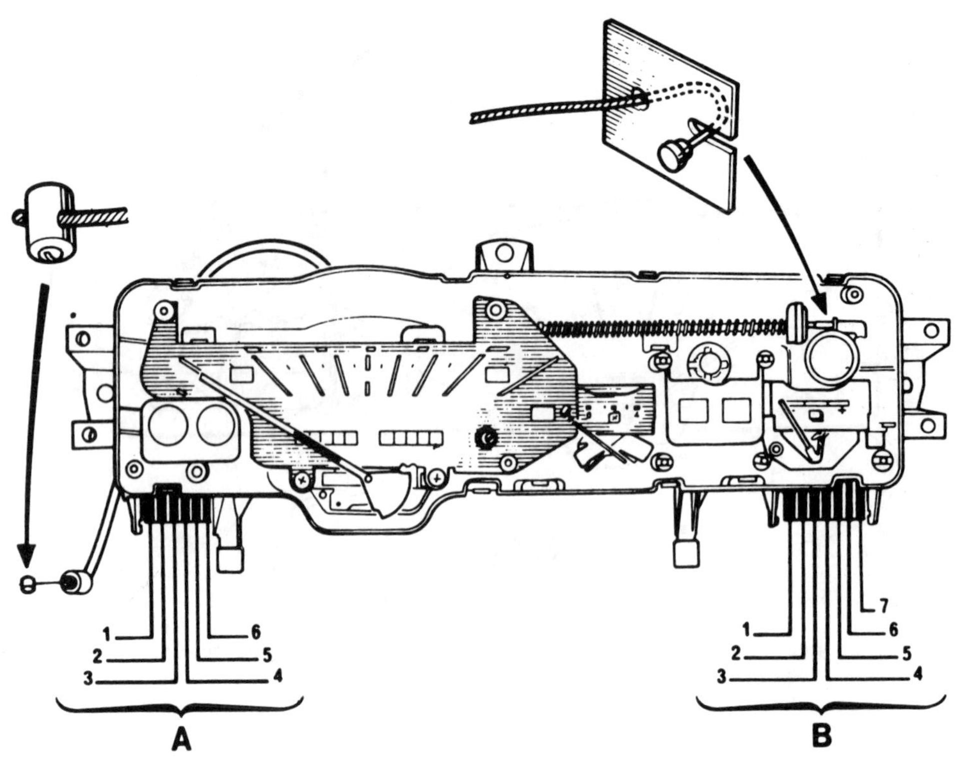

Fig. 14.99 Selector repeater cable attachment to printed circuit type Jaeger panel (Sec 13)

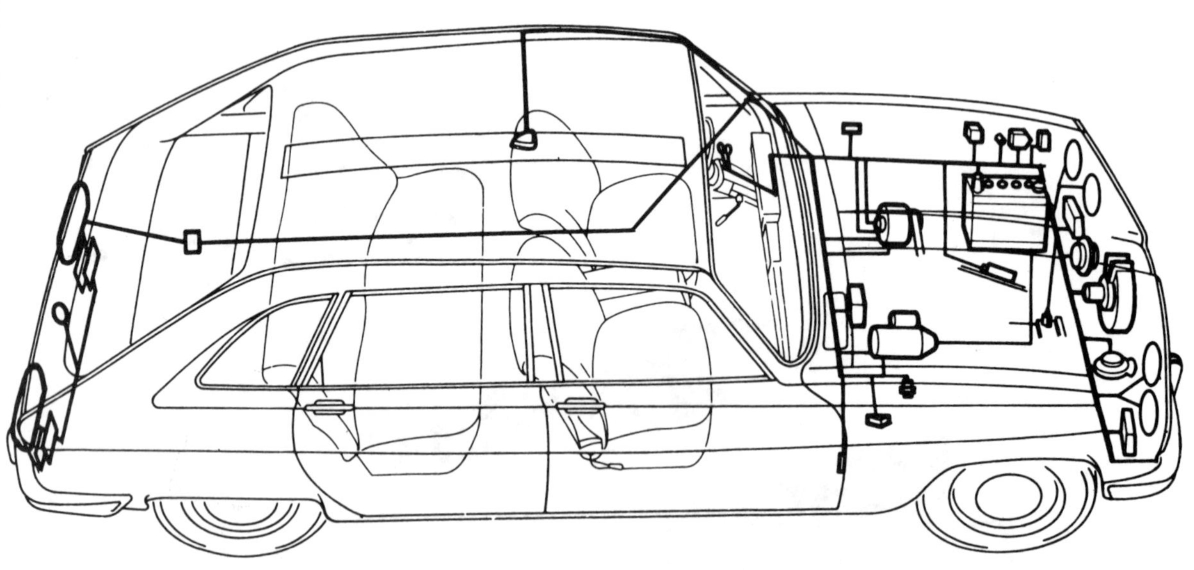

Fig. 14.100 Wiring harness layout

Key to wiring diagrams (except R1156 – 1978)

1 LH front sidelight and direction indicator
2 LH front headlight
3 LH inner headlight (R1152 - 1153 - R1155US)
4 LH horn
5 LH QI driving light (R1151 - R1154)
6 RH QI driving light (R1151 - R1154)
7 RH horn
8 RH inner headlight (R1152 - R1153 - R1155US)
9 RH front headlight
10 RH front sidelight and direction indicator
11 LH front sidelight wire junction (R1152 - R1153 - R1155US)
12 RH front sidelight wire junction (R1152 - R1153 - R1155US)
13 LH front catseye reflector (R1152 - R1153 - R1155US)
14 Reversing light switch
15 Cooling fan motor
16 Temperature switch on radiator
17 RH front catseyes reflector (R1152 - R1153 - R1155US)
18 Cooling fan motor relay
19 Battery
20 Ignition coil
21 Centrifugal switch (R1152 US)
22 Alternator
23 Oil pressure switch
24 Solenoid flap valve (R1152 - R1153 - R1155US) (fast idling)
25 Solenoid flap valve (R1153 - R1155US)
26 Front junction plate (+) (R1152 - R1154)
27 Regulator
28 QI driving lights relay (R1151 - R1154)
29 Sunroof relay
30 Window winder relay
31 Fusebox
32 Stoplight switch
33 Brake pressure drop switch (R1152 - R1153 - R1155US)
34 Distributor
35 Temperature sender switch
36 Idling speed damper (R1152US)
37 Starter motor
38 Dipped beam wire junction R1156)
39 Main beam wire junction (R1152 - R1153 - R1155US - R1156)
40 Brake warning light wire junction
42 Earth (ground) – window winder
43 LH front brake pad
44 LH front brake pad junction terminal
45 Scuttle junction plate
46 Windscreen wiper motor
47 Heater fan
48 RH front brake pad junction terminal
49 RH front brake pad
50 LH door pillar switch
51 Pedal operated dipswitch (R1152 - R1153 - R1155US)
52 Flasher unit
53 Headlight main beam ON tell-tale
54 Ignition key IN POSITION tell-tale (R1152 - R1153 - R1155US)
55 Instrument panel lighting
56 Brake pad wear/handbrake ON warning light
57 Fuel gauge
58 Choke ON warning light
59 Oil pressure/water temperature
60 Voltmeter
61 Direction indicator telltale
62 Water temperature gauge (R1151 - R1154 - R1156)
63 QI driving lights switch (R1151 - R1154)
64 Heated rear screen switch
65 Windscreen wiper switch
66 Heated rear screen telltale
67 QI driving lights telltale (R1151 - R1154)
68 Tachometer (R1151 - R1154 - R1156)
69 Speedometer
70 Sunroof switch
71 LH window winder switch (R1151 - R1154 - R1156)
72 RH window winder switch (R1151 - R1154 - R1156)
73 Clock (R1151 - R1154 - R1156)
74 Clock illumination (R1151 - R1154 - R1156)
75 Instrument panel lighting rheostat
76 Heater fan motor rheostat
77 RH door pillar switch
78 Hazard warning lights system switch (R1152 - R1153 - R1155US)
79 Brake pressure drop warning light checking switch (R1152 R1153 - R1155US)
80 Brake pressure drop warning light (R1152 - R1153 - R1155US)
81 Hazard warning lights system telltale (R1152 - R1153 - R1155US)
84 Junction block
85 Junction block
86 Combination lighting/direction indicator switch
87 Junction block (R1152) (R1152 - R1153 - R1155US)
88 Junction block
89 Flasher unit fuse
90 Junction block
91 Junction block (+ direct) (R1151 - R1154 - R1156)
92 Instrument panel junction (LH)
93 Instrument panel junction (RH)
94 LH window winder (R1151 - R1154 - R1156)
95 Ignition starter switch illumination
96 Ignition starter switch (R1151 - R1154 - R1156)
97 Choke ON switch (R1151) (R1152 US)
98 Handbrake ON switch
99 Thermal overload switch (sunroof)
100 Earth (ground) for instrument panel
101 Glove compartment light
102 Cigar lighter
103 Ashtray illumination
104 Cigar lighter illumination
105 RH window winder earth (ground) (R1151 - R1154 -
106 RH window winder (R1151 - R1154 - R1156)
107 Luggage compartment light
108 Luggage compartment light switch
109 Windscreen washer pedal (R1151 - R1154 - R1156)
110 Sunroof motor
111 Interior light
115 Map reading light
116 Fuel tank
117 Wire junctions for rear light assemblies (R1151 - R1154 - R1156)
118 LH rear illuminated catseyes reflector (R1152 - R1153 - R1155US)
119 Heated rear screen (+ contact)
120 Heated rear screen
121 Heated rear screen – contact
122 RH rear illuminated catseyes reflector (R1152 - R1153 - R1155US)
123 Reversing lamps wire junction
124 LH rear direction indicator
125 LH stoplight and rear light
126 LH reversing light (R1151 - R1154 - R1152 - R1153 - R1155 US - R 1156)
127 Push-on blade and socket for rear light wire
128 Number plate light
129 RH reversing light (R1151 - R1154 - R1152 - R1153 - R1155 US - R1156)
130 RH rear light and stoplight
131 RH rear flasher
132 Windscreen wiper switch illumination
133 Junction for water temperature and oil pressure switch wires
134 LH parking light
135 RH parking light
136 Junction for '+ direct' wires
137 Junction for '+ after ignition switch' wires
138 Parking lights switch

Automatic transmission
150 Governor
151 Computer
152 Sealed junction box
153 Connection block
154 Kickdown switch
156 Safety switch for solenoid
157 Starter solenoid safety switch

Electro-magnetic door locks
200 Junction for 4 housings
201 Earth (ground)
202 Thermal cutout
203 Inertia switch
204 LH front door junction plate
205 RH front door lock (changeover switch)
206 LH front door actuator
207 RH front door lock (changeover switch)
208 RH front door actuator
209 RH front door junction plate
210 LH rear door junction plate
211 LH rear door actuator
212 RH rear door actuator
213 RH rear door junction plate

Air-conditioning system
250 Evaporator
251 Magnetic clutch
253 Additional cooling fan

Wiring harnesses
A: Engine front harness
B: Combination lighting/direction indicator switch
C: Instrument panel harness (R1150 - R1152 - R1153)
D: Rear harness
E: Interior lights/sunroof harness
F: QI headlights relay harness (R1151 - R 1154)
G: Sunroof/electric window winder relay harness
H: LH electric window winder/LH front door electro-magnetic lock harness (R1151 - R1154 - R1156)
I: RH front and rear door electro-magnetic lock harness (R1151 - R1154 - R1156)
K: Electric window winder harness (R1151 - R1154 - R1156)
L: LH window winder motor harness (R1151 - R1154 - R1156)
M: RH window winder motor harness (R1151 - R1154 - R1156)
N: Sunroof motor harness
O: Alternator harness
P: Positive lead (+)
Q: Negative lead (–)
S: Automatic transmission harness (R1153 - R1154 - R1155)
T: LH rear door electro-magnetic lock harness
U: Air-conditioning system harness

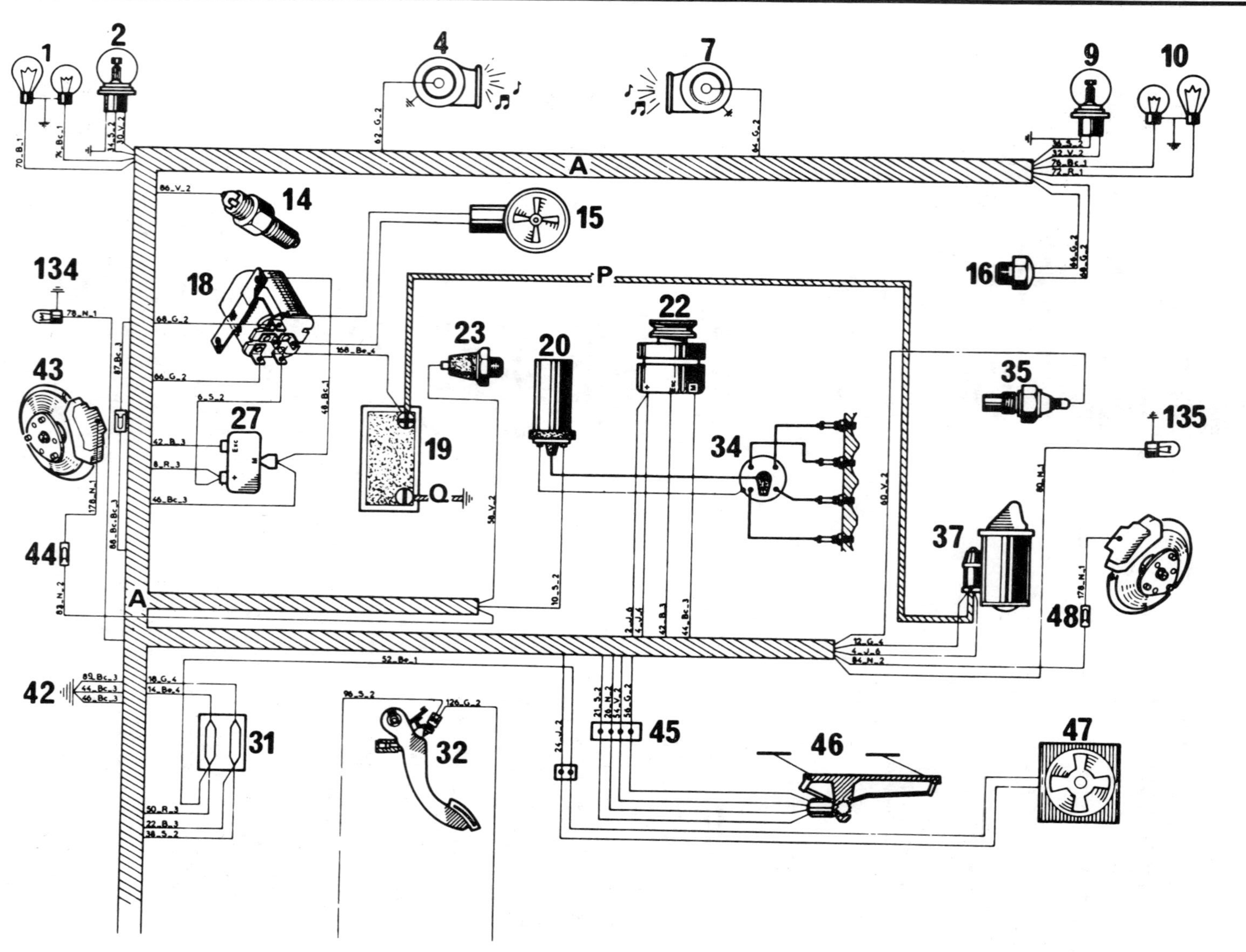

Fig. 14.101 Wiring diagram – R1150, 1969/70 – R1152, 1971/72 – R1153, 1969/72

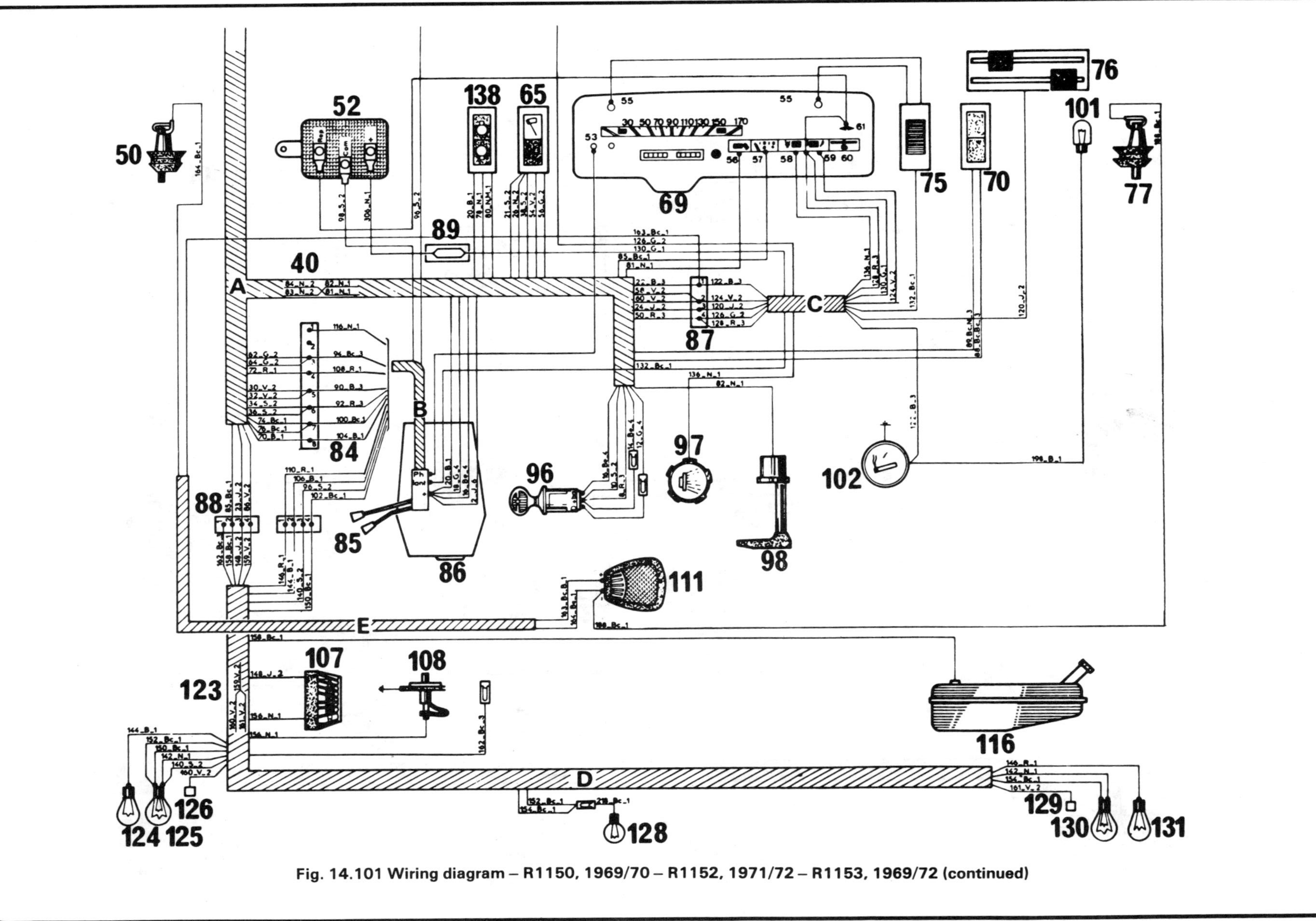

Fig. 14.101 Wiring diagram – R1150, 1969/70 – R1152, 1971/72 – R1153, 1969/72 (continued)

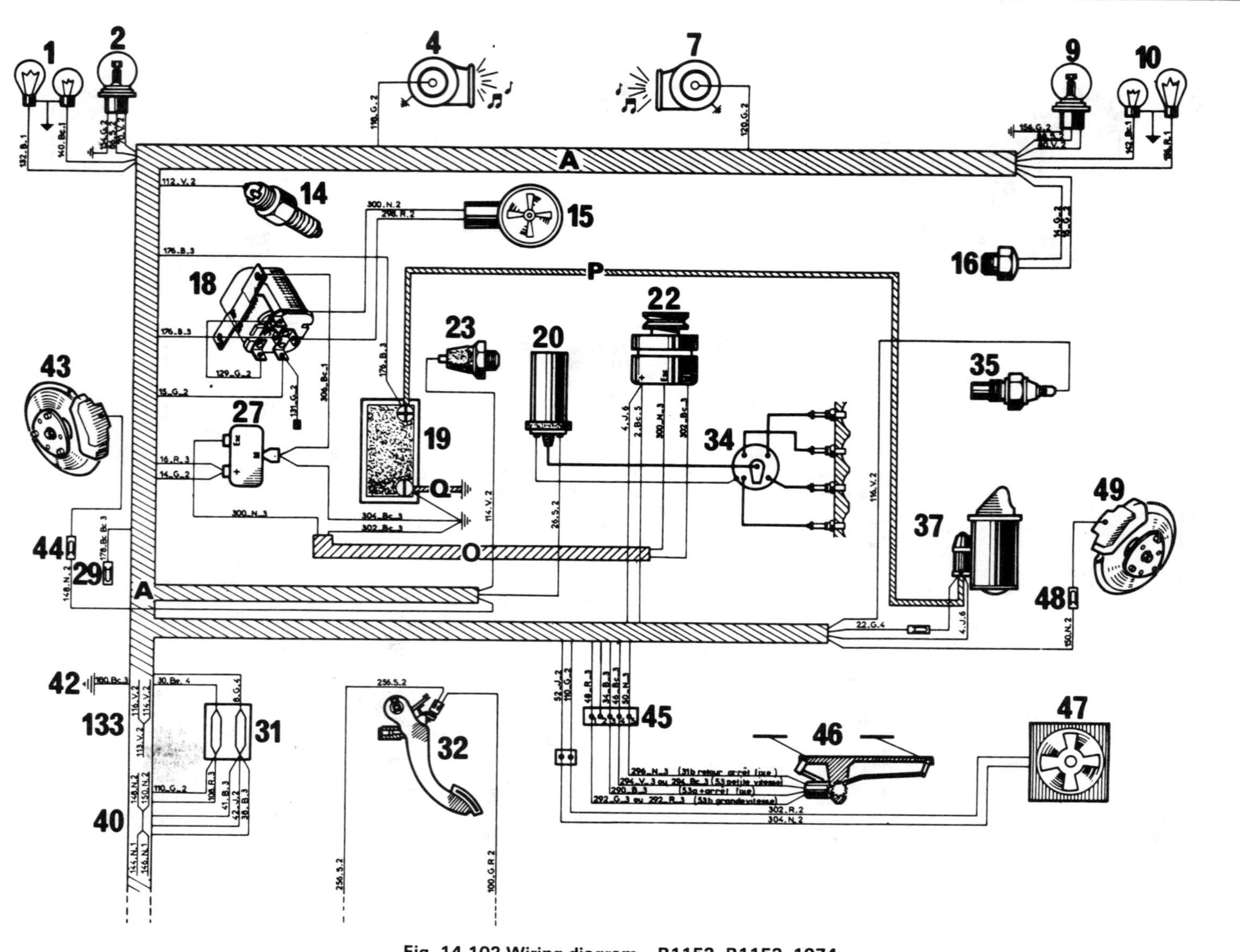

Fig. 14.102 Wiring diagram – R1152, R1153, 1974

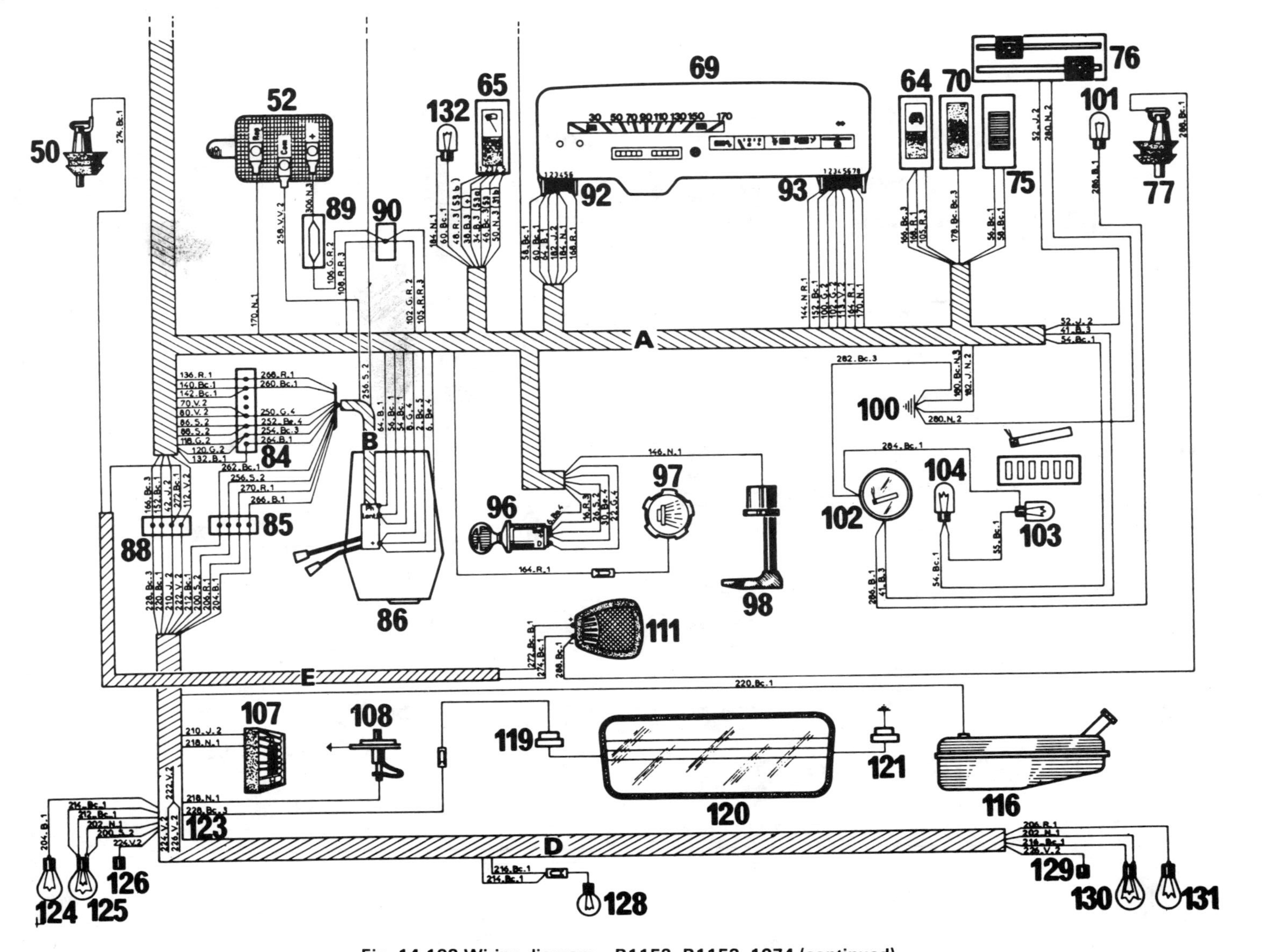

Fig. 14.102 Wiring diagram – R1152, R1153, 1974 (continued)

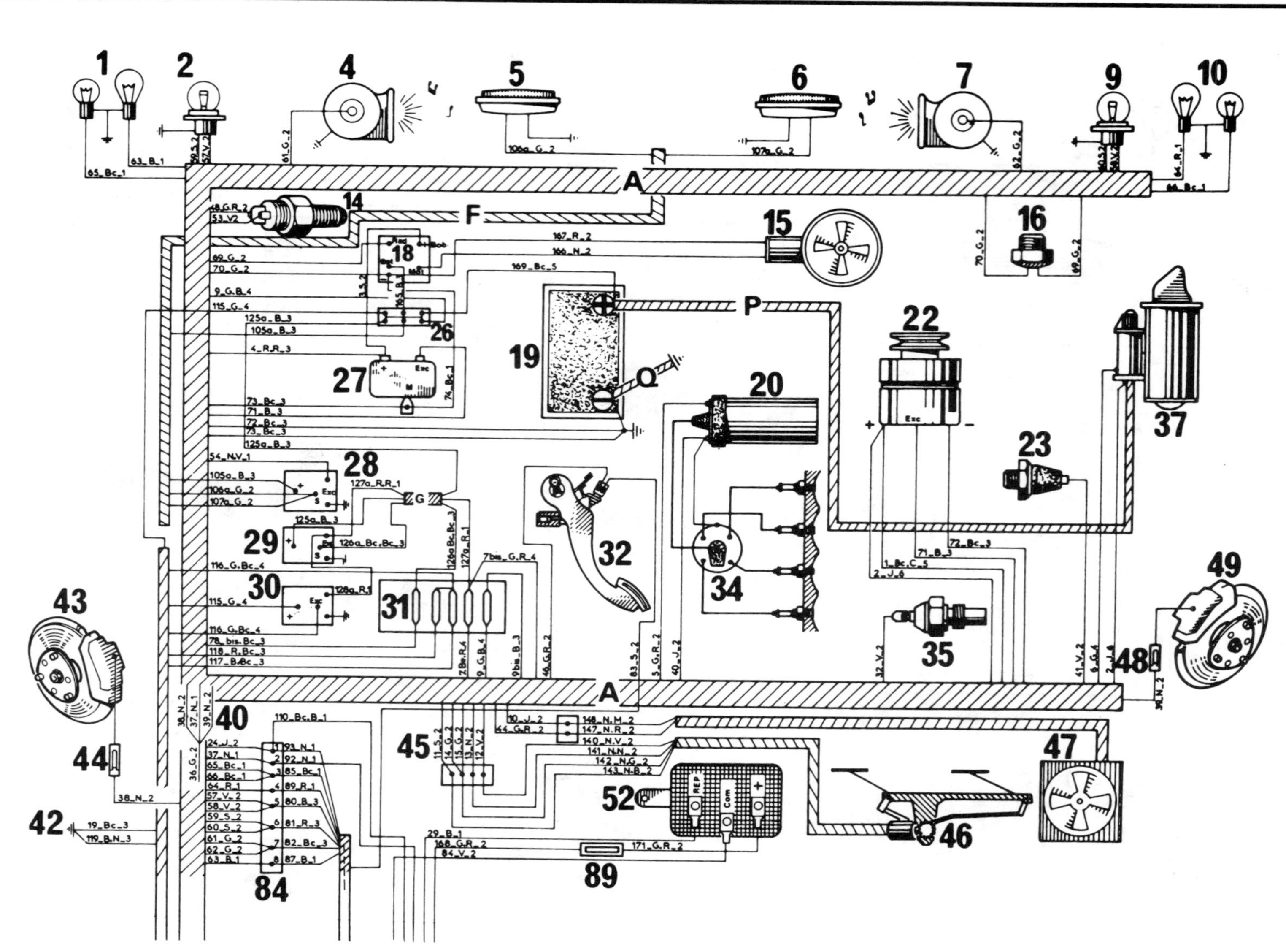

Fig. 14.103 Wiring diagram – R1151, 1970/73 – R1154, 1971/73

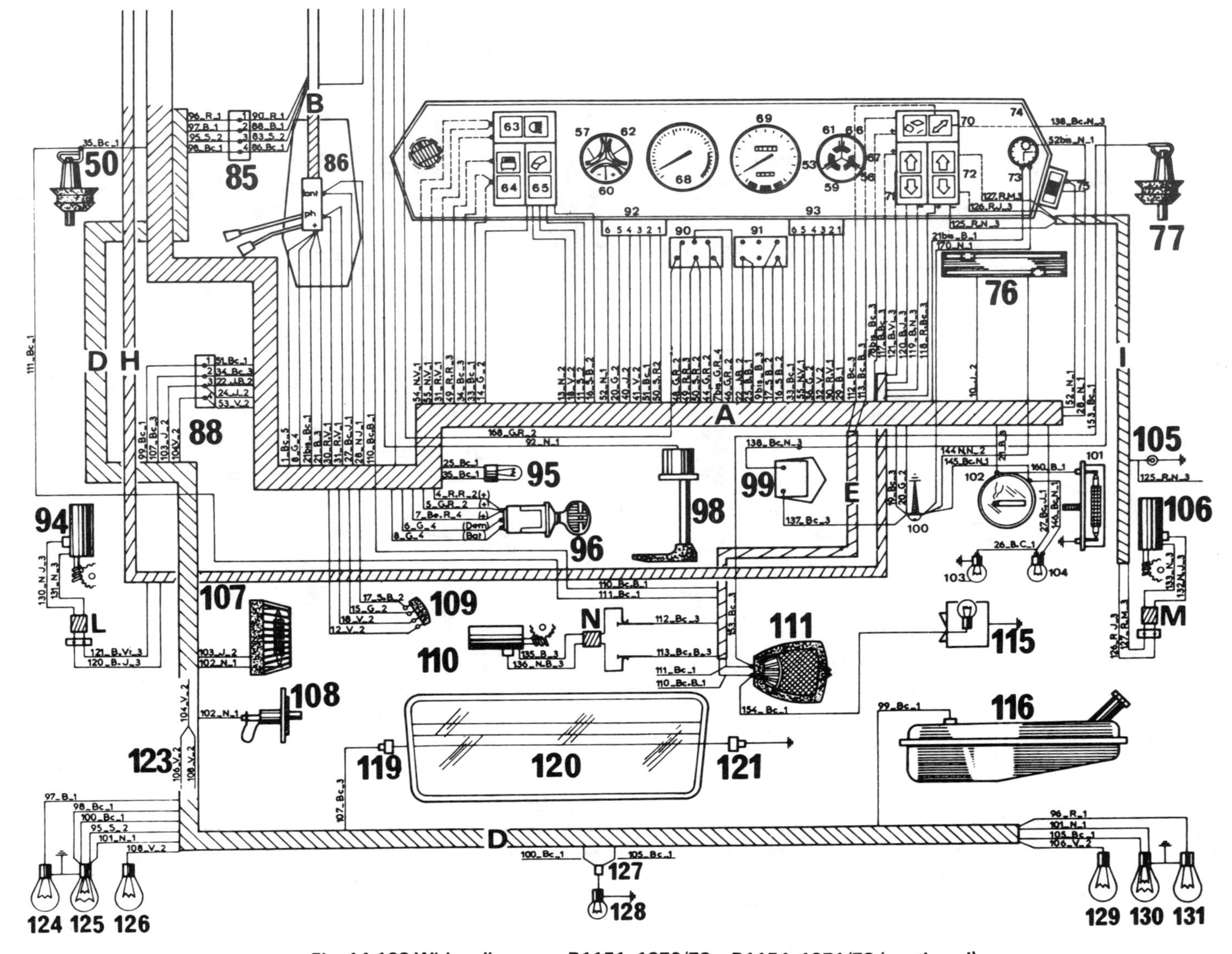

Fig. 14.103 Wiring diagram – R1151, 1970/73 – R1154, 1971/73 (continued)

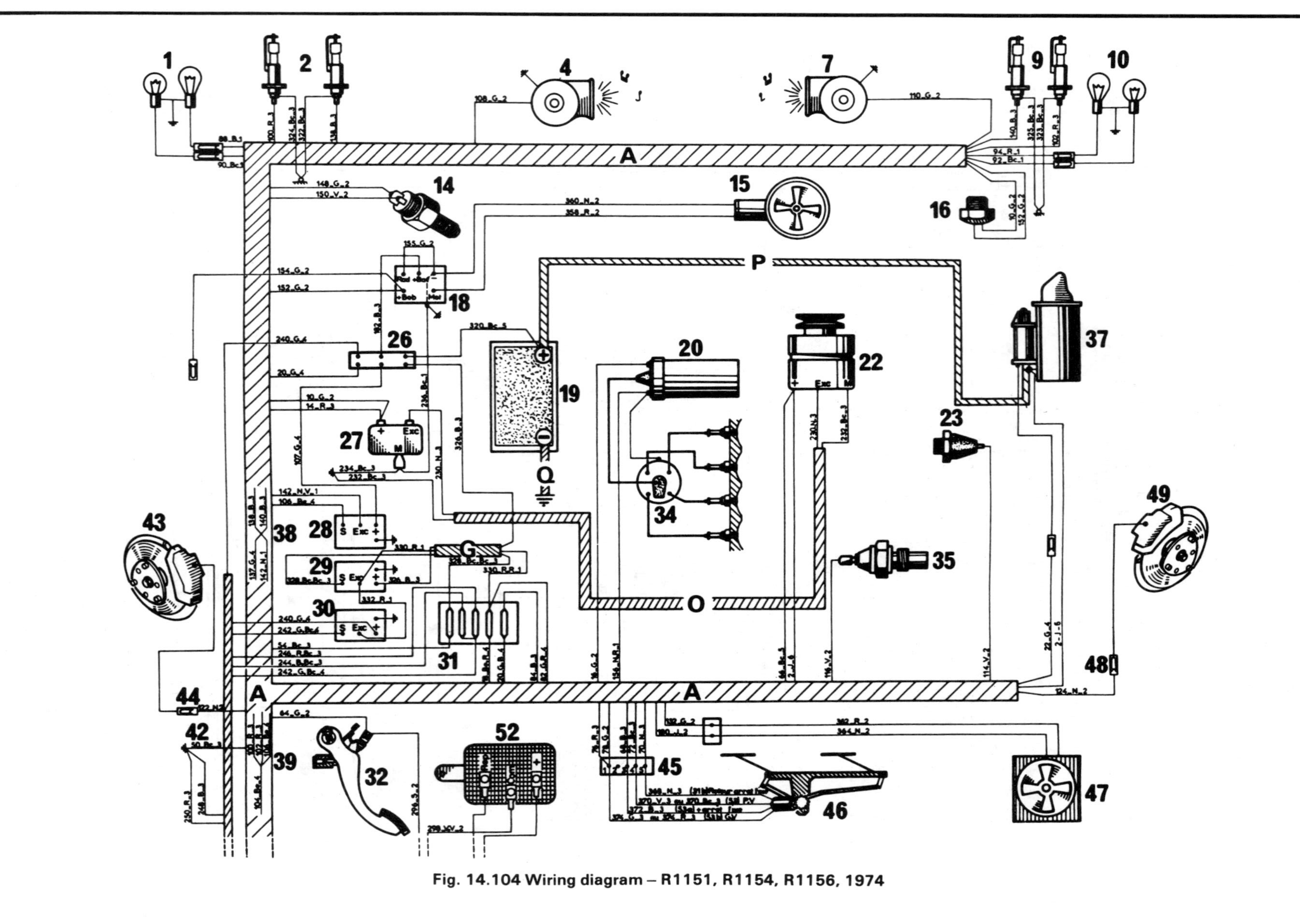

Fig. 14.104 Wiring diagram – R1151, R1154, R1156, 1974

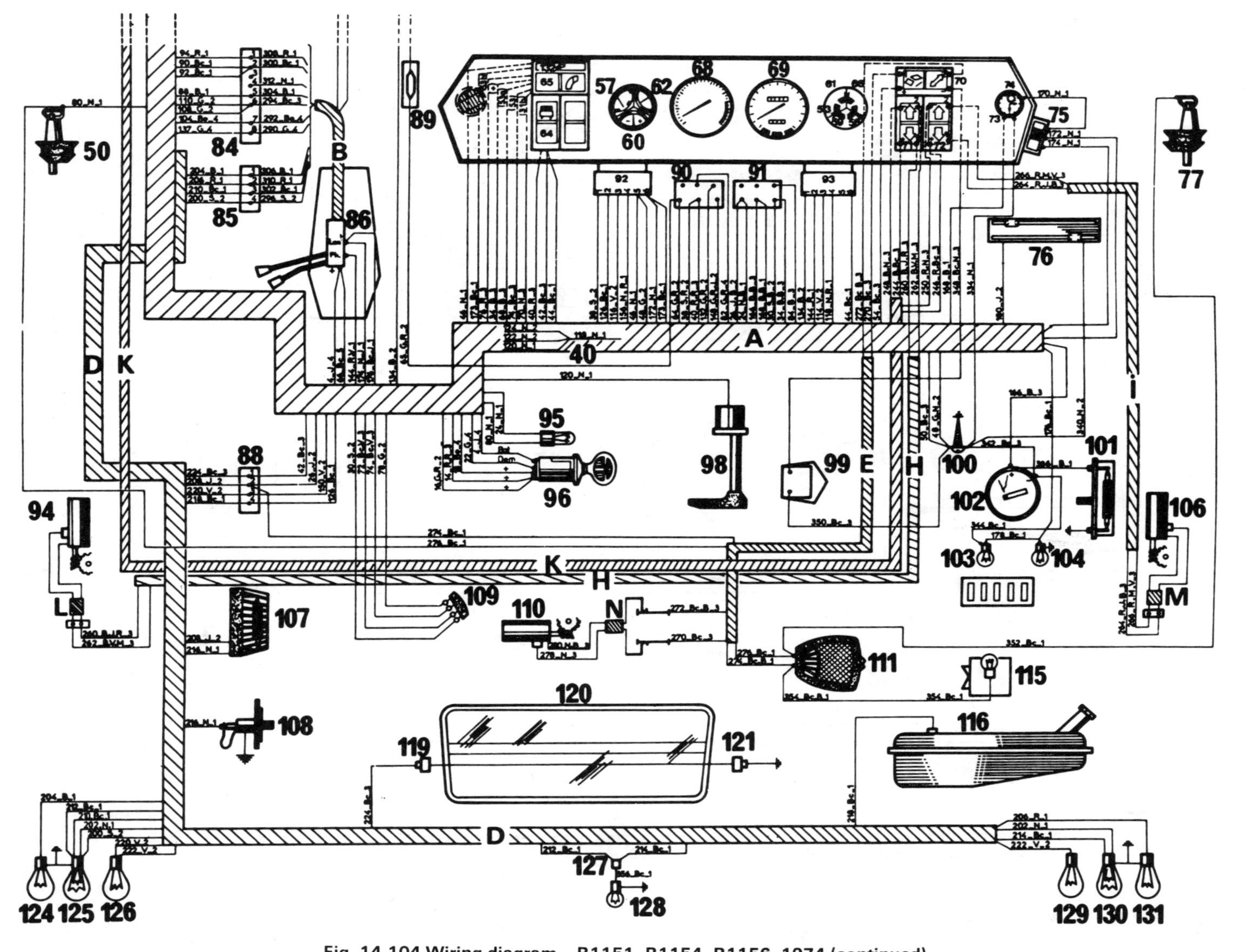

Fig. 14.104 Wiring diagram – R1151, R1154, R1156, 1974 (continued)

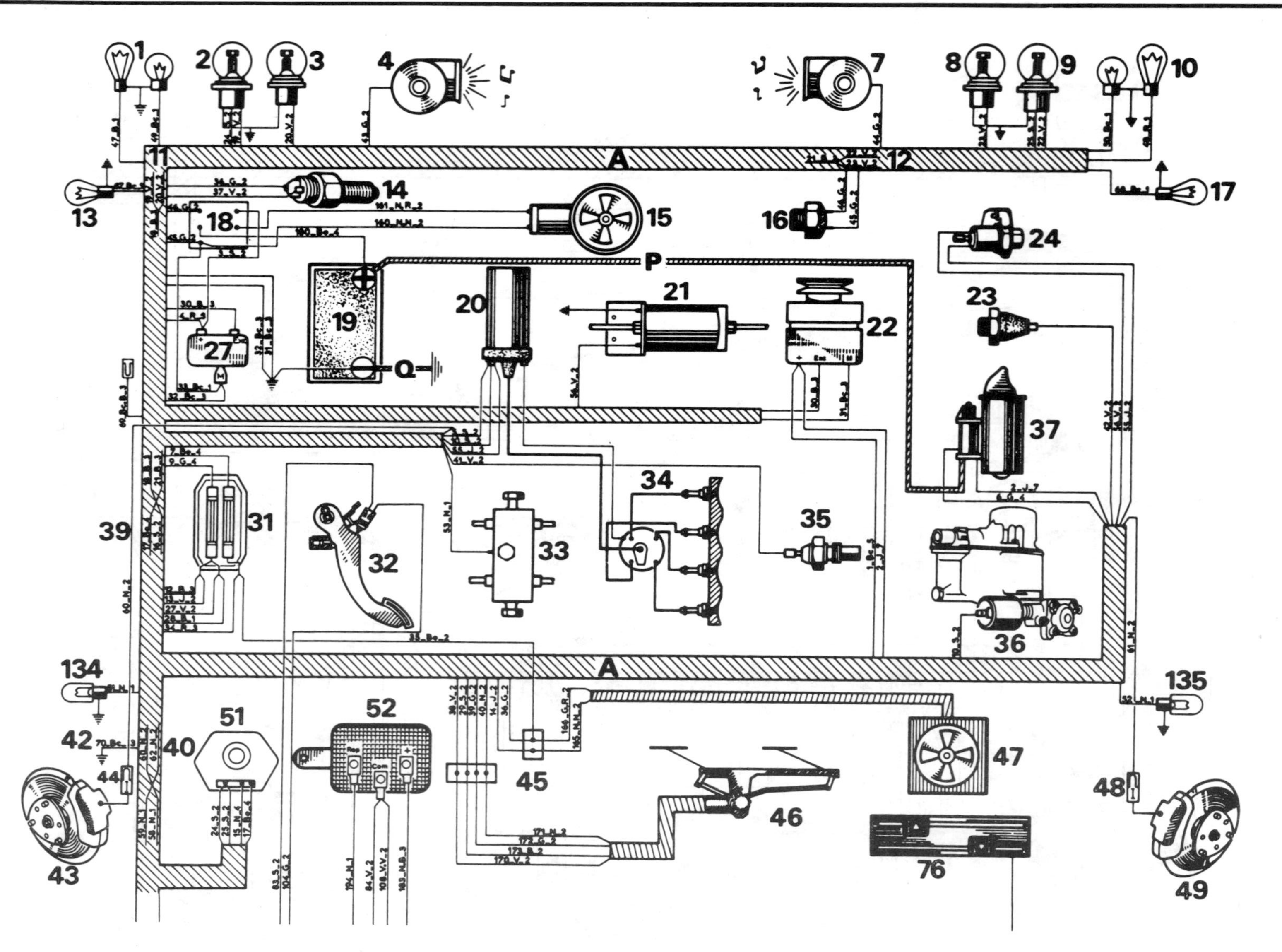

Fig. 14.105 Wiring diagram – R1152, R1153, R1155, USA Canada

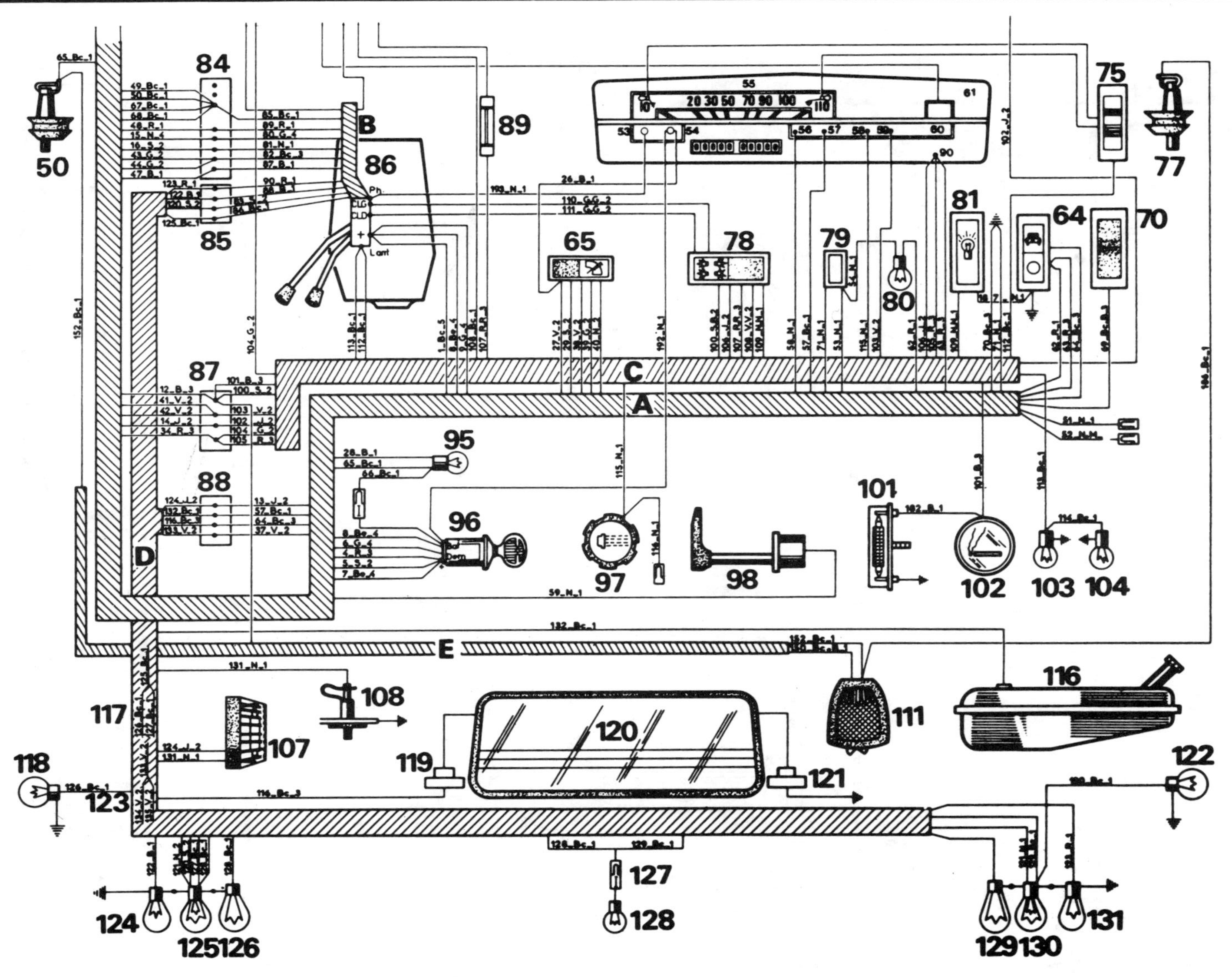

Fig. 14.105 Wiring diagram – R1152, R1153, R1155, USA Canada (continued)

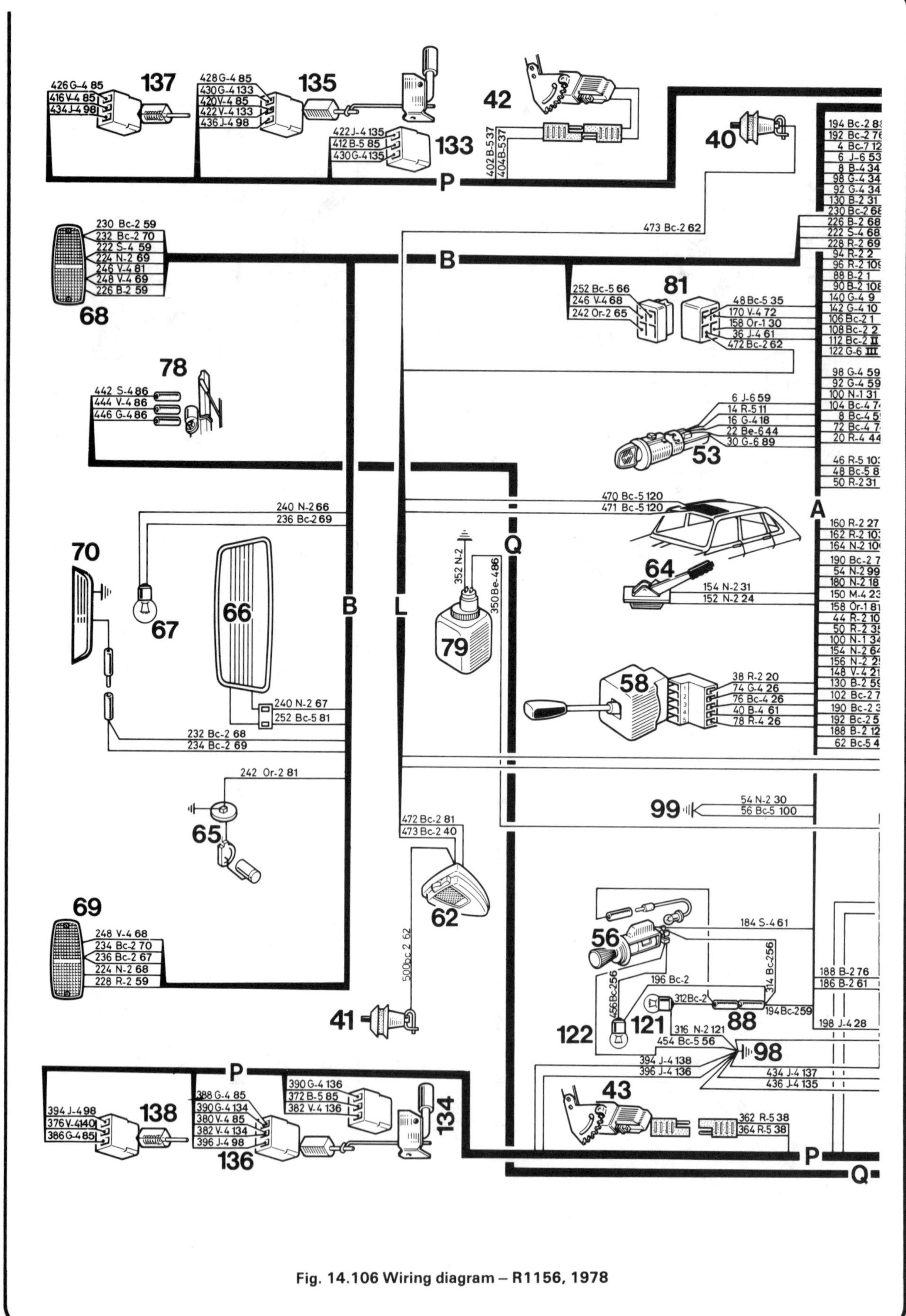

Fig. 14.106 Wiring diagram – R1156, 1978

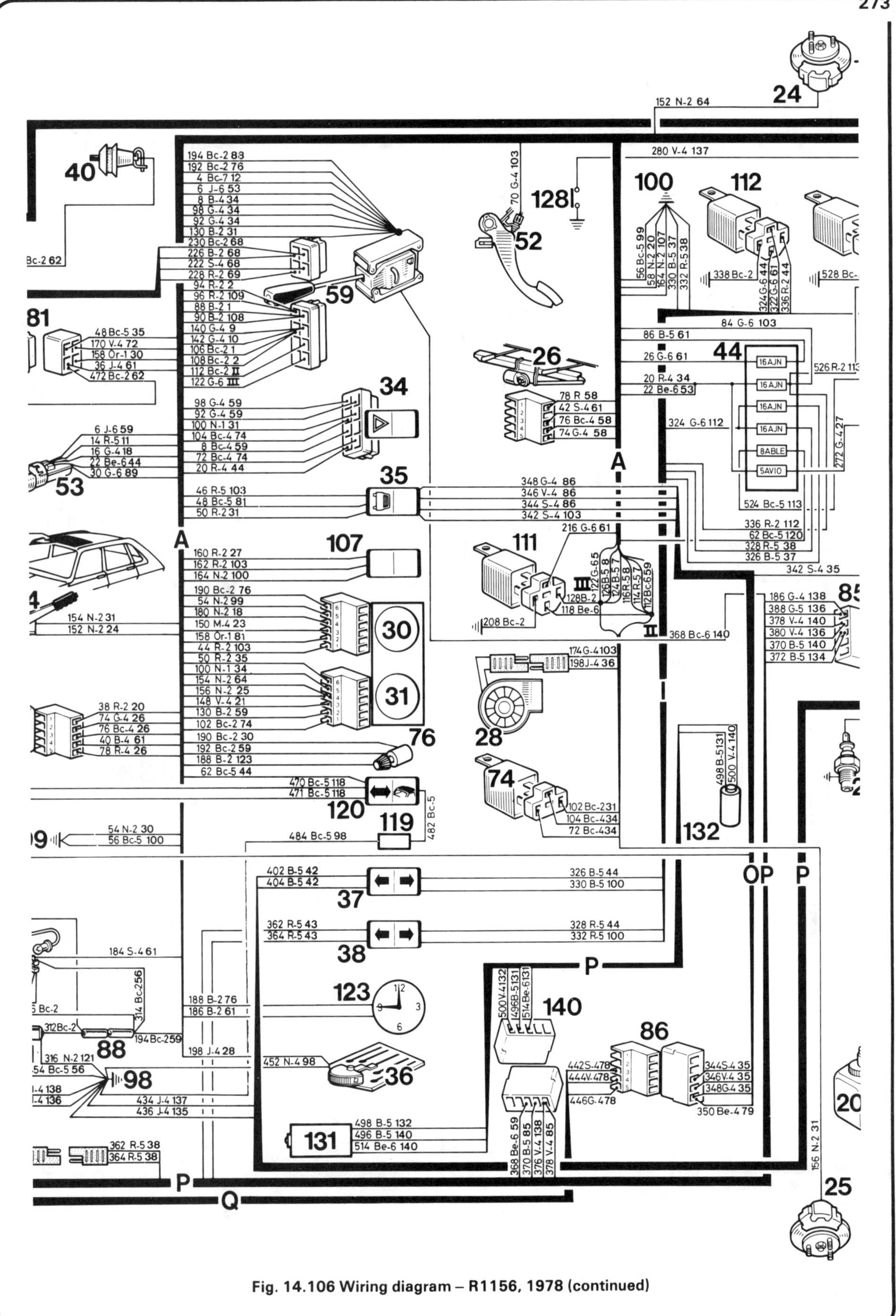

Fig. 14.106 Wiring diagram – R1156, 1978 (continued)

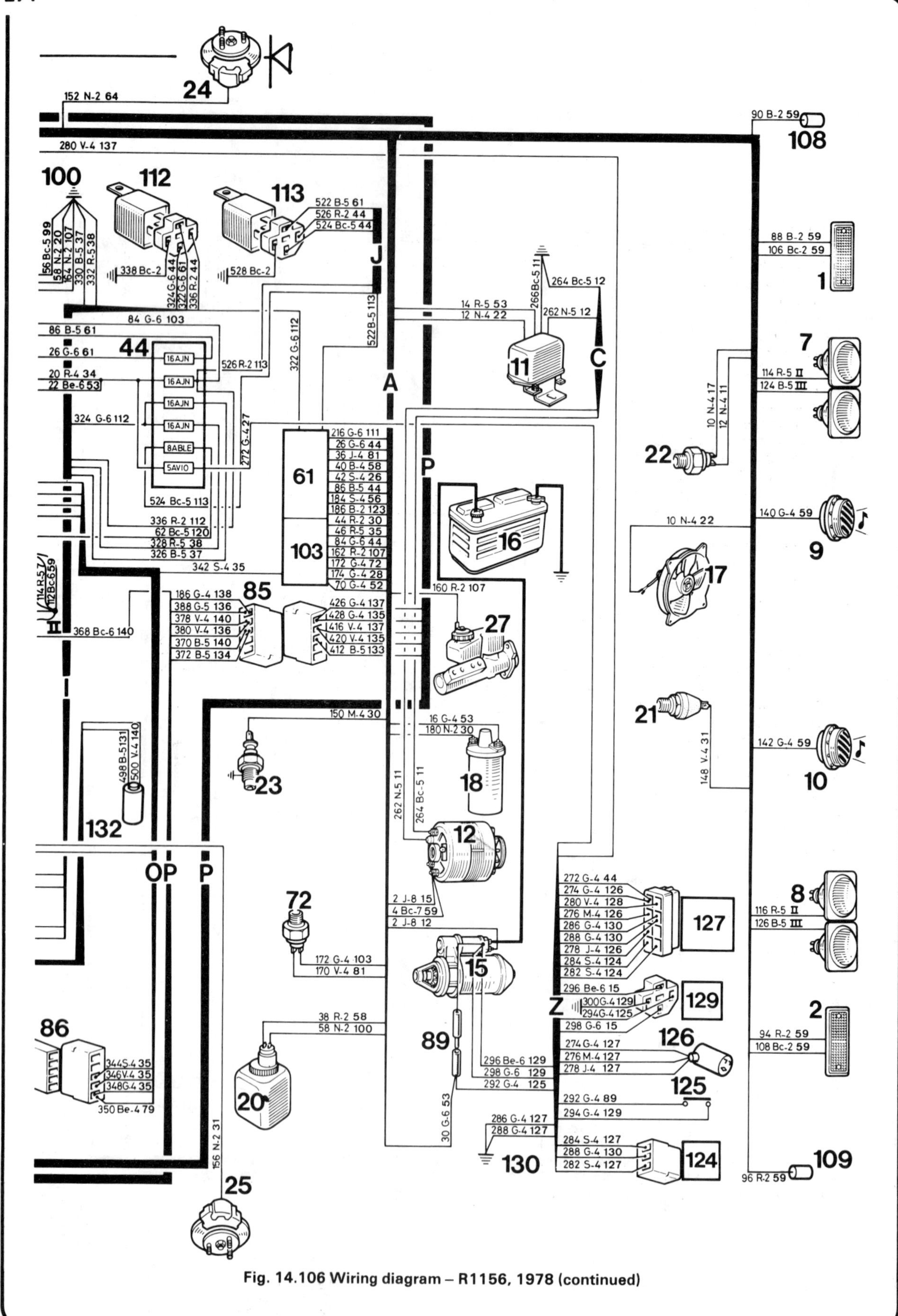

Fig. 14.106 Wiring diagram – R1156, 1978 (continued)

Key to wiring diagram for 1978 R1156 model

1 LH front sidelight and direction indicator
2 RH front sidelight and direction indicator
7 LH headlight unit
8 RH headlight unit
9 LH horn
10 RH horn
11 Regulator
12 Alternator
15 Starter
16 Battery
17 Engine cooling fan motor
18 Ignition coil
20 Windscreen washer pump
21 Oil pressure switch
22 Thermal switch on radiator
23 Thermal switch on cylinder head
24 LH front brake
25 RH front brake
26 Windscreen wiper plate
27 Master cylinder
28 Heating/ventilating fan motor
30 Connector No 1 – instrument panel
31 Connector No 2 – instrument panel
34 Hazard warning lights switch
35 Rear screen demister switch
36 Heating-ventilating fan motor rheostat
37 LH window winder switch
38 RH window winder switch
40 LH door pillar switch
41 RH door pillar switch
42 LH window winder
43 RH window winder
44 Accessories plate (fusebox)
52 Stoplights switch
53 Anti-theft switch
56 Cigar lighter
58 Windscreen wiper-washer switch
59 Lighting switch
61 Feed wire junction before switch
62 Interior light (LH)
64 Handbrake
65 Fuel gauge tank unit
66 Rear screen demister
67 Luggage compartment illumination
68 LH rear light assembly
69 RH rear light assembly
70 Licence plate light
72 Reversing lights switch
74 Flasher unit
76 Instrument panel lighting rheostat
78 Rear screen wiper motor
79 Rear screen washer pump
81 Junction block – front and rear harnesses
85 Junction block – window winder harness
86 Junction block – chassis-tailgate harnesses
88 Wire junction – glove compartment illumination
89 Wire junction – starter wire
98 Glove compartment light earth
99 Dashboard earth
100 LH inner wing panel gusset earth
103 Junction plate – + after switch
107 Brake circuit warning light bulb checking switch
108 LH front width marker light
109 RH front width marker light
111 Headlight main beam relay
112 Window winder relay
113 Sunroof relay
118 Sunroof motor
119 Sunroof cutout
120 Sunroof changeover switch
121 Glove compartment illumination
122 Ashtray illumination
123 Clock
124 Automatic transmission
125 Automatic transmission starting authorisation switch
126 Sealed multiple plug on automatic transmission
128 Kick-down switch
129 Automatic transmission starting authorisation relay
130 Automatic transmission earth
131 Electro-magnetic locks cutout
132 Electro-magnetic locks inertia switch
133 LH front door lock changeover switch
134 RH front door lock changeover switch
135 LH front door electro-magnetic lock
136 RH front door electro-magnetic lock
137 LH rear door electro-magnetic lock
138 RH rear door electro-magnetic lock
140 Junction block – electro-magnetic locks harness

Wiring harnesses

A Engine front
B Rear
C Alternator
H Window winder relay
L Interior light door switches
P Electro-magnetic door locks
Q Tailgate

Wire colour codes

Be Beige
Bc White
B Blue
C Clear
G Grey
J Yellow
N Black
S Pink
R Red
V Green
M Maroon
Or Orange
Vi Violet

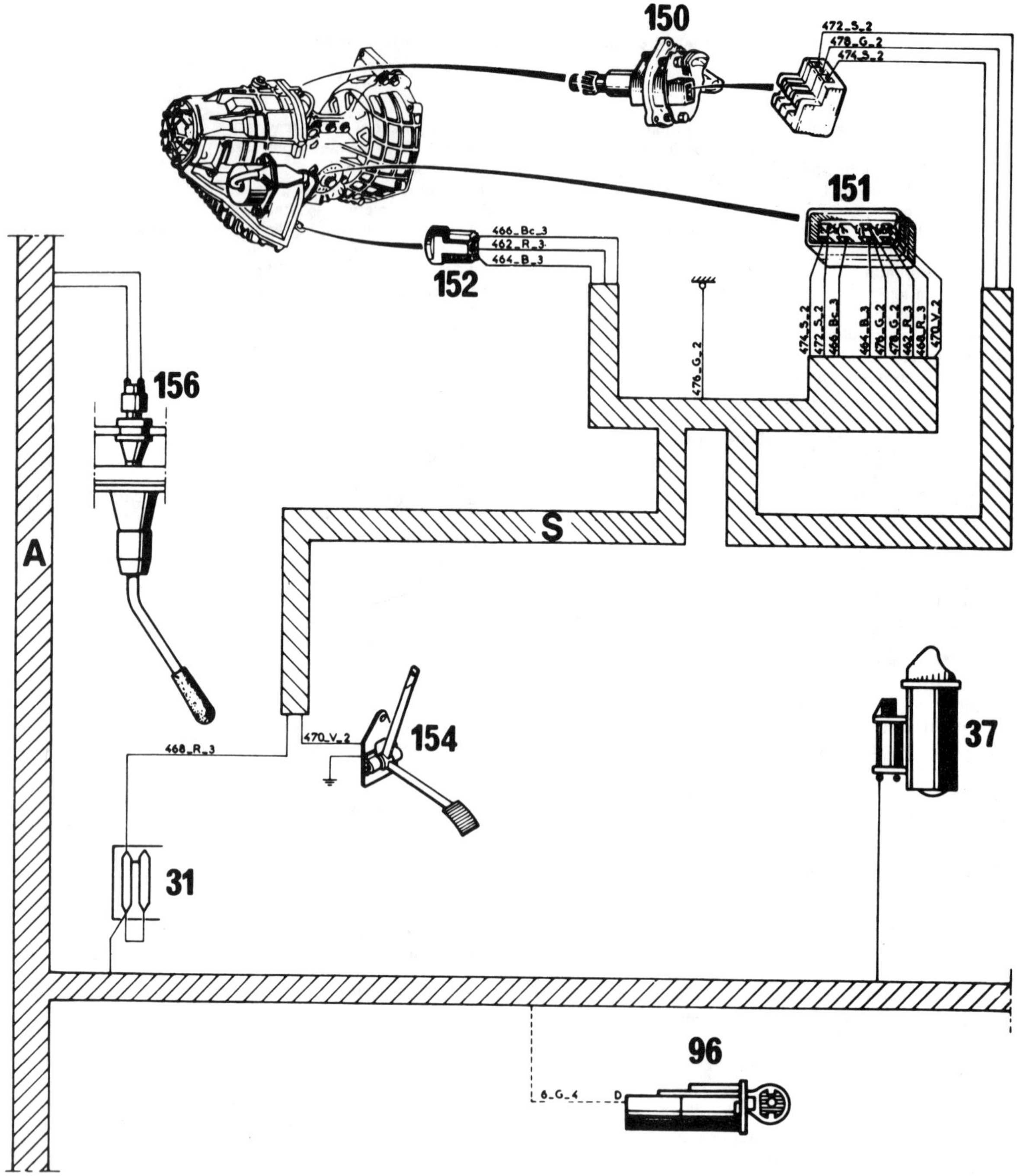

150

472_S_2
478_G_2
474_S_2

151

466_Bc_3
462_R_3
464_B_3

152

474_S_2
472_S_2
466_Bc_3
464_B_3
476_G_2
478_G_2
462_R_3
468_R_3
470_V_2

476_G_2

156

A

S

470_V_2

468_R_3

154

37

31

96

6_G_4 D

Fig. 14.107 Wiring diagram for automatic transmission – R1153, R1154, pre 1973

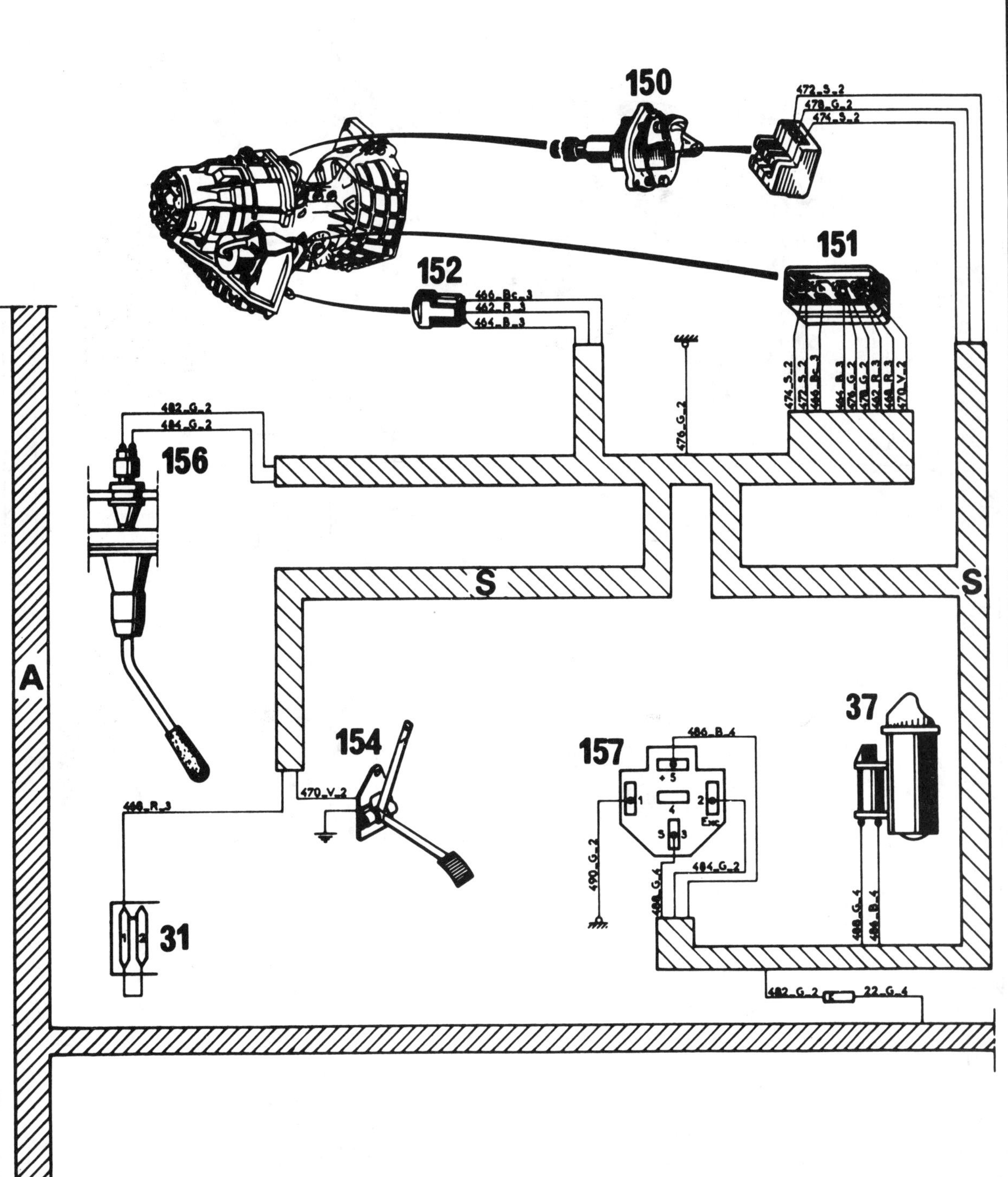

Fig. 14.108 Wiring diagram for automatic transmission – R1153, R1154, 1973/74

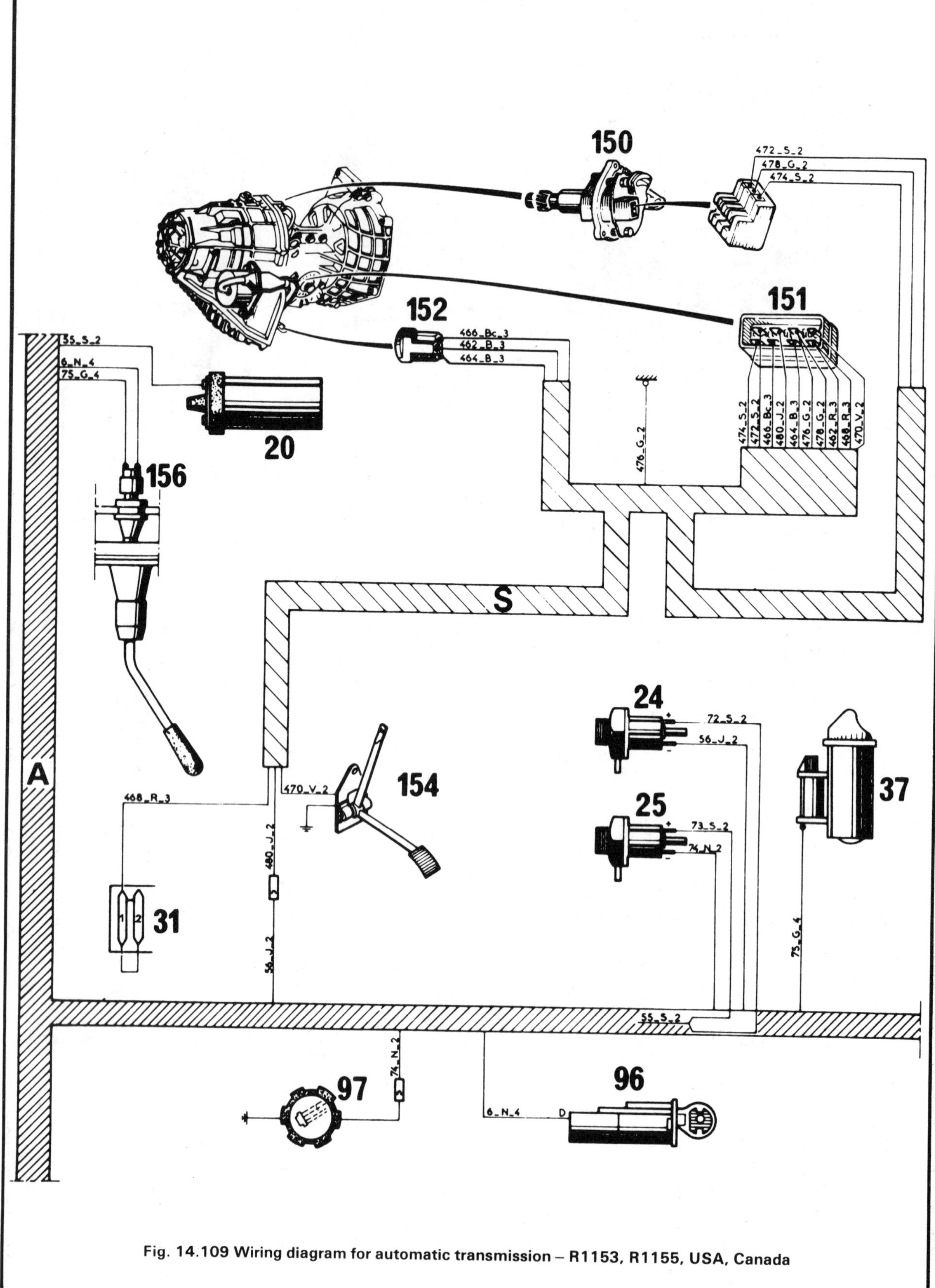

Fig. 14.109 Wiring diagram for automatic transmission – R1153, R1155, USA, Canada

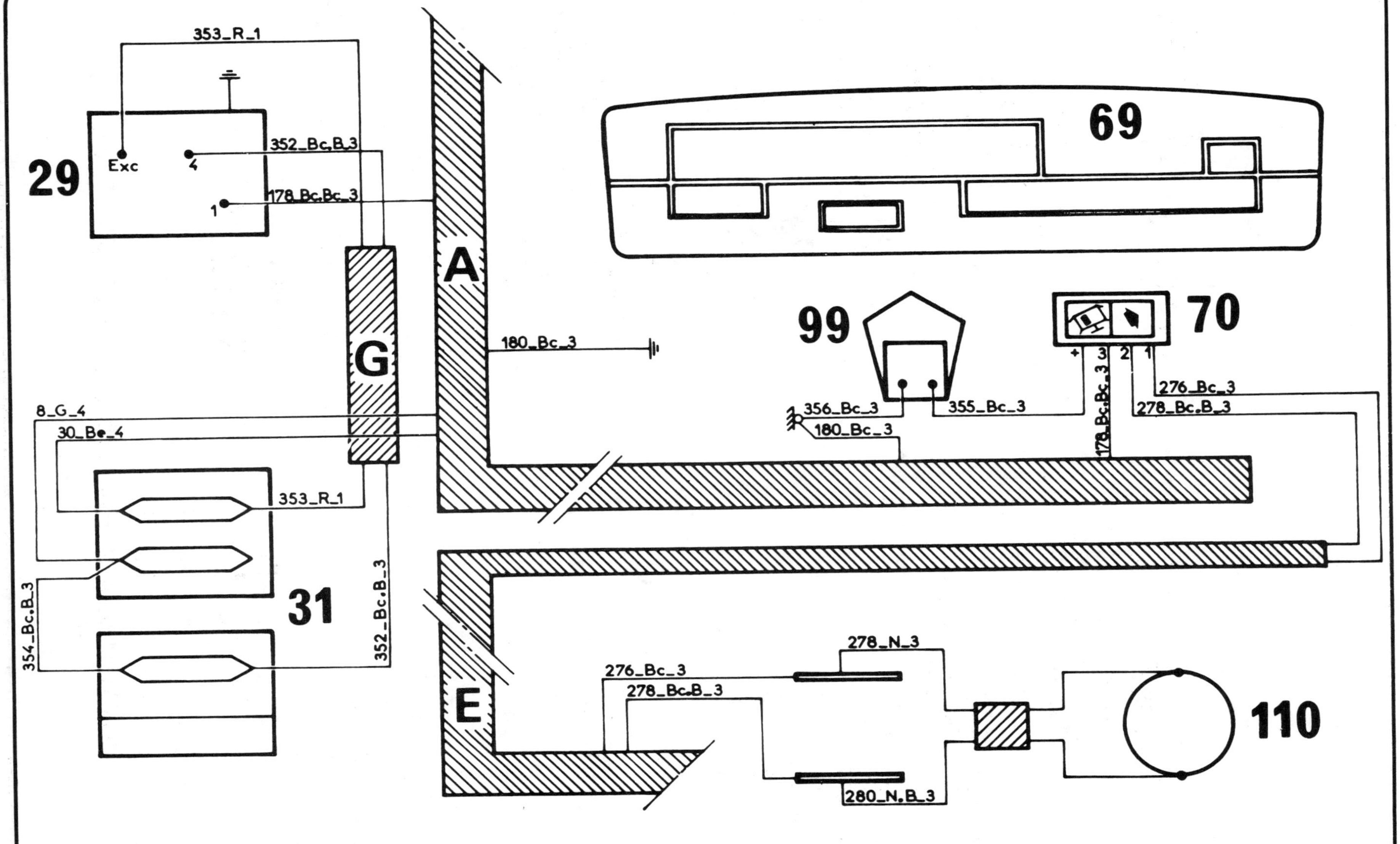

353_R_1
29
Exc
4
1
352_Bc.B_3
178_Bc.Bc_3
G
A
180_Bc_3
8_G_4
30_Be_4
353_R_1
354_Bc.B_3
352_Bc.B_3
31
69
99
356_Bc_3
355_Bc_3
180_Bc_3
70
+ 3 2 1
178_Bc.Bc_3
276_Bc_3
278_Bc.B_3
E
276_Bc_3
278_Bc.B_3
278_N_3
280_N.B_3
110

Fig. 14.110 Wiring diagram for sunroof – R1150, R1152, R1153

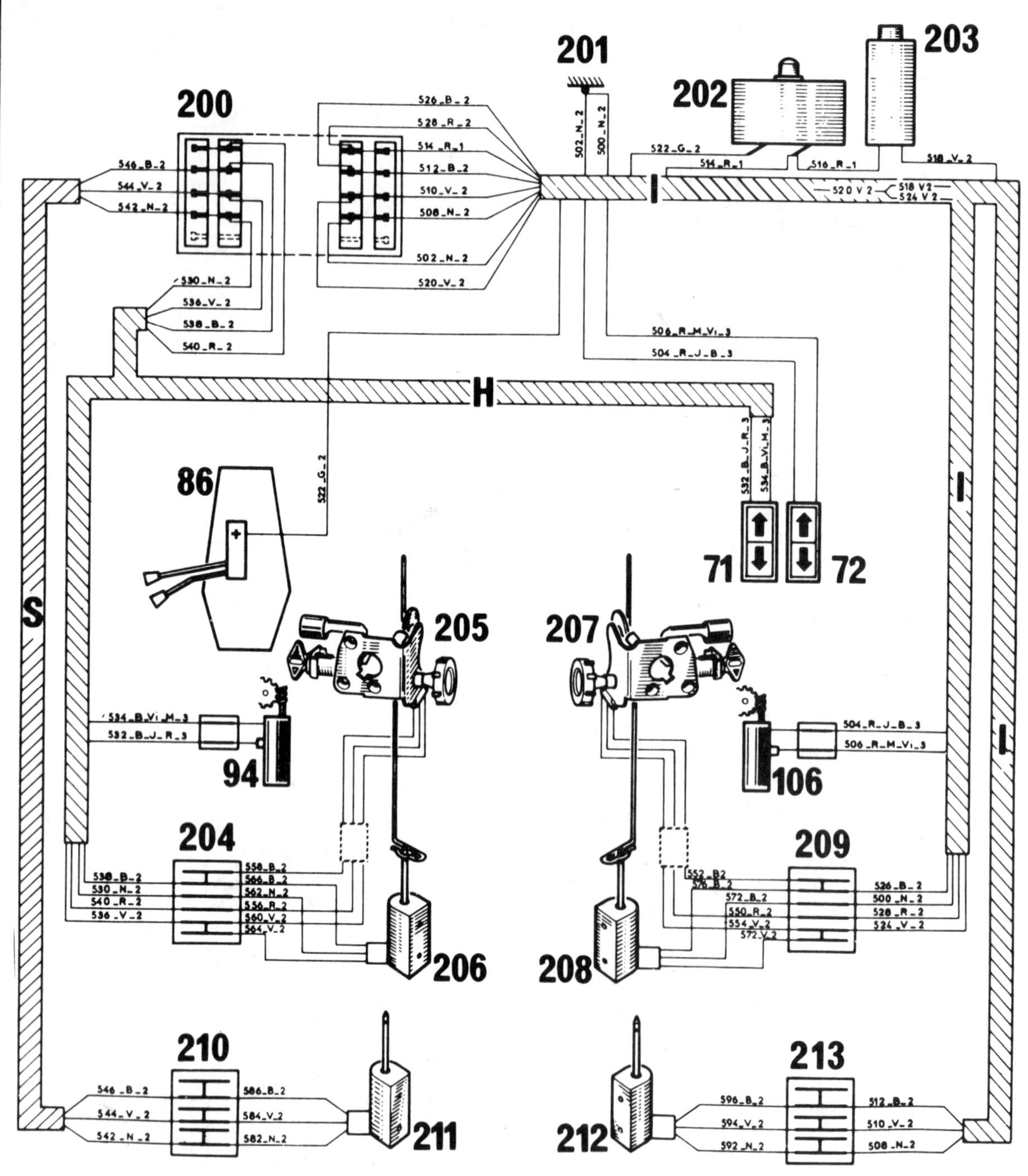

Fig. 14.111 Wiring diagram for electro-magnetic door locks – R1151, R1154, R1156

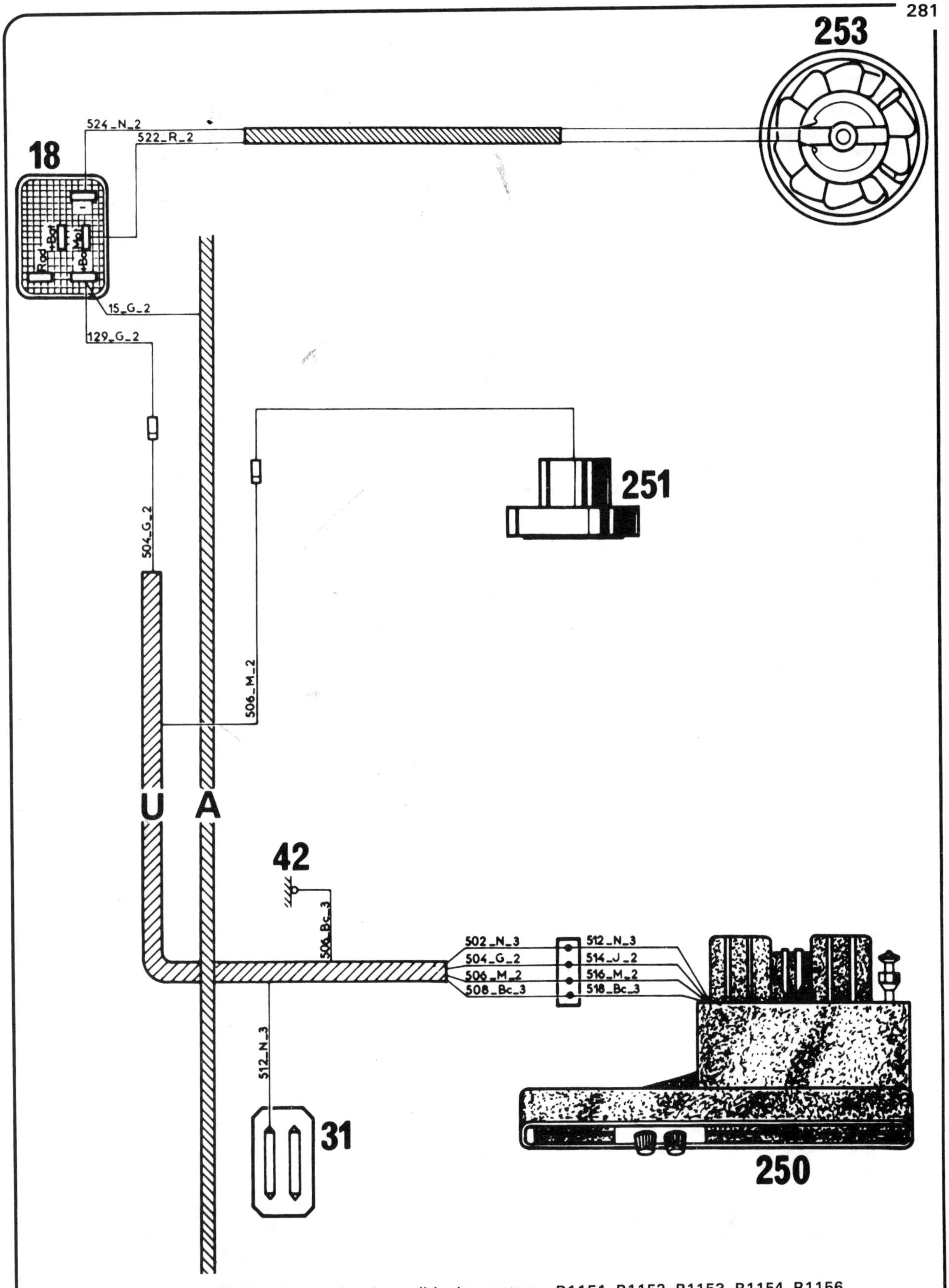

Fig. 14.112 Wiring diagram for air conditioning system – R1151, R1152, R1153, R1154, R1156

14 Bodywork and underframe

Underbody height

1 Heights must be measured when the vehicle is standing on the level, is unladen, but has a full fuel tank.
2 Tyres must be inflated to the correct pressure.
3 Measurements must be taken from the ground to the side-member on a vertical centre-line through the wheel centres.
4 The tolerance on all the H1 and H2 dimensions in the Table in Specifications is 0.4 in (10 mm), and the maximum tolerance between RH and LH sides must not exceed 0.4 in (10 mm).
5 The driver's side must not be lower than the passenger's side.
6 Adjust the brake limiter (Chapter 11, Section 6) after making any adjustment to the underbody height.

Electro-magnetic door locks - general

7 Some vehicles are fitted with a system for locking and unlocking all four doors simultaneously.
8 The system is fitted with two safety devices which are intended to override the system in the event of a crash or fire. These are an inertia switch and a thermal cut-out which are fitted to a bracket in the glovebox.
9 The thermal cut-out and the inertia switch are each secured to the bracket by two screws.
10 When fitting an inertia switch, ensure that it is fixed to the bracket securely so that it cannot vibrate and operate spuriously.

Electro-magnetic door locks - removal and refitting

11 Remove the door trim, then lower the window and remove the remote control housing.
12 With the window raised as high as possible, disconnect the two cables from the junction plate and remove the plate.
13 Remove the tumbler plate assembly (1) (Fig. 14.114) from the door frame.
14 Remove the clip (2) from inside the door frame, to disconnect the external lock control.
15 Remove the inner fixing screw (3).
16 Remove the fixing screws (4) from the actuator (5).
17 Withdraw the lock by moving it towards the lower part of the window channel.
18 The front and rear door actuators are different. The front door one has a flat (6) on the control rod which fits the bottom of the rod as shown. Always ensure that the rod is fitted with a safety clip (A).
19 The rear door actuator is identified by having a circular groove (7) on the control rod.
20 When refitting, first fit the lock assembly to the door frame and adjust the lock, then fit the actuator, leaving the fixing screws loose until the actuator has been adjusted.

Actuator - adjustment

21 Push the locking lever up as far as possible and fit a block (C) between the actuator and the control rod clip, to prevent the rod from bending.
22 Push the actuator assembly up so that its plunger is in the locked position, and tighten the actuator fixing screws.
23 Apply grease to the lock mechanism, the lock operating rod and the top of the actuator.
24 Refit the door trim, taking care that when sticking down the waterproof plastic membrane the hole for the changeover switch knob is kept free of adhesive which might subsequently cause malfunction of the switch.

Changeover switch

25 The changeover switch is swaged to the door lock, and is removed by levering it off with a screwdriver inserted between the switch and the lock plate.
26 After fitting a new switch, swage it to the lock plate.
27 When fitting the changeover switch knob, align its end with the swing lever slot and then clip it into place.
28 Only fit changeover switch knobs which have a flat L = 0.47 in (1.2 mm) wide near its end, as shown in Fig. 14.117.

Bonnet lock (R1156) - removal and refitting

29 Remove the locking assembly by removing the nut to release the centre mounting lever (1) (Fig. 14.118).
30 Remove the fixing bolts from the side plates (2) and lift away the locking assembly.
31 To remove the lock, punch out the roll pin (arrowed) and withdraw the lock barrel.
32 Refitting is a reversal of the removal operations.

Front grille (R1156) - removing and refitting

33 Remove the two outer headlights (Fig. 14.119).
34 Take out the screws (A) securing the wing mouldings.
35 Remove the two screws (B) which secure the front grille and lift off the grille by pulling it forwards and upwards. Take care not to lose the two rubber washers (C) which fit over the locating pegs.
36 Remove the screws (D) from the bottom moulding and unclip the plastic centre fixing.

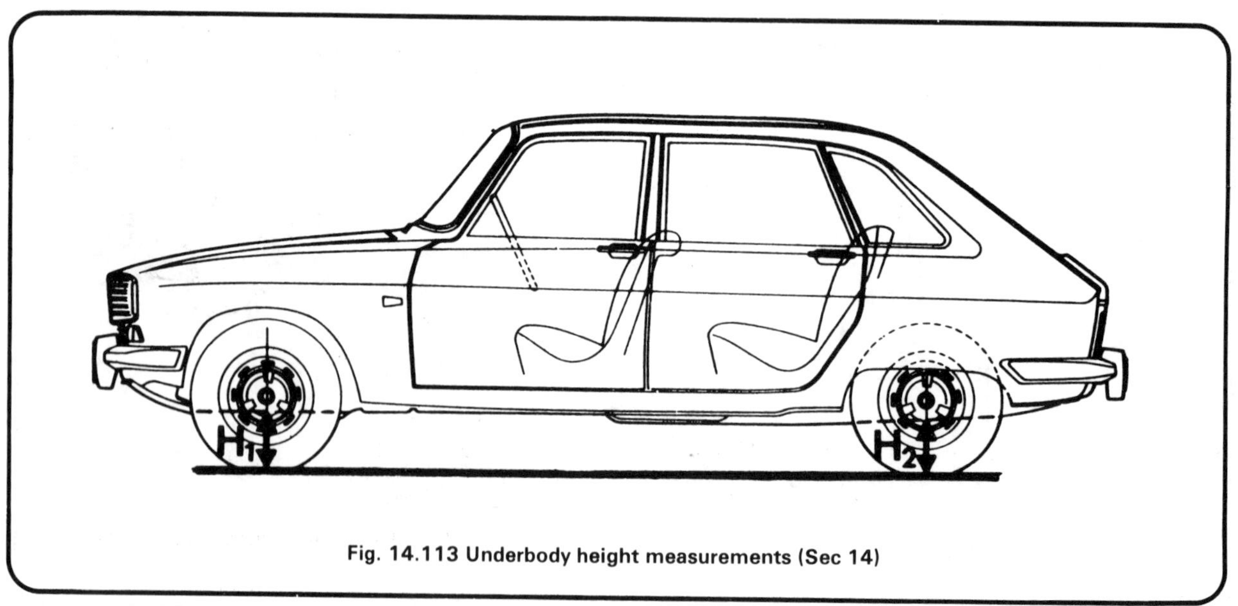

Fig. 14.113 Underbody height measurements (Sec 14)

37 Using a screwdriver blade and a piece of rag to protect the paintwork, carefully lever off the side mouldings.
38 Refitting is the reverse of removal, but remember to ensure that the rubber washers are in place on the lower fixing pegs of the grille.

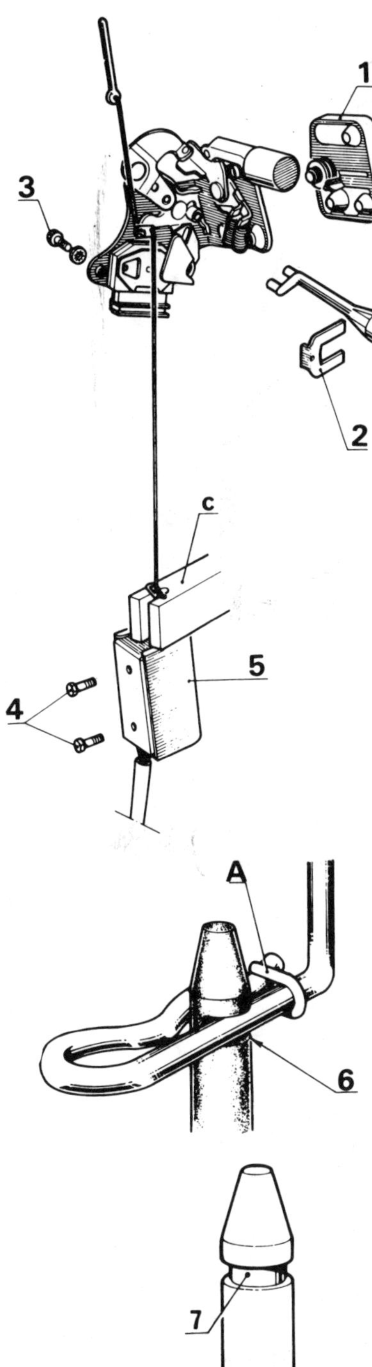

Fig. 14.114 Electro-magnetic lock components (Sec 14)

1 *Tumbler plate*
2 *Clip*
3 *Screw*
4 *Screws*
5 *Actuator*
6 *Front door actuator flat*
7 *Rear door actuator groove*
A *Safety clip*
C *Block*

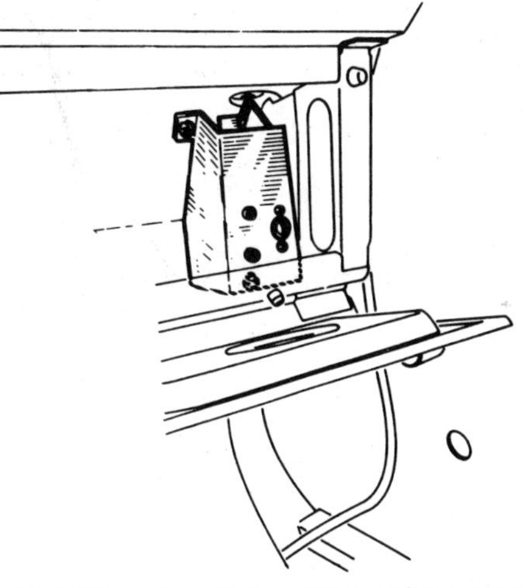

Fig. 14.115 Inertia switch and thermal cut-out positions (Sec 14)

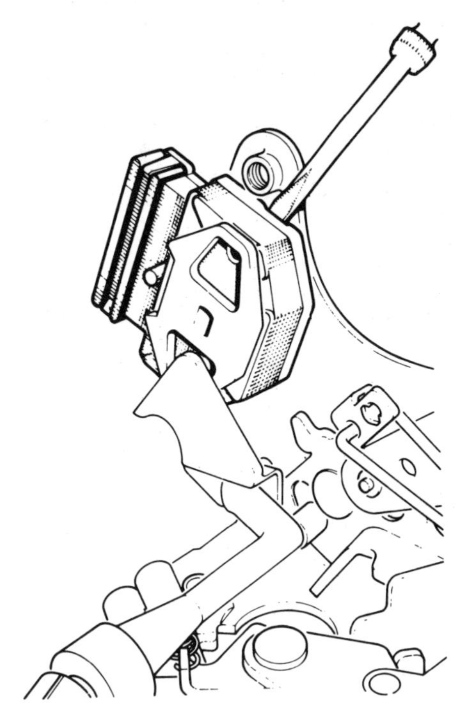

Fig. 14.116 Changeover switch removal (Sec 14)

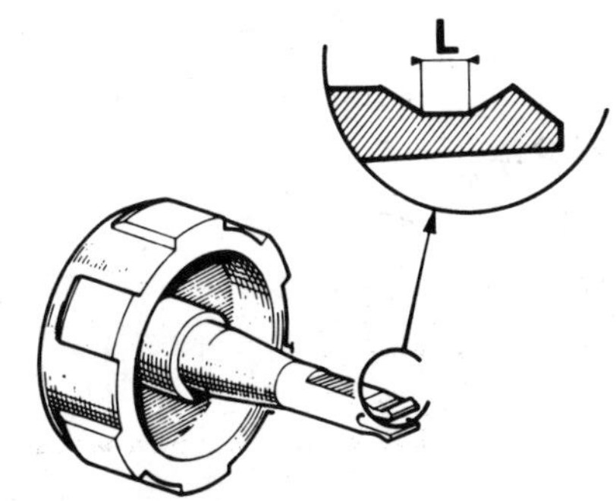

Fig. 14.117 Changeover switch knob (Sec 14)

L 0.47 in (1.2 mm)

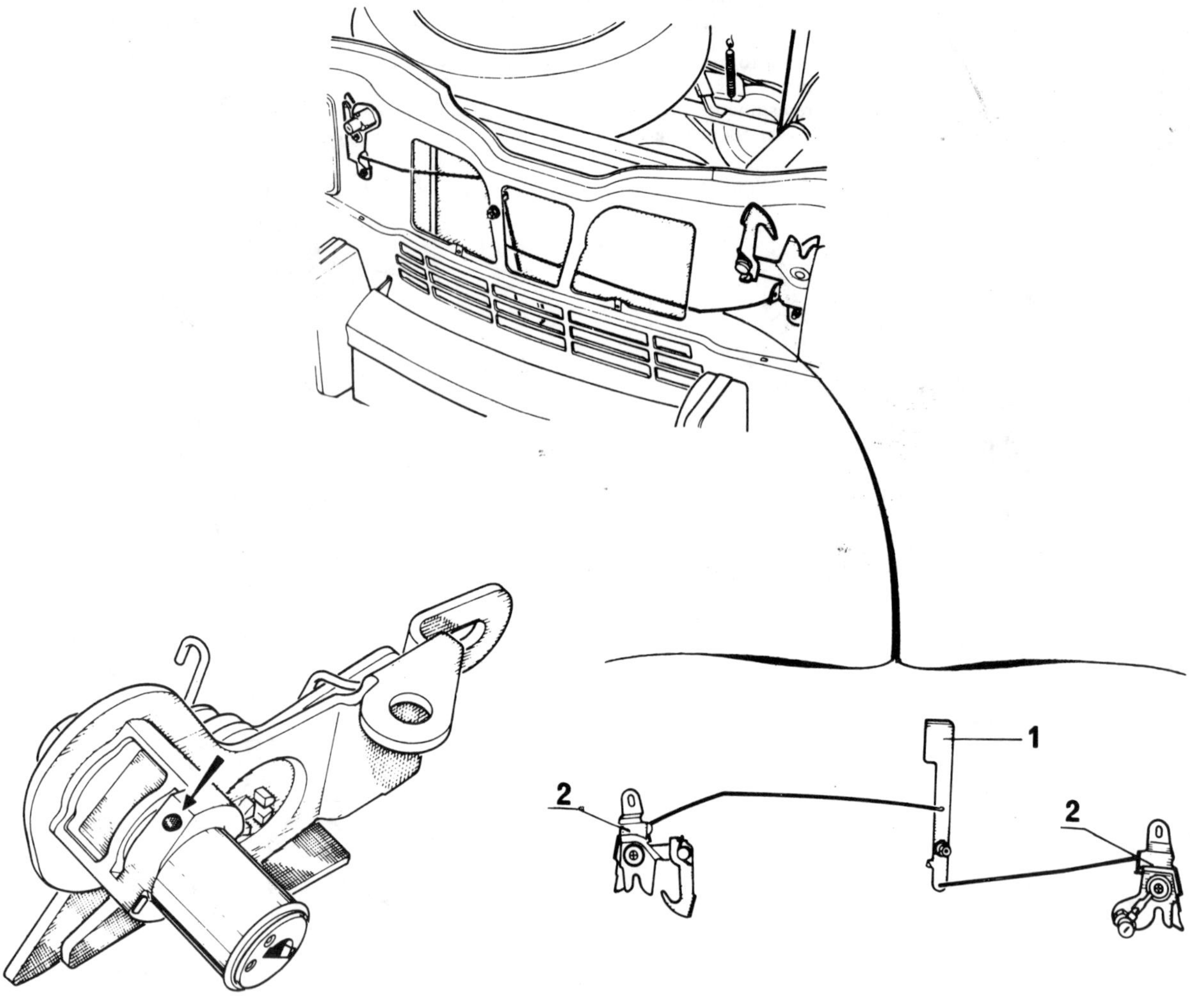

Fig. 14.118 Bonnet lock components (R1156) (Sec 14)

1 Centre mounting lever *2 Side plates*

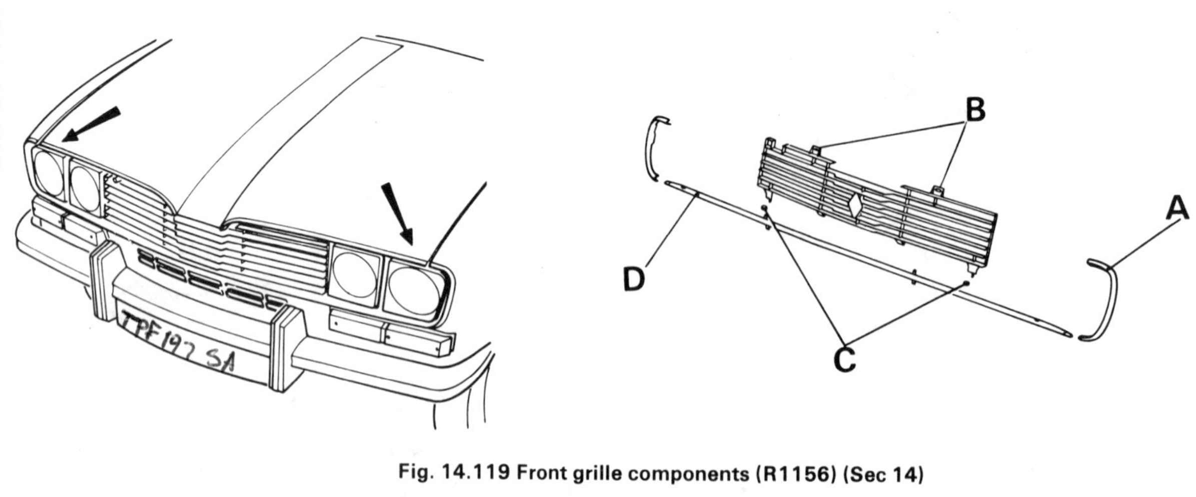

Fig. 14.119 Front grille components (R1156) (Sec 14)

A Screws *B Screws* *C Rubber washers* *D Screws*

Fault diagnosis - electro-magnetic door locks

Symptom	Reasons
Locking mechanism inoperative	Changeover switch faulty, or contaminated with adhesive Swing lever becomes unclipped when switch knob is fitted Switch shorted externally
Inertia switch is set off	Possibly caused by slamming the glove compartment lid too hard, or by loose switch fixing

Air conditioning system

Description and precautions

39 When an air conditioning system is fitted, it is necessary to observe special precautions whenever dealing with any part of the system, its associated components and any items within the engine and heating compartment that necessitate disconnection of the system.

40 The refrigeration circuit contains a liquid gas (Freon) and it is therefore dangerous to disconnect any part of the system without specialised knowledge and equipment. If for any reason the system must be disconnected (engine removal for example), entrust this task to your Renault dealer or a refrigeration engineer.

41 Whenever working on the vehicle in the vicinity of the air conditioning system, adhere to the following precautions.

(a) *Should any part of the system malfunction and cause a leakage of the liquid or gas, do not breathe in the refrigerant fumes. Should the fluid get in the eyes it can cause permanent blindness and a doctor should be consulted without delay! To reduce the effects of fluid contact with the eyes or skin, a few drops of mineral oil can be applied, then wash clean with a weak boric acid solution.*

(b) *Do not expose the system components to a naked flame, especially where a leak is suspected. The gas is not itself poisonous, but if drawn through a heat source (eg a lighted cigarette) it will produce phosgene which will kill if inhaled.*

(c) *In the event of a sudden leak in the system, switch off the engine (if running) and disconnect the compressor drivebelt. Get the system fault repaired without delay. Do not attempt to operate the system if it is known to be short of refrigerant.*

42 Fig. 14.120 shows the layout and principal components of the system. Operation is as follows.

43 The camshaft-driven compressor raises the pressure of gas in the system and pumps it to the condensor where it liquifies. From the condensor, liquid is pumped to the accumulator where it is dehydrated before passing onto the evaporator. The accumulator incorporates a sight glass so that a visual check can be kept on liquid circulation. With the system operating, the glass should display a clear stream of liquid, perhaps with occasional bubbles. A lot of bubbles, or even foam, will indicate a low liquid level. Do not delay before investigating a low or zero level.

44 Before entering the evaporator, liquid is pumped through a reducing valve which injects it into the low pressure circuit whilst at the same time regulating its entry into the evaporator by means of a thermostatically controlled probe which senses temperature variation in the evaporator outlet pipe. Air entering the vehicle is ducted across the evaporator and is cooled. The warmer liquid leaving the evaporator reverts to gas and returns to the compressor.

Component location

45 It follows that if a vehicle has to be returned to a Renault dealer for disconnection of any system component, then it is advisable to allow the dealer to change that component, especially where in the case of such items as the camshaft to compressor 'juboflex' attachment, several special tools are required.

46 The figures which accompany this text are provided as a means of component identification only, to help when relaying information to a specialist.

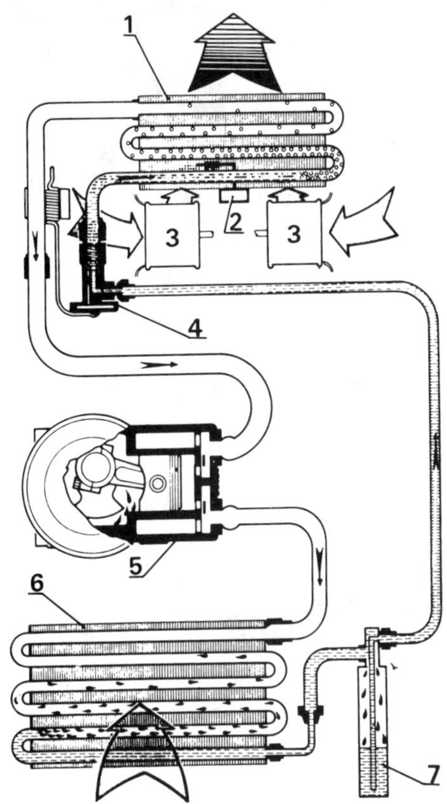

Fig. 14.120 Air conditioning system components (Sec 14)

1 *Evaporator*
2 *Thermostat*
3 *Fans*
4 *Reducing valve*
5 *Compressor*
6 *Condensor*
7 *Accumulator and dehydrator*

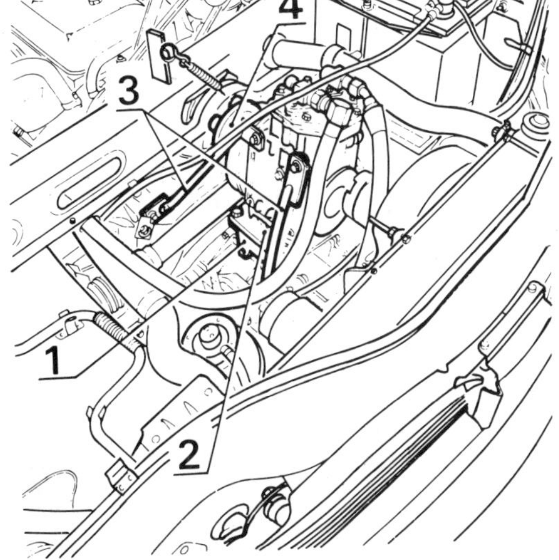

Fig. 14.121 Compressor location (Sec 14)

1 *Mounting bracket*
2 *Intermediate plate*
3 *Tie-rods*
4 *Juboflex attachment*

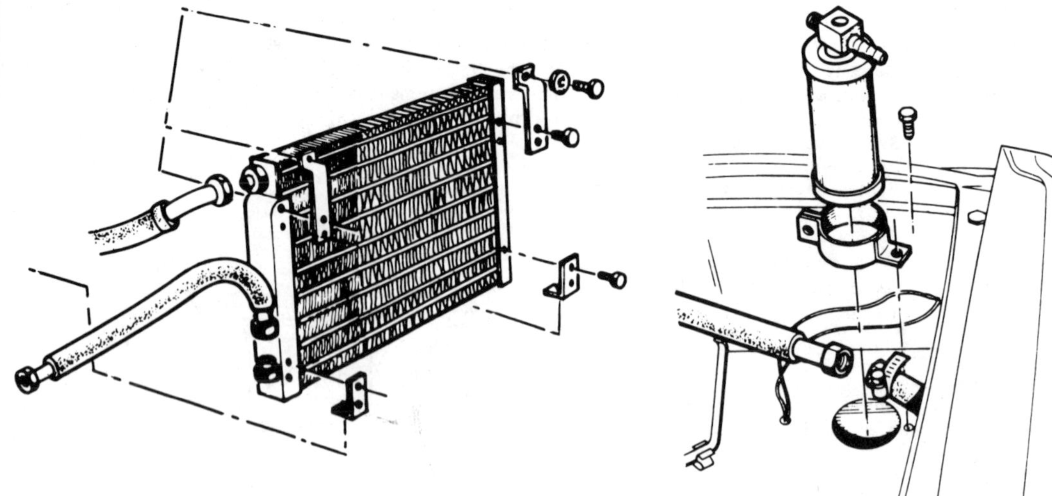

Fig. 14.122 The condensor (Sec 14)

Fig. 14.123 Accumulator location (Sec 14)

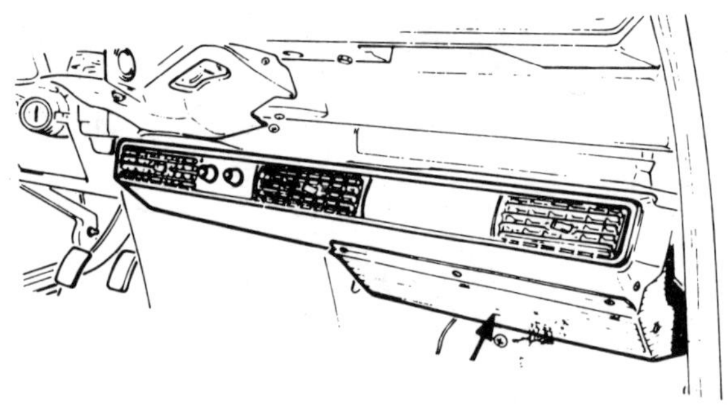

Fig. 14.124 Evaporator location (Sec 14)

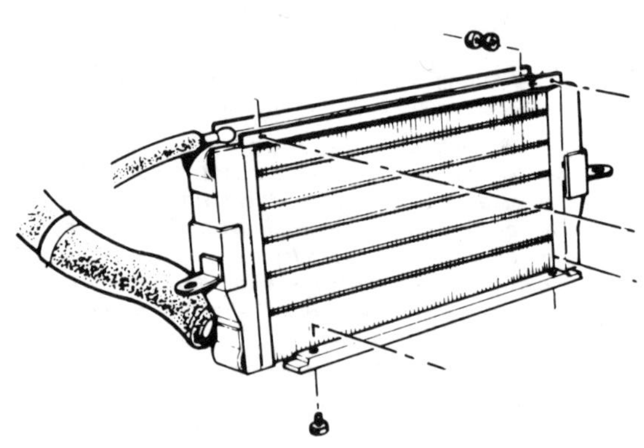

Fig. 14.125 The cooling radiator (Sec 14)

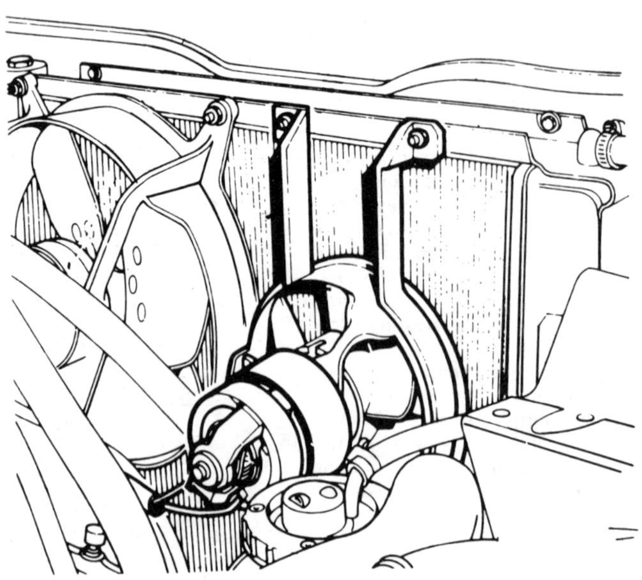

Fig. 14.126 Supplementary fan location (Sec 14)

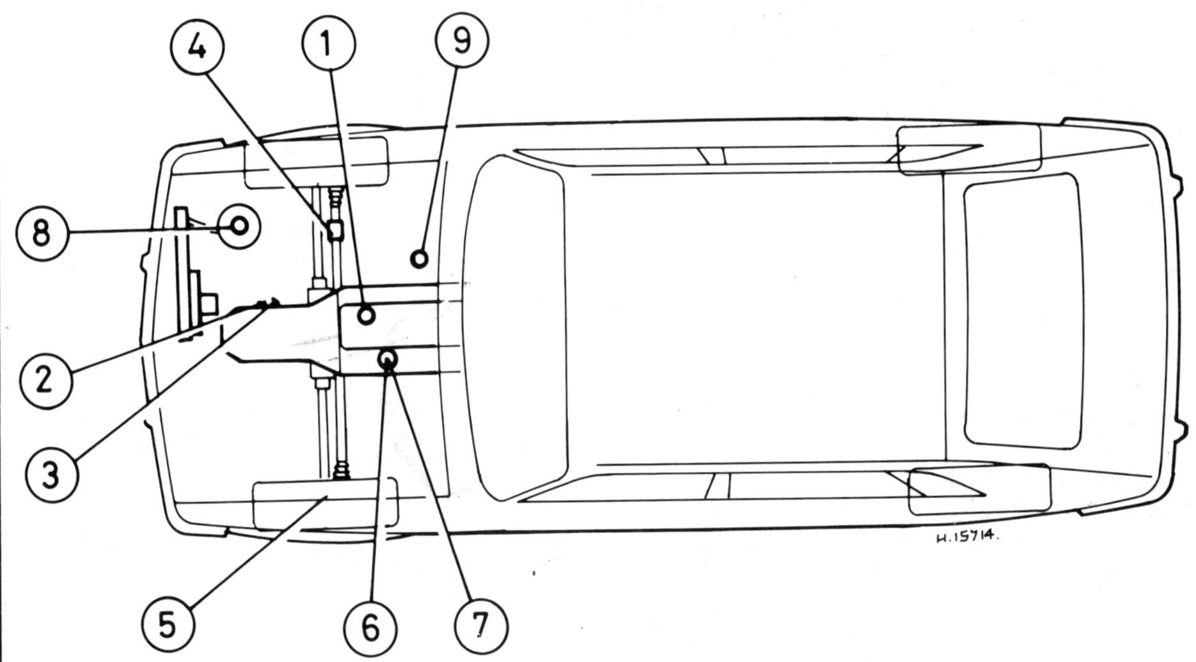

Recommended lubricants and fluids

Component or system	Lubricant type or specification
Engine (1)	20W/40 multigrade engine oil
Manual gearbox (2)	SAE 80W hypoid gear oil to API GL4 or API GL5
Automatic transmission (3)	Dexron automatic transmission fluid
Steering box (4)	Multi-purpose lithium based grease
Wheel bearings (5)	Multi-purpose lithium based grease
Distributor (6)	Engine oil
Contact breaker cam (7)	Petroleum jelly
Cooling system (8)	Ethylene Glycol antifreeze
Brake fluid reservoir (9)	Hydraulic fluid to SAE J1703 or DOT 3

The above are general recommendations only: lubrication requirements vary from territory to territory. Consult your owners handbook or a Renault dealer.

Fault diagnosis

Introduction

The vehicle owner who does his or her own maintenance according to the recommended schedules should not have to use this section of the manual very often. Modern component reliability is such that, provided those items subject to wear or deterioration are inspected or renewed at the specified intervals, sudden failure is comparatively rare. Faults do not usually just happen as a result of sudden failure, but develop over a period of time. Major mechanical failures in particular are usually preceded by characteristic symptoms over hundreds or even thousands of miles. Those components which do occasionally fail without warning are often small and easily carried in the vehicle.

With any fault finding, the first step is to decide where to begin investigations. Sometimes this is obvious, but on other occasions a little detective work will be necessary. The owner who makes half a dozen haphazard adjustments or replacements may be successful in curing a fault (or its symptoms), but he will be none the wiser if the fault recurs and he may well have spent more time and money than was necessary. A calm and logical approach will be found to be more satisfactory in the long run. Always take into account any warning signs or abnormalities that may have been noticed in the period preceding the fault – power loss, high or low gauge readings, unusual noises or smells, etc – and remember that failure of components such as fuses or spark plugs may only be pointers to some underlying fault.

The pages which follow here are intended to help in cases of failure to start or breakdown on the road. There is also a Fault Diagnosis Section at the end of each Chapter which should be consulted if the preliminary checks prove unfruitful. Whatever the fault, certain basic principles apply. These are as follows:

Verify the fault. This is simply a matter of being sure that you know what the symptoms are before starting work. This is particularly important if you are investigating a fault for someone else who may not have described it very accurately.

Don't overlook the obvious. For example, if the vehicle won't start, is there petrol in the tank? (Don't take anyone else's word on this particular point, and don't trust the fuel gauge either!) If an electrical fault is indicated, look for loose or broken wires before digging out the test gear.

Cure the disease, not the symptom. Substituting a flat battery with a fully charged one will get you off the hard shoulder, but if the underlying cause is not attended to, the new battery will go the same way. Similarly, changing oil-fouled spark plugs for a new set will get you moving again, but remember that the reason for the fouling (if it wasn't simply an incorrect grade of plug) will have to be established and corrected.

Don't take anything for granted. Particularly, don't forget that a 'new' component may itself be defective (especially if it's been rattling round in the boot for months), and don't leave components out of a fault diagnosis sequence just because they are new or recently fitted. When you do finally diagnose a difficult fault, you'll probably realise that all the evidence was there from the start.

Electrical faults

Electrical faults can be more puzzling than straightforward mechanical failures, but they are no less susceptible to logical analysis if the basic principles of operation are understood. Vehicle electrical wiring exists in extremely unfavourable conditions – heat, vibration and chemical attack – and the first things to look for are loose or corroded connections and broken or chafed wires, especially where the wires pass through holes in the bodywork or are subject to vibration.

All metal-bodied vehicles in current production have one pole of the battery 'earthed', ie connected to the vehicle bodywork, and in nearly all modern vehicles it is the negative (–) terminal. The various electrical components – motors, bulb holders etc – are also connected to earth, either by means of a lead or directly by their mountings. Electric current flows through the component and then back to the battery via the bodywork. If the component mounting is loose or corroded, or if a good path back to the battery is not available, the circuit will be incomplete and malfunction will result. The engine and/or gearbox are also earthed by means of flexible metal straps to the body or subframe; if these straps are loose or missing, starter motor, generator and ignition trouble may result.

Assuming the earth return to be satisfactory, electrical faults will be due either to component malfunction or to defects in the current supply. Individual components are dealt with in Chapter 12. If supply wires are broken or cracked internally this results in an open-circuit, and the easiest way to check for this is to bypass the suspect wire temporarily with a length of wire having a crocodile clip or suitable connector at each end. Alternatively, a 12V test lamp can be used to verify the presence of supply voltage at various points along the wire and the break can be thus isolated.

If a bare portion of a live wire touches the bodywork or other earthed metal part, the electricity will take the low-resistance path thus formed back to the battery: this is known as a short-circuit. Hopefully a short-circuit will blow a fuse, but otherwise it may cause burning of the insulation (and possibly further short-circuits) or even a fire. This is why it is inadvisable to bypass persistently blowing fuses with silver foil or wire.

Spares and tool kit

Most vehicles are supplied only with sufficient tools for wheel changing; the *Maintenance and minor repair* tool kit detailed in *Tools and working facilities,* with the addition of a hammer, is probably sufficient for those repairs that most motorists would consider attempting at the roadside. In addition a few items which can be fitted without too much trouble in the event of a breakdown should be carried.

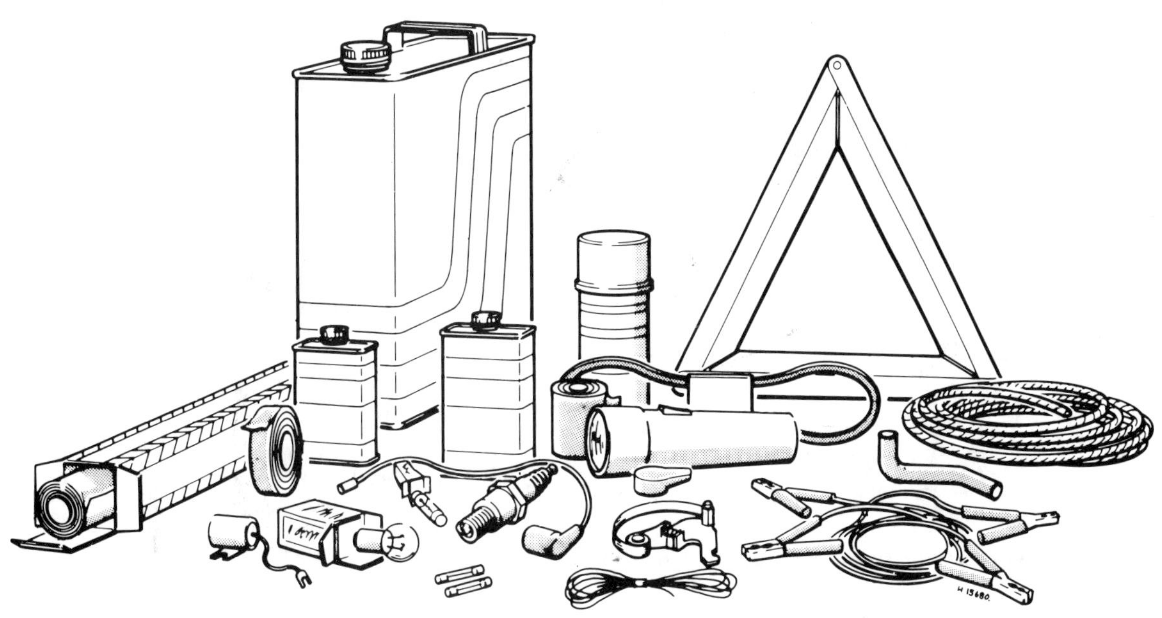

Carrying a few spares may save you a long walk!

Experience and available space will modify the list below, but the following may save having to call on professional assistance:

Spark plugs, clean and correctly gapped
HT lead and plug cap – long enough to reach the plug furthest from the distributor
Distributor rotor, condenser and contact breaker points
Drivebelt(s) – emergency type may suffice
Spare fuses
Set of principal light bulbs
Tin of radiator sealer and hose bandage
Exhaust bandage
Roll of insulating tape
Length of soft iron wire
Length of electrical flex
Torch or inspection lamp (can double as test lamp)
Battery jump leads
Tow-rope
Ignition waterproofing aerosol
Litre of engine oil
Sealed can of hydraulic fluid
Emergency windscreen
'Jubilee' clips
Tube of filler paste

If spare fuel is carried, a can designed for the purpose should be used to minimise risks of leakage and collision damage. A first aid kit and a warning triangle, whilst not at present compulsory in the UK, are obviously sensible items to carry in addition to the above.

When touring abroad it may be advisable to carry additional spares which, even if you cannot fit them yourself, could save having to wait while parts are obtained. The items below may be worth considering:

Clutch and throttle cables
Cylinder head gasket
Alternator brushes
Fuel pump repair kit
Tyre valve core

One of the motoring organisations will be able to advise on availability of fuel etc in foreign countries.

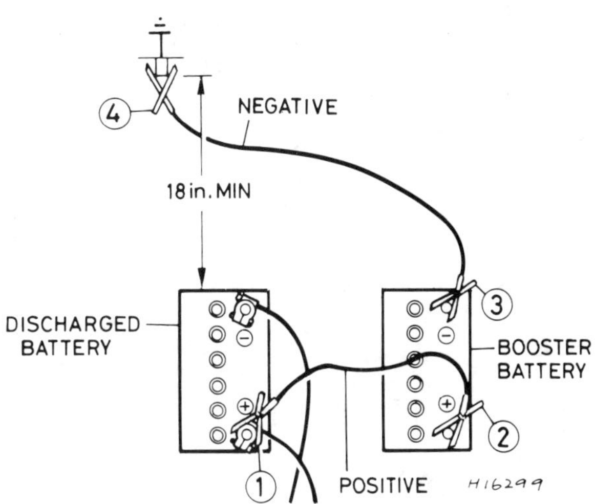

Jump start lead connections for negative earth vehicles – connect leads in order shown

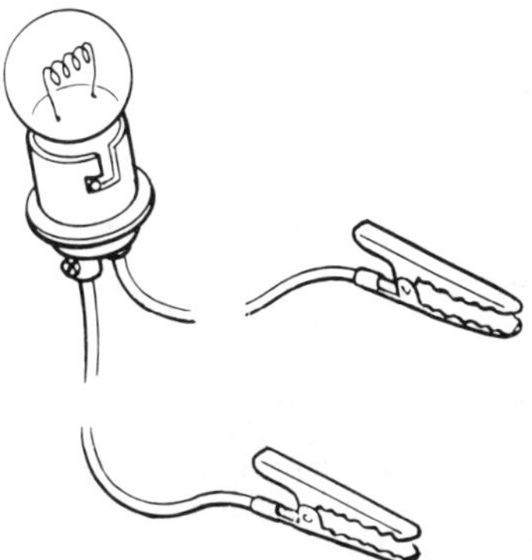

A simple test lamp is useful for checking electrical circuits

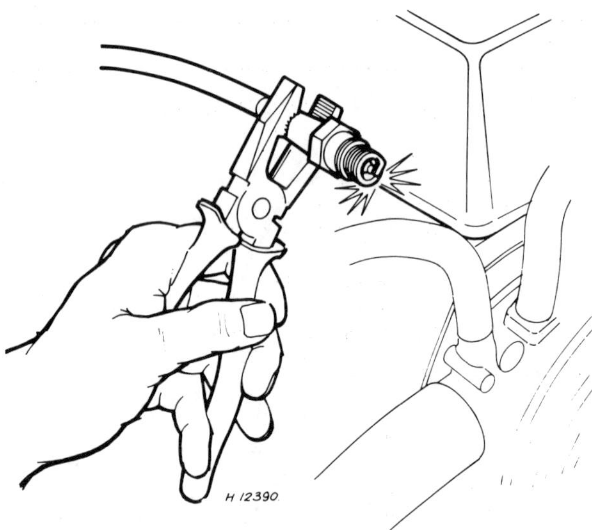

Crank engine and check for spark. Note use of insulated tool!

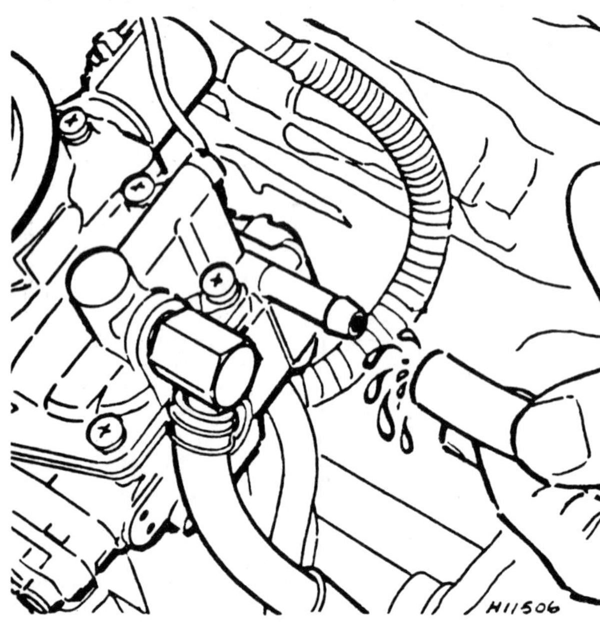

Check for fuel delivery at carburettor

Engine will not start

Engine fails to turn when starter operated
Flat battery (recharge, use jump leads, or push start)
Battery terminals loose or corroded
Battery earth to body defective
Engine earth strap loose or broken
Starter motor (or solenoid) wiring loose or broken
Automatic transmission selector in wrong position, or inhibitor switch faulty
Ignition/starter switch faulty
Major mechanical failure (seizure)
Starter or solenoid internal fault (see Chapter 12)

Starter motor turns engine slowly
Partially discharged battery (recharge, use jump leads, or push start)
Battery terminals loose or corroded
Battery earth to body defective
Engine earth strap loose
Starter motor (or solenoid) wiring loose
Starter motor internal fault (see Chapter 12)

Starter motor spins without turning engine
Flat battery
Starter motor pinion sticking on sleeve
Flywheel gear teeth damaged or worn
Starter motor mounting bolts loose

Engine turns normally but fails to start
Damp or dirty HT leads and distributor cap (crank engine and check for spark)
Dirty or incorrectly gapped distributor points (if applicable)
No fuel in tank (check for delivery at carburettor)
Excessive choke (hot engine) or insufficient choke (cold engine)
Fouled or incorrectly gapped spark plugs (remove, clean and regap)
Other ignition system fault (see Chapter 4)
Other fuel system fault (see Chapter 3)
Poor compression (see Chapter 1)
Major mechanical failure (eg camshaft drive)

Engine fires but will not run
Insufficient choke (cold engine)
Air leaks at carburettor or inlet manifold
Fuel starvation (see Chapter 3)
Ballast resistor defective, or other ignition fault (see Chapter 4)

Engine cuts out and will not restart

Engine cuts out suddenly – ignition fault
Loose or disconnected LT wires
Wet HT leads or distributor cap (after traversing water splash)
Coil or condenser failure (check for spark)
Other ignition fault (see Chapter 4)

Engine misfires before cutting out – fuel fault
Fuel tank empty
Fuel pump defective or filter blocked (check for delivery)
Fuel tank filler vent blocked (suction will be evident on releasing cap)
Carburettor needle valve sticking
Carburettor jets blocked (fuel contaminated)
Other fuel system fault (see Chapter 3)

Engine cuts out – other causes
Serious overheating
Major mechanical failure (eg camshaft drive)

Engine overheats

Ignition (no-charge) warning light illuminated
Slack or broken drivebelt – retension or renew (Chapter 2)

Ignition warning light not illuminated
Coolant loss due to internal or external leakage (see Chapter 2)
Thermostat defective

Low oil level
Brakes binding
Radiator clogged externally or internally
Electric cooling fan not operating correctly
Engine waterways clogged
Ignition timing incorrect or automatic advance malfunctioning
Mixture too weak

Note: *Do not add cold water to an overheated engine or damage may result*

Low engine oil pressure

Gauge reads low or warning light illuminated with engine running

Oil level low or incorrect grade
Defective gauge or sender unit
Wire to sender unit earthed
Engine overheating
Oil filter clogged or bypass valve defective
Oil pressure relief valve defective
Oil pick-up strainer clogged
Oil pump worn or mountings loose
Worn main or big-end bearings

Note: *Low oil pressure in a high-mileage engine at tickover is not necessarily a cause for concern. Sudden pressure loss at speed is far more significant. In any event, check the gauge or warning light sender before condemning the engine.*

Engine noises

Pre-ignition (pinking) on acceleration

Incorrect grade of fuel
Ignition timing incorrect
Distributor faulty or worn
Worn or maladjusted carburettor
Excessive carbon build-up in engine

Whistling or wheezing noises

Leaking vacuum hose
Leaking carburettor or manifold gasket
Blowing head gasket

Tapping or rattling

Incorrect valve clearances
Worn valve gear
Worn timing chain or belt
Broken piston ring (ticking noise)

Knocking or thumping

Unintentional mechanical contact (eg fan blades)
Peripheral component fault (generator, water pump etc)
Worn big-end bearings (regular heavy knocking, perhaps less under load)
Worn main bearings (rumbling and knocking, perhaps worsening under load)
Piston slap (most noticeable when cold)

Safety first!

Professional motor mechanics are trained in safe working procedures. However enthusiastic you may be about getting on with the job in hand, do take the time to ensure that your safety is not put at risk. A moment's lack of attention can result in an accident, as can failure to observe certain elementary precautions.

There will always be new ways of having accidents, and the following points do not pretend to be a comprehensive list of all dangers; they are intended rather to make you aware of the risks and to encourage a safety-conscious approach to all work you carry out on your vehicle.

Essential DOs and DON'Ts

DON'T rely on a single jack when working underneath the vehicle. Always use reliable additional means of support, such as axle stands, securely placed under a part of the vehicle that you know will not give way.

DON'T attempt to loosen or tighten high-torque nuts (e.g. wheel hub nuts) while the vehicle is on a jack; it may be pulled off.

DON'T start the engine without first ascertaining that the transmission is in neutral (or 'Park' where applicable) and the parking brake applied.

DON'T suddenly remove the filler cap from a hot cooling system – cover it with a cloth and release the pressure gradually first, or you may get scalded by escaping coolant.

DON'T attempt to drain oil until you are sure it has cooled sufficiently to avoid scalding you.

DON'T grasp any part of the engine, exhaust or catalytic converter without first ascertaining that it is sufficiently cool to avoid burning you.

DON'T allow brake fluid or antifreeze to contact vehicle paintwork.

DON'T syphon toxic liquids such as fuel, brake fluid or antifreeze by mouth, or allow them to remain on your skin.

DON'T inhale dust – it may be injurious to health (see *Asbestos* below).

DON'T allow any spilt oil or grease to remain on the floor – wipe it up straight away, before someone slips on it.

DON'T use ill-fitting spanners or other tools which may slip and cause injury.

DON'T attempt to lift a heavy component which may be beyond your capability – get assistance.

DON'T rush to finish a job, or take unverified short cuts.

DON'T allow children or animals in or around an unattended vehicle.

DO wear eye protection when using power tools such as drill, sander, bench grinder etc, and when working under the vehicle.

DO use a barrier cream on your hands prior to undertaking dirty jobs – it will protect your skin from infection as well as making the dirt easier to remove afterwards; but make sure your hands aren't left slippery.

DO keep loose clothing (cuffs, tie etc) and long hair well out of the way of moving mechanical parts.

DO remove rings, wristwatch etc, before working on the vehicle – especially the electrical system.

DO ensure that any lifting tackle used has a safe working load rating adequate for the job.

DO keep your work area tidy – it is only too easy to fall over articles left lying around.

DO get someone to check periodically that all is well, when working alone on the vehicle.

DO carry out work in a logical sequence and check that everything is correctly assembled and tightened afterwards.

DO remember that your vehicle's safety affects that of yourself and others. If in doubt on any point, get specialist advice.

IF, in spite of following these precautions, you are unfortunate enough to injure yourself, seek medical attention as soon as possible.

Asbestos

Certain friction, insulating, sealing, and other products – such as brake linings, brake bands, clutch linings, torque converters, gaskets, etc – contain asbestos. *Extreme care must be taken to avoid inhalation of dust from such products since it is hazardous to health.* If in doubt, assume that they *do* contain asbestos.

Fire

Remember at all times that petrol (gasoline) is highly flammable. Never smoke, or have any kind of naked flame around, when working on the vehicle. But the risk does not end there – a spark caused by an electrical short-circuit, by two metal surfaces contacting each other, by careless use of tools, or even by static electricity built up in your body under certain conditions, can ignite petrol vapour, which in a confined space is highly explosive.

Always disconnect the battery earth (ground) terminal before working on any part of the fuel or electrical system, and never risk spilling fuel on to a hot engine or exhaust.

It is recommended that a fire extinguisher of a type suitable for fuel and electrical fires is kept handy in the garage or workplace at all times. Never try to extinguish a fuel or electrical fire with water.

Fumes

Certain fumes are highly toxic and can quickly cause unconsciousness and even death if inhaled to any extent. Petrol (gasoline) vapour comes into this category, as do the vapours from certain solvents such as trichloroethylene. Any draining or pouring of such volatile fluids should be done in a well ventilated area.

When using cleaning fluids and solvents, read the instructions carefully. Never use materials from unmarked containers – they may give off poisonous vapours.

Never run the engine of a motor vehicle in an enclosed space such as a garage. Exhaust fumes contain carbon monoxide which is extremely poisonous; if you need to run the engine, always do so in the open air or at least have the rear of the vehicle outside the workplace.

If you are fortunate enough to have the use of an inspection pit, never drain or pour petrol, and never run the engine, while the vehicle is standing over it; the fumes, being heavier than air, will concentrate in the pit with possibly lethal results.

The battery

Never cause a spark, or allow a naked light, near the vehicle's battery. It will normally be giving off a certain amount of hydrogen gas, which is highly explosive.

Always disconnect the battery earth (ground) terminal before working on the fuel or electrical systems.

If possible, loosen the filler plugs or cover when charging the battery from an external source. Do not charge at an excessive rate or the battery may burst.

Take care when topping up and when carrying the battery. The acid electrolyte, even when diluted, is very corrosive and should not be allowed to contact the eyes or skin.

If you ever need to prepare electrolyte yourself, always add the acid slowly to the water, and never the other way round. Protect against splashes by wearing rubber gloves and goggles.

When jump starting a car using a booster battery, for negative earth (ground) vehicles, connect the jump leads in the following sequence: First connect one jump lead between the positive (+) terminals of the two batteries. Then connect the other jump lead first to the negative (–) terminal of the booster battery, and then to a good earthing (ground) point on the vehicle to be started, at least 18 in (45 cm) from the battery if possible. Ensure that hands and jump leads are clear of any moving parts, and that the two vehicles do not touch. Disconnect the leads in the reverse order.

Mains electricity

When using an electric power tool, inspection light etc, which works from the mains, always ensure that the appliance is correctly connected to its plug and that, where necessary, it is properly earthed (grounded). Do not use such appliances in damp conditions and, again, beware of creating a spark or applying excessive heat in the vicinity of fuel or fuel vapour.

Ignition HT voltage

A severe electric shock can result from touching certain parts of the ignition system, such as the HT leads, when the engine is running or being cranked, particularly if components are damp or the insulation is defective. Where an electronic ignition system is fitted, the HT voltage is much higher and could prove fatal.

Use of English

As this book has been written in England, it uses the appropriate English component names, phrases, and spelling. Some of these differ from those used in America. Normally, these cause no difficulty, but to make sure, a glossary is printed below. In ordering spare parts remember the parts list may use some of these words:

English	American	English	American
Accelerator	Gas pedal	Leading shoe (of brake)	Primary shoe
Aerial	Antenna	Locks	Latches
Anti-roll bar	Stabiliser or sway bar	Methylated spirit	Denatured alcohol
Big-end bearing	Rod bearing	Motorway	Freeway, turnpike etc
Bonnet (engine cover)	Hood	Number plate	License plate
Boot (luggage compartment)	Trunk	Paraffin	Kerosene
Bulkhead	Firewall	Petrol	Gasoline (gas)
Bush	Bushing	Petrol tank	Gas tank
Cam follower or tappet	Valve lifter or tappet	'Pinking'	'Pinging'
Carburettor	Carburetor	Prise (force apart)	Pry
Catch	Latch	Propeller shaft	Driveshaft
Choke/venturi	Barrel	Quarterlight	Quarter window
Circlip	Snap-ring	Retread	Recap
Clearance	Lash	Reverse	Back-up
Crownwheel	Ring gear (of differential)	Rocker cover	Valve cover
Damper	Shock absorber, shock	Saloon	Sedan
Disc (brake)	Rotor/disk	Seized	Frozen
Distance piece	Spacer	Sidelight	Parking light
Drop arm	Pitman arm	Silencer	Muffler
Drop head coupe	Convertible	Sill panel (beneath doors)	Rocker panel
Dynamo	Generator (DC)	Small end, little end	Piston pin or wrist pin
Earth (electrical)	Ground	Spanner	Wrench
Engineer's blue	Prussian blue	Split cotter (for valve spring cap)	Lock (for valve spring retainer)
Estate car	Station wagon	Split pin	Cotter pin
Exhaust manifold	Header	Steering arm	Spindle arm
Fault finding/diagnosis	Troubleshooting	Sump	Oil pan
Float chamber	Float bowl	Swarf	Metal chips or debris
Free-play	Lash	Tab washer	Tang or lock
Freewheel	Coast	Tappet	Valve lifter
Gearbox	Transmission	Thrust bearing	Throw-out bearing
Gearchange	Shift	Top gear	High
Grub screw	Setscrew, Allen screw	Trackrod (of steering)	Tie-rod (or connecting rod)
Gudgeon pin	Piston pin or wrist pin	Trailing shoe (of brake)	Secondary shoe
Halfshaft	Axleshaft	Transmission	Whole drive line
Handbrake	Parking brake	Tyre	Tire
Hood	Soft top	Van	Panel wagon/van
Hot spot	Heat riser	Vice	Vise
Indicator	Turn signal	Wheel nut	Lug nut
Interior light	Dome lamp	Windscreen	Windshield
Layshaft (of gearbox)	Countershaft	Wing/mudguard	Fender

General repair procedures

Whenever servicing, repair or overhaul work is carried out on the car or its components, it is necessary to observe the following procedures and instructions. This will assist in carrying out the operation efficiently and to a professional standard of workmanship.

Joint mating faces and gaskets

Where a gasket is used between the mating faces of two components, ensure that it is renewed on reassembly, and fit it dry unless otherwise stated in the repair procedure. Make sure that the mating faces are clean and dry with all traces of old gasket removed. When cleaning a joint face, use a tool which is not likely to score or damage the face, and remove any burrs or nicks with an oilstone or fine file.

Make sure that tapped holes are cleaned with a pipe cleaner, and keep them free of jointing compound if this is being used unless specifically instructed otherwise.

Ensure that all orifices, channels or pipes are clear and blow through them, preferably using compressed air.

Oil seals

Whenever an oil seal is removed from its working location, either individually or as part of an assembly, it should be renewed.

The very fine sealing lip of the seal is easily damaged and will not seal if the surface it contacts is not completely clean and free from scratches, nicks or grooves. If the original sealing surface of the component cannot be restored, the component should be renewed.

Protect the lips of the seal from any surface which may damage them in the course of fitting. Use tape or a conical sleeve where possible. Lubricate the seal lips with oil before fitting and, on dual lipped seals, fill the space between the lips with grease.

Unless otherwise stated, oil seals must be fitted with their sealing lips toward the lubricant to be sealed.

Use a tubular drift or block of wood of the appropriate size to install the seal and, if the seal housing is shouldered, drive the seal down to the shoulder. If the seal housing is unshouldered, the seal should be fitted with its face flush with the housing top face.

Screw threads and fastenings

Always ensure that a blind tapped hole is completely free from oil, grease, water or other fluid before installing the bolt or stud. Failure to do this could cause the housing to crack due to the hydraulic action of the bolt or stud as it is screwed in.

When tightening a castellated nut to accept a split pin, tighten the nut to the specified torque, where applicable, and then tighten further to the next split pin hole. Never slacken the nut to align a split pin hole unless stated in the repair procedure.

When checking or retightening a nut or bolt to a specified torque setting, slacken the nut or bolt by a quarter of a turn, and then retighten to the specified setting.

Locknuts, locktabs and washers

Any fastening which will rotate against a component or housing in the course of tightening should always have a washer between it and the relevant component or housing.

Spring or split washers should always be renewed when they are used to lock a critical component such as a big-end bearing retaining nut or bolt.

Locktabs which are folded over to retain a nut or bolt should always be renewed.

Self-locking nuts can be reused in non-critical areas, providing resistance can be felt when the locking portion passes over the bolt or stud thread.

Split pins must always be replaced with new ones of the correct size for the hole.

Special tools

Some repair procedures in this manual entail the use of special tools such as a press, two or three-legged pullers, spring compressors etc. Wherever possible, suitable readily available alternatives to the manufacturer's special tools are described, and are shown in use. In some instances, where no alternative is possible, it has been necessary to resort to the use of a manufacturer's tool and this has been done for reasons of safety as well as the efficient completion of the repair operation. Unless you are highly skilled and have a thorough understanding of the procedure described, never attempt to bypass the use of any special tool when the procedure described specifies its use. Not only is there a very great risk of personal injury, but expensive damage could be caused to the components involved.

Conversion factors

Length (distance)

Inches (in)	X 25.4	= Millimetres (mm)	X 0.0394	= Inches (in)
Feet (ft)	X 0.305	= Metres (m)	X 3.281	= Feet (ft)
Miles	X 1.609	= Kilometres (km)	X 0.621	= Miles

Volume (capacity)

Cubic inches (cu in; in^3)	X 16.387	= Cubic centimetres (cc; cm^3)	X 0.061	= Cubic inches (cu in; in^3)
Imperial pints (Imp pt)	X 0.568	= Litres (l)	X 1.76	= Imperial pints (Imp pt)
Imperial quarts (Imp qt)	X 1.137	= Litres (l)	X 0.88	= Imperial quarts (Imp qt)
Imperial quarts (Imp qt)	X 1.201	= US quarts (US qt)	X 0.833	= Imperial quarts (Imp qt)
US quarts (US qt)	X 0.946	= Litres (l)	X 1.057	= US quarts (US qt)
Imperial gallons (Imp gal)	X 4.546	= Litres (l)	X 0.22	= Imperial gallons (Imp gal)
Imperial gallons (Imp gal)	X 1.201	= US gallons (US gal)	X 0.833	= Imperial gallons (Imp gal)
US gallons (US gal)	X 3.785	= Litres (l)	X 0.264	= US gallons (US gal)

Mass (weight)

Ounces (oz)	X 28.35	= Grams (g)	X 0.035	= Ounces (oz)
Pounds (lb)	X 0.454	= Kilograms (kg)	X 2.205	= Pounds (lb)

Force

Ounces-force (ozf; oz)	X 0.278	= Newtons (N)	X 3.6	= Ounces-force (ozf; oz)
Pounds-force (lbf; lb)	X 4.448	= Newtons (N)	X 0.225	= Pounds-force (lbf; lb)
Newtons (N)	X 0.1	= Kilograms-force (kgf; kg)	X 9.81	= Newtons (N)

Pressure

Pounds-force per square inch (psi; lbf/in^2; lb/in^2)	X 0.070	= Kilograms-force per square centimetre (kgf/cm^2; kg/cm^2)	X 14.223	= Pounds-force per square inch (psi; lbf/in^2; lb/in^2)
Pounds-force per square inch (psi; lbf/in^2; lb/in^2)	X 0.068	= Atmospheres (atm)	X 14.696	= Pounds-force per square inch (psi; lbf/in^2; lb/in^2)
Pounds-force per square inch (psi; lbf/in^2; lb/in^2)	X 0.069	= Bars	X 14.5	= Pounds-force per square inch (psi; lbf/in^2; lb/in^2)
Pounds-force per square inch (psi; lbf/in^2; lb/in^2)	X 6.895	= Kilopascals (kPa)	X 0.145	= Pounds-force per square inch (psi; lbf/in^2; lb/in^2)
Kilopascals (kPa)	X 0.01	= Kilograms-force per square centimetre (kgf/cm^2; kg/cm^2)	X 98.1	= Kilopascals (kPa)

Torque (moment of force)

Pounds-force inches (lbf in; lb in)	X 1.152	= Kilograms-force centimetre (kgf cm; kg cm)	X 0.868	= Pounds-force inches (lbf in; lb in)
Pounds-force inches (lbf in; lb in)	X 0.113	= Newton metres (Nm)	X 8.85	= Pounds-force inches (lbf in; lb in)
Pounds-force inches (lbf in; lb in)	X 0.083	= Pounds-force feet (lbf ft; lb ft)	X 12	= Pounds-force inches (lbf in; lb in)
Pounds-force feet (lbf ft; lb ft)	X 0.138	= Kilograms-force metres (kgf m; kg m)	X 7.233	= Pounds-force feet (lbf ft; lb ft)
Pounds-force feet (lbf ft; lb ft)	X 1.356	= Newton metres (Nm)	X 0.738	= Pounds-force feet (lbf ft; lb ft)
Newton metres (Nm)	X 0.102	= Kilograms-force metres (kgf m; kg m)	X 9.804	= Newton metres (Nm)

Power

Horsepower (hp)	X 745.7	= Watts (W)	X 0.0013	= Horsepower (hp)

Velocity (speed)

Miles per hour (miles/hr; mph)	X 1.609	= Kilometres per hour (km/hr; kph)	X 0.621	= Miles per hour (miles/hr; mph)

*Fuel consumption**

Miles per gallon, Imperial (mpg)	X 0.354	= Kilometres per litre (km/l)	X 2.825	= Miles per gallon, Imperial (mpg)
Miles per gallon, US (mpg)	X 0.425	= Kilometres per litre (km/l)	X 2.352	= Miles per gallon, US (mpg)

Temperature

Degrees Fahrenheit = (°C x 1.8) + 32

Degrees Celsius (Degrees Centigrade; °C) = (°F - 32) x 0.56

**It is common practice to convert from miles per gallon (mpg) to litres/100 kilometres (l/100km), where mpg (Imperial) x l/100 km = 282 and mpg (US) x l/100 km = 235*

Index

A

B

C

F

P

R

S

T

U

V

W

Printed by
J H Haynes & Co Ltd
Sparkford Nr Yeovil
Somerset BA22 7JJ England